W9-BYK-772

AMERICAN PRIEST

AMERICAN PRIEST

THE AMBITIOUS LIFE AND CONFLICTED LEGACY
OF NOTRE DAME'S FATHER TED HESBURGH

WILSON D. MISCAMBLE, C.S.C.

IMAGE

NEW YORK

Copyright © 2019 by Wilson D. Miscamble

All rights reserved.
Published in the United States by Image, an imprint of the Crown Publishing
Group, a division of Penguin Random House LLC, New York.
ImageCatholicBooks.com

IMAGE is a registered trademark and the "I" colophon is a trademark of
Penguin Random House LLC.

Photography credits appear on page 425.

Library of Congress Cataloging-in-Publication Data is available upon request.

ISBN 978-1-9848-2343-4
Ebook ISBN 978-1-9848-2344-1

Printed in the United States of America

Book design: Lauren Dong
Jacket design: Sarah Horgan
Jacket photograph: University of Notre Dame Archives

10 9 8 7 6 5 4 3 2 1

First Edition

To

Dan and Mary Ann Rogers

Brian and Nancy Sullivan

&

Terry Seidler

CONTENTS

The Evolution of a Book—and a Relationship

FATHER THEODORE MARTIN HESBURGH—ALWAYS "FATHER TED" TO me—died peacefully at Notre Dame late in the evening of February 26, 2015. He lived a long and full life. *American Priest* sheds light on this life and his many and varied engagements both at the university that he led for thirty-five years and far beyond it. The book has had a long gestation, and its form and content have evolved over the two decades since I first announced to Father Ted that I planned to write about him.

One fall evening in 1994, I called Father Hesburgh and caught him at his desk in his office suite on the thirteenth floor of the Hesburgh Library. I asked if I might see him and he invited me to come right over. Five minutes later I was in his office surrounded by all the special photographs, memorabilia items, and autographed books that gave glimpses of his associations, activities, and accomplishments over his long tenure as president of Notre Dame. From its window we could see Our Lady positioned so gracefully atop the university's signature Golden Dome. Father Ted was smoking a sizable cigar and had been reading the *New York Times* with a magnifying glass and listening to classical music. Father Ted drew my attention to some of the first editions he had on his bookshelves. I then caught him a bit unawares when I interrupted him and said, as best I can recall: "Well, Father Ted, I have come to see you tonight about writing a book. I want to write a book about you." After paying a tribute to his best-selling autobiography, *God, Country, Notre Dame*, I explained that I planned to write a comprehensive biography of the "life and times" sort that would build on his memoir.

Father Ted was taken aback by this statement of my intentions. We sat down, and I must say that he momentarily was caught out for the appropriate words, definitely a rare occurrence for him. He knew I was a historian of some ability, but I was a student of postwar American foreign relations. I had no special background as a biographer, unlike my distinguished colleague Fr. Marvin R. O'Connell, whose terrific biography of Archbishop John Ireland Father Hesburgh so admired. Furthermore, he knew that I was heavily engaged in my work as chair of the history department at Notre Dame and would not be able to devote my full energies to this effort. Perhaps with such concerns in mind he puffed on his cigar, and after exhaling he offered a warning. He revealed an insightful sense of his extensive activities, and explained that it would be hard for a single historian to capture in a full and meaningful way the extent of his actions over the years since he had emerged as a prominent public figure in the United States. He even recited for me the extent of the holdings in his presidential papers housed in the University of Notre Dame Archives. Additionally, he asked, how could any single person, let alone a busy one like me, investigate with care the records of the various commissions and agencies on which he had served.

Having come to know Father Ted over the years since my ordination as a Holy Cross priest and appointment to the regular faculty of Notre Dame in 1988, I had expected something like this response. I had two rejoinders at the ready. First, I explained that a trained historian did not need to read every document ever associated with a subject to get the gist of things. Otherwise, I continued, how would biographies be written of great figures like Winston Churchill and Franklin Roosevelt, historical figures with whom he knew I was well familiar. Putting that matter to the side, I readily conceded to him that it would be a major undertaking to write a definitive biography of him. I went further and told him candidly that I planned to write another book—a study of the transition from FDR to Harry Truman and its implications for American foreign policy—before I settled down to devote myself to his biography. After that work was completed, I assured him, I would give myself fully to what I knew would be a multi-year project. Then I introduced a delicate matter and explained that I had to announce my intention now so that I might ask his cooperation and help while he still enjoyed vigorous good health. I advised that I would need to speak with him extensively while his memory was still sharp and incisive. I did not seek to be his "authorized biographer" in any way, but I recall guaranteeing him that I would tell his important story well.

Reassured by my response Father Ted thereupon promised me his cooperation and suggested that we might have a drink to mark our agreement. We walked down the little corridor off his office to the kitchen area of his suite and he produced a bottle of Cutty Sark, the blended scotch whiskey that he preferred when the Manhattans mixed for him at the Morris Inn were not available. Some tumblers soon had ice in them and healthy portions of the smooth drink. We returned to his office and talked for over two hours, refilling our glasses once or twice. I produced for Father Ted from a folder I had brought with me a title page for the biography, a title that I subsequently varied slightly. It had on it: "AMERICA'S PRIEST: FATHER HESBURGH OF NOTRE DAME." He signed it and dated it in his clear handwriting: "Fr. Ted Hesburgh, csc—10.17.94."[1]

WHY I DESIRED TO write a biography of Father Hesburgh and why I believed myself capable of doing so deserves some explanation. I first had come to know of Father Ted in a limited way when I arrived at Notre Dame from Australia as a doctoral student in 1976. I observed him at a distance, but I met him only once and that in the context of a gathering of graduate students. I focused on my own history studies and appreciated his leadership of Notre Dame from afar. I returned to Notre Dame a second time in August of 1982 to enter the Holy Cross order, and I met him occasionally during my seminary years. He kindly displayed some interest in me, knowing that I possessed a doctorate and hoped to serve in the higher education ministry of the Congregation of Holy Cross. He assured me of his satisfaction when I joined the full-time faculty of the history department after my ordination in 1988.

I began my service on the regular faculty of Notre Dame just after Father Hesburgh ended his decades as president and moved on to his new status as "president emeritus," which he held for a further quarter century. As he made his adjustment to this new role, and initially traveled far and wide, I set about my ministry as a priest-teacher. My early years on the faculty went smoothly. I loved my teaching and it was favorably recognized. My scholarly efforts reached some fruition in 1992 when Princeton University Press published my book *George F. Kennan and the Making of American Foreign Policy, 1947–1950*. The book was well received and assured my promotion to associate professor with tenure. Father Ted graciously noted my accomplishments and either in person or in writing extended congratulations. He also recognized that I was a Holy Cross priest interested in the broad direction of Notre Dame, and not one who focused only on my own scholarly interests. This was especially obvious after Father Ted's successor, Fr. Edward "Monk" Malloy, appointed me to serve on the university-wide self-study known as The Colloquy for the Year 2000, which did the bulk of its work in 1992.

The years of the early 1990s coincided with enhanced discussion of Notre Dame's mission as a Catholic university. The promulgation of Pope John Paul II's apostolic constitution on Catholic universities, *Ex Corde Ecclesiae* (From the Heart of the Church), in August 1990 gave a pointed focus to campus deliberations. Much of this discussion emerged in debates surrounding the Colloquy's draft mission statement, which included the clear statement (in accord with *Ex Corde Ecclesiae*) that "the Catholic identity of the University depends upon, and is nurtured by, the continuing presence of a predominant number of Catholic intellectuals."[2] Father Hesburgh had deep reservations about aspects of the apostolic constitution, but he was most interested in the efforts of a group of faculty, of which I was part, to promote serious discussion of Notre Dame's mission as a Catholic university. This group, dubbed the Conversation on the Catholic Character (CCC), organized a series of lively and (occasionally) even disputatious meetings in 1992 and 1993. Father Ted was very curious about these discussions and requested reports from me on them. Hoping that some of the heat generated in the CCC debates might produce some constructive light, Father Ted decided to request contributions from many of the folks who had participated in CCC debates along with some other colleagues. I advised him on contributors and wrote an essay of my own for this volume, which he edited in 1994 and entitled *The Challenge and Promise of a Catholic University*.[3]

My involvement in deliberations and debate over Notre Dame's Catholic mission and identity inexorably drew me to reflect on Father Hesburgh and his role in shaping Notre Dame into the institution it was in the 1990s. I began to think about writing of Father Ted and Notre Dame out of a presentist concern to understand for myself and, I hope, to explain to others, how events had come to pass that Notre Dame's mission as a *Catholic* university had become so contested. I wanted to understand better what had happened in recent decades such that there now existed a sizable element on the university's faculty that seemed determined to emasculate Catholicism's role in the academic heart of the university. Readers must be aware of this perspective at the outset because it still operates and unquestionably it influences the perspective of this book.

My interest in Father Hesburgh was in no sense restricted to viewing him through this lens. I realized at the outset that a study of him would afford a terrific opportunity to explore some crucial and fascinating areas, among them the growth of Notre Dame in the half century after World War II and the nature of the relationship of the university to its founding religious community, the Congregation of Holy Cross, stood out. Addressing those topics provided an opportunity to shed further light on the wide-ranging developments in Catholic higher education and in higher education more generally in the United States. But I knew well that telling Father Hesburgh's story also would allow me to explore other and broader stories including elements of the postwar American story, including such momentous issues as civil rights, overseas development, and immigration and refugee policy. I wanted to understand the nature of Father Ted's relationships with presidents from Dwight Eisenhower onward. Furthermore, I knew that telling his story would enable me to understand better the journey of the Church in which we both served as priests.

REGRETTABLY AND SOMEWHAT TO Father Ted's disappointment, I did little more than a rather haphazard gathering of materials in the initial years after my 1994 visit to his office to secure his agreement and support for my writing about him. I served five years as chair of the history department in the mid-1990s and found it difficult to balance these duties with sustained scholarly work. Nonetheless, we maintained a very friendly relationship and he always asked after my parents. He and his great collaborator Fr. Edmund (Ned) Joyce had kindly contacted them during their visit to Australia on their round-the-world cruise on the ocean liner QE2 in 1988. I lived with him as part of the Holy Cross community and enjoyed listening to him at the Corby Hall dinner table. I occasionally invited Father Ted to speak to my classes on his impressions of postwar presidents and on the Notre Dame experience during the Vietnam War era. He always graciously accepted.

For a variety of reasons I decided to resign my position as chair of the history department and to re-engage my scholarly work in 1998. I sought and was granted a sabbatical for 1998–1999 to work on my book on the transition from FDR to Truman. But I determined that I could no longer delay speaking in a systematic way with Father Ted, who after all had turned eighty on May 25, 1997. He still enjoyed robust good health, his memory remained sharp, and the hints of the macular degeneration that would later beset him did not prevent him from reading voraciously. Yet I knew I should not delay. I asked Father Ted if I might engage him in extensive interviews that summer. After some discussion we agreed to gather at a place that was deeply meaningful for him, the Notre Dame property at Land O'Lakes, Wisconsin. The interviews I completed in June of 1998 with Father Ted in that beautiful place form an essential basis of this book.

It is important for readers to appreciate that at the time these interviews occurred my relationship with Father Ted was a fraternal one with a good measure of trust between us. In preparation for my encounter with Father Hesburgh I reviewed the extensive oral history interviews that Richard (Dick) Conklin previously had completed with him (in 1982 and 1989) and that the writer Jerry Reedy then had shaped into *God, Country, Notre Dame*.[4] I conveyed to him that we must go beyond that information—to go deeper, if you will, and to pull back the curtain further on how he handled his multiple responsibilities. Perhaps Father Ted possessed some anxiety at having his story entrusted to a fellow religious who had emerged during the 1990s as a proponent of the vision for the renewal of Catholic higher education outlined by John Paul II in *Ex Corde Ecclesiae*, but he never expressed concerns. I, in turn, downplayed any disagreements over such matters and focused on getting him to open up more than he had in his interviews with Dick Conklin.

In preparation for my interviews with Father Ted I dedicated weeks to reading not only the Conklin interviews and *God, Country, Notre Dame*, but a significant amount of secondary literature and some of Father Hesburgh's writings. His numerous publications—books, articles, essays, forewords, prefaces, introductions, newspaper articles, and much more—are listed in Charlotte A. Ames's extraordinarily valuable and thorough *Theodore M. Hesburgh: A Bio-Bibliography* (1989), of which I made good use.

Much of the literature on Father Ted leaned in a hagiographical direction, but I determined that he deserved a serious and critical examination of his life. I did not want to add to the shelves of flattering (if rather superficial) summations of his life. I approached the interviews with a determination to move beyond the always positive persona of "Father Hesburgh" that he so effectively presented in *God, Country, Notre Dame*. Father Ted once explained to me that he kept discussion of divisions and disagreements and criticisms to a minimum in his memoir. The result was a charming work that neglected key conflicts and struggles. I concluded that a more authentic and honest account of his life must include them.

FATHER TED AND I flew up to Land O'Lakes in the university plane on a bright summer afternoon. He was most at peace when relaxing at that rustic and beautiful place. During his presidency he retreated there at the end of each academic year to unwind, enjoy the beauty of nature and the presence of God, and, so to speak, to recharge his batteries. While various faculty and students pursued their scientific endeavors on the part of the property occupied by the Environmental Research Center, Father Ted and I went to the Holy Cross retreat site. The wonderful caretakers, Gerry and Bonnie Schoesser, welcomed us. We were their only guests for the week from June 16 until our departure on June 22. We easily established a regimen for our work. Father Ted was very much a "night person," so we agreed to do the interviews in the late evening and to meet in the tiny cottage that was his special home when at Land O'Lakes and that, for reasons that escape me, was known to one and all as the "honeymoon cottage." We both slept late each day, although he slept much later than I did. I spent my day organizing my notes for the topics I planned to cover each evening and doing further background reading. He roused himself around noon and would read from a number of the books he lugged up with him. We came together for Mass in the small chapel on the property at 4:00 p.m. and then went up to Bonnie and Gerry's for a drink and early dinner. Then Gerry and Father Ted went off fishing for muskie, the still physically vigorous man's favorite freshwater fish for the thrilling fight it put up when hooked.

The fishermen returned somewhere around 8:30 p.m. each evening whereupon Father Ted and I connected. We made our way down a somewhat rickety path to the honeymoon cottage. After getting my small tape recorder set up we would get under way. Father Ted would immediately pour himself a generous drink. Dewar's White Label was the brand favored by the Holy Cross fishing contingent, and the liquor cabinet was well stocked with the distinctive half-gallon bottles. At times, he would light a fire to take the chill out of the still cool air. He encouraged me to also work with a full tumbler of Dewar's in hand, but I declined initially, and clarified that I needed to keep a clear head. After working for three hours or so I would agree to join him for a drink. Together we polished off a moderately impressive quantity of Scotch during six nights of interviews.

Each evening we met for roughly five hours. The questioning was never contentious. Reviewing the transcripts, I note that my approach at times bordered on ingratiating as I encouraged him to open up. I tried my best to impose a certain order to the topics covered, but one subject would lead to thoughts of a related matter, which would then spark memories of a different episode or person. At times there could be a backlog of four or five tangentially related matters awaiting attention. Father Ted's sheer sturdiness and abundant energy were on good display. The man never tired. On the first night of our meetings and well into our sixth one-hour tape I inquired of him if he could go for just another fifteen minutes to wrap up some subjects. He replied that he was fine, and then added with a flourish: "I'll wear you out. You won't wear me out. I'm only eighty-one years old."[5] I never asked again how he was holding up. There was no need to do so. No one could question his stamina.

Readers must appreciate that the interviews undertaken at Land O'Lakes, which undergird this biographical portrait, took place at a particular moment in Father Ted's life. Over a decade had passed since his retirement from the presidency of Notre Dame, yet he still brooded over the direction of the school. With a certain "lion in winter" temperament he was restless over some of the decisions his successors had made, and surprisingly critical of the failure of the Malloy administration to consult him more fully. Furthermore, Father Ted was more unfavorably disposed to certain other individuals than he normally allowed himself to be. Dare I say he let down his guard to some degree. The timing of the interviews proved critical. If I had interviewed Father Ted ten years previously, directly after he ended his presidency of Notre Dame, I suspect his responses would have been more guarded. If I had spoken to him ten years later, as he moved beyond "legendary" to "iconic" status at Notre Dame, his views would have been more limited even if more generous. As a historian I am glad that I spoke to him when I did.

I recognized the value of the interviews I conducted with Father Ted immediately. This was especially the case in that he had never kept a sustained personal diary. Of course he had kept extensive travel diaries over the years—reports on his far-reaching overseas trips that he shared regularly with university officers and trustees—but he had not aimed to make these personally revealing. The travel diaries that I have read are interesting, and a fascinating compilation of them might be undertaken in the future, but they are not central to Father Hesburgh's life and the essential themes of this work. Thus I knew that in the absence of a personal diary, his Land O'Lakes reflections had a real worth for those who want to move beyond hagiography to understand more fully Notre Dame's longest serving president.

Father Ted had some appreciation for the import of the interviews. He told me on our final night that "you are hearing some stories that no one has heard [or] very few people have heard."[6] Soon after our return to Notre Dame he wrote to me and told me that he had enjoyed our time together and noted that while "the written record is fairly complete . . . at least now you can read between the lines." He also made a further generous offer. "If my life goes on for a few more years," he suggested, "you should feel free to continue taping it at whatever time you deem necessary."[7] It was an offer I should have pursued more systematically, but I did not as I was pulled in other directions. Somewhat to my surprise I was asked to serve at Moreau Seminary and I moved there in 1998. Again I put my scholarly work on hold. Father Ted was perplexed by my agreeing to serve initially on the formation staff at the seminary and then as its rector. He believed that I should have maintained my full involvement in my university ministry, but in typically gracious fashion he wished me well.

Whatever the other responsibilities I assumed, I always made clear to him that I planned to write about him. He seemed glad of that. When Michael O'Brien's balanced and commendable biography of him appeared in 1998 under the title *Hesburgh: A Biography*, Father Ted welcomed the fact that his life had attracted the scholarly attention of a good historian, but he regretted that the book neither captured his full accomplishments nor drew much public attention to him through its publication. O'Brien's book is a fine study that I commend to serious readers, but in the words of Dick Conklin it is "workmanlike." The president emeritus felt he deserved better. After reading a generally favorable review of the O'Brien book by Sister Alice Gallin, O.S.U., which nonetheless suggested that it might stimulate further research, he dispatched a note to me on his "President Emeritus" stationery noting that "Alice Gallin says there is a lot of work yet to be done," while adding for good measure: "Thank God I don't have to do it."[8]

Our relations remained friendly, but we viewed some developments at Notre Dame differently. He still sent congratulatory notes regarding my publications. But our contacts diminished as our views of the direction of Notre Dame diverged over the next decade. He found particularly troubling my public criticisms of the honoring by Notre Dame of President Barack Obama in 2009. While I spoke at a protest rally on that commencement day, Father Ted basked in the glory of praise from the nation's first African American president. I kept our occasional conversations rather light and away from controversial topics when I saw him at Holy Cross House, the Holy Cross order's retirement home to which he moved in 2005. I had no desire to upset or to argue with him. In my last brief conversation with Father Ted he inquired after my mother and promised his prayers for her and for my father, who had died the previous year. Then with a wry smile on his aging face he added: "I'll also say a prayer for you, Bill." I laughed and thanked him and promised him my prayers. By this point Father Ted had given up inquiring about progress on my study of him. Ironically, by this point and at long last, I had something worth reporting to him.

I now found myself ready to devote more serious attention to my study of Father Hesburgh. I decided that I would not try to write the massive "life and times" biography that I had once contemplated. I began to conceive of a more accessible biographical portrait that drew on my interviews with Father Ted as well as additional research and analysis. I determined to use the material from my interviews with Father Ted to tell a compelling narrative of his leadership of Notre Dame and some of his most significant outside efforts.

In *American Priest* I first examine Father Ted's family background and upbringing and then his education and his formation in Holy Cross. These topics are covered in both *God, Country, Notre Dame* and in O'Brien's biography. I avoid lots of repetition from these works. Instead I aim to advance and deepen the Hesburgh story, and so to shed new light. The focus of the largest part of the book is on Hesburgh's meteoric rise to the presidency of Notre Dame and his notable leadership of the school from 1952 to 1987. Building Notre Dame into a "great Catholic university" was always his central mission, and the focus here is on how he operated and what priorities he established for Notre Dame, the struggles he faced in pursuing his ambitious goals, and the people he either enlisted or dismissed in order to reach them. Not surprisingly, Father Ted's attitude toward college athletics and his involvement with the fabled Notre Dame football program and the coaches who led it during the Hesburgh era also receive attention.

The second substantial section of the book moves beyond the campus to explore Father Hesburgh's numerous outside involvements. These involvements led some observers to deem him the most influential priest of the mid- to late twentieth century. This book concentrates on his contributions to presidential administrations from Eisenhower's through to that of Bill Clinton, along with an assessment of his relations with the men who led them. Father Ted loved the United States deeply, and he had reacted very positively to my proposed title for this book. He was a self-proclaimed American patriot who viewed the United States as the greatest nation on earth. He was deeply proud of his public service in the second half of the twentieth century, and I trust this book will provide readers with a richer sense of this service and the extent of his influence and real accomplishments.

Father Ted also was involved in a variety of contributions and controversies within the Catholic Church over a long period of great change and turmoil. He very much was a priest who favored the reforms of the Second Vatican Council and imbibed deeply of its spirit. He developed a close and fraternal friendship with Pope Paul VI in the years surrounding the Council and collaborated with him in a number of areas. Yet he proved very *American* in his service in the Church. He brought his American disposition and proclivities to how he served in the Church, and at times he found himself in tension with papal decisions and teaching on issues ranging from birth control to Catholic higher education.

A final chapter covers Father Hesburgh's years following his departure from the presidency of Notre Dame. They were not always easy years for him, as he struggled to define his new role at the university. Yet he remained very active for the next two decades and relished his election as chair of Harvard University's board of overseers, and his participation in the affairs of the nation's oldest and most prestigious university.

Father Ted received enormous recognition and many accolades during his life and benefited from very favorable attention from the local and national press. His appearance on the cover of *Time* magazine in 1962 and his being described as "the most influential figure in the reshaping of Catholic higher education in the United States" in the story that followed provides just a glimpse of the positive treatment he received over the decades. The pattern persisted, not surprisingly, in the obituaries and tributes that followed his death. Few reservations or criticisms were raised. This ability to attract such remarkably favorable treatment probably should be marked as a true Hesburghian accomplishment. At times it seems that Father Hesburgh cast a spell upon those with whom he associated in order to garner their praise, and that he carried an invisible shield to keep any criticism at bay. I do not claim to be fully immune to his "spell," but I have aimed to move beyond what might be termed the learned hagiography of his obituaries. Father Ted deserves a serious and critical assessment.

Soon after the completion of our interviews in June 1998, Father Ted wrote me of his gratitude for his years of service as a priest and with a flourish he explained: "Serendipity has been the order of the day and the Holy Spirit was at work mightily in most of the important matters."[9] I hope that providence more than mere luck has guided this book, and that the Holy Spirit is at work within it such that it does justice to a very American priest, Father Theodore Hesburgh of Notre Dame.

CHAPTER 1

PREPARATION OF
A PRIEST-PRESIDENT

FAMILY AND FAITH

THEODORE MARTIN HESBURGH GREW UP IN MODEST BUT COMfortable circumstances in Syracuse, New York, and enjoyed a typical boyhood for an American Catholic lad of his generation. The years spent in upstate New York from his birth on May 25, 1917, until his departure in the fall of 1934 to enter the formation program of the Holy Cross order laid firm foundations for him in terms of both his family and his faith. The roots planted remained strong and helped nourish him throughout his whole life.

In his family tree Father Hesburgh seemed most fascinated by his paternal grandfather, named Theodore, as was his father. The captivation with his grandfather grew out of the elder Hesburgh's career as a teacher and a journalist and from his having graduated from college. It gave him a sense that he had some "learning" in his background, and an ancestor who had a noted facility with languages. Perhaps there also was some special interest because of the tragedy that afflicted his grandfather and which so weighed upon his own father's childhood. Within a two-week period, Grandfather Hesburgh's wife and two of his three children died in sudden and heartbreaking circumstances. In a state of deep grief and distress, he took his remaining son, who was just three years of age, away from New York City and improbably traveled to Bellevue, Iowa, to join some distant relatives there on a large farm. He taught in a one-room school, and his son remained there with him for seven years before a concerned aunt brought the boy back to New York and raised him. After being rescued by his aunt,

Theodore Bernard Hesburgh worked hard and managed to graduate from high school, which was an accomplishment, given all he had been through. The serious and deeply religious young man then began his work with the Pittsburgh Plate Glass Company, where he remained throughout his working life. He eventually gained a promotion to serve as the manager of the company's warehouse in Syracuse, where he and his wife raised their family in a very Catholic household.

Father Ted knew that his father, Theodore Bernard, was a "highly principled man" who worked extremely hard for his family. He admired him for this, but he never managed to forge a close emotional bond with his father. He always seemed perplexed that his younger brother (Jimmy), seventeen years his junior, eventually managed to do so. Perhaps some rather simple factors offer part of the explanation. The young Ted never shared his dad's interest in either the Yankees or Notre Dame football. The boy proved a particularly inept athlete and never played on any serious teams after grade school. Rather he developed a lifelong love for hunting and fishing during these years, and his father worried about his interest in rifles. As he grew older he rarely engaged his father on political or other serious issues. The disaster of the Great Depression dominated American life during Father Ted's teenage years. The devastating collapse of the economy following the stock market crash in 1929 caused widespread unemployment and immense social hardship. It broke the presidency of Herbert Hoover and eventually brought Franklin Roosevelt and his New Deal to Washington, D.C. Given the immensity of human suffering that the Depression caused, it is surprising what little impact it had on the teenage Hesburgh's thinking. He was not shaped noticeably by this national trauma and the political turmoil it produced.

He certainly did not adopt his father's passionate political perspective. He remembered: "My dad was a very conservative guy. He hated Franklin Roosevelt. He hated the New Deal. Of course, it caused him a lot of trouble. He was managing a Pittsburgh Plate Glass Company warehouse in Syracuse, with thirty or forty people working for him. Every week, the New Deal would come in at the beginning of the week with a new list of regulations, which would drive him up the wall. . . . I can remember my father opening up those regulations every week and just about going through the roof because it just complicated his life to no end. So he hated Roosevelt. That's a strong word. I don't mean that technically, maybe 'abhorred' him would be a better word. But he was a Republican, and, if anything, more strongly when they were very conservative." The son would eventually head in another political direction, but during the 1930s he seemed rather apolitical. In this area, as in much else, he felt closer to his mother.

Ted Hesburgh always felt a deep connection to his lively and outgoing mother, Anne Marie (Murphy). She was quite short, just five foot one, but blessed with a beautiful voice and a gift for friendship. She too shared the deep religious faith of the tall (six foot two) young man whom she married and whom she complemented well. She devoted herself to forging a happy home for her husband and the children that soon came along—Mary, the oldest (in 1915), and then Ted (1917), followed by Elizabeth (1920), Anne (1925) and, after a substantial gap, James (Jimmy) in 1933. Her first son said, "I probably inherited a lot more of my mother's genes than my father's. That's probably not scientifically true, but the fact is that I was the only one in the family who had black hair like her and black eyes like her. My father was blue-eyed and so are my sisters. And, I think, temperamentally, I got more of the Irish of the Murphys than I did of the German-French of the Hesburghs. I just think that for some curious reason, I probably was closer to my mother than to my father." While not wanting to get too Freudian about it, he noted that he was the only one of the children that she nursed, and he speculated that this deepened his bond with his mother. And, no doubt, the young Hesburgh found much to love in his mother, especially her vivacious nature, the aura of joy that surrounded her, and her wonderful laugh. As he recalled: "Everybody loved mother. The nuns all liked her, the priests all liked her, the people in the neighborhood all liked her. We never had any problems with the neighbors—back and forth. She was just a very pleasant, likeable human being."[1] She also had lessons to teach her son about basic kindness and standing against prejudice such as in the way she favorably treated a young Jewish woman who was otherwise ostracized in their majority Protestant neighborhood of Strathmore.

Such lessons helped ensure that the young Ted grew up a well-mannered and generous boy. He gave his parents little trouble at any stage. He related well to his sisters, and his closest relationship was with his older sister, Mary. He built model airplanes, which presaged his adult interest in flight. In 1927 on a visit to New York he caught a glimpse of Charles Lindbergh as the young pilot who had flown his single-engine *Spirit of St. Louis* nonstop from New York to Paris and returned back to receive a hero's reception in a tickertape parade up Broadway. Seeing the adulation for Lindbergh the ten-year-old boy could have been easily forgiven if he entertained thoughts of emulating his feats. But he already had determined that he was called not to be a daring pilot but rather a Catholic priest.

Hesburgh grew up in Strathmore, a new residential subdivision in the southwest of Syracuse, and home to middle- and upper-middle-class families. The marketing materials for the new development advertised that it contained "no smoke, no dirt, no fogs, no two-family or apartment houses, no business places of any kind, nothing but homes." While their immediate neighborhood was not a Catholic enclave, the Hesburghs were part of a vibrant Catholic subculture, rather typical of the period, that centered on Most Holy Rosary Parish and School. The young Ted spent twelve years there and benefited from the devoted labors of the Immaculate Heart of Mary (IHM) nuns who taught him. The sisters helped create a veritable culture of vocations, which led to a sizable number of their graduates studying for the priesthood or becoming religious sisters. Perhaps one of the IHM sisters first planted the idea of the priesthood, although Father Ted never identified any individual as decisive. He just knew from an early age, as a surprising number of future priests do, that he was called to serve God at the altar.

When Hesburgh was in the eighth grade and assisting in his parish as an altar boy, four priests of the Congregation of Holy Cross came to preach a mission at Most Holy Rosary. Hesburgh's words can give details of how their visit influenced him: "It was a very popular mission. When one priest was out there giving the parishioners hell and damnation, as they always did in those missions, one of them stayed with us [altar boys] in the sacristy and would regale us with stories about Notre Dame, Deer Park [the Holy Cross retreat property in western Maryland], and the camps they had and all of the stuff that went on in the seminary." Fr. Tom Duffy impressed the young Hesburgh, who revealed his hopes to serve as a priest someday to the Holy Cross mission giver. Duffy took it upon himself to visit the Hesburgh household to pursue the matter further. Thereupon occurred a notable exchange that Father Ted loved to retell: "So he went out to visit my mother at the house. He said to her, 'Ted tells me he thinks of being a priest. Why don't you send him out to Holy Cross Seminary at Notre Dame? He could go to high school and the seminary.' She said, 'A young boy's place in his teenage days is home with his family.' He said, 'Yes, but if he stays here, he may lose his vocation.' And my mother, being a tough Irish gal, said, 'If he grows up in a Catholic family, all practicing Catholics and good with the sacraments, and he's going to Mass every day at school, and he is going to a Catholic high school, if he loses his vocation, let me tell you something about it: he doesn't have one.' And that was the end of that argument."[2] Father Hesburgh's mother insisted he complete high school in Syracuse, where he performed well.

The retort of Mrs. Hesburgh proved only a temporary deterrent to Father Duffy, who stayed in touch with Ted Hesburgh as he navigated his way through his high school years. He wrote two or three letters a year to keep alive the possibility of joining Holy Cross before the young man, whom he sensed to be a fine prospect for his order. His persistence eventually paid off because the future Father Ted decided to enter the seminary at the end of his senior year. The graduating senior knew that he was well prepared by his high school education to begin his undergraduate studies. Well over sixty years later he recited with pride the course of studies he had completed: "Four years of Latin, three years of French, algebra/geometry, chemistry (I skipped physics because I wanted to get a third year of French, which was probably a good bet, although I got to learn a lot of physics later), art two years, religion four years, history three years, English four years, a lot of writing." Only art caused him difficulties, and he readily conceded that his sister Mary got the measure of artistic talent that had thoroughly escaped him. He performed strongly in Latin and studied Virgil's *Aeneid*, Cicero's letters and speeches, and Julius Caesar's *De Bello Gallico* (The Gallic War), whose opening words, *"Gallia est omnis divisa in partes tres"* ("All Gaul is divided into three parts"), he relished reciting. He graduated third in his class.

His talent for languages, similar to his grandfather's, and his love for words, shared with his father, were evident at this point and always remained with him. He also possessed a genuine intellectual curiosity. As a youngster he read the *Encyclopedia Britannica* volumes his parents had purchased for their home and developed an interest in many areas. This too stayed with him, and his interests would always be wide-ranging even if his knowledge might be rather modest in a given area. He fancied himself a serious reader, preferring books with a strong moral message or that included characters worthy of emulation. Yet no particular author or body of literature grabbed him deeply and shaped his intellectual outlook at this point. Rather he possessed a breezy confidence that he could learn well, and even master, whatever came before him. He also developed his practical skills and honed his ability at using the second-hand typewriter purchased originally for Mary. By his junior year of high school he "could easily bang out an essay or a story." He was to bang out many such essays in future years.

Success in his studies, his emergence as a popular and very handsome young man, and the affirmation of his teachers all contributed something to the development of a remarkably self-assured person as he completed his final years of high school. He was neither obviously cocky nor arrogant, but his confidence combined with his earnestness to produce a readiness to proffer advice to others. In his senior year, Hesburgh helped edit *The Rosarian*, his school's newspaper. "In one remarkable article," Michael O'Brien noted in his biography of Father Hesburgh, "he brashly challenged his fellow students to elevate the quality of their reading." He counseled against the "dime novel" and instead recommended that they "read books 'that will elevate your ideas, enlarge your vocabulary, and widen your perspective.'" As O'Brien's fine account makes clear, while the student editor's intentions were undoubtedly noble, he verged toward pretentious self-importance as he challenged his classmates to avoid wasting their time on frivolous reading while the "world of adventure, history, romance and culture beckons."[3] We don't know if any of his fellow students responded positively to these Hesburghian recommendations. What we do know is that subsequently he never lost his confidence that he could address a situation judiciously and then forge positive recommendations for the betterment of others.

The confident high school senior also proved to be a young man ready and willing to take on leading roles. It was no surprise when he was cast as Christ in his school's Passion play during his final year at Most Holy Rosary. It was a demanding part in a large production. The one-time lead actor remembered: "You had to put on a moustache, and I remember putting a damn beard on and off every night with stickem. We had these crazy robes we had to wear, but the thing that was incredible was I practically had to memorize the life of Christ right out of the Bible. I went on for about two or three hours. The big pitch that everybody remembered was when I was hanging on the cross—they got a life-sized cross and they still have it there behind the altar—and I had to cry out, 'My God, my God, why have you forsaken me?' You know the whole house kind of fell through the floor. But again, it was a dramatic moment. Even to this day when I read the Passion that stands out for me, that moment." Father Ted would eventually come to stand *in persona Christi* in a real enactment of Christ's sacrifice on the cross, but his high school performance pointed to a strong disposition that never left him: to play the leading role. It would always be more difficult for him when he was cast in a minor part.

The young man's desire to play on a large stage influenced where he chose to pursue his seminary studies with Holy Cross. The order was in the process of establishing a new eastern province in the New England/New York region and had already established a formation site in North Dartmouth, Massachusetts. The Holy Cross priest recruiter offered the young man a choice between the fledgling but closer North Dartmouth and the well-established Notre Dame. This "was no contest." For Hesburgh, "Notre Dame was *the* quintessential Catholic institution in the country." Its reputation for Catholic values, athletic prowess, and the dedicated loyalty of its alumni gave the place an irresistible appeal for him. Additionally, some older boys from the parish already had entered Holy Cross at Notre Dame, and he wanted to follow along the trail they were blazing. And while he was no great sports fan, he knew that "Notre Dame was just *the* place."[4]

Although he knew only a little about Notre Dame, he knew even less about the order that ran it. He eventually came to know that the Congregation of Holy Cross was founded in 1837 by Rev. Basil Anthony Mary Moreau in the district of Sainte-Croix in Le Mans, France. In 1841 Moreau dispatched Fr. Edward Sorin, ordained just a few years before, to assist in the diocese of Vincennes in far-off Indiana in the United States. On November 26, 1842, Sorin and his brother companions arrived at a place near the tiny community of South Bend, and he christened it Notre Dame du Lac. There the ambitious young priest and his confreres began the work of transforming a small log chapel-cabin combination into a college. Sorin dreamed big from the outset. Notre Dame's founder aimed to establish what he promised Father Moreau would be "one of the most powerful means for good in this country."[5] By the early 1930s at least some progress had been made toward reaching this lofty goal. Certainly Notre Dame had developed into an institution that held a special place in the American Catholic imagination, especially as a result of the success of Knute Rockne's football teams and the unalloyed religiosity of the campus. It clearly had become the most important apostolic site for the Holy Cross order, a veritable base for the launching of other missionary endeavors.

The young Ted Hesburgh would soon learn this and much more upon his arrival on campus and his entry into the formation program of Holy Cross. First, of course, he had to bid farewell to his family and community. His high school classmates and teachers wished him well. This was a blessed time when friends rejoiced when one of their number entered the seminary. His family too gave him their full support even though they knew that they would see much less of him because of the rather cloistered approach to training religious priests that prevailed during that time. Pride in having a priest in their family far outweighed the sadness of the impending separation. Yet whatever the physical distances that thereafter would divide Father Ted from his family, their bonds always remained very strong. The deep affection he had for his sisters and his baby brother would extend eventually to their families after they married and had children. Following his ordination he would be the one who baptized his nephews and nieces as they arrived, took a special interest in their spiritual lives, and as the years passed presided at their weddings. Of course, he also anointed and said the funeral Masses for both his father and his mother, the ones who had done so much to give him a firm foundation in the faith.

FORMATION

On an early September day in 1934, Mr. and Mrs. Theodore Hesburgh brought their son Ted to Notre Dame so that he might enter the congregation's seminary and begin his formal studies for the Catholic priesthood in the Congregation of Holy Cross. Ted enjoyed the trip to the Midwest with his parents and his treasured sister, Mary, although it had not been easy to bid farewell to his other sisters and his baby brother. They traveled from Syracuse in a borrowed car and arrived safely on the expansive Notre Dame campus where the seminary was located. The young man felt a true thrill as he rode down Notre Dame Avenue and looked up to see the gleaming Golden Dome. The Main Building and Sacred Heart Church lay at the heart of the campus, which had undergone dramatic expansion in the previous fifteen years. New academic buildings such as the Lemonnier Library and impressive engineering and commerce buildings were matched by a series of attractive residence halls—Howard, Morrissey, Lyons, Dillon, and Alumni, among them. The young men who filled those halls took their meals in the magnificent Gothic South Dining Hall. The teenager from Syracuse could not help but be impressed at the spacious quads and the classic architecture. And adding to the campus vista, on its edge was the famous football stadium—the "House that Rockne Built"—which had first swung its gates open in 1930 to welcome the numerous fans of the Fighting Irish. Hesburgh had arrived at the distinctive place that would claim so much of his life from that point forward.

Unfortunately, the Hesburghs reached their destination on a Saturday only to be told that registration began on Monday and they must return then. After getting accommodation in an inexpensive hotel, the family stayed around South Bend over the weekend. They returned on Monday morning to deliver their son. The seminary registration proceeded quickly, and soon the time came for the young man to say good-bye to his parents and sister, who needed to depart promptly to make their return to Syracuse. They were not parting for a mere semester or even for an academic year. Given the rigorous approach to seminary formation pursued then, the young Hesburgh expected it would be some years before he saw his family again. His faith-filled parents believed that they had brought him to the place where he could pursue his God-given vocation. Handshakes and hugs were exchanged, and soon the Hesburghs climbed into their vehicle and drove away. We can assume that Mrs. Hesburgh shed some tears like so many mothers, before and since, who have left their sons at Notre Dame for the first time. As for her son, he recalled sixty years later: "Right there on that old porch, I watched that car go down the drive. It wasn't much fun."[6] He suffered from homesickness during his initial months, but he always used the difficult experience as a reference point when he later counseled students who were missing their homes and families. He knew what missing one's family meant.

The Holy Cross seminary program of the day was located at Notre Dame but was not fully part of the university. Set apart from the main campus on a hill on the north side of St. Mary's Lake, the seminary looked back toward the spire of Sacred Heart Church and the statue of Mary atop the Dome. It operated largely as an independent program, separated from the main thrust of campus life, so that the seminarians could follow their own strict regimen. Nonetheless, the college-level seminarians formally registered as undergraduates at Notre Dame, and so began Hesburgh's direct involvement at the university. The school in which young Holy Cross religious like Hesburgh began their studies in the fall of 1934 had developed quite a reputation over the past decade and a half. Indeed the 1920s proved a crucial decade for Notre Dame. Under the brief but brilliant leadership of Fr. James A. Burns (1919–1922), measures were initiated that finally transformed Notre Dame into a true institution of higher education.

Whatever the long-term significance of Father Burns's educational initiatives, they were completely overshadowed by Notre Dame's extraordinary football success under the legendary coach Knute Rockne. In this sports-crazed era the renowned exploits of his teams kept Notre Dame in the headlines. Father Ted's dad had followed Notre Dame's triumphs closely as did a multitude of mainly Catholic supporters across the country. Most of the young men who entered Holy Cross Seminary in 1934 would have been able to recount key episodes from the recent football past. They likely would even have been able to recite Grantland Rice's lead to his report on the 1924 Notre Dame–Army game, which began: "Outlined against a blue-gray October sky, the Four Horsemen rode again. In dramatic lore they are known as Famine, Pestilence, Destruction and Death. They are only aliases. Their real names are Stuhldreher, Miller, Crowley and Layden."[7] Even a rather ambivalent football fan like the young Ted Hesburgh would have known Notre Dame lore well enough to narrate the culmination of Knute Rockne's halftime talk to his team in the bruising 1928 encounter with Army at Yankee Stadium when he famously relayed George Gipp's request to "win just one for the Gipper."[8]

The revenue generated by football triumphs added to the general prosperity of Notre Dame during the 1920s to allow for a significant expansion of its physical plant. The decade saw the construction of some of the campus's most beautiful buildings.[9] Even the onset of the Depression failed to halt the campus expansion as the university steered its way forward in more challenging times. Enrollment declined a little, but President Charles O'Donnell, a poet and World War I chaplain, managed to keep the institution operating in a fairly normal manner, and even welcomed to campus such notable literary figures as William Butler Yeats and G. K. Chesterton.

During the twenties Knute Rockne unquestionably was the dominant figure on the campus, far outshining the various Holy Cross priest-presidents. Rockne's stirring championship seasons in 1929 and 1930 had buoyed campus spirits and made him known throughout the nation. The great coach's death in a plane crash in March of 1931 caused enormous grief both on campus and beyond. Sadly, his successors found it hard to replicate his coaching feats. As football fortunes declined, the university president emerged again as the figure who attracted the most attention, at least on campus. This arrangement prevailed during the presidency of Fr. John O'Hara, and it would be Hesburgh's preference during his own, later leadership of the university. Father O'Donnell died right at the end of the 1933–1934 academic year, and O'Hara stepped smoothly into the role. He was the president during Hesburgh's initial involvement at Notre Dame, and the seminarian-student forged his initial impressions—both positive and negative—of the presidential role in light of him. O'Hara was already well known on campus for his service as prefect of religion, in which role he put an emphasis on frequent attendance at Mass and reception of communion. His preparation of the daily *Religious Bulletin* had earned him the nickname of "the Pope" among the students whose admiration he attained. As president he proved deft at attracting notable scholars and speakers to campus, such as the leading Catholic philosophers Jacques Maritain and Étienne Gilson. O'Hara also presided over the first visit to Notre Dame of a sitting president when Franklin Roosevelt visited the campus in December of 1935 to participate in a special convocation honoring the establishment of the new Commonwealth of the Philippines. In the fall of 1936 he also hosted a future pope, Cardinal Eugenio Pacelli, who was then serving as Vatican secretary of state.

One suspects that such accomplishments gained some favorable response from Hesburgh at the time, but his later recollection of O'Hara and the university he led leaned in a quite negative direction. He admitted that O'Hara was "quite a charismatic figure" who held the regard of the students, but in retrospect Father Hesburgh criticized the emphasis on the reception of communion and O'Hara's seeming obsession with maintaining accurate counts of participation in the sacraments. From his vantage point decades afterward he deemed it rather spiritually superficial. He had little direct contact with John O'Hara in the 1930s, yet he rather harshly remembered him as "an archconservative" who led a "middle-class, middle-west, ultraconservative school."[10]

Hesburgh spent only two years as a student at the university before he received his obedience (assignment) to continue his studies in Rome, but these two years were divided by his novitiate year, which involved no formal study but demands of a quite different sort. At Holy Cross's St. Joseph Novitiate near Rolling Prairie, a small town located about twenty-five miles west of Notre Dame, the novices focused less on studies than on a deeper induction into their religious order and a sharp discernment of their call to profess vows in it. Although Father Ted later (and laughably) described the place as the Holy Cross "boot camp (not unlike the marines' Parris Island, perhaps) complete with rigorous physical training and a hard-nosed drill instructor," it did require the novices to engage in some of the tough labor involved in running a farm. The young novice from Syracuse got a good taste of everything from clearing brush and sawing wood to picking lice out of sheep and butchering pigs. Hesburgh threw himself into the work and forever after relished talking about it.[11] He found the strictures on silence during the novitiate year more difficult. His was hardly a contemplative nature. Nonetheless, Hesburgh satisfied the careful scrutiny of his novice master Fr. Kerndt Healy, who approved him to profess the initial vows of poverty, celibacy, and obedience at the end of the required canonical year. Now wearing the black serge habit of his order the newly professed Ted Hesburgh returned to Notre Dame to resume his sophomore-year studies in the fall of 1936.

Upon returning to campus the newly professed seminarians moved to Moreau Seminary (now the Sacred Heart Parish Center) on the shores of St. Joseph's Lake. Here they normally resided for three additional years in order to complete their bachelor's degree with a major in philosophy. After that lay the prospect of their formal theology studies at Holy Cross College (now O'Boyle Hall at Catholic University of America) in Washington, D.C. The essential elements of the year remained prayer and study as the young men worked to build the spiritual and intellectual foundations to sustain their ministry as priests. There were limited opportunities for developing and honing one's pastoral skills, although Hesburgh was part of the group of seminarians who in a celebrated episode planted the seeds for Little Flower parish on the east side of the university. Two seminarians, when searching for the Moreau Seminary horse that had run away, discovered a small settlement of nominal Catholics living in appalling poverty in an area known as Dog Patch. They determined to do something for these people. They provided some food and material aid, and also worked on weekends to build a makeshift chapel for Mass and for religious instruction. Hesburgh and a fellow seminarian named Patrick Peyton, who would go on to found the Family Rosary Crusade, were among those who contributed. Hesburgh enjoyed rolling up his sleeves and addressing directly the spiritual and practical needs of others.

Those familiar with seminary life in this era know that the day was structured by a regular schedule not subject to individual preference or alteration. One conformed to this set regimen. Hesburgh considered the frequent and rather lockstep moves from one activity to the next something of a trial. He found himself critical of the daily program provided for him with set times for ablutions, meditation, Mass and communal prayer, meals, classes, obediences, recreation, choir practice for Gregorian chant, study hall, and even scheduled "smoke breaks." He grew to truly dislike his obedience of waiting on tables in the seminary dining room and washing the dishes for a community of a hundred or so. Needless to say, he refrained from giving voice to these sentiments. To have done so risked a reprimand or even dismissal, and Hesburgh wanted neither. Instead he obeyed the seminary rule to the letter.

Hesburgh also silently criticized the academic offerings provided at Moreau Seminary. He judged most of his courses to be rather mediocre, although he supplemented them with his own serious reading, continuing a practice he had taken up during his time at Rolling Prairie. Few professors impressed him; however, he counted it an "amazing break" to have Fr. Leo Ward teach a yearlong course on the philosophy of literature that was built around George Shuster's well-known work *The Catholic Spirit in Modern English Literature*. This was Hesburgh's first if indirect association with Shuster, although their paths would cross again some decades later. He loved the course and Leo Ward's instruction. Father Ward, known as "L" for "Literature" to distinguish him from a philosopher-priest of the same name who was known as "R" for Rational, gave his students a rich Catholic outlook on literature in a manner resembling that pursued later by the legendary English professor Frank O'Malley. He also gave Ted Hesburgh a more specific lesson. The budding scholar had a love for florid language. He recalled that "if I could use a big, complicated, long word, I would use that rather than a simple word." It had worked well for him in the past, but it didn't pass muster with Leo Ward. The priest-teacher commented on the front page of Hesburgh's final paper in the course: "If you don't learn to simplify your style with simple words, you will wind up being a pompous ass."[12] This hit the confident sophomore "right between the eyes" and was a lasting lesson that he judged to be among "the best advice" he ever got. As it turned out, he did not get to apply this advice at Notre Dame. His superiors assigned him to continue his studies in the Eternal City.

In Father Ted's retelling, his assignment to study in Rome came as a real shock, but it was the normal practice of Holy Cross to send some of its more able students to study at the Gregorian University in Rome, and it can't have been a complete surprise to him, given his fine abilities as a student. He and his classmate Tom McDonagh joined other seminarians from the Indiana Province who already had been assigned there in previous years. The Rome-bound seminarians were told that they were both to study for double doctorates, in philosophy and theology, which might take them eight years.

After a hurried home visit to say farewell to his family, Hesburgh departed the United States on the SS *Champlain* on September 25, 1937. It was the first of his many journeys across the Atlantic Ocean. The French ship took him, McDonagh, and some additional seminarians from the nascent Eastern Province of Holy Cross to Le Havre, where a young priest named Louis Putz, then assigned to the French province, met them. He then served as tour guide for the small Holy Cross group as they took in the sights of Paris—Notre-Dame Cathedral and Sainte-Chapelle among them. Then they traveled on to Le Mans, where Basil Moreau had founded their religious order. Hesburgh found little of appeal in Le Mans. After a few days he was very glad to leave and to return to Paris. From there they took the train to Rome. He rarely returned to Le Mans thereafter, and he always identified strongly with Edward Sorin rather than Basil Moreau.

On arrival in Rome the small American contingent made their way to the Holy Cross house of studies on Via dei Cappuccini, a two-block street that ran down from the Capuchin Church close to the city center. Located between Via Veneto and Via Sistina it was but a block from the bustling Piazza Barberini and also a very easy walk to the Jesuit-run Gregorian University, where the seminarians took their classes. Italy and its capital languished under the one-party dictatorial rule of Benito Mussolini's Fascists, but national politics intruded little into the interior life of the house of studies where Fr. Georges Sauvage, a member of the French province, served as religious superior. Although the majority of residents were Americans, Father Sauvage enforced French as the house language, and he maintained a rather spartan approach to community life, although with a notable exception. He required that his new charges take some wine with their meals, even though a number of them like Ted Hesburgh had taken the pledge not to drink any alcohol until they turned twenty-one. Sauvage insisted on this against any and all protestations, but he also lectured his new charges that they should drink in moderation. Drinking to get drunk would not be tolerated. It proved a lasting lesson for Hesburgh, who held his liquor well, for the most part.

Hesburgh's experience in Rome proved formative. He took his classes in Latin at the Gregorian University and spoke French in his local community. With the help of his classmate George Di Prizio he began speaking Italian every day and gained some fluency in the language. During the summers the Holy Cross seminarians took a retreat in Tyrol, and there he learned some German. So this young seminarian acquired facility in a number of the languages that he would utilize effectively in the future. The years in Rome also were beneficial for him on an intellectual level. He read widely and also gained what the insightful Notre Dame scholar

Thomas Stritch called "a cosmopolitan polish" that would serve him well in his various international collaborations as president of Notre Dame.[13] He came to know the city well and appreciated it as the true geographic center of the Catholic Church. Living in the city during the election of Cardinal Eugenio Pacelli and being present in St. Peter's Square for the new pope's first blessing left a real imprint on him. He wrote a gushing article—his very first publication as a Holy Cross religious—in *Ave Maria* magazine on the memorable event.[14] Seeds were planted for his desire to walk the corridors of the Vatican and to engage Pius XII and his successors.

Hesburgh was a diligent student and attended all of his classes even though he found the experience less than exhilarating. Rote learning was not to his taste. Yet he came to appreciate the solid grounding he received in Scholastic philosophy and in orthodox theology. It provided him an intellectual grounding that steadied him whatever the buffeting theological winds that blew in future days. It also provided him with some limited contact with seminarians from literally all over the world and an enriched sense of the universal nature of the Church.

In addition, Hesburgh's spiritual and personal commitment in Holy Cross deepened during these years. He had the good fortune to have as his spiritual director a relatively young priest named Father Edward Heston who worked in the general administration of the order. Heston had studied in Rome from 1928 to 1936 and earned doctoral degrees in philosophy and theology just as Hesburgh intended to do. He would later serve as the English language press officer during Vatican II, and Pope Paul VI named him an archbishop in 1972. He was a zealous spiritual guide and a compassionate counselor and confessor, and under his guidance Hesburgh moved to profess final vows in Holy Cross after completing three years in temporary vows. He never had doubts about his decision beforehand and, by his own account, none afterward, whatever his battles within the order.

In August of 1939 Tom McDonagh and Ted Hesburgh made their final commitment in Holy Cross. Fr. George Sauvage, their religious superior, received their vows in the Hermitage of Camaldoli, established by St. Romuald in 1012 and located on a mountain in the Tuscan Apennines well above the Camaldolese monastery. It was a simple ceremony within the context of Mass and with only other Holy Cross religious present. Unlike McDonagh, Hesburgh did not take the so-called fourth vow, which signaled one's readiness to be assigned to the foreign missions. He had given it some consideration, and according to his own account brought the matter to Sauvage: "I went in to make my petition and I said, 'I'd like to take the fourth vow.' He said, 'You really want to go to the missions?' All we had then was Bangladesh or as it was then, East Bengal. Sauvage questioned me, 'You really want to go to the missions in East Bengal?' He'd gone there and gotten malaria; he wasn't all that hot about it. And I said, 'Well, to be perfectly honest, I wouldn't look forward to being assigned, but if I were assigned then I'd go.' He said, 'No fourth vow.' That was it. A very short conversation. And he was right, because I was doing it as a kind of extra generosity but I didn't really want to go and spend my life there."[15] So it was that Georges Sauvage abruptly helped Ted Hesburgh discern that he did not have an overseas missionary's vocation. He felt called to labor primarily in the Lord's American vineyard. World events forced his return to that domain sooner than he had expected.

Adolf Hitler's invasion of Poland on September 1, 1939, sparked the outbreak of World War II, although Mussolini's Italy stayed out of the conflict initially. The atmosphere was tense as the European continent began its descent into the terrible conflict that eventually consumed millions of lives, but Ted Hesburgh and his fellow seminarians stayed on in Rome and completed a further year of studies. By the spring of 1940, the Nazi blitzkrieg turned westward and Hitler's forces invaded the Low Countries as they struck toward France. Soon thereafter Mussolini brought Italy into the war on Hitler's side. Before he did so, American consular officials in Rome urgently advised U.S. citizens to depart immediately and to return to the safety of the United States. Hesburgh and his American confreres left Genoa on board the USS *Manhattan* on June 1, 1940. It would be well over a decade before he returned to Italy.

After a wonderful reunion with his family, Hesburgh took up his new assignment to continue his studies at Holy Cross College near Catholic University (CUA) in Washington, D.C. Although virtually on the CUA campus, Holy Cross College was a freestanding seminary staffed by Holy Cross religious. Here the newcomer from Rome reconnected with the larger cohort of men in formation engaged in the theology studies preparing them for ordination to the priesthood. He completed his academic work well and confirmed anew that he had the aptitude to pursue doctoral studies. He also made new friends among his fellow seminarians, including a colorful character named Charlie Sheedy. "We hit it off right away," Father Ted recalled.[16] They began a collaboration there that would last for the next thirty years. Hesburgh appreciated Sheedy's intellect and his creativity. They encouraged each other in various pastoral efforts including, in Hesburgh's case, starting a Newman Club at Howard University, where he had his first sustained contact with African American students and began learning something of the difficulties they confronted.

Hesburgh, Sheedy, and the other seminarians spent much of their summers at a Holy Cross property at Deep Creek Lake in western Maryland to get away from the humidity and heat of Washington. There Sheedy and Hesburgh found time to flex their apostolic muscles further by working to assist young men in a Civilian Conservation Corps camp located in nearby Swallow Falls. Their collaboration developed further after the United States entered into World War II, when they worked on booklets directed at American servicemen that addressed various topics on Christian living. These were widely circulated under the auspices of the National Council of Catholic Men, although Hesburgh did most of this work after his ordination on June 24, 1943.

On the Feast of the Nativity of John the Baptist that year, John Francis Noll, the bishop of Fort Wayne from 1925 until 1956 and the well-known founder of *Our Sunday Visitor* newspaper, ordained fourteen Holy Cross religious in Sacred Heart Church at Notre Dame. The feast celebrates the birth of John the Baptist, the prophet who foretold the coming of the Messiah in the person of Jesus. The young men who were ordained did not concentrate on the last and greatest of the prophets, however, but rather on the Messiah he proclaimed. The *ordinandi* knew that they would undergo a profound ontological change. After Bishop Noll laid his hands upon them each became an *alter Christus* (another Christ), consecrated to be Christ and to do what Christ did, especially in their celebration of the sacraments—and most importantly when celebrating the holy sacrifice of the Mass. Ted Hesburgh drank deeply of the well of this priestly understanding and spirituality. He would witness major changes in the Church and in the liturgy during his life, but the essential core of the priesthood remained fixed for him. Although decades later, in the aftermath of Vatican II, some tried to reduce the priest's role to an insipid "leader of the assembly" or a mere "gatherer of the community," Hesburgh never wavered in his understanding. When speaking to a seminary audience in the fortieth year of his priesthood, he explained "the priestly role as one of mediation. The priest stands between God and humankind and brings the blessings and graces of God to humans while also, in the other direction, bringing their hopes and needs and desires to God."[17]

Father Ted forever counted his ordination day as his happiest. It was also a day that in his retelling cemented his commitments. He explained later that as he lay facedown in the sanctuary of Notre Dame's beautiful Gothic church he was filled with a sense that the Holy Spirit called him to serve not just Catholics but all people. Further, as he put it in his memoir, after the ordination he paused "at the sculptured east side door of Sacred Heart, a memorial to the Notre Dame men who had given their lives in World War I, [and] . . . read the dedication above the door: GOD, COUNTRY, NOTRE DAME." Tellingly and accurately he continued: "I would dedicate my life to that trinity too."[18] He never experienced a day when he regretted being a priest, and he never tried to hide or disguise his special calling.

The ordination of Father Hesburgh and his classmates took place in the midst of World War II and on a campus transformed by war. Father O'Hara had left Notre Dame in 1940 at the request of then archbishop Francis Spellman of New York to take on the role of auxiliary bishop of the U.S. Military Ordinariate. Fr. J. Hugh O'Donnell succeeded him, and following the Japanese attack on Pearl Harbor on December 7, 1941, he managed to keep Notre Dame afloat by allowing the U.S. Navy to train deck officers and midshipmen on campus. Only a few regular degree students remained as most Notre Dame men marched off to fight for their country. With the nation at war the guest list was limited at the 1943 ordinations, but Hesburgh's parents, his sisters, and his now ten-year-old brother were able to attend. Of course he joyfully extended his first priestly blessings to them. And he traveled back to Syracuse with them to celebrate the traditional first Mass in the parish where his faith had been nourished. It was in Syracuse that he made a decision that he lived out with extraordinary fidelity. During his short visit home he went to the parish every morning to say Mass and he thereupon "decided I was going to say Mass every day of my life if it was humanly possible."[19] He kept this pledge even up to the day of his death.

After his brief visit to Syracuse it was back to Washington, D.C., where the newly ordained priest had been instructed to obtain a doctorate in theology at the Catholic University of America. He applied himself diligently to his scholarly labors, but this new priest was not one to lock himself away in his study. His activist temperament and desire to serve others drew him often away from his doctoral research and out into a wide variety of pastoral activities. Hesburgh savored the range of experience in priestly ministry that he gained in wartime Washington. He pushed himself tirelessly, perhaps to compensate for not serving as a military chaplain in one of the dangerous war theaters, unlike almost thirty of his fellow Holy Cross priests.

In the midst of his frenetic pastoral ministry Hesburgh completed his graduate course work and simultaneously worked on his dissertation. He desperately wanted to be a Navy chaplain assigned to an aircraft carrier in the Pacific theater, so he pushed himself to complete the three-year program in just two years. Somehow or other he completed this seemingly superhuman feat. He gained the encouragement and support of his dissertation director, the Paulist priest Eugene Burke, who helped him navigate his way around a largely conservative theology faculty led by the formidable Fr. (later Monsignor) Joseph Fenton. Hesburgh wrote on Catholic Action, the lay activist movement identified with Fr. (later Cardinal) Joseph Cardijn of Belgium, who had founded the Young Christian Workers organization in the 1920s and guided its growth through the 1930s. He wanted to demonstrate how lay activity in the world emerged from the Church's sacramental life. His dissertation title, "The Relation of the Sacramental Characters of Baptism and Confirmation to the Lay Apostolate," pointed to his central arguments. In Hesburgh's view baptism and confirmation prepared the layman (as he expressed it then) for his essential work in the world. Baptism incorporated him "into the Body of Christ and placed [him] under the life-giving influence of Christ's Headship." Confirmation deepened further this preparation because "the confirmed Christian is given a more perfect configuration to Christ the Priest, and a consequent full participation in his priestly work."[20]

The dissertation clearly placed Hesburgh among those promoting an enhanced role for the laity. After its approval the young Holy Cross priest was granted his Doctorate in Sacred Theology (STD) on May 23, 1945. Soon thereafter Ave Maria Press at Notre Dame published a thousand copies of the work under the title *The Theology of Catholic Action*. It proved to be his most sustained theological work. Most of his subsequent publications, at least prior to his retirement, were either textbooks or collections of talks and essays. This initial work had a real impact on him, nonetheless. He would later be a supporter of efforts to spread Cardijn's movement and methods to Notre Dame and beyond. And he saw the Second Vatican Council's teaching on the role of the laity in such documents as *Gaudium et Spes* (Joy and Hope)—the Pastoral Constitution on the Church in the Modern World—as fulfilling the thesis he had put forth almost two decades before. He would explain and justify major decisions at Notre Dame in the 1960s as designed to enhance the role of the laity. For him these decisions represented a culmination of what he had proposed in his doctoral work two decades before.

In the early summer of 1945, after receiving his STD degree, Hesburgh focused his immediate attention less on the role of the laity than on his own role. Demonstrating his notable gifts for making contacts with influential individuals, the eager priest used his cousin Joe Farrell, a captain in the Navy, to make a connection with the chief of chaplains, who promised to admit him to an accelerated program for chaplains and then get him out to the Pacific. The war in Europe had ended with Germany's defeat on May 7, 1945, and now all the power of the American armed forces was being directed to the brutal conflict against Japan. Hesburgh wanted to be part of it and had earlier made his desire known to his provincial, Fr. Thomas Steiner, who had insisted that he first complete his degree. Again Hesburgh wrote hopefully to him explaining that "I have done my part. I've got my degree."[21] Once more Father Steiner turned him down. He ordered him instead to return to Notre Dame while noting that the university held more naval personnel than any ship in the Pacific. Notre Dame badly needed faculty to teach the required courses in religion. So the young priest's romantic and powerful desire to serve his country remained unfulfilled. There was real regret that he had been deprived of an opportunity to demonstrate his courage in wartime, but Hesburgh manfully accepted Steiner's direction. His response gave him some legitimate grounds later to claim that he had lived out his vow of obedience faithfully and well. After a quick visit home to see his family he returned to Notre Dame in July of 1945. A little more than a month later the dropping of atomic bombs on Hiroshima and Nagasaki forced Japan's surrender and World War II came to an end. The young and charismatic Fr. Ted Hesburgh was back on campus to help welcome the returning veterans who soon descended on Notre Dame to complete their studies now that victory had been won. Full of energy and zeal Father Ted began his life's work at Our Lady's school.

PRIEST AND TEACHER

The young Fr. Theodore Hesburgh who returned to Notre Dame in the summer of 1945 brought with him not only his newly minted doctorate but a remarkable combination of self-confidence and zealous energy. He relished taking on priestly duties both pastoral and academic. He identified closely with the generation of American GIs who had done the hard fighting in the war and who returned home eager to play their part in shaping the postwar era. He planned to make his own notable mark at Notre Dame, and the few years prior to his appointment as executive vice president in 1949 proved to be of real importance in shaping his attitudes to the university. For example, he quickly found himself in conflict with the Holy Cross "old guard" led by President J. Hugh O'Donnell. The seeds of his strong convictions that Notre Dame needed serious changes were firmly planted during his initial years as a priest-teacher.

He began his service on campus during a remarkable period in the history of both the United States and American higher education. The postwar decades also witnessed a remarkable period of economic growth and prosperity and an enormous burst of scientific and technological developments that fueled the impressive increase in the research capabilities of American universities. Hesburgh's Notre Dame would benefit from these developments in the following decades. The young priest also easily acclimated to the greatly enhanced role of the United States on the world stage that World War II brought about and that the Cold War cemented.

Hesburgh quickly displayed notable pastoral gifts as he sought to attend to the spiritual, academic, and social needs of the young men who had put their lives on the line for their country and with whom he established a close rapport. His great and well-earned pride in his apostolic labors with the student-veterans, both married and unmarried, remained undiminished throughout his life. It was certainly evident in the pages he devoted to this ministry in his memoir. Furthermore, he recounted at some length his noteworthy efforts to assist the single veterans through the campus Veterans Club and his legendary service to the married vets and their young wives and children gathered in Vetville, the temporary housing village established on the east side of campus in 1946. Perhaps Father Ted had seen the 1944 Academy Award–winning film *Going My Way*, starring Bing Crosby as the unconventional and yet inspirational and compassionate Father Charles "Chuck" O'Malley, but he must have been aware of the character whom Crosby reprised in the 1945 box-office hit *The Bells of St. Mary's*. And, it must be said, the approach and accomplishments of the real Fr. Ted Hesburgh run parallel to and even exceed those of the fictional Fr. Chuck O'Malley.

Just as in *Going My Way*, where a clash occurred over the running of a parish between the young and handsome Chuck O'Malley and the aged and traditional pastor Father Fitzgibbon played by Barry Fitzgerald, so too at Notre Dame different generations of Holy Cross religious disagreed over how to regulate student life on the postwar campus. The handsome newcomer Ted Hesburgh found the existing system "like a French boarding school." He recognized that this was part of the Holy Cross heritage, but he quickly concluded that the tough discipline and firm controls were excessive. Unlike the traditional Fr. Hugh O'Donnell, he took no satisfaction when Notre Dame was described as a "Catholic West Point." The young Hesburgh wanted less emphasis on rules and more on personal responsibility. This was especially his wish for the veterans he came to know in Badin Hall, for whom "lights out" at 11:00 p.m. and Mass three times a week at 7:00 a.m. seemed too controlling. Instead of patrolling the corridors for rule violations, Hesburgh ignored minor infractions and welcomed these men—now all in their twenties—to his room for conversations late into the night, where they recalled their missions over Berlin, Hamburg, and Dusseldorf and paid tribute to the friends they had lost on those dangerous flights. The priest who had organized gatherings for service men and women during his time in Washington, D.C., also understood the need of these GI Bill students to socialize beyond campus, which included dancing and even drinking with local young women. His understanding of what they had been through and his commitment to their general well-being distinguished him from many of the older religious on campus.

While his work with the single veterans brought out his manly understanding and compassion, his work at Vetville with the young married couples demonstrated his pastoral initiative, creativity, and sheer energy. Later in life he relished recounting his ministerial accomplishments in Vetville. As he told it, he was almost all things to all the young people who lived in the housing units made over from prisoner of war barracks transported to Notre Dame from Weingarten, Missouri. Opened toward the end of 1946, Vetville and its occupants, in the words of Fr. Arthur J. Hope's centenary history of Notre Dame, caused "old Notre Damers" to chuckle at the sight of "so many young matrons [sic] on campus" and "the young book-laden fathers wheeling their youngsters under the statue of Sorin." Arthur Hope went further in his 1950 history and observed: "Although most of the married veterans have a struggle to get by on their meager allowances, they are, by their own assertion, experiencing one of the happiest periods of their lives. They tell us that a great share of that happiness has been due to the solicitude of their very special chaplain—Father Theodore Hesburgh."[22]

Solicitude barely captures the range of zealous service that the self-appointed Vetville chaplain undertook to aid these young couples starting out in life together in very challenging circumstances. He "did the rounds" most days and checked on residents. He organized social events, planned retreats for married couples, gave instruction in the Catholic faith to various non-Catholic spouses, made babysitting arrangements to allow some couples an occasional night out, and gave marriage counseling to those who were struggling. He oversaw the preparation of a village newspaper, the *Vet Gazette*, to share the community's news and boost morale. In classic priestly fashion he blessed the pregnant young women and the babies they carried and then baptized them after those children were delivered by the local doctors whom he had lined up to provide a discount rate. Hesburgh even notably served as a kind of pre-maternity nurse/de facto mother who (rather implausibly) diagnosed for some women that the nausea they suffered from each morning signaled their being pregnant! On sad occasions he rallied his community to deal with the tragic deaths of young children and he lent emotional support to the grieving parents. A more compassionate and capable shepherd of the Vetville flock cannot be imagined.

Hesburgh's early and notable pastoral initiatives with the married students attracted some criticism from Hugh O'Donnell. According to Father Ted's recollection, the burly president accosted him one night outside the Corby Hall chapel and while forcefully poking him in the chest angrily asked: "Who put you in charge of Vetville?" Apparently Hesburgh's answer sufficed because O'Donnell thereafter left him alone to labor in the Vetville vineyard, but the memory of this interrogation still rankled a half century later. It served to confirm further his dismissive attitude toward the old guard in Holy Cross. They remained for him always the ones who just didn't understand and whom he needed to maneuver around and then eventually replace.

Hesburgh's dissatisfaction with the state of affairs at Notre Dame was compounded by his initial and difficult academic experiences. Father Steiner had called the young priest back to the university primarily to instruct students. And teach he did, a full load—six two-credit-hour courses!—of the religion curriculum. He began with the required course on moral theology but eventually gravitated to the important dogmatic theology course. He found the general situation for these required courses rather inadequate. They were, he judged, lacking in content and also often poorly taught by Holy Cross priests who were untrained for the task. Father Ted struggled in his own initial efforts at teaching. Like many beginning teachers he complained about the difficult task he confronted. There was no set syllabus to work from. Further, the assigned textbook, he later claimed, "was just about the worst presentation of moral theology I had ever seen." He felt there was an egregious overemphasis on casuistry in explaining the moral life. Fortunately for the fledgling teacher his old friend from Washington, D.C., Charlie Sheedy, also was now assigned back to Notre Dame and was laboring away at the moral theology course. Hesburgh rightly noted in his memoir that "teaching was brand-new to me," but Sheedy "helped guide me."[23] Not only did the brilliant Sheedy help his neophyte colleague with teaching methods, but he also helped him refocus the content of the moral theology course. Sheedy determined to teach the virtues—theological and cardinal—as the basis of his class. He worked up lecture notes, known as "Sheedy Sheets," which he generously shared with his confreres and of which Hesburgh made full use.

The existence of these lecture notes eventually prompted the department chair Fr. Roland Simonitsch to realize that the religion courses at Notre Dame could be improved significantly if the curriculum was standardized and the course content for the required classes encapsulated in a text shaped by competent Notre Dame faculty. He first approached Sheedy to transform his "Sheedy Sheets" into an accessible text for college students and the general reader. By this point, roughly in 1947, Hesburgh had moved to the dogma courses and also now found himself on firmer ground as a teacher. So Simonitsch asked him to write a number of books in the broad area of dogmatic theology. The first would cover God's nature and His relationship to man. Among the topics eventually covered were God's existence, essence, and attributes as well as the Holy Trinity, creation, the elevation and fall of man, and the end of the world and of man. The second proposed volume aimed to treat the incarnation and redemption, while the final proposed volume would be devoted to sacramental theology.

Sheedy's volume entitled *The Christian Virtues: A Book on Moral Theology for College Students and Lay Readers* appeared in 1949. He thanked Hesburgh for his help and support. Hesburgh's initial, and as it turned out, only volume in the series came out the following year bearing the impressive title *God and the World of Man*. Father Ted explained that Sheedy's "book came out much easier than mine because he was smarter and wrote better and was a really gifted guy for doing difficult things in a very fast and delightful way." Dare one say there might be some truth in his observations regarding Sheedy. But Hesburgh was destined to be neither a teacher nor a publishing scholar. He was called to administration and to leadership.

The calls to take on the tasks of administration at Notre Dame, which would so occupy his life, came early. The principal initiator was Fr. John Cavanaugh, successor to Hugh O'Donnell as president in 1946 and leader of the university until 1952. Cavanaugh was an urbane and gracious man whom Thomas Stritch has labeled even "more than Hesburgh . . . the originator of modern Notre Dame."[24] He recognized the great need for Notre Dame to improve its academic standing, and he personally possessed a great love for the classical Great Books education then being developed at the University of Chicago by Robert Hutchins and Mortimer Adler. He represented a sharp contrast to poor Hugh O'Donnell in this regard. But Cavanaugh also retained a very practical side, as befit someone who had worked in the business world as an executive for the Studebaker Corporation prior to entering Holy Cross. He knew that Notre Dame needed to expand and to garner the resources to make such expansion possible. To this end he established the Notre Dame Foundation in order to enlarge the university's development capabilities. During his presidential term, undergraduate enrollment dramatically increased from approximately 3,200 to 5,100 students, and he built new academic facilities to house his growing university, including Nieuwland Hall of Science and O'Shaughnessy Hall for the College of Arts and Letters. Cavanaugh also realized that he needed to recruit the most talented Holy Cross priests to assist him in his ambitious efforts.

The young Ted Hesburgh admired Cavanaugh personally and fully supported his plans to improve Notre Dame. He recalled to me his appreciation for Cavanaugh's capabilities and noted that his predecessor had "graduated highest in his class at Notre Dame," and added, "so John was no dummy—he was definitely number one."[25] But according to Father Ted's well-rehearsed narrative, he displayed no eagerness to join Cavanaugh's administrator team. He reputedly rebuffed Cavanagh's early invitations to consider taking on some administrative duties, claiming that he "was perfectly happy to continue for the rest of my life doing what I was then doing—teaching, writing, and ministering."[26] Hesburgh fought off a Cavanaugh entreaty that he take over as dean of the College of Arts and Letters from Cavanaugh's brother, Frank, saying that the jump in rank from assistant professor to dean bordered on the inappropriate. His resistance flagged rather quickly, however, and in September 1948 he accepted Cavanaugh's assignment to head the religion department, although it meant that he needed to surrender his chaplaincy at Vetville.

The new head of the Department of Religion clarified quickly that he had natural gifts for administration. He brought further coherence to the religion curriculum and hired competent instructors. He also had a flair for advertising the accomplishments of the academic department he led and for displaying its importance in the overall mission of the university. After just one year in the position, Hesburgh wrote a "Mid-Century Report" for the *Notre Dame Alumnus,* in which he explained to interested alumni and parents that religion needed to be "an integral part" of each student's "education for life." He emphasized that although the prefect of religion, the office previously held by John O'Hara, bore the responsibility to guide Notre Dame men "along the practical lines of masculine religious living," the religion department sought "to impart the basic religious truths that are the necessary intellectual foundation for a mature Catholic life."[27] His deeply felt concern to shape a mature Catholic laity underlay his notable departmental efforts.

Hesburgh associated his efforts with Cavanaugh's larger aim to raise academic standards. He insisted that only Holy Cross priests with proper training could teach religion, and he pushed for all faculty to gain the Doctorate in Sacred Theology degree that he proudly possessed. He hired other religious priests—Dominicans, Franciscans, and Passionists, among others—to assist in the essential teaching until sufficient Holy Cross men could be suitably trained. He built on and strengthened the six-semester sequence that Simonitsch had overseen. The freshmen took courses on the life of Christ and Christian morals. The sophomores enrolled in an apologetics course and the first dogma course on the truths of faith, while the juniors completed the dogma sequence and also took a course on the sacramental life of the Church. The fledgling department head spoke proudly of the unified curriculum and of the carefully prepared texts that the department used to facilitate it. With a certain relish he also noted the demanding nature of the departmental exams he set at semester's end. He wanted genuine rigor in his department and for religion to be taken seriously at Notre Dame. He explained that the department still had to make further progress to achieve its goals, but he left his readers in no doubt that under his leadership they would be realized.

Ironically, by the time Father Ted's report appeared in print he no longer served as head of the Department of Religion. He received a call after just one academic year to move higher in the Cavanaugh administration—indeed John Cavanaugh arranged for him to assume the newly created position of executive vice president. Hesburgh had no advance warning of the appointment and learned of it from Cavanaugh just prior to entering the crypt chapel of Sacred Heart Church to receive his annual obedience from the provincial in June of 1949. As executive vice president he would report directly to Cavanaugh and sit right underneath him in the hierarchy of the university. This meant he would oversee the work of four Holy Cross priest–vice presidents, each of whom was older and more experienced than he was. It was a dramatic move on Cavanaugh's part. He wanted Hesburgh's assistance in his ambitious effort to advance Notre Dame. His calling on the young priest would be decisive for the future of both Father Hesburgh and the university.

Many a priest or religious when appointed to a position that they have coveted feel obliged to engage in a strange exercise designed to convey that they were truly surprised by their elevation. In Uriah Heepish tones of false humility they protest that they never sought the position but will do their best to serve well in it. Theodore Hesburgh rightly can claim that he never coveted the position of executive vice president because it had not existed prior to his holding it. But he is somewhat disingenuous in suggesting that he rose reluctantly in the hierarchy of Notre Dame—or, as he later put it, that he rose "mostly against my will."[28] He once conceded to me that although he remained surprised at how quickly he rose in influence after his early conflicts with the old Hugh O'Donnell brigade, by 1948 he could see that Cavanaugh wanted him in administration. The timing and the specific position and its responsibilities, however, did genuinely surprise him. He made no effort to back away from them. By now he realized fully that he could play an important role in bringing significant change to Notre Dame. In the evening following the distribution of obediences, Charlie Sheedy came to his room to quietly celebrate with him. According to Father Ted, the ever astute Sheedy exclaimed to him: "God, Ted—this is the whole banana." Ted, lurching a little in Uriah Heep's direction, protested that he had a job to do as executive vice president and he would stick with that, but Sheedy, perhaps with the benefit of a drink or two, persisted that "John's only got three more years to go."[29] He knew then that Hesburgh would be favored to succeed Cavanaugh, if he performed well in his new responsibilities. Ted Hesburgh resolved to do just that.

FATHER CAVANAUGH'S DEPUTY

John Cavanaugh's method of tutoring his thirty-two-year-old novice executive vice president in the ways of administration mainly involved assigning
him major tasks from the outset. Executive leadership training programs,
long preparatory periods, and other such luxuries lay in the distant future for
fledgling officers at Notre Dame. Hesburgh moved immediately from his
religion department responsibilities to an office across from Cavanaugh's in
the Main Building and took up his new duties. The older priest succinctly
told his eventual successor that administration involved making decisions
and making them because they were the "right thing to do." Hesburgh
claimed that he never forgot Cavanaugh's counsel that one must do the
right thing regardless of whether it was unpopular or hard. He deemed this
a "touchstone" that helped guide his labors first as Cavanaugh's deputy and
then after he moved across the corridor to occupy the presidential suite.[30]

Father Hesburgh quickly established himself in his new administrative
role and easily overcame some initial resistance. Fr. John Burke, in Business Affairs, treated his younger confrere like an unwelcome parvenu seeking to interfere in his personal domain. He contested Hesburgh's efforts to
draw up proper job descriptions for each functional vice presidency, part
of a larger effort to clarify administrative procedures and structure. Burke
fumed at the young priest's requests for clarification on what his duties included. But, as would become the norm, Hesburgh's careful discipline and
self-control—he rarely raised his voice in anger—easily countered Burke's
bluster and temper. The younger priest simply called on the authority of
John Cavanaugh and told Burke that if he had problems with the new
arrangements then he should take them up with the university president.
Burke eventually conceded, even if grudgingly, and the word went out that
Hesburgh operated as Cavanaugh's delegate and with his full authority.

Cavanaugh revealed quickly his full confidence in Hesburgh by sad-
dling him with a mix of responsibilities across a range of areas. The new
officer produced updated articles of administration and clarified the organizational structure of the university. He cultivated donors and oversaw
the construction of a number of major new buildings on campus. In a
demonstration of his courage he also accepted the challenge of reviewing
the administrative procedures for athletics. This brought him into serious

contact with the legendary and intense Notre Dame football coach Frank Leahy. Hesburgh had already demonstrated an impressive capacity for work during his early years of teaching at Notre Dame, but Cavanaugh's delegating him such significant responsibilities put his capabilities fully to the test.

For the most part the Cavanaugh-Hesburgh relationship remained strong. John Cavanaugh proved for a time to be something of a father figure for the younger man. Hesburgh admired Cavanaugh, although not without reservation. He bore some lasting resentment to his predecessor, feeling that Cavanaugh essentially exploited him as a battering ram of sorts to force through needed changes at Notre Dame. He also believed that Cavanaugh dispensed "impossible jobs" to him such as giving him long lists of contacts to call upon whenever he accompanied the football team to an away game, while never reducing Hesburgh's campus workload. He also noted that while he was doing the "grunt work," as he termed it, Father Cavanaugh found time to socialize in South Bend and also to take occasional trips away to visit with friends in Florida, such as Joseph P. Kennedy, with whom the Notre Dame president had become close.[31] The young priest proved too busy to let this resentment fester much at the time. In the end, he knew that someone with his temperament benefited much more by being burdened with important responsibilities than by suffering under restraints and being deprived of any authority to make decisions. His gratitude to Cavanaugh always far outweighed any resentment. They shared a vision for Notre Dame and there was never any major difference on matters of substance between them.

Hesburgh's initial years on campus had given him a meaningful taste of the classroom and of ministry in the residence halls. Now he garnered a large portion of experience in what might be termed the "other side" of the university. Symbolic of his changing role was his departure from Farley Hall and his move into his fabled room—the one overlooking the dumpster—in Corby Hall, the priests' official residence on campus, which he would occupy until his retirement. He would remain accessible to students, but he never lived among them again. A new and key constituency emerged for him: the benefactors and friends of the university. Father Ted gave himself fully to the work of fostering relations with them. He also proved enormously proficient in drawing them into support of the university with which his very person and being were becoming intimately meshed. During these important years of preparation, the university and its present and future became his life's work. Other opportunities would come for him to serve his nation and his Church, but these would all be incorporated within his primary responsibilities at Notre Dame.

Father Cavanaugh tasked his executive vice president heavily, but he also supported him generously. He began to introduce Hesburgh into the important world of Chicago Catholics who backed the university. It was Cavanaugh who introduced Hesburgh to a rising star in Chicago legal circles, Edmund Stephan, who eventually became the younger priest's key collaborator in changing the governance structure of the university. Hesburgh also became friends with a wonderful Chicago couple, Pat and Patty Crowley, who emerged as leaders of the Christian Family Movement (CFM), a group that reflected Catholic Action principles in the postwar decades.[32] He related well to this emerging generation of postwar Catholics and effortlessly enlarged his circle of influential friends and associates.

Cavanaugh also introduced him directly to some of the key benefactors of the university such as the wealthy Minnesota businessman and philanthropist I. A. O'Shaughnessy. Hesburgh's close and easy relationship with one of Notre Dame's greatest supporters right at the start of his career in administration undoubtedly convinced him not only of his ability to raise money for the university but also that he could enjoy this particular work. He soon concluded that raising money for the university and building an endowment to support its work were crucial for Notre Dame's proper development. Cavanaugh already had realized this, of course, but Hesburgh would take fund-raising to the next level, as certain contemporary development staff members might say. He threw himself into this demanding work with enthusiasm, and his ability to articulate both a broad vision and specific needs combined with his confident manner and handsome appearance made him a natural. During his retirement he once explained, perhaps a little defensively, that he never felt like a "huckster" when raising money. His characteristic self-assurance that he had long been engaged in "doing the right thing" came through as he explained that in asking for money for the university he was "just giving them [donors] a chance to do some good."[33] He supplied literally thousands of such opportunities in the decades of his presidency.

Hesburgh's friendship with Ignatius Aloysius O'Shaughnessy proved special, and the Minnesota businessman also served, like Father Cavanaugh, as a father figure of sorts for the young priest. O'Shaughnessy had made a fortune in the oil refining business and aided a number of Catholic charities and institutions. His initial contact with Notre Dame came through his youngest son, Don, who enrolled there in 1941. O'Shaughnessy gravitated immediately to the atmosphere of the campus and he attended a football game in the fall. In Don's sophomore year I. A. made an initial donation of $100,000 to the university, which established the O'Shaughnessy Fine Arts Foundation in the College of Arts and Letters. Don left Notre Dame later in his sophomore year to join the Army, but I. A.'s devotion and allegiance to the school had already been established. In 1943 he accepted election to Notre Dame's advisory board of lay trustees. He made further significant donations to the O'Shaughnessy Fine Arts Foundation and in 1949 was elected president of the Associate Board of Lay Trustees. The young Father Hesburgh moved easily into a collaborative role with O'Shaughnessy as the businessman made clear he wanted to fund a liberal and fine arts building on the campus.[34] Their work together on what became O'Shaughnessy Hall of Liberal and Fine Arts laid the basis for a true friendship that lasted until the older man's death in 1973. Hesburgh appreciated O'Shaughnessy's devout commitment to his Catholic faith and his devotion to his wife and family. He also valued the authenticity and manliness of this benefactor and his great sense of humor. O'Shaughnessy possessed a deeper affection for athletics and for Notre Dame football than did Father Ted, but they shared a love for fishing and hunting. Before long, Father Hesburgh began making trips to Florida to spend some days relaxing on the *Marileen*, O'Shaughnessy's sixty-five-foot yacht. While Father Cavanaugh gravitated to Joseph P. Kennedy, Father Hesburgh found himself much more comfortable in the company of I. A. O'Shaughnessy.

The Hesburgh-O'Shaughnessy collaboration held major implications for the future architecture and design of the campus. Upon the Minnesota benefactor's contributing over $2.1 million to construct the Liberal and Fine Arts building, the Notre Dame team of Cavanaugh and Hesburgh proved only too willing to take up his suggestion to use the St. Paul architectural firm of Ellerbe and Company to design the building. O'Shaughnessy knew the firm and its principals and he introduced Hesburgh to them. It was to be an important relationship. At the time Hesburgh was working with a number of firms as he oversaw construction of the Nieuwland Hall of Science; worked on plans to build the campus hotel (the Morris Inn) and Fisher Hall, a new residence hall; and managed a major renovation of the power plant. The young priest relished dealing with the various architects and builders, although he readily admitted he didn't have any experience in the area.

What Hesburgh did have, however, were firm opinions about how buildings should be designed. He believed that the old guard at Notre Dame and the architects they hired had paid too much attention to the external appearance of the buildings they oversaw. He determined on a different approach that emphasized the functions of the building first before giving attention to the external façade that "wraps [around] those functions and how it fits the rest of the campus."[35] Perhaps to reflect the changing of the guard on campus he welcomed more "modern or semimodern" designs that reflected the postwar era rather than staying faithful to the neo-Gothic style. O'Shaughnessy Hall accurately captured the strengths and weaknesses of his functional approach. The building terminated the east end of the beautiful South Quad on campus and provided classrooms, offices for the dean, rooms for departments and faculty, modern language labs, studio space, and the university art gallery. Although it met many needs, the building immediately faced criticism "because of its asymmetrical main entrance, its ill-proportioned clock tower, its narrow, low-ceilinged corridors, and its poorly ventilated classrooms." Harsh critics spread the (false) rumor that the architectural plans borrowed from "those drawn for a Minneapolis parochial grade school."[36]

Father Hesburgh defended his first major building then and always, and he regularly praised Ellerbe for the firm's work on campus, especially for what we know now as the Hesburgh Library and the Joyce Athletic and Convocation Center. But the criticisms annoyed him whatever his protestations to the contrary. Although he denied that the griping about the architecture of the Notre Dame campus bothered him, his later gibes that "I've never seen any two architects that agree with each other," and that "in fact, if you get five architects in a room, you get six opinions," belie this claim.[37] It can't be disputed, even by the most ardent Hesburgh loyalist, that many of the buildings he authorized during his service as executive vice president and afterward in his first term as president—such as the Morris Inn, Fisher and Pangborn Halls, Keenan-Stanford Hall, and the North Dining Hall—stand as the plainest and least interesting buildings on campus, whatever their functional contributions. Fortunately, Hesburgh engaged in no complete reversal of his predecessors' overall campus plans. He kept to the broad, open mall or quad design of the campus, and he gave a certain unity to its buildings by continuing to use Indiana limestone and so-called Notre Dame brick as principal materials. The overall beauty of the campus survived the Hesburghian functional approach.

Although Hesburgh's work with benefactors and with campus architecture and construction brought him a real sense of accomplishment and was marked mainly by success, his foray into the world of athletics—and specifically Notre Dame football—brought him challenge and eventually criticism. Soon after he appointed Hesburgh as executive vice president, Cavanaugh directed him to gain better control and direction over athletics and specifically over the way Frank Leahy managed the football program. According to Father Ted, Cavanaugh was concerned that Fr. John Murphy, who exercised nominal control over the athletic program from 1946 to 1949, "had just given Leahy everything he wanted, and Leahy wanted everything."[38] In Hesburgh's portrayal this arrangement came to an end as of the summer of 1949 when he courageously began to implement a series of reforms of Notre Dame athletics.

In his autobiography, *God, Country, Notre Dame*, Hesburgh gave lengthy treatment to his initial efforts to reform athletics, the details of which need not be repeated here. He clearly wanted to establish that he had done the right thing from the outset with college sports at Notre Dame. Father Ted also rendered his encounter with Leahy in almost David and Goliath terms by characterizing himself as a simple thirty-two-year-old priest–assistant professor courageously going up against "the most famous, most talented football coach in the country."[39] Without diminishing his genuine mettle in reining in Leahy, it must be noted that the work already had begun. Cavanaugh had reduced the number of scholarships available to Leahy in 1947, so Hesburgh built upon a foundation that had already been laid. Also Cavanaugh made it clear to him that in any conflict with Leahy he would receive presidential backing even to the point of hiring a new coach if Leahy refused to cooperate. Additionally, Hesburgh gained support from senior faculty on campus who understood that for Notre Dame to advance as an academic institution, its image as a "football factory" needed to be tempered. Hesburgh would have been familiar with sentiments such as those expressed in a 1949 issue of the influential lay Catholic magazine *Commonweal* in a review essay of two books on Notre Dame entitled "Football Capital or Intellectual Community?" Authored by Waldemar Gurian, the European émigré and renowned political scientist who joined the Notre Dame faculty in the late 1930s, the piece reflected the views of faculty members who wanted more attention given to the academic heart of the university and its "scholarly achievements" rather than to the exploits of its team on the gridiron.[40] Our young David knew instinctively that he gained the respect and support of such faculty as he worked to restrain the power and independence of the Goliath football coach.

Still, Hesburgh took on this tough assignment with amazing audacity. After all, he aimed to restrain an enormously successful coach, whose feats rivaled even those of the remarkable Knute Rockne, and who stood as a veritable Notre Dame icon. The brooding and complex Leahy led Notre Dame to four national championships (1943, 1946, 1947, and 1949) and six undefeated seasons. His postwar teams went undefeated for thirty-nine games, and four of his players won the Heisman Trophy. Leahy seemed to many to embody the very spirit of Notre Dame. One astute commentator has noted that he "often goaded his 'lads' to victory by casting them as defenders of the faith, Saturday afternoon warriors doing chivalric battle for 'God, Country, and Notre Dame.'"[41] Despite Leahy's stature, Hesburgh had the coach as a target in his sights immediately. The priest moved in a controlled but forceful manner that gave his decisions and demands a certain inexorable air to them. He clarified quickly that he was "in charge" and his decisions would rule the day. His deep conviction that football must be handled better and made less dominant at the university drove him forward.

Hesburgh separated the positions of athletic director and football coach and replaced Frank Leahy in the former role with Edward "Moose" Krause, who reported directly to the executive vice president. This choice was inspired. Krause, a two-sport all-American during his student days at Notre Dame, also embodied the Notre Dame spirit and gave Hesburgh a reliable friend in the athletics department. The good-hearted Krause gave up his role as head basketball coach and loyally supported Father Ted and then Fr. Ned Joyce in their efforts to guide athletics at the university over the coming decades. Hesburgh's efforts went beyond this important appointment. He established regulations for injured players and gave the team doctor rather than the coach the final approval on the availability of players. He enforced guidelines on the size of the traveling squad for away games and prevailed in a sharp contest of wills with Leahy on this matter. He secured a strict control of the finances of the athletics department and carefully oversaw the approval of its expenses. He also ended abuses regarding the distribution of complimentary tickets for home games and assured that all such tickets were distributed under the name of the president of the university rather than that of the football coach. In some ways his efforts paralleled those of an earlier generation of Holy Cross priests who restrained Knute Rockne's more questionable entrepreneurial endeavors.[42]

Hesburgh developed his firm views on college athletics and of football at Notre Dame during these crucial years as Cavanaugh's deputy. He began to articulate them intelligently and persuasively. A notable example occurred when he spoke at the annual football banquet in December 1951, after a solid 7-2-1 season that improved on the very disappointing 4-4-1 effort of the previous year. Hesburgh gave attention to the football season only in the conclusion of his remarks and focused instead on what he termed "the football player." His words still hold force well over six decades later. He explained that "the football player is more than a pawn in the hands of unscrupulous people who can use him to represent an educational institution without allowing him to get educated himself." In pointed language that must have made Leahy at least a little edgy, he described that player as a "person" and explained that "this means that you cannot use persons the way you use puppets to put on an exhibition; it means they can't be bargained for like beef; it means they can't be used and abused as though they were mechanical gadgets." The young priest stated plainly that "football players are to be trained and respected as men, not as circus animals."[43] This was a philosophy regarding scholar-athletes that he would develop further after he succeeded John Cavanaugh.

After their initial tense skirmishes, Hesburgh and Leahy came to a rough truce as the football coach adjusted to the new order. Father Ted claimed that he and Leahy eventually became "fairly close" and that on football trips he spent time with the coach, occasionally endeavoring to calm him down when he experienced his usual pre-game anxieties. He found himself playing "the role of friend and confidant."[44] But this role altered neither the concerns he felt about Leahy as coach nor his determination to retain control of the football program. He brought these with him to the presidency of the school that some considered the "football capital" of the country.

Hesburgh's service as executive vice president involved him in a myriad of other activities and duties beyond development, architecture and campus construction, and athletics. He handled with ease whatever came to him. He had the gift of a born administrator to balance multiple responsibilities effectively whatever the extent of the demands upon him. And the demands only increased. John Cavanaugh began to experience increasing health difficulties and concluded on doctor's orders that he needed more rest. Cavanaugh's health worries were genuine, although he actually lived another two decades and died at eighty. He wanted to relinquish his presidential duties so as to give more time to reflection on great ideas and to his service as the personal chaplain to Joseph P. Kennedy and family. Father Ted recalled that the university president called him to his office in January of 1952, admitted his health worries, and told him that he planned to go to Florida to relax and recuperate. He then explained to his deputy that "you're it for the next six weeks," and pushed a pile of unanswered mail in his direction. In effect Hesburgh served in fact if not in name as acting president of the university for much of the first half of 1952. It was hardly a surprise then when this reality was formally recognized at the annual retreat in June of that year. The Holy Cross provincial, Fr. Theodore (Ted) Mehling, assigned the thirty-five-year-old Theodore M. Hesburgh, C.S.C., the obedience to serve as president of the University of Notre Dame. The next stage in his meteoric rise to power and influence began.

PART I

LEADING NOTRE DAME

CHAPTER 2

AMBITIOUS PRESIDENT, 1952–1958

H ESBURGH'S INITIAL TERM IN OFFICE COINCIDED WITH A PERIOD of general prosperity in the United States. The social and economic status of Catholics continued to rise during this time as they left the immigrant era behind and assimilated "as full-fledged Americans." Catholic institutions of higher education also expanded rapidly in both number and size as student enrollment and faculty ranks increased dramatically. These schools also "adopted a more professional approach to such activities as admissions procedures, personnel management, and fund-raising," as Philip Gleason has noted, "while striving to improve their performance in terms of teaching and research."[1] Hesburgh pursued his efforts at Notre Dame as part of a broader movement to grow and strengthen Catholic higher education. Yet he pushed Notre Dame ahead faster and further than most peer schools.[2]

TAKING OFFICE AND BUILDING HIS TEAM

Father Hesburgh had been consulted in the preceding months about whom among the Holy Cross religious he wished to have assigned as the senior members of his administration. Mehling met all his requests for those who would serve as vice presidents and deans, which Hesburgh appreciated. He planned to continue the work Cavanaugh had begun, but he wanted his own team in place to pursue this work. He recalled being "shaken with an attack of nerves" at the announcement, but if this occurred it did not appear to be of long duration. Soon he and John Cavanaugh exited the crypt chapel, and the older man simply reached into the watch pocket of his religious habit (cassock) and handed the younger priest the key to his office. Father Ted proudly recalled, "Just like that, I was president of the University of Notre Dame." Furthermore, he added in a manner that implicitly chided the grander presidential inaugurations of more recent times, "No convocation, no installation, no speeches. Just go right to work. That's the way it was done in 1952."[3]

As if to emphasize the point, John Cavanaugh wished the new president luck and revealed that he planned to catch a train to New York that very night. But he passed along to his successor a commitment to give a talk to the Christian Family Movement over at Veterans Hall. So without preparation Hesburgh marched over to the Christian Family Movement group led by the Crowleys and addressed the gathering. In the Hesburgh mythos it became "my first official act as president of Notre Dame, and fortunately, it also turned out to be the launching of a new national movement."[4] Whatever his modest contribution in helping launch the dynamic lay movement for young Catholic couples, the occasion remained firmly lodged in his mind as his first presidential action, and it notably bonded him over the years to Pat and Patty Crowley and their endeavors. With his talk completed Father Ted returned to what was now his office. Cavanaugh had simply walked out, leaving his books on the shelves for Hesburgh's use. The new president straightened things out and began the first of many long evenings of work in the presidential suite.

As Father Ted recounted in God, Country, Notre Dame, when he reflected on the goals he wanted to accomplish for himself and Notre Dame, "the answer came silently as a kind of vision." In his telling he envisioned "Notre Dame as a great Catholic university, the greatest in the world!" He explained further that "there were many distinguished universities in our country and in Europe, but not since the Middle Ages had there been a great Catholic university." According to his later recollection, he told himself that "the road was wide open for Notre Dame."[5] All the details of this vision were not clear to him at first, but he grasped well that it would mean breaking free from the complacency and mediocrity that he believed characterized so much of the campus in the past, in everything but football and pious practices. This then was the overarching goal that would guide his activities over the six years he expected to serve as president. He would accomplish as much as possible while moving with the intensity and effort of a sprinter in a hundred-yard dash, rather than in the more measured pace of a long-distance runner. There was no time to waste, no occasion for desultory rumination.

In fashioning his principal goal for the university, Hesburgh operated as the undisputed decision-maker. He neither consulted broadly with his local Holy Cross community, nor did he confer with the provincial administration that had appointed him. Having been assigned the obedience to serve as president of Notre Dame he now claimed the right to determine Notre Dame's direction. He resented any interference from his superiors in the order. He ignored any criticism of his plans from within the Holy Cross community, and he recruited to assist him those who shared his ambitions for the university. His deep conviction that he understood what Notre Dame needed, along with an almost mystical sense that he had been singled out to serve as its leader, drove him forward.

Hesburgh's gifts for leadership were evident from the start. He possessed the essential virtues of integrity and courage. He proved to be a leader whose word could be trusted, and he assuredly was not afraid of the challenge that lay before him. He even seemed to relish addressing the multiple tasks that confronted him. In contrast to John Cavanaugh, Hesburgh also possessed what David Gergen called those "hidden ingredients of leadership," namely fitness and stamina, and they served him well throughout his presidency.[6] This man of strong character operated with a central and compelling purpose that enabled him to explain to various constituencies where he would lead Notre Dame. Not only did he articulate this purpose effectively; he also demonstrated real success from the outset in persuading others to adopt it. Those who did not were eventually dismissed or marginalized, but most approved of the vision he delineated and worked to implement it. In pursuing his presidential effort, he inspired others to share his dream for Notre Dame, and he enlisted some able associates to aid him in the work.

At the community chapter at which Ted Mehling named Hesburgh as president, he also made key appointments of the Holy Cross priests whom the new president had selected. One man of note was Edmund P. (Ned) Joyce, who succeeded Father Ted as executive vice president. Ned Joyce rose in the Notre Dame hierarchy as rapidly as did Ted Hesburgh. Born in Tela, Honduras, and raised in Spartanburg, South Carolina, Joyce entered Notre Dame in 1933 and graduated magna cum laude with a degree in accountancy four years later. He worked for some years as a CPA but returned to Holy Cross in 1941 and entered the novitiate at Rolling Prairie in

1942. Color blindness and a heart murmur prevented Joyce from joining the Navy, despite his being a fine athlete. After further studies at Moreau Seminary and then at Holy Cross College in Washington, the impressive southerner was ordained a priest in Sacred Heart Church on June 8, 1949. Presumably Father Hesburgh laid hands on his confrere during the ordination ceremony, but their first real meeting occurred later that day. Ned Joyce had called on Father Cavanaugh, whom he knew from his student days, and met Hesburgh coming out of the president's office. Hesburgh immediately asked for his blessing and recalled: "I knelt down right in the doorway and he gave me a blessing and then tore off to see somebody else."

Observers often liked to contrast Hesburgh and Joyce and then to note how well they complemented each other. Dick Conklin skillfully juxtaposed them, with Joyce being "from the bedrock of the Confederacy (the first South Carolinian to graduate from Notre Dame), a CPA at home with numbers, an athlete who loved sports and a conservative who looked slowly at all sides of a decision," while Hesburgh "was a Yankee from Syracuse, New York, trained as a theologian, leaning liberal on most issues, self-described as 'having two left feet' in terms of athletic ability, at home with words and quick decisions." Yet, as Conklin further noted in writing a perceptive tribute to Father Joyce on his death in 2004, the two Holy Cross priests balanced each other because "Hesburgh was the outside persona of Notre Dame, deeply involved in public service, traveling the New York City–Washington corridor, using his multilingual ability to give Notre Dame an international presence." On the other hand, "Joyce covered for him on campus as a quiet but powerful No. 2 (until the creation of the position of Provost in 1970) with a hand especially firm on the budgetary tiller."[7] Their clear division of labor also aided their long collaboration. In Hesburgh's view he took the lead only on academics while "Ned reigned over finances, buildings and grounds, university relations, athletics, and everything else."[8]

Hesburgh and Joyce worked well together right from the start. Their relationship, however, was not one of equals. Father Ted indisputably took the leading role while Father Ned proved content to assume an important supporting part for decades. He had real influence on university finances, and his conservative approach to taking on debt prevailed throughout his time in office. He also played a central role in athletics, although he deferred even in this area when Hesburgh intervened. But Joyce never felt himself capable of guiding the broad direction of Notre Dame. This always remained Hesburgh's domain. The new president rested comfortably knowing that his second-in-command would never seriously challenge him, and that Joyce would never consider himself a legitimate candidate to succeed him. There was never any rivalry between them, and this gave Hesburgh extraordinary security in his position.

Father Joyce became a regular on the South Bend social scene, and he also handled negotiations with city and county officials, absolving Hesburgh of such responsibilities. Hesburgh would eventually aim to solve national and international issues, while Joyce knew how to gain local approval for Notre Dame's expansion and development. Of course, being able to delegate authority at the university to the always reliable and trustworthy Joyce made it easy for Hesburgh to leave the campus to pursue duties either directly on behalf of Notre Dame or increasingly for other interests as he gained appointments to various commissions, boards, and task forces. Never did he worry about what was happening back in South Bend. Hesburgh always recognized his debt to Joyce. Fittingly he dedicated *God, Country, Notre Dame* to him.

Ned Joyce shared the book's dedication with Helen Hosinski, an "extraordinary woman" who served as secretary to Notre Dame's president for two years under John Cavanaugh and for all thirty-five years under Father Ted.[9] Just as one cannot understand how Hesburgh operated at Notre Dame without understanding his relationship with Father Joyce, so too one must comprehend his remarkable working partnership with Helen Hosinski. A woman from a Polish neighborhood on the west side of South Bend who never went to college, Hosinski had an astonishing memory for details and an enormous capacity for work. She never married and dedicated herself totally to her labors at Notre Dame. Hesburgh attempted to capture something of Hosinski's contribution in his autobiography by noting that "she ran the office and she ran much of my life with nary a misstep or mistake," but the short paragraph allotted to her hardly sufficed to encapsulate the way she facilitated Hesburgh's work both on campus and off. She was the gatekeeper of his office and the organizer of all his materials. She remembered the given names of all of his many contacts as well as those of their spouses and children, which she helpfully inserted into his correspondence, giving it a personal quality. Additionally, she performed some of those duties that might normally be undertaken by a wife in the 1950s. She told him when to get his hair cut, ordered new clothes for him when they were needed, and directed him to have his health checkup annually.[10]

Neither Joyce nor Hosinski possessed either the background or the interest to serve as crucial collaborators with Hesburgh in the central academic project at Notre Dame. Here he drew on the assistance of not a single individual but rather a number of confreres. Father Philip Moore served effectively as Hesburgh's first vice president for academic affairs. He was a capable scholar who trained in medieval studies at the Catholic University of America and at the École Nationale des Chartes in Paris. Moore served as the foundation dean of the graduate school from 1944 to 1952 and was a natural to join Hesburgh's effort to build Notre Dame's academic strength. Hesburgh admired the older priest and had real affection for him. To succeed Moore in the graduate school, Hesburgh tapped Father Paul Beichner, a Yale-trained specialist in medieval literature. Beichner was only five years older than Hesburgh but shared none of the latter's extroverted style. The younger man understood that Beichner had direct experience of an illustrious university and that he understood serious scholarship.

Hesburgh's closest collaborator in the academic domain proved to be his friend Charlie Sheedy, to whom he assigned the leadership of the College of Arts and Letters. Hesburgh described Sheedy as his "closest intellectual confidant," a man who was bright, well read, and blessed with extraordinary capabilities. Sheedy served for the first half of the Hesburgh presidency as a key person to help Father Ted in formulating proposals and in drafting speeches or statements. He notably composed important statements on Catholic universities and education that Hesburgh then presented in various meetings held by organizations such as the International Federation of Catholic Universities (IFCU). Sheedy also served as his point man on improving the quality of the departments in the college that Hesburgh saw as central in a Catholic university.

Hesburgh wanted other Holy Cross religious to contribute on his team, but they were unavailable. He particularly wanted to enlist the strengths and support of Howard "Doc" Kenna, but this sturdy priest moved to head Holy Cross College in Washington, D.C. The Hesburgh-Kenna collaboration would await another day. Hesburgh also wanted the help of his predecessor, but John Cavanaugh had other ideas. He left for Santa Barbara, California, to enjoy a scholar-in-residence arrangement with Robert Maynard Hutchins's newly established think tank, the Fund for the Republic. But his successor would not leave him in peace to think "deep" thoughts in that lovely place. He wanted Cavanaugh back in the Midwest to head the Notre Dame Foundation in anticipation of a major fund-raising drive. He considered Cavanaugh's "personal magnetism, his business acumen, and his wide network of friends" indispensable.[11] Hesburgh believed that the Foundation was "the guts of the future," and he believed that Cavanaugh was "the one guy [who] could make it work." So he didn't rely just on his own persuasive powers, but requested that the provincial, Ted Mehling, order Cavanaugh to return. John Cavanaugh thereupon returned after only six months away on the West Coast. He took over the Foundation and led it for a few years, during which time he selected and trained James Frick, a young man who soon assumed the crucial development responsibilities.[12] Once back on campus, Cavanaugh worked dutifully and never sought to overshadow his successor. He proffered advice only when asked, but was a steady and wise presence especially in difficult situations.

MAKING CHANGES AND MEETING CHALLENGES

In the mid-twentieth century, Catholic universities like Notre Dame were vulnerable to criticism for their academic limitations.[13] Waldemar Gurian's 1949 review of the Notre Dame philosopher Leo R. Ward's *Blueprint for a Catholic University* noted that American Catholic colleges had only begun to emerge from a defensive period in which "learning and scholarship were under-emphasized." Gurian optimistically observed that Catholic institutions now were engaged in efforts to address the situation and to effectively engage the secular research methods "used in great non-Catholic universities."[14] Change came slowly, however, and the upsurge of critiques of Catholic institutions and of American Catholic intellectual life only mounted as the 1950s moved along. Critics censured not only the "ghetto" status and the supposed siege mentality of Catholic universities, but also the failure of Catholic scholarship to influence the broad culture. The criticism reached a notable climax with Monsignor John Tracy Ellis's influential 1955 essay, "American Catholics and the Intellectual Life," which quoted and endorsed the view of Denis Brogan, the well-known British observer of American affairs, that "in no Western society is the intellectual prestige of Catholicism lower" than in the United States.[15] Ellis's essay set off a firestorm of self-criticism among Catholic educators. The consensus reached obviously pointed to the need for major improvements in Catholic institutions. Theodore Hesburgh followed this whole exercise in Catholic self-criticism with interest, but he felt no need to contribute directly to it.

Rather he focused his energies on addressing the specific academic limitations of Notre Dame. This represented his pragmatic response to the concerns raised by scholars like Ellis. Hesburgh did not simply bemoan the supposed mediocrity of Catholic higher education. Rather he aimed to effect real change within it.

From the outset Father Ted wanted to clarify that his focus was academic excellence, but he had difficulty getting this message across. The handsome young president desired to clarify that his concerns ranged far beyond the prospects of Frank Leahy's team in the upcoming season. This proved difficult since the reporters who attended Notre Dame media events concentrated on football. Things came to a head for Hesburgh and the Notre Dame public relations official J. Arthur (Art) Haley on a West Coast tour designed to introduce the new president and his plans. Over forty years later Father Ted still steamed as he recalled a press conference in Seattle at which Haley, who previously had worked for the athletic department, rounded up sports reporters to interview him. Inevitably the first question posed was: "How's the team going to be next year?" In Hesburgh's recollection he retorted: "Damned if I know because I am the president and I am not involved with the football team." In Father Ted's recollection: "Then I said, 'You guys want to talk about something else like education at Notre Dame?' And they said, 'Hell no. We just want to know how athletics are going.'" Afterward, they asked him to pose for a photograph passing a football to Art Haley. He refused, advising them to "go to hell." After the reporters were dismissed he told poor Haley that "if you ever stick me with an athletic reporter again, you're fired."[16]

Hesburgh delicately recalled in his memoir that "the hardest thing I had to do when I became president of Notre Dame was to shunt someone aside, or to talk someone into resigning, or, worst of all, to outright fire someone."[17] Whatever the personal angst such actions caused him he forged ahead. He was the "new broom" needed to sweep away the incompetent and the uncooperative. This is how he portrayed himself, and there is much to be said for his account. Over his initial period in office he forced the resignations of a number of the deans, including that of James E. McCarthy in Commerce [Business] and Fr. Frank Cavanaugh in Arts and Letters. He fired James Reyniers, the director of the Laboratories of Bacteriology at the University of Notre Dame (LOBUND) project, in a dispute over administrative procedures.

What warrants closer attention is the political nature of some of his personnel decisions and what they tell us of his outlook and modus operandi. A number of those he fired or reassigned identified closely with John O'Hara and his presidency. It seems clear that the vigorous new president worked to secure his power by removing or restraining these remnants of the old guard. Hesburgh noted this himself, although he denied that there was anything "systematic" about it. Hesburgh wanted to fashion Notre Dame as a more mainstream Catholic institution so as to obtain regard and respect within the broad American academy. He moved against those deemed more unconventional or extreme.

He had begun this work under John Cavanaugh when they obtained the resignation of Clarence Manion as dean of the Law School. Manion was in Hesburgh's own description "an enormously attractive man and a popular teacher," but he also had emerged as a significant conservative intellectual and spokesperson.[18] Manion had taught constitutional law at Notre Dame since 1924 and forged a worldview "organized around the premise that an overreaching government quashes individual freedom."[19] The expansion of federal power during the New Deal and World War II only confirmed him in his view. Additionally, he joined the America First Committee that opposed U.S. entry into World War II and began an association with General Robert Wood, the powerful executive of Sears, Roebuck and Company, and a major figure in American conservatism. After the war, the deeply Catholic Manion, who had taken up the deanship of the Law School in 1944, joined Woods to start the For America organization "that advocated cutting down the size of the federal government and the end of U.S. military and economic intervention abroad." Manion also supported Ohio's senator Robert Taft in his bids to secure the Republican nomination for the presidency in both 1948 and 1952. Within the Law School, Manion had promoted the importance of natural law and had formed the Natural Law Institute in 1947, but it was less these internal efforts than his outside activities and reputation that prompted Cavanaugh, with Hesburgh's support, to move against his Law School dean in his final months as president. In October 1952 Hesburgh, as the new president, filled the vacant position by bringing in Joseph O'Meara, an experienced practicing attorney. Meanwhile Manion went on to play a notable part in the growth of the conservative movement over the following decade through his *Manion Forum* radio program, his membership in the John Birch Society, and his encouragement of Barry Goldwater's run for the presidency. Such engagements convinced Hesburgh of the wisdom of the decision to remove him. Father

Ted wanted Notre Dame associated with more moderate views, and he also wanted to be the primary person who would speak for Notre Dame beyond the confines of the campus.

This concern for how Notre Dame was represented publicly and corporately prompted him to move against Fr. Edward Keller's Bureau of Economic Research. Keller has been labeled the "high priest" of pro-capitalist Catholics for his work from the 1930s through to the 1950s. A friend of Herbert Hoover, a fierce critic of the New Deal, and a sentinel against the dangers of both foreign and domestic communism, Keller promoted free enterprise capitalism and argued for its compatibility with Catholicism. His bureau at Notre Dame churned out pamphlets, articles, and books making this case and criticizing "Big Government" and "Big Labor," which were both growing rapidly in the decades after World War II. Critics on the left deemed the bureau "reactionary" and Keller an "economic royalist," and their voices registered with Notre Dame's new president.[20] Father Ted recalled that he explained to Ed Keller that "this can't go on." He assured Keller that "[you] can do your research any way you want, but you can't have a Bureau of Economic Research when you have one guy working in the bureau on a very narrow economic theory."[21]

Hesburgh held strongly to his view that Notre Dame must be perceived by various external constituencies as a serious academic institution, and one that was not wedded to a particular political or partisan perspective. He applied his thinking mainly against more conservative faculty, but not exclusively so. His reaction to efforts by liberal faculty to support Democratic candidate Adlai Stevenson in his campaign against Dwight Eisenhower in the 1952 presidential race well illustrates the point. Philip Gleason has summarized the background to the episode: "Frank O'Malley, the legendary professor of English who was also a Democratic precinct captain, drew up a pro-Stevenson testimonial signed by 65 members of the University faculty. It contained the standard disclaimer that the signers were speaking as individuals and not as representatives of the University. That distinction was hopelessly blurred when the Stevenson forces used what they called the 'Appeal from Notre Dame' in paid political advertisements across the country—and when the former chairman of the Democratic National Committee referred on network television to 'the Notre Dame Petition.'" Blindsided by the statement, Hesburgh was deeply upset by it and the criticism it generated that Notre Dame had departed "from the University's traditional policy of strict neutrality in partisan political affairs."[22] He publicly clarified that Notre Dame held to its normal nonpartisan stance, and in an address to the faculty on October 28, a week before the election, he made his displeasure known, although in a measured way. As the minutes for the meeting record: "Father Hesburgh urged the faculty to use prudential judgment in their actions and to avoid involving Our Lady's school in partisan situations; that the University is not a propaganda agency; and that its reputation had been gained by hard work of both laymen and clergy."[23] In a display of his own deftness and prudence, Hesburgh made his concerns known while he avoided any messy academic freedom dispute over the right of faculty to express their views. He recognized much better than any of his predecessors that he must respect that right.

Within Holy Cross, however, Hesburgh still faced some criticism. Most notably this came from Fr. Thomas T. McAvoy, who served not only as chair of the history department from 1939 to 1960, but also as university archivist and managing editor of the *Review of Politics* from its founding in 1942. McAvoy also wrote respected histories and had built the history department into the strongest department in the College of Arts and Letters. He could not be dismissed by Hesburgh as a "mossback," as the president described some of the more conservative faculty. McAvoy refused to simply sign on to the Hesburgh project.[24] His opposition and criticism came less from a disagreement about the need for high standards—assuredly he maintained precisely such standards in his department—but rather from the young Hesburgh's audacity in implying that he would be the one who would introduce and enforce them at Notre Dame. Hesburgh and Sheedy eventually combined forces to oust McAvoy from his leadership of the history department in 1960. The historian's dismissal represented a warning to Holy Cross religious that they either should endorse the administration's goals and actions or, at a minimum, temper criticism of them.

Inveterate critics like McAvoy could not be won over, but Hesburgh worked hard to impress the majority of faculty and to enlist them in his efforts to meet the challenge of building a great Catholic university. To this end he put special emphasis on the annual address that he gave as part of the opening Mass for the academic year. He worked hard on these formal talks, seeking to convince the assembled faculty of his learning, intellectual depth, and wide-ranging interests. He later began publishing his various outside lectures in edited collections entitled *Thoughts for Our Times*. He observed that "the faculty always think the president is a dope or an idiot or a cretin or other such things and once in a while if you send them some talks and if they read them it might give them the impression that maybe you do have a few good thoughts and you are able to express them."[25]

Hesburgh described the addresses he gave during his first term as representing "what I was thinking about at that time—about the university and its growth and things that were important to it." He allowed that these talks served as an entrée to this thinking about the university. At the end of his term he gathered these six sermon-lectures into a book entitled *Patterns for Educational Growth: Six Discourses at the University of Notre Dame*, which he "affectionately dedicated" to the Notre Dame faculty.[26] To read these lectures more than half a century later is to see a young priest earnestly outlining elements of his vision of a great Catholic university inside a packed Sacred Heart Church. The theme of "academic excellence" ran through the talks, but it was excellence driven by distinct purposes and toward much more than mere secular ends. In his 1953 address, entitled "A Theology of History and Education," he called for an incarnational approach to education. He proclaimed to his faculty listeners: "We do not rest in human reason, or human values, or human sciences—but we certainly do begin our progress in time with all that is human in its excellence. Then, after the pattern of the Incarnation, we consecrate all our human excellence to the transforming influence of Christ in our times." He explained incisively, and in words that are still applicable to Christian scholars, that "our prime concern must be to offer a worthy gift to the service of God and man." And for good measure he added that "we should not offer as our part of this divine symphony of all creation, the sour notes of intellectual mediocrity or educational complacency."[27] He deemed the quest for academic quality as fulfilling a divine mandate.

The following year Father Ted built upon these ideas and addressed his goals directly in "The Mission of a Catholic University." He pointed to the richness of the long Catholic intellectual tradition upon which Notre Dame could draw, but also noted the immensity of the immediate challenge that lay before the university to fulfill its promise. Its mission, he argued forcefully, was one "that no secular university today can undertake—for they are largely cut off from the tradition of adequate knowledge which comes only through faith in the mind and faith in God, the highest wisdom of Christian philosophy and Catholic theology." Then he brought his peroration to an apex. The more attentive faculty would have been awaiting it. "I know of no other spot on earth," he confessed, "where we might make a better beginning than here at Notre Dame, where we might inaugurate a new center of Christian culture to effect a re-awakening of the potential of Christian wisdom applied to the problems of our age."[28] For him Notre Dame could be at the heart of a Catholic intellectual revival to help redeem the time.

Hesburgh's deep love for and concern about his "beloved America" also coursed through his thinking. He acknowledged the "magnificent advance" of his country and praised its democratic charter, which guaranteed "the dignity of man and his rights and responsibilities to his fellow men under God." For him the United States, rooted in Christian and Western culture, needed to lead other democracies in the great battle of ideas being waged against totalitarian communism rooted in materialist and naturalist philosophies. But Hesburgh worried deeply about the moral and intellectual strength of the United States in this effort. He expressed the fear that Americans might allow "the soul of [their] culture to die," by turning their backs on foundational principles and instead adopting variations of the materialist and naturalist philosophies of Rousseau and Marx. Thus man (in his formulation) would be "left without any norm or sanction beyond himself and his own desires." The result would be a disastrous situation in which man would worship or serve only "himself or his false gods of money, power, nation or race." Understanding that "death comes to a culture or a civilization" more often "from the inner withering of a vital principle, from the loss of faith, from moral anemia, and from the abdication of a basic commitment to truth and integrity," he fretted that the United States was well launched on a downward slide. His vision was prophetic. Hesburgh held that his Catholic university had deep obligations to influence contemporary American society and thought for the good and to hold to "the truth that will set man free."[29]

Whatever its necessary service to the nation, Father Ted understood that Notre Dame's fundamental allegiance was owed to God and His Mystical Body, the Church. He clarified in his 1956 address, "The Divine Element in Education," that the university existed "as a work of the Church." Of this he had no doubt during his initial term. He exhorted the faculty to fully appreciate their vocation as lay members of this Church. Drawing on his doctoral thesis on the lay apostolate, he reflected on the Church as "not just a juridical organization, but a life-giving body" in which all "have the same basic dignity as members of Christ, partakers of His divine life." All were called to participate in "His work of redemption." He proceeded to outline for his lay colleagues their duties in both the spiritual and the temporal realms. Drawing on the work of Jacques Maritain he outlined the desperate need for "the integral humanist, the whole man who is really at home, temporarily in time and eternally in eternity, the man who respects both orders, and neglects neither, the man who has been completely revivified by the grace of Christ."[30]

It is crucial to comprehend that Hesburgh engaged in no facile effort to raise academic standards in accord with existing secular standards. He did not come into office determined to transform Notre Dame into some midwestern version of Princeton. Although he used that Ivy League school as a model for some elements in his planning at Notre Dame, his recognition of the limits of secular education and his blunt criticism of it stand out. He understood his life's work as being to shape a distinct institution. How exactly to do it challenged him and his collaborators.

Father Ted first explicated much of his approach to Catholic education in his *God and the World of Man*, where he described "education [as] not a series of patches sewed onto a crazy quilt, but an ordered assembly of many tight fitting parts." He endorsed the neoscholastic or Thomistic synthesis, which aimed to harmonize religious truth and secular learning. This approach emerged from the "neoscholastic revival" sparked by Pope Leo XIII's encyclical *Aeterni Patris* (1878). As summarized by scholars Philip Gleason and Michael Baxter, this intellectual approach, based on the philosophy of Saint Thomas Aquinas,

> established seven interrelated intellectual convictions: (1) that the existence of God can be known through reason, providing us with a natural theology and the preambles of faith; (2) that the mind conforms to external objects such that it is capable of discerning order and intelligibility in the universe; (3) that people are capable of discerning a divine purpose to the universe by virtue of its being implanted in creation and imprinted on the human heart, which thus provides a reliable basis for a stable, practical philosophy of life; (4) that this divine purpose provides the foundation for a philosophy of the whole of society as well, of morality, law, politics, economics, society, and culture; (5) that these aspects of life can be brought together into a unified, harmoniously ordered intellectual vision; (6) that this intellectual vision is centered on God, so that all things must be viewed, not only through reason, but also under the aspect of eternity (*sub specie aeternitatis*), thus infusing this intellectual vi-

sion with a religious dimension that can only be grasped by means of prayer, worship, and contemplation; and (7) that this religious dimension unites the philosophical, literary, aesthetic, and even mystical elements of life, thereby infusing this intellectual vision with a sense of personal piety and communal membership in the Mystical Body of Christ.[31]

He also drew heavily on John Henry Newman's *The Idea of a University* and gave theology "the first place among all the varied branches of knowledge at a University." It should "impregnate the whole field of university teaching and learning." Like Newman he lamented a world "where much attention is paid to the physical sciences like physics, chemistry, biology; [where] great favor is lavished on the social sciences, the mathematical sciences, history, languages and the like; and yet not a word is mentioned, not a class scheduled in most secular universities regarding theology." Theology, followed by philosophy, stood unquestionably in his mind at the top of the hierarchy of learning as these were the crucial disciplines that searched for the "ultimate answers." Without them there could be "no true or complete human culture, no true Christian wisdom."[32] To read such views today when theology and philosophy are largely marginalized in Catholic universities is indeed to be transported to a different time. Understanding that Hesburgh operated ardently in *that* earlier time affords a key insight into his labors.

Under his direction, Notre Dame completed a major curriculum review that affirmed the importance of theology and philosophy. Serious steps were taken to provide greater coherence and integration to these courses, which were deemed essential to synthesize the student's overall program of learning. He fervently expected Notre Dame students to engage the ultimate questions and believed deeply that this prepared them best for the world, whatever their particular field of study. Of course, he worried about the quality of the theology and philosophy courses and the quality of the faculty who taught them. He and Paul Beichner traveled in 1954 to universities across Europe—in Ireland, England, Belgium, France, and Germany—searching for Catholic faculty to boost Notre Dame's teaching ranks and academic reputation. Their joint expedition realized only modest results, but the intent reveals Hesburgh's thinking and priorities.

So too did Father Ted's efforts to draw major Catholic intellectuals into some association with Notre Dame. He recognized the major contributors in the Catholic intellectual renaissance, which had gathered strength in the 1930s and continued into the postwar years, and which included such notable figures as Étienne Gilson, Jacques Maritain, Christopher Dawson, J. R. R. Tolkien, and Frank Sheed and his wife, Maisie, along with such illustrious Christian fellow travelers as T. S. Eliot and C. S. Lewis.[33] In January 1954 he wrote to Dawson, the great Catholic historian, whose article in *Commonweal* "Education and Christian Culture" had attracted his interest for its argument that "the study of Christian culture could serve as the unifying focus" for higher education and as an antidote to the specialization that increasingly beset it.[34] He confided to Dawson that during his term as president he hoped "to re-center the emphasis at Notre Dame where it belongs—on those studies which belong to the Catholic university as Catholic." He assured him that the study of Christian culture would be important in this venture and invited the brilliant English man of letters to come to Notre Dame for lectures or seminars on the subject. He advised him that if he came he would find local scholars eager to engage him and such other regular visitors as Jacques Maritain and the leading American theologian John Courtney Murray, S.J.[35] Regrettably, Dawson never accepted Hesburgh's invitation, but the conception of Notre Dame as a forum for the advancement of the Catholic intellectual revival rested deep in him.

Dramatic moves like attracting Dawson to Notre Dame rarely came to fruition, although serendipity (a favorite word in the mature Hesburgh's vocabulary) rather than any careful planning enabled him to bring a great Catholic artist to campus in 1955. In the 1950s Father Anthony Lauck, a Holy Cross priest and artist, had enrolled at Syracuse University to study with the noted Croatian sculptor Ivan Meštrović. Meštrović, a true Croatian patriot, had been imprisoned by the Nazis in the early part of World War II, was subsequently released as a result of Vatican intervention, and spent the rest of the war as a refugee in Switzerland. After the war, in protest against Tito's Communist regime, he went into exile in the United States and took up an appointment at Syracuse. In the summer of 1954, when Father Ted traveled home to visit his family, he decided to visit with his Holy Cross confrere, who introduced him to his renowned teacher. It proved a key connection. Hesburgh loved the strength and power of Meštrović's work. When the man he eventually would address as "Maestro" indicated that he desired to spend his remaining years dedicating himself to religious art, the young Notre Dame president immediately extended an invitation to the artist to visit his campus and perhaps to make his home there. In Father Ted's account of this meeting he recalled that he put but one request to Meštrović, namely that he "create some religious art around the campus to add to the Catholic spirit of the place, because art says things that words don't."[36]

After a preliminary visit, Ivan Meštrović and his wife, Olga, decided to make the permanent move to South Bend, and his appointment under the "Distinguished Professor's Program" was announced in January 1955.[37] Hesburgh persuaded I. A. O'Shaughnessy to fund construction of a spacious, high-ceilinged studio wherein the sculptor could shape some of his larger pieces. Meštrović worked and taught at the university until his death in January of 1962. Father Ted rightly was proud that he had played a key role in bringing Meštrović to Notre Dame. He considered him "the only great artist" that he ever knew well, and he believed that they became "good friends."[38] They shared a disdain for "modern art," which Father Ted recalled that Meštrović described as "crap." He remembered that Meštrović held that "art that has to be explained is not art, [whereas] art that is authentic explains itself." Hesburgh took deep satisfaction that Meštrović's coming to Notre Dame added wonderful exemplars of religious art to the campus. The most notable piece was Meštrović's great marble *Pieta*, which Hesburgh arranged to have transferred from New York's Metropolitan Museum of Art to one of the side chapels just off the main altar of Sacred Heart Church. Hesburgh's association with Meštrović was unique. He did not become a devotee of the fine arts and never saw them as central in Notre Dame's academic development. Strengthening Notre Dame academically remained his main focus.

The university gathered momentum in the 1950s. Capable new scholars joined the faculty, new doctoral and master's programs were added, and a rapid increase in publication and scholarly activity occurred. Some of the research received the sponsorship of the federal government as well as of major foundations and industry. Hesburgh's Notre Dame appeared to be a place in motion, and Father Ted effectively advertised it as such. Privately he later acknowledged that "excellence doesn't come easily. It's step by step, person by person, and it's often in anguish," but publicly he touted the school's accomplishments and, even more so, its potential, to audiences far and wide.[39]

He worked to prevent any direct interference from his superiors in the Congregation of Holy Cross that could upset his plans. A real challenge emerged in this regard in 1954. It involved a book entitled *The Catholic Church in World Affairs*, which Waldemar Gurian and the historian Matthew Fitzsimons edited and the University of Notre Dame Press published. The volume gathered together papers from an important conference hosted at Notre Dame, including one by John Courtney Murray, the Jesuit priest who was engaged in exploring the relationship of religious freedom and the modern democratic state.[40] Murray and his views ran afoul of the Vatican's Holy Office headed by Cardinal Alfredo Ottaviani.[41] Objections arose to Murray's essay because it challenged the confessional state model, in which Catholicism held the status of the official religion, then seen in Catholic teaching as the ideal arrangement. Ottaviani advocated Catholicism as the state religion, whereas Murray embodied a Catholic embrace of religious freedom as described in the U.S. Constitution. Father Ted soon found himself engaged in a clash with Fr. Christopher O'Toole, then the superior general of the Holy Cross Congregation based in Rome. O'Toole, apparently under instructions from the Holy Office, demanded that Hesburgh withdraw the book, whose review copies already were circulating. Father Ted gave a lengthy accounting of this episode in *God, Country, Notre Dame*. He presented the dispute as not only an issue of academic freedom but also a matter of justice to Murray and the other authors. For him the case involved a "deeper principle" than even academic freedom. Rather it encompassed several questions: "Who runs this university? Is it run according to its own constitution, or can someone, because he is a higher authority in the [Holy Cross] community and the Catholic Church, just tell us to do something that is unjust?"[42] He offered his own answers in a particular way in the following decade, but in 1954 he successfully fought off O'Toole first by threatening to resign and then by persuading his nominal superior to allow him to avoid an immediate controversy while agreeing to eventually limit access to the book. He let the first print run sell down, but after a month he stored the remaining copies in the Dillon Hall attic. They later resurfaced after Murray's vindication at the Second Vatican Council.

Father Ted later portrayed himself as performing valiantly in this Murray episode, but there was an element of prudence in his quietly burying the book. In his autobiography he claimed that to let "everyone know where we stood" he granted John Courtney Murray an honorary degree at the next commencement.[43] But Murray had already received an honorary degree from Notre Dame in 1951 under Father Cavanaugh. Hesburgh made no grand public gesture in support of Murray. And there is surely some irony in Father Ted's awarding Cardinal Ottaviani an honorary degree in 1959 when the aged and near-blind cardinal visited the Notre Dame campus. Father Ted gave him "the grand tour," and undoubtedly the president also glowingly affirmed the Catholicity of the university.

While he placed significant energies into addressing the academic challenges facing Notre Dame, Father Ted gave less attention to the broad area of student life in the all-male school. Only in the 1960s did student activities become a central question for him. In his initial term he affirmed strongly the notion of "in loco parentis," and he defended the right of the university to act in lieu of parents. Although he eased up on some of the more extreme regulations and restrictions that he had criticized during his time as a rector, he did not alter what he characterized as "the unique kind of residential society that exists here." He understood that "something special" happened to a student during his four years at Notre Dame such that he became a proud "Notre Dame man," and he wanted to preserve that distinctive species.

Hesburgh never wanted the university to lose those qualities of spirit, atmosphere, and tradition that led its students to identify deeply with their alma mater. But he wanted students to challenge themselves ever more deeply spiritually, intellectually, and physically, and he took a special pride in student academic accomplishments as recognized by national awards and fellowships. Hesburgh derived greater satisfaction from Don Sniegowski's being named a Rhodes scholar in 1956 and Dennis Moran following in his footsteps in 1957 than he did from any Heisman Trophy award. He desired Notre Dame graduates to emerge as leaders who would take their values and talents out into the world.

MAKING FRIENDS, RAISING MONEY, AND SUPERVISING FOOTBALL

Father Hesburgh planned from the outset to be a different kind of Notre Dame president than his predecessors had been. He was determined to give his attention to representing the university to various constituencies far beyond the usual Notre Dame groups to whom previous presidents had connected. He viewed his presidential forebears, with the exception of John Cavanaugh, as too inward looking and parochial. The new president astutely judged the time right for Notre Dame to relinquish its defensive stance and to engage major elements of American society and particularly American higher education. Notre Dame, he thought, could be a vehicle to lead the broader Church in moving beyond the Catholic "ghetto" and making a larger mark in the United States. He concluded that he should personally spearhead this effort for the university. He had few peers in his capacity to meet people and to attract them to him. His serious purpose and winning personality impressed many. His enthusiastic willingness to accept appointments and assignments away from South Bend was soon noted, and as one appointment soon begat another, his reputation for public service grew. He eventually emerged as a member of a new generation of notable American university presidents—figures such as Robert Goheen at Princeton, Kingman Brewster at Yale, and William Friday at North Carolina. Yet none would match his ability both to engage a diverse array of individuals and groups and to gain appointments to so many significant organizations beyond higher education.

In his early years, he took the initiative and joined significant peak organizations such as the American Council on Education and the Association of American Colleges and Universities. He also signed on to participate in the activities of the International Federation of Catholic Universities (IFCU). In such groups as these he contributed vigorously and, in classic American fashion, he networked relentlessly. Hesburgh also took the initiative to invite leading figures in higher education to campus, where he could convey to them his own hopes and plans for the university. The earliest commencement speakers of the Hesburgh era testify to the new president's great interest in networking amidst and connecting his university to the elite circles of American higher education. He brought the presidents of Johns Hopkins University and of MIT to campus in 1953 and 1954.

In 1954 his initial networking paid handsome dividends. The Eisenhower administration appointed him to a full term on the National Science Board, the body founded in 1950 to establish policies for the National Science Foundation (NSF); the board advised the president and Congress on science and engineering research and education issues. Membership on this distinguished science organization gave him enhanced prestige and credibility, which he utilized to the full. Looking back during his retirement years, he remained surprised at the appointment and at some others that followed. He explained them as owing to his being not merely a priest but a special kind of priest who related so well to others and seemed so comfortable with the American way.

Father Ted began to make inroads into some of the inner citadels of the American academic establishment as he met more university presidents and leading scientists and foundation administrators. He relished every opportunity and found not only the formal meetings but the informal socializing that surrounded them much to his liking. Still, it was hard work. He once explained, although a trifle defensively, that "on these committees you had to do your homework. That's a side of me that no one knows—the innumerable hours I had to spend reading papers, doing homework, writing things, and just keeping on top of that outside work. That's why I didn't have time for a lot of other things that people would normally do on this [Notre Dame] job."[44]

Gaining access and acceptance in the elite circles of American higher education was only a part of Father Ted's "friend-making" enterprise. He grasped the importance of building connections in Washington, D.C., and in New York City. He spent many days in these cities and in particular seized every opportunity to visit Washington, D.C. He soon developed a bipartisan group of contacts including Richard Nixon, whom he first met at Notre Dame in November 1952 when the vice president–elect and his wife came to Notre Dame for the University of Southern California football game. He also aimed to bring important Washington figures to campus to be commencement speakers. In 1955 he welcomed U.S. Attorney General Herbert Brownell, Chief of Naval Operations Admiral Arleigh Burke came the following year, and Chief Justice Earl Warren came the year after that. Hesburgh's appointment to the U.S. Commission on Civil Rights in 1957 confirmed him as a frequent visitor to Washington and even made him an occasional participant in White House meetings. He savored every opportunity to enter the Oval Office. In New York he made the acquaintance of the powerful prelate Cardinal Francis Spellman, with whom he developed a friendship. Father Hesburgh was well launched as a national figure during his first term as president, but he would fully emerge once he was confirmed in the position for the long term. Then more foundation and commission appointments flooded in. So too would come the deluge of honorary degrees and invitations to deliver commencement addresses. In the 1950s he was honored by a few smaller Catholic schools including Le Moyne College in his hometown (1954) and St. Benedict's College in

Atchison, Kansas (1958). The number of honorary degrees increased as the decades marched along, and so too did the prestige of the schools that honored him.

Ranging far afield from campus did not mean that Hesburgh ignored the Notre Dame faithful. His friendship with key alumni like Ed Stephan deepened. He came to know Stephan and his wife, Evie, and their children as if they were family, and a deep trust developed between them that would be engaged in the following decade when Stephan emerged as the key legal mind to oversee the formal separation of ownership of the university from the Holy Cross order. He derived real personal support from his friendships with laymen like Stephan and I. A. O'Shaughnessy, who continued to be an enormous patron and enthusiast for Hesburgh. Ted and Ned ventured to Florida every winter to enjoy his hospitality aboard the *Marileen*. Hesburgh also recognized the need to draw more prominent figures into some engagement with Notre Dame, and he worked to bring them to campus. To this end he created advisory councils for each of the Colleges. In 1953 he announced that the leading business figures C. R. Smith, the president of American Airlines, and R. Sargent Shriver, Joseph Kennedy's son-in-law who was then running the Merchandise Mart in Chicago, had become advisers for the College of Commerce.[45] The following year came the Council for Arts and Letters, to which he recruited such public figures as the actress Irene Dunne, the conductor Fritz Reiner of the Chicago Symphony, and Senator John F. Kennedy of Massachusetts. He labored tirelessly to make new friends for the university.

Hesburgh also found time to deepen his bond with his brother, Jim, who had still been a baby when he left home to enter the seminary. Jim Hesburgh arrived at Notre Dame in 1951 and was a sophomore when his older brother assumed the presidency. Fortunately, the brothers Hesburgh found a convenient way to spend time together and they got to know each other well. Jim liked to drive, so Helen Hosinski enlisted him often to drive Father Ted either to or from Chicago's Midway airport as he set out on or returned from a trip. Jim enjoyed cruising along in the university Oldsmobile and learning of and from his brother. Despite the age gap a genuine and lasting brotherly relationship developed. Hesburgh also did his best to be a dutiful son to his parents, although his connection with his father never truly warmed. The older man maintained his very conservative political leanings and also a slight edge in dealing with his son who now led Notre Dame. In an oft-told anecdote, when the new president returned to visit Syracuse, the elder Hesburgh beat him in a game of Scrabble and pronounced that "they just don't make college presidents the way they used to." Father Ted never forgot the crack or the tone in which it was delivered. Fortunately for him his mother more than compensated with her endless pride in him and all he did.

While Hesburgh rapidly increased his range of friends and associates it must be noted that not everyone whom he met was drawn to him. Furthermore, he had reservations about certain individuals even as he engaged in efforts to enlist their support. Sister Madeleva Wolff of Saint Mary's College epitomizes the first category while Joseph P. Kennedy notably exemplifies the second. Father Ted's reaction to each of these individuals provides a deeper understanding of the ambitious young Notre Dame president. Madeleva Wolff came from a prominent St. Paul family to join the Sisters of the Holy Cross at Saint Mary's College, the sister school to Notre Dame. A brilliant woman, she earned a doctorate in English at the University of California, Berkeley, in 1925 and in 1934 took over the presidency of Saint Mary's, where she served for twenty-seven years. She was a much-published poet, a respected lecturer and intellectual.[46]

Hesburgh recognized Madeleva's accomplishments and set out to court her by awarding her an honorary Doctorate of Letters degree at the special ceremony commemorating the dedication of O'Shaughnessy Hall.[47] But no warm friendship developed. In an unguarded moment, he admitted that he was never close to her and placed the blame firmly on the great Holy Cross nun. He revealingly speculated that "she looked at me as an upstart probably, or as a small boy she could order around. She was always a little hard to get ahold of, in the sense that she was a poet and always in a different world than I was anyway." He admitted their relationship was at best "cordial" and that the Notre Dame–Saint Mary's relationship was strained at times because Madeleva resented the male "rowdiness" of Notre Dame regularly invading the feminine "tranquility" of Saint Mary's.[48] Trying to put the matter in the best possible light, in retrospect, he concluded that their relationship was a case of "very good people who just somehow don't click."[49]

One person with whom he tried to build a close relationship was Joseph P. Kennedy, Father Cavanaugh's great friend and benefactor. The patriarch of America's most famous Irish-Catholic family, Kennedy personified energy, ambition, and the quest for power. He lived to see one son elected president and two others elected to the U.S. Senate. The Kennedy family's relationship with Notre Dame and especially the friendship between

John Cavanaugh and the elder Kennedy is worthy of a study in its own right. It suffices to say here that it began with Joseph Kennedy's giving the commencement address at the university in 1941. He appreciated the gracious hospitality extended to him, and his friendship with John Cavanaugh developed from their meeting then. His warm feelings for Notre Dame led him to accept an appointment on the lay advisory board. After Cavanaugh assumed the presidency, Kennedy appreciably increased his donations to Notre Dame, usually through the Kennedy Foundation. Without any publicity he gave what Cavanaugh called "the handsome gift of $100,000" in 1949 and followed that up the next year with another gift of the same amount.[50] In the period between the two gifts, Notre Dame awarded an honorary degree to the Honorable John F. Kennedy, U.S. congressman from Massachusetts. Cynical readers might speculate that this degree and the donations were remotely related as the father eagerly sought preferments and honors for the son to boost his public standing.[51] Theodore Hesburgh later thought so, and he held that "Joe Kennedy never did anything for Notre Dame without wanting something in return."[52]

In 1950 when Father Ted was serving as executive vice president, he first met Congressman Kennedy and his sister Eunice when they drove in from Chicago for the January commencement exercises. He established an easy rapport with each of them. He soon engaged in exchanges with their father about Notre Dame. They seemed to be on the same wavelength. In 1951 the Kennedy patriarch wrote Hesburgh congratulating him on a report that detailed academic developments at Notre Dame and encouraging him to get more publicity for these achievements. In words that could only have confirmed the executive vice president in his own views, the well-connected Kennedy proceeded to tell him: "While having lunch in Rome last week with Prince Pacelli and Monsignor Montini [later Paul VI] of the State Department of the Vatican, I was talking about what a terrific job Father Cavanaugh was doing at Notre Dame and two of the Americans there, one a Jesuit and one a Bishop, in attempting to explain Notre Dame said, 'Oh yes, they have a great football team.' I then proceeded to tell them about the other great things they have. I don't ever expect that collegiate achievement can compare newspaper publicity-wise with the regular football team, but I think more people should know about the splendid work the University is doing."[53] It was music to Hesburgh's ears.

Hesburgh also was well aware of Joseph Kennedy's more publicized gift to Notre Dame to support cadets expelled from West Point for cheating.

This cheating episode occurred in the spring of 1951, the same semester that Harvard College expelled Edward (Teddy) Kennedy for the same offense. Perhaps his son's experience prompted some sympathy from Joe Kennedy for the expelled cadets, because he advised Cavanaugh to offer a place at Notre Dame to all of them and he promised to cover all tuition costs. Eventually twelve of the cadets took up the Notre Dame offer and graduated from the university. All had graduated by 1954 at a total cost to the Kennedy Foundation of $35,147.87.[54] Hesburgh hoped that this modest sum might be increased many times over in a subsequent donation, and he worked hard to secure it. Replying to Joe Kennedy's congratulations on his taking on the presidential mantle, he wrote that "because you have always shown such an unusual quality of friendship for Father John and for Notre Dame, I prized your endorsement more than any of the others I received."[55]

During his presidency Hesburgh made no effort to supplant Cavanaugh in his role as Kennedy family chaplain, and he did not serve as a Kennedy courtier at Hyannisport or Palm Beach as did Cavanaugh, but he gave considerable time to staying in touch with the millionaire and visited with him on occasion. He gained some modest dividends for his efforts. In 1953 he accepted Kennedy's suggestion to extend a Christmas bonus to faculty members with large families. Aiming to firm up his connection to the Kennedy father he also took time to praise the speeches of then senator John F. Kennedy, who had defeated Henry Cabot Lodge in the 1952 elections. All appeared to be progressing well. Father Cavanaugh's integration with the Kennedys deepened further as his associations with the Kennedy children expanded. He helped Eunice and her husband, Sargent Shriver, now residing in Chicago, to lead a discussion group on Catholic topics, and much to his pleasure he officiated at the wedding of Patricia Kennedy and the British actor Peter Lawford at New York City's Church of St. Thomas More in April 1954. In March of that year Hesburgh acknowledged with delight another gift of $100,000 to Notre Dame from Kennedy and advised him that it would be "used as the basis of the University's efforts to build a new, much-needed dining hall." Then in words that from this distance seem a trifle extravagant he expressed gratitude for the "magnificent benefaction" and went on: "The realization that there is no way on earth in which to thank you properly prompts me to have one hundred Masses offered for your intentions."[56]

By 1954 Father Ted felt that he had made real progress in his relationship with Ambassador Kennedy, as he liked to be called. That progress slowed markedly following a visit Hesburgh made to the villa Joseph Kennedy occupied that summer on the French Riviera. From there Kennedy had contacted Father Ted, who was in Paris wrapping up a tour of European universities with Paul Beichner. The onetime ambassador complained that Father Cavanaugh had been denied permission to come to join him. To placate him Hesburgh volunteered to join Kennedy at Èze-sur-Mer, a small village between Nice and Monte Carlo, for a few days. He thought it would give him the chance to pen an article for *Sports Illustrated* that he had committed to write and also to converse with Kennedy so as to lay further groundwork for a major gift. The overlap between making friends and raising money was on obvious display.

The visit didn't work out quite as expected. Father Ted arrived to be greeted not only by Joe Kennedy and his wife, Rose, but also by an attractive young woman, Janet Des Rosiers, who served nominally as Kennedy's secretary, although Hesburgh remembered her more as an "attendant." His first morning there he said Mass for the devout if somewhat disengaged Rose and then adjourned to a pleasant pergola to work on his article. Joe Kennedy went off to play golf with friends. On his return he called Father Ted to join him for a swim at the Villa's private beach. Hesburgh readily agreed yet was surprised not only that the scantily clad Janet des Rosiers joined them but also that Kennedy "was all over the young woman." He felt uneasy and resented that Kennedy was behaving that way in front of him as if to draw him into complicity in what the priest judged an inappropriate relationship. He recalled that he didn't think a married man should cavort on the beach with a young woman. A tension developed between them. The next day Hesburgh resisted Kennedy's invitation to travel to the beach at Monte Carlo.

Father Ted presented this episode as a key moment when he determined that the elder Kennedy's moral character was questionable. Although the incident might be measured as rather minor by some worldly readers, Father Ted judged it as a decisive revelation. The scales fell from his eyes and he now saw who Joseph P. Kennedy really was. In short, he explained, Kennedy pursued only his own purposes and he used religion as he used everything and everyone else: to foster the special interests of himself and his family. Father Ted also voiced, although hesitantly, his criticism of John Cavanaugh for his close association with Kennedy. Speaking in retrospect, he opined that Cavanaugh's association with Kennedy helped the Boston millionaire to maintain the fiction of being a "great Catholic family man" when he was really "a womanizer who hit on everyone."[57]

The reality was more complicated. On his eventual return to Notre Dame Father Ted made no effort to distance himself from Joe Kennedy. Instead he wrote telling Kennedy how much he "enjoyed the interlude at Èze" and how it "was a great relief to slow down for a few days and to bask in your hospitality." He enclosed a copy of his draft article for *Sports Illustrated*, suggesting that the piece "should have been dedicated to you because it never would have been written without the peaceful atmosphere on the terrace at Èze."[58] This hardly constituted getting caught in the Kennedy web, but the intrepid Hesburgh continued to fly dangerously close to it. Ironically, the elder Kennedy played the larger role in the distancing that occurred between him and Hesburgh and Notre Dame. He resigned from the lay advisory board in 1955, claiming an inability to attend the meetings in South Bend, although he continued his efforts to free Father Cavanaugh from his Notre Dame duties so that he might join him at more appealing places. Hesburgh took the resignation dauntlessly and wrote thanking Kennedy for his "wonderful counsel and thoughtful help in so many of our university projects." In a further indication that he wanted continued contact with the Kennedy clan he expressed his happiness to the patriarch that "the work you have begun is being carried on by Jack, Bob [Robert Kennedy], and Sarge Shriver, who are now active members on three of our Advisory Councils."[59] It should be noted that Robert Kennedy, then serving as chief counsel and staff director of the Senate Permanent Subcommittee on Investigations, had by this point joined the Law School's Advisory Council and had spoken on campus.

After this point Joseph Kennedy's giving to Notre Dame largely dried up with the exception of a 1956 donation to establish a chair named in honor of his British/Canadian friend Lord Beaverbrook (Max Aitken), a flamboyant businessman, newspaper proprietor, and sometime politician. Correspondence between Hesburgh and Kennedy also largely shriveled after 1956, although Father Ted didn't stop trying. In September 1957 he wrote Kennedy advising that he had been elected as an honorary life member of the advisory Lay Board of Trustees and encouraging him and Rose Kennedy to visit Notre Dame. There is no indication that Joseph Kennedy took up the invitation.

It is surely fair to suggest that Father Hesburgh would not have expended the energy he did on Joseph P. Kennedy unless he anticipated that some further massaging of Kennedy's ego might bring a large gift to Notre Dame that would provide a real boost to the school's fledgling development efforts. This hints at the burdens of fund-raising for Notre Dame in the 1950s. Raising money was not easy and potential donors of major gifts were few and far between. Some of Hesburgh's predecessors had simply accepted that Notre Dame could never raise large sums of money, and had tailored their expectations for the school in light of this. Hesburgh reversed that view with a vengeance. He established the goal of creating a great Catholic university first and then he determined that he would find the financial resources to accomplish it. He drew a direct connection between wealth and quality of institution. He later explained that "you can say that the top ten endowed universities in America are the ten best universities in America. It is almost axiomatic."[60] He dreamed of joining the company of these wealthy institutions. The prospect of doing so must have seemed daunting as the Notre Dame endowment stood at a miniscule $7.5 million when he took office, and the school faced pressing needs that had first claim on any monies that were raised. Nonetheless he gave raising money and building the endowment a high priority from his first days in office and he never relented on this goal. In our times, when as one astute observer has put it "the middle name of American higher education today isn't wisdom but money: the pursuit of alumni, foundation and federal 'research' dollars," Hesburgh's prioritizing of fund-raising seems rather obvious.[61] But it was a major shift for Notre Dame in the mid-1950s.

Many observers, in both the past and the present, have closely associated Notre Dame's ability to raise money and to attract support with its success on the gridiron. The relationship is overstated. Assuredly football proved crucial to Notre Dame. It made Notre Dame a school known throughout the country and one beloved by its devoted fans, including the subway alumni who live and die for the Fighting Irish. Hesburgh's predecessors also used very effectively the direct income generated by the football program to help build the campus. But with few exceptions, Notre Dame football failed to be the generator of sizable donations to the university during the first half of the twentieth century. Hesburgh understood this as he began his presidency, and this awareness gave him some freedom as he set about to alter the balance between academics and athletics on campus. He knew he would not be harassed by wealthy donors complaining about the state of the football program. (That would come later and mainly for his successors.)

When Hesburgh arrived in office he brought with him the reputation of asserting firm control over athletics that he had gained from his work as executive vice president. He quickly built on his earlier efforts and made clear that under his leadership the academic development of the university held priority. Criticism quickly emerged that he was de-emphasizing football. In his memoir he denied this and claimed that he "never deliberately did anything to cut back on football."[62] His denial is rather disingenuous because he had already helped implement measures to limit the size of the classes that Frank Leahy could recruit. Further, there can be no doubt of his determination to strike firm blows against Notre Dame's image as a "football factory."

Few close followers of Notre Dame football doubt that Hesburgh effectively fired Leahy. The able writer Jim Dent in his book *Resurrection* presents this perspective succinctly, noting that "when Leahy was eased out the door at the end of the 1953 season, he claimed it was the conspiratorial work of Fathers Joyce and Hesburgh" and that "practically everyone with knowledge of the situation supported Leahy's contention that he was fired."[63] Father Ted always rejected claims that he "fired" Leahy. Rather he presented Ned Joyce and himself as concerned for Leahy's health—after all, the coach had collapsed during halftime at the 1953 Georgia Tech game—and worried that his continued coaching would lead to his early death. So Father Ted "resolved to do something to keep Frank from killing himself."[64] As he made clear in his memoir, he knew he personally couldn't persuade Leahy to resign, so he cunningly enlisted the support of Art Haley, the director of public relations at Notre Dame, and the influential *Chicago Tribune* sportswriter Arch Ward, both of whom Leahy considered good friends. At a dinner in Ward's Chicago apartment after the end of the 1953 season, they persuaded Leahy to retire. Haley immediately called Hesburgh to inform him, and Leahy called soon after to make it official, much to Hesburgh's relief. In a later conversation Hesburgh offered to cover tuition for any of Leahy's eight children who could gain entry to Notre Dame; Leahy accepted this offer and moved on. Father Ted told me explicitly and somewhat defensively that "everybody for years tried to say that there had a been a terrible fight between the two of us and that I fired him." But, he explained, "I didn't fire him, rather he called up and resigned. I [indirectly] persuaded him to, but I didn't fire him."[65] He stated firmly that if Leahy had not resigned he certainly would not have acted to remove him. Leahy's resignation and departure from Notre Dame caused some distancing but no deep rupture in his relationship with Hesburgh. Father Ted wanted it known that he stayed in touch with Leahy and even visited with him in his apartment in Portland, Oregon, just a week before his death in 1973.

Hesburgh genuinely cared for Leahy's health and the well-being of his wife and children, but truth be told his satisfaction with Leahy's resignation went far beyond his concern for the coach and his family. Hesburgh realized that Leahy represented the old image of Notre Dame football, which he aimed to revise. Further, he worried that Leahy stood so prominently as a public spokesperson for the university. He wanted to clarify that the president ran things at Notre Dame. That became even clearer when Hesburgh, after briefly consulting Father Joyce, announced twenty-five-year-old Terry Brennan as the great Frank Leahy's successor.

Brennan remains the youngest head coach in Notre Dame history. He played successfully for Leahy in the late 1940s, and after graduation he coached successfully at the powerhouse Mount Carmel High School in Chicago. He returned to Notre Dame in 1953 as freshman football coach and (in Hesburgh's mind) heir apparent to Leahy. Brennan's opportunity came quickly. Hesburgh knew and liked both Brennan and his young wife, a Saint Mary's College graduate. He had taught Brennan in a religion class when he was a student, and he made a point of noting in his *Sports Illustrated* article in 1954 that "Terry majored in philosophy as an undergraduate, and I can say, after having had him as a student in class, that he performed as well there as on the field."[66] Some cautious observers at the time worried about Brennan's youth and lack of coaching experience, but Hesburgh was untroubled. Brennan seemed to him a good match for his more academically oriented Notre Dame, and as Thomas Stritch noted, it was an "engaging idea: young Hesburgh and young Brennan, energetic, ardent, idealistic, confronting the wolves of the college football world together."[67]

Hesburgh tackled head-on some of the perennial problems of college football in his notable piece in *Sports Illustrated*. Borrowing from his previous addresses at Notre Dame he emphasized the importance of placing the student's education first and foremost. If this principle was followed, he argued, most of the abuses in college football could be eliminated. He bragged that under the "watchdog" guidance of Father Joyce, the Notre Dame program now met the high ethical standards he had laid out, although he did note a couple of occasions in the quite recent past where only *his* direct intervention had prevented transgressions. In his summing up, Hesburgh argued that his basic principle regarding the student's education being the essential priority could be implemented but only if a number of other conditions were accepted. These included "if directors of athletics and coaches are not unmercifully pressured for victories, remembering that after all, even football *is* still a game, and one side always loses, even though we must always play to win."[68]

All started well. As the conventional account presents it, Brennan guided Leahy's experienced players to a fine 9-1 result in his first year and to a respectable 8-2 in his second. Then things fell apart. In 1956 Notre Dame fell to a 2-8 record, the worst record in the history of the school, although somehow or other during it the "golden boy" Paul Hornung managed to win the Heisman Trophy. Brennan quickly came under public fire, but football cognoscenti blamed the recruitment restrictions within which he operated. Hesburgh showed no desire to share any blame for the poor showing with Brennan and instead began to worry about his young coach's abilities. Early in 1957 he met with Brennan at the New York Athletic Club, where they both were staying for the presentation of the Heisman Award to Hornung. According to Hesburgh's recollection, they talked about the past disastrous season, and Brennan "made an impassioned plea that he had it under control and next year was going to be great, so couldn't he have one more year." Hesburgh agreed to this but extended a warning that "if it is bad I am going to have to give you the axe." As it turned out Brennan's 1957 squad improved significantly and the team went 7-3, including a great upset victory over Oklahoma, which broke the Sooners' record-breaking forty-seven-game winning streak. Despite the improvement Brennan lived on borrowed time. In 1958 the team would go 6-4, but after some early season defeats Hesburgh's serious concerns that Brennan wasn't up to the job re-emerged. He met with Joyce, and according to Father Ted it was "jointly decided" that "it was time for a change."[69] Making that change involved Hesburgh in a controversy that produced significant negative publicity, an experience he weathered but did not appreciate.

Hesburgh had Joyce advise Brennan of his decision to terminate him as coach early in December. They planned to announce it in the near future. Soon after the meeting Father Ted traveled to the Mayo Clinic for his health checkup. Brennan contacted him there with a request that the announcement be delayed since his wife, Kelly, was planning a big Christmas party later in the month and he did not want it ruined by news of his dismissal. Hesburgh gave in and delayed the announcement until December 21. He remembered it as the "dumbest thing I ever did." He recounted (with generous hyperbole) that "when we announced it all hell broke loose." In his words the condemnation and criticism charged that "Notre Dame fired the coach right at Christmas [revealing] that it had no Christianity, no generosity, no Christmas spirit and that it was a 'Scrooge' thing to do." His recollections withstand some scrutiny as this sample from Arthur Daley in the *New York Times* makes clear: "No college in the country, in all probability, has as many or as unrestrainedly devoted followers as has Notre Dame. Here is the 'People's Choice' in a most sentimental form, all of it packed in the roseate glow of pure idealism. Yet this was the school that gave the sack to the 30-year-old father of four children for Christmas."[70]

Mail criticizing the firing decision deluged Notre Dame, although Hesburgh managed to avoid reading it for some weeks. He had departed for a Christmas vacation on the Baja peninsula in Mexico with his new-found friends C. R. Smith, the president of American Airlines, and Charlie Jones, the president of the Richfield Oil Corporation, to enjoy some hunting and fishing. When he returned "thoroughly relaxed from his Mexican sojourn," he decided not to read the "bushel baskets" of critical letters, and he instructed that a short standard response be offered in reply. He recalled telling Fr. John "Hack" Wilson, whom he drafted to help deal with the correspondence, that "there are things more important than football fans and their fanaticism." Hesburgh withstood the criticism, although he disliked it. He felt burned by the saga of the Brennan firing and largely left the selection of the new coach to Ned Joyce. In retrospect, however, he saw the football failures of the Brennan years and those of subsequent years as backhandedly beneficial. Despite these losses Notre Dame prospered and the school's reputation grew. For him, "that was something everybody had to learn."[71]

RELIGIOUS SUPERIOR, PRIEST IN PUBLIC AND PRIVATE, AND RENEWAL

When Theodore Martin Hesburgh received his obedience to serve as president of Notre Dame in 1952 he also accepted the assignment to serve as religious superior of the local Holy Cross community. By canon law and the statutes of the congregation, the latter position was limited to a six-year term. Holy Cross had seen it as appropriate for the two positions to be jointly held because the religious superior exercised authority over all members of the local community, and it was deemed fitting that the priest appointed president should also serve as superior so there could be no confusion over who presided over and led at the university. The joint appointment also symbolized the integral nature of the Holy Cross role at the university. The Holy Cross community held a central role in the workings of the university. It was not simply one among a number of interest groups on campus. During Hesburgh's superiorship from 1952 to 1958 he bore formal responsibility for over a hundred priests and close to twenty brothers who held a variety of positions at Notre Dame ranging from senior officer positions to staffing the firehouse.

Ted Hesburgh realized quickly that he could not take on all the duties of superior while devoting his energy and committing himself to the presidency of the university. Therefore he soon delegated much of the superior's role to the assistant superior, Fr. Richard "Dick" Grimm, a good friend of his who taught in the religion department. Grimm led communal prayer and handled all the day-to-day administration out of his office in Corby Hall. As Father Ted consigned much of the daily superior's duties to Grimm, his own regular contact with the community diminished. As his travel schedule increased, he found himself frequently away from campus and from the common exercises that regulated the lives of committed religious. He prioritized his apostolic efforts on behalf of the university and saw himself as faithfully fulfilling his obligations as a Holy Cross priest in the process.

Tensions between Father Ted and the leadership of Holy Cross beyond the university emerged during these years and contributed to his sense that the interests of the congregation and those of the university diverged. Hesburgh's discontent over the budget arrangements between Holy Cross and the university troubled him. He believed that the Indiana Province relied too heavily on Notre Dame for its annual operating funds, and he resented that the provincial could simply request support from Notre Dame for various special projects. Things came to a head for Hesburgh when the Indiana Province decided to build a new seminary on the edge of St. Joseph Lake across from the main campus. Ted Mehling, still serving as provincial, pressed him for a sizable donation from Notre Dame, but Father Ted resisted. He recommended that the congregation undertake its own fund-raising drive, which it eventually did under the direction of Fr. (later

Bishop) Alfred Mendez. Father Ted explained to me that his "conscience" was bothering him about what he saw as "raids" by Holy Cross on the Notre Dame treasury. He acknowledged that "technically, the community owned and operated the place and I guess they could do what they wanted," but his priority of building Notre Dame led him to be irritated by Holy Cross requests.[72] Surprisingly, he gave little thought to the reality that over a hundred priests and many hardworking brothers labored in the Notre Dame vineyard without regular salaries and basically for their upkeep, which was the standard practice for religious in those days. In light of their largely unpaid labor, a request for the university to assist in constructing a seminary for the training of new priests seems not wholly unreasonable. But Hesburgh analyzed the situation quite differently.

Father Ted's prioritizing of Notre Dame over against Holy Cross was pursued at the same time that he developed a more individualistic approach to living his religious life. In the ideal circumstances, membership in a men's religious community means *not* serving as independent individuals but rather as part of a brotherhood. The collective effort is fuel that normally makes possible accomplishments that individuals simply could not achieve. Although Father Ted always felt part of the Holy Cross brotherhood, he increasingly charted his own course. He accepted that his formal obedience consisted in leading Notre Dame, and he didn't welcome further guidance from any superior. His growing success in the position led him to say that if Holy Cross didn't like what he was doing then the provincial could remove him. Now, and necessarily, he operated not on the personal budget of a typical religious but through university funds that Helen Hosinski regularly replenished for him. He was never ostentatious in his spending and he continued to live in his simple rooms in Corby Hall, but away from campus he often stayed in fine hotels and ate in good restaurants. In addition to his extensive travel on university business and on National Science Board excursions, he now regularly spent weeks over Christmas with his friends Smith and Jones in Baja, Mexico, then time in the late winter with I. A. O'Shaughnessy in Florida on the *Marileen*, and then he enjoyed a fishing retreat at Land O'Lakes, Wisconsin, immediately after graduation. He also began the practice of making major international trips during the summer. His initial foray to Europe with Paul Beichner had been labeled an academic mission to recruit faculty, but thereafter the big international trips became mainly occasions for his own education and to enrich his experience and satisfy his insatiable curiosity. He was never a simple "sightseeing" tourist, but an active traveler searching out people and places, especially any major universities. Extensive trips to Latin America, Africa, and the Middle East all occurred in the 1950s, and over the course of his life he would visit more than 140 different countries. He occasionally felt some resentment that his brothers in community did not fully appreciate all that he did on their behalf. Such concerns, however, rarely troubled him as many other matters claimed his attention.

Hesburgh's distancing from the community was well camouflaged in the 1950s by the emphasis he placed on his priestly ministry. Everywhere he went on campus and far beyond he was *Father* Hesburgh. On campus he was seen wearing his religious habit. Off campus he featured his clerical suit at any formal gathering. His visibility and commitment as a priest struck Catholics and non-Catholics alike. He was present on campus for all the major liturgical events, such as the opening Mass of the school year, at which he delivered his formal homily-addresses. When he traveled, his Mass kit always traveled with him. His fidelity to celebrating daily Mass and to reading his breviary withstood all the pressures and demands placed upon him. The complexities of his relationship with his own religious order were irrelevant to most observers, who saw only a zealous priest exercising his ministry energetically and effectively. And this is what he did. He served as the chief pastor of Notre Dame and as a priestly ambassador beyond.

Father Ted kept to his understanding of the priest as not only a mediator between God and humankind but also as an instrument of God's grace and mercy in the world. His ministry involved important dimensions of leadership and administration, but his presidential duties never caused him to be walled off from people. He presided at weddings, baptisms, and anniversary Masses. He visited and anointed the sick and dying among the Notre Dame family. Whatever the demands of his relentless ambition for Notre Dame, he never failed to extend kindness of one sort or another to individuals who either revealed some need to him or whose need he learned of from others. I warrant that his significant kindnesses literally must be measured in the tens of thousands over the course of his long life. Certainly he never lost the pastoral skills he applied in Vetville in his early years as a priest.

A recitation of his kind actions could fill a book, but I mention here but two from the period of his first term as president. In 1957 when a young priest–graduate student in the history department named Marvin O'Connell found the conditions of his Lingard Fellowship altered so that his continuance in studies was problematic he was instructed to see

Father Hesburgh for a final appeal. The university president heard the case, agreed that a full stipend should be restored to the Lingard fellow, said that he would take care of it, and then announced (as O'Connell recalled) in these exact words: "Downstairs they'll think me a bastard, but they already do, so that's no problem."[73] Earlier in 1957, Michael McInerny, the young son of Ralph and Connie McInerny, died of encephalitis just a few months after his third birthday. Ralph McInerny, just beginning his distinguished career in the philosophy department, and his vibrant young wife "learned the meaning of loss" when they had to bury their first child. The priests on campus sought to be supportive, but soon after the funeral Fr. Philip Moore, acting as Father Hesburgh's intermediary, called Ralph in and told him to draw up a list of all the expenses that the young couple owed and told him that the university would take care of them. Further, he advised him that the university would provide a down payment for them to obtain a house of their own. This, as McInerny recalled in his memoir, conveyed tangibly to him the meaning of the Notre Dame family, and he knew that Hesburgh guided it.[74] Both O'Connell and McInerny later would have genuine concerns about some decisions Hesburgh made regarding Notre Dame, but neither of them could ever forget the kindness he showed them.

Hesburgh's straightforward generosity on a personal level reflected his uncomplicated spirituality. He prayed that the Holy Spirit would guide him and he rested comfortably in the belief that the Third Person of the Trinity directly inspired his actions. Whatever the pressures on him, he was not given to dark nights of the soul or to spiritual crises. His devotion to the Blessed Mother deepened during these years. She was the Lady atop the Dome who presided proudly over the school he was building to honor her and her Son. He visited the Grotto to pray to her most days after arising late and before he went near his office. He continued the practice his whole life. Although his spirituality leaned in a very traditional direction, his ecclesial approach had a decidedly more liberal or reformist flavor as his support for John Courtney Murray indicated. Through the 1950s he continued to encourage the efforts and initiatives of lay Catholics and he maintained his close association with his friends Pat and Patty Crowley and their thriving Christian Family Movement.

He wanted to see the Church active in the world and engaging the world, and he wanted to play a significant role himself. He always saw his endeavors on civil rights as fulfilling a distinct religious purpose. His growing interest in and engagement on scientific matters gave a new and very modern dimension to his priestly ministry and its outreach to the world. Hesburgh understood the contemporary challenges involved in devising the appropriate relationship of science with religious faith. But he was not overly perturbed by the challenge. He recalled some momentary worries when he was first invited to join the National Science Board. According to his recollection he thought that "I'm going to be right there at the heart of the biggest and most spectacular developments in science and a lot of them probably are going to be faith-threatening, but it's reality. It [science] is not fairy tales and I have a framework into which I have been able so far to fit new kinds of knowledge that I have gained. So I'm not going to be afraid of it. I'm going into it." He did so with gusto and relished his association with leading scientists and the projects they pursued.[75]

Never did any project shake his faith, as one key later instance revealed. In the early 1960s when Dr. Frank Drake of the National Radio Astronomy Observatory in Green Bank, West Virginia, explained his Search for Extra-terrestrial Intelligence (SETI), which looked for evidence of sentient life in the universe, he warned the Catholic priest/National Science Board member that he would not like the idea. According to Hesburgh, Drake, after presenting his research program, inquired whether Hesburgh hated him. Father Ted surprised the radio astronomer by replying, "I don't hate you. I think it is a great idea." The rather stunned scientist responded, "How can you say that? You're a theologian. This threatens God." He was even more surprised to hear this reply: "On the contrary, it expands God." Hesburgh explained further: "When you look at the immensity of the universe, then you get a little inkling of the creative power of God." He concluded, in a way that backhandedly endorsed the scientist's work, that "it's a compliment to God to say we're looking to see if You did some more things that we haven't heard about yet."

Hesburgh fleshed out his ideas on science in his 1957 opening Mass homily-address, which he titled "Education in a World of Science." Here he noted the increasing dominance of science and technology and the emphasis on the scientific method. There could be no disputing that in this period, as he said, "science is the recognized darling of our day." But Hesburgh warned of the danger if science devolved into scientism—that arrogant claim that "science" exists as an interpretative worldview capable of explaining everything in empirical terms.[76] These ideas guided his solid support for scientific research and for science education throughout his presidency. They also ensured that he was not seen as being in any way backward as a priest or afraid of science. He was as eager as anyone to conquer new frontiers on earth and beyond.

In late April 1958, Fr. Theodore J. Mehling, provincial of the Holy Cross Fathers, reappointed Hesburgh as president of the University of Notre Dame for an indefinite term. Mehling advised that Hesburgh would complete his term as religious superior in June, after which a new superior would be named.[77] Father Ted often presented Mehling's decision as a real surprise to him. He recalled that Ted Mehling had simply told him the news on the way to the chapter where obediences would be distributed, "Oh by the way, you're going to stay on as president." His "hundred-yard dash" was quickly extended into a much longer race. He claimed that he had expected to go back to teaching theology and to living in a residence hall, but now he had to rouse himself to continue in office.[78] Memory plays tricks on us all, and this was a case where Father Ted's memory simply had it wrong. His reappointment was announced two months before the provincial chapter, at which other assignments were made, including those of Dick Grimm as local superior of the Notre Dame community and that of Chester Soleta as vice president for academic affairs.[79] The public announcement in April came only after significant consultation with Hesburgh. Indicative of his desire and intention to stay on as president was his important announcement on March 1, 1958, of a $66.6 million development program geared "to consolidate and further [Notre Dame's] academic excellence" over the coming ten-year period. The plan included $27 million in endowment for increased faculty salaries, $18.6 million for buildings (heading the list was a new library), $11 million for research, $5 million for student aid, and $5 million for administrative purposes. This was not presented as some guidance for his expected successor, but as his charter for where he wanted to lead Notre Dame and what he wanted to accomplish in his next phase as its president.

A number of factors complemented his desire to continue in office and led to Mehling's announcement. Father Joyce, his most obvious successor, made clear he did not want the position but preferred to stay on as executive vice president and to continue his collaboration with Hesburgh. Renewing the current president then allowed for the retention of his effective executive vice president. Hesburgh had not groomed any other Holy Cross priests to take over leadership in the way that Cavanaugh had trained him. Additionally, other possible candidates for the position remained silent. And what sensible Holy Cross priest could expect to present himself as anywhere near as qualified as the dynamic Hesburgh, whose achievements on campus and whose reputation off-campus were now so impressive?

Mehling's announcement of Hesburgh's renewal was met with an over-whelmingly positive response. There was no lamentation that this move pushed the Notre Dame presidency toward what James Burtchaell later called "a more narrowly profiled professional identity" and away from a formal ecclesial role.[80] Instead all was celebration—both of what Father Hesburgh had accomplished and of his plans for the future. His already significant list of appointments was proudly noted, especially his presiden-tial and papal service. Photos of him "conferring" with Pope Pius XII as Vatican City representative to the International Atomic Energy Agency and of him receiving his commission from President Eisenhower to serve on the Civil Rights Commission graced the pages of Notre Dame Alumnus. Faculty greeted the reappointment enthusiastically. They appreciated his emphasis on academics and particularly his efforts to raise their salaries and benefits. Students gushed over the news. Jim Steintrager editorialized in the Scholastic that "Father Hesburgh's warmth and personal charm has always been appreciated by the student body." John Glavin, Steintrager's associate editor, noted the "great strides" Notre Dame had made previously, but then predicted that "the gains we can make in the near future under the guidance of Father Hesburgh and the Notre Dame family will far sur-pass anything that has ever been realized in the past."[81] Ted Hesburgh must have read these words with satisfaction. He had made a start. But much more needed to be done at Notre Dame, and he would do it.

CHAPTER 3

FATHER HESBURGH AND THE PURSUIT OF EXCELLENCE, 1958–1966

WITH HIS LEADERSHIP OF NOTRE DAME SECURED INTO THE indefinite future, forty-one-year-old Theodore Hesburgh confidently led Notre Dame through the final years of the seemingly more placid 1950s and into the more turbulent decade that followed. The period from mid-1958 through to the middle part of the next decade proved to be one of notable success for the university and its president, who emerged as a significant American public figure. Hesburgh's stature and significance received a very public affirmation when his portrait graced the cover of *Time* in February of 1962. He received an explicit presidential ratification when Lyndon Johnson conferred on him the Presidential Medal of Freedom in 1964.

Hesburgh appeared to be a man fully in tune with the times both in his nation and in his Church. When John Kennedy assumed office intent on getting "the country moving again," Father Ted stood ready to respond. He identified easily with the pragmatic and vigorous approach of the Kennedy team, many of whose members he knew well. In conjunction with the exciting new administration at home, a fresh spirit had been unleashed by the 1959 election of Pope John XXIII and his decision to call an ecumenical council to bring *aggiornamento* to the Church. Hesburgh identified closely with the reform agenda of Vatican II, and he saw his own efforts to engage with the world and to enhance the role of the laity as sanctioned by the Council fathers.

While events beyond the campus moved along favorably and he continued to devote considerable energies to his external activities, Hesburgh also witnessed some major successes on campus that added further to the luster of his leadership. He stated his ambitions for the university with clarity when he told the student readers of the *Dome* yearbook in 1961 that he desired "one quality for Notre Dame: *dedicated excellence* in all the broad educational endeavor that goes on here: intellectually, spiritually, physically." He went further in his exhortation and proclaimed that "I would rather see Notre Dame die than be educationally mediocre."[1]

BRICKS, MORTAR, AND MONEY FOR A *MODERN* CATHOLIC UNIVERSITY

After bringing the 1957–1958 academic year to a conclusion, Ted Hesburgh spent much of the summer on an extended tour of Africa and the Middle East funded by the Carnegie Foundation. He traveled in the company of Jerry Brady, the former student body president and a recent graduate. Hesburgh intended to "visit every university south of the Sahara and [also] to see East Africa in the company of Holy Cross and other missionaries."[2] The two men traveled together first to Senegal and on to Ghana, Nigeria, the Belgian Congo (now the Democratic Republic of the Congo), South Africa, Basutoland (Lesotho), Southern Rhodesia (Zimbabwe), Kenya, Tanganyika (Tanzania), Uganda, Rwanda, Sudan, and Egypt.

Brady's account evokes numerous colorful images that capture the ease with which Hesburgh navigated through the world whatever the particular circumstances in which he found himself. Hesburgh "chatting up everyone on the luxury cruise ship [which took them across the Atlantic], drink in hand." Hesburgh telling his British hosts in Rhodesia that they were quite wrong on apartheid. Hesburgh politely declining the offer made by Masai tribesmen that he drink a special concoction "of milk and blood in a gourd sterilized with cow urine." Hesburgh enjoying the experience as "belly dancers glided by" their table in a Cairo restaurant. Nothing unsettled the Notre Dame president, and he never tired of meeting new people and seeing new places. An oft-used photo captures them looking like typical American tourists while riding camels and adorned with fezzes with one of the famous Egyptian pyramids at Giza on Cairo's outskirts providing a spectacular background.

Ted Hesburgh said farewell to Jerry Brady after their Cairo sojourn. The Notre Dame president then donned his hat as Vatican City representative to the International Atomic Energy Agency and flew to Vienna for meetings. His ability to move from one environment to another quite different situation and circumstance was on splendid display. During the almost two months he was absent from Notre Dame he made no efforts to stay in touch with developments on campus. He understood well that Ned Joyce had matters in hand. Yet Notre Dame had been on his mind as he traversed Africa. Jerry Brady recalled that his resolute traveling companion conveyed clearly to him his heartfelt conviction that "the Catholic Church knows nothing about higher education." As he saw it there were "almost no good Catholic universities in the world." When the summer ended and with his energies renewed from his impressive African experience, Father Ted returned to Notre Dame ever more determined to set things aright.

The broad charter to guide Hesburgh's undertaking had been publicly revealed back in March of 1958 when he had announced his ten-year development program designed "to consolidate and further [the university's] academic excellence." The $66 million plan called for significant funds to be committed to the endowment so as to boost faculty salaries, and it also provided money for research, student aid, and for administrative purposes. Additionally, it provided for seven new buildings to meet "essential" needs of the university's 5,800 students. Heading the building list and crucially important in Hesburgh's eyes was a new library to replace the old Lemonnier Library built in 1917 (and later known as Bond Hall of Architecture). Other new buildings specified included residence halls for graduate students and a new fieldhouse and auditorium. The increased funds to be allocated to faculty salaries reflected Hesburgh's desire to "stabilize and strengthen the present faculty as well as to attract some of the world's outstanding teachers to the campus." The enhancement of the faculty would be a focus of every subsequent development campaign that he oversaw in his quest for academic excellence. He also gave greater emphasis to research and declared that it constituted "an integral phase of Notre Dame's program for the future." He recognized that Notre Dame had some modest reputation for research in science, especially in areas like nuclear physics, radiation chemistry, and germ-free life, but he appreciated that a modern university's research enterprise had to be both broadened and deepened. It required that the humanities and social sciences be fully included in the effort. In an especially necessary action he outlined plans to raise funds to improve salaries and conditions for the university's nonacademic employees, including providing them with a "much-needed retirement plan."[3] All combined it was a bold program for the future.

Hesburgh drew support for his agenda from some loyal allies such as Fr. Philip Moore, now retired from his position as vice president for academic affairs, who in 1960 published a serious study of Notre Dame's "past, present, and future" academic development. Quite intentionally he examined what was needed "to grow into greatness as a university." Moore pointed explicitly to the importance of research and to the role of the graduate school as distinct from the undergraduate college. In direct support of Hesburgh he argued that "the future development of Notre Dame into greatness depends upon the recognition that as a university it is committed to research and the pursuit of knowledge, to 'profound and finished scholarship.'" The astute Moore called for special consideration to be given to research in areas that should characterize a Catholic university such as theology and philosophy.[4]

Father Hesburgh had thrown caution to the wind from the outset, but now with deep trust in Divine Providence he set about implementing his program. Each day on campus he continued his practice of offering Mass in one of the side chapels of the Crypt of Sacred Heart Church. He then walked the short distance to the Grotto to pray for Mary's guidance and intercession. Nothing disturbed his traditional piety, no matter how many notable boards he joined or weighty meetings he attended with sophisticated participants. Yet he assumed that the Lord and the Blessed Mother fully endorsed *his* plans.

Hesburgh's membership on the National Science Board and his specific interest in nuclear matters manifested by his work on the International Atomic Energy Agency led to his inviting John McCone, who chaired the U.S. Atomic Energy Commission, to speak at the 1959 commencement. McCone, a devout Catholic who went on to direct the CIA during the Kennedy administration, chose to highlight in his speech the work of the agency he headed. Without any inhibition he proudly announced that he led the "nation's nuclear armorer." He also explained that the Atomic Energy Commission worked to facilitate "the use of the atom for peaceful purposes."[5] His speech fleshed out the integral relationship between this government institution and the nation's major research universities. Ted Hesburgh, who remained throughout his life a dedicated proponent of nuclear power for peaceful purposes, wanted some share of the government largesse that was devoted to building the extraordinary Cold War technological/scientific/educational complex in the wake of the "crisis" prompted by the Soviet launch of the Sputnik satellite late in 1957. McCone delivered for him. He promised to fund a new laboratory facility to enable Notre Dame to expand its research in radiation chemistry. A few years later Notre Dame's very modern Radiation Research Building was completed, and it proceeded to operate largely with federal funds.

Private funding also proved crucial for Hesburgh's ambitious program. In September 1960 Henry Heald, the president of the Ford Foundation, announced that Notre Dame was one of five privately supported American universities chosen to receive major grants to assist them "to reach and sustain a wholly new level of academic excellence, administrative effectiveness and financial support." Under the terms of the Ford Foundation's Special Program in Education, Notre Dame was required over the next three years to raise two dollars from private sources for each one dollar of the $6 million Ford grant. The same terms applied when the Ford Foundation proffered a further $6 million grant in 1963. Hesburgh described the 1960 grant, the largest to date in the university's history, as "an answer to our deepest hopes." Constantly repeating his "excellence" mantra he asserted that the grant would make it possible for Notre Dame "to take a great leap forward in its striving for academic excellence."[6]

The Ford Foundation did not fortuitously pluck Notre Dame's name from a large number of possible recipients. Father Ted worked hard to secure the grant. Jim Armsey of the Ford Foundation asked Hesburgh to meet him at the Foundation offices located at that time on Madison Avenue within sight of New York's St. Patrick's Cathedral. The Foundation official asked what Hesburgh would do if he received the money. There, in the sight of the Cathedral spires, Armsey also, as Father Ted remembered, "deliberately baited me about the Catholic character of the university" and about the possibility of Catholic Notre Dame becoming a "real" university. Hesburgh recalled a sharp exchange, and he demanded that Armsey visit Notre Dame to see the place "up close." Armsey came to campus, and Hesburgh and Joyce pressed him hard throughout the day of his visit. Over drinks and dinner they won him over. The priest duo convinced the Ford Foundation representative that supporting a university whose tradition and basic inspiration were Christian would benefit higher education and the society at large. Armsey then became a true sponsor of Notre Dame within the Ford Foundation, and he secured both the first and second grants for the Catholic school.[7]

Each of the Ford Foundation grants required that Notre Dame raise $12 million in matching funds. This task drove a major part of Hesburgh's activities over the following three years. He began his Challenge I fund-raising campaign immediately and made the construction of a new library the centerpiece of it. A great university simply needed a great library. He enlisted as national chairman for this campaign J. Peter Grace, the president of W. R. Grace and Company, a business conglomerate known well for its shipping line and its Latin American interests. Grace already served as vice chairman of Notre Dame's Associate Board of Lay Trustees, although he was not an alumnus of the university. He lent considerable support to Hesburgh initially, although difficult days lay ahead in their relationship. The greatest support for Hesburgh came from two individuals. Ned Joyce stood loyally at his side throughout and joined him in various presentations and requests. Even more important to him in the fund-raising effort was Jim Frick, whom John Cavanaugh had hired into the Notre Dame Foundation during his time as director. Hesburgh revealed his faith in collaborators like Grace, Joyce, and Frick and his confidence in his own individual capacity by authorizing the groundbreaking for the new library in 1961 long before the projected $8 million dollars had been raised to cover its cost. He knew in his gut that Divine Providence and Our Lady would not allow for failure. He took great satisfaction almost four decades later in conveying that he had been right!

The university raised over $18 million in the first effort and approximately $16 million in the 1963–1966 time frame—well above the amount needed in each case to secure the Ford Foundation money. The amounts seem rather modest compared to the fund-raising targets of today, when universities boast endowments in the billions of dollars. But readers must appreciate the deep satisfaction that Hesburgh took in these accomplishments. Later campaigns raised more money, but he approached them with an unflappable assurance that these early campaigns built within him. Not only had the Ford Foundation support been assured, but 23,438 donors had contributed gifts or grants and Frick kept track of every one of them for future contact.[8] Serious and sustained fund-raising had arrived at Notre Dame. The new library, so favored by Hesburgh, was the great beneficiary of the first campaign, and Father Joyce's favorite project, the new Athletic and Convocation Center, benefited most from the second.

Jim Frick was once labeled Father Hesburgh's "alter ego in money raising," and the description captures something of the symbiotic connection between the two men.[9] When Dick Conklin asked Father Ted to comment on Frick he blurted out, "My Lord, it's like talking about Ned Joyce and

Helen Hosinski." For him Frick was a kind of "genius" and "a pillar of the place" who "should be revered for fantastic achievement."[10] The tributes to Frick at the time of his death in 2014 invariably noted that the money-raising maestro had grown up in a Catholic orphanage in North Carolina. He served in the Navy in World War II and came to Notre Dame afterward as a twenty-three-year-old freshman. After his graduation he eventually worked under Cavanaugh as Notre Dame's first full-time lay employee devoted to fund-raising. In 1961 as Challenge I gathered force he became director of development, where he built a professional operation. Four years later Hesburgh named him vice president for public relations and development, thus making him the first lay officer in the university's history.

Hesburgh appreciated that Frick quite literally poured out himself at the expense of his health to serve Notre Dame, so he subjected himself to the extensive demands that Frick's fund-raising schema placed on him. No other person at Notre Dame ever gave Hesburgh more instructions and never had anyone had them obeyed so completely as did Frick. In the midst of the various campaigns they traveled constantly together. Frick established the schedule and even forced Hesburgh to rouse himself for breakfast meetings. In a given city he lined up events and appointments with potential benefactors for the priest-president throughout each day and into the evening. Then they moved to another city and did it all over again. Always Frick provided the carefully researched details of the potential benefactors and their interests and capacity to donate to the university. Hesburgh made the case and spelled out his vision; Frick then directly asked for money. Perhaps it might be more accurate to say that he demanded support. The Hesburgh-Frick partnership brought the priest's charisma together with an aggressive and meticulous "closer." It worked effectively through the Challenge campaigns and then the SUMMA campaign (1967–1972), which raised $62.5 million, and finally the Campaign for Notre Dame (1975–1981), which procured over $180 million. In 1983 Frick, who had suffered several serious heart attacks, retired. Hesburgh awarded him an honorary degree as a token of gratitude. He knew how much he owed to the one-time orphan from North Carolina who drove the fund-raising that made the advances of his administration possible.[11]

Father Hesburgh demonstrated his deep desire to make Notre Dame more contemporary in the design of the buildings the Challenge I campaign underwrote. This proved the case with the Memorial Library—the building now named in his honor. From the beginning of his presidency he had railed against the inadequacy of the existing library, which housed an embarrassingly small 250,000 volumes. When the chance came to rectify the situation he decided to build in line with the pragmatic "form follows function" approach that he and the Ellerbe architects from St. Paul had utilized in the preceding decade. Rather surprisingly Ellerbe initially drew up a bizarre (in retrospect) proposal for him in 1958 that involved the demolition of the Main Building—which admittedly was in need of major and expensive structural repair—and its replacement with a particularly garish and ugly boxlike building set in the very heart of the campus. The architectural historian Margaret Grubiak insightfully has noted that "the early library schemes" are "so striking" because of the "unabashed modernism" advanced in the reconception of the central campus. That Hesburgh entertained this possibility even for a moment communicates something of his intention to modernize his institution. Fortunately for Notre Dame and Hesburgh's reputation regarding the campus design, "the architects could not design a new building and still retain the original [golden] dome, the destruction of which was not an option given the inevitable vociferous protests of the alumni."[12] Thank God, might we say, for the alumni. With this idea stymied, Hesburgh and Joyce looked eastward to the inviting open space of the old Cartier Field, where the football team practiced. The idea of a new East Campus quickly gained their endorsement.

With the library's spacious location now determined, Hesburgh abandoned the boxlike structure and encouraged the architects to design a truly large library. He wanted to make a statement and so he did. The new library rose over the campus and was by far its largest structure to that point and, as a Notre Dame press release boasted, "one of the larger buildings in the state of Indiana."[13] The first two floors housed the undergraduate library, and each occupied an area of nearly two acres. The central cruciform tower rose a further twelve stories (including the penthouse level), devoted to the research library and to many specialized research units such as the Medieval Institute, the Jacques Maritain Center, and the offices of the newly formed Committee on International Studies. Designed to house over 2.5 million volumes, it clearly spoke of Hesburgh's strong future commitment to research and graduate study. In the basement the architects provided 250 individual offices for the growing liberal arts faculty, a marked improvement over the cramped and shared spaces they had endured previously, whatever the faculty complaints about the absence of natural light in the new space. The most striking feature of the new library was the soaring multicolored *Word of Life* mural on the central axis of the tower. It rises nine stories above the library's main entrance and faces the football stadium to dramatic effect, as the legions of football fans who branded it "Touchdown Jesus" so readily appreciated.

Hesburgh suggested the idea for the striking mural, and he always maintained emphatically that he did so without any reference to its possible relationship to the football stadium. He had agreed to the basic tower design but recalled saying that "it looks like a damn grain elevator in the middle of the prairies, so we've got to do something to dress it up apart from doing it in marble and limestone." Here, he recalled, all his "tootin' around the world" came into play. He remembered the spectacular murals that graced the exterior of the Central Library of Universidad Nacional Autónoma de México, and he grasped that something similar would work on his huge building. With Charlie Sheedy's help he provided the basic ideas for the eventual mural completed by the artist Millard Sheets, which depicts the Risen Christ with arms outstretched and "surrounded by his apostles and an assembly of saints and scholars who have contributed to knowledge throughout the ages."[14] Father Ted loved the mural, despite his later regret at his mistake in not including even one woman in the tableau of saints.[15]

The elaborate dedication ceremonies for the new library took place on May 7, 1964, Ascension Thursday, and they have been wonderfully captured in Bill Schmitt's beautiful commemorative study *Words of Life*.[16] Hesburgh counted that day and the preceding day, during which he convened a symposium entitled "The Person in the Contemporary World," as among the favorites of his whole life. He relished being in the midst of it all. He opened the symposium, which brought together a psychiatrist, a theologian, a scientist, and a philosopher as its lead speakers, with a characteristically optimistic discourse that defined the conference theme as not only the human person's "estrangement and alienation in today's world, but also his inner dignity and enduring hope for a better tomorrow." He decried negativism and argued that "over and above the pessimistic vision is the challenge to greatness that still confronts every person—every modern man."[17] He basked in the praise that conference participants showered upon him. Kenneth Thompson, the vice president of the Rockefeller Foundation and a symposium cochair, led the way by thanking Notre Dame for sharing "the remarkable originality and creativity of your great president." Hesburgh derived especial satisfaction from the presence as honorary chair of the symposium of Cardinal Eugène Tisserant, dean of the Sacred College of Cardinals and prefect of the Vatican Library. The next morning Tisserant presided at the Solemn Pontifical Mass and Chicago's Cardinal Albert Meyer preached. In the afternoon Cardinal Joseph Ritter, archbishop of Saint Louis, performed the formal blessing of the library building. An exquisite final touch came when a Notre Dame honorary degree recipient from 1960 who now served as Supreme Pontiff, Pope Paul VI, sent a message of blessing to the university community through his "beloved son," Theodore Hesburgh.

This occasion served to spur Hesburgh onward to implement further his program. In moving forward he accentuated his intention to give Notre Dame a very modern appearance. Even before his library was dedicated it was flanked by two buildings that spoke to Notre Dame's commitment to modern science and research. The Radiation Research Building took its place on the developing quad across from a new if nondescript building that accommodated mathematics and computer science. Father Ted also had announced detailed plans for two other buildings designed to enable his university to engage the world better by hosting visitors of varied sorts to the campus. Generous support from the Kellogg Foundation of Battle Creek, Michigan, made possible the construction of the Center for Continuing Education (later McKenna Hall) on Notre Dame Avenue across from the Morris Inn. This building with its auditorium and various seminar and lecture rooms provided a space for scholars and others participating in academic conferences and all kinds of meetings. It proved a boon for Notre Dame.

So too did the Athletic and Convocation Center (ACC) that Hesburgh authorized in late 1963, which opened in 1968. In this wonderful facility the "form follows function" approach at last enjoyed a notable success. The dual-domed building replaced the decrepit Field House and met numerous university needs. Convocations, conventions, the basketball program, ice hockey, and other varsity athletic teams as well as intramural sports all found space in the complex. Ned Joyce and "Moose" Krause took the lead in planning for the ACC, but Hesburgh placed a restriction on them. He recalled telling Father Joyce that "you can't put more money into the athletic thing than I am putting into the library."[18] The library's final cost reached $12 million. The initial plans for the ACC costed out at $13 million. Indicative of the Hesburgh-Joyce relationship, the executive vice president came to the president and asked him what should be taken out. Hesburgh without any great deliberation decided that the proposed swimming pool could be removed and the campus could make do with the existing small pool in the Rockne Memorial building.

Hesburgh's fixation with modern architecture and his openness to some of the faddish designs that the Ellerbe firm drew up reached its culmination in the late 1960s, although the planning had begun as part of the preparations for the SUMMA fund-raising campaign. In 1967 the Minnesota architects proposed a new "mod quad" stretching north of the Memorial Library. Five new eleven-story student resident halls/towers were tentatively projected to form a semicircle around a proposed modern chapel. The rather futuristic chapel, supposedly designed in the spirit of Vatican II, was shaped as a swirling conch shell rising to a high spire. Someone in the Main Building possessed a sense of humor, because the chapel was designated to be named the John Cardinal O'Hara Chapel in honor of the former president who was known for his traditional theological outlook and piety. The chapel was never built and only two of the five towers (Grace and Flanner Halls) were constructed and eventually opened in 1969. By that point Hesburgh had much else on his mind aside from architecture.

NAVIGATING FORWARD ON CAMPUS AND BEYOND

Holy Cross priests still dominated the leadership of the university during the 1960s, and they did so right through to the mid-1970s. Ned Joyce and Father Jerry Wilson, vice president for business affairs, remained pillars of stability in their domains. In 1961 Hesburgh appointed Fr. Charles McCarragher as vice president for student affairs, and somehow the priest known as "Black Mac"braved the coming storm of turbulent change in student life sparked by protest of the Vietnam War and the social upheaval of the late 1960s. He held the position until 1970. Fr. Chet Soleta served as vice president for academic affairs until 1965. By that point, he had experienced quite enough of academic administration. Hesburgh replaced him with the engaging Fr. John Walsh, who had served as vice president for public relations and development starting in 1961, thereby freeing that role for Jim Frick. Walsh would journey closely beside Hesburgh through the challenges and changes of the late 1960s, including the formulation of the Land O'Lakes Statement. Although both Soleta and Walsh possessed real abilities, neither proved capable of truly putting into meaningful practice

Hesburgh's broad vision of a modern Catholic university. This task proved problematic through the 1960s and, sadly, well beyond. Indeed, the challenge in meeting this vision is a recurring theme in Notre Dame's story during the Hesburgh years.

Hesburgh's heightened national reputation led to increasing numbers of invitations for him to address various audiences and topics away from campus. He became a mainstay on the commencement address circuit and began racking up more honorary degrees. In 1962 he published a booklet entitled *Thoughts for Our Times*, which contained two speeches on science and technology delivered appropriately enough at MIT and Cal Tech as well as his address before the winter convocation of the University of Chicago, in which he examined the phenomenon of "rapid and all-pervading change in our times."[19] The booklets then kept coming. In 1964 *More Thoughts for Our Times* appeared, which included an important address entitled "The Moral Dimensions of the Civil Rights Movement," delivered before the American Academy of Arts and Sciences in Boston.[20] In 1966 he circulated *Still More Thoughts for Our Times*. In addition to providing an invitation to parody the title, the volume included talks that convey something of the changing political, social, and cultural ground that he traversed. In March 1966 at the University of Michigan he gave a talk entitled "The Social Sciences in an Age of Social Revolution." Just a few months later he delivered the commencement address at the University of Illinois under the title "Our Revolutionary Age."[21] Rare was the topic on which he felt he could not pronounce, whatever the limits of his specific expertise and training.

As he moved about the country for various meetings and to give these addresses, his range of contacts kept growing. He knew "as personal friends" most of the distinguished formal participants who gathered in the symposium for the opening of Memorial Library. They were essentially professional contacts, but such was his skillful way of engaging others that he gave an extra dimension to these limited relationships. Many of his interlocutors wanted to feel some connection to him beyond mere acquaintanceship and he deftly allowed it. He rarely revealed much of his true inner self to any of these occasional associates. They received the public "Father Hesburgh" persona, and most remained impressed and grateful for that. Such contacts and his reputation as a noted public figure gained him quick admittance to eminent scholarly bodies such as the American Academy of Arts and Sciences and the American Philosophical Society.

His accommodations away from Notre Dame indicated something of his stature as a public figure and his ease with his status. From the 1950s right through to the 1980s he continued to stay during his regular visits to New York City at the Commodore Hotel across from the Chrysler Building in Midtown Manhattan. The hotel always assigned him a spacious suite and he never received a bill. This rather agreeable arrangement came about through his friendship with Frank Walker, the former postmaster general and chair of the Democratic National Committee. Walker told the manager, "Look after Father Ted," and so the hotel did for a quarter century! Only in his later years as president of Notre Dame, and after the Commodore had been transformed into the Grand Hyatt New York, did he migrate to the more modestly priced University Club, where he finally paid for his stays in New York City (unless his accommodations were covered by the organization/foundation he had come to address). In Washington, D.C., he made the historic and luxurious Mayflower Hotel his regular domicile. There too he received preferential treatment because the manager had a son who graduated from Notre Dame.

Hesburgh believed that his work attending all his meetings and conferences and giving addresses was done ultimately for Notre Dame and the larger good. He resented any implication that he participated in them in any way for his own indulgence or enjoyment. But he reveled in leaving campus to engage the challenging matters of the day. In some ways Hesburgh drank deeply of the same elixir as Nelson Rockefeller, whom he had come to know, and who proclaimed that "there is no problem that cannot be solved."[22] Perhaps he would have accepted a qualification of sorts proposed by President Johnson, who averred that "there are no problems we cannot solve together." Father Ted relished getting together with the "right" people and developing plans to address issues like world hunger, domestic poverty, and the like. He showed no hint of being cautious in light of the limits of human capacities nor did he give any indication that Niebuhrian realism might lead him to reflect upon constraints on what could be accomplished. Rather, as Kenneth Woodward perceptively noted, Father Ted tended to "put too much trust in the wisdom of 'the best and the brightest' who bulked so large among his incredibly wide circle of friends."[23]

The confidence that Father Hesburgh possessed in his capacity to contribute to solving major problems and to forge Notre Dame into an institution that could address them in meaningful ways received a real boost through his appointment of George Shuster to serve as his special assistant.

Hesburgh delighted in awarding the Laetare Medal to Shuster in 1960 at that notable commencement featuring President Dwight Eisenhower and Cardinal Giovanni Battista Montini. He deemed it a coup when he persuaded this distinguished Catholic intellectual and educator to return to Notre Dame in 1961 and to finish out his career on the Notre Dame campus, which he had left disconsolately almost forty years before. Shuster had graduated from Notre Dame in 1915, served in the U.S. Army in World War I, and returned to Notre Dame, where he earned a master's degree in English. He then joined the faculty and wrote his classic *The Catholic Spirit in Modern English Literature* (1922), which Hesburgh read as a seminarian and treasured. In 1924 Shuster left Notre Dame in protest against what he deemed its oppressive academic atmosphere and traveled to New York. There he was among the early writers for *Commonweal*, the recently founded independent and liberal Catholic journal, for which he served as managing editor from 1929 to 1937. After breaking with *Commonweal* over its failure to oppose Franco in the Spanish Civil War, Shuster completed a doctorate at Columbia and then was appointed president of Hunter College, where he served from 1939 until 1960. Widely published and highly respected, Shuster epitomized the best of American liberal Catholicism.

Shuster had numerous other attractive opportunities upon his retiring from Hunter College, but Hesburgh's vision and person convinced him to give up the allures of New York to return to South Bend. Shuster also wanted to help create a modern Catholic university. In addition to his special assistant duties, Father Ted named Shuster to direct a new institute, named the Center for the Study of Man in Contemporary Society. He played a valuable role in boosting research at Notre Dame in the social sciences and the humanities, especially in international and area studies. He served as something of a campus elder statesman who was widely consulted by faculty and who encouraged new intellectual endeavors and projects.[24] Hesburgh recalled that George Shuster "was at the core of things, always a voice of wisdom, always a voice of restraint in extreme situations, always a voice of moderation and yet courage moving forward."[25] The depth of affection that Hesburgh had for Shuster and the high regard in which he held him is striking. He began a foreword to an edited volume of Shuster's writings with the uncharacteristically demonstrative question: "How can one write adequately about another human being whom he loves?" He admitted that he looked on Shuster as a cherished father figure and then, with an implicit clericalism at work, he proclaimed Shuster as ready for immediate ordination because there was "something essentially priestly about his relationship to others."[26] After Shuster's death in 1977, Hesburgh numbered him in the select company of Jacques Maritain and the Christian Family Movement's Pat Crowley as those whom he believed "could be classified as saints" from among all the many people he had known in his life.

Whatever Shuster's credentials for canonization, he played a crucial role in relieving Hesburgh of certain duties. Those faculty and others who requested appointments to see the president could adroitly be referred to meet instead with his esteemed special assistant. Shuster became a fixture at the Morris Inn, enjoying lunch and discussing either a research project with a faculty member or a thesis topic with a student while sipping on "a dry Manhattan" and smoking a cigarette in a holder such that Father Ted thought "he looked like FDR."[27] He represented Hesburgh at academic meetings in a way that Ned Joyce could not. And Shuster also operated as a trusted adviser and confidant for Hesburgh on the larger questions regarding the future governance of the university. Here his liberal Catholic outlook made him both a strong advocate for and a supporter of the moves to distance Notre Dame from formal ecclesiastical control.

Shuster's generous engagement with various campus constituencies and Father Hesburgh's frequent absences ironically contributed to the creation of what Thomas Blantz described as "a movement among some student leaders to have Father Hesburgh removed as president—and replaced by George Shuster!"[28] A lead editorial in the *Scholastic* in February of 1963 rather impertinently declared that "that the student romance with Fr. Hesburgh is over" and then argued that it was "imperative" that Father Hesburgh be removed from his post as president and "be designated Chancellor," in which capacity he could attend to his activities away from campus. Shuster as his replacement would "govern the internal affairs of the university," assuring a liberation from the supposedly oppressive weight of the Holy Cross order.[29] A somewhat embarrassed Shuster laughed off the suggestion and quickly dismissed it.[30] Hesburgh found himself annoyed by it, and his testy dealings with students in this period tells us much about him at this time.[31]

Hesburgh had received a shock over Thanksgiving 1960 when "a mob of more that 1,500 angry students milled in front of old Corby Hall [the priests' residence on campus], hurling abuse at the Holy Cross fathers within." The students wanted major changes made to the disciplinary system that led to vivid criticism of what they called a "concentration-camp atmosphere" prevelant at Notre Dame, which allegedly more resembled "an Inquisition jail tempered by paternalism" than a modern university.[32] The following year Hesburgh and McCarragher made some concessions. The requirement that students attend Mass three mornings per week was abolished, as was the "lights-out" policy. Students could now sleep in and stay up as long as they wished. The practice of priests patrolling the downtown South Bend bars for boozing students also ended, and "the bulky student manual [was] streamlined and rewritten to convey a more positive attitude toward student behavior."[33] Such modest reforms hardly placated the more activist students, who still complained about "an oppressive system of discipline and indoctrination." Their continued complaints angered the Notre Dame president and contradicted claims about his imperturbability. An encounter with an able sophomore (and 1965 Rhodes Scholar) named Jack Gearen suffices to illustrate the point. Gearen exchanged letters with Hesburgh over the president's rejection of student suggestions to adopt a "stay" hall system, which would allow for a residence hall community made up of all classes from freshmen through to seniors. Students could then stay in the same hall all four years rather than moving each year as was the existing practice. Hesburgh replied to an initial letter, but the sophomore responded and forcefully refuted Hesburgh's arguments. Two able chroniclers of the period, Joel Connelly and Howard Dooley, reported that this "letter infuriated Hesburgh, who had never before been addressed in this tone by a student, and Gearen was threatened with expulsion." Even after he "had recovered his cool, Hesburgh wrote to Gearen suggesting that since he didn't like Notre Dame, perhaps he should complete his education elsewhere." Apparently he even offered to write him a personal letter of recommendation.

Although Hesburgh wanted to transform Notre Dame into a modern university and even though he increasingly associated with progressive reformers beyond the campus, he displayed no willingness to dismantle the well-established in loco parentis approach to student life that prevailed at Notre Dame. He had complained about some of its harsher features when he served in the dorms in the late 1940s, yet he believed deeply not only that Notre Dame held a responsibility for the moral and spiritual formation of its students, but also that the good character and religious convictions of its graduates spoke eloquently to the success of the university's approach. He wrote to the students of the special quality of Notre Dame in the 1961 yearbook, and tellingly he invoked one of his heroes, the medical doctor

Tom Dooley, quoting him as saying: "Notre Dame is always in my heart. That Grotto is the rock to which my life is anchored. Do the students ever appreciate what they have, while they have it? I know I never did."[34] His rather paternal message rang out clearly, but the less docile students of the 1960s refused to simply accept it and increasingly mocked his "Father Knows Best" approach. In March 1963 they drafted a "Declaration of Student Rights and Grievances," which called for an end to the in loco parentis system and challenged the role of the Holy Cross order in guiding student life at the university.

This student government declaration, which McCarragher preemptively banned from being distributed on campus, came at the exact same time as the call for Shuster to replace Hesburgh as president. Both actions manifested similar student discontent with his leadership. How did the university president respond? Connelly and Dooley claimed he had only two choices—either to crack down or to restructure how Notre Dame ran student life. With some insight they suggested that he "was personally forced to choose between the understandable desire to be popular with his students and the equally compelling need to show himself a strong executive, a man capable of hard decisions when the chips were down. The whole episode prompted Fr. Ted to address the various issues involved in a long and quite personal letter, the first of a number of such missives that he wrote during this unstable decade, and which came to be known as the 'Epistles of Hesburgh to His Constituencies.'"[35]

The letter Hesburgh sent, dated April 8, 1963, to the university's 6,700 students during the Easter vacation period addressed "the Winter of our discontent."[36] He deftly suggested that the discontent on campus be seen in the context of "the total spiritual malaise that afflicts so much of our world today." Its causes, he explained, not only rested with local circumstances, but consisted of a larger impulsive willingness to challenge authority. Then he fixed on the Notre Dame scene and directly lambasted the editors of the *Scholastic* for what he described as their misrepresentations, lack of integrity, and general irresponsibility. He defended the role of the Holy Cross order and the sacrifice and dedication of the priests and brothers over the previous 120 years. He stated his belief that the primary role for students was "to learn, not to teach," and he encouraged the undergrads to understand this distinction. He also pounded home the message that if any students couldn't handle the discipline of Notre Dame then "the only honest reaction is to get free of Notre Dame, not to expect Notre Dame to lose its unique character and become just another school with just another quality of graduates." Father Ted assured students of his love for them but also told them that he assumed that they didn't need him around to constantly pat their heads. He needed to be away often "raising money and trying to involve Notre Dame in many crucial areas where no Catholic university has been involved before." He concluded with a typical call for students to serve others so that "the Winter of our discontent may be forgotten in the flowering of a new Springtime of hope." The student protest and complaints did not compel him to make any major changes either in how he led Notre Dame or in how he pursued his numerous activities off campus. But they made him less naïve about students and they toughened his skin in dealing with complaints.

IN PURSUIT OF ACADEMIC EXCELLENCE

The commitment to excellence that Father Hesburgh made a featured part of his design for a self-consciously modern Notre Dame was hardly original. The issuance in 1958 of the Rockefeller Brothers Fund report entitled *The Pursuit of Excellence* set off what Philip Gleason has described as a "near-mania for excellence" across the country.[37] Catholics in higher education inevitably got caught up in it, especially in light of the recent harsh criticisms by John Tracy Ellis and others on the weakness of Catholic intellectual life. Hesburgh had served on the Rockefeller Fund panel that issued the report and on the special task force that wrote it, so it is hardly surprising that he adopted the pursuit of excellence as a goal for his university. Yet as Gleason has noted in his magisterial study, although "Catholics joined in what some would sardonically call 'the excellence binge,' they were not in a position to *define* academic excellence." If their schools didn't measure up they would need "to look elsewhere for models to emulate," and these would be the leading secular schools with their impressive graduate programs and research activities. In the process, Catholics increasingly lost confidence that (even on the undergraduate level) they could provide "a distinctive intellectual vision that enabled them to integrate the student's learning experience more effectively" than could secular schools. By 1960 the concern for "curricular integration that loomed so large in the early 1950s had lost its dynamism," to use Gleason's astute phrasing.[38] This situation prevailed at Hesburgh's Notre Dame. During his first term Father Ted had ably defended the benefits and rationale of a distinctively Catholic education. But he altered course abruptly in the 1960s, although sadly without realizing the full implications of his new emphasis and direction.

In Atlantic City in April 1961 Hesburgh addressed the National Catholic Education Association on the subject of Catholic higher education in twentieth-century America and made explicit his updated commitments. He told his fellow educators that "our efforts must be measured against the reality of life on the great American plain. Our objectives in Catholic higher education today must have relevance to a new age in a new land." Then in a direct assault on the traditional approach he explained: "Personally, I have no ambitions to be a medieval man. . . . It is futile comfort for a Catholic university in the second half of the twentieth century in the United States of America to point with pride to the lively intellectuality and critical vitality of the Catholic university of Paris in medieval France. Let the dead bury their dead." He admitted that these were "hard words" but argued that they were "true ones," and then borrowing from Matthew 19:12 he concluded "*Qui potest capere capiat* [Let him accept it who can]."[39]

Eye-catching remarks such as these contributed to his appearance on the cover of *Time* and to his being lauded for his role in the "reshaping of Catholic higher education." Yet what is so obvious in retrospect is that the critique of the old approach was not accompanied by a well-conceived schema for what might take its place. Hesburgh certainly had no desire simply to move to some secular model in his educational approach. He understood that a Catholic university must differentiate itself from its secular peers because of its convictions regarding "the Truth" with a capital *T*. He tried to explain this to the *Time* magazine audience when he declared that "we are men committed to Truth, living in a world where most academic endeavor concerns only natural truth, as much separated from supernatural truth, the divine wisdom of theology, as sinful man was separated from God before the Incarnation." His predicament is captured in his own words in the *Time* story: "We must somehow match secular or state universities in their comprehension of a vast spectrum of natural truths in the arts and sciences, while at the same time we must be in full possession of our own true heritage of theological wisdom."[40]

It is impossible not to sympathize with Father Hesburgh in his dilemma. He wanted Notre Dame to be a place where the truth in its many aspects was pursued—the truth about the world and nature, the truth about the human person, the truth about God. He did not intend to radically separate faith and reason. The gigantic mural he placed on the library spoke powerfully to his belief that Jesus Christ was "not one teacher among many, [not] one more in the long line of prophets and sages, but the very truth that every teacher, prophet, and sage sought."[41] His faith held that Jesus was the Logos, the Word made flesh, the One who brings the ultimate and definitive answer to the question of human meaning. And yet he failed to keep the challenge of combining natural and eternal truths clearly before him, and without making a major and formal decision he began to allow what might be called the pursuit of excellence approach to supplant the pursuit of the truth. It proved a telling failure on his part in terms of maintaining Catholicism in the academic heart of the university. It was one he neither completely recognized nor ever really admitted.

This crucial change did not happen immediately, but the die was cast in the early 1960s. In 1961 Father Hesburgh approved another major review of the curriculum at Notre Dame to strengthen the program provided its undergraduates, but he failed to provide good direction for curricular revisions. Resistance emerged to the whole concept of an integrated and coherent curriculum. As Gleason masterfully summarized, "the faculty clearly placed a higher value on departmental autonomy, which implied that academic quality was a function of scholarly competence in specialized disciplines." This then "represented a significant movement in the direction of secular norms of excellence and away from the older belief that Catholic higher education should embody and make available to its students a distinctive Catholic intellectual vision whose most characteristic mark was its synthesizing power."[42] Hesburgh acquiesced in this fundamental change, which worked its way through the Notre Dame academic regimen over the decade and culminated in a curriculum reform in 1970 that ratified the approach and merely adopted various distribution requirements for certain subjects. Philosophy and theology were included among the others but gone was any sense that they either held some essential integrative role or guided students toward a Catholic understanding of truth. Father Ted continued publicly to assert the importance of both theology and philosophy in aiding students to confront the ultimate questions about life and belief, but he simply became more detached from what actually occurred in the classroom. His attention lay elsewhere.

Rather than confront head-on the problems created by the shunting aside of the Thomist approach by enlisting able associates to help him address them, Hesburgh quickly moved onward in his pursuit of excellence—

however defined. He engaged in a certain amount of denial, but he was also excited that new methods in education could be tried that would pre-empt the condescending criticism of Catholic education with which he was all too familiar. After all, he was helping Notre Dame to break out of the Catholic confines that his Holy Cross predecessors had been content to live within. This assimilationist instinct was powerful not only with Hesburgh but across the realm of Catholic educators, all of whom celebrated the increased acceptance of Catholics in America as symbolized by JFK's election. In his view the times demanded that Catholic universities give new emphasis to facing the great issues of the day and so liberate themselves from their supposed narrowness.

Hesburgh's eagerness to move forward and his frustration with those who continually carped about the need to provide traditional Catholic intellectual formation to students came through strongly in an essay he published in *America* magazine in March 1962 entitled "Looking Back at Newman."[43] After making an inaccurate criticism of John Henry Newman by suggesting that "it is easier to write about what a Catholic university should be [read Newman] than to create and administer one in reality [read Hesburgh]," he went on to imply with an unbecoming smugness that Newman's university model simply didn't measure up to meeting the contemporary challenges. Newman held that the university should educate "the intellect to reason well in all matters, to reach out towards truth, and to grasp it," but in Hesburgh's presentation this became students residing in an ivory tower gaining general knowledge. He, by contrast, strongly endorsed university faculty and students going outward to tackle real problems in the world through their specific research endeavors. He readily conceded the importance of philosophy and theology in confronting these problems, although he never adequately explained the manner in which this could be done. However that may be, he wanted his university to address "such problems as racial equality, demography, the world rule of law, the deteriorating relationship between science and the other humanities, the moral foundations of democracy, the true nature of communism, the understanding of non-Western cultures, the values and goals of our society, and a whole host of other human problems that beset mankind caught in its present dilemmas of survival or utter destruction, life or death, civilized advance or return to the Stone Age." Merely listing this catalogue of grave problems sufficed in his mind to win his imaginary argument with Newman's supposedly insular approach. But it also disguised the intellectual

transition that was under way on his own campus, and it focused less attention on what happened in the classroom and more on activities beyond it.
Father Hesburgh would maintain this emphasis through to the end of his
presidency, and he gave notable expression to it by establishing and promoting various institutes and centers aimed at solving major world problems.

In making his case that philosophy and theology contributed to the solution of major challenges, such as achieving racial equality and maintaining
the rule of law, Father Ted made very clear that those two departments
in a Catholic university needed to be "as competent as its departments of
history, physics, and mathematics." Philosophers and theologians should
be "fully skilled in their science." Neither loyalty to the inspiration of Saint
Thomas Aquinas nor mere membership in the Holy Cross order would
suffice. Excellence should be the order of the day for them as for scholars
in every other department. This rationale led to significant changes in both
departments at Notre Dame. Hesburgh delegated the authority to make
these changes although he approved them. In the philosophy department
the Irish-born priest Ernan McMullin took the lead. In theology a suc-
cession of Holy Cross priests culminating in James Tunstead Burtchaell
attempted to advance the department so as to gain respect not only at Notre
Dame but in the broader academy—an academy that increasingly looked
on religion with suspicion and that prioritized empirically verifiable knowledge as in the natural sciences. To do this, of course, the university needed
to hire faculty who primarily possessed academic credentials validated by
secular peers. Less important was faith [as in "faith seeking understanding"], loyalty to and membership in the Church, and a willingness to speak
of truth.

Ernan McMullin, a brilliant philosopher of science, had earned Hesburgh's regard and trust since his arrival at Notre Dame in the mid-1950s.
He became chair of the philosophy department in 1965 and "unveiled his
plan for a pluralist department in which Thomism would take its place as
one philosophy to be taught on an equal basis among many others."[44] This
departmental strategy prompted objections from those like Ralph McInerny who believed that Notre Dame should be the center for a renewed
Thomism in light of the teachings of the Second Vatican Council.[45] But the
winds of the proverbial spirit of Vatican II filled the sails of McMullin's pluralistic project and his approach prevailed. Philosophers were hired whose
expertise reflected what was in vogue, notably analytical and continental
philosophy. The practice of doing philosophy in a distinctively Catholic

way faced increased marginalization. Yet under McMullin's leadership and with a much increased emphasis on graduate education and research, the academic reputation of the philosophy department rose among its secular peers. It stood out at Notre Dame as a "top-twenty" department in national rankings, something few other departments in the university could match. The philosophy experience seemed to confirm its success in the quest for excellence. Yet, sadly, in its effort to climb in the rankings, the department gave less attention to what was taught on the undergraduate level. The pursuit of excellence seemed to come at the expense of the pursuit of wisdom. Father Ted didn't appear to notice.

The theology department expanded its mission notably in the 1960s from a primary focus on the teaching of standard and required courses to undergraduates (which had been its concern when Father Hesburgh chaired the religion department) to being a place where theological education took place on all levels and theological research was expected of its faculty. The place for serious Catholic theological investigation shifted decisively in this decade away from the major seminaries to colleges and universities. Notre Dame became an important venue of this shift. Under the leadership of Fr. Robert Pelton, who guided the department from 1959 to 1964, efforts were made to devise undergraduate courses that were more acceptable to restive students who were aware of the turbulence in the Church occasioned by Vatican II.[46] Under Pelton's successor, Father Albert Schlitzer, the department took further steps designed to strengthen its academic credibility. A new undergraduate major was launched in 1965, and 1966 saw the inauguration of a formal doctoral program in theology. Notre Dame recruited the well-regarded Benedictine monk Aidan Kavanagh, an expert in liturgical studies, and the well-known Jesuit biblical scholar John L. McKenzie to enhance the reputation of its theology faculty. Schlitzer also appointed new and well-trained Holy Cross priests to the faculty. In the *Time* magazine piece on Father Hesburgh, the theology department was branded the "worst" on campus, but Hesburgh held out hope for its improvement once younger Holy Cross priests returned from graduate studies.

In 1966 Father Burtchaell, the future chair of the department and the first provost of Notre Dame, began his service at Notre Dame. His impressive credentials included a Licentiate in Sacred Scripture from the Biblicum in Rome and a doctorate from Cambridge University. Burtchaell and confreres like the philosopher David Burrell, with his doctorate from Yale, represented a new breed of Holy Cross scholar trained at highly ranked graduate schools who readily signed on to the modernizing project. When Burtchaell replaced Schlitzer as chair of the department just two years after his arrival, he completed the dismantling of whatever remained of the old system of required classes with clearly defined content. A new day had arrived for theology at Notre Dame. Students soon were asked to take few courses and the content of those courses became largely a matter of the instructor's choice. These courses were simply on a par with other requirements in the core curriculum like history, mathematics, and English. The courses naturally aimed to be proudly "academic." The notion that they should enrich the faith of students and encourage them truly to encounter Christ as "the Way, the Truth and the Life" was resisted as proselytizing. So it went. Father Hesburgh endorsed all these changes because he desired a respected theology department, and from his distance it seemed to be under construction.

While Hesburgh still held to his own very traditional fundamental theological convictions, he seemed very much a modern priest operating in the spirit of Vatican II. He loved the call of *Gaudium et Spes,* the Council's Pastoral Constitution on the Church in the Modern World, to engage and serve the world. He actively placed the university on this course. Furthermore, he energetically took up the request of his friend Pope Paul VI to establish an ecumenical institute for scholars of varied Christian denominations in the Holy Land. At Tantur, near Bethlehem, he worked in a very practical way to create a center for dialogue among all Christians— Catholics, Protestants, and Orthodox. He also reached out regularly to other Christian denominations eager to bring about the greatest degree of reconciliation possible. In like manner he took to his heart the Second Vatican Council's *Nostra Aetate,* the Declaration on the Relation of the Church to Non-Christian Religions, with its emphasis on the unity of all peoples and its strictures against religious discrimination. He had especially extensive dealings with Jews and spoke out forcefully against anti-Semitism. His views on these important matters certainly influenced the campus atmosphere for the good.

In pursuing excellence at Notre Dame Father Ted exhorted the faculty but did not deeply engage them. When asked about his friendships among the faculty, he spoke more in terms of scholars whom he admired such as the political scientists Stephen Kerterz and John Kennedy, the historian Matthew Fitzsimons, and the philosopher Fred Crosson, whom he eventually selected to replace Charlie Sheedy as dean of the College of Arts and Letters.[47] Shuster effectively served as an emissary of sorts for him. Hesburgh did admire the legendary Frank O'Malley for his remarkable impact on students, even though he judged him an awful lecturer because of his mumbling and stuttering. But by the 1960s he looked on O'Malley and his course Modern Catholic Writers in much the same way that he looked on Newman. O'Malley, however handicapped by his heavy drinking, conveyed powerfully to his students that "Jesus Christ is a force greater than knowledge and more terrible than truth." He gave them a basic charge to "cherish [their] Catholic heritage and to redeem the time."[48] But Father Ted viewed him more as a relic of a bygone era, the period of the interwar Catholic renaissance. Reading Romano Guardini, Léon Bloy, Georges Bernanos, and T. S. Eliot was fine, but familiarity with such literature hardly solved problems. He considered that he had a better way to "redeem the time" and it meant addressing the great issues head-on. A perfect case study for Hesburgh was his own early Peace Corps work, done in collaboration with Walter Langford, the chair of the Department of Modern Languages, which involved training young Peace Corps volunteers at Notre Dame and dispatching them to Chile for service.[49]

The pursuit of the vaunted excellence required furthermore that Notre Dame be seen and respected as a more open institution in which academic freedom functioned without any restraints. Hesburgh made a point of trying to hire faculty who would demonstrate his openness. When Morris Pollard came in 1961 to assume the directorship of LOBUND he recalled meeting Hesburgh and expressing "some trepidation about how I, as a Jewish person, might fit in at Notre Dame." In Pollard's retelling he heard in reply: "You'll fit in fine. All of us are trying to get out of our own ghettoes."[50] Around the same time Hesburgh aimed to highlight the freedom that prevailed at Notre Dame by appointing a controversial historian, Samuel (Sam) Shapiro, who had been fired by Oakland University in Michigan and subsequently blackballed from appointment at other schools for his sympathy for Castro's Cuba and for his call for the restoration of diplomatic relations with the Havana government. When Frank Mankiewicz, who handled public relations for the Peace Corps, called Hesburgh to object to Shapiro's teaching Latin American history to Peace Corps volunteers, he met a firm response. Hesburgh clarified that Notre Dame would determine "who would teach what" and to whom.[51] He savored conveying to Mankiewicz and others that Notre Dame stood stronger for academic freedom than did many of its Big Ten neighbors.

Hesburgh's dedication both to ensuring academic freedom and to utilizing the university to address major issues received obvious demonstration in his support of George Shuster's organization of a series of annual meetings at Notre Dame from 1963 to 1967 aimed at addressing the "population problem." The Ford and Rockefeller Foundations sponsored these meetings, which Shuster organized in close collaboration with Cass Canfield of the Planned Parenthood Federation. They brought together liberal Catholics with representatives of Planned Parenthood such as Alan Guttmacher and also with various foundation and public policy officials. Readers of a certain vintage may recall that by the 1960s the "population issue" had begun to gain major national attention. The issue would get dramatic attention in 1968 when the neo-Malthusian Stanford biologist Paul Ehrlich published *The Population Bomb*, which began: "The battle to feed all of humanity is over. In the 1970s and 1980s hundreds of millions of people will starve to death in spite of any crash programs embarked upon now."[52] Long before Ehrlich's hysterics, John D. Rockefeller and the Population Council, which he funded, had worked to implement population control measures and to persuade governments to adopt family planning regimens. The Catholic Church stood as a fierce opponent of such policies. Father Hesburgh's position on these questions and his deep and controversial involvement in the work of the Rockefeller Foundation will be explored subsequently. It is important to clarify here that Notre Dame's president raised no objections to these meetings even though they were clearly intended, as the historian Donald Critchlow has argued, to establish "a liberal forum to create an oppositional voice within the Catholic Church on the issue of family planning."[53] Academic freedom, Hesburgh thought, must be given its due.

"DOC" KENNA, ED STEPHAN, THE O'GRADY GIRLS, AND ARA PARSEGHIAN

Howard J. (Doc) Kenna served as provincial of the Indiana Province of the Congregation of Holy Cross from 1962 until 1973. During this time he also acted as some combination of father figure/elder brother for Father Hesburgh in a similar manner to George Shuster.[54] Kenna also collaborated closely with Hesburgh on the transfer of ownership of the University of Notre Dame from Holy Cross to an independent board of fellows. Without

Kenna's decisive support and full backing, this transfer could never have been accomplished. Kenna, who was sixteen years older than Hesburgh, gave his younger confrere essential encouragement to proceed down his course of building a modern Catholic university. He also gave him personal sustenance during challenging days.

Ted Hesburgh voted for Doc Kenna at the provincial chapter in 1962 that brought the older priest to his leadership of the Indiana Province and hence to his role as a religious superior of all the Holy Cross priests and brothers in that province. He had first met Kenna during his seminary days but had come to know him well after he returned to teach at Notre Dame in 1945. Kenna, who had done graduate work in mathematics at Johns Hopkins in the 1930s, although without completing his doctorate, was director of studies (broadly overseeing academic affairs) at Notre Dame from 1944 to 1949, and then the first vice president for academic affairs for the 1949–1950 academic year. Father Ted remembered that Kenna proved a good sounding board for him. Kenna held a number of important posts—first as assistant superior general (1950–1953), then as superior of the Holy Cross College theologate in Washington, D.C., for a couple of years thereafter, and finally for seven years as president of the University of Portland, the college owned by the congregation in Portland, Oregon. Hesburgh appreciated the wide experience that Kenna possessed and especially valued his knowledge of Catholic higher education.

Doc Kenna holds a special place in the memories of Holy Cross religious who endured the turmoil of the 1960s. His time as provincial largely coincided with the great exodus of priests from the order in the wake of Vatican II. These departures pained Kenna greatly, but he won the regard of all for the compassion and good judgment he brought to dealing with the tumult that beset the Holy Cross congregation and most other religious orders. He helped hold Holy Cross together through a time of some upheaval. Among the seminarians of the day his nickname was "Yahweh" because "he evoked the same admiration and response as God did."[55] Father Ted did not see him in quite so exalted a way, but he greatly admired him. In the homily he preached at Kenna's funeral Mass in 1973 he described him as "a person totally given to the good of the Community, with little thought to his own desires or preferences."[56]

Kenna certainly was a steadying rock for Hesburgh. They traveled a lot together. On their travels they talked at length on all kinds of subjects. They both read widely and could address many subjects. They devoted considerable time to reflecting on the relationship between the Holy Cross order and its educational institutions (Notre Dame and the University of Portland) in light of the teachings of Vatican II. Those were consequential conversations. In his homily at Kenna's funeral, Father Hesburgh observed that long before Vatican II, Kenna "was mindful of the true role of the laity of the Church." In this context he proceeded to make the extraordinary claim of his deceased brother in Holy Cross that "more than any other person, it must be said that the vital new role of the laity in the governance of our universities was his dream and of his doing."[57] Doc Kenna assuredly played an important role in enabling an enhanced participation for the laity at Notre Dame, but his was without question a supporting effort to the man who preached his funeral homily.

Father Ted always cast the transfer in ownership of Notre Dame away from the Holy Cross order as part of an effort to empower the laity. Needless to say, his motives were more complicated. His previous clashes with his Holy Cross superiors such as Christopher O'Toole honed his desire to remove himself from under their direction. Also he increasingly saw the university as distinct from Holy Cross, as the episode over the funding of the new Moreau Seminary building clarified. He preferred clearer lines of demarcation.[58] Furthermore, he increasingly felt a deep frustration with the high-handedness of a lot of the Roman authority in the Church. The brusque efforts of the conservative Cardinal Giuseppe Pizzardo, the prefect of the Sacred Congregation of Seminaries and Universities (renamed the Congregation for Catholic Education in 1967), to block Hesburgh's appointment as president of IFCU in 1963 further aroused his suspicion of Church authorities. (Only the personal intervention of Pope Paul VI resolved this matter in Hesburgh's favor.)[59] He wanted to free his university from any canonical oversight or intervention that might be applied by the likes of Cardinals Pizzardo and Ottaviani, and that placed at risk the academic freedom and credibility of the university.

His experiences with the foundation officials and the fellow university presidents with whom he now associated and who looked askance at the old Notre Dame governing structure also weighed upon him. Additionally he judged that the size and complexity of Notre Dame had "reached the point where [it] could no longer be run by a handful of Holy Cross priests."[60] The talents of the lay (advisory) trustees and lay administrators needed to be tapped more copiously.[61] The sense of renewal in the Church that Vatican II released provided the needed context for rethinking the governance structure. With Kenna's election as provincial Hesburgh had the key ally who could help him gain Holy Cross approval for governance changes within the university.

Kenna and Hesburgh began their initial discussions and then involved others in their deliberations as they proceeded forward, both at Notre Dame and beyond. Father Hesburgh regularly consulted with the Jesuit president of Saint Louis University, Father Paul Reinert, who had begun to plan for a similar transfer at his school. Reinert proved another valued ally for him, and these activist presidents schemed together quietly about the best means to reach their objective. Hesburgh realized that he also would need the crucial support of the head of his congregation based in Rome to gain approval for the formal canonical process known as alienation of property, which would allow for the formal transfer of ownership of the university. Here fortune, if that is the term, smiled on his efforts. Father Christopher O'Toole would have proved an implacable foe of the arrangements Hesburgh planned, but his successor, Rev. Germaine-Marie Lalande, readily supported the proposals.

In the summer of 1965 Hesburgh gathered all the university vice presidents, several key (advisory) trustees including Ed Stephan and George Shuster, as well as Lalande and Kenna, and thrashed out the governance issue.[62] They met around the large table on the front porch of the summer house at Land O'Lakes, Wisconsin. The consensus, not surprisingly, favored a move toward greater lay control. Lalande conveyed his view that "the principal commitment of the order was in sanctification of people in the Church and not in the administration of education institutions."[63] With the superior general in full agreement, the task then moved on to framing new governance arrangements. Here Hesburgh and his colleagues were navigating in uncharted waters and without obvious models. It was not normal behavior for religious orders to surrender the ownership of their major apostolic endeavors. In this process Ed Stephan, the prominent Chicago lawyer and Hesburgh's close friend, made crucial contributions. He examined the civil documents with care and determined that the original charter given to Father Sorin by the State of Indiana allowed the current board composed only of Holy Cross priests to elect any number of lay members to the board with equal status. Stephan mapped a way forward without the need to resort to any request to the state for revision of the existing charter.

In the summer of 1966 Hesburgh convened another gathering in the beautiful surrounds of the Land O'Lakes property. Lalande and Kenna attended again, as did Fathers Joyce and John Walsh. On this occasion a larger group of lay advisory trustees participated. Shuster and Stephan both returned, but a number of leading trustees joined them, including Paul Hellmuth, Robert Galvin, Newton Minow, Joseph O'Neill, Al Stepan Jr., and Bernard Voll. Although Hellmuth chaired the meeting, Hesburgh took the lead in explaining the broad proposal and its background and purpose. On a couple of occasions Kenna emphatically interjected that "we must make sure that Notre Dame retains its essential [religious] character."[64] There was "unanimous agreement" on his point. After much discussion and deliberation, the proposals offered by the prudent and judicious Stephan garnered consensus support. As a result of his initiatives a two-tier structure emerged that assured a continued crucial role for the Congregation of Holy Cross. There is perhaps some irony in that Stephan, a layperson, initiated these efforts that explicitly guaranteed the order's continued significant role in university governance. In what is best described as a shared governance arrangement Stephan set the ownership of the university in a board of fellows consisting of six Holy Cross religious and six lay trustees. This board would need a two-thirds vote to make any changes to proposed statutes and bylaws. It also had responsibility for electing trustees and for maintaining the Catholic character of the university. In addition to the members of the board of fellows there would be a larger board of trustees of thirty to forty members on which laypersons would predominate. All present accepted that the president of Notre Dame would be a Holy Cross priest of the Indiana Province. In order to select that person, Father Hesburgh proposed that "the Provincial would submit the name of a member of the Congregation to the nominating committee of the Board who in turn would present the name to the full board for approval." So all understood that a Holy Cross priest would serve as Notre Dame's president, and they appreciated equally well that for the foreseeable future that priest would be Theodore Martin Hesburgh.

Although the governance issue decidedly held priority for Ted Hesburgh in 1965 and 1966, it was not the only major matter to which he gave attention. He oversaw the running of the university at a time when undergraduate enrollment continued to increase and new graduate programs were added, with all the attendant pressures such expansion triggered. Buildings and budgets and development efforts all claimed his attention, as we have seen. With arguments for coeducation increasingly in the societal air, Hesburgh authorized discussions with neighboring Saint Mary's

College regarding cooperative programs. Sister Madeleva had retired in 1961 and died in 1964, so he no longer worried about dealing with that formidable woman. Still, he kept his own direct involvement to a minimum and delegated Shuster and others to take the lead on this sensitive matter.[65] In 1965 and 1966 representatives from both campuses developed a "co-exchange" program that allowed upper-division students from each school to take classes on the other campus. Hesburgh encouraged Shuster to build on these initial efforts and to draw up a master proposal for "the best possible plan for future intellectual cooperation between the two schools."

In the midst of pressing demands he found solace and support from family and friends as well as from some unlikely sources. He continued both his annual Christmas excursion to the Baja peninsula with C. R. Smith and Charlie Jones and his Land O'Lakes retreat after the end of each academic year. Doc Kenna's return to South Bend meant he had a Holy Cross confrere with whom he could travel and converse easily. Ned Joyce, his ever loyal deputy, always backed up his decisions. When on campus he socialized with the larger Holy Cross community at Corby Hall. There he continued to dominate conversation at meals and other gatherings that he attended. Few of his fellow religious engaged him in genuine discussion on the direction in which he led Notre Dame. Most simply deferred to their famous confrere, who, after all, had appeared on the cover of *Time*. Further, it was considered bad form to question the president on "business matters" when he was enjoying community time. Also to dissent openly was to risk a reassignment from Notre Dame. The fear was expressed that one might be sent to Portland or to the dusty missions of Texas.[66]

Father Ted remained devoted to his family—his mother and his siblings and their children—and he attended to them as best he could. These years notably provided an opportunity for him to grow even closer to his brother, Jim, and his wife, Mary, and their growing family. Jim Hesburgh served in the Navy for three years after his graduation and then attended Harvard Business School before beginning a business career. In the 1960s he took a position as a vice president for the Wheelabrator Corporation, which was headquartered in Mishawaka, Indiana, the neighboring city to South Bend. Father Ted loved having his brother's family so close for some years. He remembered this "as one of the nicest times of my life."[67]

Even before Jim and Mary Hesburgh arrived back in close proximity to Notre Dame, Father Ted had begun a friendship with another family that provided him with a treasured experience of being a foster father for some lively young undergraduates. As recorded in some detail in his memoir, Hesburgh met an American couple on a visit to Buenos Aires in 1956, Charles O'Grady and his "vivacious" wife, Victoria. They had five daughters and a son whom they planned to send back to Saint Mary's and to Notre Dame for college. Victoria enlisted Hesburgh to serve as their "father" during their college years because they would not be traveling back and forth often to Argentina during their undergraduate studies. To say that Father Ted took up this responsibility with relish probably understates the case. He recollected in *God, Country, Notre Dame* that "Robert O'Grady became like a son to me, and all the O'Grady girls were like daughters. I shared their joys and sorrows, nurtured and guided them as best I could, and watched them do a lot of growing up."[68] There were O'Grady children around Notre Dame from the late 1950s through the mid-1960s, and Father Ted somehow found time to take the young women (and eventually their younger brother) to the movies or for a dinner at the Morris Inn and to discuss all kinds of subjects with them from boyfriend problems to their course and career choices. Anne O'Grady, the oldest daughter, later observed astutely that their foster father benefited greatly from the relationship. She thought he elicited a lot of information from them, while they "brought a whole lightness and charm" through being women. "Yet it was safe. It was nice for him to be able to be seen with us . . . and no one would say anything."[69]

Meanwhile, after the controversy surrounding the firing of Terry Brennan, Father Hesburgh stepped back and let Father Joyce take the lead in the selection of Brennan's successor. They agreed that they had made a mistake in selecting a young coach without real experience at the intercollegiate level. The obvious solution was to enlist an experienced coach. Joyce settled on Joe Kuharich, a South Bend native, who had played at Notre Dame in the 1930s under Elmer Layden and coached both at the college level and in the NFL in the years after World War II. Joyce recalled, "I knew Joe for many years. I was one year behind him at Notre Dame. He was a good student, fine football player and an intelligent guy."[70] Kuharich also wanted the job and readily gave up the head coaching position at the Washington Redskins to return to his alma mater and his hometown. His four-year tenure turned out to be a terrible stretch in Notre Dame's fabled football history. He compiled a 17-23 record, and he holds the unfortunate distinction as the only Notre Dame football coach to have an overall losing record. In 1960 the team finished 2-8, which included a school record eight-game losing streak. As the sportswriter Jim Dent later noted: "Knute Rockne had lost twelve games in thirteen seasons. By the end of the 1960 season, Kuharich had lost thirteen games in *two* seasons." At the end of the 5-5 1962 season Joyce indicated to him that the next season likely would be his last. With the die thus cast Kuharich decided to leave on his own terms. In March of 1963 he resigned and took a position created for him in the office of his old friend the NFL commissioner Pete Rozelle. The Notre Dame experiment with experience had not produced excellence on the gridiron.

Things didn't change under Hugh Devore, whom Joyce named interim head coach after Kuharich's unexpected departure. Devore, affectionately known as "Hughie," had also played at Notre Dame in the 1930s and gone on to a long coaching career at both the college and professional levels, including at Notre Dame for the 1945 season while Leahy served in the U.S. Navy. Devore coached the Philadelphia Eagles in the 1956 and 1957 seasons but was fired after two losing campaigns. In 1958 he returned to Notre Dame as the freshman coach and assistant athletic director. He assumed the head coaching task right before the beginning of spring practice in 1963 knowing full well that he was likely a stopgap until a full search could be undertaken in the fall. Apparently the likable Devore initially boosted morale on the Notre Dame squad but not its performance on the field. Notre Dame's woes continued. Devore led his team to a 2-7 record with the scheduled game against Iowa canceled because of the assassination of John F. Kennedy, a cancellation that Hesburgh insisted upon.

According to Father Ted, Ned Joyce always kept a list of two or three coaches around as possibilities for the future. As the fall of 1963 moved along, two names came to the fore—Dan Devine, the successful coach of Missouri, and Ara Parseghian of Northwestern. Notre Dame fans knew Parseghian well. His teams had defeated the Irish in the previous four seasons. Parseghian knew Notre Dame planned to hire a new coach and he took the initiative and contacted Joyce to express his interest. According to Hesburgh, "it was like a man offering a sirloin steak to a hungry dog," although it is not clear who he thought was the man and who was the dog. Hesburgh and Joyce decided to interview Parseghian. They recognized that he had no previous Notre Dame connection and that he was not a Catholic, but they readily grasped that he was a terrific football coach. If he could replicate in South Bend what he had done in Evanston, they knew their football worries would be resolved. Things moved quickly.

After preliminary meetings with Joyce, Parseghian met secretly with the Hesburgh-Joyce duo at a hotel on the north side of Chicago at 9:30 on a wintry December night. There Father Ted interrogated his coaching prospect on his willingness to abide by the articles of administration he had written for athletics at Notre Dame and on his commitment to run an honest program. He heard the reassuring response: "You run an honest show and I will run an honest show." Hesburgh told Parseghian right then that he was their choice, although they needed to gain the formal approval of the faculty board in control of athletics. Hesburgh gained that and thereafter left Ned Joyce and Parseghian to work through the contractual details and the public announcement. Although these details proved almost comically complicated, Ara Parseghian eventually signed his contract and took up his duties as head football coach at Notre Dame as of January 2, 1964. Hesburgh had done his main part by bringing this extraordinary coach to his university.[71]

The students on campus and the alumni and many supporters of the football team greeted Parseghian's appointment with a combination of delight and relief. One student wrote that "after suffering through four disastrous years . . . I received the news of Parseghian's hiring in much the same way as I imagine Americans must have received news of VJ Day after suffering through World War II."[72] The "Era of Ara" had begun and it began with a bang. Under the undoubtedly helpful gaze of "Touchdown Jesus," Ara Parseghian took Hugh Devore's downtrodden team and worked a miracle in the 1964 season. Effectively exploiting the passing talent and heroics of the quarterback John Huarte, the team went undefeated through to its final game. Only a 20–17 away game defeat at the hands of traditional rival USC deprived them of a national championship. In just one season Parseghian brought Notre Dame to the winning ways that prevailed throughout his celebrated tenure as coach. As Jim Dent would have it, Ara oversaw the "resurrection" of Notre Dame football.[73]

Father Hesburgh watched the restoration of Notre Dame football with mixed emotions. He savored the team's success on the field. He had no liking whatsoever for defeat. He knew that winning was good for student morale and that it engaged the alumni at a time when he was eliciting their support. He grew to value Ara Parseghian as a person and came to know him and his wife, Katie, and their children well. Ara signed on to the Hesburgh project and spoke always of his conviction "that academic excellence and football excellence are compatible."[74] He also never sought to upstage

Hesburgh and always gave him deference. In taking on the coaching duties he paid tribute to the "great progress" that Notre Dame had made academically under Father Hesburgh.

Still, Father Ted always remained slightly uneasy about the football program and worried that the football tail could once again begin to wag the central academic dog (if that unfortunate metaphor might be excused) of Notre Dame. He kept a certain distance from the day-to-day running of the football program. That remained Father Joyce's domain. His resolve did weaken once during the excitement of the 1964 season. He accepted an invitation to speak at the Friday night pep rally prior to the much-anticipated game against Duffy Daugherty's highly regarded Michigan State Spartans. While the crowd, fueled in the usual manner by excessive drinking, chanted Ara's name, Father Ted gamely took the microphone and began to speak of Notre Dame's accomplishments not only in football, but in academia. It was not exactly what the crowd had come to hear, and student and alumni fans alike showed no particular deference to *Father* Hesburgh. Some "enthusiasts" close to the stage even disrespectfully shouted out "bowl game" as he tried to talk—a reference to the Notre Dame ban on participation in postseason bowl games. The Notre Dame president wrapped up quickly and turned things over to Ara, whom the fans actually wanted to hear. As he left he spoke to Frank Gaul, the student organizer of the pep rally, and assured him "that this will be the last time I will ever speak in this place."[75] Despite his annoyance in this instance, he went along with Joyce's request to increase the number of football scholarships, which made Ara's recruiting task easier. He supported Ara's having a strong cadre of assistant coaches and improved training facilities. Whatever his reservations, Hesburgh found winning at football much easier to deal with than losing. And Parseghian gave him many victories.

In 1966 Ara guided his Irish team to a national championship, the first since Frank Leahy had held the reins at Notre Dame. The famous tie with Michigan State in the "game of the century" and then a 51–0 thrashing of USC in the final game of the season assured that Notre Dame was crowned national champions by both wire service polls. The decade-long wandering in the wilderness following Leahy's departure had come to an end, and Notre Dame fans readily reignited their ample expectations that Our Lady's team should compete regularly for the national championship.

Memories of Father Ted's supposedly negative attitudes to the football program began to fade, and he passed over into the phase of being an elder statesman among college presidents arguing for integrity in athletic programs. Immediately upon winning the 1966 national championship he offered a serious reflection extolling the virtues of sport above and beyond the win-loss record in the *Scholastic*'s Football Review issue. He ponderously intoned that "the display, the spectacle, the color, the excitement lingers only in the memory. But the spirit, the will to excel and the will to win endure. These human qualities are larger and much more important than the passing events that occasion them." While defending football as part of the "mid-twentieth-century American way" he warned that "the football season in our land" could be "overdone." In this article, meant to celebrate the 1966 team's success (and which was soon reprinted for the larger *Sports Illustrated* audience), he bluntly and colorfully cautioned that football "could be wrenched out of all perspective, so that even the fantastic becomes the phantasmagoric, as is done by prolonging the season unduly, indulging in an increasing orgy of bowl games, the psychedelic dream makers of collegiate football."[76] This challenge of keeping sound perspective regarding football was one he would face in the next decade of his presidency. It was but one of many tests he confronted, but hardly the most pressing as he strove to enhance Notre Dame's standing among American universities.

CHAPTER 4

CHANGES, CHALLENGES, AND TURMOIL, 1967–1977

I N 1967 THE UNIVERSITY OF NOTRE DAME MARKED THE 125TH AN-
niversary of its founding with modest celebrations. The commemorative
events started on December 8 with an academic procession and pontifical
Mass for the Feast of the Immaculate Conception, at which Archbishop
Luigi Raimondi, the apostolic delegate to the United States, served as principal celebrant. Then followed a two-day symposium during which a number of academic notables offered learned reflections on the theme of "The
University in a Developing World Society." The commemorative events
likely would have passed quickly into the realm of foggy memory except for
the presentation Father Hesburgh gave at the convocation, which he entitled "The Vision of a Great Catholic University in the World of Today."[1]

When he published the talk the following year Hesburgh rightly described it as "in many ways . . . the most important talk I have ever written,
since it deals with the heart of all our efforts during these recent years and,
hopefully, it is a realistic blueprint of what we hope to realize at Notre
Dame, as a great Catholic university, in the years ahead."[2] Hesburgh's December address drew heavily on earlier talks and articles that he had written, especially a May 1967 address to the faculty entitled "Why Are We
a Catholic University?" His convocation address reflected the important
recent changes that had taken place in the governance of the university.
It also drew upon the discussions on the nature of Catholic universities
encapsulated in the so-called Land O'Lakes Statement of July 1967. He
believed that these developments laid the foundations for achieving his
goal of creating "a great Catholic university." But as he looked ahead he
also realized that the university confronted "dangers and difficulties." At

the convocation he exhorted his listeners not to succumb to timidity or defensiveness in light of them. Rather, he earnestly called upon them to adopt "the qualities of the pioneer" as they proceeded forward—"vision, courage, confidence, a great hope inspired by faith and ever revivified by love and dedication."[3]

The decade from 1967 to 1977 tested to the full Father Hesburgh's "pioneering" qualities. This period constituted the most stormy span in the university's modern history. Hesburgh faced dangers and difficulties aplenty that strained his remarkable composure and stamina. Yet with his usual self-assurance intact he led his university on a journey over a perilous trail of change and contention.

TRANSFER OF OWNERSHIP AND NEW GOVERNANCE FOR NOTRE DAME

Ted Hesburgh, Ed Stephan, and Doc Kenna completed most of the planning for a transfer of ownership from the Holy Cross order to a joint lay-religious board of fellows in the summer and fall of 1966. Hesburgh had no reservations or second thoughts about this weighty action. He believed that it would give Notre Dame a more reputable governing structure and make it more presentable in the eyes of the broad academic community. Stephan and Paul Hellmuth drew up the essential legal documents for the new structure and Hesburgh eagerly wished to implement them, but he faced a final hurdle. He needed to secure the agreement of his fellow Holy Cross religious gathered in the special provincial chapter that Kenna scheduled for late January of 1967 to consider and vote on new arrangements for both Notre Dame and the University of Portland.

Prior to the meeting of the provincial chapter Hesburgh broached the whole subject with the Holy Cross priests and brothers who constituted the Corby Hall community at Notre Dame—all those who served at the university. With Stephan at his side he presented the details of the new structure and the process of effecting it. Ed Stephan recalled that it was "a long meeting with lots of questions and comments." He further recalled that although a consensus in favor began to emerge, a number of the Corby Hall members "were not at all happy with the idea."[4] News of the proposed changes and the disagreements within the Holy Cross order soon began to leak out into the wider university and beyond. In an effort to squelch the rumor mill and also to give a "preordained conclusion" quality to his pro-posal, Father Ted seized the initiative on January 18 and wrote a letter to the whole university community—over 80,000 persons including faculty, alumni, students, parents, and friends—explaining the changes that were under way. He emphasized the perceived benefits of the proposed new ar-rangements and pronounced the change an "inevitable development" that was part of an effort to recharge the institution for a new age.[5] The Holy Cross priests and brothers who were opposed to the transfer of ownership had no similar vehicle to make their views widely known to the various Notre Dame constituencies. They were mainly more traditional and older religious including Louis (Lou) Thornton, the director of placement at the university; Ralph Davis, who taught chemistry; Anthony (Tony) Lauck, who chaired the art department; and Cornelius (Con) Hagerty, who had recently served as chaplain at Saint Mary's. None had the capacity to ef-fectively counter the Hesburgh initiatives. Nonetheless, they determined to make their case, and their willingness to do so still annoyed Father Ted thirty years later.

The essential arguments of each side of the debate were well captured in a "special report" in *Ave Maria* magazine, which appeared right before the chapter meeting. Entitled "Control of Catholic Universities," and writ-ten by its editors John Reedy, C.S.C., and James Andrews, the piece began provocatively: "'How can you consider giving away 100 million dollars worth of real estate?' [and] 'How can you consider abandoning a century of labor and love which a whole community of priests, brothers and sis-ters have poured into an institution?'" Reedy and Andrews then noted that "these questions are being asked with honesty, deep concern, and a sense of urgency by religious of the Congregation of Holy Cross as they reexam-ine their community's relationship to two institutions which were born and nourished on the zeal, dedication and labor of their Congregation." Reedy and Andrews initially outlined Kenna's perspective in calling the chapter, gave some details of the respective and somewhat different proposals for Notre Dame and Portland, and then offered a "sampling of opinions from both sides." The piece gave some voice to the opponents who feared that this was but a first step to full secularization and who believed the risks too great to proceed forward at a time when the institutions were performing well. Hesburgh's antagonists argued further that some kind of revocable experiment should be tried first, and they especially objected to the haste with which the new arrangements were being forced through. Reedy and

Andrews highlighted the latter issue in their summation. They observed that the leaders of the two universities and of the congregation believed that the time for decision had come and "that the cost of delay—even a delay of six months—would be so great that the issue must be put to a decision now." As they outlined it, "the question is whether they will be able to convince their fellow religious, many of whom would prefer to avoid the responsibility for this decision, that the values inherent in the opportunity are great enough to justify the acknowledged risks." With some care they concluded that "no one can confidently predict the outcome at this time."[6] Ted Hesburgh begged to differ. He was determined to prevail, and he did.

The special chapter opened on Monday morning, January 23, 1967, with a concelebrated Mass of the Holy Spirit in Sacred Heart Church at which provincial Howard "Doc" Kenna presided. The forty-two chapter delegates (capitulants) then made a profession of faith, after which "an accusation of faults" followed wherein some delegates publicly admitted to their sins and transgressions, an indication that some of the norms of religious life from before Vatican II still operated. The afternoon session was held in the plush, UN-style main auditorium of the Continuing Education Center. Father Ted held real pride in this well-appointed room, which he saw as a key venue for making Notre Dame the site for discussions of the great issues of the day. The high quality of the amenities (for the time) spoke silently but forcefully to all the delegates of what Hesburgh had accomplished at Notre Dame. While blizzard conditions beset the campus outside, the chapter delegates plunged into the special work at hand.

In the morning session on January 25 Hesburgh presented the comprehensive proposal for changes in the ownership and administration of Notre Dame. He forcefully tried to correct "misconceptions in the press" that his proposal was in any way similar to the secularization that had recently occurred at Webster College in St. Louis, a school previously run by the Sisters of Loreto. For him both "the Catholicity of the university" and "the role of the community at the university" were to be preserved "at all costs." Somewhat misleadingly, he claimed that in the initial stages of discussion he "was hesitant," but that Fathers Kenna and Lalande had urged him forward. Rather amusingly, in one of the drafts of his presentation found in the records of the chapter he went so far as to describe himself as "a reluctant bridegroom" in the marriage of the two boards, lay and religious. Of course, he always had been the leading advocate for the union, and his deep commitment to this "marriage" stood out as he outlined at length the evolution of the proposal, the reasons for it, and its implications. Furthermore, Father Ted could indicate that the superior general favored the proposal and that his good friend Father (later Archbishop) Ed Heston in Rome had given assurances that there would be no difficulties in gaining approval for the transfer from the Congregation for Religious (the competent Vatican authority). He conceded that there was some opposition among the local religious, but he concluded by assuring the delegates that the plan he offered "will give us the opportunity to build a truly great Catholic university with an impact on the modern scene." And then he offered a final peroration that it would "fulfill all the good purposes that first brought Father Sorin to found the institution."[7]

In Father Hesburgh's recollection, after he gave his lengthy presentation, he and Doc Kenna let the opponents of the transfer of ownership have "the rest of the week" to express their opposition. He claimed that "they fought incessantly and violently against it and spoke against it." He later described the opponents as "mossbacks" who thought he planned to give away "the crown jewels." He aimed a special venom at Lou Thornton, whom he dismissively branded as "a great protégé of John O'Hara," and as one who held that the transfer would bring on "Sodom and Gomorrah."[8] Thornton certainly opposed the Hesburgh proposal. Although not a chapter delegate, he was granted special permission to address the capitulants. He did so in the afternoon session of January 25. He warned about undue haste, raised concerns about the irrevocable nature of Hesburgh's proposal, and argued that there were other ways to involve the laity without transferring ownership. A perusal of the minutes of his address reveals no mention of either Sodom or Gomorrah, although Thornton, who presumably knew his cause was vanquished, waggishly compared the situation of the Holy Cross community at Notre Dame "to that of our first parents in the Garden of Eden." He begged the delegates "not to make an irrevocable mistake as they had done." His biblical reference failed to persuade his confreres. Contrary to Father Ted's recollection, few others spoke out in opposition to his proposal. Attention focused more on the details of the arrangements.[9]

The discussion was serious yet it reached no particular heights, and it would not qualify as a genuine debate over the issue. Father Hesburgh easily handled the various questions that were raised to him, although his good friend Father Arnold Fell, who ran the Holy Cross Foreign Mission Society, did surprise and alarm him by asking why Holy Cross should even stay in the higher education apostolate. In light of Hesburgh's argument that the laity should play a larger role in the governance of the university, Fell asked whether "when others can do the work shouldn't the religious community move on to some other work?" This idea involved rather more of a transfer of authority and responsibility to the laity at Notre Dame than Father Ted thought advisable. He quickly responded that the Holy Cross community had a special role to give leadership in the intellectual and pastoral areas and to show that "Catholicism and freedom are not incompatible and [that] priests and laymen can work together." On January 26, with no further interventions forthcoming, the question was called. In a secret ballot, thirty-eight religious voted in favor of the proposal while four opposed it.[10]

With approval gained from the provincial chapter Hesburgh moved swiftly to secure formal consent from Father Lalande and his council and then to obtain the rescript, or official permission, from the Vatican for the alienation of property involved in the new arrangement. With Father Heston, the procurator general of the Holy Cross order, oiling the wheels of the notoriously slow Vatican bureaucracy, the rescript came quickly. Then documents were signed, meetings convened, elections held, and appointments made with Father Ted and Ed Stephan being the decisive contributors at every step. By early May of 1967 Hesburgh and Stephan could stand with Paul Hellmuth and Doc Kenna at a press conference at the Continuing Education Center and announce the full realization of the new arrangements. The formal ownership of the university was now vested in the board of fellows consisting of six Holy Cross priests and six laypersons. The fellows in turn had elected a predominantly lay board of trustees and delegated important powers to it. The fellows also had adopted new statutes and bylaws to govern the university. The new board of trustees elected Ed Stephan as its first chair and Paul Hellmuth as secretary. The trustees also confirmed Father Hesburgh and the other university officers in their positions and approved a new faculty manual.

In his prepared remarks at the press conference Hesburgh stressed the responsibilities of the fellows to maintain "the essential character of the university as a Catholic institution of higher learning," and he emphasized that the newly adopted statutes provided that "the University shall retain in perpetuity its identity as such an institution." He noted further, and in a manner meant to reassure those who worried that the new arrangements represented a step along the slippery slope to secularization taken by so many one-time Protestant universities, that "the trustees would always elect a Holy Cross priest as the president of Notre Dame."[11] In explaining the new arrangements, Father Ted accentuated that they provided an enhanced role for the laity in light of Vatican II and also that they accorded better both with the more public character of the university, as evidenced by the diverse variety of its funding sources, and with its recent dramatic growth. On the whole, the changes were well received. Ed Stephan even remembered that on a visit with Pope Paul VI at Castel Gandolfo after the IFCU meeting held in Kinshasa in 1968, Father Ted had him outline the details of the new governing structure to the Holy Father. After hearing Stephan's description, the Notre Dame honorary degree recipient gave them each a kiss on the cheek and pronounced it all a "fine idea" that had his wholehearted approval.[12]

Father Hesburgh forever after described the transfer of ownership in terms of a far-reaching move to lay control of the university, whereas it clearly was a transition into a shared governance arrangement. But the new structure certainly allowed for much greater participation by laypersons in the affairs of Notre Dame through their membership as fellows and trustees. Under Stephan's leadership they contributed more effectively than during the period when their role was merely advisory. What the changes also provided was some guarantee that the administration of the school would not be subject to direct ecclesial interference on an institutional level. Father Hesburgh appreciated this greatly and presented the new structure as an insurance policy against efforts by any Church authorities to censor discussions or publications on campus. He incorporated into the new faculty manual a commitment to academic freedom, and thereafter he consistently championed the concept in response to secular critics who questioned the extent of free discussion at his Catholic university.

Whatever the significance of the new structures over the longer term, one could hardly describe them as bringing some dramatic immediate change to the governance of Notre Dame. Father Hesburgh dominated the administration of the university before the transition and he dominated it afterward. The board of trustees proved generally pliable to his wishes, especially during the period when Stephan chaired the group and worked so intimately with him. The first board chair intimated this himself in an interview in 1983 when he noted that Father Hesburgh "with his brilliance, reputation and background, tends to dominate any group that he is in." So it was with the trustees. Yet it exaggerates matters somewhat to say as does Michael O'Brien that "Notre Dame was still a one-man show."[13] Rather

Hesburgh remained the captain of the ship who determined its course, but he now could draw more directly on lay trustees such as Stephan and Hellmuth to assist him in important ways just as he drew on the support of loyal subordinates such as Ned Joyce and Jim Frick within the university.

Father Hesburgh never admitted that his continued domination of the administration of Notre Dame might necessitate a qualification regarding his claims of transferring the university to "lay control." The fact that he successfully removed the university from direct clerical control as exercised through the Holy Cross local council and that he gave it a presentable two-tier governing structure (that conveniently bore some resemblance to that of Harvard's) sufficed for him. As the years passed, he found it more necessary to clarify that the transfer of ownership meant no retreat from Notre Dame's Catholic mission and identity. In his memoir he noted that "the board of fellows has an enormous amount of power, and if a crisis came up, they would use that power to solve it. For example, if several members of the board of trustees got up and said that they no longer wanted Notre Dame to be a Catholic university, the board of fellows could fire those trustees on the spot. And my guess is that they would."[14]

LAND O'LAKES AND THE CONTEMPORARY CATHOLIC UNIVERSITY

A little over two months after the press conference announcing the change in governance arrangements at Notre Dame, Father Hesburgh convened twenty-six North American educators at Land O'Lakes to prepare a position paper for the International Federation of Catholic Universities (IFCU) meeting scheduled to take place the following summer. The meeting produced a relatively brief statement entitled "The Nature of the Contemporary Catholic University." As James Burtchaell later noted, this statement quickly became "the classic doctrine on how modern Catholic universities were to be defined primarily by their membership in the modern educational establishment, sharing the same autonomy, academic freedom, functions, services, disciplines, public and norms of academic excellence."[15] In the document's classical formulation: "To perform its teaching and research functions effectively the Catholic university must have a true autonomy and academic freedom in the face of authority of whatever kind, lay or clerical, external to the academic community itself."[16] This apparent "declaration of independence" by these Catholic educators has been the source of much controversy and commentary ever since.

The Land O'Lakes Statement reflected the same desire for institutional autonomy that motivated schools like Notre Dame and the leading Jesuit institutions to change their governance arrangements. As the major figures such as Father Hesburgh and Father Paul Reinert of Saint Louis University made very clear, they needed to provide their universities with an identity appropriate for the age. The problem of potential interference by Vatican officials or other church authorities, who (Hesburgh thought) knew little about contemporary higher education, needed to be clearly addressed and resolved so as to secure appropriate credibility for American Catholic universities. But the Land O'Lakes meeting had no formal authority, and it certainly did not intend to rupture the connection of the signatories with the Catholic Church. The majority of those who signed were priests and religious (mainly Jesuits), and two were members of the hierarchy: the scholarly archbishop Paul J. Hallinan of Atlanta, and Bishop John J. Dougherty, the president of Seton Hall University and the chair of the U.S. bishops' committee for Catholic higher education. Those whom Father Ted gathered in northern Wisconsin wanted to define better what a *Catholic* university should be.

The seeds of the Land O'Lakes meeting were planted in August 1965 at the close of the Tokyo meeting of the International Federation of Catholic Universities, of which Hesburgh now served as president. The delegates adopted "the nature and role of the contemporary Catholic university" as their theme for the next meeting, planned for the summer of 1968 at the Lovanium University in Kinshasa in the Democratic Republic of the Congo.[17] In preparation for that full gathering in the Congo, regional seminars were planned for 1967 to develop preliminary papers for discussion. In March of 1967 Father Ted gathered a planning committee at Notre Dame to consider what approach the North American region should take. To assist him he drew upon the talents of the able Jesuit priest Neil G. McCluskey, who had come to Notre Dame as a visiting professor of education after serving some years as vice president for academic affairs at Gonzaga University in Spokane. McCluskey, a close friend of Notre Dame's vice president for academic affairs John Walsh, stayed "on loan" at Notre Dame for the next few years and assisted Hesburgh with IFCU and other education projects. With McCluskey helping facilitate relations with the major Jesuit institutions and Hesburgh's close friendship with Paul Reinert also contributing in that regard, the members present at the March meeting decided on a follow-up seminar at Land O'Lakes.

The participants whom Hesburgh assembled in July were a mixed group in terms of the responsibilities they held, but broadly similar in outlook. The Jesuit heads of Boston College, Fordham, Georgetown, and Saint Louis joined Notre Dame's leader in the contingent of university presidents. The American assistant general of the Jesuits, Vincent T. O'Keefe, (himself a former president of Fordham), came with Fathers Lalande and Kenna to represent the religious orders. Hallinan and Dougherty flew the flag for the hierarchy, while the Canadian contingent included Monsignor Alphonse-Marie Parent and Fathers Lorenzo Roy from Laval and Lucien Vachon from Sherbrooke. Fr. Theodore McCarrick, then president of the Catholic University of Puerto Rico, represented schools from the Caribbean. A small number of laymen were present including George Shuster and the newly named chairmen of the boards of trustees of Notre Dame and Saint Louis, Ed Stephan and Daniel J. Schlafly. Rather surprisingly Hesburgh invited John Cogley, a onetime editor and columnist for *Commonweal* and later the religious news editor at the *New York Times*, who in 1967 was associated with the Center for the Study of Democratic Institutions. No women were present, although it must be said one particular woman had forced her way into Father Ted's thinking prior to Land O'Lakes: Miss Jacqueline Grennan.

Grennan began 1967 as a Sister of Loreto and the president of Webster College in St. Louis. By the summer she had announced that her institution would become a lay and legally secular institution and that she would be laicized and leave her religious order. Grennan attracted much attention for her rejection of any kind of shared governance arrangement. She really did want a full declaration of independence and claimed that if the founding religious congregation remained involved then "the final responsibility and authority still remains with the Church."[18] She recognized that her vow of obedience could actually mean something at some point. Thus she presented the notion that any connection to the Catholic Church was incompatible with the norms of American higher education. Grennan was hardly the only one raising questions and giving a certain credence to the George Bernard Shaw canard that a Catholic university was a contradiction in terms. In fact, the aforementioned John Cogley had published an article in *Commonweal* in June 1967 entitled "Catholic Universities: The Future of an Illusion," which revealed that he did "not believe the Catholic university as such has any future." Cogley declared that the Church would undergo drastic change in coming years and that in such circumstances the "Catholic university," such as those that existed in 1967, would "one day seem as anachronistic as the papal states."

The men gathered with Father Ted brimmed with confidence that they could answer effectively "two simple but all-important questions: What makes a modern university Catholic? How does a modern university act Catholic?"[19] They worked hard each day but took some time off in the afternoons to enjoy their beautiful surroundings and each other's company.[20] Whatever the intermittent merriment, the participants toiled so that at the end of four days they adopted their joint statement without dissent and, in fact, with "some excitement" as Neil McCluskey recalled. Father Robert J. Henle, S.J., the academic vice president at Reinert's Saint Louis University (and later president of Georgetown), was the principal drafter of the document. Father Ted admired greatly Henle's skill as a wordsmith and his ability to capture the essential points made during the freewheeling discussions. Hesburgh endorsed fully all that emerged in the document, especially the foundational case that a Catholic university "must be a university in the full modern sense of the word, with a strong commitment to and concern for academic freedom." But he also approved strongly that "Catholicism" would be "perceptibly present and effectively operative" on these campuses. Regrettably, however, aside from emphasizing an enhanced role for the theology faculty, little detailed attention was given to recommending effective measures to make Catholicism so integrally operative and present. The end was stated, but the means were not well addressed.

John Cogley pointedly pressured the group to release the statement to the public, and all the participants agreed to do so. In his capacity as both the chair of the meeting and as president of IFCU, Father Hesburgh circulated the brief statement. His name quickly became closely identified with it, certainly more so than any other of the signatories. He offered a brief explanatory preface in which he described it as a "study document" and expressed the hope that it would widen and deepen discussion on the contemporary Catholic university. He furthermore invited both "individual and group comments" on it.[21] Whatever his efforts to clarify that the document did not stand as "holy writ," the Land O'Lakes Statement quickly took on a special place in debates over Catholic higher education. Not surprisingly, as McCluskey noted, "those sections of the statement that spoke of the Catholic university's need for autonomy and academic freedom" received notable attention in the secular press and tough criticism among more conservative elements of the Catholic press.[22] In the face of such criticism Hesburgh doubled down. He defended "Land O'Lakes" (as it quickly came to be known) and promoted the approach it outlined.

Father Hesburgh maintained his commitment to the Land O'Lakes Statement throughout the rest of his life, and it is important to gain a clear grasp of his perspective. When interviewed at the Land O'Lakes property over three decades after the educators had gathered there, he still proudly recounted their accomplishment and gladly pointed out the table they had sat around. For him Catholic universities had to be seen as independent from Vatican authority and from their founding religious congregations so they could be genuine universities first. Yet he denied vigorously that there was any intention to follow the great majority of once Protestant universities and colleges down the secularization path. "We didn't intend to be that way," he held, "and we said that right in the opening statement, but at the same time we had to operate in that milieu [the American academy], . . . and if there was any thought at all that a Catholic university would be under the thumb of some monsignor in Rome who wouldn't know a university from a cemetery, we would lose our credibility and we would have no influence."[23] This quintessentially American priest clearly wanted to guarantee that his university would garner respect among American universities. At the same time, he still wanted universities like his to serve the Church. He would regularly proclaim that the Catholic university was where "the Church" did its thinking.[24] Yet he never effectively reconciled how the very entity that supposedly did the Church's "thinking" was somehow independent of the body it supposedly thought for.

Father Hesburgh and his colleagues in northern Wisconsin in 1967 regrettably directed most of their energies to stymieing possible future Vatican interference in their schools and on placating liberal critics like Cogley who were concerned about academic freedom in Catholic institutions. In retrospect they seem rather like generals preparing for the wrong kind of conflict with the wrong foe. They seem to have learned nothing from the sad example of secularization experienced by so many Protestant schools.[25] As a result they gave little serious attention to fashioning a curriculum appropriate for a modern Catholic university and almost no consideration to the task of recruiting capable and committed faculty to teach it. They gave no critical analysis to whether the still evolving theology departments could carry the heavy load assigned them in the new world they envisaged.

They made no strong commitment either to the pursuit of truth or to drawing upon the magisterial teachings of the Church. They refrained from making clear that they wanted students to encounter the person and message of Christ.

Ironies abound in examining Land O'Lakes and its aftermath. Notably, when government agencies and departments and various private instrumentalities, like accrediting agencies and foundations, increased their oversight and regulation of higher education, the Catholic educators acquiesced meekly so as to assure their access to financial support and secular approval of their programs. Yet they found it necessary to declare their liberation from possible interference from the Vatican and Church authority. Father Ted never fully appreciated the contradiction. Instead, he resented criticisms that the Land O'Lakes declaration had started Catholic schools down the slippery slope of enervated Catholic identity. Suggestions that he and his collaborators had severed the branches from the very vine that ultimately secured their Catholic integrity made him angry.

Much had changed from the beginning of 1967 when the provincial chapter had met during the January blizzard to the time when Father Ted delivered his December address at the university's 125th convocation. He now spoke with enhanced authority as the president of a university whose autonomy was established and where academic freedom prevailed. For him, Notre Dame needed to be "a *beacon*, shining with the great light of intelligence illumined by faith and faith seeking ever-greater understanding and expression of what we believe, in words that really speak to modern man." He sincerely hoped that it would be "a great light in the all-encompassing darkness that engulfs our world today."[26]

While Father Hesburgh understandably gave significant attention to the mission of his university, his purview extended far beyond it because of his leadership of the International Federation of Catholic Universities. He worked hard to shape the organization into something meaningful. At various IFCU meetings through the 1960s Hesburgh sought to gain clarity about the nature and purpose of a Catholic university. Hesburgh was one of the forty elected delegates who traveled to Rome for a week in late April of 1969 to continue the discussions under the auspices of the Sacred Congregation for Catholic Education. Here he helped secure approval of a statement that held that "the purposes of the Catholic university can be pursued by different means and modalities according to diverse situations of time and place."[27] He worked hard to secure a more expansive and less legalistic definition of Catholic universities. It is crucial to appreciate that both 1968 and 1969 were especially demanding years on campus with all the challenges of the student upheaval. Yet Hesburgh's willingness to leave Notre Dame for considerable stretches of time for meetings speaks to the unrelenting seriousness he gave to this matter. He might be likened to the proverbial bulldog who won't let go in his tenacity. He refused to yield in his determination to gain official Church approval for the kind of arrangements that he had implemented at Notre Dame and that Land O'Lakes expressed. He never found any irony in the spectacle of his dogged efforts to get formal Church approval of arrangements to declare as genuine Catholic universities those institutions that neither were erected canonically nor came under any direct ecclesial jurisdiction. That he poured so much effort into this undertaking, however, does complicate any simplistic portrayal of him as intent on distancing his university from the universal Church.

The end result appeared in November of 1972 as "The Catholic University in the Modern World." The document broadly supported the "American" position on institutional autonomy and academic freedom and thus did not outline formal juridical norms. Hesburgh especially valued the document's introduction, which outlined the essential characteristics of a Catholic university—such as "Christian inspiration not only of individuals but of the university community as such," and "fidelity to the Christian message as it comes to us through the Church"—and then stated plainly that "all universities that realize these fundamental conditions are Catholic universities, whether canonically erected or not."[28] He saw this as a victory in his long battle to establish what Catholic universities were. Almost a decade of his life had been given over to the project to define the nature of and appropriate structure and governance for the contemporary Catholic university, and he felt deep satisfaction with what he accomplished. Only if one appreciates the depth of his gratification can one in turn grasp the extent of his disappointment and even anger when in 1973 the wily Cardinal Gabriel-Marie Garrone, prefect of the Congregation for Catholic Education, resurrected the issue and expressed concerns about "university institutions without statutory bonds linking them to ecclesiastical authorities."[29] Garrone's apprehensions set off a lengthy dialogue between the international community of Catholic universities and the Vatican that culminated in the publication of *Ex Corde Ecclesiae* in 1990. Father

Hesburgh played some role in this dialogue, but his effort was always to defend the understandings he thought were properly established in "The Catholic University in the Modern World."[30]

STUDENT PROTEST, ACADEMIC DEVELOPMENTS, AND THE BURTCHAELL APPOINTMENT

In 1968 Christopher Jencks and David Riesman published *The Academic Revolution,* their influential study of American higher education. In their book the distinguished Harvard sociologists presented the "Harvard-Berkeley model" of the research university as the academic pacesetter for the United States. When examining Catholic universities, they observed that "the important question" was not "whether a few Catholic universities prove capable of competing with Harvard and Berkeley on the latter's terms, but whether Catholicism can provide an ideology or personnel for developing alternatives to the Harvard-Berkeley model of excellence." Jencks and Riesman went on to speculate, with some prescience it must be said, that "the ablest Catholic educators will feel obliged to put most of their energies into proving that Catholics can beat non-Catholics at the latter's game. But," they noted, "having proved this, a few may be able to do something more." Throwing down a gauntlet of sorts before Catholic educators like Ted Hesburgh, they asserted that "there is as yet no American Catholic university that manages to fuse academic professionalism with concern for questions of ultimate social and moral importance." They challenged Catholics to make "this distinctive contribution to the over-all academic system."[31]

Notre Dame's president eagerly wished to accept and meet this challenge. His quest to build his great *Catholic* university equaled in commitment that of any Arthurian knight seeking the Holy Grail. Yet Jencks and Riesman might well have had Father Ted in mind when they predicted that the ablest Catholic educators would place great emphasis on trying to replicate the Harvard-Berkeley model. In a way the quest for "excellence" that propelled Notre Dame right through the 1960s essentially guaranteed this, because the major research universities established the criteria for assessing excellence. Hesburgh wanted Notre Dame to be respected as a university by its secular peers. So he worked largely in light of their criteria to develop its academic strengths and reputation during the late sixties and early seventies. Of course, he additionally wanted to enhance Notre Dame's standing as a Catholic institution, but his work on his own campus proved less focused in this area. There existed no intact model to replicate. In retrospect, Father Ted failed to influence his campus community to fashion a coherent educational ideology that could replace the old Thomist synthesis. Nor, on a practical level, did he ensure that careful attention would be given to hiring faculty and developing the content of the curriculum, both key elements in building a distinctive institution. He grasped something of the importance of these tasks but could neither marshal the energy nor recruit the associates to address them efficaciously. Other more immediate challenges demanded his attention.

American universities in the late 1960s became the prime locations for the full-fledged youth revolt, which emerged from the Berkeley Free Speech Movement and especially from the antiwar struggle. On elite campuses across the country baby boomers charged that something was fundamentally wrong with America's political system and its institutions, including the very universities in which they studied. They questioned and contested authority of all sorts and sometimes violently. It is occasionally noted that campus unrest at Notre Dame was relatively modest compared to what happened at institutions like Berkeley and Columbia, but Father Ted did not experience these years as tranquil ones just because his Domer students were less rebellious than were their peers on Morningside Heights. He tried to keep a steady hand on the tiller to guide his institution forward as a place for genuine academic exchange, but it was difficult for him. He made this very clear in 1974 when he reflected on the question of "what really happened to American universities in the sixties?" One can sense his anguish at the whole ordeal. After assuring his readers that it "was a most unpleasant experience," he ratcheted up the tempo: "Everything became unhinged at once. Support was nowhere. The unheard of and unprecedented happened daily. Nothing seemed right and everything seemed wrong." Then tellingly he revealed, "Moreover, almost nothing one tried worked and one had the feeling in the pit of one's stomach of being perpetually the small boy with his finger in the dike, holding back the flood, precariously."[32] While it is not easy to picture the always resolute Hesburgh as some equivalent of the little Dutch boy stopping the flooding torrent, he definitely meant what he said about the anxiety in his gut.

Michael O'Brien and Robert Schmuhl have provided fine accounts of Father Hesburgh's engagement with the student protests at Notre Dame.

O'Brien rightly notes that Father Ted initially "underestimated the strength of the burgeoning student rebellion" at Notre Dame. In 1966 and 1967 there were hints of the troubles to come. Robert Sam Anson and others founded the *Observer*, an independent student newspaper, and used its pages to regularly criticize the Hesburgh administration, although probably not as harshly as Hesburgh remembered when he claimed that he "got fried in oil every day."[33] The appearance and mores of the students were changing. Longer hair, faded army jackets, and blue jeans made their appearance along with a greater willingness to challenge the still fairly strict regulations governing student behavior on campus. The redoubtable Father McCarragher still enforced the rules in a vigorous manner and the majority of students grudgingly acquiesced. As O'Brien noted, as late as October 1967, Father Ted "confidently pointed out that Notre Dame was having no serious problems with drugs, hippies or protestors—'just a few beards and I have nothing against beards.'"[34]

The following year brought a dramatic change in his perspective. He began the year intent on maintaining order on his campus so that the real work of the university could proceed. He conceded that protests such as those against the presence on campus (in order to conduct job interviews) of the napalm producer Dow Chemical Corporation were acceptable, but he laid down his "ground rules" for such protests. These included "First, respect for the freedom of others. Second, they ought to be peaceful. Third, the ordinary operations of the University should not be disrupted."[35] Such thoughtful guidelines were no longer operative in many leading schools across the country. In May at Columbia, student protestors held a dean hostage and occupied the office of President Grayson Kirk, looting his files. Similar activities occurred at campuses large and small. Occupying buildings and destroying property became customary, and ROTC programs were particular targets.

Hesburgh watched these occurrences with dismay. He tried to be a voice of reason, although that task became more arduous in a country that writhed in tribulation. The Tet Offensive in January and the assassination of Martin Luther King Jr. in April had Americans on edge, to put it mildly. On June 6, 1968, Father Hesburgh was in Los Angles to deliver the commencement address at the University of Southern California. He spoke just a few hours after Sirhan Sirhan shot and killed Senator Robert Kennedy. He told the graduating students that on his way across town to their campus he stopped at Good Samaritan Hospital where RFK had died and visited "with his brother Ted, and the widows of John and Bob." He reported that he told the grieving Kennedys "that I would dedicate my remarks this morning to the memory of these two brothers, with the prayerful hope that their example might be much more persuasive than my words." He titled his address "In Defense of the Younger Generation" and argued that "the uneasiness of modern youth has some legitimate bases and, hopefully, some better outlets than those we are presently seeing all over the world." He attempted to understand the causes of "the unrest, the protest, the revolt of young people today." He suggested that we [folk like himself] "have to get the young back into the human family," and even conceded that a place to begin would be by "devising new structures in the university for the activities and meaningful participation of students in their university life and education."[36]

Hesburgh's high-minded sentiments, like so many of those uttered in commencement addresses, soon floated away. The summer of 1968 saw continued political turmoil and radical students and other protestors battling it out with Mayor Richard Daley's police at the Democratic National Convention in Chicago. When classes resumed in the fall, the campus mood had soured further. Hesburgh approved the creation of a Student Life Council (made up of faculty, students, and administrators), but this did little to placate the angrier students. He mainly held on tight as the protest skirmishes roiled the campus. He found the demonstrations of African American students and their supporters particularly upsetting. At the Georgia Tech football game in November 1968, about fifty students took to the field carrying banners with pointed slogans like "Ara, the day of lily-white backfields is past," and "Hesburgh of the Civil Rights Commission: Check on your own backyard."[37] The hostile reception accorded the protestors by the crowd, including racist slurs and booing, further disturbed him. Complaints that his efforts on the Civil Rights Commission were not matched by practical commitments at home especially troubled him. He recognized the need to improve enrollment numbers, financial aid, and the hiring of African American faculty and staff, but he aimed to pursue this gradually. This hardly placated the protestors. He always expressed gratitude for the contribution of Bayard Rustin, the noted civil rights campaigner whom he appointed to the board of trustees, for his assistance in de-escalating some of the confrontations with African American students.[38]

The Hesburgh gradualist approach met criticism from student leaders like Richard Rossie and David Krashna. Rossie won election as student body president in 1968 with the slogan "Student Power." They worked to force concessions from Hesburgh and were unafraid to challenge his decisions. As O'Brien has summarized: "For them ROTC must go; parietal rules must go; Dow Chemical must go; fat-cat trustees must go; and the Vietnam War must go."[39] In the end it was disputes over the Vietnam War, the great gaping wound in the American body politic by 1968–1969, that caused the greatest contention on campus. In November 1968, around the same time as the African American protests broke out, demonstrations took place against the presence at Notre Dame for purposes of recruitment of both Dow Chemical and the CIA. On Wednesday, November 20, a group of demonstrators engaged in a "lie-in" in front of the placement office on the second floor of the Main Building. Hesburgh issued a letter soon after criticizing those involved because "they used their freedom of action to obstruct the freedom of others and impose their own personal convictions on others."[40] He wanted to cut off any movement toward the kind of behavior that had so damaged Columbia, and his trustees encouraged him in this regard. His concerns deepened early in the new year when some members of Congress warned him of the growing backlash against campus unrest. He "worried about a major threat to higher education in the form of repressive legislation from federal and state governments."[41]

Father Hesburgh began to prepare a long letter to his university community to address the whole subject of legitimate protest while maintaining appropriate order in the university. He consulted the various college councils and the academic council on his broad proposals and then composed his letter. Before he could release it an episode occurred to add something of the exotic, or perhaps more accurately the erotic, to the overall scene of campus unrest. Students organized a conference entitled "Pornography and Censorship" for February 5–10, 1969, with a variety of speaker presentations and the showing of various films. After receiving complaints from antipornography campaigners, Father Ted banned the showing of two films—imaginatively titled *Flaming Creatures* and *Kodak Ghost Poems*—deemed hard-core porn. Indicative of the changed campus mood, this prohibition failed to deter over two hundred students from crowding into a classroom in Nieuwland Science Hall on a Friday afternoon to view the forbidden films. What followed is a worthy subject for a student film—a comedy or a farce to be sure. In Tara Hunt's re-creation of the episode it unfolded as follows: Plainclothes policemen from South Bend "burst into the room"; they eventually seized the film reels from a Saint Mary's student, who tried to conceal them under her miniskirt [presumably a difficult task]; the police left but with a student mob in pursuit pelting the officers with snowballs and yelling "Pigs!" and "Fascists!" As the small police contingent neared O'Shaughnessy Hall the crowd surged at them, knocking the officer with the reels to the ground. Thus provoked, the cops retaliated by spraying mace at the students. More student abuse and confusion followed until the police eventually beat a harried escape.[42] Rossie denounced the police for their "Gestapo [tactics]." Father Hesburgh, as O'Brien notes, "was shaken by the awareness that he almost had a major riot on his hands."[43] The incident reinforced his determination to act to guarantee more stability and civility on campus. He told Dick Conklin that he feared "we were really coming to a point where the university was going to be destroyed."[44]

In a letter addressed to students and faculty and dated February 17, Father Ted referenced the disturbances of the previous week but went on to set out a practical policy on dealing with campus unrest. He acknowledged the validity of student protests if such actions neither infringed on the rights of others nor disturbed the normal functions of the university. However, he wrote in a sentence that garnered nationwide attention: "anyone or any group that substitutes force for rational persuasion, be it violent or non-violent, will be given fifteen minutes of meditation to cease and desist." A failure to end disruptive actions would lead to suspension or expulsion. He drew a clear line in the sand.[45] Father Ted effectively issued a blunt warning that Notre Dame would not go down the Columbia University path. His office would not be occupied nor his files looted. He would not run "scared" of the students as he judged that many of his fellow university presidents had done.[46]

The Hesburgh letter received a quite mixed reception, but it certainly evoked an enormous response. Father Ted remembered that "within two days of being sent to the students, the letter was reported in every newspaper in the country. The *New York Times* carried the full text." Commentators debated the pros and cons of his "15-minute rule." Critics like the recently graduated Robert Sam Anson, now working for *Time* magazine, called on Hesburgh to resign. In contrast President Nixon sent a personal letter on February 22 in which he applauded Hesburgh's stand. He also requested that the Notre Dame president proffer advice to Vice President Agnew in advance of his meetings scheduled with the nation's governors to discuss measures "to cope with the growing lawlessness and violence on our campuses."[47] The Nixon request worried Hesburgh and caused him to fear that

Agnew might push for the very repressive legislation his letter had been composed to avoid. He made direct representations against any such interference. Yet he remained troubled that he had become "a kind of folk hero among the hawks, who saw the solution to the student revolution in terms of truncheons and police actions."[48] He decidedly didn't want such status. Furthermore, he quickly found rather embarrassing the comparisons made between his "strong" actions and the seeming "pusillanimous" behavior of so many other university presidents with whom he remained friends. He had sought to preserve what he believed they all stood for—civility and rational discourse on campus—but he hardly wished for his efforts to lead to any rupture between himself and the likes of Yale's Kingman Brewster, who pursued a more conciliatory approach to student protestors on his campus.

In order to avoid being too closely identified with the Nixon administration and with the hard-liners on this issue, Hesburgh deftly tacked back toward a stance more sympathetic to student concerns. He won some kudos from students opposing the Vietnam War by approving and funding a program on nonviolence in the spring of 1969.[49] He also recognized that he needed to make further concessions regarding the restrictions that governed student life. When the Student Life Council voted in favor of women visitation in the dorms, he "yielded without a murmur," as O'Brien noted, whatever his own personal reservations and the complaints of old guard Holy Cross priests who worried what young men and women might do together if left unsupervised in their dorm rooms. Hesburgh saw such concessions as necessary to build a stronger community on campus and to pacify the majority of students while holding the extreme forces of violence and disruption at bay.

In the end, he staggered through to the end of the academic year enduring plenty of angry criticism but not having his new fifteen-minute rule directly tested by some student occupation or violent action. He knew that the problems with the antiwar students and the African American students would be festering over the summer and would break out again in the fall. He also knew that he was close to exhaustion. He no longer slept well and his Mayo Clinic checkup had revealed some early worries with angina. He concluded that he would be hard put to survive another year like the one he had just completed. This was the view he put to Doc Kenna. As he recalled, he told his friend and provincial: "I don't think I am going to make it through another year of this." His solution to address his difficult circumstance was "just to get the hell out of here and to go to a bunch of places I've never been to flush my mind out of all this student business." So it was that the intrepid travelers, Hesburgh and Kenna, set out in early July on a six-week round-the-world trip. Surely it reveals something of our protagonist's spirit that he rejuvenated himself while visiting Tahiti, Auckland, Sydney, Alice Springs, and Ayers Rock (Uluru), which he climbed; Jakarta, Kuala Lumpur, Delhi with an excursion to the Taj Mahal; Kathmandu, Karachi, Lahore, Peshawar, Kabul after a road trip through the Khyber Pass; Addis Ababa, Nairobi with visits to the famous game reserves; Geneva, and Paris before returning to the United States on the SS *France*.

After his extensive travels Father Ted returned to his leadership of Notre Dame and continued his efforts to address what he saw as the more legitimate grievances of his student critics. He worked actively to improve Notre Dame's record on minorities. He lobbied President Nixon and Congress to lower the voting age from twenty-one to eighteen to give students a greater sense of participation in the political system. He began to carefully indicate the extent of his own opposition to America's continued involvement in the Vietnam War. On the eve of the nationwide Vietnam Moratorium on October 14, 1969, he cosigned a letter with other college presidents calling for the withdrawal of U.S. forces from Vietnam. "Were I in a position to do so," he said, "I would end this war tonight before midnight."[50] Still, troubles continued on campus. In what Father Ted later thought an "idiotic" move the placement office proceeded with a reprise of 1968 and scheduled three days of interviews with recruiters from Dow Chemical and the CIA. This red rag to the proverbial bull drew a predictable response. On November 18 students tried to block the entrances to the Main Building and lie down in front of the office where the interviews were to take place. Father James Riehle, the dean of students, invoked for the first and only time Father Hesburgh's "fifteen minutes" cease and desist order. Ten students were suspended after a sizable ruckus. The following day's *Observer* carried a photo on its front page of South Bend riot police arrayed outside the administration building waiting for a call to enter if needed—they appear to have truncheons at the ready, although mercifully they were not wielded.[51]

The turmoil of the fall weighed on Hesburgh. Robert Schmuhl, then a student reporter on retainer with the Associated Press, filed a story on October 29 with the headline "Hesburgh Considers Quitting." His story mentioned that Notre Dame's priest-president at a press conference the previous day declined to "deny rumors that he would like to give up the position." Schmuhl quoted Hesburgh as saying: "I think I'd be an absolute fool if I didn't think about stepping down. You're constantly in the middle."[52] But Father Ted later denied that he ever seriously considered resigning from his position. As he explained: "I don't remember ever thinking of quitting because you don't quit when you're on the bridge and there's a hurricane going on outside." He believed that he had "to see it through and it was an agony."[53] "Captain Hesburgh" on the bridge did see it through, but he increasingly realized he needed greater support. Ned Joyce kept himself apart from student matters, and the once tough Fr. Charlie McCarragher now increasingly sided with the students so that he simply passed issues up to the president rather than dealing with them as vice president for student affairs. Out of his need for more support emerged Hesburgh's eventual decision to create the provost's position and to appoint Fr. Jim Burtchaell to fill it. He simply didn't want every "student crisis or problem to come immediately to the president's office."[54]

The student protests continued in various manifestations over the next few years and occasionally reached explosive levels. Richard Nixon's decision in late April 1970 to invade Cambodia to target North Vietnamese sanctuaries located there prompted demonstrations on campuses across the country. On Friday, May 1, students at Notre Dame invaded the Center for Continuing Education building and disrupted the year-end meeting of the university trustees. Further confrontations followed over the weekend. Rumors circulated that the ROTC building would be firebombed. On May 4 Hesburgh addressed a large crowd of students. He made his opposition to the Cambodian invasion clear, pleaded for an end to violence at home, and outlined a six-point program (which became known as the Hesburgh Declaration) to address the national circumstance. Dave Krashna, then the student body president, also addressed the crowd and called for more strident actions including a student strike. Into this maelstrom came the shocking news that the Ohio National Guard had shot and killed four students at Kent State University. Classes subsequently were suspended, further meetings held, and speeches given. On May 6 over five thousand students marched from campus to Howard Park in South Bend to protest the war and the slaying of the Kent State students. On May 7, Ascension Thursday, Hesburgh presided at Mass in Sacred Heart Church. The packed church heard him "eulogize the slain students at Kent State and plead for a society in which 'ballots replaced bullets' for American youth." Hesburgh's actions helped keep these days of protest from taking a violent turn. The following week classes began to return to something approaching normal. On Monday, May 11, as O'Brien records, "students at the Stepan Center gave Fr. Ted a one-minute standing ovation when he appeared on the platform to introduce a speech by [anti-war] Indiana senator Vance Hartke."[55] Student regard for Hesburgh increased even more when the Nixon administration effectively fired him as chair of the Civil Rights Commission in November of 1972 because of his pointed criticisms of the administration's failures to make progress in this area. It became difficult for students to condemn the man who had been fired by Nixon.

Although preoccupied with confronting the campus turbulence of the late sixties and early seventies, Father Ted also worked to advance his university's academic strengths. The general atmosphere hardly proved conducive, but he doggedly continued his efforts to make Notre Dame a more respected academic institution. The pursuit of "excellence" remained the general goal and he worked hard to raise the financial resources to further that pursuit. In the midst of everything he faced he regularly traveled across the country in support of the "SUMMA: Notre Dame's Greatest Challenge" fund-raising campaign, and he did everything Jim Frick asked of him. A focus of the new campaign was strengthening the faculty. By 1971 Notre Dame had established its first four endowed professorships— one in each of the major colleges; the appointments were intended to raise the research profile of the university.

It was a time of real transition. The "bachelor dons" of old were a dying breed. The most famous of them, Frank O'Malley, died in 1974, and, sadly, so too did the distinct type of Catholic teaching he contributed to Notre Dame. Greater emphasis began to be placed on faculty research in order to secure tenure and promotion, and this was especially so after Burtchaell assumed the provost's position in the fall of 1970. With the new provost running interference for him, Father Hesburgh easily rode out some faculty grumbling about changing expectations. Faculty members now actually had more forums in which to air any grievances. The university-wide academic council and the five college councils along with a somewhat more contentious faculty senate began to operate and to influence in some ways the academic direction of the school. In normal measurements like budget, buildings, and research funding, the university continued to grow. Major weaknesses persisted, such as the library's modest holdings for a university with serious research ambitions. Father Hesburgh found it irritating to have the library's shortcomings constantly raised to him. Rather naturally he preferred to read positive news such as the high retention level of first-year students, which was attributed to the work of Emil T. Hofman as dean of the Freshman Year of Studies. He also appreciated the steady development of study abroad programs, and he gave special attention to the Tantur program. It was not all growth, however. Burtchaell led the way in eliminating the graduate education school, which was deemed not to be meeting the scholarly standards of the modern Notre Dame.

Reflective of his efforts in negotiations with the Vatican over the need for independence for Catholic campuses, Father Hesburgh worked to convey that genuine academic freedom prevailed on his campus. He supported the continued efforts of Shuster and others who organized conferences related to birth control and family planning.[56] That controversial topic attracted much attention in anticipation of Pope Paul VI's expected encyclical on the matter. When in the fall of 1968 Paul's letter rejected the contraceptive use of artificial birth control, Hesburgh's soon-to-be provost gave him a further opportunity to demonstrate his commitment to academic freedom. Just a few months after his appointment as chair of the theology department, "Burtchaell created a sensation by denouncing Pope Paul's birth control encyclical before a student audience in the library auditorium." According to the account of Joel Connelly and Howard Dooley: "Entitling his lecture 'The Bitter Pill,' Burtchaell called *Humanae Vitae* [Of Human Life] 'grossly inadequate and largely fallacious,' and papal marriage views an example of 'sexual plumbing.'" Unbeknownst to Burtchaell, a student named Bill Mitchell, who served as a campus reporter for both the *New York Times* and the *National Catholic Reporter*, was in the audience, and soon he gave Burtchaell's incendiary comments some nationwide attention. Not surprisingly, complaints followed the priest-theologian's harsh criticism of Paul VI's encyclical. In response, Hesburgh took the occasion to clarify his commitment to the free exchange of ideas. At a lengthy news conference he explained: "I'm against half the stuff said around here, but that is irrelevant. The faculty here are perfectly free, as everyone knows." Then he pointedly took on the objectors, noting that "there are always a lot of people around who want to get [the university] into trouble. As soon as something comes out, they put it in an envelope and send it over to Rome. It happens all the time. We are in the world of ideas; ideas are going to be discussed. No ideas are out of bounds."[57] Hesburgh's defense of the free exchange of ideas and his support for dialogue on campus and beyond influenced the American Association of University Professors to confer on him its Alexander Meiklejohn Award for Academic Freedom. He relished receiving this award. It represented precisely the kind of recognition that confirmed he had won the regard of secular educators.

Despite his quite liberal approach on academic freedom, especially when viewed from the perspective of traditional Catholic teaching, Hesburgh did not seek to throw on the full mantle of liberal attitudes. He reacted negatively to much of the agenda that emerged out of the sexual and social revolutions of the 1960s. He thought most universities conceded far too many of their responsibilities in response to these developments. In 1974 he explained that "in the name of scrapping the age-old attitude of *in loco parentis*, most universities not only gave up all and every measure of adult supervision of student mores, but also gave students the impression that they do not care how students live, what their real values are as regards drugs, sexual activity, drinking and the disciplined life in general." In his view "peer pressure by a few made the bohemian life in student residence halls the absolute norm for all." He argued that "one should be able to eliminate petty *in loco parentis* discipline without abandoning *in loco parentis* caring for students and their inner-life values." This was the approach he adopted at Notre Dame in hopes of warding off "student anomie [and] moral rootlessness."[58] Consequently he strongly defended and maintained the traditional residential hall system at Notre Dame and emphasized the importance of building community on campus. After Notre Dame moved to coeducation he robustly defended single-sex dorms against the complaints of those who judged them retro and not in keeping with a modern university. His influence was strong in preserving important elements of what Alfred Freddoso has labeled the "Catholic Neighborhood" of Notre Dame—including "a set of faith-inspired rules governing campus life, e.g., single-sex dorms, parietals, restrictions on parties and alcohol consumption, various regulations governing the nature and funding of student organizations, etc."[59] He encouraged efforts to sustain the religious life of students on campus and promoted the various initiatives for students to participate in service projects. Clearly he wanted Catholicism to be perceptibly present and effectively operative at Notre Dame, although that turned out to be easier to apply in the dorms than in the academic classrooms.

As has already been alluded to, the academic project increasingly came to replicate what was offered at secular schools as Notre Dame pursued the goal of excellence. With all the turmoil on campus along with the "spiritual earthquake" of Vatican II as context, changes came quickly. A consistent claim was made that a concern for ethics and values pervaded the university, but no one could clarify whose ethics or which values. Discussion of the unity of knowledge and the pursuit of truth began to be seen as rather outdated. The various disciplines pursued their own agendas in a decidedly compartmentalized way, and individual departments operated with greater independence in determining faculty hires and course offerings. The doctorate was established as a requirement for most faculty appointments. Faith and reason were clearly separated, with faith largely "reduced to a private emotive principle" that might influence the sphere of one's personal life but certainly not the broad scholarly agenda of the university.[60] In the 1970 core curriculum revision, as has been noted, the requirements for theology and philosophy were reduced to just two courses each, and these were accorded the same status as all other core requirements.[61] They played no effective integrating function and soon were viewed by most students as introductory subjects to "get out of the way." There was no considered effort given to introducing all students either to the Catholic intellectual tradition or to the richness and beauty of Catholic culture. Courses in these areas continued to be taught, but increasingly (as now) it became the task of those students who were serious about a Catholic education to discover them.

Father Hesburgh hoped that Holy Cross priests would continue to contribute effectively to the teaching mission of the university, and the late 1960s saw a number of them return to campus to take up faculty appointments after training in elite graduate schools. The most prominent among them were David Burrell, who was trained at Yale in philosophy, Ernest Bartell from Princeton in economics, Thomas Blantz from Columbia in history, and Burtchaell from Cambridge in theology. They collectively became known as the generation of the "Bs." Burrell, Bartell, and Burtchaell often received mentions from observers of Holy Cross internal politics as likely candidates for high office in the university, including as possible successors to Father Hesburgh. Hesburgh quickly narrowed the list. He judged Burrell as too intense and also too erratic in his protest actions on campus. Although he admired Bartell's intellect, he believed that his temperament was ill suited for upper administration at Notre Dame. Hesburgh soon focused on Burtchaell, who had soon gained some reputation on campus following his return there in 1966.

Burtchaell, as Connelly and Dooley noted, became "a campus personality" on his return from Cambridge. He rode the wave of excitement in the wake of Vatican II with his dialogue homilies at late-night Masses in

Fr. Hesburgh with his family on the beach at Selkirk Shores, Lake Ontario, 1943.

Congregation of Holy Cross Ordination Class of 1943, with Ted Hesburgh (back, third from left).

Four Notre Dame presidents gather together (John O'Hara, on left, and Matthew Walsh, seated; Theodore Hesburgh and John Cavanaugh, standing), 1956.

Fr. Hesburgh and Fr. Edmund Joyce looking over an architectural model map, planning the expansion of the campus, 1960.

Fr. Hesburgh celebrating Mass at the university's Sacred Heart Church, 1961. The church would be raised to the status of a minor basilica in 1992.

Notre Dame's 1960 honorary degree recipients and Laetare Medalist, Dr. George Shuster (first row, left). President Dwight Eisenhower and Cardinal Giovanni Montini (later Pope Paul VI) on either side of Fr. Hesburgh.

Fr. Hesburgh and Ivan Meštrović in the artist's studio, 1961.

Fr. Hesburgh presenting Fr. Charle Sheedy with an honorary degree, 1968

Fr. Hesburgh in his office with his longtime secretary, Helen Hosinski, June 1971.

Fr. Hesburgh's 25th anniversary celebration with Fr. Hesburgh and Fr. Joyce shaking hands in front of a large cake with the Golden Dome on top, 1977.

Portrait of Fr. James Burtchaell, provost 1970–77, c. 1970s.

Fr. Hesburgh dances with student Mary Blazek during a campus picnic celebrating his silver jubilee as president of Notre Dame, spring 1977.

Fr. Hesburgh with outgoing football coach Frank Leahy and incoming coach Terry Brennan, 1954.

Notre Dame's acceptance of the 1973 Orange Bowl bid in Fr. Hesburgh's office, 1973. Fr. Hesburgh, Coach Ara Parseghian, Fr. Joyce.

Football coach Lou Holtz and Fr. Hesburgh pose inside Notre Dame stadium, 1986.

Hesburgh and Jerry Brady (Notre Dame student body president, 1957–58) in Egypt with the pyramids in the background, c. 1960.

Fr. Hesburgh fishing at Notre Dame's retreat center–research facility, Land O'Lakes, Wisconsin, 1980.

Fr. Hesburgh and Provost Timothy O'Meara meet with Mother Teresa in Seychelles, summer 1984.

Fr. Theodore M. Hesburgh stands in front of the Hesburgh Library, 1987.

Dillon Hall and his demanding Bible-based courses. He established a high reputation as both teacher and preacher. Hesburgh tapped him to chair the theology department, which he did with a distinctive cachet. After the controversy over his "The Bitter Pill" speech, Burtchaell reputedly "became notably more restrained in his public pronouncements." Speculation developed that he had begun to campaign for the presidency of Notre Dame. Connelly and Dooley claimed that "by year's end, Burtchaell practically had the bumper stickers printed up."[62] Perhaps so, because Burtchaell refrained from joining Burrell and Bartell in some of the more public protest efforts against the war. Furthermore, he defended the in loco parentis approach to student life at Notre Dame, believing, as he later put it, "that the university held a responsibility to help boys and girls grow into manhood and womanhood."[63]

Hesburgh admired Burtchaell's intellectual brilliance and impressive academic pedigree. He also appreciated his notable skills as both a writer and a speaker. He didn't know his younger confrere all that well, but recognizing that he needed greater support in the upper levels of the administration, he quickly gravitated to recruiting the priest-theologian. George Shuster encouraged him to adopt the Columbia University model of having a president flanked by a strong provost, and he fashioned a position that gave the provost authority over both academic and student affairs. In the spring of 1970 he secured the trustees' approval for the administrative reorganization and also their enthusiastic endorsement of his choice of Burtchaell to fill the provost post. Hesburgh explained to Burtchaell that in the new organization the president would supervise the work of the provost and the executive vice president, who would be co-equals on the organizational chart. Burtchaell bluntly rejected that arrangement. As Father Ted recalled: "He was apodictic that there was no way he would take the job unless he was number two and Ned was number three."[64] Hesburgh had not been prepared for such an insistence, but he thereupon laid out the situation for Ned Joyce. Ever the good soldier, Father Ned encouraged the man whose deputy he had been for almost twenty years to promote Burtchaell as the new second officer of the university. And so it happened. In mid-July Hesburgh announced the changes in a letter to the university community. Burtchaell would be in charge of the "total academic enterprise" and indirectly in charge of student affairs. Other changes occurred. The reserved history professor Thomas Blantz replaced Father McCarragher as vice president of student affairs. Hesburgh also named Philip J. Faccenda, a capable lawyer who had assisted him in recent years, to another newly created position, that of vice president and general counsel.[65]

From the outset Hesburgh found his dealings with Burtchaell rather strained. The two strong-willed men had differing temperaments and interests. Hesburgh remembered being struck not only by Burtchaell's arrogance and brashness but also by the fact that his provost was observing him "like a butterfly on a pin" and also "judging me under a magnifying glass." He clearly did not welcome such close scrutiny. The two of them maintained a cordial if cool relationship, but no simpatico developed between them. Burtchaell never reached out to include Hesburgh in any of his famed social gatherings. The new provost fancied himself a gourmet chef and regularly organized dinner parties. Hesburgh had enough dinners to attend, so failing to garner an invitation to Burtchaell's epicurean occasions hardly bothered him. He was perhaps more perturbed by Burtchaell's driving around in a Mercedes and appearing in expensive suits, typically with his Cambridge tie rather than a traditional clerical suit. But he made no public comment on any of this, putting it down, as he recalled, to Burtchaell's possessing a "flair" that he did not have. He remained convinced that Burtchaell "was the best person whether I liked him or not," and he let his provost take on a heavy share of the load of running Notre Dame.[66]

With memories of how John Cavanaugh had so heavily burdened him during his service as executive vice president possibly in mind, Father Hesburgh stood somewhat above the fray as Jim Burtchaell addressed a whole range of crucial matters. The provost injected himself—and not all that successfully—into a lead role in negotiations with Saint Mary's College over a possible merger. He also took the leading part on academic planning and on faculty appointments. Hesburgh always reviewed new hires and final tenure decisions with Burtchaell, but he largely went along with Burtchaell's exacting recommendations. The provost welcomed the opportunity to make decisions, and, even if they proved unpopular, he remained firm in his own judgments. Hesburgh never had to worry that Burtchaell would duck a decision and trouble him by passing the buck up to the president's office. When Notre Dame began an extensive self-study in 1972, Burtchaell rather than Hesburgh chaired it. The Committee on University Priorities (COUP) aimed to identify Notre Dame's "traditional strengths that were worth maintaining and to recommend new priorities deserving the future attention of the institution."[67] Burtchaell wrote the COUP report, and the avid gossipmongers on campus speculated that he drafted the report to guide his own leadership of the university after he replaced Father Ted. According to Father Ted's recollection, he never explicitly indicated to Jim Burtchaell that he would be named his successor, but he believed that the younger priest simply assumed it and with good reason. No other Holy Cross priest enjoyed his prominence. He was the "crown prince," as the campus wits put it.

Whatever may have been Burtchaell's personal assumptions and ambitions, he demonstrated a willingness to address the key issue that Notre Dame faced, namely how to secure its Catholic identity in a very challenging environment. In a notable sermon on September 10, 1972, at the Mass inaugurating the academic year, Burtchaell addressed the topic of "Notre Dame and the Christian Teacher." He made clear that Notre Dame was committed to be and remain a Catholic university. Putting to the side definitional questions, he honed in on a practical matter of great importance and posed this question: "In the unpredictable and surely surprise-laden future of belief and higher learning, no matter what a Catholic university turns out to be, how can we best assure ourselves that Notre Dame will be one?" He had an answer to his own question and it revealed his incisive judgment. "Before all else," he responded, "by preserving a faculty which sustains our commitment. The key to the character of a university lies in a consciously dedicated company of teachers." He went on to express the need for a "critical mass of Christian teachers" and explained that "if Notre Dame is to remain Catholic, the only institutional way for assuring this is to secure a faculty with prominent representation of committed and articulate believers who purposefully seek the comradeship of others to weave their faith into the full fabric of their lives." Other Christian scholars and those of other faiths or none could join the scholarly community so long as they shared "a common desire that this school retain its wonderful and special character." Additionally, he included this precise goal of having a faculty "among whom Catholics should predominate" as a major recommendation of the COUP report.

While Hesburgh found himself in agreement with Burtchaell on the general principle of hiring Catholic faculty, he was increasingly disturbed by Burtchaell's treatment of individual faculty. He noted that Burtchaell had "an imperial style" and that "he liked to fire people." He observed but did not interfere as his provost targeted and then moved to dismiss a number of faculty and staff. Then he discerned that Burtchaell planned to terminate Dr. Thomas Bergin from his position as director of the Center for Continuing Education. He confronted Burtchaell and, according to his recollection, told him: "Tom Bergin has been a very faithful, decent, steady guy here for a long time and you're not going to fire him. And if you try to fire him you're going to find me trying to fire you. Now, it is that serious, so knock it off." Burtchaell backed off, presumably thinking that he would be in charge soon enough and not wanting to provoke a major conflict with the man he hoped to succeed.[68] This relatively minor clash is of particular interest because Hesburgh recalled it as "the only really tough words I ever had with him." But there was another matter that concerned him, and it must be mentioned, although I do so with some caution and due reservation. To pass by it would be to engage in a cover-up of sorts.

Father Hesburgh admitted in our late-night conversations that some years into Jim Burtchaell's provostship he began to hear rumors and vague allegations that Burtchaell engaged in sexual misconduct with male Notre Dame students. He was distressed by these reports but unsure of the validity of the accusations. In his recollection he eventually raised the difficult issue directly with Burtchaell, who assured him that the complaints were "a bunch of nonsense" and a "fabrication" designed only to damage him and his role at Notre Dame. Hesburgh said, speaking with some remorse, that he took Burtchaell's word as a priest and agreed not to pursue the matter further. In light of the validity of subsequent accusations brought by of-age students, and Burtchaell's forced resignation from the university in 1991, Father Ted understandably realized that he "should have been tougher." But he affirmed strongly that he engaged in no effort to conceal any details of Burtchaell's deeply inappropriate behavior in order to protect him. He held that "I did what I thought was proper to do at the time," although he recognized by 1998 in the context of the growing clergy sexual abuse crisis in the Catholic Church that he should have investigated further.[69] Taking a fellow priest's denial, however convincingly made, as sufficient cause to drop concerns about accusations of sexual misconduct now seems remiss, although it is always much easier to reach such conclusions in hindsight.

As the 1976–1977 academic year came to a close, Hesburgh completed a quarter century of service as Notre Dame's president. He turned sixty on May 25, and his health reports again were positive. He indicated no desire to leave his position and make way for Burtchaell. Father Ted denied that Jim Burtchaell's breathing down his neck made him uneasy. He also insisted that he did not take any initiative to influence the board of trustees' decision to cut short Burtchaell's service as provost and so to remove this obvious rival to the present occupant of the Notre Dame throne. Rather he claimed that the trustees themselves determined to terminate Burtchaell because of their concerns about how he related to people in the university community and because they had lost confidence in him as the likely successor to the presidency. Ed Stephan explained in his 1983 oral history interview that he judged that Burtchaell had "a basic difficulty in dealing with people and especially subordinates." As Stephan saw it, Burtchaell, despite his brilliance, "did not understand . . . how to use power in an academic setting."[70] It is easy to accept that many trustees had concerns about Burtchaell and his arrogance and condescending manner. Yet whatever the trustees' concerns about the provost, they hardly would have moved to replace him without knowing that this step would receive the ready acquiescence and approval of Father Hesburgh.

What is known for sure is that Hesburgh was authorized to convey the board's decision to Burtchaell that he would not be renewed as provost. Because of their varied travel schedules over the summer, Father Ted waited until almost the beginning of the 1977–1978 academic year to convey the "bad news." He revealed the trustees' decision and also that he supported it, but averred that he did not initiate the action. He also recalled that he told Burtchaell, although he couldn't "swear to it," that this decision "had nothing to do with the allegation we discussed some years ago," which must have added further tremors to the room. According to Hesburgh's account, Burtchaell sat and listened without emotion. He vividly described him as "steely-eyed" and "almost like a snake." The news must have come as a shock to Burtchaell, who had received no forewarning of any sort. After Hesburgh concluded, his provost responded with something of a surprise of his own. He indicated that he would finish as provost immediately. Hesburgh pleaded that the school year was about to begin and that the provost's important duties needed to be covered, but Burtchaell indicated that Hesburgh had created the problem for himself and so he could deal with it. He got up and walked out of the office with disdain for Hesburgh presumably issuing from him.[71]

Thereafter the Hesburgh-Burtchaell relationship remained glacial, and the tension between them bothered Father Ted for the rest of his presidency and afterward. He barely mentioned Burtchaell in *God, Country, Notre Dame*. He found discussing his first provost's contributions as too sensitive and too difficult. Perhaps he shared something of his friend Ed Stephan's view that "the Burtchaell thing was a kind of tragedy."[72]

ADMITTING WOMEN, PLACATING DONORS,
ADDRESSING ISSUES,
TROUBLESHOOTING ATHLETICS

Notre Dame's decision to admit women as undergraduate students unquestionably counts as among the most consequential of Father Hesburgh's presidency. He took considerable pride in the decision and basked in the praise that came to him as a result of it. Two decades after the historic change from an all-male institution he noted that coeducation "had a marvelous effect on Notre Dame." In his rather traditional way he observed that "the women brought their great gift of femininity to our campus" and helped create a "much more normal and healthier atmosphere."[73] Additionally, admitting women doubled the applicant pool and allowed for a significant rise in admission standards. The decision benefited Notre Dame in multiple ways. It also proved very popular.

Father Hesburgh played a decisive but hardly heroic role in the decision to admit women. He was in no sense a leader in the movement for coeducation, but he basically moved in synch with a group of leading higher education administrators in the late 1960s who determined that coeducation was necessary for the well-being of their institutions. Nancy Weis Malkiel's recent exploration of the introduction of coeducation at America's elite colleges and universities in the late 1960s and early 1970s demonstrated, somewhat ironically, that a key factor motivating coeducation in Ivy League schools such as Princeton and Yale was competition for the best male students, who preferred a co-ed environment. Father Hesburgh's good friends such as Kingman Brewster at Yale and Robert Goheen at Princeton made this case directly to their various constituencies. Brewster even went so far as to tell a 1967 gathering of Yale alumni that "our concern is not so much what Yale can do for women but what women can do for Yale."[74] Yale and Princeton admitted women in 1969, and Harvard began a difficult integration of its nearby women's college, Radcliffe, the same year. Hesburgh watched their progress with interest, and he was well aware that "in an era of rising sensitivities to rights and inequities, being single-sex was increasingly equated with being backward."[75] Given his efforts to make Notre Dame a modern Catholic university he could hardly afford such a designation. Furthermore, he was well aware that student sentiment favored coeducation. As Susan Poulson and Loretta Higgins noted in their examination of coeducation in Catholic higher education: "Nearly a third of accepted Notre Dame students chose not to enroll because of its single-sex status, and a 1968 poll indicated that nearly three-fourths of all Notre Dame students considered transferring to a coeducation school." Father Hesburgh later guessed that 95 percent of students favored coeducation. In some sense then the decision to admit women bubbled up from below. Hesburgh's challenge lay less in deciding to adopt coeducation than in determining how best to do it.

At an early stage Father Ted floated a scheme designed less to integrate women organically into the university than to have various women's colleges (Barat College from Lake Forest, Illinois, was often mentioned) move to Notre Dame and associate themselves with it. This harebrained scheme fortunately went nowhere. His most serious effort in the late 1960s revolved around an effort to merge with Saint Mary's College. He wanted to build on the cooperative arrangements (the co-exchange program) that were already in place with Saint Mary's. George Shuster encouraged him strongly in the merger option with the Holy Cross Sisters at Saint Mary's, and Hesburgh genuinely hoped to make it work.[76] He remembered it as "the most logical and correct way to go," so as to introduce coeducation to Notre Dame. Initially, developments seemed promising for the happy union of the two schools. The Saint Mary's College trustees had removed their president, Sister Mary Grace, C.S.C., in November of 1967, partly because of her opposition to a merger, and replaced her with Monsignor John J. McGrath—the first non-sister to hold the position—who supported expansion of the co-exchange arrangements as well as negotiations on a full merger. Tangible developments, including the full merging of their speech and drama departments, gave clear evidence of the serious purpose of the two schools at this time. In early 1969 a Notre Dame–Saint Mary's Dual Council was formed. Father Ted and Ed Stephan sat on it with their Saint Mary's counterparts. In May this council publicly announced the goal of the two schools becoming "substantially coeducational with each other." Notably, however, although the council envisioned "one educational entity," the goal would be accomplished "with the preservation of the individuality and integrity of Saint Mary's College as a women's college."[77] Although it was not fully appreciated at the time, the seeds for the failure of the merger and thus in turn for Notre Dame's move to genuine coeducation were planted in the desire of Saint Mary's to preserve its own integrity.

Outside consultants were hired to fashion a detailed implementation plan for the merger. The consultants' report presented in late 1969 recommended that Saint Mary's join Notre Dame "as a separate and distinctive entity operating within the larger university framework." The report of the well-meaning consultants troubled some on the Notre Dame side, including Father Joyce, who worried that the distinct identity afforded Saint Mary's in the proposed merger would leave too much duplication and not achieve real economies of scale. Discussions continued through 1970, and Hesburgh remained faithfully wedded to the amalgamation with Saint Mary's. But by the end of that year new participants had entered the discussions, and they decisively influenced the direction of them. After Monsignor McGrath died suddenly of a heart attack, Sister Alma Peter, C.S.C., assumed responsibility as acting president of Saint Mary's. She favored the merger and related well with Father Hesburgh, who held her in high regard. But the dominant negotiators on the Saint Mary's side ultimately proved to be Mother Olivette Whalen, the superior general of the Sisters of the Holy Cross, and her tough-minded treasurer, Sister Gerald Hartney. On the Notre Dame side an important actor had arrived on stage—Provost James Tunstead Burtchaell. Matters headed for a climax.

Father Hesburgh wanted to make the merger with Saint Mary's succeed partly out of his regard for the Holy Cross Sisters and out of a sentimental regard for the shared history of the two neighboring schools stretching back to the time of Father Sorin. Such sentimental feelings found no place in Burtchaell's makeup. The new provost recognized that Notre Dame held the stronger hand in negotiations, and he preferred to show his cards. Early in 1971 he bluntly laid out his position in a memo to the trustees of both Notre Dame and Saint Mary's. He asserted that Notre Dame "does not need to merge with Saint Mary's, but wants to. Saint Mary's needs to merge, but is hesitant." With the power differential established he proceeded to introduce the idea that Notre Dame "could decide independently to admit female undergraduates," a move likely to be quite damaging to its sister school. He stated his essential position with force and clarity: "What is needed is not the merger of two equivalent institutions, but the incorporation of one into another."[78] The Holy Cross Sisters resisted the idea of their absorption into Notre Dame, but the momentum still seemed favorable to merging the two institutions. In May 1971 the board chairs and the presidents signed a "Joint Statement on Unification" that made clear that the "ultimate goal" was "a single institution with one student body of men and women, one faculty, one president and administration, and one Board of

Trustees." No one doubted that Father Ted would continue as president. The unification process was scheduled to begin in the fall of 1972 and to be completed by the 1974–1975 academic year. It seemed as if the direct pressure applied by Burtchaell had secured a good result for those who hoped to join the two schools.

But plans for the merger began to collapse almost immediately upon the signing of the unification statement. Father Ted captured it well when he recalled that just two weeks after the signatures had been affixed to the joint statement, "our negotiations crashed in flames."[79] Sister Gerald had continued to raise demands regarding the financial details of the settlement between the two schools, and Mother Olivette worried that the Holy Cross Sisters would be frozen out of the new joint venture. Burtchaell's imperious and aggressive negotiating stance especially bothered them. Ed Stephan recalled that one of the senior Holy Cross sister-negotiators (probably Mother Olivette or Sister Alma Peter) told him that she would be enthusiastic about the merger if he and Hesburgh would always be in their positions, "but if Father Burtchaell is going to be president [of Notre Dame in the future], I'm not sure I want any part of it."[80] With real sorrow, Hesburgh slowly came to adopt his provost's position. According to his account in *God, Country, Notre Dame,* he then said: "Sisters, we've been talking about a merger for two years. To me a merger is like a marriage, but I have the impression that a merger means something different for you. You're saying you want to marry us, but that you don't want to take our name and you don't want to live with us." Perhaps the sisters held a less traditional view of marriage, for one of them shot back: "That's exactly right." He then responded candidly that "the merger's off."[81]

Father Hesburgh regretted the failure of the negotiations with Saint Mary's, and he especially blamed Sister Gerald and Jim Burtchaell for their collapse.[82] Yet he realized that the end result proved to be very beneficial for Notre Dame. Burtchaell's arrogance and aggression in the negotiations, which so upset the Holy Cross Sisters, led ultimately to a better course for the university. Notre Dame could now pursue its own coeducation course unencumbered by the vast sensitivities involved in a merger. Hesburgh's later awareness of the tensions involved in Harvard's effort to absorb Radcliffe College only confirmed him in this view. He still tried to be sensitive to Saint Mary's as he moved Notre Dame forward on the co-ed path. He continued the co-exchange program and always wanted to include the fifteen hundred Saint Mary's students in any calculations of gender balance at Notre Dame, meaning that the targeted Notre Dame student ratio eventually would be roughly 60:40 male to female students (an arrangement that ended soon after his presidency and somewhat to his dismay). He largely delegated the work of arranging for Notre Dame to admit its first small class of female students for the fall of 1972. Reflecting his paternal concern that Notre Dame women not live in unsafe housing off-campus, he insisted that residence halls be prepared to accommodate them. The vice president for student affairs, Blantz, had the delicate task of determining which of the men's dorms would become home for the first generation of female Domers. Hesburgh strongly resisted—both then and thereafter—any suggestion that co-ed residence halls be established.[83]

The transition to coeducation went quite smoothly given all the challenges involved in the shift. "We're Glad You're Here" read a sign posted across the entrance to the South Dining Hall at the beginning of the semester, and it captured the attitudes of most of the male students, who did not find it burdensome to share their campus with women. Whatever the myriad difficulties female students faced in entering the male bastion of Notre Dame, most of them quickly developed the same deep love for and loyalty to the school that their male peers had.[84] Sister John Miriam Jones joined the provost's office and took a special responsibility for the integration of women. Dean Emil Hofman in Freshman Year of Studies also worked tirelessly to aid the adjustment of the first classes of women. Father Ted played his role as an occasional counselor for the young female students who worked up the nerve to visit him in his office. The faculty quickly appreciated the improvement that female students brought to the quality of work expected in their courses. Even the rather traditional Notre Dame alumni accepted the decision with relative good grace and, in Father Ted's opinion, much more willingly than did some of the alumni of Yale and Princeton. The alums readily adjusted to the idea that their daughters now might attend Notre Dame. And, after all, it was a school dedicated to Mary, the Blessed Mother.

In the midst of such demanding tasks as confronting the student turmoil of the late 1960s and early 1970s and overseeing negotiations such as those with Saint Mary's, Ted Hesburgh continued his constant labors to raise money for Notre Dame. He worked tirelessly to build relations with new members of the board of trustees, and he cultivated the members of the advisory councils of the respective colleges. Most of these individuals were selected, then as now, less for their knowledge of Catholic higher education than for their giving potential. That potential had to be tapped, and he did it. With Jim Frick as its primary strategist, the public phase of the SUMMA campaign began early in 1968 and ran through to 1972. The launch program alone involved visits by Notre Dame teams to thirty-nine cities. Father Hesburgh headed one team and Father Joyce the other. They executed a well-developed road-show formula of first educating their mainly alumni audiences about the plans for Notre Dame and then selling them on the need to contribute to the realization of those plans. They made the case for such key categories of the SUMMA campaign as faculty development, the growth of the graduate program, and support for special research programs.

Hesburgh believed strongly in the value of the residential experience for undergraduates and favored keeping as many students in on-campus accommodation as possible. Plans were developed for some high-rise residence halls with an expected cost of $6 million each. Father Ted felt great satisfaction when a leading university trustee, J. Peter Grace, pledged to provide the lead gift for a hall named in honor of his father, Joseph P. Grace. Peter Grace was a conservative businessman who had advised the Kennedy administration on the Alliance for Progress, its aid and development program for Latin America. A devout Catholic, Grace had received the Laetare Medal in 1967. Although he worried that Hesburgh acted in too lenient a manner toward the student radicals on campus, Grace generously committed to funding the building, which was constructed in 1969. Among the events planned to celebrate its dedication Fr. David Burrell organized a symposium of sorts to discuss developments in Latin America, where Grace's shipping and chemical firm had sizable interests. Burrell invited Grace to what the businessman thought would be an occasion for him to outline his views on how best to address Latin America's social problems. The event turned out to be something quite different, and in the aftermath Father Hesburgh was left with a donor whom he could not placate despite his best attempts.

When Grace arrived at the library auditorium for what he expected to be a civil occasion with himself as the main speaker, he discovered that he was part of a panel including a former (and now married) Maryknoll priest and nun duo who spoke of their revolutionary efforts in Guatemala. According to Father Ted's recollection, David Burrell had brought these onetime missionaries to Notre Dame so that they might upbraid Peter Grace for the abuses of American multinational corporations in Central America. Hesburgh relied on Grace's account of the episode, and in his recounting he described the audience as a "bunch of jeering students." Soon, he claimed, "Peter was being pilloried by this group of idiots."[85] Grace emerged from the ordeal furious and demanded that the Grace name be removed from the newly opened residence hall. Also he made clear that he would not complete the unfulfilled part of his significant pledge toward the tower building. Hesburgh, in turn, was furious with Burrell. Nonetheless, he displayed considerable restraint and never allowed the incident to rupture his relationship with the Holy Cross philosopher. His major effort was focused on repairing the breach in relations with Peter Grace. His struggle to do so reveals the extent of his commitment to raising funds for his university.

Hesburgh traveled to New York and met Grace in his office looking out over the Avenue of the Americas. He recalled saying: "Peter, I had nothing to do with this. I know that you claim that Father Burrell told you that you would be the only speaker, and if he did I apologize for him. I think it was unfortunate that you did agree to go to that rabble-rousing group of wild people. We have a few at every university. But all I can do is to say that I am extremely sorry, and I apologize profusely, and if there is anything I can do to rectify it then I will do it." Grace was not in a gracious mood. He told Hesburgh that he didn't believe him. Poor Father Ted in full penitential mode persisted and wrote out on a piece of paper: "As God is my witness, I apologize." He handed it to Grace, who responded "rubbish" and threw the sheet of the paper in his waste bin. In what must have been a near-comic moment Hesburgh (again according to his own account) then jumped to his feet demanding to know if the windows of the office opened, and he asked Grace: "Do you mind if I jump out of one of them?" Grace described him as "crazy," and Father Ted said it was a way to prove his seriousness about his apology. The offended businessman eventually gave a grudging acceptance of Hesburgh's statement of contrition. They shook hands and Hesburgh left. But Grace did not relent on his decision to withdraw his support for Grace Hall. He moved off the board of trustees and distanced himself from the university. Hesburgh regretted this and tried to stay in touch with other members of the Grace family. Later he made a point of attending Peter Grace's funeral in 1995. The whole episode burdened him, and his anger at Burrell still simmered years later. He described the row as resulting from his "being sideswiped and murdered by my own guys."[86]

The debacle with Peter Grace did not slow Hesburgh in any way. He demonstrated a marked willingness to continue speaking on other campuses. In the decade covered by this chapter he received over thirty honorary degrees, and at most of the commencements he delivered the principal address. He derived a special satisfaction when he was recognized by Ivy League institutions. Yale honored him in 1971, and he and his fellow honorees, including Chancellor Willy Brandt of West Germany, crossed the picket lines of striking Yale workers to accept their degrees.[87] Hesburgh did not speak at Yale, but two years later he gave the commencement address at Harvard. He took such honors as a validation of his work at Notre Dame. In many of his talks in the late sixties he spoke about the divisions in society and the turmoil on campuses. By the early 1970s and especially after the national debate over the Vietnam War receded, he turned his attention to major global issues and questions. He titled his 1973 Harvard address "A New Vision for Spaceship Earth" and loftily called for a vision "of social justice, of the interdependence of all mankind on this small spaceship."[88]

In December 1973 Father Hesburgh delivered the prestigious Dwight Harrington Terry Foundation Lectures at Yale. He worked hard on these Terry lectures, which Yale University Press later published as *The Humane Imperative: A Challenge for the Year 2000* (1974). In some ways these lectures marked a transition in the focus of his concerns. During his service on the Civil Rights Commission his key concern was race relations in the United States and the effort to make the promises and pledges of the Declaration of Independence and the Bill of Rights a living reality for African Americans. He ranged across other matters as well, especially through his work at the International Atomic Energy Agency and with the Rockefeller Foundation. Yet after his dismissal from the Civil Rights Commission by Nixon he turned much greater attention to world problems and issues. He had agreed to serve as chair of the board of the Overseas Development Council in 1971, and he found himself intrigued by the research it conducted on third world nations and international development issues. He readily drew upon this scholarship in encouraging U.S. policymakers and citizens to support international aid programs. Hesburgh's efforts were characterized by his innate optimism and his deep conviction that there were feasible answers to major problems if only good men and women would cooperate to address them. He believed that science and technology, if properly harnessed, could provide the wherewithal to tackle such huge problems as global peace, hunger, and illiteracy.

When recollecting the Terry lectures Father Ted introduced a particular incident from his lecture entitled "Human Dignity and Civil Rights." In this lecture Hesburgh spoke eloquently about civil rights, and then he continued by saying that he also needed to "speak for those who have no voice at all, the unborn children who are so cavalierly deprived of the most basic right of all, the right to life, without which all other human rights are meaningless." He explained to his audience that "each of us once was what these unborn children, of whatever stage of development, now are. No one of us would like to have been deprived of the days and years of human life we have enjoyed. Millions of unborn children are now, within the law—the law of man, not of God—being so denied."[89] This critical reference to the Supreme Court's recent decision given on January 22, 1973, in *Roe v. Wade*, which essentially legalized unlimited access to abortion in the United States, prompted a negative response from some of the female members of his audience. They began hissing at their Terry lecturer. According to Father Ted, his friend Kingman Brewster, who was seated in the front row, turned "three shades of purple" with embarrassment, but Father Ted took a different tack. He stopped speaking and remained silent until long after the hissing stopped. Thereupon he took the chance to deliver an ad-lib lecture on freedom of speech and civil exchange in a university. He recalled saying: "I don't mind at all that you disagree with me, but to hiss because I say something that you don't agree with, well that strikes me as not worthy of a great university." Thereupon he completed his reprimand of his Ivy League listeners by reminding them that the university should be "a place where people can disagree without being disagreeable."[90]

This ultimately proved a subject of some controversy for him. Whatever his response to the hissing Yale feminists, he thereafter failed to make abortion and the right to life one of the great issues that he chose to address forcefully. To have pursued it vigorously would have put him at odds with the liberal establishment figures with whom he wanted to associate in tackling global poverty and world peace. Rather than positioning himself strongly as a defender of what he knew to be a fundamental human right, he tacked away from a forthright position. Instead, he looked for compromise and for "common ground" on the issue. This was evident in his willingness to make Notre Dame a venue for wide-ranging discussions of the abortion issue. With his encouragement the philosophers Edward Manier and David Solomon and the sociologist William Liu organized two conferences on various aspects of abortion—the first in the fall of 1973 and the second in the spring of 1975.[91] In response to concerns about the initial gathering expressed by Leo Pursley, the bishop of Fort Wayne–South Bend, Father Hesburgh (and the chair of the board of trustees Edmund Stephan) replied to the disturbed local ordinary that "if this country is to find a better legal policy and practice in the matter of abortion than it now has by Supreme Court decree, it would appear fairly obvious that we must discuss our differences with those who proposed and have promoted the present situation."[92] In their response to the bishop, however, they never clarified the possibilities of "compromise" on this deeply divisive issue. Instead, Father Hesburgh only extended his desire to make Notre Dame a hub for discussions on major public policy questions.

While Father Hesburgh enthusiastically involved himself on major global issues he always preferred to leave Notre Dame athletic matters safely in the hands of Ned Joyce and Moose Krause. For the most part that worked quite well for him, although he injected himself on major decisions and in dealing with crisis situations. Father Joyce and his legendary athletic director shared the responsibility to implement Title IX of the Education Amendments of 1972 mandating a redistribution of resources so that women would have greater access to athletic programs. Neither man welcomed conforming their athletic programs to federal mandates, but they eventually allowed for the establishment of solid programs that would bring Notre Dame notable success especially in women's soccer and basketball. Hesburgh left such matters alone. Earlier, however, he had made the final decision to overturn a longstanding tradition by agreeing that Notre Dame athletic teams could participate in postseason bowl games. What he had fiercely opposed in his 1966 *Sports Illustrated* article became acceptable by 1969. The reason was simple—Notre Dame wanted the money. Father Joyce and Ara Parseghian favored accepting a bid to play in a bowl game, and Father Hesburgh eventually agreed, with the proviso that the game's proceeds would be applied for much-needed minority scholarships. Thus in January 1970 Notre Dame played the Texas Longhorns in the Cotton Bowl (losing 21–17). Under Joyce and with Hesburgh's broad endorsement, Notre Dame moved to benefit financially from the further commercialization of college sports, although they resisted calls to expand and modernize the football stadium. Father Ted judged the message that such an expansion would convey as antithetical to his vision for the modern Notre Dame.

Hesburgh's decision on participating in bowl games reflected his concern to recruit more African American students to Notre Dame. The student protest at the 1968 Georgia Tech game had publicly highlighted the need for more black students at Notre Dame, including more black football players. Hesburgh occasionally raised to Ara the need for more African Americans on the football team, and the football coach always responded that the difficulty lay with the high academic admissions standards set by Notre Dame. There are some suggestions that Father Ted eased admissions standards for some athletes in the early seventies, although he maintained that he allowed the recruitment of only students whom the admissions office affirmed could succeed academically at Notre Dame.[93] Hesburgh always admired Notre Dame's young and flamboyant men's basketball coach Richard "Digger" Phelps, not only for his successes on the court—such as ending UCLA's eighty-eight-game winning streak in 1974—but also for his strong record of graduating his players. Even though money and television were coming to dominate college football, Father Ted maintained that Notre Dame could never return to the "football factory" days. Players would need to be genuine students who studied in real courses and earned their degrees.

In 1973, Notre Dame under Ara Parseghian's expert guidance had a perfect season, and Ara won a second national championship for Notre Dame after his team overcame Bear Bryant's Alabama squad in the Sugar Bowl 24–23. Parseghian was named coach of the year, and expectations were high for the 1974 season. Instead that year turned into something of a nightmare for Notre Dame's team and its football coach. Father Hesburgh could not avoid involvement. Before the year started, six Notre Dame players, four of them likely starters, were accused of gang-raping an eighteen-year-old South Bend girl in a university dorm. The story had a racial dimension because all the players were black and their accuser was white. The university handled the matter internally and suspended the individuals involved for a year for "a serious violation of university rules." No legal charges were filed by the local authorities, and the university never acknowledged the nature of the rules violations that necessitated the suspensions. It gave no indication that a rape had occurred, implying that the young woman involved had participated willingly in the sexual activity as the players presumably alleged. Father Hesburgh signed off on the Notre Dame actions and he said rather defensively that his football coach thought he had been too tough on the players.[94] Hesburgh was embarrassed by the episode and the damage it did to Notre Dame's good name.

The expectations of Notre Dame fans for another undefeated season were dashed early on when Purdue upset the Irish in the third game of the year. Their disappointment reached even higher levels when the USC Trojans pulled off an amazing comeback victory against Parseghian's team in their game at the LA Coliseum. Notre Dame led 24–0 right before half-time, but USC won the game 55–24 with their star back Anthony Davis running wild in the second half. Although rumors circulated that there had been some kind of racial conflict in the Irish locker room during halftime, Hesburgh totally dismissed this based on Ara's assurances.[95] The defeat by USC and the weight of the season had taken a toll on the Notre Dame coach. Later news reports suggested that he decided to retire in midseason, but it was only after the USC game that he consulted with Father Hesburgh. According to Hesburgh's account the splendid coach admitted to serious health worries. "Father Ted, I want to confess something to you," he explained. "I'm at a point where I'm taking pills to go to sleep at night and other pills to wake up in the morning." The stress of the job could be read on Parseghian's face. He later admitted to being "physically exhausted and emotionally drained." Perhaps with memories of his experience with Frank Leahy still resonating, Hesburgh remembered saying: "Ara, that means one thing. It's all over." Hesburgh assured him of his love and concern for the Parseghian family and then told him that he must resign.[96]

During his tenure as coach from 1964 through 1974, Parseghian played an important role in Father Hesburgh's success. Whatever the turmoil on campus or off, Notre Dame's football team enjoyed a notable achievement that rallied their loyal fans and kept discontent limited only to those who demanded perfection. Hesburgh readily went along with Father Joyce's suggestion of Dan Devine as Parseghian's successor. Devine had been considered for the Notre Dame job at the time of Ara's appointment. He enjoyed impressive accomplishments at the collegiate level and then had gone on to coach the Green Bay Packers, although not with great success. This experienced coach gladly returned to the college ranks at Notre Dame, where he maintained Parseghian's strong program and secured yet another national championship for Notre Dame in 1977. Yet, as Father Hesburgh noted in *God, Country, Notre Dame*, "Dan just was never accepted at Notre Dame. I don't think it was his fault. It was just something to do with the chemistry, or lack of it, between him and the fans."[97]

RELIGIOUS LIFE, PRIESTHOOD, AND FRIENDSHIPS IN FLUX

Pope Paul VI declared the 1967–1968 Church year as a "Year of Faith." In order to inaugurate Notre Dame's celebration of the Year of Faith, Father Hesburgh preached a sermon at Sacred Heart Church on November 5, 1967. He included it in his collected *Thoughts* for that year, explaining that "the Faith created this place, still inspires it, and gives strength both to the institution and to all of us."[98] Alluding to the changes that beset the Catholic world in the aftermath of Vatican II, Hesburgh noted that "in the post-Conciliar world, many things are changing and, in a time of rapid change, there needs to be a few things which do not change. Faith is one of these." Being a supporter of the need for reform in the Church, he readily conceded that "how we express it [faith] may be different and with what cultural trappings it is clothed may change from age to age." But he clearly stated his foundational position that "what we believe most deeply and most fundamentally as Christians is not a matter of change." Father Ted went on to speak of faith as his "most precious possession," the one reality that he would willingly "follow, even unto death."[99]

Catholics of a certain vintage might recall Septuagesima Sunday of 1965. On that day almost every altar in Catholic churches in the United States was turned around. For the first time in a millennium, the priest said Mass facing the congregation and he said it partially (soon totally) in English. The traditional Latin liturgy's quick disappearance can stand as a symbol of the dramatic changes implemented in a space of five years that reordered Catholic worship and practice. The American bishops even decided to change the discipline of abstaining from meat on Fridays. The spirited priest-sociologist Andrew Greeley later deemed this "the most unnecessary and the most devastating" change because it removed a visible symbol that distinguished Catholics from their fellow Americans. In making such changes and others similar in nature, Church leaders assured the faithful, as Greeley noted, "that nothing had *really* changed." They offered assurances that such reforms did not touch on "the essence of Catholic doctrine." Yet as the astute Greeley noted, such distinctions were easily lost as "the immutable had mutated."[100] In circumstances where established Church practice seemed up for grabs it hardly took long for the essential authority of the Church to be challenged.

Religious orders and their distinctive way of living the Christian life experienced major disruption. Vatican II's Decree on Religious Life, *Perfectae Caritatis*, called for religious orders of all kinds to renew themselves and their unique rules (i.e., their constitutions and statutes) in light of Christ's call in the Gospel and in accord with the spirit of their founders.[101] Such an expansive call soon facilitated major changes. The old style of religious life, built on hierarchy, tradition, and authority, provided for a clearly defined mission, a central commitment to common prayer and the sacraments, and fidelity to the common rule especially as lived out through the vows of poverty, chastity, and obedience. It certainly represented a very institutional view of the Church. No doubt there was some need for a modernizing of elements of religious orders' rules to allow for greater responsibility and individuality in members of the respective orders. But once the Pandora's box of renewal was opened, religious orders succumbed to a barrage of change that eventually pushed some communities in the direction of extinction.

As already noted, Father Hesburgh identified fully with Vatican II and its teachings. He eagerly adopted the new approach on ecumenism and used the Council's teaching on the role of the laity as an essential justification for his changes to the governmental structures of Notre Dame. On a more personal level he transitioned easily to the new liturgy. Yet he never allowed himself to succumb to extremes. While the younger generation of Holy Cross religious doffed their religious garb and adopted secular attire (i.e., expensive suits for Burtchaell, rather plain campus wear for Burrell), Hesburgh always appeared in public in his clerical suit or in a clerical shirt with his distinctive Notre Dame blazer. He rejected some of the more wacky aspects of what was presented as reform. His deep love for the Mass and his typical reverence when presiding at the Lord's table made him a skeptic regarding experimental liturgies. When he received word from one of his nieces at Saint Mary's that a visiting priest from Texas was purportedly celebrating the Mass at Notre Dame using the elements of pizza and Coca-Cola (the "supper" food of the time!), he called the priest up and warned him that a repeat performance would lead to his dispatch so fast "that his teeth would rattle." When he discovered that a number of young Holy Cross religious recently back from studies in France were "taking girls to the movies in town," he approached them directly. According to his account they responded that "we do this in France," to which he retorted with admirable clarity: "My God, you are not in France. You are in South Bend, Indiana, at the University of Notre Dame and it ain't [*sic*] done here."[102]

Despite such specific interventions he mainly tried to ride through the changes without direct confrontations. His own very individualistic approach to the formal practices of religious life, such as common prayer and table, which he crafted to meet the demands of his presidential office, hardly put him in a position to exhort others on greater fidelity to communal life. He continued to abide by his established interpretation of the vows, which afforded him considerable independence from the community. Nonetheless, he lent support as best he could to his friend Doc Kenna, who, as the provincial, carried the heavy burden of dealing with the many departures from the Holy Cross ranks at the time. He also aimed to help Kenna face the inevitable closures and withdrawals that the order's reduced numbers soon necessitated. In June 1967 the Indiana Province chapter voted to close its minor seminary, and it also authorized the provincial to begin discussions to close Holy Cross College, its theologate in Washington, D.C., where Father Ted had completed his seminary studies after returning from Rome. The low vocation numbers could not justify the site, and, additionally, Hesburgh argued, if they consolidated efforts back at Notre Dame it would lead both to improved training for seminarians and to an improvement in the theology department in the university.[103] This move then took place in 1969.

Yet even the Kenna-Hesburgh relationship suffered some tensions. Father Ted passed over it quickly in our interviews, but he admitted that Doc Kenna once wrote to him complaining forcefully that he was "downgrading the Community" at the university on matters regarding faculty appointments and the like. Hesburgh recalled defending himself calmly and attributing Kenna's criticisms to the provincial's reflecting the voices of "the discontented in the community who for a lot of reasons felt they were not getting all that they had coming to them."[104] After the transfer of ownership in 1967, the Holy Cross religious at Notre Dame formed an "Association" to provide themselves with some formal voice so as to make representations to the administration if need be. The body proved ineffective. In theory the Holy Cross order should have been a major force within the institution, but in practice it served as an adjunct to the president, who made all the major decisions. Corby Hall essentially became a location for community life and prayer sustained by the older members. Father Ted felt comfortable with this arrangement.

When delivering the homily at Doc Kenna's funeral in September 1973, after the provincial's sudden death, Father Hesburgh paid tribute to his friend's having "held the Community together and moved it forward with a minimum of tension, rancor, or division through a very difficult period in all of our lives."[105] Kenna merited the tribute. There had been no major rupture in the community, and the order had not followed the suicidal course pursued by some religious orders of withdrawing from their major institutions. Whatever the limits of its communal influence the Holy Cross order remained deeply committed to Notre Dame. As the expression went, the blood of its members was embedded in the bricks. In the 1968–1969 academic year, the academic Holy Cross head count consisted of fifteen full professors, twenty associates, and twenty-two assistants. Holy Cross also provided a sizable number of priests and brothers in the student and residential life arenas. It was a substantial contingent, and Father Hesburgh certainly expected this cadre of religious to play a crucial role in the spiritual life of the campus. He never doubted that Holy Cross should take the lead in what increasingly was called "pastoral care" at Notre Dame. He wanted good Holy Cross priests who would inspire students in the midst of the campus confusion and change to continue to practice their faith, although he recognized that the approach to reaching out to students would need to be renewed.

A paradigm shift in the approach to the religious lives of students occurred on Hesburgh's long watch. In the old paradigm lasting through to the early 1960s, John O'Hara stood as the iconic figure with his emphasis on the regular reception of the sacraments and especially Mass attendance. From the mid-1960s onward the new emphasis was on service. This approach conformed well with how the reformers interpreted *Gaudium et Spes*, and it found an eager cheerleader in Father Ted. He even delivered a commencement address in 1967 at Manchester College entitled "Service: The Great Modern Prayer." There already was a well-established tradition of Christian-inspired volunteer service at Notre Dame, especially through the Council for the International Lay Apostolate, which had sponsored activities like summer service projects in Latin America since the early 1960s. But over the next decade new initiatives like the Office of Volunteer Services and the Center for Experiential Learning in the Institute for Pastoral and Social Ministry involved greater numbers of students. Whatever the limitations of the curriculum in shaping the intellectual and faith lives of Notre Dame students, Father Ted drew some considerable satisfaction that the students engaged in service in the world.

Father Hesburgh's emphasis on service did not dampen his hopes that students would avail themselves of the sacraments. He accommodated sensible campus liturgical changes meant to attract students to Mass. Late-night Masses became standard in the dorms with the same Saint Louis Jesuit hymns sung with gusto in chapels across the campus on Sunday nights. He presided at such Masses when he could. Fortunately for him, a Holy Cross priest named Bill Toohey took over the directorship of campus ministry in 1970. A dynamic homilist and a charismatic figure, Toohey helped make going to Mass almost fashionable on campus. One observer has noted that he "exemplified Catholic activism in an era of earnest and faith-filled engagement" with his idealistic calls for students "to work for justice and peace."[106] During these years the liberal Catholic ethos cemented itself in liturgy and pastoral care at Notre Dame and this would continue throughout Father Hesburgh's administration.

The significant changes that took place within Holy Cross and in the religious practices of the campus were paralleled in Father Hesburgh's personal life. Old friends either died or moved on and he needed to adjust in light of that. Doc Kenna's death meant the loss of one of his closest friends within the order, and he never found a real successor. William (Bill) Lewers took Kenna's place as provincial, but although Hesburgh judged that he performed well in the role, they established no close personal relationship. Hesburgh maintained his close working relationship with Ned Joyce, but they rarely socialized together outside of work-related events, and especially as Hesburgh grew more liberal in the 1970s and Joyce went in the other direction. No one in the younger generation of Holy Cross emerged as a genuine personal friend, certainly not Jim Burtchaell.

Among his lay friends, Ed Stephan remained very close and Hesburgh always felt a part of his family. He also felt some connection with such senior trustees as Paul Hellmuth and Tom Carney. He occasionally traveled with Hellmuth and correctly suspected that the Boston lawyer did undercover or courier work for the CIA.[107] George Shuster remained a valued friend and adviser but his involvement on campus tapered off after 1970. The man that Father Hesburgh referred to as his "Father Confessor" died early in 1977.[108] Father Ted felt the loss hard just as he did with Doc Kenna. He never found a suitable replacement for the layman who served as his counselor for over a decade of profound change at the university. Hesburgh also missed greatly the friendship and support of I. A. O'Shaughnessy, who died in 1973. Father Ted delivered the eulogy at his funeral in St. Paul and paid tribute to his generous benefactor's "great heart." Yet with his typical resilience

Hesburgh continued on. He had a wide range of friendly contacts beyond the university, ranging from the advice columnist Ann Landers to David Rockefeller at the Chase Manhattan Bank. In the years after 1977 he established new and sustaining friendships at Notre Dame, one with Timothy O'Meara, whom he selected to replace Burtchaell as provost, and another with Richard P. McBrien, the priest he charged with "re-Catholicizing" the theology department. But that is a story for our next chapter.

DID THE CENTER HOLD?

In 1977 Father Hesburgh completed his twenty-fifth year of service as president of Notre Dame. He gave no indication of any desire to retire. The absence of any obvious successor after Burtchaell's departure as provost made the trustees insist that he continue in his leadership of the university. He possessed a renewed energy to do so. He took some personal satisfaction in knowing that he had been the captain who did not desert his post but guided his ship through rough seas and stormy weather into more tranquil waters. Somehow he had navigated Notre Dame through the student and sexual revolutions, the divisions over the Vietnam War, the challenges to authority of all sorts including within the university, the widespread disillusionment with most social and political institutions, and the upheaval within the Catholic Church. It surely must be judged a bravura performance and one not equaled by any of his contemporaries. That he did this while maintaining a full range of outside involvements including with the IFCU, the Civil Rights Commission, and the Rockefeller Foundation only adds to the virtuoso quality of his accomplishment.

Recognition of his achievement grew and the awards and honorary degrees piled up further. As early as 1972 Joel Connelly and Howard Dooley sensed his success and they titled their book *Hesburgh's Notre Dame: Triumph in Transition*. They recognized that Hesburgh possessed rare abilities as a "survival artist," and that he had proved willing to make necessary concessions to his "crew" and to alter his course on occasion—and especially so after the Cambodian invasion/Kent State crisis on campus. They understood that he had proved pragmatic enough to revise his methods and direction, and they further recognized that his firing by Nixon from the Civil Rights Commission added to his reputation on campus as did his admirable fidelity to his priestly ministry. They concluded that Hesburgh had enhanced Notre Dame as a modern university while ensuring that it remained "identifiably Catholic."[109] This represented for them his essential triumph. He transformed Notre Dame by changing the governmental structure, reforming student life, and especially through the move to coeducation, yet he did not allow for secularization.

The praise for his accomplishments rained in from outside the Notre Dame community as well. In a preface provided for the published version of Father Hesburgh's Terry Lectures at Yale, Kingman Brewster predictably noted that his invited speaker's "contribution to the continuing and unfinished effort to make the Declaration of Independence and the Bill of Rights a living reality for all Americans is so widely appreciated that it needs no embellishment." More noteworthy was his tribute to Hesburgh's leadership during "the harassed late sixties" when the Yale president asserted that his Notre Dame counterpart "combined firmness and flexibility, authority and openness, which set a standard for us all." Finally, and even still more notably, Brewster declared that Father Hesburgh "has brought the University of Notre Dame to the first rank of the nation's universities; without betraying the sponsorship of his church and his order, Father Hesburgh has achieved both the hospitality to controversy and the highest standards of rational rigor that every free university requires."[110] How Father Ted relished such praise, which acknowledged the realization of his long-stated goal of creating a great Catholic university. He took it as a validation of his success in leading Notre Dame through these very hazardous years for American higher education when, as he vividly portrayed it, "a life of reason was suddenly smothered by blind emotion, when a place of calm civility was engulfed by violence, bombings, burnings, vandalism and vulgarity."[111]

Father Hesburgh hardly was one to rest on his laurels. The physical growth of his campus and the enhanced prestige accorded it failed to satisfy him. His ambition led him to give even greater expression to his university's service as bridge, beacon, and crossroads, and he personally placed himself in the very forefront of this effort. With remarkable deftness he quickly pivoted away from the turmoil of the late sixties and early seventies and pronounced himself excited to face the challenges of the present and future. He subtitled his Terry Lectures as "A Challenge for the Year 2000," and in them he looked forward rather than backward. In the prelude to his published lectures he declared himself a "Christian optimist" who was hopeful for the future because of "my firm faith that the Holy Spirit is at work in the world, that the great powers and forces of the religious and secular orders can find new and fruitful directions if we nudge them at the right time toward better goals."[112]

Father Hesburgh's achievements in holding Notre Dame together, in advancing its reputation as a modern research university, and in seeking to develop it as a force for good in the world deserve praise. Yet one cannot ignore that his leadership over the period from 1967 to 1977 was not simply a triumph to be lauded. Any honest assessment must note that his creation of the modern Notre Dame came at some cost. To overlook this is to airbrush history by neglecting to examine central elements of the university, namely the faculty and the curriculum. Although Connelly and Dooley praised Hesburgh for keeping Notre Dame identifiably Catholic, they largely referenced key elements of the Catholic "neighborhood." As we have seen, Father Ted supported the religious and liturgical life of campus and encouraged students to engage in service. He maintained a somewhat conservative approach to student life and firmly resisted entreaties for co-ed dorms. He defended in loco parentis, understood as "caring for students and their inner-life values." He cared deeply about the moral lives of Notre Dame students. As a good priest he truly worried for his students' souls. He helped preserve the distinctive residential system and sense of community that gave the student experience at Notre Dame such a unique quality.

Given his forthright striving to maintain the Catholic neighborhood, it remains somewhat surprising that Father Hesburgh did not replicate those efforts in preserving and enhancing the Catholic "school" at Notre Dame—its intellectual and academic heart. Sadly, he did not. In consequence, while the center held at Notre Dame, it turned out to be somewhat hollowed out. During the late sixties through the mid-seventies Notre Dame gave up on any effort to provide students with a truly distinct and coherent Catholic education that would guarantee them some introduction to a Catholic worldview. There was a significant loss of Newman's sense that a university might "form a habit of mind in its students enabling them to see things in relation and to form a right judgment about complex realities."[113] The transcendental values of goodness, truth, and beauty were left largely unexplored. Many students at what Father Hesburgh began to think of as a great Catholic university, rather ironically, could move through their studies without seriously engaging the Catholic intellectual tradition and without any introduction to the rich works of the Catholic literary and artistic imagination.

The increasing compartmentalization that occurred at Notre Dame and the surrender of any serious effort to provide an integrated educational experience largely replicated what had occurred at most of the major research institutions. Father Hesburgh was vaguely aware of it but didn't effectively address the change, which occurred gradually rather than as one sharp rupture. His desire to have Notre Dame gain respect in the world of American higher education led him to give up on the old Thomistic approach, even though he realized the valuable benefits it had provided to him in thinking about an individual's place in the world, the nature of the good, humanity's final end, and the existence of God. But he surrendered easily and without making any major efforts to provide a genuine replacement that might incorporate both faith and reason. This surrender occurred at most of the other major Catholic (all Jesuit) universities. They all abdicated on the two key questions of who teaches and what is taught. It was a costly mistake, and many students subsequently have paid a high price because their intellectual formation has been pursued largely in isolation from the other elements of their life.

It is still surprising that Father Hesburgh did not fight harder against the prevailing trends to shape some replacement for the old Scholastic synthesis. He and Charlie Sheedy had worked in the early days in the department of religion to revise the curriculum to make it more accessible and relevant for students. Then and always Hesburgh wanted students to understand the essential tenets of their Catholic faith. But by the 1970s his attention and abilities were so diffused he could hardly have been expected to contribute to the hard intellectual work of updating Thomism. He did not seek help either on campus or beyond it. Within the university he mainly favored those like Ernan McMullan who placed the requisites for academic prestige over the requirements of an integrated curriculum. Perhaps if he had had some equivalent of Mortimer Adler at his side to influence him as Adler had influenced Robert Hutchins at the University of Chicago, events might have developed differently, but John Walsh and Neil McCluskey were incapable of playing such a role. Burtchaell understood the crucial importance of hiring faculty for mission in a Catholic university, but even he failed to put a real stamp on the curriculum. If Hesburgh had done so, Notre Dame would have really stood out in how it saw its purpose as a university and how it taught its students.

The verdict on Father Hesburgh's major structural reforms at Notre Dame must also be rendered in mixed tones. There were both positive and negative consequences of the transfer of ownership of Notre Dame from the Congregation of Holy Cross and the declaration of independence from ecclesial authority represented by the Land O'Lakes Statement. The Hesburgh changes assuredly meant a much larger role for the laity on the board of trustees. This role in turn brought much increased support for the university and allowed for notable institutional growth. But in the Hesburgh model, which has been continued, trustees largely were selected for their giving potential and not for their knowledge of Catholic universities. Most trustees either absolved themselves from concern about the academic heart of the university or they misunderstood the distinct nature of a genuine Catholic university.[114] They were not competent to honestly address essential matters of Catholic identity and mission. If they had been, then Notre Dame trustees would have challenged the assertion of the absolute autonomy of the university from the Church made at Land O'Lakes. Father Hesburgh's own obvious confusion regarding the nature of the relationship of the university and the Church remains even more arresting. He wanted to be "of" the Church but not formally "in" it in terms of accepting ecclesial authority. Further, it must be said that the 1967 arrangements meant some diminution in the corporate role of Holy Cross at Notre Dame. The president assumed major responsibility and in effect no longer answered in any way to the larger community. This allowed significant autonomy for Father Hesburgh's leadership, but it also meant he distanced himself from the founding religious community and the collective wisdom it might offer.

In 1977 Father Hesburgh gave little thought to such vital matters. He judged that the changes he had overseen had made Notre Dame vastly better off than the institution he had led in the mid-1960s. He was ready to move forward on major new initiatives. There were still immediate challenging issues to face on campus. Finding a new provost headed his list of key priorities, but in the fall of 1977 he confronted challenges that reflected that Notre Dame was truly a more modern university. The faculty and some workers attempted to unionize. The Hesburgh administration fought off both of these bids. The faculty effort collapsed quickly, although a modest American Association of University Professors chapter continued on campus. The faculty action attracted little attention or sympathy from the students or the interested public, which contrasted sharply to what happened in the case of twenty-one groundskeepers who tried to join Teamsters Local 364.[115] The university played hardball, as the expression goes, against the groundskeepers and enlisted the services of a high-powered law firm to defeat the workers' efforts to organize. In early October 1977 the administration, with General Counsel Philip Faccenda taking the public lead, announced that the groundskeepers would be permanently laid off and their work subcontracted out to an outside firm (Cromwell Management). This announcement sparked protests on campus and the inevitable question as to whether Notre Dame (read Father Hesburgh) would put into practice the dictates of justice that it preached beyond the campus.[116]

The sharp criticisms of the administration's actions annoyed Father Ted. He had absorbed the charges of hypocrisy from the African American students at the height of the student protest, but now he resented having his bona fides as a champion of justice questioned. He responded in an open letter to faculty and students on October 14 and engaged in a deft display of damage limitation. Indicative of Hesburgh's enduring political skill, he determined that because of the "gross misunderstanding" of the university's intentions he would "go slower in this entire matter."[117] Soon thereafter the university shifted gears in its approach. Wage increases and fringe benefit improvements for all employees were announced for January 1, 1978. The Teamsters charged that the university had engaged in a blatant attempt to "buy off its employees" to discourage their unionization initiatives. In the end the carrot worked better than the stick and unionization faltered. Hesburgh found the whole experience distasteful because he recognized full well that Notre Dame's tactics linked it to the broad-scale employer assault on organized labor occurring at the time. He also knew that he had ignored Catholic social teaching on the benefits of properly organized trade unions. Nonetheless, he defended his actions as a "kind of act of self-defense" against "the most corrupt union in America." Still sounding a little defensive two decades later, he argued that the need to prevent the Teamsters' gaining an inroad at Notre Dame warranted his acting against "his deeper conviction that labor ought to be able to organize if they wanted to."[118]

CHAPTER 5

BUILDING A DISTINCTIVE LEGACY, 1978–1987

A POWERFUL PROVOST AND ACADEMIC EXCELLENCE

THE SUDDEN RESIGNATION OF JIM BURTCHAELL AS PROVOST led to the creation of a search committee tasked with finding a successor to fill this crucial position. This group included such important Notre Dame figures as the former dean of the College of Arts and Letters Fred Crosson and the distinguished historian Philip Gleason. Timothy O'Meara, the Kenna Professor of Mathematics, chaired the committee. The committee members worked hard over the 1977–1978 academic year identifying candidates and undertaking preliminary interviews in order to present a list of three finalists to Father Hesburgh for his consideration. O'Meara kept Hesburgh abreast of the progress of the search. Eventually the committee members met with him to discuss the strengths and weaknesses of the three candidates whose hefty files he had already examined. According to his recollection he told them: "I can't take any of these guys." He explained that he thought "each one of you is better than these characters." Then he told the committee members that he wouldn't waste more of their time. Father Ted asked Tim O'Meara "to call your wife and say you're not going to be home for dinner tonight." He and O'Meara adjourned down to the Summit Club, then a private restaurant on the twenty-fifth floor of what became the Chase Tower in downtown South Bend. There over drinks and a fine dinner Hesburgh recruited O'Meara for the position.

In Father Ted's recollection he put a question plainly to the brilliant mathematician: "Tim, didn't it ever occur to you that you're better than any of these other three guys?" With commendable frankness O'Meara agreed that he was in fact better. So Hesburgh asked him to take the job. O'Meara balked, exclaiming, "I am the chair of the search committee and if I wind up getting the job, I'd be the laughingstock of the university." Hesburgh was in no mood for laughter. He needed a provost and he now wanted Tim O'Meara. He quickly devised a scheme wherein the outside candidates would be dismissed and an internal search pursued in which O'Meara would be a candidate matched against a couple of sacrificial lambs. After securing the endorsement of the Academic Council, Hesburgh then would present O'Meara's name to the trustees for formal approval. And so it came to pass. The press release announcing O'Meara's appointment quoted Father Hesburgh's effusive praise for his "outstanding scholarly and administrative credentials." O'Meara certainly fulfilled Hesburgh's hopes for him. There was never a day that Hesburgh regretted his decision to appoint O'Meara as his key associate at Notre Dame. They quickly formed a close personal bond and an intimate working relationship

The man who so impressed Father Hesburgh had journeyed far to come to Notre Dame. Born in Cape Town, South Africa, in 1928, O'Meara was one of five children of an Italian mother and an Irish father. He once described himself as "half Irish, half Italian, all South African," and since his naturalization as a U.S. citizen in 1977, as "all American."[1] He grew up in a faith-filled Catholic household and received his early education from the Sisters of Loreto and then from the Christian Brothers in Cape Town.[2] Thereafter he attended the University of Cape Town for his bachelor's and master's degrees, where his superb talent for mathematics impressed his teachers and won him a fellowship for doctoral studies at Princeton. In 1950 he sailed from Cape Town to begin his doctoral work. After completing his doctoral work, O'Meara taught first at the University of Otago in New Zealand; then he returned for a stint at Princeton before he moved on to his distinguished service at Notre Dame. A committed Catholic, O'Meara was deeply sympathetic to the changes wrought by Vatican II.

With all the strengths—such as his powerful intellect and boundless energy—that O'Meara brought to the provost's position, it might seem churlish to note that he also had a notable limitation for which neither he nor Father Ted ever managed to compensate. The new provost knew little about the humanities. Unlike some scientists, he was not dismissive of the liberal arts. Indeed, he wanted to see the major departments in the College of Arts and Letters improve and rise in the rankings. He worked hard to provide resources to this end. But he had no real knowledge or experience in how the humanities should help shape a Catholic university. His emphasis on strengthening Notre Dame would not be focused in this area. In retrospect it is clear that Tim O'Meara, despite his own admirable Catholic faith and practice, was better equipped to help Father Ted achieve the goal of becoming a "great university" in line with existing secular institutions, as distinct from its becoming a "great Catholic university."

When Tim O'Meara accepted the appointment as provost he asked for a four-year term so that he could return to his teaching and research. In his mind, presumably, also rested the likelihood that Father Ted would retire in 1982 after thirty years as president. When Hesburgh stayed on another five years, O'Meara agreed to continue in the role, and he went on to serve for a total of eighteen years (1978–1996) as provost. Over that time he established himself as in many ways the most powerful figure at Notre Dame. Edward "Monk" Malloy, who worked for five years as vice president and associate provost under O'Meara, and then succeeded Hesburgh as president, recalled from his close observation that within the officers group of the university, "Ted was the dominant figure in terms of rank and prestige, but Tim O'Meara basically set the agenda and assigned responsibility for reports and follow-through." As Malloy learned, "Notre Dame was run in its daily operations by Tim," who met independently with Father Ted about major matters. Malloy observed that even though Ned Joyce continued as executive vice president and Tom Mason served as vice president for business affairs, Tim O'Meara was "the real determiner of the University's spending priorities."[3] Hesburgh accepted this arrangement because O'Meara, who possessed none of Burtchaell's arrogance and sense of superiority, attended to their relationship and proceeded forward on any major matter only after securing Hesburgh's approval.

Monk Malloy's description of Tim O'Meara as "Mister Inside" with Father Ted as "Mister Outside" captures something of the president-provost relationship during the final decade of Hesburgh's leadership at Notre Dame, but it needs some qualification. Explicating the modus operandi that Hesburgh and O'Meara developed sheds important light on how Father Ted operated as president during his final decade. In Hesburgh's recounting, he allowed Tim O'Meara to do "all the background work," in terms of preparing reports and proposals. Then each evening sometime around 10:00 or 10:30 p.m. Tim O'Meara would come up to Hesburgh's office to meet. They would pour drinks for themselves and get to work.

Father Ted recalled that "some nights he would come up with half a foot of papers on things that he would give me to read or discuss, and sometimes he had already sent them up and wanted to discuss them. And we would make our decisions at that meeting—10:30 to 11:30 at night." He admitted that it was "kind of unusual, I guess," but he explained that they had "very blunt, no-holds-barred discussions at all times."

Father Ted emphasized that these discussions covered the full range of policy matters. He wanted to clarify that he wasn't some absentee landlord who let Tim O'Meara manage the estate as he wished. Rather he, as president, played a crucial role as the final decision-maker. In fact he emphasized that they would disagree "reasonably often" and "especially on appointments" for everything from department heads to new faculty. He stressed, however, that they talked out every issue. He didn't just sign pieces of paper that his provost placed before him. He recalled that he would say, "No, Tim, I'm not going to approve this," and he would give his reasons. O'Meara, who had something of the bull terrier in him, would energetically argue his case and, if rebuffed, occasionally ask to discuss the matter further on a subsequent night after he had the chance to recalibrate his arguments. Only occasionally did Hesburgh recall saying, "No, Tim, that's the end of it." According to Father Ted's recollections, in these situations Tim O'Meara would accept his decision even though "he wouldn't agree with me and he wouldn't like it." They never raised their voices but rather they talked "reason" to each other.[4] Thus were the key decisions made at Notre Dame from 1978 through 1987.

Father Ted's partiality for this close and rather exclusionary working relationship with Tim O'Meara only deepened as the years progressed and his personal friendship with his provost grew closer. He explained in simple but meaningful terms, "I really liked him and I liked Jean and I liked his kids." The O'Meara household became a place he willingly visited in South Bend. He began to travel extensively with Tim and Jean O'Meara. They not only attended IFCU meetings, but also went on a number of other major overseas trips including one to China and Nepal. He found Jean O'Meara a "very thoughtful person" who sent him interesting books to read as well as little travel kits when he was readying for a big trip. His deep affection and easy rapport with the O'Mearas continued long after his retirement from the presidency of Notre Dame. In March 2008 he was called upon to celebrate the funeral Mass for Jean O'Meara and to offer words of consolation to her grieving husband and family. He meant what he said when he later noted that "there is nobody within the whole university, apart from Ned of course, whom I have been closer to as a friend and confidant than Tim O'Meara."[5]

Despite their close bond Hesburgh initially objected to a central pillar of O'Meara's plan to strengthen Notre Dame academically, namely his scheme to markedly raise faculty salaries. O'Meara calculated in rather elemental fashion that to attract the superior faculty to undertake the desired superior scholarship he would need to offer superior salaries. His objective became to firmly lodge Notre Dame faculty salaries and total remuneration securely within the top quintile (as he loved to say) among major universities. Hesburgh thought many Notre Dame faculty members already received compensation beyond their performance. His irritation at O'Meara's efforts to improve faculty compensation only festered as he learned that faculty teaching loads across the colleges were being dramatically reduced. But Tim O'Meara wore him down in the end and won the argument. Father Ted told me with some seeming regret, "I went along with Tim's ploy." Over his time as provost and with his influence over budget priorities, O'Meara more than tripled the salaries of Notre Dame faculty from assistant to full professor ranks. He especially gave excellent compensation to the endowed chair professors whom he recruited in increasing numbers as a result of Notre Dame's fund-raising success, and whom he and Father Ted tasked with providing real academic leadership in the university.

Although O'Meara emerged victorious on the issue of faculty salaries he had more mixed success with Hesburgh in the contested area of faculty appointments. O'Meara recognized the need to hire capable Catholic faculty, but he wanted to balance that with hiring faculty who brought with them impressive academic reputations and active research agendas. Hesburgh remembered that he had to push O'Meara on this crucial matter. He claimed that he rejected certain candidates that his provost had approved. He even continued to express reservations about granting endowed chair positions to faculty members who were divorced and remarried, including, it is reported, the acclaimed philosopher Alasdair MacIntyre, who came to Notre Dame only in 1988 after Hesburgh's retirement.[6]

By 1998 when we spoke at Land O'Lakes, the issue of faculty hiring and its integral connection to the university's mission had stirred some controversy on campus. The percentage of Catholic faculty had dropped markedly, and Father Ted exhibited some defensiveness on the matter, but he commented that "when I walked out [of the president's office] there was two-thirds Catholic faculty on the numbers," although he conceded that "the reality" in terms of their actual practice and commitment might have been less. Whatever the percentage of actual Catholic faculty as of 1987, it must be said that the trends were well set in place by then that led to what Philip Gleason described as "a hollowing-out of the Catholic character of the faculty, in numbers, self-identification, and group morale."[7] Tim O'Meara and other administrators issued occasional statements of concern about the long-term maintenance of Notre Dame's Catholic identity. Yet he and his administrator colleagues devised few creative and workable answers to the question of how to recruit committed faculty across the whole range of disciplines who would embody and express openly the fundamental purposes of the institution.[8] Taking serious action on the matter risked a clash with an increasingly assertive faculty. That was a battle he preferred not to fight.

The difficulty that Hesburgh and O'Meara had in effectively confronting the faculty hiring issue signaled a broader and ongoing problem that they also failed to address effectively. We need not belabor the point already examined at some length in the preceding chapter, but during the decade of the Hesburgh-O'Meara partnership they undertook no sustained effort to overcome the intellectual fragmentation and compartmentalization at Notre Dame that resulted in what Don Briel termed with telling accuracy "an incoherent and un-integrated educational experience."[9] While the new breed of faculty focused on their specialized research, Hesburgh and O'Meara rested on the laurels of the university's established reputation for undergraduate education. O'Meara's emphasis was on expanding and strengthening Notre Dame's graduate programs and gaining improvement in the doctoral program rankings provided by the National Research Council. Here, to his considerable satisfaction, Notre Dame enjoyed success. This validated his superior scholarship by a superior faculty strategy. It also emboldened him to take actions that seemingly affirmed his commitment to an ever more modern Notre Dame. Notable among such moves was his willingness to support the plot in 1985 to oust Ralph McInerny, Notre Dame's leading Thomist philosopher, from the directorship of the renowned Medieval Institute. McInerny apparently appeared too parochial, too politically conservative, and not sufficiently concerned with the rankings to merit retention. There were some casualties in the quest for excellence, but Father Hesburgh focused less on them than on his distinctive initiatives for the university.

DISTINCTIVE PROJECTS, JOAN KROC, AND A PERSONAL LEGACY

Tim O'Meara's energetic supervision of the day-to-day management of Notre Dame afforded Father Hesburgh the opportunity to give more attention to special areas in the university that held his personal interest. During his final decade as president he gave notable consideration to a number of institutes or centers to which he felt a close connection. His intellectual curiosity ranged from environmental research in northern Wisconsin and ecumenical dialogue in the Holy Land to civil and human rights and, especially, the efforts to secure peace and avoid nuclear war. Institutes and centers were hardly new to Notre Dame during this period. Father Philip Moore had helped establish the Medieval Institute in 1946, and LOBUND gained independent institute status in 1950. Nonetheless, a host of new centers and institutes were launched in the 1970s and 1980s, usually as a way to bring scholars from a range of disciplinary backgrounds together to focus on a broad theme or subject from a variety of perspectives. Father Ted played a decisive role in the establishment and/or development of at least five projects in which he maintained a personal interest long after he retired from the presidency.

His initial commitment, and one that remained close to his heart all his life, came about as a result of a request from his friend Pope Paul VI. The pope had been much taken by a suggestion offered to him in October 1963 at a meeting of the Orthodox, Anglican, and Protestant observers present in Rome for the Second Vatican Council that "an international ecumenical institute for theological research and pastoral studies" be established. After the pope's pilgrimage to the Holy Land in January 1964 and his meeting there with Patriarch Athenagoras of Constantinople, he expressed the hope that an ecumenical center might be established in that sacred if troubled place to further the important dialogue begun during his historic meeting with the Greek Orthodox leader. Eventually Paul requested Father Ted's assistance to make his dream a reality. The Notre Dame president eagerly accepted the assignment and expended much time and energy to finding the site, constructing appropriate buildings, and obtaining funding for what became the Tantur Ecumenical Institute for Theological Studies. Through this particular effort he deemed that he and Notre Dame contributed both to the larger search for Christian unity and to deepened understanding between Christians, Jews, and Muslims.

Hesburgh took the initiative in establishing a civil rights center that eventually evolved into the Notre Dame Center for Civil and International Human Rights. After Nixon fired him from the U.S. Civil Rights Commission he determined he would found a body on campus to foster learning on advancing justice and dignity for all people. It was partly a defiant response aimed at continuing the fight he had waged within the Nixon administration, which had cost him his position. He housed this center in the Notre Dame Law School and lodged in it all his papers and books on civil rights that he had accumulated over the preceding fifteen years. Additionally, he brought to campus Howard Glickstein, his staff director and key aide during his service as chair of the Civil Rights Commission, who served as the center's first director. Hesburgh and Glickstein combined forces to obtain a sizable grant from the Ford Foundation, and the energetic Glickstein expeditiously began to put it to use. He planned major conferences and submitted legal briefs across a range of areas. He took an expansive view of "civil rights" and planned a conference in April 1975, entitled "Beyond Civil Rights: The Right to Economic Security," which featured the Reverend Jesse Jackson as keynote speaker.[10] Hesburgh backed Glickstein's efforts, and his capacious view of civil rights influenced the views Father Ted expressed in *The Humane Imperative*.[11] By 1976 the Ford Foundation grant was depleted. Glickstein departed Notre Dame to pursue a career in legal education culminating in his deanship of the Touro Law Center. To replace him Hesburgh recruited an existing Notre Dame faculty member and specialist in German constitutional law, Donald Kommers, who had a joint appointment in political science and law. Fortunately, Kommers also brought an existing faculty budget line and salary with him to the center and he was charged primarily with keeping the doors of the now ill-funded operation open. As Father Ted expressed it, the center "ran out of money and [we] put it on hold."[12]

Ironically, Hesburgh's reputation in the civil rights area, burnished by the center's existence, was used against him in the late 1970s and 1980s during the campus debate over divestment from firms having holdings in apartheid South Africa. On this matter Father Ted, backed by the trustees, pursued a moderate course much favored by schools with sizable endowments. Notre Dame adhered to the "Sullivan Principles," named for the Reverend Leon Sullivan, a member of the board of General Motors, which held that universities could invest in American companies with divisions in South Africa if they desegregated their plants in that country. This approach hardly satisfied the increasingly vocal critics who charged that this did nothing to challenge in any systemic way the racist structures of a brutal apartheid regime. An articulate professor of political science named Peter Walshe, himself born in Rhodesia although educated in England, emerged as Hesburgh's bête noire on the issue. Walshe went for Hesburgh's jugular and harshly asked in 1986: "What has happened to Father Hesburgh of earlier civil rights days? Why is he now totally out of step with civil rights leaders in America and deaf to the voices of South Africa?" Hesburgh opposed apartheid but genuinely believed in the validity of the Sullivan approach. He thought that complete divestment would damage the black workers employed by American subsidiaries, and would also inflict further suffering on the country's black majority. He described the radical divestment pushed by Walshe as "phony," and, with the trustees' backing, he held to the Sullivan approach.[13] Yet the attacks of Peter Walshe and his allies wounded the former chair of the Civil Rights Commission. He alleged that Walshe "slaughtered me in half a dozen ways" and that he did "everything he could to blacken [sic] me in many ways."[14] Hesburgh maintained civil relations with Peter Walshe, but he neither forgot nor completely forgave what he saw as his unfair attacks.

Hesburgh took some considerable satisfaction in being able to make use of the Center for Civil and Human Rights—whatever the limits of its funding—to counter the charges Walshe made against him that he cared little for the South African people and their anti-apartheid struggle. In the mid-1980s Hesburgh met with Richard Goldstone, a white South African judge and prominent opponent of apartheid, and asked the courageous jurist what Notre Dame could do to contest the apartheid system and to promote justice in South Africa. Goldstone quickly responded: "Educate our lawyers." With this prompting Hesburgh saw a new role for the center, and fortuitously he also found in Bill Lewers the person who could realize his vision. Lewers, a Holy Cross priest and a professor in the Notre Dame Law School, made a special effort to recruit students from South Africa and to train them to return home to work for justice.[15]

The Kellogg Institute for International Studies got under way with a generous endowment that secured its financial future, something that never happened for the Center for Civil Rights. Father Hesburgh's actions played a crucial role in ensuring that good fortune. Through the 1970s Father Ned

Joyce had elicited support from the elderly widow of John Kellogg, the son of the breakfast cereal magnate, who had made a considerable fortune of his own. Father Ned wanted some share of the over $30 million (in Father Ted's recollection) held by the John L. and Helen Kellogg Foundation. Despite his solicitations Joyce was never quite able to consummate a formal commitment on Helen Kellogg's part to support Notre Dame before she died in 1978. In her will Mrs. Kellogg "specified a 'precatory' wish [one that need not be obeyed in a will] that money should be donated to the university." The actual decision on distributing the foundation's resources lay with a group of trustees. They promptly made a major contribution to Northwestern University, which named its school of management in honor of the Kelloggs. Hesburgh (and Joyce and Frick) watched nervously as the total dwindled down to $10 million as further distributions were made. In the end he decided to act. He recalled saying, "Ned, we've got to put our foot down on this. There is that precatory thing in the will, yet they haven't given five cents to Notre Dame." He had Ned Joyce intervene with the chair of the trustees, whom he knew, and the chair invited Father Hesburgh and Joyce to attend the next board meeting to make their case. Hesburgh flew from New York to Chicago early in the morning of the meeting day and "wrote my pitch on the airplane." Although feeling "half dead" from his travels he "was put up to bat first and I made a pitch on what we could do with international studies with an institute for social, economic and political development, especially in the Third World."[16] It proved another strong performance. When the trustees came out of the board room they told the waiting (and slightly anxious) Fathers Ted and Ned that they had voted to assign the whole $10 million to Notre Dame. Thus the Kellogg Institute quickly emerged as one of the best endowed academic enterprises in the university.

Father Hesburgh recruited Fr. Ernie Bartell as the founding executive director of the Kellogg Institute. For the most part Hesburgh left the energetic and somewhat temperamental Bartell to shape the new outfit. He approved the focus on Latin America that Bartell gave it and applauded the efforts that the Kellogg Institute undertook to promote democratic institutions and social and economic development. During a time when he was personally working to foster democracy in Central America and while many Latin American nations writhed to liberate themselves from military governments or authoritarian regimes of both the Left and the Right, Father Ted saw these emphases as most appropriate.

The involvement of Father Hesburgh in initiatives like the Kellogg Institute and the Center for Civil and Human Rights reflected his major public commitments. His deep allegiance to the University of Notre Dame Environmental Research Center at Land O'Lakes, Wisconsin, grew out of a much more personal connection. He simply loved the Land O'Lakes property that Martin Gillen had deeded to Holy Cross in the 1930s. It was his favorite place in the world, aside from the Notre Dame campus. He used it as his personal retreat, and as the location where he brought guests for major meetings. Until the 1960s only limited scientific research had taken place in the area, carried out by biologists and lake ecologists from the University of Wisconsin. Land O'Lakes was a rustic retreat place much favored by those in Holy Cross given to fishing. Also the seminarians had spent summers there in the 1950s and thereafter. With the 1967 transfer of ownership of the university to the board of fellows, the property came under the purview of the university, which pleased Hesburgh. But it was not until the following decade that he was able to encourage Notre Dame scientists to undertake serious research there. Watching the gradual transformation of Land O'Lakes from primarily a summer camp for priests and seminarians into a modern research facility brought Hesburgh great pleasure.

Before we turn to the last of the five entities to which he devoted special attention, we must note another center that was established around this time. Father Hesburgh took special pride in its activities. Those familiar with Notre Dame will not be surprised to know of his true gratification in the work of the Center for Social Concerns (somewhat confusingly known as the CSC, the same initials used to refer to the Congregation of Holy Cross). The Center for Social Concerns aimed to combine the traditions of both service and learning developed by the Notre Dame Office of Volunteer Service, previously lodged in the Office of Student Activities, and the Center for Experiential Learning, which had been a part of Monsignor Jack Egan's Institute for Pastoral and Social Ministry. In 1983 the new Center for Social Concerns under the direction of Fr. Don McNeill, C.S.C., opened its doors in the partially renovated building previously occupied by WNDU-TV, the university-owned television station, which had moved to a new facility on the edge of campus. Because the building was a prime location, located just to the west of the library, a number of different university units had expressed strong interest in occupying the building. The lobbying reached all the way to Hesburgh, who made the final decision in favor of the Center for Social Concerns. He took pride in providing such a prominent home for the social service and social justice efforts of the students at the university. Under McNeill's creative leadership, students during the regular academic year engaged in all kinds of activities in the local area—serving at food banks and soup kitchens, tutoring disadvantaged kids, comforting the sick and the elderly, teaching religious education in poorer parishes, visiting prisoners and assisting those released on parole— and then sought to reflect upon their experience. Hesburgh applauded the students' work, often quoting from the Gospel of Matthew, "I was hungry and you gave me something to eat. . . ."

McNeill and his staff built the Center for Social Concerns into a thriving operation that touched the lives of many students. Father Hesburgh trumpeted the service work undertaken by the Notre Dame undergrads. It confirmed for him the Catholicity of the university and clarified that the Notre Dame that he had shaped took seriously the call of *Gaudium et Spes* to engage and serve the world. As he came to the end of his presidency he contrasted the situation of the university with what he had inherited. In a somewhat unfair comparison he opined, "I don't know how many students back in 1952 were working for the less fortunate. But if there were any doing so, I didn't know about them. Today [circa 1985] about a third of our student body is working for the less fortunate, and about ten percent of our graduates are going into such work for a year or two of their lives after they graduate."[17] He wanted students not only to serve on the local level, but also to address the big issues of the day. This is surely what he tried to do in the 1980s, and it by chance led to the creation of an institute at Notre Dame devoted to peace.

Concern for peace had been a fixture on some American campuses from the time of the Vietnam War. As the nuclear arms race intensified in the 1970s, peace studies became a proverbial "hot topic" on American campuses. The failure of the Carter administration to secure ratification of the SALT II Treaty it had negotiated with the Soviet Union, followed by the decisive election of Ronald Reagan, were deemed major setbacks to arms control efforts. The Catholic bishops of the United States certainly thought so, and they decided in November 1980 to prepare a pastoral statement on nuclear war and peace, which eventually appeared after wide consultation in May 1983. The nuclear freeze movement garnered much public support and organized large demonstrations demanding an end to the nuclear arms race. Public concern about the dangers of nuclear war was confirmed when over 100 million people watched the TV movie *The Day After* in 1983, which portrayed the consequences of full-scale nuclear exchange between the United States and the USSR.

From the early 1980s onward Father Ted made the nuclear issue his primary public concern. As the Reagan administration engaged in a major defense buildup in both conventional and nuclear forces and as arms control efforts faltered, Hesburgh became genuinely concerned. He had some knowledge of the terrible consequences of a nuclear exchange going back to his work as Vatican representative on the International Atomic Energy Agency. He feared that such an exchange was likely, and he felt a deep moral obligation to do all he could to prevent this. Over the coming years he became agitated and even shrill in warning that the nuclear issue was "the number one problem" of the day. "We are not far from utter disaster," he told a Notre Dame audience in 1985. He explained: "We are in proximate danger of destroying everything we hold dear [and] not just our homes, not just our loved ones. We are in danger of destroying not just this whole world but this whole species, which means destroying all those lives which have not begun."[18] He saw the nuclear arms race as evidence of human insanity. Given such views it is hardly surprising that he spoke and wrote constantly on the issue. He saw it in very personal terms and once explained "that everything else that I've been working on all my life would literally be wiped out by a nuclear attack."[19]

In May 1985 Father Ted accepted an invitation to deliver an endowed lecture at the University of California San Diego named in honor of his old doctoral mentor at Catholic University, the Paulist priest Gene Burke. In terms of practical consequences it was one of his more successful endeavors in public speaking. Before a packed auditorium he "talked on the obligation of universities to train their students on the realities of and the solutions to the nuclear threat to humanity." He remembered not reading a prepared text but "doing it out of my head," having given variations of the talk previously. He noticed a "very handsome blonde lady" sitting in the front row paying close attention. He estimated that she was in her fifties but admitted to me that "with blondes it's hard to say." This woman came up to him after his address as people were milling around him and she said simply, "I really believe in what you're doing and I'm going to help you." Father Ted replied, "Well thank you very much. I sure need help." So ended their conversation. Hesburgh's host, Richard Atkinson, the chancellor of UC San Diego, said to him: "That's Joan Kroc," to which Hesburgh remembered that he responded: "And who is Joan Kroc?" He would come to know Joan Kroc, the wealthy widow of Ray Kroc, who had made a fortune through the McDonald's Corporation.

So began the Father Ted courtship of Joan Kroc, or perhaps it was the Joan Kroc courtship of Father Ted. Over the subsequent months there were some limited overtures between them, although Hesburgh did not pursue Mrs. Kroc but rather allowed her to come to him. Joan Kroc eventually came to visit the campus in the fall. She met with Hesburgh and also with former Ohio governor John "Jack" Gilligan, who now served on the law school faculty and who encouraged "peace" initiatives on campus. Gilligan gave her an estimate of $6 million dollars to establish a peace institute. Joan Kroc clearly took the number to heart. On the Wednesday before Thanksgiving Hesburgh was visiting Ed Stephan's home and Joan Kroc tracked him down around 8:00 p.m. In breezy fashion she mentioned that she was calling from her kitchen where she was making gravy for Thanksgiving. Then she caught the Notre Dame president's attention by informing him that she planned to send him ninety-eight thousand McDonald's shares. She then explained that "when you sell them you will have six million dollars and you can start your program."[20] Hesburgh appointed Gilligan as the founding director and what would become the Kroc Institute for International Peace Studies began. In contrast to his somewhat detached relationship with the Kellogg Institute, Hesburgh threw himself into the work of the peace institute, where Gilligan welcomed his every contribution. A feature of the new institute was the master's degree program in international peace studies, and the aim was to recruit an array of students from around the world. Hesburgh, in classic fashion, took it upon himself to travel to both Moscow and Beijing to persuade each of the respective education ministers to send two students for the initial cohort of students, who were forced to live together in some dilapidated space rented from the Holy Cross Brothers off of Columba Hall. Inevitably it was titled Peace House.

In the midst of the initial struggles to get the peace institute up and running, Joan Kroc contacted Father Ted and asked to visit Notre Dame again. She came in the fall of 1987 and Hesburgh introduced her to his successor, Edward Malloy. They enjoyed a Notre Dame football victory against Michigan State and then went on to a dinner where the discussion focused on the work of the new institute. At the dinner that evening they met up with Eppie Lederer, also known as Ann Landers. Father Ted invited both women to meet the students at the Peace House the next morning. There, in his recollection, "they had a great two-hour discussion with the kids."

What the various international students made of their conversation with the largest shareholder of the McDonald's hamburger chain and America's most famous advice columnist has not been recorded, but the meeting had some impact on Mrs. Kroc. After a further meeting with some of the peace institute faculty Hesburgh and his honored guest returned to his office. There, sitting demurely on his couch, she asked him if he needed "something else." According to the well-known account included in his *God, Country, Notre Dame,* Father Ted replied that he needed a place that would give "the international dimensions of Notre Dame visibility and impact." Mrs. Kroc asked if he meant a building, and he said yes. She then said that she didn't "believe in giving money for buildings." She asked him why he didn't spend the $6 million she had already given to him on a building. He explained that "then I would have an empty building because I put the [original] six million into endowment," and that covered the annual program costs. Joan Kroc apparently replied that she didn't believe in endowments either. This prompted a telling response: "Well, if you were an outgoing president at Notre Dame you would believe in endowment because you have your own bright ideas and you start things and if they aren't endowed they'll be gone in two or three years. But this thing [the peace institute] is going to go on forever. It's my legacy if you will." Joan Kroc made no decision in Father Ted's office, but instead announced that she must return home to San Diego. Father Ted insisted on driving her to the airport and blessing her brand-new Grumman Gulfstream IV jet, and they said their good-byes.[21]

Joan Kroc did not delay long. She called him the next day and promised $6 million for the building on condition it be named the Hesburgh Center for International Studies. He protested that the main library already was destined to carry his name, but the teasing Mrs. Kroc said: "no name on building, no money." Hesburgh put up but a modest protest before succumbing quickly. He wrote later, "I agreed because I did want that building, even if it had to have my name on it."[22] In the greater scheme of things it hardly seemed a high price to pay. Soon Hesburgh and Mrs. Kroc were wielding shovels as ground was broken in 1988 for the Hesburgh Center on Notre Dame Avenue. That building housed both the Kroc and the Kellogg Institutes.

In his retirement Father Ted kept up his engagement with the Kroc Institute. He felt deep satisfaction that his chance encounter with Joan Kroc had led to the creation of the peace institute that now bears her name. This sentiment only deepened when he learned in 2003 of the $50 million bequest that "Saint Joan" had made to Notre Dame to further the work of peace studies at the university.[23] It was the largest gift to that point that the university had received, and Ted Hesburgh knew that neither it nor any of the preceding gifts that Mrs. Kroc had made to Notre Dame would have happened without him and his antinuclear activities. Riding the peace train had paid rich dividends on the Notre Dame campus.

Notably missing among the range of important issues that Father Hesburgh chose to secure his legacy at Notre Dame was the blight of abortion. By the 1980s it was clear that the people involved in the pro-life movement were not going to fade away and allow the Supreme Court's *Roe v. Wade* decision to prevail uncontested. This movement saw Justice Harry Blackmun's demarche to impose a national ruling on when personhood began and to remove this fundamental matter from the purview of state legislatures as the equivalent of the Dred Scott decision, which had denied U.S. citizenship to African Americans. The various elements of the pro-life movement demanded that *Roe v. Wade* be overturned. Even by 1976, abortion had become a divisive issue that affected national politics. Hesburgh originally attempted to address this matter by calling for dialogue and discussion of the sort that resulted in the "National Conference on Abortion" organized by Jim Burtchaell in 1979. He also made clear that he didn't think this issue bore such significance that it should outweigh other major public issues. While he gave his primary attention to the nuclear issue because of the potential "danger of destroying not just this whole world but this whole species, which means destroying all those lives which have not begun," he seemingly worried less about the increasing millions of unborn lives decimated by abortion. He objected to "single issue" voting if the issue was abortion. In his preface to Burtchaell's book *Abortion Parley*, which assembled the papers from the 1979 conference, Hesburgh wrote critically of "the fact that political candidates who agree 95 percent with Catholic principles of social justice in most issues of public policy have been defeated by their opposition on this one issue and have been replaced by candidates who, agreeing superficially on this issue of abortion, disagree with us on almost every other issue bearing on justice and equality."[24]

Hesburgh always made his own personal opposition to abortion clear. Yet he often seemed unenthusiastic about the grassroots efforts of the pro-life movement. In a similar way to the "seamless garment" approach later promoted by Cardinal Joseph Bernardin, the archbishop of Chicago, he held that "if we really respect the right to life we must respect it right across the board for everyone, from the beginning of conception to the end of life." Rather dismissively he noted that the pro-life effort could not be "just a little narrow crusade."[25] Perhaps his continuing extensive involvement with the Rockefeller Foundation lay behind some of his reticence, but we must simply note here that he instigated no substantial academic initiatives on campus to assure sustained research on abortion. There was no pro-life institute that might counter the policy analysis and social science research undertaken by the "pro-choice" Alan Guttmacher Institute, the research affiliate of the Planned Parenthood Federation of America. Father Ted largely left it to the students of Notre Dame Right to Life and to a few dedicated faculty to carry the pro-life cause on campus. One of those faculty, Professor Janet Smith of the Program of Liberal Studies, actually founded (off-campus) the Women's Care Center to assist pregnant women and to provide options other than abortion. Father Ted occasionally spoke favorably of the venture and gave modest support to its fund-raising appeals, but he did not adopt this as his cause.[26] It didn't seem to fit well with his other issues and they held priority for him.

DICK MCBRIEN AND THE TRIUMPH OF LIBERAL CATHOLICISM

At the time of Pope Benedict XVI's election to the papacy, Father Hesburgh recalled that some decades before, during the years of Vatican II, he had tried to recruit Joseph Ratzinger, the then young German theologian and Council *peritus*, or theological adviser, to the Notre Dame faculty. Sadly for Notre Dame, he declined, explaining that he lacked a sufficient command of English to take up such an appointment.[27] One wonders how the Notre Dame theology department might have evolved if Ratzinger had left Bavaria and made his academic home in northern Indiana. Perhaps he might have helped fashion a department committed to the "hermeneutic of continuity," which aimed to implement the teachings of the Council in some fidelity to sacred tradition as opposed to those promulgating a "hermeneutic of discontinuity" that called for a "new Catholicism" largely divorced from the pre–Vatican II Church. The great theological contest over the legacy and correct understanding of Vatican II eventually pitted such figures as Ratzinger, Hans Urs von Balthasar, and Henri de Lubac, who were identified with the journal *Communio*, against a larger group who helped found the journal *Concilium* in 1965 and were fully intent on keeping "the spirit of Vatican II" alive in the church. Numbered among the luminaries in the latter group were Johann Baptist Metz, Yves Congar, Karl Rahner, Edward Schillebeeckx, and Hans Kung. Although Kung proved the most successful self-promoter among the latter group, the brilliant German Jesuit Karl Rahner was the most influential. In 1974 Rahner published *The Shape of the Church to Come,* in which he outlined his vision for the future Church. His recommendations convey key elements of what would come to be known as liberal Catholicism, an outlook that would have a major impact in the Church, including at Notre Dame in the 1970s and 1980s (and in fact beyond).

Rahner's formulations have been succinctly summarized as follows: "The pastoral should have priority over the dogmatic. Christ asks for an internal, existential decision in the deepest recesses of our being, not assent to doctrinal propositions. The Church needs to open her doors and reach outsiders, meeting them on their own terms rather than addressing them with legalistic moralizing. In fact, the Church needs to rethink the way morality is taught. Social criticism is the true purpose of the Church's magisterium, which must seek engagement with the modern world rather than walling off the Church from outside influences."[28] Not surprisingly in light of this broad approach, Rahner's positions on particular issues leaned in a progressive direction. He foresaw an end to priestly celibacy and favored lay-led Christian communities. He recognized the possibility of female priests and called for more democratic structures in Church governance. In his enthusiasm for ecumenism he encouraged open communion.[29] It all combined, we might say, into a rather full agenda, and one that obtained a sizable following of those who wanted to fulfill what they saw as the full promise of Vatican II.

Mentioning Ratzinger and Rahner here and their differing understandings of Vatican II's mandate serves as a brief preface to noting the obvious point that Catholic theology by the early 1970s was in a state of flux and dispute. It was hardly an easy time to chair a theology department. Nonetheless, when Burtchaell left to become provost in 1970, David Burrell boldly took on the responsibility at Notre Dame. Burrell had displeased Father Ted with his ambush of Peter Grace, but Hesburgh still believed a Holy Cross priest should chair the theology department. So after Burtchaell's promotion Burrell stood out as the obvious choice based on his scholarly credentials, although his eccentricities gave some people pause. Burrell was a yoga devotee and occasionally did exercises during committee meetings. Whatever his personal quirks, Burrell possessed genuine intellectual independence and integrity. He rested comfortably in neither of the theological camps described above. He worked in the somewhat esoteric area of philosophical theology, and acknowledged the influence of Bernard Lonergan and Ludwig Wittgenstein.

Burrell took up his post in the fall of 1971 (after Charlie Sheedy served as acting chair for a year), but without any specific directions from Hesburgh or anyone else. He knew well only that the department needed to be strengthened so as to improve its academic reputation. Further, he needed to jettison any remnant of its past reputation as a Catholic catechetical operation. The predictable course of action, which Burrell pursued, was to hire theologians—Catholics and Protestants alike—on the basis of their academic training and accomplishments. Given the vocation crisis and resignations from the priesthood, the pool of possible clerical appointments was much reduced, and sizable numbers of his hires were laypersons including some women. Burrell resisted the temptation to fully go down the modern path and to transform the theology department into a department of religious studies, which would examine religion from the outside, so to speak, from a supposedly neutral stance. He believed genuinely in operating from within a given faith tradition, but he found it interesting and creative to have a number of faith traditions represented. As one of his then colleagues, Stanley Hauerwas, explained it: "Under David's leadership we came to understand ourselves not as a Catholic department but as a 'theology department in a Catholic context.'"

In retrospect one can see that Burrell and some of his colleagues tried, in Hauerwas's words, to "avoid the sterile 'liberal' and 'conservative' alternatives that seemed to shape the theological world" at the time, but they never made fully clear their intention.[30] They wanted "to form a theology department that took God seriously," but ultimately their efforts were not fully appreciated.[31] As the decade progressed some critics began to allege that the department possessed the qualities of an "ecumenical department" whose leading figures were non-Catholics. Attention especially focused on the charismatic ethicist/moral theologian Stanley Hauerwas (nominally Methodist, although he often worshipped at Sacred Heart), the brilliant church historian Robert Wilken (then a Lutheran), and the prominent pacifist theologian John Howard Yoder (a Mennonite, who taught regularly as an adjunct).

Father Hesburgh developed serious concerns about theology at Notre Dame as the decade progressed. He recalled that he realized by the end of the 1970s that the theology department had become "an awful mess." As he saw it, under Burrell's chairmanship Notre Dame was "quickly developing a Protestant faculty of theology."[32] While Father Ted genuflected regularly before the sacred cow of ecumenism, what was happening at the theology department was a step too far and on his very own campus. He claimed that he confronted Burrell and challenged him on the direction of the department. He remembers saying that "somewhere in the damn country there has got to be a Catholic theology department and we are it."[33] He resolved to rectify the situation and he knew exactly whom to enlist for the mission.

Burrell finished his nine years as chair in the spring of 1980 and soon left for a sabbatical. By that point Tim O'Meara had announced that Fr. Richard McBrien would take Burrell's place as chair, and that he also would occupy the newly established Crowley-O'Brien endowed chair in theology.[34] Father Ted told me, "I really looked the country over and I found a guy who was both productive as a theologian . . . and who had good political sense." In reality he had decided on McBrien after reading his two-volume synthesis entitled *Catholicism* prior to its formal publication. Thereafter he and O'Meara worked to bring McBrien, a diocesan priest from Hartford then teaching at Boston College, to Notre Dame. Hesburgh said he told McBrien, "I want you, with all the guile you've got, to change that department from a Protestant department to a Catholic department with predominantly Catholic scholars." In Hesburgh's recounting the new chair came into "a real messy situation," but with "enormous political skill" he "turned that department around."[35] There can be no doubt that when McBrien retired as chair in 1991 he had turned the department in a different direction, and one much to Hesburgh's liking. Indeed, McBrien brought about the triumph of liberal Catholicism in the theology department at Notre Dame.

McBrien arrived at Notre Dame as a well-known public figure, at least in the Catholic world. He appeared regularly on television as a commentator on various Catholic issues and on events like papal elections, and he wrote a syndicated column that many Catholic newspapers carried. Unlike many academics he handled the media with consummate ease. Although he sometimes featured the Roman collar in his television work, he normally dressed neatly in gray slacks, a blue blazer, and a sensible tie. Articulate and occasionally witty, McBrien brought with him impressive organizational gifts and, as Hesburgh noted, an undeniable talent for academic politics.

As a theologian, McBrien stood in complete contrast to the philosophical Burrell. McBrien had pursued his doctorate at the Gregorian University in Rome in the heady days leading up to Vatican II. The Council proved the defining event of his life, and he liked to present his work as fulfilling the vision established by the Council fathers, as did Father Hesburgh. McBrien accorded Pope John XXIII heroic status—he later proclaimed him with some possible hyperbole "the most beloved pope in history"—and viewed the work of his papal successors, including Paul VI after 1968, with dismay.[36] In his columns and in the numerous lectures he gave around the country, McBrien regularly addressed contentious issues including a married priesthood as well as the ordination of women. Like his good friend Charles Curran he also dissented vocally from *Humanae Vitae*. He sought greater accountability within the Church and was unafraid to criticize episcopal actions of one sort or another. As he saw it, he mainly challenged the structures of the Church and the way it should fulfill its mission, but he accepted her doctrines. He demanded that the Church work for "justice" in society. This invariably lined him up in support of politically liberal causes and politicians.

Hesburgh and McBrien formed a deep bond that lasted until they died just a month apart in 2015. They became not only intellectual comrades in the cause of liberal Catholicism but also close personal friends. They both wanted the Church to engage and serve the world, to further the cause of justice as they understood it. McBrien exercised significant influence over Hesburgh and confirmed his increasingly liberal instincts and positions. Beginning in the 1980s and continuing right through his retirement years, Hesburgh dined regularly with McBrien and the theologian's close friend Beverly Brazauskas. He loved their company and their lively conversations, which combined serious discussion of theological and political matters with gossipy speculation as to who was up and who down in the Church and how it all connected to them and Notre Dame. McBrien viewed the Church in very political terms. There was a division between the "white hats," who were the liberals and progressives, and the "black hats," who were conservative or even (much worse) "restorationist."[37]

McBrien pursued his leadership of the theology department while engaging in a constant critique of Pope John Paul II and his actions and appointments. He portrayed the Polish pope as somewhat intolerant and as clearly unable to relate to such American practices as openness, tolerance, and free discussion.[38] There was some irony in these complaints given that

McBrien worked rather deftly and behind the scenes to impose his control over the theology department. Within a few years Hauerwas and Wilken found the department's climate so unfriendly that they decided to move on to positions elsewhere—Hauerwas at Duke and Wilken at the University of Virginia. Yoder, whom McBrien actually hired full-time in 1984, and Burtchaell were easily marginalized as the new chair began to hire theologians cut mainly from his liberal Catholic cloth. Hesburgh did everything he could to facilitate McBrien's campaign to redirect the department. McBrien thus benefited from the opportunity to fill a number of new endowed chair positions. His access to enhanced resources was aided further by Tim O'Meara, who also emerged as a close friend and ally. By the mid-1980s the department increasingly reflected the liberal Catholic outlook of its chair.

Dick McBrien's political approach in no way disturbed Father Hesburgh. He extended his prestige and support to all the efforts of his chosen appointee. This became patently clear when he fully endorsed McBrien's invitation to New York Governor Mario Cuomo to visit campus in 1984 to defend his position on abortion. This invitation was made after Cuomo had clashed with Archbishop John J. O'Connor over the responsibilities of Catholic politicians on this crucial issue. McBrien enthusiastically provided Cuomo with a Catholic platform at Notre Dame to broadcast his disagreement with the voluble O'Connor. After consulting with his favored theologians (among whom McBrien was numbered), the New York governor announced that while he accepted the teaching authority of his church and its doctrine on abortion, this did not lead him to support actions that might limit or ban abortion (contra O'Connor). He appealed instead to "Catholic realism" and argued that any ban on abortion would be divisive and would not work. Thus he stated as his fundamental principle: "The values derived from religious belief will not—and should not—be accepted as part of the public morality unless they are shared by the pluralistic community at large, by consensus."[39] Dick McBrien served as a veritable cheerleader for the New York governor, thus providing the spectacle of the chair of the theology department in the nation's best-known Catholic university essentially endorsing a position at fundamental odds with that promulgated by a leading member of the Catholic hierarchy. Father Hesburgh did nothing to either restrain or caution McBrien. He accepted that it was quite appropriate for the theology department chair to apply his liberal views not only in the world of religion, but also in the world of politics.

Liberal Catholicism eventually proved influential and even dominant in most theology departments in the major American Catholic universities. Notre Dame was hardly unique. But Dick McBrien, with Father Hesburgh's backing, played a key role in assuring the ascendancy of this approach on what Father Ted still called Our Lady's campus. The impact of liberal Catholicism rippled out forcefully through campus ministry and agencies like the Center for Social Concerns. It affected the Congregation of Holy Cross on campus, and it reached many of the other institutes and centers touched on earlier, such as the peace institute. Those who failed to accept liberal Catholicism as the dominant paradigm, such as Ralph McInerny still holding on in his Maritain Center redoubt, were viewed censoriously. Liberal Catholicism, however, never served as a stirring force to rally the campus in a needed renewal of its Catholic mission. McBrien's focus on intra-ecclesial issues and his harsh criticisms of the pope and the hierarchy hardly provided the right fuel to power Catholic life on campus. Father Hesburgh failed to grasp that reality. He left the presidency still deeply reassured that the theology department rested securely in what he deemed McBrien's good hands.

Father Hesburgh and Father McBrien genuinely believed that they had succeeded in "re-Catholicizing" the theology department. They judged that they had rescued it from the peril of a nebulous ecumenical approach. In light of that it is somewhat ironic that both priests remained deeply opposed to either the theology department or the university maintaining any formal connection to the Catholic Church. They agreed fully that there should be no outside interference in the university, if "outside" meant any kind of Church authority. McBrien relentlessly confirmed for Hesburgh the sagacity of the Land O'Lakes declaration and the necessity to maintain it. McBrien's negative disposition toward the hierarchy worked in synch with Father Ted's pride in his own handiwork in securing for himself free rein within the university. Much to their dismay the Polish pope, who knew something of universities, began speaking of the bond between the Church and institutions that claimed the Catholic mantle. On his first visit to the United States in October 1979 he addressed the presidents of Catholic colleges and universities and explained that "if then your universities and colleges are institutionally committed to the Christian message, and if they are part of the Catholic community of evangelization, it follows that they have an essential relationship to the hierarchy of the Church."[40] The pope also introduced here "the role of theologians and the importance of their fidelity to the magisterium."[41] This latter area proved of real concern to Father Ted, especially in the early 1980s as those in Rome involved in drafting a revised Code of Canon Law (governing Church procedures, etc.) insisted on including in their draft document provisions that Catholic theologians in Catholic universities obtain a canonical mandate from their local bishop.

Hesburgh and McBrien bristled at this attempt at "interference." As Alice Gallin explained, Father Ted wrote "a circular letter to all of the [American] bishops, recounting in detail the story of American Catholic higher education and its interaction with church authorities and urging them to defend the way in which the universities had benefited from the American system of government." He went on to argue—somewhat hyperbolically—that the proposed "provisions of the new Code would do irreparable harm and would force the universities out of a relationship with the church."[42] Hesburgh maintained his strong opposition to the concept of a mandate, although the revised Code included a provision (Canon 812) for theologians to obtain such an authorization. Hesburgh and McBrien essentially ignored the provision as irrelevant to Notre Dame.

Having thus dispensed with the Code of Canon Law issue, they faced a new challenge. The Vatican decided to produce some kind of document on the mission and purpose of Catholic higher education. Hesburgh organized opposition to this document and presented his contrary arguments to the appropriate congregations in Rome.[43] He eventually transferred to his successor the responsibility for Notre Dame's contributions to the lengthy discussions, which led to John Paul II's apostolic constitution *Ex Corde Ecclesiae* (1990) and the subsequent deliberations over the norms to implement it.[44] Thereafter he and Dick McBrien let no opportunity pass to express their opposition to what they saw as a dangerous challenge to the institutional autonomy of Notre Dame and a wrongheaded assault on the American approach to higher education adopted by Catholic universities. Standing strong against "Rome" assuredly was what liberal Catholics did—at least back then.

FINISHING STRONG WITH BILL SEXTON AND LOU HOLTZ

With Tim O'Meara handling the daily operations of the university and Dick McBrien engaged in his rescue mission of the theology department,

Ted Hesburgh felt increasingly ebullient as the decade of the 1980s moved along. The momentum of affairs on campus appeared to flow in a favorable direction. Additionally, his national reputation continued to grow. In the 1960s his profile had graced the cover of *Time*. In the 1980s television dominated, and now his older but still handsome visage translated well onto the screen; he appeared on such programs as *Nightline* with Ted Koppel and *60 Minutes* with Dan Rather. He continued to give lectures and interviews all over the world as well as writing op-eds for newspapers large and small.

Sometimes these addressed important public policy issues such as immigration in major venues like the *New York Times*, while in other instances he wrote thoughtful responses to personal questions that Ann Landers then packaged in her column. His honorary degrees and other awards and honors piled up further.[45]

On campus he made himself available for major events such as the occasion he introduced the famed writer, Holocaust survivor, and (future) Nobel laureate, Elie Wiesel, who came to Notre Dame to deliver a series of lectures, eventually published (with a foreword by Father Ted) as *Four Hasidic Masters and Their Struggle Against Melancholy*.[46] He relished that speakers like Wiesel were sharing their intense learning on his campus. But the celebrated priest-president also willingly accepted invitations to speak to informal late-night gatherings in dorms across the campus. When his schedule permitted he presided at hall Masses on Sundays, where usually he preached at some length but still managed to connect with students. He continued to work late at night in his office, and occasionally students would visit him there and benefit from his counsel. The turmoil of the 1960s and 1970s had more than satiated his appetite for any sustained involvement in student affairs. He gladly left this domain to his vice presidents—first, to Father John Van Wolvlear (1978–1982) and then to Father David Tyson. Occasionally he expressed concern about a particular issue concerning students, such as grade inflation, but undergraduate curricular concerns didn't preoccupy him. Particular programs did gain his attention, however. He notably remained committed to the continued presence on campus of the Reserve Officers' Training Corps (ROTC), despite the criticism of some campus peace activists who argued that this ROTC presence tied the university too closely to the military actions of the Reagan administration. The priest who had wanted to serve as a Navy chaplain in the Pacific during World War II still recognized the necessity of conventional armed forces, whatever his support for nuclear disarmament and peace studies.

While Father Ted dabbled in academic and student matters where his interests drew him, he remained at the center of the effort to raise money to develop the university. In April 1977 a five-year development program, known simply as the Campaign for Notre Dame, was launched. This new endeavor focused heavily on increasing the permanent endowment. At the campaign's inaugural event Father Ted explained this focus in a rather blunt fashion by noting: "If you take the ten universities in this country with the largest endowment, you will have the ten best universities in this country."[47] He wanted to enter that exalted company. As if to confirm the point, the publicity materials surrounding the launch indicated that this was the ninth largest fund-raising campaign in progress among American universities. To save the reader from any suspense, the fund-raising effort more than met its target. But as the campaign wrapped up in 1982, Jim Frick, suffering from health problems, came to see Hesburgh and advised him that he would have to "pack it in."[48]

Father Joyce took initial charge of searching for Frick's successor and employed a noted headhunter company. This search firm's efforts produced a number of finalists who were brought to campus for interviews with Hesburgh and Joyce. The president found these candidates presented to him through the normal search process inadequate. He sat down with Father Ned after the final interview and declared that he couldn't hire any of them. He recalled saying that "compared to Jim Frick they are children." Father Joyce agreed. But his ever loyal deputy went on to suggest that they change the focus of the search away from people with technical fund-raising experience. Rather, he suggested, they should look around the university and "get a guy who is totally convinced that Notre Dame is the greatest thing in the world and is prepared to work hard to make it better." Father Ted asked him if he had anyone in mind, and Joyce offered him the name of Bill Sexton, an outgoing professor in the business school. Joyce spoke glowingly of Bill Sexton's virtues and emphasized that he was a man totally dedicated to Notre Dame. Hesburgh recalled that he needed no persuasion. He remembered pronouncing Joyce's suggestion a "genius idea." He then took control and arranged to have dinner at the Summit Club with Bill Sexton and his wife, Ann. He laid out an attractive offer for the rather surprised Sexton to become vice president for development.[49] The Sextons decided to throw caution to the wind and to take up the position. It proved an enormously beneficial appointment for Notre Dame.

Bill Sexton's easy public presence and extroverted nature presented something of a contrast to the intense Jim Frick, but he proved just as brilliant a fund-raiser as his predecessor. Hesburgh loved traveling with Bill and Ann Sexton on fund-raising and other trips. He glowingly described her as "an absolute gem and an angel" who never seemed to get flustered or worried.[50] As for her husband, his grace and constant amiability—even on days when he made a hundred phone calls—impressed the university president who prided himself on keeping his own equanimity whatever the pressures he faced. Soon Sexton was gearing up for the next fund-raising campaign. Hesburgh and Joyce did everything that Sexton asked of them. They traveled widely and hosted "fly-in" weekends for major donors. Father Ted took to heart his own prayer, which derived from Reinhold Niebuhr's famous "Serenity Prayer." Hesburgh's variation went like this: "Lord, give us the ambition to do as much as we can, as well as we can, as long as we can, and the resolve not to despair over the things we cannot do." No one accused him of not doing all that he could in the realm of fund-raising. Notre Dame began the silent phase of meeting the $300 million goal of the Strategic Moment campaign in 1985. This campaign's formal inauguration in the spring of 1987 was tied directly to all the celebrations surrounding the dual retirements of Fathers Hesburgh and Joyce. Contributing to the effort meant doing them honor and showing them gratitude for all they had done. When the public phase of the campaign concluded in 1990 it had raised $463 million, a truly remarkable result. Bill Sexton by this point had long passed the trial period, after which he could return to teach in the business school. He stayed in his position for twenty years and oversaw campaigns that raised over $1.5 billion for Notre Dame.

It did not prove quite as easy for Fathers Ted and Ned to oversee changes and transitions in Notre Dame's football program as they did in the development domain. This was a time of real challenge in college athletics. There was action aplenty both on and off the field during the last decade of the Hesburgh-Joyce partnership, and Notre Dame was in the midst of it. In 1976 Father Joyce played a key role in the formation of the College Football Association (CFA), which aimed to wrest a bigger share of television football revenue for its major football school members away from the iron grip and monopoly control of the National Collegiate Athletic Association (NCAA). After successful legal action, the CFA emerged as the dominant voice in college football. Father Ned was an important figure within the organization and very close to its executive director, Charles (Chuck) Neinas. Joyce, Neinas, and their colleagues aimed to derive more income for their schools from football, and in Father Ned's case this meant not only television revenue but also enhanced returns from royalties, licensing fees, and advertising. The college football juggernaut that "monetizes every aspect of the game" was dramatically enhanced during this period.[51]

Meanwhile, Father Hesburgh still maintained the seeming high ground and gave earnest talks extolling the virtues of intercollegiate athletics. In his speech at the annual Notre Dame football banquet in 1981 he lamented the number of schools that were under NCAA disciplinary probation for cheating of one sort or another. He argued that university presidents had to help keep athletics in perspective. Speaking as if using his old notes from the 1950s when he dealt with Coach Frank Leahy, he rather blithely noted to the assembled players and coaches that "it is a game, no more, no less." Most of them thought differently and rightly so, given the time and commitment they devoted to this "game." Father Ted emphasized that the players were "first and foremost students," and he argued that Notre Dame should serve as a model for intercollegiate athletics in maintaining high standards.[52] He presented himself as the defender of college athletics done right, and he worked to that end. Yet he never confronted effectively the contradictions involved when big money dominated college sports and markedly increased the pressure to win. He was fully aware of all of Father Joyce's activities, but he seemed to operate on a separate track that allowed him to maintain an air of innocence as to what was really happening in the world of big-time athletics, where various interests were ravenous for ever greater returns on investments. That said, he did operate on occasion as a brake on Father Ned's plans to derive ever more revenue from football. Joyce proposed a major expansion of the venerable but aging stadium and recommended funding it through the sale of skyboxes and premium seating to corporations and wealthy individuals. Hesburgh told me, "I never let him go ahead with [the proposal] because it didn't feel right." As he saw it, to focus such attention on the football stadium risked "jeopardizing the academic [mission] at the price of promoting athletics."[53] He refused to pay that price. Father Joyce also placed some restraints on his own revenue generating efforts. According to Allen Sack, he "turned down two opportunities [in 1984 and 1987] for Notre Dame to negotiate separate agreements with the television networks out of loyalty to the CFA."

While the business side of the football juggernaut rolled on, the performance of the team on the field was uneven during Father Ted's final decade in office. To a superficial observer the late 1970s constituted yet another glory period for Notre Dame. Ara Parseghian's experienced successor Dan Devine compiled an impressive 53-16-1 record (.764), which put him in the same vicinity as the truly great Notre Dame coaches. After solid seasons in 1975 and 1976, Devine's 1977 team under the brilliant guidance of quarterback Joe Montana went on to win the national championship. That season featured the famous "green jersey" triumph against USC, which entered into Notre Dame folklore. Devine's teams provided other thrilling victories, and such successes should have endeared Devine to the Irish faithful. But the needed chemistry between coach and fans simply failed to develop. Devine lacked charisma and from the outset seemed somehow lacking when compared with his popular predecessor. The "dump Devine" signs could be held at bay during his successes, but the least sign of faltering brought his critics out of the woodwork. Devine also failed to gain the full respect of his players, and, according to the team chaplain Fr. Jim Riehle, morale became an issue. Riehle remembered that both Moose Krause and Father Joyce began to express private concerns about whether Devine was a good fit for Notre Dame.[54] Apparently Devine reached the conclusion that he was not, and on August 15, 1980, he announced that the upcoming season would be his last as head coach. General relief greeted his announcement, and great anticipation awaited the naming of his successor. Hesburgh had built no close relationship with Devine and stood apart from the deliberations concerning him. He made no effort to persuade Devine to stay, and he too seemed glad to move Notre Dame football on to its next chapter.

In the fall of 1980, Father Joyce made two major appointments. On October 10 Moose Krause stepped down as athletic director and Joyce announced that Gene Corrigan, the athletic director at the University of Virginia, would take his place. Father Ted recalled that Corrigan and his wife "were very dear friends of Ned's." Joyce and Corrigan had come to know each other over recent years through their various associations in college athletics. Hesburgh described Gene Corrigan as "a wonderful guy," and the new athletic director brought to Notre Dame a more modern appreciation of the developments in athletics. Joyce knew exactly whom he wanted as athletic director, and it seems he was equally sure whom he wanted to replace Devine. Hesburgh readily acquiesced in his decision. On November 24 their selection of Gerard Anthony (Gerry) Faust as Notre Dame's football coach was announced. Not deterred by Hesburgh's failed experiment with Terry Brennan, Joyce recruited Faust despite his total lack of head coaching experience at the college level. Faust's stellar record as the football coach at Archbishop Moeller High School in Cincinnati, where he racked up a number of high school state championships, won the day. Additionally, Joyce wanted a good fit as coach—someone who would reflect the values and spirit of Notre Dame and with whom the Irish alumni and extended fan base would readily identify. Faust, a devout Catholic, whom Father Ted described "as totally dedicated to Notre Dame, almost with a passion," appeared cut out for the role.[55] He had always dreamed of coaching Notre Dame, and after he signed a five-year contract he had his chance. Sadly, for him and for Notre Dame, his golden dreams of winning national championships never became a reality.[56]

Gerry Faust won his opening game at Notre Dame in 1981, but thereafter defeats occurred with regularity. Notre Dame finished the season 5-6, the school's first losing season since Parseghian took over as head coach. Four more mediocre seasons followed as Faust's teams went 30-26-1 from 1981 through 1985. Calls for the coach's dismissal grew, and after the end of his fourth season Faust went to see Father Ted seeking reassurance. As is noted in *God, Country, Notre Dame*, Faust petitioned, "Padre, I'd love another season. I think this [coming] year's going to be great." Hesburgh reassured him that he did not need to ask for a fifth year. In the Hesburgh account Faust expressed surprise and observed that "at any other school in the country, they'd buy me out." This was the perfect setup line for Hesburgh to proudly reply: "I know, Gerry, but we aren't any other school. We said five years. Five years it is." In retrospect Hesburgh believed that staying with Gerry Faust benefited Notre Dame: "It showed people that when we made a contract, we stood behind it, and that while winning was important to us, it was not the only thing we cared about." Faust resigned the following year. If he hadn't, Hesburgh and Joyce planned to fire him, despite their continued personal affection for him. They had already determined who would take his place. Two days after Faust revealed his decision to resign, Lou Holtz, then the head coach at Minnesota, was named as his successor.

Hesburgh always regarded Gerry Faust with deep affection, but he grew to love Lou Holtz. Father Joyce took the lead in selecting the new coach. Holtz had dreamed of coaching Notre Dame just as had Gerry Faust. But unlike Faust he had extensive head coach experience, having overseen football programs at William & Mary, North Carolina State, Arkansas, and Minnesota before coming to Notre Dame.[57] He even tried his hand at coaching in the pro ranks, but his unhappy experience with the New York Jets in 1976 convinced him that college coaching was his forte. He brought enormous gifts as a motivator with him and a track record for rescuing flailing programs. He did not need to be persuaded to come to Notre Dame to salvage its football reputation. Lou Holtz coached Notre Dame for only one season under Hesburgh's presidency, and it was a losing season. The wiry and wily coach undertook to resuscitate the program, and it was apparent from his first day that he would do it. In his second season Holtz improved to 8-4 and won a bid for the Cotton Bowl. Then his 1988 team went undefeated, and after a victory over West Virginia in the Fiesta Bowl it claimed the national championship. Notre Dame football was back on top under the coach whom Joyce had selected and Hesburgh had approved. Memories of the failed experiment with Gerry Faust soon receded. If Hesburgh and Joyce had retired in 1985 during the Faust years they would have been remembered for leaving the football program in sad condition, but Holtz's rapid success gave them the opportunity to depart with a sense that the program was well launched on a return to glory, to borrow a phrase much favored by Notre Dame fans.

Additionally, Hesburgh understood immediately that Holtz truly was a tremendous fit for Notre Dame. He loved that the coach was a daily communicant at the 6:30 a.m. Mass at the Crypt at Sacred Heart. Furthermore, Holtz was a terrific speaker—both witty and moving—who quickly won the student body and the alumni to his side. Holtz articulated the spirit of Notre Dame effectively. In a letter he wrote to his team in the spring of 1987, he exuded heartfelt sentiments, which may seem schmaltzy to anyone but the Notre Dame true believers. He explained to his players, of whom probably half were not Catholic, that Notre Dame was "founded as a tribute to Our Lady on the Dome." He quoted Father Sorin to the effect that "I've raised Our Lady aloft so that men will know without asking, why we have succeeded here." He proceeded to lecture his team on the Notre Dame mystique: "When we do what is right, we bring glory and honor to Notre Dame. When we win in football, we help this university. To reach your potential, you must learn to love this university. Put your faith, confidence and belief in Jesus. That is what this university is all about. It's your decision, but I firmly believe that Our Lady on the Dome will watch out for you. Spend some time at the Grotto, and you'll discover that this school is special. There is a special mystique about it. You are special for being here, a student at Notre Dame."⁵⁸ Holtz also extolled the virtues of loyalty, respect, discipline, brotherly love for teammates, courtesy, perseverance, and the need to strive for perfection. Father Ted lapped it all up enthusiastically and soon established a bond with Holtz.

Hesburgh and Joyce began the practice of taking Holtz and his wife, Beth, out to the Summit Club on a somewhat regular basis for dinner and good conversation. They began this custom during Holtz's initial year as coach and continued it in their retirement. Hesburgh loved these occasions, and, according to him, Beth Holtz would call him up to say thank you and would report how much her husband treasured these dinners. Hesburgh believed he and Joyce were providing emotional support for the always-intense coach in a way that their successors did not. He also appreciated that Holtz supported his postpresidential efforts. Hesburgh drew special attention to Holtz's providing a substantial donation to cover the publication expenses and honoraria for all contributors to his edited volume *The Challenge and Promise of a Catholic University* (1994).⁵⁹ He remained forever proud that he and Joyce had brought Lou Holtz to Notre Dame, and he was delighted that Holtz's impressive success eventually won him a place beside Rockne, Leahy, and Parseghian as a Notre Dame coaching immortal.

CHOOSING A SUCCESSOR AND SAYING GOOD-BYE

In February 1979 Father Hesburgh gave an extended interview to two editors from the *Observer*, Chris Stewart and Tony Pace. The student journalists pushed him with surprising vigor on a number of fronts, including whether he had "any intention of stepping down in the near future." Father Ted parried them with the rather cute response that he "retired" every year, but that "the board of trustees refused to accept his resignation." He claimed that he had alerted the trustees that he was on the "downswing," and advised his questioners that "I'm not eternal by any means." While assuredly not immortal, Father Ted had no intention of entering into retirement at that time. Earlier in the interview he defended his commitment on campus as president, despite his many off-campus duties. He spoke of the students he saw, the residence halls he visited, and the guest lectures he gave in classes, and he argued that "I'm more involved around here than most college presidents I know are in any way."⁶⁰ Truth be told, he was giving some thought to transitioning from the president's role. The question of determining who would replace him surfaced periodically over the coming years. It proved difficult to answer.

While Burtchaell was serving as provost and was seen as the unofficial heir-apparent from 1970 onward, the matter of a smooth transition in the leadership of Notre Dame seemed in place. But his dismissal in 1977 cast such plans to the wind, and neither Hesburgh nor the trustees had a ready backup option. Hesburgh's friend and confidant Ed Stephan remained chair of the board of trustees, and he gently began to inquire of Hesburgh as to who might succeed him. Once Tim O'Meara was in place and clearly handling the daily operations of the university, Father Ted began to give some renewed consideration to a proposal that had been first raised in the 1960s. It had been suggested at that time that George Shuster succeed him as president and that Hesburgh would move to the position of chancellor. He had rejected that possibility, but now he revisited the idea and concluded that his ascent to the role of chancellor would allow him to devote even more time both to representing the university to external constituencies and to pursuing his broader public commitments. In 1980 Father Ted announced that he would retire as president in June of 1982 upon the completion of three decades of service in the position. The task then was to find a capable Holy Cross priest to take on the presidential duties, as required by the university statutes. Although the trustees formed an ad hoc committee that held nominal responsibility for a search to replace him, Father Ted involved himself directly. He vetoed both David Burrell and Ernie Bartell as simply not suited for the position for reasons that need not be repeated. In this situation Hesburgh then focused his attention on Father Thomas Blantz, who had served for some years as vice president for student affairs but was now content to teach popular courses in the history department.

According to the Hesburgh account, one night he approached Blantz and explained: "Tom, we've got a board discussion coming up on the future, and looking over the whole crowd I think you are the most stable, steady, responsible kind of guy in this whole community." He went further and told his confrere, "I would like to put your name forward as a candidate to succeed me. And the odds are, if I put you forward as the only candidate, that's what will happen." Father Ted confidently expected that the trustees would do as he recommended. Blantz, in Father Ted's recollection, was surprised by his request and asked for time to think about it. Hesburgh believed that Blantz would be a steady hand on the tiller, and he further believed that the broad direction of the university was well set and required more of a manager than an innovator. In his mind, it would be the task of his successor to simply build on what he had accomplished and to consult him for any guidance. In practice this offer potentially involved a redefinition, even a diminution, of the presidency because a new occupant of the office would be situated between a strong provost and a much-celebrated chancellor. In Hesburgh's recollection he awoke the morning after his conversation with his chosen successor and found a note under the door of his Corby Hall room. In it he recalled that Blantz had written: "I walked this campus all night long and now as the sun is rising I must tell you that I can't under any circumstances do this."[61]

Blantz's refusal of his offer surprised Father Hesburgh, but he accepted it. He conveyed the situation to Edmund Stephan, who was still the chair of the board of trustees. They had no other options to pursue, and neither did other members of the trustees' committee who were waiting for directions from Hesburgh. After the trustees' meeting in October 1981, Stephan announced that Father Hesburgh would serve a further five years and would retire in June of 1987 rather than in 1982. He clarified that the trustees' committee had received "recommendations from numerous sources" and determined that the present "great leadership" of the university needed to continue. He explained for the benefit of any doubters that Father Hesburgh was a man "who is in rigorously good health and as intellectually alive as I have ever seen him." Putting the best light on the failure to find a suitable successor, he asserted that the trustees had concluded that they simply could not change "such a winning situation" as presently existed at Notre Dame. Hesburgh displayed a certain resigned obedience to the call of duty. According to the *Observer* report that was published shortly after the October trustees' meeting, he commented that he was "not 'jumping for joy' over the trustees' decision because he felt that now would be a good time to 'get out.'" He explained further, "I had pretty much psychologically prepared myself to be Chancellor and someone else President," but said that he had to respond favorably to the trustees' request.[62] Acceding to the request presented him with no great difficulties. He remained in vigorous good health as Stephan noted, and took some satisfaction in being required to continue on.

The news of Father Ted's further renewal hardly surprised the people on campus. The *Observer*'s cartoonist Michael Molinelli, in his comic strip *Molarity*, poked gentle fun at the trustees conducting a search that selected Father Hesburgh to replace himself.[63] Most other campus observers reacted with equanimity. The faculty knew well from Father Ted's lengthy disquisitions about his activities at the annual end-of-year banquets just how much he relished his presidential role. Tim O'Meara seemed especially pleased by the news. Yet some concerns existed among the trustees. According to Father Ted they chided him on failing to groom a successor and clarified that this would be an essential task that he must undertake in the upcoming five-year term. As an initial step in this regard a number of younger Holy Cross religious were identified as potential leaders and given new assignments to provide them with more administrative experience. Right after the announcement of his five-year renewal Hesburgh made a number of notable appointments.[64] Edward "Monk" Malloy was named vice president and associate provost to succeed Fr. Ferdinand Brown. William (Bill) Beauchamp was assigned to assist Father Joyce in his duties and to learn from him. David Tyson came to Hesburgh's office as his special assistant. In addition to these younger religious, Ernie Bartell was included on the list as executive director of the Kellogg Institute. Knowledgeable observers appreciated well that the trustees had formed a pool of candidates from which Hesburgh's successor would be named in five years or so.

In the spring of 1986 Thomas Carney, who had replaced Ed Stephan as chair of the board of trustees, began the formal search process to select a new president for Notre Dame. He requested input from faculty, students, and alumni and, of course, he also formally consulted the Congregation of Holy Cross. Father Richard (Dick) Warner had by this point succeeded Bill Lewers as provincial of the Indiana Province, and he served as an active member of the nominating committee of the board. In the fall of 1986 the nominating committee released the names of five candidates who had been selected for formal interviews. Father Michael McCafferty joined the list of Malloy, Beauchamp, Tyson, and Bartell. McCafferty taught in the Law School and possessed notable qualities, but he had rather recently battled lymphatic cancer. By the fall of 1986 Don Keough, the president of the Coca-Cola Company, had succeeded Tom Carney, and he oversaw the final stages of the search. He and Stephan and Carney (as former chairs) along with Andrew McKenna, the new vice chair of the board, and Dick Warner were joined by four other trustees on the nominating committee. Hesburgh technically belonged to the committee, but he formally removed himself from the process of choosing the priest who would succeed him. Informally, however, he gave his input especially through the conduits of Keough, Stephan, and Carney. According to Father Ted it was not a difficult

choice. He judged Bartell as too much of "a nervous Nellie" to be considered seriously for the post. McCafferty's previous ill health and concerns for
his future health ruled him out. Hesburgh liked Tyson but found him lacking in intellectual heft and seriousness. The choice as he saw it lay between
Malloy and Beauchamp. Hesburgh judged Beauchamp to be "personable
and bright," but more suited for Ned Joyce's position as executive vice president. He knew that Malloy "desperately wanted the job" and that he was,
in fact, the best suited for it. In his telling, the inner core of powerful trustees felt likewise, but, upon his recommendation, they conveyed to Malloy
that his selection bore the "condition that Tim O'Meara [receive] the same
time appointment that he did." Hesburgh later resented what he labeled
Dick Warner's exaggerated claims of having played a key role as provincial
in the nominating committee deliberations so as to secure the presidency
for Malloy. In Father Ted's telling, Keough, Stephan, and Carney were the
decisive players, and he was a kind of gray eminence consultant for them.[65]

On November 13, 1986, the nominating committee settled on Father
Edward Malloy as its choice. The next day the full board of trustees endorsed their recommendation and elected Malloy as the sixteenth president
of the university. Malloy immediately asked that the trustees appoint Tim
O'Meara to serve the same five-year term to which he had just been named.
Malloy also asked that Bill Beauchamp be elected executive vice president
for a five-year term beginning July 1, 1987.[66] He clearly had given thought
to who would fill the major positions in his administration. According to
Father Ted's recollection, Father Joyce initially had not wished to end his
service as executive vice president and thought he might stay on under a
new president. But Hesburgh clarified for his longtime associate that having come in together they needed "to walk off together," thereby allowing
the new president at least some leeway to establish his own administration.[67]

With their successors announced, the long farewell by the priestly pair
that had served together since 1952 could begin in earnest. Monk Malloy
enjoyed only a brief moment in the spotlight before attention reverted back
to Father Hesburgh. Over the next six months special issues of campus
publications appeared extolling "The Hesburgh Years."[68] Father Ted gave
seemingly endless interviews and was the subject of numerous articles and
personal profiles all seeking to capture the accomplishments and contribution of Notre Dame's fifteenth president. In his interviews he stressed
the importance of the 1967 decision to transfer ownership of the university
from the Congregation of Holy Cross to the board of fellows and the 1972

decision to admit undergraduate women as the key ones during his tenure. He also focused attention on the sheer growth of the school during his long presidency. He could recite various statistics with ease. Undergraduate enrollment had risen from approximately 4,400 in 1952 to over 7,500 in 1986. The expansion of the graduate and professional schools was even more notable, jumping from less than 600 students in Hesburgh's first year to over 2,100 in his last. He could also quote readily the impressive growth across a wide array of categories including the annual operating budget, total faculty, endowment, physical facilities, library holdings, and financial aid.

Hesburgh did not choose to go quietly into the good night. He welcomed and enjoyed the numerous farewells, despite his occasional modest protests that it was all too much. He especially enjoyed the rousing picnic send-off that the undergraduate students gave him and Father Ned. The two priests surprised them by arriving at the event on the South Quad riding red scooters and wearing matching helmets and motorcycle jackets. The formal opening of the Strategic Moment campaign on May 9 doubled as a giant farewell celebration for Fathers Hesburgh and Joyce. Hesburgh's farewell speech was broadcast via satellite to alumni groups not only throughout the United States but around the world. The university already had honored him by naming the Memorial Library for him, just as the Athletic and Convocation Center was named for Father Joyce. The honors continued. In the spring of 1987 Hesburgh received the university's Laetare Medal, awarded to American Catholics of distinction. It appeared a little unseemly that the university was using this award to reward its own—Ed Stephan and his wife had received it in 1983 and Tom Carney and his wife in 1986—but few commentators complained about Hesburgh. Clearly he had been a prominent figure in American Catholic life for over three decades, and he stood out for his influential contribution in American Catholic higher education. Only serious conservatives like Monsignor George Kelly, founder of the Fellowship of Catholic Scholars, raised questions about the cost side of the ledger on the Hesburgh balance sheet.[69] They pointed to Land O'Lakes and the distancing of the university from the Church and asked at what price to the Catholic mission had all the measurable progress occurred. Such criticism was dismissed as ill-founded carping among the vast majority of the Notre Dame faithful, including Father Hesburgh.

Harvard's president Derek Bok agreed to travel to Notre Dame to give the commencement address at the final graduation exercises over which Father Hesburgh would preside. Bok had a policy of not giving commencement addresses but overruled himself in order to honor Hesburgh. Bok gave a thoughtful address, but all the attention at the gathering focused on the legendary retiring president. Father Hesburgh's charge to the graduating class of 1987 would be the last time he addressed the whole university community assembled together. He began with one of his favorite quotations, from Alyosha's "Speech at the Stone" at Ilusha's funeral from *The Brothers Karamazov*: "Let us agree that we shall never forget one another, and whatever happens, remember how good it felt when we were all here together, united by a good and decent feeling which made us better people, better probably than we would otherwise have been." Then as "a kind of father figure" he offered some brief parting wisdom. "The days ahead will also have their lessons," he intoned in his still strong voice, "some easily and joyfully learned, and some will etch your very souls in the strong acid of sorrow and adversity. We trust that the values you have learned here—the joy of truth, the exhilaration of beauty, the strength of goodness, the passion for justice, the quiet courage born of prayer, the love and compassion we owe our fellow men, the modesty and humility that our human frailty dictates, the reverence for the inner dignity of all things truly human, for human life from its beginnings to its end—we trust that all of these intellectual and moral qualities will take deeper root and grow in you throughout the days ahead, to enrich you as a person and to add luminosity to your life in a world often dark." Then he offered the graduates as a "parting thought" yet another of his favorite quotations, taken from Winston Churchill's eulogy for Neville Chamberlain delivered in the House of Commons in 1940. He relished reading the passage in his best Churchillian manner: "The only guide to a man is his conscience; the only shield to his memory is his rectitude and sincerity of his actions. It is very imprudent to walk through life without this shield, because we are so often mocked by the failure of our hopes and the upsetting of our calculations; but with this shield, however the fates may play, we march always in the ranks of honor." Finally, the audience heard him say his familiar words: "May Our Blessed Lady, Notre Dame, bless you ever with Her Divine Son—and may each of you ever be a true son or daughter of Notre Dame."[70] Thunderous applause erupted. The alma mater was sung. Soon the stage party processed off the platform and Father Theodore Hesburgh moved down the steps and out of the Joyce Center arena. His long service as president lay behind him. A new stage in his life was about to begin.

PART II

SERVING POPES AND PRESIDENTS

CHAPTER 6

OLD AND NEW:
Dwight Eisenhower, Pius XII, John XXIII, and John F. Kennedy

IKE, SCIENCE, THE ROCKEFELLERS, AND CIVIL RIGHTS

FATHER HESBURGH'S TIMING COULD NOT HAVE BEEN BETTER TO take up opportunities for public service, given developments in the United States. America's participation in World War II had a socially unifying effect and helped break down religious barriers and prejudice against Catholics. Furthermore, in the context of the Cold War that soon followed, Catholics assimilated even more into the mainstream of American society. And Catholicism flourished in the America of the late 1940s and 1950s in most obvious measurable categories. The Catholic middle class increased, and with it the capacity to send sons and daughters to growing Catholic schools and colleges, including, of course, to Notre Dame. Parishes proliferated as Catholics left the confines of defined ethnic neighborhoods and moved to burgeoning suburbs, where they mixed more easily with people of other faiths. One writer has colorfully suggested that Catholics engaged in the "pursuit of suburbia, wealth, respectability, and a place in the American sun."[1] Ted Hesburgh readily participated in his own variation of this Catholic quest to play a larger role in the American story and to secure a firmer role in American society.

Looked at in the long view—and also through the lens of the tumultuous 1960s—the immediate postwar era has taken on a rather rosy glow. There undoubtedly existed an atmosphere of optimism and possibility about what progress American science and technology could accomplish. Yet the period was not without its anxieties. The historian George Marsden has insightfully observed that best-selling books like David Riesman's *The Lonely Crowd* (1950) and Sloan Wilson's *The Man in the Gray Flannel Suit* (1955) evinced a postwar "crisis of liberal belief," communicating concern that "'modern man' had become alienated, inauthentic, conformist, and phony."[2] In addition to this general disquiet, there remained a strong undercurrent of anti-Catholic sentiment that held that Roman Catholicism was incompatible with American democracy. Paul Blanshard gave popular voice to this view, which retained significant influence among more secular American liberals as well as some Protestants (as JFK discovered in 1960).[3]

Father Ted found himself well equipped to navigate his way through the tensions of the age. He loved and believed in America and unashamedly described himself as "a great American patriot." He believed in the promise and potential of America and held that the nation he loved could resolve most problems if only people of goodwill applied themselves to developing proper solutions. He shared the optimism of the age but did not partake of its deepest anxieties. Through the 1950s this Catholic priest assuredly associated with individuals who worried about the influence of clerics like Cardinal Spellman and the power of the Catholic Church, but who felt no such concerns about Notre Dame's handsome young president. His earnest charm, easy openness, and willingness to collaborate with non-Catholics and non-Christians while still holding firm convictions won him respect and friends. His declaration that he was politically independent also gained him regard with moderates on both sides of the political divide who valued him as a potential ally. Without obvious deliberate calculation he allowed himself to become a most acceptable Catholic to non-Catholics while still retaining the confidence and high regard of his fellow Catholics. His political instincts were such that he knew the time was right for such acceptable Catholics to move more fully into the corridors of power in the national government and in America's leading institutions and organizations, which had long been dominated by the Protestant establishment. When the summons came he intended to be ready. He didn't have to wait long.

Sherman Adams, Eisenhower's chief of staff, called Hesburgh one Sunday morning in 1954 and requested that he accept appointment to the twenty-four-member National Science Board, which governed the National Science Foundation. In Hesburgh's recollection he protested mildly that he lacked a sufficient scientific background to make a useful contribution. Ike's key White House assistant quickly explained that the president wanted to appoint him so that he might bring a moral perspective to the board's deliberations. Father Hesburgh accepted the invitation. He took the place on the National Science Board of a Notre Dame faculty member, Dr. James Reyniers, a microbiologist who directed LOBUND (and whom Hesburgh later fired).[4] He embraced the role. A great admirer of General Eisenhower, Hesburgh had voted for him.[5] Although he formally registered as an independent, he favored Eisenhower's internationalist wing of the Republican Party over the more isolationist/nationalist wing identified with Senators Robert Taft and John Bricker. His support for the removal of Clarence Manion as dean of the Law School surely indicated where he stood in that contest. Hesburgh felt very much at ease with moderate Republicans like Nelson Rockefeller. He welcomed the chance to use the national government as an instrument for good, and he understood that Ike, despite his reservations about the excessive growth of the national government, believed the same.

Although Father Ted's initial governmental role was then as one of the two dozen members of the National Science Board, he seized all the possibilities of this appointment and played them to the full. There can hardly have been a more enthusiastic member of the board that oversaw the national government's effort to encourage basic scientific research. The National Science Foundation (NSF) had emerged from recommendations in Vannevar Bush's landmark 1945 report *Science: The Endless Frontier*. It helped create a new federal science establishment built on research contracts with universities, research institutes, and engineering and industrial laboratories. Hesburgh proved a wholehearted supporter of funding scientific research of all sorts. It was an almost dizzying period of discovery as the frontiers of knowledge were extended in atomic energy, space, physics, chemistry, and biology. The energetic and intellectually curious Hesburgh never contented himself with attending the occasional board meeting and reading the lengthy reports of the NSF staff. Instead, he traveled widely, inspecting major projects and research facilities and engaging the scientific and engineering researchers in discussion of their work. He served for two six-year terms on the National Science Board and loved every moment, especially his on-site inspection tours. Although he was a most cooperative member of the board, there appears to be little evidence that Father Hesburgh had any major impact on the NSF's key policy directions regarding scientific research. Nonetheless, he regularly affirmed the compatibility of science and religion, and perhaps the mere presence of a Catholic priest on the board played a beneficial role. In the end his experience on the National Science Board was enriching for him personally, and it gave him a platform to "more effectively promote science at Notre Dame."[6]

Father Hesburgh recognized that serving on the National Science Board not only proved a valuable experience for him but was also a beneficial introduction to government service. He deepened his understanding of how the government bureaucracy operated and how funds were allocated, and this proved of practical benefit on future assignments. His service also functioned as a launching pad for him into further assignments and appointments. As a member of the NSF's supervisory group he was recruited to serve on the executive body of the Midwestern Universities Research Association and on the advisory board of the Argonne National Laboratory. One appointment led to another and soon Father Ted was increasingly known as the able Catholic priest who was very well connected in the worlds of higher education and scientific research. Given his ambitions for Notre Dame, Father Hesburgh determined to parlay these initial appointments into entry into the upper reaches of the American establishment. His formidable confidence and drive left him in no doubt that he could contribute in these elite circles, which at least until World War II had been dominated by mainline Protestants. The Rockefeller family provided him with an entrée that brought him into contact with major figures in the U.S. political, intellectual, and cultural establishment. Here he made the acquaintance of and became friends with the so-called best and brightest.[7] In fact, here he became a full-fledged member of this establishment himself.

John D. Rockefeller III invited Father Hesburgh to join the board of the Rockefeller Foundation in 1961. When he did so he noted that they had never had a Catholic on the board before, much less a Catholic priest. The reason that Rockefeller invited this particular Catholic priest from Notre Dame lies in Father Ted's previous associations with him and his brothers Nelson, Laurance, and David, and especially through their various involvements with the Special Studies Project initiated in 1956 by Nelson Rockefeller. This was a major seven-panel planning group funded by the Rockefeller Brothers Fund. It aimed to draw on the best minds and leading experts so as to identify the central problems of the day and to outline how they should be addressed. The ambitious project sought to clarify national purposes and objectives, and in the process it coincidentally aimed to lend Nelson Rockefeller a certain intellectual gravitas and to lay policy foundations for a Rockefeller presidential run in 1960. Rockefeller, as his capable biographer has noted, held the "conviction that any problem could be mastered, if only one assembled the right people and plans."[8] He recruited Ted Hesburgh to join his assembly of "right people" and he gained a most eager participant.

Nelson Rockefeller enlisted a brilliant young Harvard academic named Henry Kissinger as director of the project. The future secretary of state and his small staff did much of the grunt work involved in the preparation of the various reports, and Kissinger's recent biographer has argued that "the experience of managing the Special Studies Project was transformative" for him.[9] The central or overall panel of approximately thirty members, on which Father Hesburgh served, then divided into six groups, each of which was supplemented by further notables and experts. The specialist panels addressed such crucial areas as "International Security Objectives and Strategy" and "U.S. Economic and Social Policy."

Father Ted relished being among "the top people in the country," as he later described them.[10] He met people such as Dean Rusk and John Gardner, with whom he associated regularly in the following years when they became cabinet members. Early in 1957 he wrote to Nelson Rockefeller about the future of the Special Studies Project and intoned that "whatever might result as written conclusions to our discussions, the most important result would be to keep the discussions going, in some permanent form." He praised Rockefeller for bringing together a group "that represents such a broad and comprehensive point of view: academic and 'practical' people, men of experience and wisdom, hard-headed thinkers and intelligent dreamers, philosophers, scientists, theologians, diplomats and military men."[11]

Hesburgh communicated his comments on various draft panel reports either to Kissinger or to the capable executive secretary of the endeavor, Nancy Hanks.[12] He regularly attended the meetings of his own panel and of the full committee. On one issue in particular he felt the need to lay out his concerns directly to Nelson Rockefeller, who planned to run for governor of New York in 1958. In a substantial letter written in April 1958 he wrote about a section on "the economic development of under-developed areas" included in the preliminary report of the panel on "International Economic Objectives and Strategy." This draft suggested that American development support should be conditioned on agreement to adopt population control measures. Hesburgh branded the proposal "completely unrealistic apart from any moral considerations of it." He did deem it immoral, of course, but he tried a more pragmatic argument in hopes of connecting with Rockefeller. He branded it "ridiculous" to tell other countries "that either they must take efficacious steps (whatever these may be) to control their population or we will refuse to help them." He asked what Soviet propaganda would make of this proposal, and argued that the Russians would portray it to developing nations as a case where "the imperialistic forces of the Western World are no longer satisfied merely to exploit them, but now want to put them out of existence." He admitted to "Nelson," whom he admired, that he didn't want to minimize the problem of overpopulation but that the proposal in question ran contrary to the "great human and spiritual qualities" that distinguished American foreign aid programs.[13] Apparently Hesburgh's concerns registered with Rockefeller and other members of the panel. The section on "The Lesser Developed Nations: Rising Expectations and Population Growth" in the final report contained no recommendation that aid be conditioned on the adoption of population control, although it emphasized the challenges posed by "the explosive increase in the world's population."[14]

Hesburgh's amazing ability to make himself liked and appreciated by his fellow Special Studies Project members and to forge friendships stands out. Through these Special Studies Project meetings he came to know other members of the Rockefeller family, including Nelson's older brother John and his younger brothers Laurance and David, each of whom participated in some aspect of the endeavor. He built a rapport with each.[15] Laurance replaced Nelson as chair of the overall panel in May 1958 when Nelson resigned to launch his ultimately successful campaign to unseat Averell Harriman as governor of New York. Father Ted found him quite easy to relate to, but he gravitated especially to the youngest brother, David, and formed a friendship with him that lasted for decades. But his relationship with John D. Rockefeller proved the most consequential in these initial years because the oldest brother recruited him to join the board of the Rockefeller Foundation, the appointment that confirmed his establishment credentials.

In his letter to Nelson Rockefeller objecting to tying foreign aid to population control measures, Father Hesburgh emphasized that he deeply believed in "bringing the benefits of science to the good of humanity everywhere with, I hope, some concern and compassion for the aspiration that every human has some dignity as a creature of God." His confidence in the power of scientific research to benefit the less fortunate drew the older

Rockefeller to him. Nonetheless he sounded out Father Hesburgh about his being a Catholic priest when he invited him to join the foundation board. He observed to his potential recruit: "You might not agree with everything we're doing." According to a revealing interview he gave in 1996, Father Hesburgh remembered replying: "I know I agree with about ninety percent of what you're doing, but there are some things you're doing that I don't agree with like abortion. Every time it comes up I'm going to vote against it and do what I can to change the policy." Rockefeller must have found such terms quite acceptable, knowing full well that Hesburgh would always be a minority voice on the foundation board on these matters. Father Hesburgh was always reticent to discuss any misgivings he might have had about accepting this invitation. Whenever the topic of the Rockefeller Foundation came up in the future, he rushed to emphasize the organization's valuable work in agriculture and education in the developing world. He could provide statistics on how the Green Revolution boosted food production and addressed the problems of world hunger. He engaged in some denial regarding the extent of the foundation's work with population control measures in the developing world and in support of birth control measures and abortion in the United States.

After World War II John D. Rockefeller had emerged as a major proponent of population control and family planning. In 1952 his wealth helped create the Population Council, a key population-control advocacy group that represented itself as being engaged in a "noble effort" to eradicate world hunger and to save the environment by limiting the growth of the world's population. Over the next two decades this group, with the support of the major foundations like Ford and Rockefeller, pushed major population control measures both at home and abroad, as the work of scholars like Donald Critchlow and Matthew Connelly have revealed.[16] Father Hesburgh knew of these efforts but he consigned them to the ten percent of Rockefeller Foundation projects with which he disagreed. Presumably, he hoped that he might be able to influence the foundation to move away from its population control efforts.

Father Hesburgh's willing embrace of the Rockefeller invitation might be seen as involving a problem of what the ethicists term "dirty hands." He accepted the association with population control activities, which from the perspective of a Catholic priest were gravely immoral, because he thought that his contribution to the work of the Rockefeller Foundation would further more important moral ends such as fighting world hunger. It was not exactly a "deal with the devil" in which Father Hesburgh sold out on his opposition to both abortion and enforced population control in order to gain access to the prestige of the Rockefeller Foundation boardroom. He wanted to change the Rockefeller stance on population control and was never at ease with it. In addition to downplaying the Rockefellers' association with population control and to agencies that promoted and funded abortion, Father Ted overestimated his own likely contribution on the foundation board. In essence he acquiesced in the substantial continued support that the Rockefeller Foundation gave to groups like the Population Council and to the Planned Parenthood Federation of America. Fortuitiously for Father Hesburgh and his overall reputation, he did not become best known for his work on the Rockefeller Foundation and his associations with the Rockefeller brothers. Instead, a second appointment from President Eisenhower was the defining assignment of his life beyond Notre Dame.

On September 9, 1957, President Eisenhower signed into law the Civil Rights Act of 1957, the first civil rights legislation passed by Congress since Reconstruction. The legislation sought with quite modest measures to address the entrenched disenfranchisement of African American voters throughout the South. It also established a six-member Civil Rights Commission in the executive branch to gather information on the deprivation of citizens' voting rights. The act required this commission to submit a final report to the president and the Congress within two years, after which it would cease to exist. Eisenhower appointed Hesburgh as one of the six members. In so doing he drew Hesburgh into what had become one of the most important domestic issues of the 1950s, and one that stands in retrospect as the great moral-political issue of the postwar era.

African Americans led the way in challenging the Jim Crow system and in asking the nation to live up to its declared ideals of justice and equality for all citizens. After the war the civil rights cause began to attract greater support among both Republicans and northern Democrats. During Eisenhower's first term, two major developments occurred. First, in May 1954 the Supreme Court unanimously decided in *Brown v. Board of Education* that segregated schools violated the equal protection clause of the Fourteenth Amendment. The court thereby explicitly reversed the *Plessy v. Ferguson* decision (1896), which provided the legal basis for the segregation system in the South. The *Brown* decision met with fierce resistance in Southern states. Eisenhower eventually needed to dispatch units of the 101st Airborne Division to Little Rock, Arkansas, to maintain order when nine black students enrolled at Central High School. Shortly before the crisis in Little Rock, in December 1955, in Montgomery, Alabama, Rosa Parks famously refused to give up her seat to a white man and move to the back of the bus. Her action precipitated the astonishing Montgomery Bus Boycott, which marked the emergence of Dr. Martin Luther King Jr. as a leader in the civil rights movement. He quickly became an inspirational figure for both blacks and whites. He also fashioned the strategy of nonviolent protest and resistance that characterized much of the African American challenge to segregation over the next decade. Thus by the time of the Civil Rights Act of 1957, two of the main streams of the civil rights effort were advancing— the legal challenges with appropriate government enforcement as well as the direct protest by African Americans throughout the South.

Father Hesburgh had observed all these developments from a consider-able distance. Other matters claimed his attention both on and off campus, as we have seen. He supported the modest efforts of integration that oc-curred at Notre Dame in the 1950s, but only very small numbers of African Americans enrolled at the university, and Hesburgh made no special efforts to alter this situation. He gave no particular attention to the broad issue of racial justice, in contrast to priests like the Jesuit John LaFarge, who had formed the Catholic Interracial Council in New York in the 1930s, or Rev. John Cronin of the National Catholic Welfare Conference's Department of Social Action, who drafted the U.S. Catholic bishops' 1958 pastoral let-ter, Discrimination and Christian Conscience, calling for an end of seg-regation. Up through 1957 Father Hesburgh had virtually no contact with those who were directly involved in the civil rights movement, and none with figures like Martin Luther King.[17]

His very lack of involvement in the civil rights movement up to 1957 and the reality that he had no activist leanings on the issue help explain his eventual appointment to the Civil Rights Commission. The White House staff, still led by Sherman Adams, prepared lists of possible candidates for appointment. The group was balanced both geographically and by tem-perament. As Eisenhower requested, three were from the South and three from the North; three were Democrats and two Republicans, with Father Ted listed as independent. All were men, as the historian of the Eisenhower administration and civil rights Robert Burk put it, of "moderate persua-sion" who seemed to accept the restrained Eisenhower approach on civil rights.[18] Ike asked John Hannah, the president of Michigan State University and a former assistant secretary of defense, to chair the group. Civil rights activists tended to discount the potential value of the commission. As Harris Wofford observed in his insightful account of the early years of the Civil Rights Commission, the critics noted that it "was entirely a fact-finding and recommending agency, with no enforcement powers of its own."[19] What, they asked, could possibly result from further study? Still, the Southern segregationists led by Senators Strom Thurmond (South Carolina) and James Eastland (Mississippi) feared any probing into the real situation in the South. Eastland used delaying tactics in the Senate Judiciary Committee to slow confirmation of the commission's members and to restrict its staff. It was hardly an auspicious beginning.

Because of Eastland's delays the commissioners were not formally confirmed until March 1958, but the designated members held an initial meeting in January 1958. Immediately after that meeting Hesburgh called Wofford, a young civil rights lawyer then working at the prestigious Washington firm of Covington and Burling, and asked to meet him in Lafayette Park just across from the White House. Hesburgh asked Wofford if he thought "the Commission could do something important." They talked over the prospects that this new body just possibly might provide "the missing dialogue at the highest level that the racial problem required." The two men established an immediate rapport. Wofford, who grew to love Father Ted, discovered in this priest from Notre Dame "a man of curiosity, compassion, conviction, and courage." Although he judged Hesburgh to be "quite conservative," he discerned that he was so open and direct that he made "a promising participant in any dialogue."[20] After further "long talks" Hesburgh asked Wofford to serve as his legal counsel on the commission. The young lawyer agreed and so began an intense working relationship and a half century of friendship. Harris Wofford helped guide Father Hesburgh in the area of civil rights and helped him emerge as an effective member of the commission.

After initial skepticism about the commission's bona fides, African American complainants began to come forward to testify to the vast discrimination and intimidation that existed to prevent their registering to vote. The commission traveled south to hold hearings and to gather direct testimony. When the commissioners traveled to Montgomery, Alabama, they were forced to seek direct White House intervention to allow them to stay at Maxwell Air Force Base, because there were no integrated accommodations in the city, and Ernest Wilkins and African American staff members needed to be able to stay with the rest of the group. This particular experience had a deep impact on Hesburgh. So too did the "depressingly repetitive testimony of denials of the right to vote" delivered by African American witnesses. The hearings in Alabama and across the South opened his eyes to the extent of the challenge to secure basic rights for African Americans. The racism and injustice they faced appalled him, but he worked thoughtfully within the commission to try to build links with his fellow northerners and his Southern colleagues and to fashion a consensus. Here he followed the lead of John Hannah, whom Michael O'Brien aptly describes as "cool, tough, and competent, accomplishing things through quiet, effective pressure." Hannah set the tenor for the commission while Father Ted lent his full support.

Father Ted loved to tell the story of how he played a pivotal role in building a consensus among the commissioners for their report, which was due to Eisenhower in early September 1959. As the familiar account goes, the commission was meeting in the stifling July heat on an Air Force base outside Shreveport, Louisiana. With the need to make progress on final recommendations for their report now pressing, Hesburgh persuaded Hannah and his colleagues that a change of venue would be beneficial. He called on I. A. O'Shaughnessy, and his generous benefactor sent his private DC-3 plane, which flew the commissioners and staff to Notre Dame's Land O'Lakes property in northern Wisconsin. There, according to Hesburgh, over July 14–15 the well-mixed martinis, the charbroiled steaks, some successful fishing, and the crisp Wisconsin air combined to help a consensus to emerge. Under Father Ted's carefully planned orchestration the six "fishermen" broke through the barriers that divided them.[21] The commission members reached near unanimous agreement on the recommendations that the staff had prepared as the commissioners enjoyed the bonhomie brought on by their pleasant surroundings. Northerners and Southerners enjoyed such harmony that it seemed almost as if the lions and the lambs now lay down together.

It is a wonderful story, but one that needs some qualification. It confuses correlation and causation. Although the agreeable atmosphere of Land O'Lakes undoubtedly helped the commissioners in their deliberations, it was hardly decisive in fashioning their agreement. The crucial ability of John Hannah to forge consensus carried much greater significance. Furthermore, the impact of the commission's hearings throughout the South had more impact on the Southern commissioners than did the crisp Wisconsin air. Two of them, Governor Doyle Carleton and Dean Robert

Storey, recognized that they needed to make some concessions to address the awful circumstances they witnessed. Their willingness to agree to some substantial recommendations made it possible for a report of some consequence to be written. The surprisingly broad consensus reflected in the eventual report does not match the virtual unanimity described by Father Hesburgh. The historian of the early years of the Civil Rights Commission, Foster Rhea Dulles, commented that while there was "an unexpected degree of unity on broad principles," the eventual report "reflected sharp differences of opinion between the Commission's northern and southern members."[22] The staff cleverly fashioned the report, however, to play down the differences over recommendations.

What then of the commission's impact? Dulles's measured assessment "that through authoritative, factual revelations of the discriminations against Negroes so widely prevalent throughout American society, and strong, unequivocal support for the basic principle of equal protection of the laws, the Commission gave significant impetus to the whole struggle for civil rights" seems apposite.[23] The commissioners played a part in the long, cumulative effort of building pressure for national action to be taken on civil rights. Their report provided, as one reviewer noted, "sobering factual confirmation" that "vast numbers of United States citizens suffer crippling disadvantage in housing and education solely by virtue of race; and, most inexcusable of all, even the precious right of franchise is denied to many for the same shameful reason."[24] The report supplemented the efforts of Martin Luther King and his collaborators to make Southern realities known, although it hardly equaled them in stirring the forces to take on entrenched segregation. Nonetheless it was a start for the Civil Rights Commission and a significant one, although Eisenhower largely shelved the report and took no major action in light of its recommendations. The president did recommend (and the Congress subsequently approved) a continuation of the commission. The impact of the body would increase in subsequent years as its internal divisions declined. Dulles argued that in 1959 it was "still the Commission *on* Civil Rights," but it eventually would become "the Commission *for* Civil Rights."

Father Hesburgh's specific contribution and the impact of his commission work upon him needs comment. Without question he became a strong voice within the commission, arguing for actions to address the grievous abuses and indignities suffered by African Americans. His first two years on the commission constituted a crucial learning experience that transformed him into a tireless advocate for civil rights. Father Ted wrote his own supplemental statement to the full commissioners' report, and it gives one an opportunity to ascertain the clarity of his appreciation of what the situation demanded. After explicitly outlining his philosophical and theological convictions that God endowed every human person ("a sacred reality") with innate rights and dignity, he argued that his beloved America needed to fulfill its obligations to supply such rights to all its citizens. He made it clear that America could no longer evade or deny the reality of the issue. And he revealed that he wanted to go far beyond the consensus recommendations of the commission's report—and, in fact, he, John Hannah, and George Johnson (who had replaced Ernest Wilkins) favored a constitutional amendment assuring universal suffrage to all Americans in all elections.

There can be no doubt whatsoever about the admirable nature of Hesburgh's convictions, but his good intentions and actions were not noted by historians of the Eisenhower years. Father Hesburgh is barely mentioned in Robert Burk's study of civil rights and the Eisenhower administration, and Taylor Branch does not comment at all on Hesburgh's specific efforts during the late 1950s in his magisterial *Parting the Waters*.[25] Though Hesburgh's initial impact on the overall civil rights movement may have been modest, his involvement on the Civil Rights Commission had a decisive impact on him and his career. Hesburgh's gravitas as Notre Dame president deepened as he left the campus not simply to hobnob in Manhattan but to hold hearings in Mississippi and Alabama. He began to make the civil rights cause a focus of his speeches in varying contexts and especially with Catholic audiences. Being a commissioner gave him standing to speak with some authority, and he took full advantage of it. He provided good copy and received increasing media attention and exposure. As the Eisenhower administration came to an end, and Ike prepared to pass the presidential baton to JFK, Father Hesburgh had become an increasingly well-known figure in the nation's capital. Hesburgh gladly accepted an extension of his term on the commission. He remained forever grateful to Dwight Eisenhower for tapping him for this worthy national service.

Hesburgh's affection for the president had grown over the years, and it grew further when the president graciously came to Notre Dame as the 1960 commencement speaker. How Hesburgh savored the 1960 graduation exercises with Eisenhower and Cardinal Montini as the featured players, Dr. Tom Dooley and George Shuster in key supporting roles, and himself in the middle directing it all. He orchestrated a meeting in a room at the Morris Inn after the formal ceremonies ended to bring Eisenhower and Montini together. There Father Joyce presented Ike with Notre Dame memorabilia, but Montini introduced a more serious tone by presenting the D-Day commander with a bronze angel statuette that was holding several chains and had a Latin scriptural quotation at its base: *"Et abstulerit vincula de medio eorum"* (He took the chains from their midst). Montini explained to the leader of the "Great Crusade" that "you freed us [Europeans] and we are deeply grateful."[26] President Eisenhower was deeply touched, but so too was Father Ted.

AMBASSADOR FOR PIUS XII AND JOHN XXIII: ATOMIC ENERGY, PEACE, AND *AGGIORNAMENTO*

By the time of the 1960 Notre Dame commencement, Hesburgh not only held his presidential appointments from Eisenhower, but also served as an official ambassador for the Vatican. Father Hesburgh had no deep personal affection for Eugenio Pacelli, whose election to the papacy he had witnessed as a seminarian in Rome on March 2, 1939. He found Pius XII "very formal, stiff, unapproachable, sitting ramrod straight in a chair while receiving visitors." He characterized the pope as constantly "striking a pious pose" so as to appear as "the fourth person of the Blessed Trinity."[27] But it bears saying that his qualms about Pius XII had nothing whatever to do with the scurrilous campaign launched to defame the pope's name and historical reputation. This deliberate campaign to trash Pius's standing began in the West—it was already a staple of Soviet propaganda—with the production in 1963 of Rolf Hochhuth's play *The Deputy,* which charged that Pius had failed in his duty by not speaking out more forcefully against the slaughter of Jews in the Holocaust. It culminated with the disgraceful labeling of Pius by John Cornwell as "Hitler's Pope."[28] Hesburgh was aware of these calumnies and resented them. Whatever his reservations about the persona of Pius XII, he appreciated the pope's wartime interventions to save persecuted Jews, which rightly garnered him both praise and gratitude in the 1950s.

The so-called Pius Wars remained well in the future when Hesburgh began his service for the Vatican. Representing Pius XII therefore bore no whiff of opprobrium at that stage. Quite the opposite, in fact. He had first met Pius XII in a group setting along with all the Holy Cross priests and brothers attending the congregation's general chapter in Rome during July of 1956. A photo of the encounter captures Father Ted solemnly bowing before the pontiff while his occasional antagonist Father Christopher O'Toole hovers right behind him.[29] This brief meeting hardly established a personal relationship, and as Father Ted made clear in his recounting, the initial call to serve as a Vatican delegate came from Cardinal Francis Spellman, New York's powerful archbishop. Pius XII had authorized the cardinal to choose some delegates to the general conference to establish the IAEA, whom the pope would then appoint.

Spellman immediately called the young president of Notre Dame whom he had come to know and like through various social and fund-raising events in New York stretching back to Hesburgh's service as executive vice president of the university. Father Ted acceded to the request. Soon Spellman arranged for Hesburgh and his co-delegate, Dr. Marston Morse, a mathematician at the Institute for Advanced Study in Princeton, to receive instructions giving them "full power to discuss, approve and sign any document of the conference in the name of the Vatican without prior instructions."[30] At the gathering's conclusion Hesburgh and Morse signed the completed statute for the IAEA along with the representatives of over eighty nations. It called for an agency "to accelerate and enlarge the contribution of atomic energy to peace, health and prosperity throughout the world." These efforts were not to facilitate a military purpose in any way.[31] Hesburgh enthusiastically endorsed the goal. From this time forward he became a true believer in the benefits of the peaceful use of nuclear power.

At the close of the New York conference Marston Morse brought his service as a Vatican delegate to an end, but Father Hesburgh continued his. He had enjoyed immensely fraternizing with his fellow diplomats. He even had reached out and befriended a member of the Soviet delegation, Vasily Emelyanov, with whom he established a firm bond. He confidently believed that he had something to contribute on this issue. Hence when Cardinal Spellman called again to ask him to accept an assignment as the Vatican's permanent delegate to the IAEA there was no need for any arm-twisting. That the IAEA would be headquartered in Vienna, and that the general conference of the IAEA would meet for only two weeks each year in September sealed his commitment. With Morse out of the picture Hesburgh suggested Frank Folsom, the recently retired president of the Radio

Corporation of America (RCA), as his co-delegate and got Spellman's immediate approval.[32]

Serving on the IAEA was not an especially taxing assignment for Father Hesburgh. It differed considerably from the heavier demands that his work on the Civil Rights Commission placed upon him, and certainly the accommodations and entertainments in the Austrian capital were more pleasant than those on Air Force bases in the American South. Hesburgh embellished both his efforts and those of the IAEA in his memoir by presenting them as laying essential foundations for the peacemaking efforts that supposedly resolved the Cold War. This, to be kind, oversimplifies matters. The IAEA played a role in certain specific instances, but Father Ted's personal role and that of the Vatican were marginal to the overall work of the IAEA. The official history of the first forty years of the organization mentions neither Hesburgh nor Folsom, although this is understandable. The main work of the organization was undertaken by the professional staff of the IAEA Secretariat, and the primary policy-making body of the organization was the board of governors, which met five times yearly and set most of the direction for the organization. The main function of the general conference to which Father Hesburgh belonged was to act simply as an annual forum for debate on current issues and to allow for a public airing of views.[33] Father Ted's main contribution within the IAEA seems to have come in his notable ability to serve as a social bridge among delegates and as a trustworthy associate for them. He even maintained a formal but friendly relationship with the Soviet resident representative to the IAEA from 1960 to 1961, one Vyacheslav Molotov, and managed to turn a blind eye to all that Molotov had done as one of Josef Stalin's most loyal lieutenants. Hesburgh once served as a valuable go-between in calming differences between John McCone, the head of the U.S. Atomic Energy Commission, and Vasily Emelyanov, by this point the head of Russia's atomic program.[34] He earned McCone's gratitude for doing so.[35]

When Hesburgh and Folsom finished their two-week sojourn in Vienna they then normally traveled to Rome to report on what had transpired before returning home. In 1957 they had a brief formal meeting with Pius XII. Folsom dressed in formal wear with white tie and tails for the occasion, while Hesburgh donned not only his Holy Cross habit but a full-length cape that added to the solemnity of the occasion. The following year it is unlikely that they met the pope as Pius was in ill health and residing at his summer residence, Castel Gandolfo, where he died on October 9. Perhaps they met with Monsignor Domenico Tardini, Pius XII's longtime aide, whom John XXIII made secretary of state. At some point, in Father Ted's telling, Tardini berated them for socializing with Russians like Emelyanov, but they easily deflected him by taking recourse in the Lord's instruction to "Love your enemies." Tardini apparently walked out on their meeting.

The deeply divided papal conclave that met to replace Pius XII eventually settled on the nearly seventy-seven-year-old Patriarch of Venice, Angelo Roncalli, a longtime Vatican diplomat. It appeared that the cardinals looked around for "an interim, seat-warming pope" and resolved upon the rotund Roncalli, who had "a reputation for peaceable holiness and pastoral warmth."[36] The bells of Sacred Heart Church at Notre Dame, Indiana, began to peal soon after 11:00 a.m. on Tuesday, October 28, 1958, to signal the election of a new pope. The campus chaplain, Fr. Glenn Boarman, conveyed the news at the 11:30 a.m. Mass that Cardinal Roncalli had chosen the name John XXIII. Few on campus knew much about the new pontiff, but a *Scholastic* commentary later in the week informed Notre Dame students with some accuracy that "as a tactful diplomat, distinguished author, and vigorous member of several Church departments, Cardinal Roncalli won the respect of the many divergent parties and factions of postwar Europe. But his greatest assets are a jovial and even-tempered sense of humor and a friendly spirit of good will—he has been referred to as the 'optimistic cardinal.'"[37] Pope John's earthy manner and warm personality presented a marked public contrast to his aloof predecessor.

Father Hesburgh held John XXIII in high regard. Looking back from the perspective of the 1990s he stated his belief "that the Holy Spirit worked through John XXIII in extraordinary ways. Vatican Council II was exactly what the Church needed." As he saw it, "John XXIII did more for the Church, the faith, the cause of reform, and the acceptance of Catholicism than anyone since the Reformation." He noted that "having lived about half of my life before Vatican II, I much prefer the half that I have lived since then. John XXIII made the difference."[38]

While his admiration for John XXIII increased as the years passed, Father Hesburgh was immediately caught up in the excitement generated by John's papacy. On January 25, 1959, just ninety days after he had been elected, Pope John surprised the world when he announced he would call an ecumenical council. Hesburgh, like most other Catholics, wondered what exactly might emerge from such a gathering. And wondering about it and praying for it remained all that Father Ted was required to do. He was not drawn into the more than three years of deliberations involved in preparing for the Council, which opened on October 11, 1962. But he resonated fully with the appeal of Pope John for *aggiornamento*—for updating and for opening up the windows of the Church to let in some fresh air. He applauded when Pope John opened the Council and disparaged "the prophets of doom who are always forecasting disaster." He endorsed fully the pope's plea to the Council fathers that "what is needed, and what everyone imbued with a truly Christian, Catholic and apostolic spirit craves today, is that [Church] doctrine shall be more widely known, more deeply understood, and more penetrating in its effects on men's moral lives." Clearly this was not to be a defensive council to combat heresy or to marshal the Church to combat hostile forces. Rather John asked that the "immutable doctrine, be studied afresh, and reformulated in contemporary terms" so that the Church might preach Christ's Gospel more effectively.[39] This was music to Hesburgh's ears.

Father Hesburgh met the pope he so admired only once, probably in 1961, when he and Frank Folsom visited Rome to deliver their IAEA report. Folsom had dropped his formal wear for a regular suit and Hesburgh had discarded his full-length cape, but they lined up on either side of the pope just as they had done with his predecessor. Father Ted told me that speaking to Pope John XXIII was like "talking to the farmer at the corner of the road," perhaps an allusion to Roncalli's peasant background and wit.[40] Father Ted mentioned to the pope that he was from the University of Notre Dame. Pope John, who had never traveled to the United States, asked him if this was the Catholic university in Washington, D.C. Presumably Notre Dame's striving president set the pope straight on his university's location.

Pope John XXIII inaugurated the Second Vatican Council, but he did not live to see it through to completion. He died of stomach cancer on June 3, 1963, less than five years after his election. Yet he had set in motion the processes that would bring enormous change to the Catholic Church. He had given the Council its pastoral and evangelical direction, but only the first session of the great assembly had been completed at the time of his death. Whether the reform process set in motion by convoking an ecumenical council would continue was more in doubt. Father Hesburgh, like others, worried whether the promise of John's papacy would be fulfilled. They took great heart when Giovanni Battista Montini, the holder of an honorary doctorate from Notre Dame no less, was elected as his successor. Pope John's optimism had helped characterize the early years of the 1960s and encouraged those sympathetic to reform like Father Hesburgh. Father Ted's hope for the future undoubtedly owed much to the presidency of the other "John" who loomed large in the early sixties. This was the man who succeeded Eisenhower as president of the United States, and Father Hesburgh knew him well.

TRIALS AND TRIBULATIONS WITH A CATHOLIC IN THE WHITE HOUSE

Father Theodore Hesburgh welcomed the election of John F. Kennedy to the presidency. He voted for him and took some satisfaction that Kennedy's entry into the Oval Office seemed to shatter the last political barrier obstructing America's acceptance of Catholicism. Father Ted hoped to help make JFK's administration fulfill its promise. He exercised his influence in two main areas. The first and most important was civil rights, where he continued his notable service on the Civil Rights Commission. Here he clashed occasionally with the president's brother, Attorney General Robert F. Kennedy (RFK), for whom he bore little affection. Hesburgh also played a role in the launching of the Peace Corps, working cooperatively with JFK's brother-in-law, Sargent Shriver, the member of the Kennedy clan whom he liked and admired most. He knew the Kennedy brothers and Shriver far better than he did any officials in the Eisenhower administration. Yet, surprisingly, his familiarity did not lead to his becoming a Kennedy courtier who thrilled to be allowed access to "Camelot." In fact, he found himself critical of the Kennedys, and he felt a decided preference for both JFK's predecessor and his successor.

In his memoir, Father Hesburgh glided over his relations with JFK. He simply noted that "from time to time I would see Kennedy in the Oval Office on business, but more often we would greet each other at social functions." Then he deftly added with some understatement: "Though we were friendly, I wouldn't say we ever became close friends."[41] The two men, so close in age—Hesburgh born on May 25, 1917, and JFK on May 29 of the same year—shared certain qualities. Ken Woodward, the religion editor at *Newsweek* for four decades, has listed among them "charm, good looks, abundant energy, unusual leadership skills, a gift for sizing up people and situations quickly, optimism and a devotion to public service." Woodward also speculated that Hesburgh recognized that both he and JFK "broke through barriers—of parochialism and of prejudice—to embody, in very different ways, the coming of age of American Catholicism." But Woodward also astutely recognized the "instructive" differences between them. Whereas for political reasons JFK "of necessity had to distance himself from the Church," Hesburgh was "always, everywhere and above all a Catholic and a priest."[42] He saw himself as working from a religious and moral framework, whereas he viewed the Kennedy brothers as guided essentially by political motives, which allowed little space for anything else. Theodore (Ted) Sorensen once clarified for Harris Wofford during the 1960 campaign that "the Kennedy staff's definition of good and bad" was "whatever helps assure the nomination and election of John Kennedy is good; whatever hinders it is bad."[43]

Hesburgh first met John Kennedy at Notre Dame in January 1950 when the young congressman received an honorary degree at the midyear commencement. John Cavanaugh had organized this at Joseph Kennedy's request, and, in retrospect, Hesburgh resented the award. He judged that JFK was a "lousy congressman" who "never showed up" at anything and hardly deserved the award. Indeed, he said that Kennedy was "the last guy in Congress that you'd give an [honorary] degree to at that point."[44] Nonetheless, he played the game that university administrators feel obliged to play in the interest of fostering support for their institutions. Upon becoming president of Notre Dame he followed Cavanaugh's lead and, as already mentioned in Chapter 2, cultivated a relationship with the Kennedy family. John F. Kennedy was appointed to the Arts and Letters Advisory Council (1954), Sargent Shriver joined the Commerce Advisory Council (1953), and RFK was added to the Law School Council (1956). But Hesburgh's attempts to nurture closer relations produced little. Despite Father Ted's efforts, Joe Kennedy distanced himself from both Hesburgh and Notre Dame from the mid-1950s onward, although the Kennedy patriarch retained his close connection with John Cavanaugh. Not much more happened with the new Kennedy generation, although JFK came to campus on occasion. A photo taken in October 1953 captures Senator Kennedy with his beautiful new wife, Jackie, and his sister Eunice Shriver in box seats taking in a game at the Notre Dame football stadium.[45] More notably Kennedy returned in 1957 to accept the Patriot of the Year award from the Notre Dame senior class. His political ambitions had been raised by this point, but Hesburgh did not take him seriously as a presidential contender. He instead gave time and energy to Nelson Rockefeller's Special Studies Project.

After his appointment to the Civil Right Commission and his association with Harris Wofford, Hesburgh came into more regular contact with JFK in Washington, D.C. He remained unimpressed, although Wofford had friendly connections with Kennedy through his chief aide, Ted Sorensen, and he did some informal speech writing for the senator in the area of foreign policy. Hesburgh focused on civil rights and saw Kennedy's record in the area as undistinguished. This influenced his general perception. Although Hesburgh was unaware of it, Kennedy sought to recruit Wofford to join the campaign team he was forming in 1959 in anticipation of a run for the Democratic Party nomination in 1960. Wofford had already committed to join the Notre Dame law faculty at Father Ted's invitation. As Wofford recalled in his memoir, Hesburgh's "skepticism about the Senator, magnified by his reactions to the highhandedness he had experienced from the Senator's father, left him in no mood to release me from my obligation. Knowing how he felt and wanting to carry out his plans, I did not ask him to do so." But declining a request from the Kennedys was no easy task as the young lawyer soon discovered. Joe Kennedy enlisted John Cavanaugh, no less, to go behind Hesburgh's back to pressure Wofford to return to Washington. In the end Hesburgh's chief assistant on civil rights matters agreed to lend part-time assistance to Kennedy from South Bend.[46] He was drawn full-time into the campaign the following year.

Wofford was not the elder Kennedy's only target at Notre Dame. He also wanted to secure the support of Father Cavanaugh to advise on the religious issue, which promised to create difficulties for a Catholic candidate. As early as May 1958 he wrote Hesburgh asking him to release Cavanaugh from his work at the Notre Dame Foundation to assist JFK's senate re-election campaign. In typical quid pro quo fashion, as David Nasaw noted, the elder Kennedy assured Hesburgh of the possibility "that in these discussions with Father Cavanaugh, I might come up with some ideas that might be beneficial to Notre Dame and that would help pay my debt to you for the loan of his services."[47] Hesburgh declined the implicit bribe for Cavanaugh, but late the following year Kennedy went over his head and wrote directly to Superior General Christopher O'Toole seeking Cavanaugh's "assistance to us on ecclesiastical questions in Jack's campaign."[48] Cavanaugh's poor health prevented him from doing much, although this did not inhibit Joseph Kennedy from pressuring him to come up with a list of Notre Dame alumni who could assist his son's campaign in the Wisconsin primary.[49]

In the midst of these various requests and maneuvers, it is notable that neither Joe Kennedy nor his son attempted to enlist Father Hesburgh's support or his counsel. Perhaps they sensed his reservations regarding JFK's stance on the religious question. When JFK's interview in *Look* magazine in 1959—in which he stated his position that "whatever one's religion in his private life may be, for the officeholder, nothing takes precedence over his oath to uphold the Constitution and all its parts including the First Amendment and the strict separation of church and state"—produced some Catholic backlash, Hesburgh remained publicly silent much to Joseph Kennedy's displeasure.[50] The elder Kennedy apparently expected those who had benefited from his donations to rise to his son's defense. Hesburgh chose not to take up that task. Privately he agreed with some of the reservations expressed by the editors of *Ave Maria*, the magazine published by the Holy Cross Order at Notre Dame, who clarified that a man's conscience took precedence even over the obligation to uphold the Constitution. "A man's religious faith was never solely a private matter," the editorial argued, "and always had a bearing on his actions in the public sphere."[51] *Ave Maria* further explained: "No man may rightfully act against his conscience. To relegate your conscience to your 'private life' is not only unrealistic, but dangerous as well . . . because it leads to secularism in public life."[52] Hesburgh recoiled against the absolute separation of church and state that Kennedy proclaimed, and the way in which the politician emphasized his opposition to aid for Catholic education in order to pander to Protestant voters. He also found it somewhat troubling that Kennedy accentuated that he had "attended non-Catholic schools, from elementary grades through to Harvard." Undoubtedly Hesburgh asked what this implied about Catholic schools like Notre Dame and the education they provided.

Whatever his reservations, Hesburgh determined that he had to support JFK. He admitted once that there was some element of tribal loyalty involved. He did not want to see a repetition of Al Smith's 1928 campaign, after which the lesson would be inevitably drawn that a Catholic could never be elected president of the United States. Hesburgh's favorable reaction to Kennedy's visit to Notre Dame in April 1960 confirmed his decision. After defeating Hubert Humphrey in the April 5 Wisconsin primary, JFK planned a couple of days of campaigning in Indiana in anticipation of the state's early May primary. The visit would culminate in a fund-raising "Victory in '60" dinner in the North Dining Hall at Notre Dame to aid the re-election campaign of John Brademas, the young South Bend congressman who was seeking his second term. Kennedy called off most of his campaigning on April 8 and flew back to Washington to vote in favor the 1960 Civil Rights Act, which strengthened federal inspection of voter registration and extended the life of the Civil Rights Commission for a further two years. Kennedy arrived back very late for the dinner at Notre Dame but received a standing ovation and gave a stirring speech. He apologized for being late but explained that he knew everyone was concerned with civil rights and he needed to vote on the legislation.[53] Hesburgh sensed that Kennedy had truly emerged as a campaigner and also had gained some real substance. After the dinner the candidate and the Notre Dame president retired to a corner room at the Morris Inn with a few close aides and talked until around 1:00 a.m. In Father Hesburgh's recollection Kennedy "let his hair down" and made a number of unfiltered observations. He told Hesburgh bluntly that "we're going to steal your professor, Harris Wofford." He also discussed his prospects in the campaign and noted that he had a tough time in Wisconsin on the religion issue, despite his victory. He even wondered aloud if he had made a mistake coming to Notre Dame given the salience of the religion issue, and the upcoming primary in heavily Protestant West Virginia, which he expected to lose.[54] Soon after Kennedy's departure Hesburgh confided to Wofford his support for Kennedy, explaining, "I guess I will opt for vigor and youth." Wofford in turn alerted Hesburgh that JFK had renewed his appeal to him to join his full-time staff and that he had agreed to move to Washington as soon as classes ended.[55] He proved a valuable conduit for Hesburgh into the Kennedy administration, as well as playing a key role in the campaign as a skillful liaison for Kennedy to black and liberal voters.

On May 10, 1960, Kennedy won the West Virginia primary, aided by heavy and well-distributed injections of his father's money. The victory tightened his grip on the Democratic Party's nomination, which he eventually won on the first ballot. Hesburgh remained only an interested observer during the subsequent fall campaign that pitted JFK against Vice President Richard Nixon, whom Father Ted also knew quite well. Hesburgh welcomed Kennedy's extremely close victory over Nixon, but unlike John Cavanaugh, he was not present with the Kennedy family in Hyannisport as they nervously watched the votes come in from crucial states like Illinois. Although he did not have his predecessor's intimacy and easy access to the Kennedy family, once the result was confirmed, he drew satisfaction that a Catholic had broken through the presidential barrier. Also, by that time he knew the president and his family lieutenants quite well, and he expected that his being conversant with them would benefit the cause to which he had become devoted: civil rights. He was in no doubt that he and his colleagues such as John Hannah from the Civil Rights Commission stood in a position to tutor the Kennedys on civil rights issues given all they had learned from their hearings in Alabama, Mississippi, and beyond.

Other matters concerning the president-elect quickly intruded upon Father Hesburgh. Soon after Kennedy's election the prospect of Notre Dame's honoring him with its Laetare Medal, which recognized outstanding service to the Church and society, was raised directly to Father Hesburgh. James (Jim) Murphy, the director of public information, wrote to Father Ted and noted that Kennedy would have to be considered for the award. He rightly noted that the award would "dramatize the advance of the Catholic layman in the nation's affairs," but he recommended against awarding the medal to Kennedy in 1961. The careful Murphy observed of Kennedy that "conceivably he might not appreciate being singled out for such an award so early in his administration." And, he added, "from our own point of view, it might be better to view his leadership as President with some perspective."[56] Hesburgh mulled over the matter, but he appreciated the significance of JFK's election for Catholics and found it difficult to ignore Kennedy's accomplishment when deciding on the Laetare winner. Also he understood the attention that would come to Notre Dame through the award. In a sense he was thinking not only of what he could do for the Kennedy administration, but what the new president could do for Notre Dame. The new year brought some testy moments in each of these domains.

The first meeting between Father Hesburgh and the new president occurred on February 7, 1961. The excitement of the inauguration day had subsided, and JFK was engaged in a round of necessary appointments with officials from various agencies and commissions. Kennedy received Father Ted and John Hannah, who still served as chair of the Civil Rights Commission, and requested that these two Eisenhower appointees continue their service. "He considered them to be highly qualified," as Taylor Branch observed, but he also "did not wish to see expectations of new civil rights policy raised by their resignation and replacement." Branch keenly noted that "the race issue was intruding on Kennedy's early presidency so persistently as to be irksome," especially since "he had been forced to pass over his first choice for secretary of state, Senator J. William Fulbright of Arkansas, because of Fulbright's segregationist voting record."[57] Although it may have been irksome, the "race issue" certainly did not reach the level of a priority for the Kennedy administration. What is more, the president and his brother wanted it that way. Harris Wofford remembered that Robert Kennedy conceded in 1964 that the new team "didn't lie awake at night worrying about [the race issue.]"

In their meeting with JFK, both Hannah and Hesburgh agreed to stay on and continue their work on the commission. But they pushed the president to appoint a White House assistant on civil rights in order, among other duties, to ensure that the president received the commission's views. "I already have a special assistant who is working full-time on that," Kennedy replied quickly, "Harris Wofford." This was news to both commissioners, who had seen Wofford right before their meeting with the president, and the young lawyer had told them he did not have a permanent White House assignment. (Wofford had worked with Sargent Shriver on the talent search to staff the new administration after the election, and now he was assisting him with initial planning for the Peace Corps.) After their Oval Office meeting, John Hannah immediately called Hesburgh's former assistant, who again explained that he had heard nothing of the civil rights position. Just minutes afterward, however, Harris Wofford received a summons to the White House, where he was hastily sworn in as special assistant to the president on civil rights. The visit of Hannah and Hesburgh should receive some credit for JFK's appointment of a staff assistant on civil rights.[58]

Harris Wofford was something of an all-purpose contributor to idealistic causes in the Kennedy administration as evidenced by his appointment on civil rights and also by his work with Shriver in developing the Peace Corps idea. John F. Kennedy had famously proposed during his presidential campaign to a crowd of enthusiastic students at the University of Michigan that he would create "a volunteer corps of Americans to serve the cause of freedom by helping to fight poverty, disease, hunger, and ignorance in the developing nations of the world."[59] Wofford recalled that Hesburgh argued that universities could play an effective role in the recruitment, selection, and training of volunteers and that his views influenced the idea that the overseas projects of the Peace Corps might be administered through contracts with universities and other educational institutions.[60] Hesburgh welcomed the idea of this international volunteer program. As he recalled in his memoir, he believed it to be "a brilliant idea, just the kind of thing this country needed."[61]

Shriver and Wofford did not enlist Father Ted to serve formally on the task force that debated the shape of the Peace Corps through February of

1961 and helped Shriver compile the report that he submitted to JFK on February 28. But Father Ted undoubtedly welcomed JFK's issuing of an executive order the following day that created the Peace Corps "on a temporary pilot basis" as a separate agency within the State Department. And he greeted enthusiastically the naming soon thereafter of Sargent Shriver as its first director.[62] Hesburgh admired not only Shriver's commitment and abilities but also his capacity to navigate his way successfully within the Kennedy clan. He told Scott Stossel, Shriver's biographer, in 2002 that "Sarge is one of the very, very few people who could have married into the Kennedys and survived. The family tends to attract people who are hangers-on or who are looking for shared glory. Sarge kept his independence, which is not easy to do, since they tend to subjugate people."[63] Shriver approached Father Ted even before the executive order was signed and asked for practical help. He wanted Hesburgh and Notre Dame to suggest "a pilot project with which to begin the work of the Peace Corps." Hesburgh gave them three possible locations—Bangladesh (still East Pakistan in 1961), Uganda, and Chile—in each of which Holy Cross missionaries were present. Chile was selected, and Hesburgh began work with Latin American specialists on campus to formulate a plan to put to Shriver and his nascent group.[64]

Coincident with his very early involvement with the Kennedy administration, Father Ted weighed the award of the Laetare Medal for 1961. It did not require lengthy deliberation. On February 14 he wrote directly to JFK that at the first meeting of the award committee "it became obvious that there could be no other first choice this year but your own good self." For Kennedy's benefit he explained that "both from your present position and from the fact that you have demonstrated that a Catholic may become President, you merit this award to the outstanding Catholic layman in a fuller sense than anyone to whom it has previously been given in the long list of distinguished Laetare Medalists."[65] Hesburgh and his committee wanted to recognize JFK for his remarkable political accomplishment.

The issue for Hesburgh in 1961 was not whether Kennedy was worthy of the award, but whether the new president would accept Notre Dame's highest honor. Although Joe Kennedy had hectored Notre Dame in the past to extend various awards to his son, times had changed and Father Ted realized it. So he asked the president whether he would accept the award and leaned on him to do so. He laid out "the alternatives," as he saw them, for Kennedy's benefit. He admitted that "some vocal non-Catholics might raise their eyebrows"; then he quickly added, "on the other hand, I am sure it would be rather incomprehensible to the more than forty million Catholics in this country if anyone but yourself were given the award this year." He left the decision to Kennedy but asked for a quick response, especially if the president declined, because his award committee would need to resume its work. Father Ted highly recommended acceptance, and to encourage that result he offered that "the time, place, and circumstances surrounding the award would be entirely up to your good judgment." And with a final flourish he predictably added an assurance "that we are very proud of your wonderful performance and are continuing to offer a daily Mass for your intentions here at the University."[66]

Whatever the depth (or lack thereof) of JFK's religiosity, he possessed sufficient sensibility of a cultural Catholic of his time to recognize that this was not an easy award to decline. Nonetheless, some kind of debate occurred among his White House inner circle about the correct course. That very pragmatic group knew that certain Protestant "watchdogs" waited like circling vultures to accuse the president of favoring his own faith. Kennedy's team undoubtedly wondered how this recognition from Notre Dame would appear. According to Hesburgh, Ted Sorensen raised the most questions. He questioned the significance of the award, and apparently asked Hesburgh whether Kennedy could get it the following year. Hesburgh told JFK's counselor that "if he doesn't take it this year, he doesn't get it."[67] Perhaps that clarification aided the White House deliberations. Kenny O'Donnell, a close Kennedy aide and a member of the so-called Irish mafia, called Hesburgh and advised that JFK would accept the honor, although no decisions were yet reached on where it would be presented. On March 3 Father Ted sent a handwritten note to "Dear Mr. President" and expressed his "delight." He also reassured him that he had "tried to phrase the announcement this year in a manner that emphasizes the 'university' character of the award."[68]

The announcement of the award of the Laetare Medal to President John F. Kennedy came on March 12. Father Hesburgh kept his word and played down the explicitly "Catholic" dimensions of the award. Kennedy was described as an exemplar for the period—"a kind of landmark for the place of young men in our times, as a symbol of the new energy, vision, and dedicated service of youth to the public welfare." Notre Dame, so the citation read, conferred the award upon him "because of what he has accomplished in so few years, because of his unique position in the long list of distinguished American Catholic laymen, and because of the sincere hope placed in his vision, energy, and dedication by so many Americans of all races and faiths." More emphasis was paid to JFK's energy than to his faith, and this apparently garnered the approval of Pierre Salinger, JFK's press secretary, who vetted the statement. Not surprisingly, the Notre Dame press release advised that the formal presentation would be held at a time and place to be announced later.

The White House eventually allowed Father Hesburgh to present the Laetare Medal to President Kennedy on November 22, 1961, in a brief ceremony in the Oval Office. The president had already had a well-publicized meeting in the late morning of that day with Chancellor Konrad Adenauer of West Germany, and then he met with the members of the Civil Rights Commission, including Hesburgh. After the conclusion of this meeting with the commissioners—around 1:10 p.m.—Father Ted stayed on for the presentation and was joined by Father Joyce, Jim Murphy from public information, and Congressman John Brademas. Father Hesburgh handed the medal to JFK and then read an ornate statement that included such effusions as: "The leader of our land, you understand with warm heart and conscience the relationship between power and responsibility as you design and direct a new course of life and action for a new era in civilization."[69] The president had examined the medal during the reading of the citation and on its completion he simply thanked Hesburgh for the honor. Some photos were taken including some fine shots with Hesburgh and Joyce on either side of JFK. During the photo-op time the conversation focused on informal matters, including the recent controversial Notre Dame–Syracuse football game. Soon the Notre Dame party took its leave. Hesburgh then returned to join his fellow Civil Rights Commission members.[70] He was disappointed by the low-key nature of the event. There was no reception and no serious response from the president upon receiving the award. As the years passed and his criticism of the Kennedys on other issues increased, his resentment of what he saw as a kind of disrespect for the Laetare award deepened. Hesburgh once observed that the furtive nature of the ordeal reminded him of "Nicodemus in the night." As he saw it, Nicodemus chose to meet secretly with the Lord out of fear of his fellow Pharisees, while Hesburgh had the subdued Laetare presentation imposed on him because of the fears of the Kennedy White House of a negative Protestant reaction.

By late 1961 and the time of the Laetare Medal presentation, Hesburgh's efforts to support Sargent Shriver's Peace Corps effort had advanced well, although not without a notable flare-up. Notre Dame's president got heavily involved in the preparation of the proposal to put to the Peace Corps. Eventually, the Notre Dame group settled on the idea of using radio to teach reading and writing to the rural people in the central valley of Chile. After submitting the idea to the Washington headquarters of the Peace Corps, Hesburgh heard nothing for over a month. This caused him some irritation. Then on a trip to Washington for a National Science Board meeting he heard from Shriver, who wanted to see him. When they met, Shriver expressed his enthusiasm for the idea and told Hesburgh that he wanted to get moving on it right away. He asked Hesburgh to go down to Chile to gain the Chilean government's approval, since every project had to be done at the invitation of the foreign government involved. Then the rather heated clash occurred. William Josephson, the legal counsel of the Peace Corps, complained, according to Father Ted's recollection, that the Chile proposal "was our [Notre Dame's] pet project and that the Peace Corps would be involved only to foot the bill." Hesburgh reacted angrily and told Josephson that Notre Dame had developed the proposal at the request of the Peace Corps director, but he needn't worry since he would end the project immediately. Hesburgh got up and walked out on Josephson. Shriver intercepted him before he left the Peace Corps offices and sought to calm down a steaming Hesburgh, a man not noted for public displays of anger. The Peace Corps director confided to Hesburgh that the staff "were gun-shy about the 'Catholic factor.'" As Father Ted explained it later: "He was Catholic, I was Catholic, the President was Catholic, and the project had been put together by a group of Catholics at a Catholic university." Shriver asked if the project could be made less "exclusively Catholic." With a practical problem before him, Hesburgh swung into action and resolved the issue by gaining the support of the Indiana Conference of Higher Education for the project. That secular body then formally sponsored it, although it was based at Notre Dame as previously planned.[71]

Hesburgh involved himself directly and ardently in the Peace Corps project in Chile. He personally negotiated approvals from the Chilean government during a complicated two-week trip to the country. He then selected Walter Langford, from Notre Dame's modern languages department, to be the in-country director. He threw himself willingly into encouraging and supporting the first group of forty-five volunteers who arrived at Notre Dame in the summer of 1961 for their training.[72] Furthermore, illustrative of his pastoral gifts, he stayed in touch with them and future cohorts of volunteers as they pursued their service in Chile, and he visited them on site whenever he could, always saying Mass when he was with them.[73] He truly caught the spirit of the Peace Corps. It reflected his deeply held belief that if education, training, and assistance could be provided from the United States to developing countries, the circumstances of the poor in these nations could be immeasurably improved. He saw the Peace Corps as reflecting the best of the America he loved, and he was truly proud to have played a part in the inception and early stages of the program.

The same deep desire to obtain dignity for men and women in developing countries through the Peace Corps also drove Father Ted's continued efforts to improve the plight of African American citizens in the United States through his work on the Civil Rights Commission. On this issue he found his interlocutors in the Kennedy administration less open to his assistance than was Sargent Shriver. He had held high hopes for the Kennedy team based on Harris Wofford's assurances that JFK was well informed on the issue. By the end of 1961 he had grown more pessimistic as he realized that the new administration gave civil rights legislation a low place on its priorities list, whatever its claims to the contrary. He made little effort either then or in subsequent discussions of the Kennedy administration to hide his disappointment and disagreements. In his oral history interview for the Kennedy Library taped in 1966 he described Theodore Sorensen's favorable portrait of JFK's civil rights endeavors as a "complete misrepresentation of what really happened." As he saw it, "the civil rights issue really imposed itself upon them, rather than they imposing themselves on civil rights."[74] He noted in a lecture at Notre Dame in 1997 that the Kennedys resisted doing much on race issues because of their political concerns about retaining Southern support for JFK's expected re-election bid in 1964.[75] In an interview given in 2011 the then elderly Hesburgh lamented that "the Kennedys put [the commission reports] in the drawer."[76] He had earlier told Dick Conklin that "Jack Kennedy never took a very pleasant view of our commission."[77] In his memoir he simply summarized that he thought JFK "was too cautious in leading the country on civil rights because of the perceived political liabilities inherent in such a battle."[78]

Hesburgh's recognition of the tepid commitment of the Kennedys on civil rights grew demonstrably after the commission presented the president with its five-volume second report at a meeting on November 22, 1961, right before the Laetare Medal presentation. The extensive report— addressing in turn voting, education, employment, housing, and justice—

was based on hearings that had taken place in 1960 and 1961 and outlined in copious detail the brutal discrimination endured by a majority of African Americans across the range of major areas.[79] Commission members (now with a strong majority favoring civil rights efforts) sought to influence the president to take further action and to adopt their recommendations. Hesburgh now viewed the commission as "a kind of national conscience in the matter of civil rights."[80] He also believed that he and his fellow commissioners could serve as "a burr under the saddle of the administration."[81] Yet they found the president in no mood to be goaded along by them. He parried most of their recommendations, and according to Hesburgh's recollection he explained at some length that he could not at the time pursue their proposal for the complete integration of the National Guard and the Army Reserves in the South because of his concerns about the dangerous situation in West Berlin (which he had just discussed with Konrad Adenauer). He could not have these military units in turmoil if he needed to use them in Europe. Hesburgh tried to appreciate the range of issues the president needed to balance, but he drew the conclusion that the commission had received a polite brush-off.

Hesburgh's moral outrage at the worsening situation in the South led him to again append a personal statement to the full commission report. In 1961, arrests, beatings, and bombings had met the efforts of the Freedom Riders of the Congress of Racial Equality (CORE) to challenge segregation in public transportation and facilities. White resistance seemed to be stiffening across the region. Such violence prompted Hesburgh to ask: "Why does America, the foremost bastion of democracy, demonstrate at home so much bitter evidence of the utter disregard for human dignity that we are contesting on so many fronts abroad?" Linking his Christian faith and his deep American convictions, he preached that the "sacredness of the human person" was what separated America from "the communistic belief that man is merely material and temporal, devoid of inherent inalienable rights and, therefore, a thing to be manipulated, used, or abused for political or economic purposes." He decried "the reign of terror" designed "to deter Negroes from registering and voting." He pointedly quoted the scriptural command to love God and neighbor, and noted that there was "no mention here of a white neighbor." But the statement was not simply a cri de coeur and an outpouring of his personal frustration and moral indignation. He also included a pointed barb at the priorities of the Kennedy administration. In memorable words he expounded: "Personally, I don't care if the

United States gets the first man on the moon, if while this is happening on a crash basis we dawdle along here on our corner of the earth, nursing our prejudices, flouting our magnificent Constitution, ignoring the central moral problem of our times, and appearing hypocrites to all the world."[82]

Hesburgh's personal statement and the Civil Rights Commission report failed to have any real impact on the Kennedy administration except to cause it significant irritation, and especially so for Attorney General Robert Kennedy. Robert Kennedy saw John Hannah and his colleagues as always interfering in his oversight of civil rights. He thought of them, in Harris Wofford's words, as like "a runaway grand jury that might suddenly at a critical juncture propose something he didn't want proposed, or turn and criticize him in a sensitive situation."[83] He resented the commission's increasing willingness to call for across-the-board action through both legislative and executive means. In a 1964 interview he admitted his annoyance with the commission and tellingly revealed, "I didn't have any great feeling that they were accomplishing anything of a positive nature." In short, he had "no confidence in them."[84] He directed his anger at the whole commission, but Hesburgh seemed to aggravate him the most on a personal level. When expressing his irritation he noted archly, "and there was always Father Hesburgh coming around the corner telling me what I was doing wrong."[85]

Robert Kennedy aimed his animosity at the commission and worked successfully to control and restrain its activities and investigations. Three times during the turbulent year of 1962 he blocked the commission from holding hearings in Mississippi, where it wanted to expose the vicious tactics being used to prevent blacks from registering to vote.[86] After the commission's third attempt he claimed that such hearings would prejudice the criminal contempt proceedings that the Justice Department was bringing against Governor Ross Barnett for his role in preventing James Meredith from registering as a student at Ole Miss. The commissioners declined to flout the U.S. attorney general's instruction, but they increasingly came under fire from civil rights organizations, who "castigated" the commission "for failing to live up to its obligations and abjectly submitting to the Department of Justice in postponing the Mississippi hearings." The commission's own advisory committee in Mississippi documented "a mounting wave of violence against Negroes and civil rights workers" in the state.[87] It became increasingly difficult for Hannah, Hesburgh, and the other commissioners to stand by mutely. Taylor Branch captures their sentiments well in noting that by late March 1963 "the six commissioners were incensed that their silent submission to the Administration had stretched into a shameful record of complicity."[88] On March 29 the commission met and decided to issue an immediate statement on the situation in Mississippi based on staff research; their statement outlined the state's "flagrant disobedience" in complying with the law. After being advised of the commission's plans, Burke Marshall, head of the Civil Rights Division at the Justice Department, anxiously wrote to his boss. He added a warning that "at least four members [of the Commission] are very doubtful, however, for the long pull, and we may at some point have to face resignations from Hannah, Hesburgh, [Erwin] Griswold and [Robert] Story."[89]

The commissioners did not resign. They continued to urge strongly the need for federal action. Hannah presented their statement on Mississippi to JFK. The president was unhappy with it and alleged to Berl Bernhard, the commission's staff director, that it would "poison an atmosphere that is already pretty bad."[90] Nonetheless, the commission members released their statement on April 16, 1963, to significant public controversy. The report painted a vivid picture of American citizens who "have been shot, set upon by vicious dogs, beaten and otherwise terrorized because they sought the right to vote." But it was the commission's recommendations that stirred the proverbial hornet's nest, for they offered for serious consideration the need to withhold federal funds from Mississippi until it complied with the laws of the United States.[91] Southern senators rose in outrage against the idea, and JFK publicly disagreed with it. All the subsequent details need not detain us, except we must note that in all of this the courageous and steadfast John Hannah held the reins for the Civil Rights Commission with Father Hesburgh in loyal support.

While the Civil Rights Commission aimed to pressure the Kennedy administration through its reports and recommendations, Martin Luther King and his Southern Christian Leadership Conference (SCLC) associates applied much more public pressure. In April 1963 they brought their nonviolent direct action campaign to Birmingham, Alabama, a city generally considered the capital of Southern racism. King led sit-ins and marches aimed explicitly at provoking mass arrests and filling the Birmingham jails. King was imprisoned for nine days before being bonded out, and during that time he wrote his "Letter from a Birmingham Jail." The sight on network television of Bull Connor's police unleashing German shepherd dogs and using cattle prods, clubs, and fire hoses against youthful protestors began to stir the nation's soul. It became harder for the issue to be postponed to a more expedient time. The events in Birmingham, along with the antics of Governor George Wallace in standing in a "schoolhouse door" to prevent the enrollment of two African American students at the University of Alabama, finally forced Kennedy to speak out. On June 11 he addressed the nation and made an eloquent case for civil rights as a moral issue. He called on the Congress to pass a new civil rights bill.

Hesburgh greeted the announcement cautiously. He wanted actions not words. Father Ted sympathized with King and the members of the civil rights movement who continued their protests in an effort to compel the Congress to act. He admired the March on Washington, which took place on August 28, where King delivered his famous "I Have a Dream" speech, but he could not attend it. His efforts remained more formal and were exercised through the Civil Rights Commission. He rarely crossed the line into direct protest actions, no doubt intent on maintaining the decorum deemed appropriate for a commission member. His direct contacts with the major civil rights leaders remained minimal through 1963. When Martin Luther King came to Notre Dame for a fund-raising event at the Stepan Center in late October, neither Hesburgh nor Joyce was available to extend him an official welcome on behalf of the university. Apparently Hesburgh was out of town, and Joyce was required to attend a meeting of the Advisory Council of the College of Business.[92] That King received no formal welcome to campus from a university official struck some in the crowd as a slight.[93] Ironically, the university's president missed a chance to be photographed on his own campus with the noted civil rights leader.

As 1963 neared its end, civil rights had become the major issue facing the country. It had climbed the rungs on the Kennedy administration's priority list. But JFK's call for civil rights legislation gained little traction in the Congress. At the time of Kennedy's death his civil rights bill was bogged down in various congressional committees. Of course, it is possible that he might have redoubled his efforts later and secured something like the Civil Rights Act during 1964, but that must remain in the realm of speculation. Father Hesburgh remained unconvinced as to that possibility.[94]

Given his unfavorable views of JFK on civil rights, it is hardly surprising that Hesburgh also viewed President Kennedy as reluctant to put his faith into action. The Laetare Medal episode clarified for him the political sensitivities of the Kennedy administration about appearing to be too closely associated with Catholicism. Father Ted noted that very few Catholics occupied cabinet-level positions in the Kennedy administration, aside from relatives. Furthermore, he complained that JFK awarded very few Catholics the Presidential Medal of Freedom. He once observed that the president hardly moved in Catholic intellectual and cultural circles, a point substantiated by David Holmes in his fine examination of JFK's religiosity. (Holmes noted how few Catholic friends JFK had, unless you counted his paid retainers of the Irish "mafia," such as Kenny O'Donnell and Dave Powers.)[95] Hesburgh saw that the Kennedys worked out of a political as opposed to a moral or ethical framework. Perhaps he also appreciated to some degree that the Kennedys adopted what James Wolfe described as "modern pragmatism" wherein "they suspended questions of right and wrong and concentrated on what would work in the competent hands of the best and the brightest."[96] In the end, as Hesburgh saw it, administration actions were determined by what would further the political success of JFK and assure his re-election in 1964. But Kennedy would never face re-election. Lee Harvey Oswald's rifle shots ended his life. Father Hesburgh, like every American, was stunned to learn of it.

November 22, 1963, found Father Hesburgh on a mountain outside Boulder, Colorado. He and other members of the National Science Board were inspecting the site for a National Atmospheric Research Laboratory. They returned from the site to the home of the University of Colorado president Joseph Smiley for lunch and there learned that President Kennedy had been shot in Dallas, Texas. Hesburgh tried to pray, but soon discovered that some of the scientists on the board had "the sensitivity of a horseshoe." They planned to continue their deliberations. Hesburgh sat in the afternoon session for a few minutes and then according to his recollection he simply stood up, apologized, and said that he must leave. He got back to Denver late on Friday afternoon and caught a plane to Chicago. Back in Chicago he stayed the night at Notre Dame High School in Niles, Illinois, which was close by O'Hare airport. There he worked with Jim Murphy and released a brief formal statement passing along the sympathy of the Notre Dame community to Mrs. Kennedy, her children, and the entire Kennedy family. The statement noted that it was two years to the day since JFK received the Laetare Medal, and it quoted from the medal citation in praising his "calm determination and imaginative courage."[97] Hesburgh then spoke with Ned Joyce and clarified for him that Notre Dame would *not* be playing the University of Iowa in their scheduled game the next day under any circumstances. Joyce had explained that the Iowa officials still wanted to play the game, that they wanted to have some kind of remembrance ceremony during halftime. Hesburgh directed him to get the team on the charter plane that had brought them to Iowa and to head back home to Notre Dame. Joyce, as always, complied with Hesburgh's instruction.[98]

Hesburgh returned to Notre Dame on the sad Saturday where the campus, like the whole nation, was beset by grief. Father John Cavanaugh already had been flown to Washington the previous night by private plane. The old priest spoke with Jacqueline Kennedy at the White House late that night, when she was still wearing the blood-stained outfit she had worn in Dallas. He offered what consolation he could. The next morning in the East Room and right near JFK's coffin, he offered a Mass for family members and close friends. He prayed for the eternal repose of the slain president's soul. The family thereupon asked Cavanaugh to fly to Hyannisport to console and accompany Joseph Kennedy, who was confined to bed after a severe stroke. Cavanaugh left that afternoon and stayed with the stricken family patriarch for the following three days.[99] Together they watched the funeral and burial of Kennedy's second son, whom he had so relentlessly promoted for high office. At some point after Father Cavanaugh's departure from Washington on Saturday, November 23, Hesburgh spoke with Ethel Kennedy, the wife of Robert Kennedy. She encouraged him to come to the nation's capital to be of support to the family. He readily agreed and flew down on a commercial flight on Sunday. The Mayflower Hotel provided a room for him that overlooked Connecticut Avenue. He greeted Ethel and members of the Skakel family there and had dinner with them. Late in the evening a police detective arranged for him to go over to the Capitol to pray at the president's body, which lay in state in the Rotunda. Riding in a police cruiser and wearing a golden police badge he traveled the short distance to the Capitol. There he was guided by back stairways to the Rotunda. He was allowed to pray right at the side of the coffin, in contrast to the long lines of grief-stricken citizens who passed on either side of it at some distance. In his recollection he met with no other members of the Kennedy family that night or the next day.[100] The need for his assistance to the family apparently had been exaggerated by Ethel Kennedy. However, she arranged a ticket for him for the funeral.

Early on Monday morning, November 25, Father Ted walked the short distance to St. Matthew's Cathedral to say his own Mass for the day. His planned attendance later at the requiem Mass for President Kennedy did not preclude that obligation. At the cathedral he met Boston's Cardinal Richard Cushing, who was to preside at the funeral. Cushing had officiated at the marriage of John Kennedy and Jacqueline Bouvier in 1953 and had baptized their two children—Caroline and John Jr.—and just a few months before had celebrated a Mass for their third child, Patrick Bouvier Kennedy, who had died two days after birth. Cushing also had offered an invocation at JFK's inauguration. There was no question about his being the person to preside at the funeral, although Jackie asked that the auxiliary bishop of Washington, Philip Hannan, deliver the eulogy. The former paratrooper chaplain had known JFK since his earliest days as a congressman after World War II. Father Ted was assigned no role in the service, but was pleasantly surprised when the aging but always friendly Cushing thanked him for coming for the funeral and invited him to attend the Mass and to join him in the sanctuary of the cathedral. So as a result of this fortuitous encounter, Father Ted found himself placed to the side of the main altar occupying a prie-dieu (kneeler) for the ceremony, and with a close view of the congregation during the whole funeral. (He gave his ticket to his sister-in-law Mary, who sat next to Richard Nixon at the service.)[101]

Father Hesburgh's memories of the funeral were a series of mental snapshots. He recalled John Jr. tearing up a program and getting restless and being taken to the back of the church to be cared for there. He remembered Caroline, just five years of age, trying to console and support her mother, who seemed overcome by grief at times. Cushing—battling asthma and emphysema—moved with dispatch through the Latin recitation of the low requiem Mass, celebrated at Mrs. Kennedy's request. Hannan's eulogy consisted mainly of his reading in English five of JFK's favorite scriptural passages, which Jackie Kennedy had approved, and then of a substantial section of JFK's inaugural address.[102] Whatever Hesburgh's reservations about the commitment of Kennedy on civil rights, it would have been nigh impossible for him not to be deeply moved at the president's funeral. And indeed he was stirred emotionally, although unlike so many others he was not so overcome as to shed any tears. His always remarkable self-control prevailed, even in the confines of the dim cathedral on that day when the nation bid farewell to its fallen leader.

Father Hesburgh did not join the Kennedy family, the various national and international dignitaries, and the prelates like Cushing and Hannan in the journey to Arlington National Cemetery for the graveside service. Instead he caught up with his sister-in-law Mary and returned with her to his room at the Mayflower Hotel from where his brother, Jim, and his nephews and nieces had been able to watch the funeral procession pass by on the march from the White House to the cathedral. Without any further calls upon him, Father Ted returned to Notre Dame later that day. Subsequently, he maintained friendly relations with members of the Kennedy family, and especially with Sargent and Eunice Shriver, but he was never an intimate with any of them in the manner of Father Cavanaugh with Joe Kennedy. He was asked neither to provide spiritual counsel nor to extend explicit priestly ministry to any family members.

Back on campus Father Ted tried to make some sense of Kennedy's death for his community. His lead article for a special edition of the *Scholastic* dedicated to the memory of President Kennedy, which appeared on November 26, placed JFK's death in the larger context of the struggle of good against evil. "In this very real world of shining good and blackest evil," he explained, "everyone who works for what is good and noble can expect to unleash against himself, all of the dark irrational power of evil—anger, hatred, and violence." Then in dramatic fashion he proclaimed that "John Kennedy, in a very real sense, was a martyr to these evil forces because he stood without compromise for their opposite realities, peaceful understanding and constructive human fellowship, here and abroad." Having decreed JFK's martyrdom, Hesburgh aimed to use the president's sacrifice to inspire others to walk the road trod by the forces of good. Targeting his Notre Dame student audience he noted that "human rights and human dignity require new champions today and tomorrow" to help take the place of the "great champion" who had been struck down. He asked if the Notre Dame community was "willing to get on the road, or at least prepare well for the day when the road will be ready for us."[103] In some ways Hesburgh's local initiative at Notre Dame paralleled what Lyndon Johnson aimed to do on the national stage, where as he later put it he had "to take the dead man's program and turn it into a martyr's cause."[104] Hesburgh wanted to channel the grief and sadness surrounding Kennedy's death and to guide it into a greater commitment to serve in the world. This coincided well with his hopes for how the more modern university he sought to shape would serve society.

Hesburgh did not continue in this lionizing vein for long. He was not one who succumbed to the notion that the deaths of JFK and John XXIII had combined to change and darken the whole world because of the work they had left unfinished. Rather he held high hopes for their respective successors and believed that the works that good Pope John and President John Kennedy had begun could be continued well by Paul VI and Lyndon Johnson.

CHAPTER 7

THE HEIGHT OF INFLUENCE:
Paul VI, Lyndon Johnson, Richard Nixon, and Gerald Ford

POPE PAUL VI AND PRESIDENT LYNDON B. JOHNSON DIFFERED considerably in temperament and personality. Paul saw himself as a humble servant struggling to guide his church to serve a suffering humanity. Others saw John XXIII's successor—the man whom Pope Francis beatified on October 14, 2014, confirming his life of heroic virtue—as an uncertain leader torn by the divisions in the church that emerged during and after Vatican II. The charge that he was cautious, indecisive, and given to holding contradictory positions earned him "the title 'amletico,' a waverer like Hamlet," although such claims seem overstated.[1] Rather than being burdened by paralyzing doubt, Paul seemed taxed by the sheer weight of responsibility involved in completing the work of the ecumenical council that his predecessor had called, as well as in implementing its decisions.

In contrast, Lyndon Johnson derived an energy and even dynamism from succeeding John Kennedy. He craved the opportunity to occupy the Oval Office. He set about with enormous skill to implement the program that his slain predecessor had outlined, and then he made plans to move beyond it. He wanted to secure his reputation as a great president by declaring war on poverty and building a truly great society. Rarely was the virtue of humility attributed to the man labeled by a capable biographer as a "flawed giant."[2] Proud, ambitious, and indefatigable are just a few of the more positive descriptions applied to LBJ's personality.

Lyndon Baines Johnson and Paul VI shared a parallel experience during the time they held their respective high offices. Each enjoyed initial triumphs or significant accomplishments followed by tragic failure and public denigration. Father Theodore Hesburgh admired both of these complex men. Whatever their travails in office or the vicissitudes of their reputations subsequently, he never lost his regard for either of them. Yet, although Hesburgh admired Lyndon Johnson more than any other president, he was personally much closer to LBJ's successors, Richard Nixon and Gerald Ford. Nixon assigned Hesburgh more responsibilities than any of his predecessors. He appointed Notre Dame's leader to serve as chair of the U.S. Civil Rights Commission and also called on him to serve on a commission to explore an all-volunteer army. Father Ted related very well with Gerald Ford after the Watergate scandal and cover-up forced Nixon's resignation. He valued the new president's valiant efforts to heal the nation's wounds, which were deep by the time Ford took office.

A FRIEND IN ROME: VATICAN II, TANTUR, AND *HUMANAE VITAE*

Upon his election as pope, Cardinal Montini chose the name Paul, after the great apostle to the Gentiles, to indicate his commitment to the Church's mission to evangelize the world. He made a number of overseas journeys, beginning with his pilgrimage to the Holy Land in 1964, and eventually he visited all the inhabited continents to preach the Gospel. He made a noteworthy, if brief, visit to New York City in 1965, the first reigning pope ever to travel to the United States. For most American Catholics the highlight of his visit was the outdoor Mass at Yankee Stadium in the Bronx attended by over sixty thousand people. His itinerary concluded after a hurried stop at the Vatican exhibition at the 1964–1965 World's Fair. By midnight he departed to return to Rome. In Father Ted's view, he did not allow enough time in America.

By 1965 Notre Dame's president did not need to wait for Paul VI to visit the United States to catch a glimpse of him. He saw the Holy Father regularly during his visits to Rome. He had made a genuine connection with Cardinal Montini during the future pope's visit to Notre Dame in 1960. Hesburgh had been his principal host, and they had walked the campus together conversing in Italian as they went. Montini even ventured into the chapel of each of the residence halls to pray. In their conversations Hesburgh shared his hopes for Notre Dame and advised the future pope of his plans to build a great library. This prompted Montini to speak of his favorite library, the Biblioteca Ambrosiana in Milan. Hesburgh seized the chance to say how he would welcome the opportunity to microfilm—the reigning technology in those days—some of its important collections and to make them more available. The Milan cardinal undertook to help arrange it. When Cardinal Montini left the campus at the end of his visit he presented Father Hesburgh with a limited edition quarto volume containing 248 drawings and sketches by Renaissance masters from the Biblioteca Ambrosiana collection. In the moving inscription he wrote to Father Ted he described himself as "bound forever with chains of esteem, devotion and friendship to a glorious American Catholic University in gratitude and benediction."

Hesburgh's relationship to Pope Paul VI is better characterized as that of a friend rather than as an adviser, although he gave advice on some issues. Hesburgh drew upon his friendship with the pope when Cardinal Pizzardo attempted to block his election as president of the International Federation of Catholic Universities in 1963. He appealed directly to his friend, and the newly elected pope intervened and ordered that Father Ted be allowed to serve in this capacity, thus opening the way for his three terms leading the IFCU. As president of IFCU Hesburgh briefed the Holy Father occasionally on the changes he sought to make regarding the governmental structures and ecclesial arrangements for Catholic higher education. He obtained the pope's broad sanction for his proposals that, as has been noted, aimed to reduce the oversight by Vatican officials of Catholic institutions. Father Ted also continued to brief the pope on the discussions that took place at the annual meetings of the International Atomic Energy Agency in Vienna. Paul VI worried about the dangers of the nuclear arms race, and he found Hesburgh's optimism about the potential for the peaceful use of nuclear power reassuring. On his annual visits to Rome to report on the IAEA meetings, Hesburgh saw the pope not just in a formal session but informally in the papal apartments. Their discussions were more wide ranging in the less formal setting, and Father Ted recalled lobbying the pope to engage in "some degree of détente with the Soviet-bloc nations."[3] He took some credit for planting the seeds of the later *Ostpolitik* efforts of the Vatican's secretary of state Cardinal Agostino Casaroli to improve relations between the Holy See and certain Eastern European nations such as Hungary and Czechoslovakia—efforts that unfortunately made matters much worse for the Catholic Church in those countries.[4]

But for the most part Hesburgh did not take advantage of his privileged access to Pope Paul to push particular issues. Perhaps that was what made it so easy for their friendship to continue. Hesburgh recalled that Pope Paul on occasion asked him: "What can I do for you? What do you want me to do for you?" Hesburgh would reply that he sought nothing; he would advise his papal interlocutor that they should just pray for each other and "that should take care of it."[5] Paul, however, wanted to demonstrate his gratitude for Hesburgh's friendship. In special appreciation for Hesburgh's willingness to assist in launching the ecumenical institute that the pope had conceived, he gave to his American friend the episcopal ring that had been presented to him on his appointment as archbishop of Milan. "I give you my ring," he said as he handed over a beautiful gold ring with a large central emerald surrounded by diamonds. Father Ted thanked his friend but indicated that he would not wear it. Instead he would hold it at Notre Dame. This prompted the pope's secretary, Pasquale Macchi, to berate him later as a "*pazzo Americano*" (a crazy American), but Paul was less troubled.

Paul VI and Ted Hesburgh shared a love of space exploration, and Hesburgh drew on his friendship with NASA administrator James (Jim) Webb to get photos and films recorded by the Ranger and Apollo missions and to show them to the pope. Few are the priests who can record in their memoirs that "over the years I spent many a pleasant evening having dinner with Paul VI and watching space movies afterwards."[6] He recalled that Paul "watched the movies with the innocent delight of a little boy." In this setting he referred to Paul as "Mon Père" instead of the more formal "Très Saint Père" (Very Holy Father) as befit their ease together. On one occasion Paul even celebrated Father Ted's birthday with a cake and a bottle of I. W. Harper Kentucky bourbon so that his friend could have an "American drink." Paul VI poured him a full tumbler, and Hesburgh needed to explain the difference between drinking a glass of table wine and drinking a full tumbler of bourbon, much to the pope's amusement.[7]

The familiarity evident in these harmonious social occasions reflected the fact that Hesburgh endorsed and supported Paul VI's important work bringing Vatican II to a conclusion and implementing its reforms. After John XXIII's death, Paul resolutely saw the Second Vatican Council through its major stages. Hesburgh remembered encouraging him onward and especially during the final session in 1965 when so many important documents were approved. The American priest relished *Gaudium et Spes*, the Pastoral Constitution on the Church in the Modern World, which he viewed as a strong affirmation of his own public efforts to engage and serve society. And he rooted his efforts to change the structures of his university in his understanding of Vatican II's enhancement of the laity's role in the Church. For him "Vatican II was a great motion of the Holy Spirit."[8] It was one he watched as a close-in spectator rather than as a direct participant. Father Ted never directly expressed public disappointment that he had not garnered any role at Vatican II, but his regret prompted him to complain to Pope Paul that in previous Church councils Catholic university rectors had been invited ex officio. To address his complaint Paul instructed Archbishop Pericle Felici, the secretary general of the Council, to welcome any Catholic university leader as an unofficial observer to its deliberations. Father Hesburgh took advantage of the invitation to visit St. Peter's Basilica on the day when the draft declaration on Christian unity was presented to the Council fathers.[9] This was yet another area where Hesburgh welcomed Vatican II's initiatives. He saw the eventual Decree on Ecumenism (*Unitatis Redintegratio*), with its clear commitment to promote "the restoration of unity among all Christians," as a major advance for the Catholic Church.[10] So too did Pope Paul, and he enlisted Father Hesburgh to help establish "an ecumenical institute" to foster the dialogue that had begun at the Council with the various official Protestant, Anglican, and Orthodox observers.

In the Terry Lecture he gave at Yale in 1973 entitled "The Power of Ecumenism," Hesburgh recounted how ten years earlier Paul VI had been inspired to make his request because of two major experiences: first, his meeting in Jerusalem with Athenagoras, the Orthodox Patriarch of Constantinople (Istanbul); and, second, his meeting with the non-Catholic observers at Vatican II. At the latter meeting, in Hesburgh's account, the great Protestant theologian Oscar Cullmann of Basel suggested that "the Holy Father should capture the magic of the hour by creating a place where the Christian theological fraternity born during the council might be continued—an institute where the mystery of salvation, which we all share and cherish, might be studied together in an atmosphere of brotherhood and prayer."[11] Such an institute is what Hesburgh accepted the challenge to establish. During Thanksgiving of 1965 he assembled an international group of theologians from various Christian churches and they agreed to form a council to realize the project. In reality Hesburgh oversaw the project from the beginning to its completion. The end result—the Tantur Ecumenical Institute, occupying a hilltop covered with olive and pine trees between Jerusalem and Bethlehem—always held a special place in Hesburgh's heart.

Examining how Father Hesburgh brought the Tantur project to completion provides further insight into his close relationship with Pope Paul VI.

Upon accepting the charge by the pope, Father Ted turned to raising the funds necessary to construct a building in which the institute would be housed. He wrote to I. A. O'Shaughnessy in August 1964, saying that the project was "most important in the present state of the church in the modern world." He had arranged to bring O'Shaughnessy to Rome to meet the pope, and he assured his generous donor that Paul VI was "a wonderful person," and that the planned project "seems to be uppermost in his mind at the moment."[12] Hesburgh and O'Shaughnessy met the pope at Castel Gandolfo on August 29, 1964, and they discussed the ecumenical endeavor. O'Shaughnessy, according to Hesburgh's memo on the meeting, expressed his support "for promoting the union of Christians in our day," and he encouraged quick movement on the scheme "while the memory of the Holy Father's visit to the Holy Land was still fresh in the minds of the world's people." Paul VI agreed and gratefully received O'Shaughnessy's assurance that he should not "worry about the means of realizing the idea once it was thought out." That meeting at the pope's summer residence wedded O'Shaughnessy to the venture, and he pledged $1 million toward the project. When construction costs far overran the initial estimates, Hesburgh went back to O'Shaughnessy and asked for another million dollars. The Minnesota industrialist simply replied, "Oh well, Ted it's just money. You need it. I got it. You can have $2 million."[13] In the end the project cost significantly more, and O'Shaughnessy came to the rescue each time.

Although the fund-raising proved rather easy, there were difficulties in most other aspects of the Tantur project. Hesburgh remembered that "everything conspired against the project," but it was the Six Day War and its troubled aftermath that caused major delays in fulfilling Paul's ecumenical dream. Nonetheless, demonstrating his resilience, Hesburgh pressed on. Yet, because of the confluence of events outside his control, it took until 1972 to deliver the reality of Tantur. Despite the delay, Hesburgh took pride in the result. He had enlisted Frank Montana, then the head of the Notre Dame architecture school, to design the building. Montana conceived an attractive structure that blended with the land and its history; in fact some observers noted that parts of its exterior resembled the Crusades-era castle that probably stood upon the hill centuries before.

By the time the Tantur Ecumenical Institute opened in 1972, Hesburgh's friendship with Paul VI had been severely tested. Partly this was because of their disagreement over birth control. In the years following the conclusion of Vatican II, Hesburgh applauded Paul's reforms in such major areas as liturgy and Church governance. He welcomed some reduction of the Italian dominance of the Vatican bureaucracy as well as the establishment of permanent Vatican Secretariats for the Laity, the Family, Christian Unity, and Non-Christians. He also supported Paul's efforts to promote world justice and peace. He saw his own efforts to improve the lives of people in the Third World, such as those pursued through his support for Rockefeller Foundation projects, as in synch with the teaching of Paul VI's 1967 encyclical *Populorum Progressio* (The Development of Peoples). But this broad swath of agreement foundered on the rocks of *Humanae Vitae* (Of Human Life), issued on July 25, 1968, in which Paul affirmed the Catholic Church's traditional view of marriage and marital relations, and its continued prohibition against the use of artificial birth control.

There had been some sentiment that the participants at Vatican II should address the related issues of population, family planning, and birth control, but the question had been tabled when Pope John XXIII established a special papal commission to deal with them. Paul VI had affirmed that decision, and he referred the matter to a much enlarged commission that included not only theologians and ethicists, but doctors, scientists, and married couples, including Hesburgh's close friends Pat and Patty Crowley of the Christian Family Movement. The pontifical commission met in a number of secret sessions during 1964 and 1965.[14] Hesburgh was well aware of the meetings. He had a sense from the Crowleys of the way in which the commission's deliberations were moving.[15] It did not surprise him when the majority of the commission wrote a report favoring significant modifications in the Church's traditional teaching so as to allow for birth control in certain circumstances.[16]

It was Paul VI's decision not to accept the majority recommendation that caught Hesburgh by surprise. Notre Dame's president had worked quietly over the previous five years to facilitate a change in Catholic teaching, and like so many Catholics caught up in the reforming spirit of Vatican II he had expected it to be delivered by his papal friend. He was persuaded of the argument that responsible parenthood should mean some limit on family size, although he never publicly made this case himself. Instead, he effectively worked to enable others to build and make the case for the lifting of the Church's ban on contraception. Under his leadership and with his full approval Notre Dame became a special venue for those calling for a change in Church teaching. With Ford and Rockefeller Foundation financial support he had allowed George Shuster to organize the various conferences on the "population problem" at Notre Dame from 1963 through 1967.[17]

In addition to supporting Shuster's work, Hesburgh lent encouragement to a number of other individuals at Notre Dame who were prominent in the birth control debate. He quietly supported the campaign of the Catholic "apologist" Rev. John A. O'Brien, who published various popular articles and pamphlets challenging Church teaching on birth control. On a more local level, Hesburgh also endorsed the efforts of the Notre Dame sociologist William V. D'Antonio, who worked with Shuster in shaping the Committee on Population Growth and Responsible Parenthood. In the spring of 1964 D'Antonio began to speak publicly in favor of contraception, and, in his recollection, "the Holy Cross administrators [of Notre Dame] were quietly supportive."[18]

Such latitude on Father Hesburgh's part must be understood as reflecting his conviction that the Church's teaching on birth control would soon be changed. Significant indications pointed in that direction, including reduced Catholic opposition in the public sphere to liberalized birth control measures. The muted Catholic reaction to the U.S. Supreme Court's 1965 decision in *Griswold v. Connecticut*, which invalidated the Connecticut restrictions on use of birth control, gave evidence of this. And Hesburgh knew that Catholic public officials were dropping their opposition to family planning programs either because of genuine concerns about the issue or in the face of pressure from the population control activists.[19]

Such support for family planning must surely explain his willingness in 1967 to call William D'Antonio to alert him that Mrs. Ernestine Carmichael—the wife of O. C. Carmichael, the South Bend business leader and Notre Dame trustee, as well as the daughter of Notre Dame benefactors Ernie and Ella Morris—planned to establish a Family Planning Center in South Bend. He asked D'Antonio to lend assistance to Mrs. Carmichael and her committee in their effort, which he gladly did.[20] In November of that year the Family Planning Center of St. Joseph County began its operations in offices provided by Memorial Hospital. Within two years the agency underwent a name change to become Planned Parenthood of North Central Indiana, and it sought affiliation with the national Planned Parenthood organization.[21]

The depth of Hesburgh's commitment to the population and birth control issues also was manifest in his continued and deepening involvement with the Rockefeller Foundation. In 1966 he accepted appointment to serve on its executive committee. Again he made clear that he would abstain from voting on issues involving contraception, sterilization, and abortion, but he understood well that the foundation was a major funder of population control projects throughout the world. His efforts to facilitate some aspects of these projects even led him to arrange a confidential meeting between John D. Rockefeller and Pope Paul VI in which Rockefeller presumably explained to the pope the supposed dangers of global overpopulation and the need to take measures to control population growth. Rockefeller consulted with LBJ's national security adviser, McGeorge Bundy, before this trip, and Bundy conveyed how helpful it would be for the Johnson administration if Rockefeller could persuade the pope to take "a more liberal stand on population control."[22] Bundy, whom Hesburgh had invited to Notre Dame to deliver the commencement address in 1965, would have been aware of Hesburgh's role in facilitating the confidential meeting with Pope Paul.[23]

It does not appear that Father Hesburgh personally lobbied or petitioned Paul VI on the birth control issue. He assumed that Paul would accept the recommendation of the majority of his appointed commission. By contrast, the redoubtable American Jesuit John Ford, who served on the birth control commission, "immersed himself in a campaign to persuade Pope Paul VI to uphold the traditional teaching."[24] Although Father Ted enjoyed occasional pleasant evenings with the pope watching space movies, Ford and the formidable Cardinal Ottaviani convinced Paul VI that he must stay faithful to the teachings promulgated by his predecessors, especially Pius XI in his 1930 encyclical *Casti Connubii*. That, in essence, is what *Humanae Vitae* did. Issued on July 25, 1968, the Feast of St. James the Apostle, Paul's long-awaited encyclical acknowledged worldwide rapid population growth and other contemporary challenges, but held that they might be met through greater concern for the common good and by respecting true human values. Holding to such values necessitated his continued defense of the moral law prohibiting artificial birth control.[25]

The extent of Hesburgh's support for family planning and of his efforts to move the Church's teaching on birth control, along with his expectation that change was in the offing, helps explain the shock he experienced when he learned of Paul VI's decision. It came in the midst of the awful summer of 1968, when so many Americans were on edge following the assassinations of Martin Luther King and Robert Kennedy, racial turmoil, Vietnam War protests, and the upheaval in Chicago during the Democratic National Convention. Anxiety was already high, and Paul's decision came as a further blow to those who saw themselves as seeking constructive change in the world. Hesburgh shared in the shock of many American Catholics, like the Crowleys, who felt betrayed by the encyclical. As Critchlow noted, "the American reaction to the encyclical was severe."[26] Protest and challenge were widespread. Hesburgh reacted in a more measured way than did some of his Notre Dame associates. But his failure to express his dismay in a public manner should not be seen as mitigating his disappointment. He profoundly disagreed with Paul's conclusion and could never reconcile himself to the distinction *Humanae Vitae* made between "artificial" and "natural" birth control. He believed that "the moment they say that natural birth control—all that cycle stuff—is okay, then they can't say that it is immoral to have sexual relations when conception is impossible."[27]

Hesburgh blamed Ottaviani for pressuring Paul VI. He explained that "Paul VI, who I love dearly, [was] not a strong guy. He [was] not going to stand up and fight with Ottaviani, and [so] he gets rammed into this corner and he comes out with *Humanae Vitae*." Hesburgh's anger was directed to those who, as he saw it, compelled his timid and irresolute friend to decide against changing Catholic teaching. He believed that they and the decision Paul rendered did serious damage to the Church in the United States. Indeed, in 1998 he stated that "more than anything else I know of, [this] is what has led to the rather perilous position of the Catholic Church in America."[28] He endorsed Andrew Greeley's thesis that the widespread dissatisfaction over the birth control encyclical led to a breakdown of the Church's teaching authority and a greater willingness to ignore papal teaching across the board.

Although Father Ted indicated his continued support for population control efforts, he never directly criticized Pope Paul. He had gladly served as head of the Vatican delegation to a UN conference in Tehran, Iran, held in April–May of 1968 to review the progress made in the twenty years since the adoption of the Universal Declaration of Human Rights. He believed he had contributed well at the gathering, and he saw a possibility of continuing to serve Paul's papacy in similar ways, despite his regret over *Humanae Vitae*. He and Frank Folsom continued their annual labors at the IAEA in the fall of 1968. But Father Ted's disappointment with the birth control encyclical and his belief that Paul had been intimidated to issue it by certain Vatican officials led to concern on his part about where the process of reform was headed in the Church. He found himself in essential agreement with the views of Cardinal Leo Josef Suenens, the archbishop of Malines-Brussels and the primate of Belgium, and a leading progressive figure at Vatican II and thereafter. In the spring of 1969 Suenens gave a lengthy interview to *Informations Catholiques Internationales,* a Catholic newsmagazine published in Paris. The interview was soon translated and published in the United States in the *National Catholic Reporter.* In the interview Suenens blamed the Roman Curia for the crisis of authority in the Church. According to Hesburgh's recollection, Suenens told him of his speaking out: "This is going to cook my goose with the Curia, but I think it is my duty as a cardinal to speak out when I can see that the church is not going the way it is supposed to in light of what happened at Vatican II." Soon thereafter Father Ted left the campus after the difficult 1968–1969 academic year. He and Doc Kenna aimed to revive their spirits with their round-the-world travels. So it was that Father Ted came to be asked for his view about Suenens's comments by a reporter in New Zealand. He responded that "Suenens was a kind of prophet and a very courageous man," and he endorsed the Belgian cardinal's criticisms of the Vatican bureaucracy. His remarks were picked up by the international religious news service, and we must assume that they made their way back to Rome.[29] Herein lay the immediate trigger, although hardly the root cause, of the rupture in his relationship with Pope Paul.

Sometime after Hesburgh's return to Notre Dame from his extensive summer travels he received a call from his good friend Archbishop Edward Heston, who was visiting the United States. Heston, who had served as Father Ted's spiritual director during his seminary days in Rome, had gone on to play an important role as the English language press officer at Vatican II and at this point in time directed the Vatican press operation. Hesburgh saw him often when he passed through Rome. Heston now informed his one-time directee that a senior Vatican official had directed him to advise Father Ted that his interview with the New Zealand reporter "had gravely offended the pope by taking Suenens's side against him." Heston relayed a request that Hesburgh write to the pope explaining that he had been misquoted and apologizing. He also noted that the Vatican official accused Hesburgh of "ingratitude," given the kindness the pope had extended to him. Hesburgh rejected the accusation and clarified that he had endorsed Suenens's criticisms of the Vatican bureaucracy, and that he had never complained against the Holy Father. Heston, attuned to Roman ways, encouraged Hesburgh to overcome his "stubbornness" and to offer an apology so as to smooth over any offense he had caused Paul VI. Hesburgh refused.

He was in no mood to turn the other cheek in response to charges that he deemed ill founded and unfair. His friend warned him that "you better get used to being in the doghouse."[30]

Rather than traveling to Rome to seek some reconciliation with the pope and to clear up any misunderstandings between them, Hesburgh took the occasion of Heston's call to begin a kind of self-ostracism. There was no dramatic break, but he began to reduce his commitments that involved contact with the Vatican. Following the death of Frank Folsom early in 1970 he resigned as Vatican representative to the International Atomic Energy Agency, and soon thereafter he declined to seek a further term as president of IFCU. He reduced his visits to Rome, and he gave up on the social calls that had characterized his relationship with Paul VI. He continued his work on Tantur, but he operated rather independently of the Vatican in doing so. Nonetheless, he still felt able to send Paul VI a lengthy telegram in August 1970 asking for his help in gaining the release of Robert Sam Anson, the former editor of the *Observer*, who had been captured by the Khmer Rouge while reporting for *Time* magazine in Cambodia. The pope assigned the Vatican diplomatic corps to the matter and through its intervention with Prince Norodom Sihanouk's exiled government in Beijing the release of the onetime student journalist and critic of Hesburgh was secured. But such direct requests were rare.

Father Hesburgh always played down the extent of the fracture in his friendship with Paul VI and attributed it to a misunderstanding. He noted an occasion of limited reconciliation when the pope greeted him at the end of a general audience with other Holy Cross religious gathered in Rome for a general chapter. Paul VI, according to Hesburgh, sought him out and complained that he had heard that Hesburgh had been in Rome but that he had not come to visit him. He asked Hesburgh to resume his visits and assured him, "I want to see you."[31] But their brotherly connection could not be restored. It was not possible to resume what they had shared in the first five years of Paul's papacy.

ALL THE WAY WITH LBJ: CIVIL RIGHTS, ESTABLISHMENT PILLAR, VIETNAM

Prior to Lyndon Johnson's assuming office as president, Father Ted had observed the Texan politician at a distance when he served as Democratic

Party majority leader in the Senate, and then as vice president. Hesburgh had not built any close personal relationship with the man who now occupied the Oval Office. Although Notre Dame's president now moved in establishment circles befitting his membership on the Rockefeller Foundation Board, LBJ maintained a resentment of the "East Coast" crowd that he believed held him in disrespect because of his Southern roots. Also Johnson had been kept on the periphery of the Kennedy administration, and Father Ted had not encountered him much in his own work on subjects such as civil rights and the Peace Corps. Thus, he had little grounds to inject himself into any role to assist the new president in carrying the heavy burden that he took up following JFK's assassination. Because a close friendship never developed between them, Father Ted saw the president mainly in larger public settings. He never gained a close awareness of the "difficult, overbearing personality who struggled with inner demons that drove and tormented him."[32] Instead, Hesburgh admired how Johnson skillfully adopted the role "as self-styled executor of the [Kennedy] legacy," who "assumed responsibility for transforming Kennedy's proposals into legislative victories." He came to have a sense of Johnson's persuasive, yet sometimes ruthless and questionable, political tactics, but he accepted that "winning by fair means and foul" was justified by the good ends that Johnson pursued.[33]

In retrospect Father Hesburgh especially admired how the new president was able to strengthen and then bring to fruition JFK's proposed civil rights legislation, although it took some time for this admiration to emerge fully. At first Hesburgh and his colleagues on the Civil Rights Commission found themselves unsure of the new president and his plans regarding their area of special interest. LBJ indicated in his first speech to Congress on November 27, 1963, that he wanted to honor Kennedy's memory through the passage of the proposed civil rights bill. But he made no effort to consult the Civil Rights Commission on that or any other matter. The commission already was in some disarray at the time of Kennedy's death, with turmoil among both the commissioners and staff over the commission's proper role going forward in light of the tensions with Robert Kennedy and his Justice Department. Now, with Johnson heading the administration, the group seemed in "a state of suspended animation." John Hannah, as chair, immediately wrote to the president and eventually received a written response indicating LBJ's desire that the commission continue, but giving the commissioners no real guidance. When the commission met in February of

1964 the group seemed dispirited and confused. Father Hesburgh, according to the minutes of the meeting, deplored the fact "that the Commission did not have at this time—as it had in the past—a clear-cut awareness of what it wanted to do." He indicated his desire for the commission to become more active in Johnson's antipoverty program.[34]

In light of the discouragement among the commission members and Hannah's lack of success in arranging a meeting with the president, Erwin Griswold, a northern member of the commission and the well-connected dean of the Harvard Law School, decided to act. He contacted Abe Fortas, a longtime legal associate who was known to be a Johnson intimate, and "told him of our problem." Proving the adage that, at least in Washington, who one knows is more important than what one knows, Griswold received a call soon thereafter inviting the commission members to visit with the president that very evening.[35] The members made their way from the Mayflower Hotel to the White House around 5:30 p.m. Johnson had been occupied all day with meetings with British Prime Minister Alec Douglas-Home and associated ceremonies, and he still had a formal dinner with the British prime minister and his party scheduled for that evening.[36] The civil rights commissioners passed the British delegation and American officials walking down the corridor away from the Oval Office just as they arrived. Hesburgh took the chance to greet his old friend Secretary of State Dean Rusk. Then the commissioners went in to see the president. Johnson was wedging this meeting in during time that he might have been resting in preparation for the dinner. LBJ admitted that he was "awfully weary" and asked his visitors if they wouldn't mind meeting in a smaller office to the side as he stretched out on a couch.

Johnson invited comments, and beginning with Hannah the commissioners gave him their views on the situation in civil rights and what should be done. According to Father Ted's account, by the time he got his turn he felt most of the civil rights issue had been adequately covered. He asked the president if he might address another topic. Johnson agreed and Hesburgh suggested that Johnson's antipoverty program needed to be framed and named more positively. He argued that it should be called the "Equal Opportunity program rather than the Poverty Program." Johnson roused himself on this topic and spoke of his commitment to lift people out of poverty. The strength of Johnson's commitment never left Hesburgh's memory. Hesburgh was further convinced of Johnson's sincerity when the president appointed his friend Shriver to run what became the Office of Economic Opportunity, which was charged with waging the war on poverty.

The president gave the commission almost an hour of his time and then left to prepare for his dinner. Somewhat surprisingly this was not only the first but also the last meeting he held with the full commission for the next three years. Johnson saw it as his task to implement reform in the civil rights area. He did not need the Civil Rights Commission to act as a "burr under the saddle" to prompt action on his part. The actions of the civil rights movement in places like Selma later provided him with prompting aplenty, and revealed the need for national action to provide full and equal citizenship for African Americans. In the spring of 1964 Lyndon Johnson needed pressure or encouragement from no one. Displaying great commitment, consummate legislative skill, and a liberal use of threats and cajoling, he ensured that the civil rights bill passed both houses of Congress. He signed this landmark law on American race relations into law on July 2. Finally, discrimination in accommodations, public institutions, and employment were outlawed and the system of Southern segregation was confronted directly.

On July 4, just two days after the signing of the Civil Rights Act, Hesburgh learned that Lyndon Johnson had awarded him the Presidential Medal of Freedom, the highest civilian honor bestowed by the President of the United States. Hesburgh found himself in some extraordinary company. Dean Acheson, one of the great secretaries of state of the twentieth century, led off the list alphabetically, but the group honored by Johnson included some of the major figures in American intellectual, cultural, and public life. What more need be said about a group that included Aaron Copland, Walt Disney, T. S. Eliot, Helen Keller, Willem de Kooning, John L. Lewis, Walter Lippmann, Edward R. Murrow, Reinhold Niebuhr, Leontyne Price, A. Philip Randolph, Carl Sandburg, and John Steinbeck.[37] Hesburgh was honored as an "educator," and he thought the broad effort upon which he was engaged to modernize and improve Catholic higher education attracted the attention of those who selected the honorees for LBJ. His appearance on the cover of *Time* in 1962 and his familiarity with those who walked the corridors of power and influence in Washington and New York contributed to his selection. In contrast to a figure like Acheson, who had reached the twilight of his active career, Hesburgh seemed to be selected as much for what he represented and for his future potential as for the extent of his accomplishments thus far. But LBJ's bestowing on him this prestigious award deepened his regard for the president and his loyalty to him. He appreciated that LBJ had included a Catholic on his list, and a priest into the bargain.

In the year prior to the announcement of his award, Hesburgh had demonstrated his continuing concern for the civil rights cause at a number of public events. He wanted to move beyond the rather formal, legal confines of the Civil Rights Commission hearing rooms to demonstrate his commitment. Perhaps the sense that the commission's labors were now more marginal also motivated him to act more publicly. The presence of Alabama's segregationist Governor George Wallace on the Notre Dame campus for a speech in the spring of 1964 might have stirred him further. Hesburgh gave quiet encouragement to a group of faculty to protest the Wallace visit, but he made no public comment himself.[38] His silence drew some student criticism, and one senses that this may have been a turning point at which he decided to speak out more publicly to clarify where he stood.[39] In May 1964 he participated in a march and rally in downtown South Bend to commemorate the tenth anniversary of *Brown v. Board of Education*. The orderly march of blacks and whites formed a column five blocks long and moved from Howard Park to the steps of the South Bend courthouse. There the crowd heard Father Hesburgh, the principal speaker, explain that "after ten years of frustration . . . we are facing, as a nation, the moment of truth. Tear gas, cattle prods, police dogs, and a long hot summer will not give us the real answer." After supporting the passage of the civil rights bill (then being debated in the Senate) and offering his endorsement of the planned voter registration campaign during the upcoming "Freedom Summer," Hesburgh emphasized the need for internal conviction on the part of all Americans regarding the dignity of men. He brought matters closer to home by noting that "here in the North I think in all honesty we must say we have been mainly hypocritical and smug, looking South, rather than at ourselves." He concluded with a call for "equality of opportunity across the board today."[40]

On June 21, 1964, Father Hesburgh had the chance to address, even if briefly, a much larger gathering at Soldier Field, Chicago. The Illinois Rally for Civil Rights was planned to put pressure on Congress to pass the civil rights bill. Martin Luther King took time off from the demanding campaign he was leading in St. Augustine, Florida, to come north to serve as the main speaker.[41] Father Hesburgh drove from Notre Dame for the occasion to show support. He was identified and asked to join the plat-form party. A large and diverse crowd of over 50,000 people participated, although that disappointed the organizers, who wanted to fill the stadium to its capacity of 100,000 at that time. Some thought the rally rather anti-climactic in its purpose, as the civil rights legislation now had passed the Congress and only awaited LBJ's signature. Nonetheless, the charismatic King clarified that passage of the bill "does not mean that we have reached the promised land in civil rights." He called for the vigorous enforcement of the new legislation, and also for a continued effort to end racial discrim-ination and poverty. His fine address in 1964 had nothing of the charged quality that characterized his speech at Soldier Field two years later on what came to be known as Freedom Sunday (July 10, 1966). On this later occasion he vowed to challenge the racism and discrimination of Mayor Richard Daley's Chicago, which locked so many blacks in poverty.[42] In the more calm atmosphere of 1964, however, when asked to say a few words, Hesburgh simply focused like Dr. King on the work still to be done. He declared that "a long road and a hot summer are ahead of us." Then he ad-dressed the African Americans who were present: "Every Negro American who does not use his opportunity now is a traitor to his race. Be proud to be a Negro. Demand respect by being worthy of respect. We want to strive for human dignity with you."[43]

After the speeches were completed the platform party linked arms and sang the anthem of the civil rights movement, "We Shall Overcome." The moment was caught by a photograph. Father Ted is on one side of Dr. King and Msgr. Robert J. Hagarty, a great Chicago priest and chancellor of the archdiocese at the time, is on the other. On the other side of Hes-burgh stands Rev. Edgar Chandler, the executive director of the Church Federation of Greater Chicago, an ordained Congregational minister, and a leader in the Chicago civil rights movement, who worked closely with Martin Luther King and also taught and encouraged the young Rev. Jesse Jackson. It is a wonderful photo and captures four men committed to the civil rights cause who lived out their commitment in quite different ways. Neither the photo nor the rally garnered much national attention at the time. Dr. King returned south to the myriad challenges that awaited him in St. Augustine and elsewhere. Only in 1988 did Hesburgh become aware of the photo when a cropped version of it that cut out Hagarty and Chandler was presented to him following his talk at a King remembrance event at Emory University. That cropped photograph has now been added to the permanent collection of the Smithsonian's National Portrait Gallery and has taken on a certain iconic quality. It conveys the dual dedication of both Dr. King and Father Hesburgh to racial justice in America.

Father Hesburgh flew back from the IAEA meeting in Vienna in September for the presentation ceremony of the Presidential Medal of Freedom awards. He invited his proud mother and his sister Betty to join him for the ceremony in the East Room at the White House. President Johnson first offered some general remarks at the gathering, and then under secretary of state George Ball, the chairman of the Distinguished Civilian Service Awards Board, introduced each recipient to the president. LBJ presented the award and read a brief citation for each person. When George Ball read out, "The Reverend Theodore M. Hesburgh," the president responded: "Educator and humanitarian, he has inspired a generation of students and given of his wisdom in the struggle for the rights of man."[44] He placed the medal around Father Hesburgh's neck. After the recipients had received their awards, Dean Acheson responded to the president's remarks on behalf of the awardees. The president went to the Blue Room to receive the guests, and Father Ted was able to introduce his mother and his sister to him and Mrs. Johnson. He recalled that LBJ was "very gracious" and "made them feel at home in the White House."[45]

By the time the Medal of Freedom presentation took place, the 1964 presidential campaign was well under way. After a bitter convention contest the Republicans nominated a western conservative, Senator Barry Goldwater, to run against Johnson. Goldwater had defeated Nelson Rockefeller, the New York governor. Given LBJ's demonstrated commitment on civil rights there was never any doubt for whom Father Hesburgh would vote. Johnson's selection of Senator Hubert Humphrey only strengthened Hesburgh's resolve. Hesburgh liked Humphrey, whom he had come to know through his civil rights work, and he deeply admired the Minnesota senator's dedication to the cause of racial justice.[46]

Goldwater's selection of New York Congressman William E. Miller complicated Hesburgh's stance in the 1964 campaign. Miller was a 1935 Notre Dame alumnus and a faithful Catholic, indeed the first Catholic to appear as a vice-presidential candidate on a major party ticket. Although Miller had represented his upstate New York district since 1950, and had also served as chair of the Republican National Committee from 1961 to 1963, he was not well known. His candidacy generated no great excitement among either Catholics or anyone else. Nonetheless, Hesburgh treated

Miller with considerable respect. When Miller returned to campus on October 3, 1964, to take in the Purdue game and to deliver his standard campaign speech, Hesburgh joined him at his rally on the steps of Sorin Hall. According to a young observer who witnessed the event, "without suggesting a personal endorsement or institutional support, Father Hesburgh told the crowd, estimated in news reports at 2,500, that the university was proud to have a graduate running for national office for the first time in history."[47] The tugs of loyalty to Miller that Father Ted experienced as a result of the congressman's Notre Dame connection and his Catholic faith were far outweighed by the regard and admiration in which he held the Johnson-Humphrey ticket. He cast his ballot to give LBJ the chance to build his Great Society at home, and he was hardly alone in doing so. In November the Democratic ticket won one of the great landslide victories in American history, receiving over 61 percent of the popular vote.

LBJ had hoped to address the education and health care issues as initial priorities after his election, but events in Selma, Alabama, pushed voting rights to the forefront. A planned march from Selma to the capitol building in Montgomery was stopped on the approach to the Edmund Pettus Bridge and brutally dispersed. The day quickly became known as "Bloody Sunday."[48] Television cameras recorded the whole vicious incident, making the entire nation eyewitness to the levels of violence to which the demonstrators were subjected in their quest to gain the right to vote. The national conscience could not ignore what it witnessed.

Lyndon Johnson determined to act. He convened a joint session of the Congress on March 15 to announce his support for a voting rights bill. In his great and memorable speech, televised to the whole nation, he powerfully concluded: "Their cause must be our cause, too. Because it is not just Negroes, but really it is all of us, who must overcome the crippling legacy of bigotry and injustice. And we shall overcome." The voting rights legislation that Johnson proposed banned the literacy tests, poll taxes, and other devices that Southern states had used for generations to prevent blacks from registering to vote. And it contained provisions for federal intervention to supervise registration and voting processes in obvious cases of disenfranchisement. At long last a serious effort was being made to secure for all African Americans the right to vote.

The Civil Rights Commission did not directly participate in drawing up the Voting Rights Act of 1965, but the legislation conformed to the recommendations the commission had made over the previous years as a consequence of its hearings across the South. Father Hesburgh testified at length in support of the legislation before a subcommittee of the House Judiciary Committee. Speaking for the commission he told the House committee members, "For the past six years we have recommended such legislation. We have done so in the belief that nothing less will suffice to root out the evil of discrimination in voting."[49] Such testimony as well as the various hearings and reports of the Civil Rights Commission played a part in securing the Voting Rights Act.

On August 11, 1965, at the end of the week that LBJ signed the Voting Rights Act, a major riot broke out in the Watts neighborhood of Los Angeles. The upheaval was sparked by accusations of police brutality after a traffic violation confrontation involving blacks. Over the next six days, part of the black community erupted with acts of arson and looting. The upheaval was quelled by police aided by four thousand members of the California National Guard. Thirty-four deaths and enormous property damage resulted. Lyndon Johnson had difficulty coming to terms with what he witnessed on the TV news reports. "How is it possible," he asked, "after all we've accomplished? How could it be? Is the world topsy-turvy?" Poor Johnson! He reeled back, disappointed. He still wanted to support and improve the lives of African Americans, but the course to pursue seemed unclear.

Father Hesburgh shared something of LBJ's quandary. He was taken aback by the violence of the urban upheavals and saw them as exercises in self-harm. Yet he had always taken an expansive view of the needs of African Americans in their quest for equality. In a major speech to the prestigious American Academy of Arts and Sciences in Boston in November 1964 he had focused on the "moral dimensions" of the civil rights movement. He cast the issue as one demanding that each person be treated with the proper dignity befitting God's sons and daughters possessed of immortal souls. He spoke of the need to secure specific political rights for African Americans, such as the right to vote and equal treatment before the law, but he went much further. He outlined the need for decent education, economic opportunity, and adequate housing to overcome "the litany of inequality" under which blacks lived.[50] He believed that government at all levels could still play a role in addressing the challenging issues that African Americans faced.

Hesburgh also felt some sympathy for the views put forward by Daniel Patrick Moynihan in the 1965 report he wrote for Johnson from his position as a political appointee in the Department of Labor.[51] Moynihan, whom Hesburgh came to know well and considered a good friend, was charged with developing ideas to pursue the war on poverty. He famously pointed to the collapse of the nuclear family among the black lower class. He directed attention to the high out-of-wedlock birthrate (then 25 percent) and warned of the danger of the continued disintegration of the black family. His solution was decent jobs and a meaningful role for black men in their families and communities. Without this, he warned, there would be higher numbers of female-headed households, and higher rates of poverty, lower educational outcomes, a sharp growth in welfare dependency, and an endless cycle of poverty. At the time, critics attacked Moynihan and his report as patronizing and racist in its stereotyping of the black family and black men. Moynihan found few friends willing to support him publicly, and he soon navigated himself out of the line of fire brought on by his well-intentioned analysis.

In his 1964 address on civil rights, Hesburgh had held "that there is needed a new moral revolution within the deprived Negro community itself, based on a new pride in what human dignity and human equality can mean in America." Such sentiments helped him recognize the validity of much of what Moynihan had argued. In February of 1966 he wrote to the future New York senator that he had read his report "with the greatest of interest and thought you had unearthed something that needed to be said." But Hesburgh advised Moynihan that the report was not being discussed much by either the Civil Rights Commission or in preparation for a planned White House Conference on Civil Rights. He advised Moynihan with regard to the latter that "many of the Negroes were anxious not to have the White House Conference focus on the family problem, and were somewhat resentful of the implications of your report." He admitted to understanding such sensitivities, but noted that "one gains nothing by being blind to facts." As he continued, "if the facts hold up, then we have a serious problem that needs consideration and action."[52]

Father Hesburgh identified closely with and supported mainstream civil rights leaders such as Dr. King, A. Philip Randolph, and Roy Wilkins who proved willing to work in collaboration with the Johnson administration. He could not relate to and felt no sympathy for the more militant advocates of "black power." Young separatist leaders such as Stokely Carmichael and Huey Newton rejected working within the system and seemed to be advocating for some kind of violent revolution. Such rhetoric offended Father

Ted and he attempted no outreach to such radicals. He still toiled along much more conventional avenues. He lent some assistance to LBJ's aide on civil rights, Clifford Alexander, who was preparing for the White House Conference on Civil Rights held June 1 and 2, 1966. The conference, titled "To Fulfill These Rights," aimed to build upon the accomplishments of the Civil Rights Act and Voting Rights Act.[53] Over twenty-four hundred people participated in the unwieldy event held at the Washington Hilton, although the Student Nonviolent Coordinating Committee (SNCC) radicals boycotted it. A long report emerged from the conference calling for legislation to ban discrimination in housing and other areas. Hesburgh's contribution was marginal, although commission reports provided some basis for the conference discussions.

Lyndon Johnson worked to maintain his commitment to the civil rights effort, but by the end of 1966 he was entangled in the Vietnam conflict and the struggle in Southeast Asia consumed more of his attention. In January 1967, LBJ at last met again with the members of the Civil Rights Commission, among them Father Hesburgh, who presented him with their report on the problems of de facto school segregation.[54] The next month the president and a number of his cabinet members met with a larger group of civil rights leaders, among them A. Philip Randolph, Clarence Mitchell, and Whitney Young, to discuss proposals he planned to present in an upcoming civil rights message. Father Hesburgh and a number of other supporters of civil rights, including Washington's archbishop Patrick O'Boyle, joined the discussion.[55] Two days later the president sent the Congress his proposals for "the Civil Rights Act of 1967." He asked the Congress "to bar discrimination in housing, and to secure other very basic rights for every citizen."[56] The legislation stalled on Capitol Hill. Only on April 11, 1968, did Johnson sign the Civil Rights Act (known as the Fair Housing Act) into law. It came in the immediate aftermath of the assassination of Martin Luther King in Memphis one week earlier. The news of Dr. King's murder set off major violence in over forty cities across the country. Johnson could not placate the rioting and anger among members of the African American community by assuring them that this new law would end racial discrimination in the sale and rental of homes and apartments. It seemed ancillary to the crisis at hand. Yet Father Hesburgh appreciated the value of this further legislative accomplishment for civil rights.

By April of 1968, however, LBJ's political support had diminished. Protests against the Vietnam War grew, and many liberals turned against him because of it. Johnson viewed himself as trapped between the challenges of the home front and the demands of the war. He could not obtain both "guns and butter" simultaneously. Hesburgh sympathized with the president's plight. In August 1967 he had accepted a presidential appointment to serve on the General Advisory Committee on Foreign Assistance Programs.[57] In the beginning of March 1968 he went to Washington and held the Bible at the swearing-in ceremony for his friend C. R. Smith as secretary of commerce. He had the chance to speak with the president on that occasion and found him "cordial," as always.[58] Yet Father Ted gained no sense of the enormous pressure the president was under as a result of the Tet Offensive, which led him to withdraw from the 1968 presidential race at the end of the month.

The mood of the country had changed from hopefulness regarding the possibilities of reform in 1964–1965 to disillusionment and division by 1967–1968. Lyndon Johnson's great dreams had turned into something of a nightmare by the summer of 1968. Ted Hesburgh rode out this change in national mood, and he deftly firmed up his place as a prominent figure in American public life. An indication of the regard in which he was held came early in 1968 when the NASA administrator James Webb (who supplied the space movies for him to show to Paul VI) called him to a meeting. Hesburgh knew Webb well from "a number of councils [and] committees" on which they had served. Webb's deputy, Robert Seamans, had just resigned, and he asked Hesburgh to take his place in the number two slot, with the implication that he would succeed Webb when he retired. Webb's offer took Hesburgh aback. Webb explained to him, in Hesburgh's recollection, that "we're coming to a point in this space program where we're coming up against some very tough philosophical and theological questions," and that Hesburgh could address them effectively. Furthermore, Hesburgh possessed a familiarity with both the educational and scientific communities. Finally, the always energetic Webb noted that "there's a kind of crisis of leadership around this town today," and that NASA needed "a man that no one can have any possible thoughts that he wouldn't merit the highest confidence" and be "noted for his integrity." Having made his case he put Hesburgh on the spot and advised him: "If you're willing, we'll go to the White House and nail it down right away." Father Ted was not willing.

Notre Dame's president was flattered by Webb's raising this possibility, and by the compliments Webb had extended in encouraging him to take on the position. Yet he balked, explaining that he didn't consider the position as "necessarily the place for a priest." Webb countered by asking if he wanted to exercise "moral influence in the world." Hesburgh said he did, but not "as head of the space agency." He explained that he saw it as more appropriate for a priest to exercise his influence in an advisory capacity rather than having authority over a major agency with a budget of over $6 billion. He recounted for Webb the large amount of time he had devoted to government service over the past fifteen years, but explained that this work was quite different from full-time service running a specific government agency. He was doubtful that such work would combine well with his priestly ministry, and he stated unequivocally, "I am a priest and I always want to be a priest."[59] He was also the president of Notre Dame and he would not contemplate leaving that post, especially given the challenges on campus at the time.

So it was as "Father Hesburgh" that he continued his march into some of the inner citadels of the American establishment, even as that establishment was fracturing in disagreement over Vietnam. The "best and the brightest" went bust in Vietnam, and by 1968 LBJ's Democratic Party and much of the nation were riven by the conflict. But Father Hesburgh circumvented much of the bitter contention because he avoided taking hard stands—either pro or con—on Vietnam during the years from 1965 to 1968. He supported the American effort in Vietnam in the early stages and endorsed the Cold War consensus that communist expansion needed to be contained. This support continued when Johnson and his advisers took the momentous decision to "Americanize" the war in 1965 with the commitment of major ground forces. He saw it as his patriotic duty.[60] Although he made no explicit statements, certain of his actions indicated his position. Inviting National Security Adviser "Mac" Bundy to give the 1965 Notre Dame commencement address, just months after the launching of a sustained bombing campaign against North Vietnam, suggested his endorsement. Even more striking was his writing to General William Westmoreland, the U.S. military commander in Vietnam, at the end of 1966 to encourage him to accept the Class of 1967's Patriot of the Year Award. Westmoreland could not come to campus to receive the award in February 1967, but Col. Jack Stephens, the Army ROTC unit's commanding officer, stood in for him with Hesburgh's approval.[61] Hesburgh's insistent support for a continued ROTC presence on campus also was taken as an unspoken signal of his support for the American military effort in Southeast Asia.

It is easy to understand why Hesburgh lent implicit support for the

Johnson administration's policies. First, he admired Johnson and endorsed his domestic agenda. Although Father Ted never discussed Vietnam with LBJ, it seemed natural to extend his support to the administration's foreign policy initiatives as the president dealt with the conflict he had inherited from JFK.[62] Additionally, Father Ted knew all the major civilian officials— McNamara, Bundy, Rusk—who developed and implemented Johnson's policy of graduated pressure on North Vietnam. Always a believer in the wisdom of "experts," he was impressed with their supposed brilliance and accepted the efficacy of the strategy they pursued in the years after 1965. He was like the majority of American Catholics who supported the American war commitment. Cardinal Spellman led the way and portrayed the conflict as just another battle in the long fight that pitted America and Catholicism against communism.[63]

Even when some of his good friends began to express their concerns about the trajectory of the war and the costs of it, Father Hesburgh maintained his own counsel. In March of 1967 a group of Catholic educators and college presidents signed an open letter asking all American Catholics to review the country's role in Vietnam. In their letter they cited "indiscriminate bombing, the needless destruction of human life," and the massive injury to the civilian population, and clearly implied that the war was immoral. Hesburgh's friends George Shuster and Bishop James Shannon were signatories.[64] Whatever reservations Hesburgh might have had, he kept them to himself. He focused on preserving appropriate order on campus in light of the growing student protests against the war. Only in 1968 in the aftermath of the Tet Offensive, and with growing public frustration with the lack of progress in the war, did Father Hesburgh make his own initial and tentative public criticisms of the American commitment in Vietnam. When pressed by student interviewers about the use of napalm in Vietnam he glided past that specific question and answered broadly: "What bothers me is we are living in a world where 80% of the people make less than $500 a year and 50% make less than $100. One-third of the world can't read or write. They are cut off from all human culture. There is an enormous gulf between the haves and the have-nots. As long as people die of hunger, die at an early age, it becomes humanly impossible to spend thirty billion dollars a year blowing up landscapes in Vietnam."[65]

As 1968 progressed it became easier for Father Hesburgh to express further reservations about the war and the way in which it was being fought. He admitted in an interview that he moved "slowly" on Vietnam, but the combination of Johnson's withdrawal from the presidential race on March 31 and the subsequent U.S. diplomatic initiative to engage the North Vietnamese in peace talks opened an acceptable avenue for Father Ted. In the summer of 1968 he associated himself with Negotiation Now!, the group headed by Clark Kerr of the University of California, which encouraged a negotiated end to the conflict, but made clear that the group had no sympathy for Ho Chi Minh or his government. The group included some classic Cold War liberals such as Pat Moynihan, Walter Reuther of the United Automobile Workers union, Arthur Schlesinger Jr. (for a time), and Zbigniew Brzezinski. Hesburgh felt secure in this company. He appreciated that Clark Kerr reached out to offer the group's counsel to the candidates of both major parties, and that the group did not focus all its criticisms on LBJ.[66] Hesburgh's membership revealed his optimistic hope that the United States could somehow extricate itself from its involvement in Vietnam without consigning South Vietnam to communist control. It was a hope that would not be fulfilled.

By the time Hesburgh lent his name to Negotiation Now! the 1968 presidential race was in full swing. Even before Johnson appeared on national television on March 31 and shocked the nation by announcing that he would not seek re-election in November, it was clear there would be a contest for the nomination of both parties. Senator Eugene McCarthy had announced in November 1967 that he planned to run for the presidency and to challenge the sitting president for the right to carry his party's banner. He gave voice to those who opposed the Vietnam War within the Democratic Party. His surprising and strong performance in the New Hampshire primary drew another antiwar senator into the race, Robert F. Kennedy. After LBJ's withdrawal, Vice President Humphrey joined the fray as the candidate most closely identified with the president and his policies. Hesburgh knew each of the three major Democratic contestants. He also knew three of the four candidates for the Republican nomination. Richard Nixon had resurrected himself after his defeats in 1960 and in the 1962 California gubernatorial race and was now the front-runner. Nelson Rockefeller decided to have yet another shot at the political prize he craved, but George Romney, the three-term governor of Michigan, competed with him for the moderate Republican vote. Father Ted did not know well Ronald Reagan, the conservative governor of California, who picked up something of Goldwater's mantle. Beyond the two major parties stood another consequential candidate—George Wallace, the governor of Alabama, who ran as the nominee of the American Independent Party.

The Democratic race presented Hesburgh with a situation where two Catholic senators were competing hard for the nomination. Hesburgh held McCarthy in good regard and had invited him to serve as the Notre Dame commencement speaker in 1967, but he shared no close personal relationship with the thoughtful Minnesota senator. Father Hesburgh respected McCarthy's antiwar position, but his loyalty to Johnson and concerns about any unilateral withdrawal from South Vietnam caused him major reservations. Nor could he get on the emotional bandwagon for Bobby Kennedy. His recollection of the conflicts between RFK and the Civil Rights Commission lingered on. Furthermore, he was never completely convinced of Bobby Kennedy's supposed conversion experience, which transformed him, in the words of his sympathetic biographer, into the "tribune of the underclass," deeply committed to social change and willing to confront injustice, racism, and poverty.[67] Hesburgh's support for the goals RFK professed never overcame his reservations over the person professing them. Both Kennedy and McCarthy spoke at Notre Dame during April of 1968 while campaigning for the May 7 Indiana primary, but Hesburgh wrapped his arms around neither candidate.[68] Perhaps ironically the president of Notre Dame felt most sympathy for the non-Catholic in the Democratic race, Hubert Humphrey, whom he admired greatly for his personal decency and his dedication to civil rights.

In the midst of the 1968 race Father Hesburgh focused more on whom he did not want to see as president than on his personal choice for the position. George Wallace's candidacy troubled him greatly. The Alabama governor presented himself as the "law and order" candidate, and the issue of race was always in play as he exploited fear of busing and of housing integration. Father Ted worried about the extent of Wallace's appeal not only in the South but among working-class whites in the North in the climate of national turmoil. He wanted to overcome the divisive threat that he believed Wallace represented. Acting on such understandable motives, he explained to a group of *Newsweek* editors, brought together by Kenneth Woodward, "his idea . . . to bring 50 of the nation's leaders together, from David Rockefeller to César Chávez, the Chicano labor leader who was battling California fruit-growers." As Woodward recalled, "they were all, of course, friends of Father Ted." Hesburgh argued that this group should settle on "one candidate and get behind him, and together we'll reunite the nation." The good intentions of its proponent can't disguise the naïve impracticality and nature of the proposal. According to Ken Woodward, the *Newsweek* editors rolled their eyes, and one of them pointed out: "That's the surest way to elect Wallace."[69] Father Hesburgh dropped the idea, although he could not shake his anxiety about Wallace's appeal. There were to be no simple and easy solutions to unite the nation in 1968.

President Johnson retired in virtual disgrace to his Texas ranch after Richard Nixon took office. He rarely showed his face in public thereafter. He died of a heart attack on his beloved ranch on January 22, 1973, at the age of sixty-four. Hesburgh praised him at a press conference thereafter and opined that "the verdict of history will probably make Johnson the greatest of Presidents, [because] he did more for practical emancipation, for civil rights, than any other President."[70] He was somewhat more measured when on January 24 he conducted a memorial service in Sacred Heart Church at Notre Dame for LBJ. He offered a heartfelt eulogy, but he conceded that Johnson was "a complicated man." Nonetheless he held that Johnson was "simple in his devotion to people." He explained to the gathered congregation that "it was a tragedy that President Johnson's work in helping the underprivileged was overshadowed by our country's involvement in Vietnam."[71]

RISING AND FALLING WITH RICHARD NIXON: CIVIL RIGHTS, WAR, ABORTION

Father Hesburgh had described President Johnson as "a complicated man," but LBJ hardly matched his successor in his contradictions and torments. Richard Nixon arrived in office in a calm mood, yet the race against Humphrey proved much closer than expected, and that fueled his insecurity. He already sensed that the press and the "Nixon haters" would oppose him at every turn. Additionally, he "bore the scars, real and imagined, of a single-minded thirty-year ambition to win the presidency."[72] He could never put past wounds and insults fully aside.

Whatever his personality flaws, the new president took office well disposed toward Father Ted. The Nixon-Hesburgh friendship had got off to a fine start during Nixon's visit to Notre Dame for the USC game in November 1952. Nixon's wife, Pat, had graduated from USC and at her request

Nixon had contacted Hesburgh and asked if they might attend the game between the second- (USC) and seventh- (Notre Dame) ranked teams. Notre
Dame's new, young president agreed to host the vice president–elect. He
met the Nixons himself when they arrived on a regular North Central Airlines flight at South Bend airport. He remembered that they weren't even
the first passengers to leave the plane, and that Pat was wearing her simple
cloth coat on a chilly November day. Hesburgh also recalled that there
were "no secret service agents, no advance people, no press." The Nixons
enjoyed the game, despite the Trojans losing 9–0. After the game Father
Ted arranged for them to go to his office for drinks, after which Father
Joyce drove them into Chicago to catch a late evening flight at Midway airport. Nixon gave no hint of social awkwardness or shyness but related well
with Hesburgh. They had what Hesburgh described as "the widest ranging
conversation." At one point the topic of confession came up and Hesburgh
asked Nixon if he had ever seen a confessional. He had not. So Hesburgh
told him, "Well, you're going to see one right now." The four of them left
their drinks on the table in the president's suite and marched over to Sacred Heart Church. Hesburgh got into the priest's cubicle in the confessional and invited Nixon to go into the penitent's place and to kneel down,
which he did. Then Father Ted slid the screen over and he invited Vice
President Nixon to confess his sins. It was in jest, of course, although one
regrets that no photographic record exists of Richard Nixon on his knees in
a confessional at Notre Dame. Hesburgh explained the normal procedure
for confession, including absolution, to him. Then they returned to finish
their drinks. Soon Ned Joyce raced "Richard and Pat" into Chicago. It was
a short visit, but a connection was established.[73]

On his future trips to Washington, Father Hesburgh would drop in to
see the vice president in the office Nixon kept in the Capitol Building.
Their discussions were of a broad and philosophical sort involving law and
especially natural law and its implications for individuals and society. He
attended a few functions as Nixon's guest and maintained a good relationship with him, although Hesburgh's gravitation toward the Rockefeller circle must have been noted by Nixon. Father Ted did not recall doing any
specific policy work for Nixon. The vice president made use of another
Catholic priest in that regard, the Sulpician priest John F. Cronin, a staff
member of the National Catholic Welfare Conference. Nixon counted
Cronin "as one of his closest friends, political advisors, and speechwrit-
ers."[74] Hesburgh contented himself with his more limited relationship with

the vice president. This survived the 1960 election contest even though Hesburgh recognized that Nixon, or at least his surrogates, attempted to exploit the "Catholic issue" for political advantage.

In November of 1968 Father Hesburgh sent Nixon a congratulatory telegram upon his election victory, which Nixon acknowledged in a "Dear Ted" note.[75] Hesburgh sent another telegram to the new president after his inauguration, advising that he had offered Mass for Nixon and the success of his presidency. Nixon replied on February 4 expressing his gratitude, and admitting that it was "truly heartening that you were remembering me spiritually as I assumed the duties and responsibilities of high office."[76] Hesburgh assumed that his service on the Civil Rights Commission would come to an end, and both he and his longtime colleague John Hannah appeared quite ready to relinquish their responsibilities. But Richard Nixon had other ideas for both Hannah and Father Ted.

President Nixon first met with the Commission on Civil Rights on February 14, 1969, for a briefing. After the meeting he spoke with a couple of the commissioners individually, including the commission's chair, John Hannah, whom he soon named to serve as director of the U.S. Agency for International Development. According to the White House daily diary, he met with Father Ted from 5:08 to 5:20 p.m. The president asked Hesburgh: "What would it take for you to come full-time with the government? Do I have to see the Pope?" Hesburgh indicated that permission from the pope was not necessary and asked what he had in mind. Nixon requested him "to take over the poverty program," the very position that Sargent Shriver had held in Johnson's administration. Hesburgh explained that he did not think he would be a good appointment because if he took on the role he would have to "destroy the patronage system used by [big-city] mayors" to distribute government largesse. He did not think Nixon would benefit from having a Catholic priest undertake that controversial course of action. Nixon accepted his argument.[77]

Hesburgh asked Nixon if he could introduce some other matters. In the space of a few minutes Hesburgh spoke to the president on some major issues. He advised Nixon to end the war in Vietnam and quickly. He recommended an end to the draft and the creation of an all-volunteer army. He pushed for eighteen-year-olds to be given the vote. And, to facilitate access for qualified candidates to higher education, he supported a federal student loan program. In time Nixon made progress on some of these recommendations. Hesburgh also let the president know that he believed it was time for someone with fresh ideas to come on board the Civil Rights Commission, and that he would tender his resignation.[78]

After his return to Notre Dame, Hesburgh wrote to the president on February 17 to thank him for the meeting. He noted how he was "much touched by the generosity and openness of the proposal" made to him. He again explained that appointing a priest to head the poverty program might be problematic and "potentially troublesome" for Nixon. "The growing openness of our society is leading toward this kind of service by clergy in the future," he continued, "but my instinct tells me that you are ahead of the times at the moment, and I would not want for the world to be any cause of embarrassment for you and your administration." Hesburgh's declining to work full-time for Nixon did not mean that he was unwilling to contribute in the new Republican administration. Although many liberals castigated Pat Moynihan for his willingness to serve with Nixon, and tried to create an expectation that a "good liberal" would keep well away from any White House appointment, Hesburgh shared no such animus. He outright announced his availability and informed the president, "I am sure there are many other ways in which I can be of assistance to our country and to you personally, and I need not assure you that I am willing to assist in any way compatible with my time and ability."[79] Nixon soon took him up on his offer, but first he was more interested in a letter that Father Hesburgh wrote and released on February 17—his famous "15-minute warning" policy for handling student unrest.

As we have noted, Nixon wrote Hesburgh soon afterward, applauding the "forthright stand" he had taken. He shared his view that "a fundamental principle of any great university is that the rule of reason and not the rule of force prevails." He held further that "whoever rejects that principle forfeits his right to be a member of the academic community." Then he asked Father Ted to make suggestions to Vice President Agnew in advance of meetings the vice president had scheduled with the nation's governors to address the "growing lawlessness and violence on our campuses."[80] Hesburgh tacked back from being a resource person for Spiro Agnew and was somewhat embarrassed by Nixon's praise and endorsement. He wanted to work with Nixon, but not to be too closely identified with him. Otherwise his relations with his liberal friends would be put under real strain.

With Pat Moynihan's encouragement Nixon then decided to ask Hesburgh not only to stay on at the Civil Rights Commission, but also to take over John Hannah's role as chair. Moynihan communicated the offer, and

Hesburgh wrote to Nixon on March 6 to accept the new appointment. Hesburgh noted for the president his belief that "important as the work of the Commission has been in the past, . . . its role in the future years may be of even greater significance." He reviewed the challenges the commission faced regarding its membership, budget, and staffing. He made an explicit request that the acting staff director, Howard Glickstein, be confirmed in that role. He assured Nixon of the commission's willingness "to assist you in every possible way in identifying and resolving the problems of civil rights." He invited the president to "call upon us to carry out any assignments which are within our special capacity." Finally, he informed the president, as he had already told Moynihan in their conversation, that he planned to stay on only for one further year as chair.[81] Father Ted's letter crossed one to him from Nixon dated the following day in which the president expressed his delight "to learn from Pat Moynihan that you have agreed to serve on the United States Commission on Civil Rights for an additional year as Chairman." He added, "I want you to know that I consider your decision a great favor to me personally as well as a considerable boon to the Commission."[82] The Nixon-Hesburgh relationship seemed to be off to a fine start with a healthy dose of mutual regard as a good foundation.

Hesburgh also accepted another Nixon appointment around this time. Hesburgh had been dismayed at how Robert McNamara had enforced the draft during his leadership of the Pentagon by engaging in a tragic social experiment wherein poorly educated and unqualified men were taken into the armed services. Hesburgh never again wanted to see those who had difficulty passing a basic literacy test being forced into military service.[83] So when Hesburgh's friend Thomas Gates, who served as Eisenhower's secretary of defense from 1959 to 1961, invited him to join the commission Nixon authorized to explore an All-Volunteer Armed Force, Hesburgh agreed. This commission met over the next year and presented its report to the president at the White House on February 21, 1970, with Father Hesburgh in attendance.[84] The report detailed how the United States should end the draft and move to an all-volunteer force. The driving intellectual force on the committee was the University of Chicago economist Milton Friedman, who had made the case for a volunteer force throughout the 1960s. His were the arguments that were taken up and developed in the Gates Commission report. Nixon adopted them and persuaded the Congress to implement them. Hesburgh felt satisfaction that he had played a part in effecting the change.[85]

Hesburgh's service on the Gates Commission proved to be smooth sailing compared to his four-year odyssey as chair of the Civil Rights Commission. His term in the latter role involved a number of perilous adventures. Michael O'Brien captured the situation well when he observed that by Hesburgh's "agreeing to become chairman he was embarking on four years of confrontation with the man who appointed him."[86] Initially it appeared that Pat Moynihan would be his liaison with the White House staff, and that was promising. Hesburgh appreciated Moynihan's intellect and enjoyed his impish wit and puckish Irish manner.[87] He recruited Moynihan to deliver the Notre Dame commencement address in May of 1969, and the Nixon adviser made provocative remarks asking for more careful delineation about what government could and could not do.[88] As the Nixon administration settled into place, however, Moynihan's influence was exercised more over policy than over personnel, as soon became obvious to Father Ted.

In what should have been an early indicator to Hesburgh of troubles ahead, he immediately engaged in a dispute with Nixon's staff over the appointment of the commission's staff director, the person who would command the day-to-day work of the commission under his guidance. Hesburgh wanted Howard Glickstein, whom he knew well. The political operatives in the White House had other ideas, no doubt judging Glickstein to be too liberal. Hesburgh wrote to Nixon on April 1 informing the president that he "would find the job impossible without [Glickstein's] assistance and [that] staff morale will go to the bottom if he is not named soon." He asked Nixon "to deliver this one for me."[89] No quick approval came. When the White House political staff pressured Father Ted to agree to their candidate, a person with no civil rights background, Hesburgh refused and an impasse developed. Hesburgh went to see Moynihan late one afternoon and they discussed matters while each emptied two tumblers of Scotch. Then Moynihan suggested they repair to the White House staff mess to dine. Moynihan retrieved two bottles of fine red wine from his cabinet, which they enjoyed with their dinner. Hesburgh retreated back to the Mayflower Hotel after the meal to get some rest while resolving to be cautious in drinking with this friend in the future. Hesburgh valued that Moynihan was "always understanding," and he prized the camaraderie that he shared with the future senator. But Moynihan could not resolve the staff director issue for him. So Hesburgh went to see his old friend John Hannah, then working at USAID. He admitted to Hannah that he had his "first big problem" and asked for advice on tactics. Hannah told him bluntly: "Ted, your problem is that you don't know your own power." He advised Hesburgh to tell the White House political operatives that he had to have the right appointment for this key position, and that it was Glickstein. So encouraged, Hesburgh explained that if he could not have Howard Glickstein as staff director he would advise the president that he could not serve as chair of the Civil Rights Commission. His ultimatum was not appreciated, but it was effective. Howard Glickstein was appointed and so continued his close collaboration with Hesburgh on civil rights issues.[90]

In the months following Hesburgh's appointment as chair, he and Moynihan participated in a healthy exchange covering a variety of civil rights matters. But this exchange halted on June 26, when Hesburgh and all the other commissioners sent a telegram to Nixon complaining about reports that "the school desegregation guidelines are to be weakened." They warned that any such weakening "would reward those school districts that had resisted compliance with the law of the land and betray those who have taken steps to obey the law."[91] That same day Moynihan wrote to Hesburgh advising that the White House had determined that from that point forward, all civil rights matters would be handled by Robert J. Brown, a special presidential assistant and the only African American on Nixon's White House staff.[92] Clearly a decision had been made that Moynihan was not the one to work with Hesburgh and the commission. Brown was an associate of John D. Ehrlichman, and he worked on various projects including black business development. No close rapport developed between him and Hesburgh, and the commission was kept at arm's length from policymaking in the White House. Eventually, Chairman Hesburgh found Leonard (Len) Garment, a special consultant to Nixon, to be the one person on Nixon's staff with whom he could communicate constructively.

Far from contributing to the development of policy on civil rights, Father Hesburgh and the Civil Rights Commission quickly took on the role of administration critic. The formulation of Nixon's civil rights agenda was influenced by his attorney general, John Mitchell, whom Father Ted grew to dislike. James Patterson and other historians have demonstrated how Mitchell, acting with Nixon's approval, was "moved by political considerations" to placate conservative white voters in the South and border states. This was the "Southern strategy" to bring such voters, who voted for Wallace in 1968, into the Republican fold.[93]

In response to the Nixon administration's retreat on major elements of the civil rights agenda it had inherited from Johnson, Hesburgh grew upset. After completing his first year as chair of the commission, Father Ted later said, he "felt I could not resign; it would be like abandoning a sinking ship." As he noted, by then "Nixon's people and I were deeply into an adversarial relationship." He knew at that point "that civil rights had few friends in the Nixon administration"; nevertheless, Hesburgh and the commission did not back off from their efforts. Over the course of 1970 the commission staff investigated the manner in which the federal government enforced the civil rights laws. On October 12 the commission issued its lengthy report and lambasted most departments in the executive branch. Hesburgh made sure not to turn the report into a personal attack on Nixon. He went out of his way to give credit to the president on some issues, while also noting the glaring failures of John Mitchell's Justice Department.[94] Hesburgh gave a copy of the report to Len Garment prior to its public release, and Nixon's counselor requested that it be held in abeyance until after the upcoming congressional elections. According to Hesburgh he exclaimed: "My God, what are you trying to do to us?" Hesburgh ignored the request and proceeded ahead. He even held a press conference to highlight the report's main findings, at which he also revealed that the White House had pressured him to delay release of the report. Little wonder, as Michael O'Brien commented, that "release of the report embarrassed and angered the Nixon Administration." Ehrlichman dismissed it as "nothing but another sermon from Father Hesburgh." The animosity between Hesburgh and the Nixon staff now ran deep.[95]

Garment and other administration staffers believed that Hesburgh was "politicizing" the race issue and deliberately seeking to damage the administration.[96] Father Ted saw his actions as the equivalent of the "burr under the saddle" treatment he had tried to mete out to the Kennedy administration. But the tension and acrimony in this instance ran much deeper than in the case of Hesburgh's clashes with Robert Kennedy. Although Len Garment proved willing to "mend fences" with Hesburgh, when he sought to line up a meeting between Hesburgh and the president, so that they might exchange views, it was blocked. Hesburgh recalled that Garment told him that he could not get him past the barrier of "the Katzenjammer Kids," Ehrlichman and the president's chief of staff, Bob Haldeman. Haldeman, who controlled access to Nixon, had no interest in facilitating a meeting for Hesburgh. And so the stand-off between the White House and the commission continued, and the gulf between their visions for civil rights widened. While Hesburgh's standing with the Nixon administration deteriorated, his stock rose to the heights with northern Democrats and the liberal press.

By the time of the issuance of the commission report that so upset Nixon's White House team, Father Ted already had criticized the Nixon administration over Vietnam. In the fall of 1969 he joined the presidents of seventy-eight private colleges and universities in signing a petition calling on President Nixon for a "stepped-up timetable" for withdrawing from Vietnam.[97] Compared to some of the demonstrations that simultaneously took place as part of the nationwide Moratorium campaign, this could be classified as polite protest. Father Hesburgh wanted to burn no bridges with Richard Nixon. Around the time when the Gates Commission presented its report to the president in February 1970, Nixon invited both Fathers Hesburgh and Joyce to dinner. There Father Ted presented Nixon with a set of gold cuff links, for which he received a generous note of thanks including the promise "that I will wear your gift with a great deal of pride."[98]

Nixon's decision on April 30, 1970, to widen the war in Vietnam with his "incursion" into Cambodia could not be covered over. On May 4, with emotions running high on campus, Hesburgh addressed a protest rally and condemned the decision, although in measured tones. He told the students and faculty gathered on the main quad, "I have carefully read and reread the President's statement, as I hope you have, and I recognize both his sincerity and his courage in deciding as he did. But I do not agree with him." He also counseled against a student strike and presented his six-point "Hesburgh Declaration" calling for an end to the conflict.[99] He indicated that if others would sign it he would convey its contents to President Nixon. Unlike some, he chose not to hurl abusive rhetoric at the president. A week later he wrote to Nixon and informed him that fifteen thousand people from the university and the surrounding community had signed the statement. What is striking about this moving letter is the sympathetic tone in which Hesburgh addresses Nixon, despite the national turmoil over the Cambodian invasion and the subsequent campus upheaval, including the tragedy at Kent State. He noted that he had spoken of Nixon's sincerity and courage, and he conceded that Nixon possessed knowledge that he did not have. He also informed the president that he had kept him "fervently in my prayers each morning at Mass for all the wisdom and courage you need to lead this country towards unity," which he deemed "our greatest need at the moment."

Hesburgh's fear that his treasured America was coming apart drove his entreaty to Nixon. "Whatever else one says about Southeast Asia," he explained, "I cannot convince myself that the whole matter is important enough to divide our country and to polarize it so decisively when our greatest need is for unity." He asked Nixon to take De Gaulle's decision on Algeria as a model and to back out of Vietnam promptly. He made clear that he sent his views in good faith, because "the best part of friendship is honesty and frankness." He ended his letter with a ringing assurance of "my sincere friendship, my dedication to our beautiful country, and my willingness to do whatever I can to help you and our country achieve the greatness for which it is destined."[100] Nixon must have appreciated this final testimony of patriotism, but perhaps he felt somewhat besieged by all the criticism that was pouring in on him. He does not appear to have replied to Hesburgh's heartfelt letter. Presumably he found himself burdened with matters of state. He did not take up Hesburgh's offer of help, and he does not appear to have been influenced in any specific way by either Hesburgh's public or private counsel. The correspondence between the two men was sparse and very businesslike after this point.

In the end, disagreements over civil rights rather than over the Vietnam War led to the decisive fissure between Hesburgh and the Nixon White House. There was never a personal clash between Hesburgh and Nixon. They still maintained some limited communication over the coming months. Hesburgh even extended an impulsive invitation to Nixon to attend the Notre Dame–USC game as late as October 1971. This rather bizarre offer can't have been given with any thought it would be accepted, but presumably it was made as an indication of continuing friendship and to evoke memories of their meeting almost two decades before.[101] Yet the release of the October 12, 1970, Civil Rights Commission report was a turning point. After that there was little chance that Hesburgh could engage the Nixon staff on civil rights. In this situation Hesburgh decided to continue his public criticism of Nixon's policies. The Nixon administration gave him plenty to criticize as it pursued the strategy of "benign neglect."

Throughout 1971 and 1972 Father Ted, backed by the commission staff, maintained a critical stance toward Nixon's administration. He censured the administration for failing to put the weight of the federal government behind the fight to secure rights for minorities. He defended busing as a necessity to facilitate the desegregation of schools.[102] In July 1972, before the House Committee on Education and Labor, Hesburgh criticized the anti-busing legislation that Nixon proposed "in the guise of the Equal Opportunities Education Act." He blasted the proposal as burning "the last bridge out of the ghetto," and as a "racially reactionary policy which will end inevitably in disaster for all."[103] His criticisms had little impact on the Nixon policymakers except to annoy them, and Hesburgh realized this. The commission no longer played any constructive role, outside of mounting a continuous critique of the Nixon approach. Hesburgh thought of resigning but decided against it. As Michael O'Brien explained, "staff members worried that if he resigned, President Nixon would replace him with someone unsympathetic to civil rights."[104] The commission's staff were perceptive in this regard. As it turned out, the Nixon staff would make the decision for Hesburgh.

By the fall of 1972 Hesburgh's public stature as a champion of civil rights was well acknowledged. The Notre Dame Law School inaugurated an annual lecture series on civil rights in honor of the university president in 1972. Earl Warren, former chief justice of the United States, traveled to South Bend to deliver the lectures as a mark of his regard for Hesburgh. U.S. Representative John Brademas introduced the former chief justice and took the occasion to say he was "proud to represent" Father Hesburgh in Congress.[105] Awards and honors continued to be showered upon Hesburgh. In 1970 the National Conference of Christians and Jews bestowed on him the Charles Evans Hughes Award. The American Jewish Committee awarded him its American Liberties Medallion the following year. In 1972 Union Theological Seminary chose him to receive the award it had established in honor of the great theologian and social philosopher Reinhold Niebuhr. Hesburgh traveled to New York in September to receive the Niebuhr Award. He delivered a lengthy and well-crafted acceptance speech to his Union Theological Seminary audience in which he tried "to get to the heart of the problem" of race relations in America.

Perhaps he had an intuition that this might be his valediction as chair of the Civil Rights Commission. He launched a full-scale broadside on the American failure to confront the "color" issue, which he argued had seared the nation from its founding through to the present. In dramatic language he detailed: "Reds were murdered like wild animals. Yellows were characterized as a peril and incarcerated en masse during World War II for really no good reason by our most liberal President. Browns have been abused as the new slave labor on farms. The blacks, who did not come here willingly, are now, more than a century after their emancipation by Lincoln, still suffering a host of slave-like inequalities." It was a damning indictment of the nation he so loved, and it reflected the frustration he felt at the Nixon administration's drawing back from civil rights. Hesburgh outlined a full program of reform measures across education, housing, and employment. He warned against the United States becoming a "polarized, divided nation," and asked that every person be accorded "human dignity." It was a powerful speech and the *New York Times Magazine* published a version of it on October 29, just a week before the election.[106] The Nixon staff saw the talk differently. It confirmed their appraisal of both Hesburgh's enmity and his implicit support for Nixon's political opponent. They determined to oust him.

The Nixon White House tapes reveal that Haldeman and Ehrlichman met with Nixon on October 16 and complained to him about "the problem of Hesburgh," who was "always attacking us." They expressed the desire to get him off the Civil Rights Commission. Nixon, in typical fashion, remembered that he had felt obliged to reappoint Hesburgh as well as "that Jew [Glickstein] who was head of the staff." The two aides were looking to the future rather than the past, and they focused on forcing Hesburgh's resignation. If the priest refused to resign, Haldeman suggested that they should "kill the Goddamn commission." Ehrlichman agreed that would be the best thing to do, but he noted that Congress had authorized the commission and only a congressional vote could dispense with it.[107] Nixon's aides saw Father Hesburgh as a partisan figure, and Haldeman complained that Hesburgh "threw his arm around [Sargent] Shriver" when George McGovern's running mate visited the Notre Dame campus with his wife, Eunice, on October 11. Nixon made no formal decision at this meeting to dismiss Hesburgh, but a clear consensus prevailed that he had to go.

Haldeman's complaint of Hesburgh's partisanship would have offended Hesburgh, who aimed to maintain his independent status throughout the presidential campaign. In late August, after the party conventions, he wrote to the major candidates inviting them and their running mates to visit campus "to discuss the issues of the current campaign." In his letter to Nixon, Father Ted tried some conciliatory words. While admitting that "we have had our differences in the area of Civil Rights," he assured the president, "I have admired your initiatives in foreign policy and have over the past four years prayed for you daily by name at Mass each morning."[108] A staff assistant replied a week later expressing appreciation for the invitation but indicating it was not likely to be accepted during the fall campaign. Shriver did take up the invitation for the Democratic ticket, and Hesburgh greeted his old friend warmly on his visit to campus, although he gave no formal endorsement. Hesburgh introduced Shriver to a capacity crowd that assembled in Stepan Center, and he traced the candidate's significant associations with Notre Dame and with himself.[109]

It is occasionally noted that Father Hesburgh was himself considered as a potential running mate for George McGovern in 1972, and this might be cited as additional evidence of his partisanship, but the reality is more complicated. McGovern first chose Thomas Eagleton, but when the Missouri senator was forced to withdraw from the ticket, a viable replacement was desperately needed. Father Hesburgh recalled that Sargent Shriver called him to elicit his willingness to run with McGovern.[110] Hesburgh explained to Shriver that he could not possibly run on a national ticket, but he encouraged Shriver to do so. McGovern eventually selected Shriver for what an observer described as "a suicide mission," after at least four other leading Democratic politicians turned him down.[111] Shriver's presence on the Democratic ticket disposed Father Hesburgh toward it, although he never revealed whether he voted for McGovern. It is inconceivable, however, given his Niebuhr Award speech, that he chose Nixon.

Nixon won a landslide victory and his staff did not waste time. On November 13, less than a week after the election, Hesburgh was in Washington and conducting a formal meeting of the commission, when John Buggs, the executive director who followed Glickstein, received a call from the secretary of Fred Malek, who worked in the White House with Haldeman. The message was blunt. All the commissioners were to submit their resignations. Buggs was especially instructed to tell Hesburgh that Malek wanted him out of his office by six o'clock that night. Hesburgh resented the abrupt dismissal, and the offensive way it was conveyed. He recounted the episode in detail in his memoirs, and the firing always stuck in his craw. He realized, as he later told me, that Haldeman and Ehrlichman "really hated my guts."[112] He conveyed to the White House that he would vacate his office by the end of the week and proceeded to finish up his work. So ended his fifteen years of service for the U.S. Civil Rights Commission. Nixon, and even more the White House staff, were glad to see him go. In mid-December the president discussed civil rights issues with Ehrlichman, who advised him, "we're well rid of Hesburgh." Nixon had inquired why Hesburgh couldn't understand their position better, and Ehrlichman described him as a "captive" of the civil rights community, which resembled the "Georgetown elite" in that they all talked only to each other and confirmed "certain accepted assumptions."[113] Nixon sought no meeting with Hesburgh to thank him for his service. Instead, a month later he wrote Hesburgh a letter of thanks, which noted that the Notre Dame priest had "worked courageously and tirelessly to advance the civil rights of every American."[114] Hesburgh assumed that Len Garment had drafted it and then persuaded Nixon to sign and send it. He did not reply. As he later noted with some understatement: "There was a spell of coldness between Nixon and me after I was sacked."[115]

Hesburgh's dismissal by Nixon served to elevate his stature further. Praise showered down upon him as a man of principle. Much to his pleasure the *New York Times* editorialized that "Father Hesburgh was never one to cower before, much less cater to, the tides of popular prejudice dictating retreat in the fight against racial injustice."[116] That and numerous other praise-filled testimonials gave him enhanced credibility for dealing with students and faculty back on campus. He wore the dismissal as a veritable badge of honor, and as the Nixon administration descended into the imbroglio of the Watergate scandal, the luster of that badge grew brighter.

The U.S. Supreme Court's decisions in the companion cases of *Roe v. Wade* and *Doe v. Bolton* on January 22, 1973—the day of Lyndon Johnson's death—presented Hesburgh with an unexpected test for how he would use the enhanced moral leadership credentials that his firing by Nixon had gained him. The court disallowed state and federal restrictions on abortion, and arrogated to itself the right to determine what law should prevail across the nation on this contested matter. In a decision written by a Nixon appointee, Harry Blackmun, the court held that a right to privacy under the due process clause of the Fourteenth Amendment covered a woman's right to choose to abort her fetus. Some state regulation of abortion was permitted, although only in the third trimester of a pregnancy. In this combined decision the court imposed on the United States one of the most liberal abortion regimes in any democratic society then or since.

The abortion issue had been roiling the politics of certain states during the mid- and late 1960s. The efforts of Planned Parenthood, the National Organization for Women (NOW), and what became the National Abortion Rights Action League (NARAL) paid dividends by the decade's end, by which time a number of states had passed laws repealing some of the restrictions placed on abortion. These included both New York under Governor Nelson Rockefeller, who pushed the repeal legislation, and

California under Governor Ronald Reagan, who signed his state's legislation with some reservations. Right to Life organizations expanded to contest the activities of the abortion rights movement. These built on an anti-abortion movement fashioned in the decades previously, which asked that the unborn child be accorded human dignity and a right to live. This was a quite diverse movement and included many traditional Democrats. Catholics were in the forefront of the movement, but by no means alone in it.[117]

Some priests such as Monsignor James McHugh, who headed the Family Life Bureau of the bishops' conference, took a leadership role in advancing the pro-life cause, and he organized the National Right to Life Committee. Father Hesburgh was not associated with such efforts. He maintained a studied silence in response to *Roe v. Wade*. He opposed abortion, but he chose not to use his impressive reputation to take any leadership role in contesting and condemning the Supreme Court's decision. Only at the end of the year did he speak up during his Dwight Terry Lectures at Yale to connect his efforts on civil rights with the need to protect "the unborn children, who are so cavalierly deprived of the most basic right of all, the right to life."[118] He decided not to make opposition to abortion one of the great issues in which he would engage. At the very moment he had reached a pinnacle in his accomplishments on civil rights and had won the regard of key groups in the society, he refrained from using his power and influence to fight for the unborn.

To speak out on abortion would have put him at odds with so many of his friends in the American establishment—with the Rockefellers, with Bob McNamara at the World Bank, with Mac Bundy, who was then heading the Ford Foundation. It was not simply a concern about putting at risk the personal status and acceptance he had won; he represented Notre Dame, and his university was in the midst of striving to improve and to build its reputation as a modern American university. To speak out on civil rights brought favorable recognition to Notre Dame from the people who mattered in academe, the media, and the foundations. But abortion was quite different. What might they think of Notre Dame if its leader stood to the fore of the pro-life movement? Also, and all too quickly, he saw many of his liberal Democratic friends who had been pro-life, such as Edward Kennedy, shed their principles and begin their procession to the pro-choice side. But these were people—friends—with whom he still agreed on so many other issues. He wanted to be with them on issues like peace, arms control, assistance to the poor, and overseas aid. Better then to mute the disagreement over abortion and to cooperate in the many areas where agreement was possible. When he addressed the abortion issue, his position was always qualified by the need to respect life "right across the board." He promoted the "seamless garment" approach long before Cardinal Joseph Bernardin popularized the term. He disliked giving the abortion issue any priority, and he recommended against determining one's vote on a single issue.[119]

America's attention was soon distracted from the Supreme Court's decision on abortion to reports of the happenings in other courtrooms in the nation's capital. On January 30, 1973, a week after *Roe* and just three days after the peace treaty designed to end American involvement in Vietnam was signed in Paris, Watergate burglars James McCord and G. Gordon Liddy were convicted of conspiracy, burglary, and wiretapping. Their convictions began a veritable procession of resignations that culminated with Nixon's announcement on August 8, 1974, that he would resign the presidency the next day. A strained but defiant Nixon mounted the steps of *Marine One* and left the White House the following morning. His presidency ended in the personal humiliation he had struggled throughout his life to avoid.

Father Hesburgh exercised commendable restraint as Nixon's presidency unraveled. He claimed in his memoir that "when Watergate happened, I did not rejoice. As President, Nixon had accomplished some good things, too." Dick Conklin recalled that when Nixon resigned Father Ted was besieged with requests for interviews by reporters who were "after the most condemning of quotes they could get from old foes of the president." Hesburgh declined them all, explaining, "I don't want to kick a man when he is down."[120] Some years later Hesburgh and Nixon had a moment of reconciliation at a football Hall of Fame banquet at the Waldorf-Astoria in New York. They shook hands and Hesburgh greeted him with respect. Thereafter, Hesburgh received a signed copy of each book the former president wrote as part of his unceasing effort to recover from his great disgrace. Hesburgh always acknowledged them and he read most of them.[121]

Although he held no government appointment during the period from his dismissal from the Civil Rights Commission until Gerald Ford assumed the presidency, Father Hesburgh found many other activities beyond campus to occupy himself. He was now virtually addicted to service away from Notre Dame, and he needed both the stimulation that serving on various boards and committees brought him and the satisfaction of knowing that he was addressing major issues of the day. He began a transition in his interests from civil rights at home to international issues, especially through his chairing of the board of directors of the Overseas Development Council. The ODC was an independent, nonprofit agency that promoted consideration of development issues by the public, policymakers, and the media through research, conferences, and publications. Hesburgh began a fruitful association with president of the council James (Jim) Grant. With Grant's backing he transformed himself into a spokesperson on develop- ment issues and on the need for the United States to relate better to Third World countries so as to address such major challenges as world hunger.

A rather different kind of appointment came after he decided to accept David Rockefeller's invitation to join the board of Chase Manhattan Bank. He had earlier turned down an invitation from Thomas Gates to join the board of Morgan Guaranty Trust. But when a Rockefeller called he found it hard to resist, especially because David Rockefeller explained that the bank had a "lot of clout" worldwide and that Hesburgh could do a lot of "moral good" from the board.[122] Father Ted never questioned whether such an appointment might involve him in conflicts of interest with his duties as a priest and as president of Notre Dame. He never considered that the rea- son that Rockefeller wanted him on the board was not for his banking ex- pertise but to signal to various constituencies that Chase Manhattan Bank took ethical issues seriously. Father Hesburgh's presence on this board also revealed that whatever his calls for increased aid for the poor at home and overseas, he meant to make no systemic challenge to American capitalism and to the role that major financial institutions played in it.

Although Hesburgh had found much to criticize in Nixon's civil rights policies, he had found elements of the administration's foreign policy more to his liking. He approved of the strategy of détente with the Soviet Union, and the arms control negotiations that were a key feature of it and that led to the signing of the Strategic Arms Limitation agreements (SALT I) in 1972. His work on the IAEA had convinced him that dialogue with the Soviet Union could produce good results and prevent the arms race from breaking out beyond control. Similarly, Father Ted viewed favorably the opening to China that Nixon and Henry Kissinger had so dramatically en- gineered. As American contacts with China expanded in the late 1970s and into the 1980s, he looked for opportunities to make his own visits and to de- velop contacts with the Middle Kingdom. Hesburgh had criticized Nixon's delay in extricating the United States from Vietnam. Although he approved of Vietnamization as a strategy to throw the burden of war-fighting back on to the South Vietnamese, he considered that its implementation had been flawed. Surprisingly, and without much basis, he blamed Kissinger and excused Nixon for most of this policy.

Hesburgh held a jaundiced view of Kissinger, whom he thought to be "egotistical."[123] His critical view resulted in part from the negative view he took of the Nixon administration's support for the 1973 Chilean coup d'état. Chile was the nation that had been the pride of Latin American democracy, and Father Ted had worked successfully to place Peace Corps workers in the countryside there. The sheer brutality of the Chilean military in executing their violent grab for power troubled Father Hesburgh. But he was also concerned about the well-being of his fellow Holy Cross religious in Chile, and with the plans of the Chilean military regime to seize control of St. George's College, the prestigious school that Holy Cross ran in Santiago. He traveled to Chile with Father Richard Warner in the months immediately after the coup to protest the Chilean military's intervention at St. George's. He and Warner secured an interview with Pinochet at the Diego Portales, the headquarters of the Chilean military. There, in the coup leader's office with its commanding views of Santiago, Hesburgh insinuated to the general that if his regime did not return control of the school to Holy Cross, he would use his many financial and political contacts to interfere with Chile's access to arms and credit. Pinochet indicated his hope that they could "negotiate" some arrangement. In the end Pinochet gave only an assurance that the school would not be sold. Father Ted's representations could not prevent the military's assertion of its control of the school for a number of years.[124] Hesburgh held Nixon and Kissinger responsible for that travesty.

In the end, although Father Hesburgh took no joy in Nixon's downfall, he knew that his resignation was best for the country. The atmosphere in Washington had become poisonous and the whole machinery of government fixated on Watergate. Father Ted shared in a sense of national relief when Nixon resigned. He was eager to move on.

GERALD FORD AND NATIONAL HEALING:
CLEMENCY AND CONVOCATION

Hesburgh greeted hopefully the prospect of a new president. He sent Gerald Ford a thoughtful message and an assurance of his prayers, to which

Ford replied expressing his gratitude.[125] Father Hesburgh had met Jerry Ford on a few formal occasions but had not developed any close relationship with the former congressman from Grand Rapids, Michigan. Nevertheless, Hesburgh developed a favorable view of Nixon's successor from the start. He appreciated Ford's sunny and optimistic disposition as well as his desire to bring reconciliation to a nation torn apart by both Vietnam and Watergate. Even Ford's having played football at the University of Michigan contributed to Hesburgh's positive impression of him.

Ford's decision on September 8, 1974, to grant Richard Nixon a full and unconditional pardon for any crimes he might have committed against the United States while serving as president took Father Ted, as it did most Americans, by surprise. It also brought Ford's honeymoon in office to an abrupt end. The president had wanted to put the whole Watergate saga to rest and to avoid a possible long and tumultuous trial of Nixon; harsh criticism of the decision followed. Many critics noted that although Ford had pardoned his predecessor he had not extended pardons to those who had dodged the draft or deserted their military duties during the Vietnam conflict. Father Hesburgh refrained from any public comment on Ford's pardon of Nixon. In private he shared something of the sentiment of those who believed that if the new president found it necessary to pardon the man who had selected him, then he should extend his mercy to those who had evaded or fled from military service during the Vietnam War. His views made him receptive to a further call to government service.

Smarting from the negative reactions to his pardon of Nixon and eager to regain some of the public's goodwill toward him, President Ford announced on September 16 plans for a conditional amnesty program for Vietnam War draft dodgers and military deserters. Ford's executive order established a nine-member Clemency Board to review the records of the deserters and draft evaders and to make recommendations for their receiving either a presidential pardon or a change in military discharge status. Ford explained his clemency program as the fulfillment of his promise "to throw the weight of [his] Presidency onto the scale of justice on the side of leniency and mercy." It constituted a key part of his effort to "bind up the nation's wounds" and to bring reconciliation and unity to the American people.[126] The new president called on Father Theodore Hesburgh to assist him in this endeavor, and he found the Notre Dame president ready to join in working toward national healing.

Earlier, Father Hesburgh had made clear his preference for the granting of full and unconditional amnesty to draft dodgers and military deserters as a way of washing out "the residue of Vietnam," but indicative of his pragmatic approach on public policy, he recalibrated and accepted Ford's offer to join the nine-member board. For Hesburgh a partial amnesty program was better than none at all. He welcomed "the opportunity to help administer a conditional amnesty, because I feel it is an important step forward in reuniting many young men with their country and, in many cases, with their families."[127] The commitment demanded an enormous amount of his time over the subsequent year, but it proved one of his most rewarding experiences in public service. After a year of work on the Presidential Clemency Board he wrote to Ford and admitted that there had been times during the preceding months when he had regretted his decision to say "yes" to the invitation to serve, especially "when problems mounted and decisions became very difficult." Yet he deemed that "in retrospect" it had proved a "great experience," and he expressed his gratitude to the president for "making it possible."[128] Hesburgh's deep satisfaction with his service on the Clemency Board emerged from a clear recognition that he had proven to be a crucial and decisive member who influenced the body to be more forgiving and generous in its recommendations.[129]

Ford appointed former U.S. senator Charles E. Goodell, a Republican who had opposed the Vietnam War, to chair the Clemency Board. He then tried to balance its membership with individuals who leaned toward either a lenient or a more harsh approach toward those who would petition for clemency. Hesburgh placed himself at the lenient end of the board's spectrum, and he soon found himself at odds with another notable member, retired Marine Corps general Lewis W. Walt, who maintained a tough approach in considering cases. Walt's approach was motivated by a desire to deter draft evaders and military deserters in the future. Walt had been a Marine Corps commander in Vietnam and later assistant commandant of the Marines. Almost from the outset he and Father Hesburgh found themselves antagonists in a contest to influence their colleagues. While Hesburgh maintained a cordial personal relationship with General Walt and could talk about hunting and fishing with him over cocktails at the end of a day of hearings, he conceded nothing to the retired Marine on the direction of the board. The days of Father Ted needing to be advised by John Hannah to recognize his own influence were long gone.

In the initial stages of the Clemency Board, as it determined its direction and procedures, Hesburgh and Walt debated vigorously.[130] Then when they began to consider actual cases requesting clemency, "the result was a virtual standoff . . . which often erupted into angry exchanges of great intensity." As John Lungren noted, "their diverging moral approaches to clemency could not be approximated, let alone negotiated."[131] The depth of disagreement between the two men even threatened the good working order of the entire board and was such that Goodell called on another board member, James Maye, executive director of the Paralyzed Veterans of America organization, to mediate between the "four-star general and the renowned Father Hesburgh." Maye found it a challenging task. He recalled that they were "both men of strong will and immense self-discipline." He saw that each man was "capable of violent indignation and compassion at the same time."[132] In the end his intervention brought some reduction in tensions and enabled the Clemency Board to pursue its mission, despite ongoing disagreements. Hesburgh succeeded in influencing his colleagues to pursue a more lenient approach. Lungren concluded: "Hesburgh emerged as the board's conscience, moving the members by his eloquent pleas and commanding presence."[133]

The Clemency Board had been directed to complete its work in one year, but the sheer volume of cases made that difficult even after Ford enlarged the body to eighteen members. Nonetheless, Hesburgh forged ahead, arguing strenuously for amnesty to be granted in almost every case. In the end the vast majority of the thousands of men who petitioned the board received either outright pardons or pardons on condition that they perform some kind of alternative service.[134] Father Ted's determined efforts played an important role in securing this result. They also brought him back into the Washington environs. It excited him to again travel regularly to D.C. for board meetings held at the Old Executive Office Building right next to the White House. He also did a series of radio and television interviews publicizing the work of the Clemency Board and encouraging individuals to come forward to petition for a pardon.[135] His work gave him some direct contact with Gerald Ford. Hesburgh met with Ford as a member of the Clemency Board on just a few occasions, but he wrote to Ford quite often.[136] His goal was to build a personal relationship with the appointed president, and he succeeded in doing so.

Father Hesburgh had taken advantage of his limited early contacts with President Ford to extend an invitation to him to visit Notre Dame. He saw this as a further step on the path of national healing. He recalled that he observed to the president: "There hasn't been a single president on a single campus, except the military schools, in the last ten years." He wanted to rectify this situation. Ford was worried that the presidential office would be damaged by a visit marred by protests, and he asked for a guarantee that "the presidency [would] not be embarrassed." Hesburgh gave his assurance, and, perhaps embellishing his response in his retelling, he told Ford: "I get to speak first. Notre Dame students are a great group but you can play them like an organ, and I guarantee when I finish you're going to have no problem."[137] So Jerry Ford agreed to come to Notre Dame for a special convocation on March 17, 1975—St. Patrick's Day, no less.

The special convocation during which Notre Dame conferred an honorary doctor of law degree on Gerald Ford brought Hesburgh immense satisfaction. He believed the occasion contributed in a meaningful way to the work of national reconciliation. He relished every moment of Ford's twelve-hour visit, during which the U.S. president enjoyed a warm welcome and Hesburgh was able to showcase his university. Father Ted was on hand to welcome Ford when *Air Force One* touched down at South Bend's airport at 10:00 a.m. He accompanied the president straight to the Athletic and Convocation Center for the special academic convocation. The event was covered live by the major television networks, so Hesburgh and Ford spoke not only to a packed crowd of twelve thousand students and faculty, but to a far larger audience across the country.

President Ford and Father Hesburgh took the stage to an enthusiastic welcome as the Notre Dame Marching Band played "Hail to the Chief." Hesburgh, as arranged, spoke first and presented the honorary degree to Ford. Special mention was made of Ford's clemency program as "a way back from a limbo of alienation for thousands of young people." Then Hesburgh played to the students and told them how he had assured Ford that he would receive a warm and wholehearted reception from the most welcoming student body in the whole world. With that he invited Ford to the podium, and, as he promised, the president was greeted with rousing enthusiasm. After the applause had stopped Ford delivered a fine speech that addressed the concerns about world poverty and hunger that Father Hesburgh had been highlighting in his recent lectures and speeches. Before getting to the substance of his remarks, Ford went out of his way to pay tribute to the Notre Dame president for his many contributions in government service. He noted his pride to be on Hesburgh's campus "that looks up to God and out to humanity at a time when some are tempted to turn inward and turn away from the problems of the world."[138]

The day went splendidly and Ford expressed his gratitude to Father Hesburgh. It had brought the exact result for which Father Ted had hoped and prayed. On March 27 in reply to a letter from Hesburgh thanking him for his visit, Ford assured Father Ted, "I had an unforgettable day at Notre Dame, and, at the risk of losing my Michigan passport, I'll even go so far as to say that I felt very much at home there."[139] The friendly relationship between Ford and Hesburgh was reflected in their correspondence over the subsequent months. In May Hesburgh wrote to Ford encouraging him and assuring him of his prayers and friendship, and Ford responded gratefully. On June 24 Ford wrote extending his congratulations to Hesburgh on the thirty-second anniversary of his ordination to the priesthood. He affirmed that Hesburgh's life was "one of dedication and service." Hesburgh made sure to have a book of photographs of Ford's trip to Notre Dame assembled and dispatched to the White House. Ford replied warmly and spoke of his "most pleasant" visit to the campus.[140] In May 1976 Hesburgh's name was included on the list of luminaries at the state dinner for President Giscard d'Estaing of France during his visit to celebrate America's Bicentennial. The invitation was an indication that "the Reverend Theodore M. Hesburgh, C.S.C.," as he was entered on the White House guest list, had earned a place among the pillars of the American establishment.

Going forward, Hesburgh used his connection to Ford to raise awareness on a number of issues, especially a world hunger crisis brought on by failed harvests in India and Bangladesh. Hesburgh had drawn significant public attention to the hunger crisis in an open letter to President Ford on November 22, 1974. He called on Ford to increase U.S. food aid "to alleviate present conditions of critical starvation."[141] Ford took the Hesburgh entreaty seriously and replied at length assuring him that "although I am not able now to give you a final determination on this year's food aid program, I am exploring all means of meeting humanitarian needs abroad."[142] Father Hesburgh continued his lobbying of Ford on this matter into 1975 and maintained a constructive correspondence with the president on the subject. Ford assured Hesburgh in January that he would aim to ensure that the food aid program was implemented urgently and in a way that worked with private aid efforts in meeting the "food shortage problem." By March he wrote giving a progress report on his efforts to get American grain shipped to the countries that needed it most.[143] Ford acknowledged in his convocation address at Notre Dame that Hesburgh's advocacy efforts were a factor in his decision to provide enhanced food aid. There seems little doubt that Father Ted's impassioned but thoughtful appeals influenced the president to intervene in humanitarian efforts to address situations of famine and starvation in 1974–1975.

Hesburgh found himself supportive of many of the Ford administration's foreign policy initiatives. He backed the efforts of Ford and Kissinger to continue the détente with the Soviet Union that Nixon had initiated. His concern for peace and nuclear arms control assured that he favored the Vladivostok Accords that Ford and Soviet General Secretary Leonid Brezhnev signed in November 24, which aimed to extend the arms control provisions of SALT I. Similarly, he favored the July 1975 Helsinski Accords in which the West formally recognized the postwar division of Europe and the Soviets promised to respect human rights. This agreement seemed to run parallel with Cardinal Casaroli's *Ostpolitik* efforts, which Hesburgh endorsed. Hesburgh also praised Ford for his continued negotiations with the Panamanian dictator Omar Torrijos, which aimed at ceding to his nation ownership and control of the Panama Canal. In April 1976 Hesburgh wrote praising Ford's position on the canal, and Ford replied gratefully, noting that his approach on negotiations "has been the consistent policy of my predecessors."[144] While Ford's pursuit of détente and a treaty with Panama pleased Father Hesburgh, it aggravated the conservative wing of the Republican Party. The anger over these and other issues prompted Ronald Reagan, the former governor of California, to challenge Ford in the 1976 Republican primaries. Hesburgh was perplexed by Reagan and at odds with him on many issues. He was pleased when Ford withstood the conservative insurgency at the Kansas City convention.

The 1976 election campaign took place during the year in which the United States celebrated its bicentennial. Father Hesburgh maintained a busy schedule over the course of the year giving talks and accepting honors. He had become one of those well-known and well-regarded figures who are sought after as keynote speakers, someone whose presence added a certain gravitas to an occasion and helped attract an audience. In April he spoke in Philadelphia at the Bicentennial Conference on Religious Liberty. On July 4 he was back in the City of Brotherly Love, where the Declaration of Independence had been signed, to address the National Citizens' Assembly on a favorite topic for him: "Justice in America: The Dream and the Reality." He had prepared major talks on justice, religious freedom, and American aspirations. He cut and pasted from these in fashioning his speeches to various groups, including university and college graduation ceremonies. He always displayed his deep love for the United States while acknowledging that it was still a work in progress. He wanted to counter some of the pessimism brought on by Watergate and Vietnam, and he expressed "the firm hope that if we are true to our original dream, God will give us the grace to go farther than any nation ever has along the highroad of freedom and justice under the law." He made clear his rejection of gloomy claims that America was "a thwarted experiment, a burned-out case, a fading hope." For him, his nation remained "still the most exciting human experiment in all the world."[145]

Hesburgh appreciated opportunities to reflect on the strengths of America and its possibilities for the future. He also drew a special satisfaction from Ford's request that he provide suggestions for the president's bicentennial addresses.[146] This request together with his receiving recognition such as the Jefferson Award for Public Service in the company of Alan Greenspan and John D. Rockefeller elevated further his sense of his capacity to contribute to the nation in a meaningful way. He kept pressing his case with the Ford administration on a number of key issues like amnesty and the need to increase foreign aid. But Ford could not focus on Hesburgh's advocacy in the summer and fall of 1976. After completing his bicentennial duties, the president turned to political survival. Hesburgh had little to do with Ford during the campaign he ran against the Democratic candidate, Governor Jimmy Carter. In contrast, he maintained substantial contact with the Carter campaign. Hesburgh invited both candidates to visit the Notre Dame campus during the fall, but only Carter took him up on it. Father Ted maintained his neutral stance in public, but he was increasingly drawn to Carter. Although he liked Ford he now found himself aligned with the Democrats on most issues. He cast his ballot for Carter on November 2, 1976, and so too did a narrow majority of Americans, so that Carter garnered 50.1 percent of the popular vote to Ford's 48 percent. Soon after the election results were announced Hesburgh wrote thanking Ford for his service, and the president replied back conveying his "deepest gratitude for your wise counsel and valuable assistance during the past two years."[147] Hesburgh knew that Ford had played an important role in aiding the United States' transition through a difficult period. He found it very appropriate that President Carter used the first words of his inaugural address to pay tribute to Ford, when he stated: "For myself and for our nation, I want to thank my predecessor for all he has done to heal our land." Father Hesburgh believed he had assisted Ford in the work of national reconciliation. But Hesburgh's focus now shifted to the Carter administration and the ways in which he might serve within it.

CHAPTER 8

FROM INSIDER TO OUTSIDER (OF SORTS):
Jimmy Carter, John Paul II, and Ronald Reagan

THE SECOND HALF OF THE 1970S COMPRISED SOME CHALLENG-
ing years for the United States. While the nation grappled with the
aftermath of the Vietnam War and Watergate, a new range of trials arose
including the energy crisis, a combination of high inflation and stagnant
economic growth that was branded as stagflation, and a raft of challenges
overseas including the nuclear arms race, the Iran hostage crisis, and the
Soviet invasion of Afghanistan. These were only some of the challenges
that Jimmy Carter faced during his one term as president. The American
people judged his performance harshly. In 1980 they unceremoniously
booted him out of office and replaced him with Ronald Reagan, the onetime governor of California. Reagan faced similar difficulties in both the
domestic and foreign policy realms, but his actions secured greater public
endorsement.

Reagan's two terms in office coincided with much of the first decade of
the pontificate of Karol Józef Wojtyła, otherwise known as Pope John Paul
II. He was elected at the second papal conclave of 1978, the "year of three
popes." Pope Paul VI died in August and was succeeded by Pope John
Paul I, but he died after barely a month in office. Cardinal Wojtyła adopted
his predecessor's name as a tribute to him, but the name was entirely fitting
as he embodied both the rich mystical spirituality associated with Saint
John and the true evangelist's commitment of Saint Paul. The first non-
Italian to serve as pope for four centuries began his papacy on October 16,
1978, and served until his death on April 2, 2005.

Father Theodore Hesburgh completed his final decade as president of
Notre Dame during the presidencies of Carter and Reagan and the papacy

of John Paul II. His influence was significant during Carter's administration. Thereafter, he found it a difficult time to serve the Church and his nation on the broader stage because he disagreed with decisions made in both Rome and Washington, D.C.

GOOD FRIENDS WORKING TOGETHER

Jimmy Carter first visited Notre Dame while campaigning for the May 4 Indiana primary. The onetime Georgia governor addressed an enthusiastic crowd of over three thousand at the Stepan Center and also dropped in on a Notre Dame football practice where he asked Coach Dan Devine and his players to "take it easy on Georgia Tech next fall."[1] Father Hesburgh was out of town at the time of Carter's visit, so he missed a chance to take the measure of the Democratic front-runner in person. Carter tried to garner support on this Catholic campus by emphasizing his own personal opposition to abortion and that he would work to minimize the need for abortion. Yet even as he explained that the government should not do anything to encourage abortion, he also confirmed his willingness to abide by the Supreme Court's rulings on it, namely *Roe v. Wade*. This position, which he outlined throughout his campaign, eventually caused some Catholics to express reservations about his candidacy.

The U.S. Catholic bishops wanted the Democratic nominee to act more explicitly on the religious and moral convictions that led him to believe that abortion was wrong. The bishops had strongly condemned the unrestrained abortion license granted by *Roe v. Wade* and had called for a constitutional amendment prohibiting abortion. They entreated both major parties to support that measure. President Ford indicated his support for an amendment that would return the abortion issue to the states for their decision. Carter firmly resisted the pressure to support any constitutional measure. Aware of the increasing strength of pro-choice supporters in the Democratic Party after McGovern's nomination in 1972, Carter fully endorsed his party's platform, which held that whatever the religious and ethical concerns that Americans had on the subject of abortion, there would be no "attempt to amend the U.S. Constitution to overturn the Supreme Court decision in this area." Archbishop Joseph Bernardin of Cincinnati, then serving as president of the National Conference of Catholic Bishops, denounced the Democrats' abortion plank as "irresponsible."[2] The extent of the bishops' criticisms worried the Carter campaign sufficiently that the candidate sought to placate the bishops at a meeting on August 31 with Bernardin and a number of his episcopal confreres. The meeting was civil but Carter made no serious concessions. Rebuffed by Carter, Bernardin publicly stated: "We continue to be disappointed with the Governor's position." The bishops' criticisms unnerved the Carter team, especially after the substantial lead the onetime Georgia governor enjoyed over Ford in the opinion polls in the summer began to evaporate as the fall campaign moved along. Candidate Carter decided to reach out for help and advice. He called Father Hesburgh.

One Sunday night in late September or early October Father Ted was in his office catching up on work. His phone rang and "a man with a Southern drawl" asked to speak with him. It was Jimmy Carter. He said he was calling from the kitchen in his home in Plains, Georgia, because he needed help. Hesburgh recalls asking what kind of help, to which Carter responded, "I think I'm in trouble with Catholics." Carter recalled that Father Ted replied, "I know." Thus began their relationship. After his customary clarification that he was nonpartisan and never endorsed any candidate, Hesburgh addressed the issue of Carter's stance on the question of a constitutional amendment. He adopted the stance of a campaign adviser and counseled Carter that "from a purely political standpoint" he should make no comment on the constitutional amendment regarding abortion as he had no authority on the matter. As Hesburgh recalled, "I advised Carter not to put himself in the middle of that debate when there was no reason for him to be there." Carter was grateful for the pragmatic advice and indicated that he would welcome any additional counsel that Hesburgh might offer.

Carter's request is not surprising as he wanted to draw on Hesburgh's experience and wisdom. What is more notable about Hesburgh's conversation with the Democratic nominee is how Hesburgh addressed the abortion issue as a political problem that Carter needed to downplay. He did not address it as a priest who saw abortion as a moral blight on the United States that should be ended. Rather than suggest that Carter give further consideration to his political stance on abortion in light of his personal claim to oppose the practice of destroying life in the womb, Father Ted treated the issue as one to be circumvented. Far from wanting to engage Carter in a serious discussion of the challenging moral issue that divided the country, Hesburgh turned their attention to another topic. He passed along a message from the Panamanian leader Omar Torrijos, whom he had seen during his recent travels, stressing the need for the U.S. government to make progress on a Panama Canal treaty.[3]

Father Ted continued to counsel Carter over the following weeks and also conversed occasionally with Walter "Fritz" Mondale, Carter's running mate, whom Hesburgh knew well. Furthermore, Hesburgh quickly determined that he wanted to do more for Carter than simply offer advice. He decided to provide some cover for Carter from the kinds of criticism he had received from the Catholic bishops over abortion. He arranged a visit by Carter to the nation's best known Catholic university, while always maintaining publicly that he favored neither candidate. Carter came to Notre Dame on Sunday, October 10, less than a month before the election. He gave a speech that might have been written by Father Hesburgh. Carter told his select audience of four hundred gathered in the Center for Continuing Education that he wanted to bring a "new spirit of optimism, patriotism and self-sacrifice" to the United States. He called for a renewed commitment to civil and human rights on both domestic and international levels.[4] Carter refrained from any reference to the rights of the unborn. That subject came within Father Hesburgh's purview. In introducing Carter, Hesburgh made a deliberate effort to reduce the significance of abortion as a political and campaign issue. He held forth that a compromise solution on the issue could be reached "in the kind of rational and civil atmosphere that the university represents."[5] He offered Notre Dame as the venue for such deliberations and promised to organize a national conference on the subject. Carter welcomed the Hesburgh proposal, which made him appear more willing to compromise on abortion than his firm commitment to abide by *Roe v. Wade* allowed. In effect Hesburgh aimed to limit the political damage that the abortion issue might cause Carter.

In the end Jimmy Carter won a small majority of the Catholic vote in 1976. Whether Father Hesburgh's efforts influenced the votes of any wavering Catholics in Carter's favor cannot be conclusively determined, but that the Notre Dame president intended to sway such voters is clear. Carter understood this and felt he was in Hesburgh's debt. This gave their relationship a different quality compared to what Hesburgh had experienced with any of Carter's predecessors. With previous presidents Hesburgh had accepted their invitations to assist with specific tasks through formal appointments. He had attempted to make suggestions in other areas, but only when a rare opportunity arose. Carter's visit to Notre Dame had deepened their bond. Hesburgh knew thereafter that Carter trusted and respected him as well as felt indebted to him. He also understood that Carter welcomed his advice and support for the broad human rights objectives outlined in the October 10 address. They shared something of the same moral outlook on the world. Hesburgh seized his chance to counsel the incoming president. During the Carter presidency he was tapped to assist on a greater variety of issues than in any previous administration. Yet, he ultimately judged Carter's presidency critically, indeed even harshly, despite his own involvement with the administration.

Father Hesburgh wasted little time contacting Carter after his election victory. He called him at his home in Plains while the president-elect was still resting after the demanding campaign. He indicated that he had an important matter to bring to Carter's attention. Carter revealed his willingness to engage Hesburgh by agreeing to see him the next morning prior to a meeting he had scheduled with the congressional leadership at Blair House in Washington, D.C. Hesburgh arranged with McGeorge Bundy, the president of the Ford Foundation, to join him so that they could together make the case for pardons for those thousands of draft resisters and deserters whose cases had not been handled by the Clemency Board during the Ford years. Hesburgh received a "jolt" at 7:30 a.m. the next morning when an aide at Blair House introduced "Father Bundy and Mr. Hesburgh" to the incoming president. After their designations were clarified, the two men outlined for an attentive Carter the results of studies funded by the Ford Foundation indicating the number of men still in need of a presidential pardon. Bundy covered the broad details while Hesburgh put a human face on the issue by giving details of a young serviceman who had deserted from Vietnam after being denied medical treatment for a detached retina.[6] Their direct representations produced quick results.

Hesburgh did not limit his counsel to this particular matter into which he had invested such time and energy. Other issues attracted his attention during the interregnum from Carter's election to his taking office. He joined a number of other establishment grandees including Sargent Shriver, George Kennan, and Charles Yost in seeking to influence Carter's stance on arms control and East–West relations. Hesburgh had earlier affiliated with the United States Committee for East–West Common Existence, which aimed to push nuclear arms reductions. In December he added his signature to a committee letter that alerted the president of the signatories' concern "that one of the most important challenges confronting America as you take office is to restore momentum to the effort to improve Soviet-American relations."[7] Hesburgh would take on this issue as of particular concern over the next decade as we have seen with his work on campus with the peace institute.

Hesburgh brought various issues to Carter's attention, and he also accepted with enthusiasm the president-elect's invitation to suggest qualified individuals to be considered for senior appointments in the administration. He signed on as a member of the National Advisors' Group for Presidential Appointments, along with liberal and labor heavyweights such as Lane Kirkland of the AFL-CIO, Vernon Jordan of the National Urban League, and the chair of the Democratic National Committee, Robert Strauss.[8] Over the weeks of the transition Hesburgh recalled transmitting close to a hundred names for consideration by Carter and his two principal advisers during the transition, Walter Mondale and Hamilton Jordan, who would serve as Carter's chief of staff. Hesburgh's role was well reported in the media, which only added to his reputation as an intimate of the new president.[9] Hesburgh did not keep quiet about his role. He passed through New York and met with Cyrus Vance, a veteran of the Kennedy and Johnson administrations who served as chair of the Rockefeller Foundation board. Hesburgh alerted the gentlemanly Vance that he was "at the top of my list." Hesburgh had no desire to bring "outsiders" to Carter's attention. He brought forward East Coast establishment figures like Vance for consideration, and many eventually took up appointments.

Jimmy Carter was sworn in on a cold but sunny January 20, 1977. On his first full day in office Carter manifested his concern for mercy by issuing a proclamation granting an unconditional pardon to all those who had evaded the draft during the Vietnam War. Later in the year he made it possible for veterans who had been dishonorably discharged to have their cases reviewed. His actions reflected Hesburgh's influence, and they deepened Hesburgh's regard for the new occupant of the Oval Office. They confirmed his commitment to work hard for Carter's success.

Hesburgh's desire to promote Carter and his policies led him to request that the president return to Notre Dame to speak at the 1977 commencement exercises and to receive an honorary degree. He wanted the president to give a truly substantial speech and Carter agreed to do so. The occasion was memorable for featuring not only the president but also House Speaker Thomas P. (Tip) O'Neill, who also received an honorary degree, and former Senate majority leader Mike Mansfield, who received the Laetare

Medal for his distinguished public service. The citation read to accompany Carter's honorary degree praised the new president for "offering a generous amnesty to those caught in the misadventure of Vietnam," for his willing- ness to use foreign aid "as a leverage to improve conditions of human dig- nity," for warning Americans that they must alter "a wasteful lifestyle," and for his commitment to strategic arms limitations. Carter reciprocated in his speech by extolling the president of Notre Dame for his twenty-five years of service during which he "has spoken more consistently and more effec- tively in support of the rights of human beings than any person I know."

Carter fulfilled Hesburgh's request to give a speech of substance. He outlined his administration's new approach to international affairs by call- ing for a "foreign policy that is democratic, that is based on our fundamen- tal values, and uses power and influence for humane purposes." Carter argued for a foreign policy that would move beyond the established postwar strategy of containing the Soviet Union. He memorably proclaimed—in words he would come to regret after the Soviet invasion of Afghanistan two years later—that Americans were "now free of that inordinate fear of communism which once led us to embrace any dictator who joined us in our fear."[10] Most notably Carter declared that a cardinal premise of Amer- ican foreign policy must be a "basic commitment to promote the cause of human rights." Indeed he affirmed human rights as a "fundamental tenet" of his foreign policy. Hesburgh loved the content of the speech, and once observed that Carter honored Notre Dame by delivering such a significant address there. Just days after Carter's visit, Father Ted wrote to National Security Adviser Zbigniew Brzezinski lauding "the wonderful speech." He waxed rather eloquent that Carter's "message really broke the bonds of the past, opened up new vistas based on principle rather than expediential ma- neuverings, and I think gave the nation and the world a new vision, a new hope, and a burst of optimism which is badly needed in our day."[11]

Hesburgh thereafter played a supportive role in seeking to realize the new Carter vision. He was not involved directly in the major foreign policy formulation efforts of the Carter team, and never found himself caught in the crossfire that eventually developed between Vance and Brzezinski over the direction of that policy. Rather he lent his public and private sup- port to a number of important Carter initiatives, some of which attracted considerable opposition. An important instance was Hesburgh's backing of the Panama Canal treaties that Carter signed with General Torrijos on September 7, 1977, which provided for the return of the canal to Panama as of midnight on December 31, 1999. Carter saw the treaties as positive for American security and trade, and he also held that they would improve U.S. relations with other Latin American countries. Hesburgh agreed fully and in doing so had the encouragement of Archbishop Marcos McGrath of Panama City, his friend and confrere in Holy Cross. On the day of the signing ceremony in Washington, D.C., Hesburgh joined a group of a hundred proverbial "opinion leaders" for a briefing from Carter and other officials on the treaties.[12] It was a Who's Who of the aging establishment with Clark Clifford, C. Douglas Dillon, W. Averell Harriman, Lady Bird Johnson, John J. McCloy, George Meany, and David Rockefeller all in attendance as well as many corporate leaders.[13] At Hesburgh's suggestion the Carter administration eventually orchestrated a major public relations campaign that mobilized citizens committees to support the treaties and that held hundreds of forums where policymakers explained the benefits of them.[14] Hesburgh regularly indicated his support for the treaties and took some satisfaction when the U.S. Senate ratified them by a vote of 68–32 in the spring of 1978.

Hesburgh made clear his support for Carter's efforts on human rights as well as his initiatives to further arms control and promote peace in the Middle East. He welcomed Carter's refusal to continue the past American practice of overlooking human rights abuses by U.S. allies. He approved the administration's tougher stance toward South Korea, Argentina, and South Africa, and cheered the decision to end political and military support to the vile regime of the Nicaraguan dictator Anastasio Somoza. On both arms control and the Middle East, a mix of naïveté and hubris, as well as a deep desire not to be seen as merely building on the Ford-Kissinger policies, led Carter to pursue faltering initiatives and to make outright mistakes. But Hesburgh was untroubled by the Carter administration's specific decisions, preferring to focus on the good intentions of Carter's team. He had signed on with Jimmy Carter and there was no easy turning back. In fact, he already had accepted a formal diplomatic role in the Carter administration.

When Carter came to Notre Dame for the May commencement exercises in 1977 he requested that Father Ted accept appointment with the rank of ambassador while he served as chairman of the U.S. delegation to a planned United Nations Conference on Science and Technology for Development scheduled for 1979. The conference was organized to determine how developed countries could best help meet the "technical needs and demands of the developing nations." Frank Press, Carter's science adviser and the director of the Office of Science and Technology Policy, prepared the talking points for Carter to use in offering the position to Hesburgh. He advised the president to explain to Hesburgh that he would serve as head of the U.S. delegation and could "help select delegates and plan the general approach on the policy problems." But, well aware of Hesburgh's resolve to continue serving as president of Notre Dame, Press emphasized in his briefing memorandum the flexibility of the appointment. Hesburgh would be able to "travel as much or as little as he wishes," and could "tailor his involvement to suit his interests."[15] A State Department–appointed coordinator and staff would assume most of the representational duties. Hesburgh gladly accepted the appointment on these terms. It gelled with his interests as chair of the Overseas Development Council, and it gave him the freedom to roam over the whole development portfolio from a position within the administration. The position suited him further because it gave him a staff that handled much of the day-to-day burden of conference preparations.

The State Department initially expected that Father Hesburgh would play a primarily ceremonial role in his position. A memorandum to Carter recommending that Jean Wilkowski, an experienced foreign service officer who would coordinate the U.S. delegation, also be accorded ambassadorial rank, explained that Hesburgh "will serve only to open and close ceremonies and as a pre-conference advisor." Wilkowski was expected to carry the heavier burden of preparing for and representing the United States not only at the UN gathering but also at various preliminary meetings.[16] The State Department officials knew little of whom they wrote. Hesburgh was incapable of just playing a minor role for public show. He threw himself into the work of preparations for the conference in collaboration with the capable Wilkowski, with whom he cooperated well.[17] Drawing on his many connections he put together a delegation of over eighty people.[18] This was the group he led to the conference that assembled in August 1979 in Vienna.

The actual conference proved a great disappointment to Hesburgh. By 1979 it had evolved into yet another vast "global problem-solving mega-conference" that was almost beyond coherent management. Over five thousand people attended the meeting and its associated activities. Delegates from 142 countries as well as representatives from various UN secretariats and programs were the official participants, but they were joined by individuals representing over 330 nongovernmental organizations. Even a friendly evaluation of the conference concluded that its results were "exceedingly modest."[19] The developing nations, gathered under the umbrella of the Group of 77, demanded nothing less than a "new international economic order" facilitated by the transfer of billions of dollars from the North to the South. These demands could not be met by the developed nations, and the end result was a tepid "Programme of Action consisting of 65 diplomatically worded resolutions" designed to achieve some lowest common denominator consensus. A new interim fund was created as a compromise measure, and its target was to raise a modest $250 million through voluntary contributions.

In reality the conference was a laborious ordeal. Wilkowski thought it resembled a "circus," and she was glad when it "came mercifully to an end." She judged it a "hollow conclusion" after all their extensive preparations.[20] Hesburgh more optimistically claimed that the conference had "taken the first step to overcome the worst aspects of poverty" and to create a better world.[21] But on his return to the United States he found that the Carter administration refused to contribute $25 million to jump-start the interim fund. He could not gain Carter's attention because the president was focusing on other matters. He judged Carter harshly for rejecting what he thought a "viable solution," and he concluded that the administration "blew it." His attempts to get the "Vienna conference off the hook" by securing some American support failed. He attributed the failure to the president's losing "interest because he was more concerned about being re-elected and more concerned about political things."[22] Hesburgh felt disillusioned about the outcome of the UN conference. His ambassadorship had hardly resulted in some kind of notable breakthrough in addressing world development issues. Quite the opposite, in fact. Despite all his efforts the UN Conference on Science and Technology for Development meeting simply passed into memory as the UN bureaucrats and the NGO staffs moved on to their next meetings

Hesburgh's extensive work for the UN conference reflected the priority he now gave international over domestic concerns. Only occasionally did he seek to bring specific matters regarding domestic policy to Carter's attention. At the request of McGeorge Bundy and Harvard University president Derek Bok, he wrote to Carter regarding a case pending before the Supreme Court, namely *Regents of the University of California v. Bakke*. The *Bakke* case was seen as calling into question the affirmative action programs for racial minorities that had recently been developed in American universities. In his letter and in conversations he conducted with Vice

President Mondale, Hesburgh defended preferential admission based on race but opposed the use of any system of racial quotas. He effectively wanted institutions like Derek Bok's and his own to be left alone on the matter. As he wrote to Carter: "where an institution undertakes voluntary efforts to remedy the effects of discrimination in our society, the implementation of affirmative action programs should be left to the demonstrated good will and wisdom of each educational institution."[23] There is little evidence that his letter had much influence, but the episode still holds significance. It surely serves as something of a marker of Catholic assimilation when the president of the Ford Foundation and the president of Harvard University called upon the priest-president of Notre Dame to make representations for them on this highly contested legal matter.

Although Hesburgh responded promptly to the appeals of Bundy and Bok to intervene on the issue of affirmative action, he remained missing in action on the issue of abortion. He made no deliberate move to hold President Carter to his commitments against both federal funding of abortion and its permissive use. He was cool to the efforts of the American bishops to pressure Health, Education, and Welfare secretary Joseph Califano on matters such as restrictions on abortions, the federal funding of sterilizations, and his opposition to tuition tax credits for Catholic schools. Califano recalled that Hesburgh understood the lines he drew "between personal religious and moral convictions and sound public policy." Hesburgh invited Califano to deliver the 1979 commencement address at Notre Dame to give him a forum to reply to his critics in the hierarchy. According to Califano's recollection, Hesburgh told him: "Maybe we can get them to understand your position and that of other Catholics in public life."[24]

Whatever his claims to be an "independent" in terms of party affiliation, by the late 1970s Father Ted found himself firmly aligned with liberal Democrats. The Rockefeller Republicans were a dying breed, and he felt no rapport with the conservative drift of the Republican Party. He had no sympathy with Phyllis Schlafly's grassroots campaign against the Equal Rights Amendment, and the direction and political impact of Jerry Falwell's Moral Majority troubled him. He had more regard for traditional conservatives like William F. Buckley Jr., the renowned editor of *National Review* and host of *Firing Line*, a program on which Hesburgh had appeared in 1974 to discuss world hunger. Hesburgh even invited Buckley to give the commencement address at Notre Dame in 1978, but was surprised when the leading light of the modern conservative movement took the opportunity to offer a pointed rebuttal to Carter's address given the previous year from the same dais. Buckley contested the benign view of communism that Carter presented, and he noted the critical challenge of communist power in Cambodia and China. He called for continued commitment in the Cold War.[25] Buckley's melancholy tone hardly pleased the graduates and their parents, who expected a more exuberant speech for the occasion, but it was the content of Buckley's address that bothered Hesburgh. Like Carter, the Notre Dame president wanted to move beyond focusing on the danger communism represented and instead to pursue East–West negotiations on arms control. This position set the scene for Hesburgh to find himself at odds with Carter's successor, whose views aligned with Buckley's.

Hesburgh's positions endeared him further to his friends in the liberal establishment. His prestige grew as he now chaired the Rockefeller Foundation Board and accepted compliments regarding his ambassadorship. He appeared regularly on serious television programs, where he invariably emanated a measured and authoritative presence. He now counted media luminaries such as Walter Cronkite as friends, and he received favorable treatment in the press. Occasionally he received a mild challenge, as when Bill Monroe of NBC's *Meet the Press* inquired in late 1977 about why a priest should serve on the board of Chase Manhattan Bank. Hesburgh responded that he aimed to serve as "a kind of conscience," someone who could get involved "when a moral problem arises."[26] Monroe proceeded no further with his questioning and didn't probe into whether Hesburgh believed that he had experienced any success in this role. Few journalists ever probed him forcefully. It would have appeared unseemly.

In November 1978, Father Hesburgh accepted appointment to the President's Commission on the Holocaust. The twenty-four-member body, chaired by Elie Wiesel, was primarily charged with making recommendations to establish "an appropriate memorial to the victims of the Holocaust." Hesburgh was not a major contributor on the commission, but he fully endorsed its recommendation that a "National Holocaust Memorial Museum" be erected in Washington, D.C. He thereafter accepted appointment to the U.S. Holocaust Memorial Council, also chaired by Wiesel, which worked to implement the commission recommendations.[27]

Hesburgh played no role in Carter's heroic efforts to negotiate a peace settlement with Anwar Sadat and Menachem Begin at Camp David, but he was called upon to help celebrate it and to pray for its successful implementation. Early on March 26, 1979, the day that Begin, Sadat, and Carter gathered at the White House to sign the Egypt-Israel Peace Treaty, Hesburgh helped lead an ecumenical prayer at the Lincoln Memorial. He was joined by a rabbi, an imam, and an evangelical preacher named Ruth Carter Stapleton, the president's sister. The national leaders were unable to attend the service, but representatives of all three countries were present. They heard Father Ted observe that "if religious persons are committed profoundly to one simple reality all around the world, it must be peace." It was a fitting start to a historic day when bitter enmities were cautiously put aside.

Although Carter could work personally with the leaders of Egypt and Israel to reach a settlement of their differences, he needed to involve a much larger group of individuals to seek resolution of the controversial question of the "policies and procedures governing the admission of immigrants and refugees to the United States." To search for a settlement that might secure strong bipartisan support, Carter agreed to the establishment of a sixteen-member commission made up of four House members, four senators, four ex-officio cabinet members, and four members appointed by the president. The law creating the Select Commission on Immigration and Refugee Policy was signed on October 5, 1978, and Carter appointed Florida governor Reubin Askew to serve as chair. A year later he asked Askew to serve as U.S. trade representative, and Askew resigned as chair of the immigration commission. Arnie Miller, who headed the White House Presidential Personnel Office, recommended Hesburgh as his successor. In a memo to Carter he explained that the "Commission Chairman must have the stature and prestige to command the respect and involvement of Cabinet officers and Members of Congress and possess the leadership necessary to build a workable consensus about the immigration issue." Miller argued that Hesburgh met these criteria and that he could provide "strong moral leadership." Carter approached Hesburgh and conveyed his belief that the Notre Dame priest could build consensus on the vexing question of immigration. Hesburgh agreed immediately, and so began his long campaign to obtain immigration reform by devising "a national policy that would with fairness control the millions of illegal aliens who were crossing our borders every year and playing havoc with the labor supply and economics of the country."[28]

Father Ted threw himself into the work of what became known as the "Hesburgh Commission," while relying heavily on an able staff headed by Lawrence (Larry) Fuchs. Over the remaining fifteen months of the Carter administration the immigration commission held public hearings, heard expert testimony, and waded through volumes of reports and surveys. The commission submitted its lengthy report on the last day of Carter's administration. Hesburgh summarized its main recommendations as "widening the front door to immigration—[by] allowing 550,000 legal aliens to enter the United States each year, or about double the [existing] 230,000 quota—and closing the back door to illegal aliens." The latter was to be achieved by making it illegal to knowingly hire or recruit illegal immigrants. The recommendations also contained provisions for illegal aliens who had resided in the United States continuously for at least five years to have some pathway to legal status. Hesburgh played an important role in reaching this consensus and collaborated especially with Vice President Mondale in doing so. He regretted his failure to persuade the committee to adopt his proposal for a national identity card to be used in employment, which would be a barrier to the illegal hiring of aliens, but the elimination of his idea assured that liberal pressure groups like the American Civil Liberties Union did not outright oppose the commission's conclusions. He believed the recommendations were "moderate, doable, and effective," and that Congress would enact a law. But the political situation had vastly altered by the time the immigration commission submitted its report. Ronald Reagan had defeated Carter, and he preferred to appoint a new group to review immigration policy. Hesburgh found this setback frustrating, but he had developed a steadfast commitment to immigration reform and refused to give up on his efforts. Although he held no official role during the Reagan years, he persisted in lobbying for the main recommendations made by his immigration commission. In doing so he developed close relations with Senator Alan Simpson of Wyoming and Representative Romano L. Mazzoli of Kentucky, who happened to be a Notre Dame graduate. After almost six years of debates, aggravations, and legislative compromises the Congress passed the Simpson-Mazzoli Act and Reagan signed it into law as the Immigration Reform and Control Act on November 6, 1986. Hesburgh rightly deserves credit for helping lay important groundwork for this legislation, whatever its strengths and limitations.[29]

Although it took some years for Father Hesburgh's endeavors on immigration reform to come to some fruition, his efforts to raise funds to provide aid to desperate Cambodians in 1979 had a more immediate impact. Regrettably, the world largely had stood aside from 1975 to 1979 as the ghastly Pol Pot and his brutal Khmer Rouge regime perpetrated a genocide against their own people. The killing fields of Cambodia claimed over a million (and perhaps two million) lives out of a total population of eight million. In December 1978 the Vietnamese army, with Soviet backing, invaded Cambodia and drove the Chinese-backed Khmer Rouge toward the Thai border. There Pol Pot and his remaining forces mounted guerrilla military resistance relying on access to supplies transferred through Thailand by China. In this disastrous political and military disarray hundreds of thousands of distressed Cambodian refugees fleeing both Pol Pot's death camps and the Vietnamese military were struggling for survival. In short it was a terrible humanitarian disaster, and it looked likely to get even worse as the summer of 1979 passed into fall. Starvation and disease threatened to decimate further the surviving Cambodian population. In this distressing situation Hesburgh's friend Jim Grant, president of the Overseas Development Council and soon to assume the leadership of UNICEF, visited the Thai border and observed the appalling plight of the refugees. He knew that immediate aid was needed to sustain these people, and he knew whom to contact to help arrange it—his friend Theodore Hesburgh.[30]

With Grant's prompting Hesburgh gathered together leaders of forty religious and relief organizations at the office of the Overseas Development Council on Massachusetts Avenue. Within a few hours they had resolved to mobilize resources and to coordinate their efforts to help the Cambodians. They also directed a letter to President Carter urging greater assistance by the U.S. government to address the needs of the Cambodian people. Carter met with the group that same day, October 24, and immediately committed significant aid to the relief effort.[31] Hesburgh was the clear leader of the nongovernment aid agencies and spoke on behalf of them.[32] Both Carter and Hesburgh declared the need to avoid a Cambodian holocaust, although there was not much recognition that one had already occurred in that tragic land. Carter decided to dispatch his wife, Rosalynn, to the Thai-Cambodian border to draw publicity to the deepening humanitarian crisis. On Mrs. Carter's arrival back in Washington in November, Hesburgh returned to the White House to join her in broadcasting loudly the need for greater assistance. He appreciated his association with Rosalynn Carter and credited her with influencing her husband's supportive actions on this matter.[33]

Hesburgh became cochair of the National Cambodian Crisis Committee, an umbrella organization that raised private money to assist the refugees caught in the virtual no-man's-land near the Thai border as well as to transport aid into the area controlled by the Vietnamese army. He was at his best in this campaign. Two of the associates who worked with him on the Cambodian relief campaign remembered his "irrepressible and magnanimous spirit," and that "his recognized humanitarian leadership and his moral authority were indispensable in giving immediacy and gravitas to this effort."[34] Over the following months, which incidentally coincided with his demanding work on the commission on immigration reform, he poured his energies into this effort. His capacity for work seemed boundless.

In July 1980 Hesburgh made another trip around the world. During his travels he met up with Jim Grant and his wife, Ethel, in Bangkok and they joined a Royal Australian Air Force relief flight into Cambodia traveling on UN passports, which Grant obtained as director of UNICEF. Hesburgh relished being able to tread where few Americans had been in recent years, and he was able to visit both Phnom Penh and the ancient temples of Angkor Wat. The situation in the majority of Cambodia under Vietnamese control had stabilized, and a rice crop had been planted. Hesburgh wrote after the trip in the cover letter distributing his travel diary to various friends that he saw a "rather dramatic recovering from death and destruction, averting total holocaust for the Khmer people in their ancient land." He shared the story "with a sense of hope and a glimmer of success," while admitting that "much remains to be done."[35] He thought much more could be done on the Thai border where aid to genuine refugees was sometimes interrupted and covert assistance was still extended to the Khmer Rouge.[36] Hesburgh was impatient with the Cold War geopolitics, which led Western nations not only to refuse to recognize the Vietnamese puppet regime in Phnom Penh, but also to retain formal recognition of the Khmer Rouge government. Hesburgh understood that Pol Pot was a butcher with the blood of many of his countrymen on his hands. He made this point in a frank exchange with King Bhumibol of Thailand. It is likely that the king took some offense at the candor with which the forceful American priest expressed his views.[37] Hesburgh was not thinking of Thai cultural practices in addressing the king nor of attending to diplomatic niceties. His goal was to obtain relief for the suffering Cambodians. Perhaps Hesburgh exaggerated the impact of the aid supplied by Western agencies when he claimed in his memoir that the aid helped "a whole nation to survive."[38] Still, he had influenced the Carter administration to act, and he led the American private aid effort to raise funding for Cambodia with those crucial humanitarian purposes in mind. It was a stellar performance.

Hesburgh visited the White House quite often during the fall of 1979 to address difficult matters like Cambodian aid, and he was especially glad to be present there for the uplifting ceremony when President Carter hosted Pope John Paul II at the conclusion of the pope's historic six-day visit to the United States. This visit came just four months after the Polish pope's dramatic visit to his homeland during which over a million Poles in Victory Square in Warsaw had chanted, "We want God," in response to his great homily at the Mass he celebrated there. His visit had culminated with an outdoor Mass at Blonie Field in Krakow that was attended by upwards of three million people.[39] The extraordinary nine-day visit had stirred the hearts of his people and sparked what George Weigel has called a "moral and cultural revolution," which ultimately challenged the communist domination of Eastern Europe.[40] That enormous contribution was still to be fully realized when the successor to Saint Peter came to the United States in October, but he was greeted with enormous enthusiasm. Americans sensed his courage and powerful commitment, and Carter was one of them. The Southern Baptist president eagerly welcomed the Roman pontiff and engaged him in private talks over matters such as world peace and justice. After their private meeting the pair emerged and greeted a large crowd gathered on the South Lawn. There the president and pope addressed each other warmly, and John Paul's specific statements of support for arms limitation and for efforts to address world hunger surely pleased Father Hesburgh. Father Ted, who was seated close to the front of the animated crowd, remembered being struck that everyone was straining and reaching out for the pope when he and the president walked by. He made a point of reaching out to Carter and assuring him: "We love you too, Mr. President."[41] He followed up by writing to Carter to thank him for his "splendid remarks." Writing "as one Catholic who greatly enjoyed the historical moment and the splendor of the occasion," he assured him of his gratitude. Carter wrote him a brief note in reply noting that "it was one of the best days of my life."[42]

Although the discussions between the pope and the president ranged widely, it seems unlikely that Jimmy Carter acted on a suggestion regarding Father Hesburgh made by Congressman John Brademas, now the House majority whip. Brademas drew to Carter's attention that Hesburgh was "widely respected among Americans of all religious backgrounds for his outstanding leadership in a remarkable variety of fields." He described the Notre Dame president, whom he knew well, as "the most prominent

Roman Catholic in the United States and one of the two or three most influential religious leaders." With this as background he asked if the president would "raise with the Pope the possibility of Father's Hesburgh's being named a Cardinal of the Church."[43] We must assume that Carter judged this unusual request as crossing the line into state interference in church affairs. He did not act upon it, despite the high regard in which he held Father Ted. But Carter had proven much more willing to demonstrate his esteem and affection for Hesburgh by granting a request the priest made directly. Earlier in 1979 in a meeting with Carter, the president expressed his gratitude to Father Ted for his help and asked if there was anything he could do to reciprocate. Hesburgh was ready. He responded: "I happen to be an aviation nut, and my fantasy is to someday ride the shuttle and say Mass in space. That probably won't happen very soon, so in the meantime I'll settle for a more attainable fantasy. I'd like to ride in the world's fastest airplane." Carter knew he meant the SR-71 Blackbird, a high-flying reconnaissance plane that had set a world speed record of 2,193 miles per hour. Carter gently tried to dissuade him, but Hesburgh astutely challenged him to demonstrate that he was in fact the commander in chief. It soon came to pass that on February 29 Hesburgh flew out of Beale Air Force Base outside Sacramento on the Blackbird. He devoted over ten pages of *God, Country, Notre Dame* to describing the experience in loving detail. It happened to be Ash Wednesday, but it was one of Father Ted's perfect days and not because he found the experience penitential even though as the plane burst through Mach 3 he "could feel the flesh on my face pulling against my cheekbones and trying to move around to the back of my head." The day was one of sheer exhilaration as the Machmeter registered 3.35: "Major Tom Allison and Father Theodore Hesburgh had just set a new world speed record!" It was not an official record, but Father Ted knew that he had topped over 2,200 miles per hour, establishing himself as the priest who had traveled faster than any other.[44]

Although Hesburgh always maintained a high personal regard for Jimmy Carter, by the end of 1979 he increasingly worried about the president's capacity to lead the country effectively. Hesburgh was hardly alone. Political scientists and media commentators even raised questions as to whether the demands of the presidency had moved beyond the competency of any one person. Carter's woes only multiplied during the election year of 1980. After storming the U.S. embassy in Tehran in November 1979, Iranian militants took more than fifty Americans hostage and held them through the following year. This action along with the brazen Soviet invasion of Afghanistan seemed to convey a sense of American weakness. Both the fruitless negotiations with Iran and the bungled hostage rescue mission in April 1980 added to a feeling of national humiliation.

Carter's political prospects appeared difficult. Senator Ted Kennedy had earlier attempted to take advantage of the American people's declining confidence in Carter and challenged him in the Democratic Party primaries. Carter eventually won renomination at the August convention in New York City, but Kennedy's challenge had wounded his campaign. Support for Carter remained lukewarm. Some liberal Democrats deserted him to support the independent candidacy of Illinois congressman John Anderson, a liberal Republican who refused to back the official Republican candidate, Ronald Reagan. Carter decided that a fear campaign was his only route to victory. He attacked Reagan as the proponent of "radical and irresponsible" policies that "could put the whole world in peril." Reagan's sunny, engaging manner blunted the Carter charge. More telling was Reagan's invitation to voters to choose between the two major candidates on the basis of the question "Are you better off than you were four years ago?"[45] American voters responded by inflicting a crushing defeat on the incumbent.

Father Hesburgh showed much less willingness to involve himself in the 1980 presidential campaign than he had in 1976. As recently as August 1979, following a private meeting between the two, Carter had sent Hesburgh a photo of them shaking hands. The president inscribed it: "To my good friend Father Ted Hesburgh."[46] But the friendship they shared did not suffice to secure Hesburgh's political loyalty through 1980. True, he knew Ted Kennedy and had worked with him on the immigration commission, but he shrewdly avoided giving any encouragement to the Massachusetts senator's campaign. Even so, he had soured on Carter during the election year. His disillusionment over Carter's failure to follow up on the UN Conference on Science and Technolgy for Development meeting opened his eyes to the president's limitations. In the interviews he did with Dick Conklin in the 1980s for God, Country, Notre Dame, Hesburgh described Carter as someone with "very good fundamental ideas" who turned out to be "a terrible manager." He went so far as to describe Carter as "fundamentally a bad president," whatever his good ideas. Indicative of his strong opinion that a president must deliver effectively on his policies, he told Conklin that "when all is said and done and he came up for re-election, I didn't feel I could vote for him because I felt he really had blown it." He knew that this was "a sad thing to say because he is a good man."[47]

In 1980 Hesburgh focused on an election closer to home. His good friend and longtime local congressman John Brademas was in trouble. The general mood of the electorate that eventually elected Reagan put liberal Democrats like Brademas in political jeopardy. The third-ranking Democrat in the House of Representatives faced a well-funded and competent local businessman named John Hiler, who worked to link the sitting congressman with the failures of the Carter administration. Father Hesburgh recalled that he and Brademas were "very close."[48] Brademas had long served as a key contact for him in Washington, D.C., and when Hesburgh faced a problem dealing with the bureaucracy, he would either consult Brademas for advice or request direct intervention by him. Invariably, Brademas came to his aid. Brademas also had introduced significant legislation on education at all levels, and Hesburgh thought of him as "one of higher education's best and most effective friends."[49] Ever the pragmatist, Father Ted wanted to secure the re-election of this man who held seniority in the Congress and who wielded his power effectively in support of causes that were important to Hesburgh.

Hesburgh did everything short of a formal endorsement to try to save the day for his friend. In a meeting held at the Center for Continuing Education at Notre Dame, Hesburgh welcomed Brademas to campus and provided some supposedly nonpartisan remarks. He spoke of their long and fruitful association, as well as the congressman's outstanding work on behalf of education. After the meeting CBS correspondent Dan Rather came over to Hesburgh and jovially remarked: "Boy, if that was a non-endorsement I'd love you to endorse me sometime."[50] Hesburgh's words may have impressed Dan Rather, but it appears that they had less impact on the voters of Indiana's third congressional district. Hiler won the race and thereafter held the seat for five terms.

AT ODDS WITH THE MILLENNIAL POPE

During the first decade of John Paul II's pontificate, Hesburgh met the pope only infrequently, and he made no particular contribution on any of the myriad significant matters that occupied John Paul II's attention. Father

Ted represented himself as being both guided by the teachings of Vatican II and in favor of its full implementation. He had utilized his understanding of these teachings to advance an agenda at Notre Dame that not only separated the university from the direct control of the Holy Cross order but also pushed the university to emulate increasingly the reigning secular paradigm among American universities. He also placed himself very much in the category of those who wanted further reform in the Church in the "spirit" of Vatican II.

The election of Albino Luciani on August 26, 1978, heartened Father Hesburgh, who interpreted John Paul I's friendly demeanor as a sign of his openness to further reform in Rome. He eagerly accepted Vice President Walter Mondale's invitation to travel to Rome as part of the official American delegation for the new pope's installation, and he recalled that they "had a wonderful trip over and back." He felt bad that John Paul I died for want of better treatment for his serious health problems. Yet, when he learned of the election of Cardinal Karol Wojtyła on October 16, his spirits rose. Hesburgh recalled being "delighted," and he told Dick Conklin in the early 1980s that he "felt it was high time we had a non-Italian there."[51]

Once the plans for John Paul II's visit to the United States were announced, Hesburgh made a point of traveling to Rome. His old connections were still such that despite the complaints of a brusque papal master of ceremonies, he was able to get on the list for a brief private audience. Hesburgh had a list of items he wanted to discuss. In particular, he wished to advise the Holy Father of how he should prepare for his visit to the United States and, not surprisingly, wanted to invite the pope to come to Notre Dame. As soon as he was formally presented, he gave the pope a framed photograph of Notre Dame and a copy of his own recently published *The Hesburgh Papers: Higher Values in Higher Education*. Father Ted then made a pitch for the pope to come to campus on his way to his scheduled stop in Chicago, given the university's close proximity. Much to Hesburgh's disappointment the pope explained that his schedule was full. Hesburgh then took on the role of adviser regarding the American church and the United States itself. He emphasized that the Holy Father must appreciate that the United States was not a "Catholic country" like Poland, and so he should give his visit an ecumenical dimension. It was Hesburgh's briefing on his recent visit to China in preparation for the UN Conference on Science and Technology for Development meeting rather than his observations about the United States that captured the pope's attention. John Paul asked him about the situation of the Chinese Church and how Catholics might regain standing in the country. Hesburgh adopted Matteo Ricci as a model, and recommended that any Westerners who entered China should adopt the Chinese language and culture before undertaking explicit evangelization. Despite the pope's interest in Hesburgh's firsthand account of his visit to the Middle Kingdom, no close relationship developed.[52]

Father Hesburgh experienced the new pope's charisma firsthand from his vantage point at the White House during John Paul II's visit with Jimmy Carter. But from rather early days he found himself not so much directly at odds with the new Holy Father as operating on a different plane. He simply did not connect easily with the pope's profound Christian humanism. Hesburgh also discerned that John Paul would emphasize the authority of the magisterium, and this stirred his concerns about academic freedom as he defined it. By 1981 some of Father Hesburgh's reservations emerged, although he gave them no public expression. The pope's insistent defense of life in the womb and his criticism of birth control and abortion emphasized areas to which Hesburgh gave less attention. His own chosen priority was nuclear arms control and disarmament, and he watched with some concern as John Paul II began to develop a friendly relationship with the new American president, Ronald Reagan, whose approach on nuclear arms, at least as perceived by Hesburgh and other arms control advocates, was troubling. But this was hardly the time for any public comment, and especially after both Reagan and Pope John Paul struggled to recover from the frightening assassination attempts that nearly took their lives.

A chance to re-engage Rome came when John Paul appointed Father Ted to membership on the newly created Pontifical Council for Culture. The pope hoped to promote a genuine dialogue among ideas as part of his larger effort to transform cultures with the message of the Gospel. He sought to shape a culture built upon the central reality of the inalienable dignity and value of the human person. His tireless evangelism was directed to forming cultures inspired by the Christian concept of the human person.

Hesburgh traveled to Rome in 1983 for his first meeting of the council, which was overseen by Bishop Paul Poupard, the former rector of the Institut Catholique de Paris, who was later made a cardinal. On the morning of the meeting Hesburgh slipped and hurt his back. Despite being in considerable discomfort, he attended the gathering. But his pain only increased at the meeting. In a later conversation he described it as a typical

European-style meeting heavy on the exchange of ideas but short on the discussion of practical measures. He listened for a time but then burst forth into a questioning of the value of the whole proceedings. By that point, he had suffered enough and he got up and left. He did not formally resign from the council, but thereafter he did not make its deliberations a priority. Hesburgh's reservations about John Paul II's papacy soon became obvious in other areas as well, especially with regard to the relationship of Catholic universities to the institutional Church. Hesburgh felt animosity toward Pope John Paul II for daring to suggest that universities wearing the Catholic mantle should be in some ways accountable to the Church. He wished that Vatican officials would simply accept the 1972 document "The Catholic University in the Modern World," which incorporated his own understandings of academic freedom and institutional autonomy, as the essential and acceptable schema for universities.

Hesburgh's frustrations came to a head on a visit to Rome in 1984. He planned to argue against the requirements in the revised Code of Canon Law that Catholic theologians obtain a mandate from the competent ecclesiastical authority (i.e., the local bishop) in order to teach in a Catholic institution of higher learning. Father Ted viewed such a requirement, which in retrospect seems less than onerous, as a terrible imposition with vast implications. He wanted to convey that "the whole future of Catholic universities in America" was at stake. In his view, the mandate "would kill us because it says that we are not independent in America as we have said we are."[53] He tried to tell anyone who would listen that such a measure would put at risk the enormous financial support that Catholic colleges and universities received from the federal government. The problem was that he had a hard time getting anyone to listen to him. Cardinal William Baum, the prefect for the Congregation for Catholic Education, avoided him, and his conversations with other officials of the Curia were unsatisfactory.[54] He hoped to have the opportunity to make his case directly to the pope as part of an American delegation including Bishop James Malone of the NCCB. But his commitment to participate as an election observer in El Salvador required him to depart from Rome before such a meeting could be arranged. He left the Eternal City deeply dissatisfied with the direction that deliberations on the relationship of the Church and Catholic universities had taken. He thereafter carried a seething resentment toward those who wanted to maintain a more formal relationship. He felt aggrieved that officials in Rome failed to appreciate the achievements of the Catholic educational system in the United States, and that they refused to grasp what he personally had accomplished at Notre Dame. He mentioned in an interview that in the early 1990s, well after he had left the presidency of Notre Dame but during the rather heated debate over *Ex Corde Ecclesiae*, he had suggested assembling a special booklet to send to the pope listing all the "Catholic" activities that occurred on campus. It is notable that most of the items he mentioned for inclusion—the Masses, the retreats, the choirs—reflected the "neighborhood" of Notre Dame. He drew less attention to the academic heart of the university.[55] The drafter of *Ex Corde Ecclesiae* demonstrated a deep interest in both areas.

From 1984 onward Father Hesburgh found himself increasingly traveling in the company of the critics of John Paul II who branded the pope a "restorationist" or worse. Hesburgh recognized some of the pope's signature achievements. He understood at some level that John Paul II was a voice of conscience and that he was guiding the Catholic Church to become a key defender of basic human rights all around the world. He also conceded the strengths of John Paul's encyclical on Catholic social doctrine, *Laborem Exercens* (On Human Work), which eloquently defended the dignity and rights of all who worked, and which portrayed human work as an act of co-creation with God. Despite John Paul's placing the system of advanced capitalism under a more searching critique than Hesburgh ever attempted to do himself, the Notre Dame president began to label the pope as conservative. It was not so much the pope's teachings but his political actions (as Hesburgh saw them) both inside and outside the Church that caused his apprehensions about Wojtyła's papacy to deepen.

Father Hesburgh came to view Pope John Paul II as too concerned with imposing theological orthodoxy and doctrinal discipline. This divergence manifested itself clearly in the disputes over Catholic higher education, but it also surfaced in his reaction to a number of the pope's specific decisions regarding leadership in the Church. Hesburgh was especially worried about developments in the United States. John Paul appointed Archbishop Pio Laghi as apostolic nuncio to the United States in 1980, and Hesburgh soon came to see him as engaged in a campaign to reverse the liberal flavor of the American hierarchy that had been fostered under his predecessor, Archbishop Jean Jadot. He saw the appointments of Bernard Law to Boston and John O'Connor to New York City as sufficient evidence that a conservative push was in play, although he downplayed the simultaneous appointments of theological liberals like Joseph Bernardin and Roger Mahony to major archdioceses. Hesburgh worried that the National Conference of Catholic Bishops might fall out of the control of the progressives who had promoted the bishops' pastoral teaching on nuclear arms control. In response to the Vatican's 1986 decision to transfer some important elements of Seattle Archbishop Raymond Hunthausen's episcopal authority to Bishop Donald Wuerl, Hesburgh showed his concern for the more progressive bishop. He objected to what he saw as the mistreatment of Archbishop Hunthausen, who had emerged as a dedicated antinuclear activist. He wrote a letter of support to Hunthausen and told him, "You are my ideal of the best kind of archbishop, courageous, idealistic, dedicated, fearless, and, most of all, unambitious."[56]

In the spring of 1987 Fr. Richard McBrien published an article in the *Notre Dame Magazine* entitled "The Hard-line Pontiff." It encapsulated much of the liberal American Catholics' developing critique of Pope John Paul II. It portrayed the pope as pursuing a "restorationist agenda" through the forceful imposition of preconciliar orthodoxy, although given that Karol Wojtyła had participated at Vatican II and helped to draft *Gaudium et Spes,* it was a little unclear as to what he aimed to restore. In the McBrien portrait, Wojtyła was a product of his harsh Polish experience in which "dissent within the church was simply out of the question." He contrasted the pope unfavorably with the U.S. Catholic Church, which McBrien presented as more open, pluralistic, and diverse, and he then highlighted the supposed tensions in the relationship. Although he did not predict outright conflict between the Vatican and U.S. Catholics, he encouraged the American bishops to stand strong against Rome and to defend "their own democratic traditions and pastoral experiences."[57] The McBrien article appeared the very semester that Father Hesburgh completed his long tenure as president of Notre Dame, and it captured in broad terms his own views of the pope.[58] Father Ted was especially aggravated that the pope and the Vatican Curia appeared to take seriously the complaints of "right-wing" Catholics who wrote detailing the "loose" pastoral practices of bishops like Hunthausen.

Hesburgh also found himself at odds with both the strong anticommunist stance of John Paul II and his determination to move beyond the *Ostpolitik* approach in challenging Soviet control of Eastern Europe. Hesburgh's temperament disposed him to favor the approach that Agostino Casaroli had implemented on Paul VI's behalf during the late 1960s and 1970s. From his early days as Vatican delegate on the International Atomic

Energy Agency he had accepted that the Soviet Union and the division of Europe were here to stay, and he tried to negotiate with the communist powers in light of that belief in hopes of securing modest agreements. His rather naïve idea of having students from the Soviet Union and various other countries living together in the Peace House at Notre Dame under the auspices of the peace institute typified his approach. John Paul II looked at matters differently; he sidetracked the Casaroli diplomacy and instead led "a morally driven campaign of resistance to communism."[59] Right from the time of his first dramatic visit back to his homeland in 1979 he proclaimed the powerful message that faith matters, the truth matters, and freedom matters. He inspired and lent true encouragement to dissidents like Lech Wałęsa and Václav Havel to challenge the sordid system of lies on which communism depended for its survival. He effectively signaled that the Iron Curtain would have to be brought down.[60]

Father Hesburgh's concerns about the pope's profound anticommunism were mirrored in much of the liberal establishment in the United States, which was focused on nuclear arms control negotiations with the Soviet Union. Far from wanting to confront the Soviet domination of Eastern Europe, they acknowledged it as a given so as to reach accommodations with the USSR on nuclear weaponry. Hesburgh worried about any ideas or measures that might risk such agreements. He directed his major apprehensions in this area toward the Reagan administration and its anti-Soviet rhetoric and major arms buildup, but he recognized that Reagan and John Paul II appeared to complement each other in their willingness to denounce communist human rights abuses. The obvious friendliness exhibited at the personal meeting between President Reagan and Pope John Paul II on June 7, 1982, only stoked Hesburgh's disquiet. He feared what confrontations the anticommunist efforts of the pope and the president might provoke.

CONTENDING WITH THE GIPPER

Ronald Reagan left office with the American economy substantially improved from the stagflation he had inherited from Carter, and with America's position in the world standing markedly higher. At the end of his term in 1989 his public approval rating stood above 70 percent. Reagan's arrival in Washington in 1981 had not been greeted with the same favorable applause as was the successful completion of his two terms in office.

Especially in establishment circles—the very sort that Father Hesburgh traveled in—Reagan was often mocked as a cowboy and a B-movie actor.

Hesburgh had developed no relationship with Reagan prior to the former California governor's taking the oath of office as president, and he found it impossible to forge a deeper relationship once Reagan began his service in Washington. Father Ted failed to connect with Reagan on anything but a superficial level. Perhaps in different times and circumstances Reagan and Hesburgh might have connected better. After all they both loved America deeply and believed that their nation had a special role in God's providential plan. They both possessed strengths as leaders and felt comfortable in their own skin. And Reagan had a special bond with Notre Dame occasioned by his having starred as George Gipp in the fabulous (at least for mature-age Notre Dame fans) 1940 film *Knute Rockne, All American*. Gipp, the outstanding halfback, was stricken with a fatal illness, but on his deathbed he made a request of his great coach. "Rock," he said, "sometime when the team is up against it, when things are wrong and the breaks are beating the boys, tell them to go in there with all they've got and win just one for the Gipper." As all who are familiar with Notre Dame lore know well, Rockne told his 1928 team of Gipp's dying wish at halftime in their bruising encounter with Army at Yankee Stadium, and the team proceeded to do just as he had asked. "Win one for the Gipper" entered the lexicon. Reagan loved the part of Gipp and relished playing opposite Pat O'Brien as Rockne. He spent time on the Notre Dame campus in May 1940 for the filming and then returned to South Bend for the premiere of the film in October of that same year. When he returned to campus thirty-six years later, he was playing a different role—that of candidate for the Republican presidential nomination. In early May of 1976 he addressed a lively crowd in the Stepan Center in anticipation of the Indiana primary, and he was greeted by a large "Welcome Back Gipper" sign. Father Hesburgh was absent from the event, but Robert Cahill, the business manager of Notre Dame athletics, presented Reagan with a football helmet from the Gipp era, which the amiable candidate tried on—albeit a little reluctantly.[61] Four years later the Gipper won the presidency.

In November 1980, soon after Reagan was elected, Hesburgh oversaw the opening of the Snite Art Museum on the Notre Dame campus. Walter Annenberg, the wealthy philanthropist who had made a contribution to support the construction of the museum, was in attendance at the opening festivities, and he raised the possibility to Father Ted of inviting Reagan to give the commencement address at Notre Dame the following year. Knowing the value of a presidential visit to bring attention and prestige to Notre Dame, Hesburgh reacted favorably to the suggestion. He recognized at the same time that he had no lines into the Reagan camp, so he "pretty much turned it over" to Annenberg to let him "scout out" the possibility.[62] Annenberg received an immediate positive response. Reagan indicated to his wealthy friend that he would be excited to come to Notre Dame to reprise his role as the Gipper. His serious injury at John Hinckley's hands put the visit in question for a time, but Reagan's remarkable recovery enabled him to come to campus on May 17, his first venture outside of Washington to deliver a major speech since the assassination attempt. Hesburgh was delighted and hoped that the visit would afford him the chance to build a relationship with the new president.

Even though Reagan's visit was somewhat tense and rather brief, it was nonetheless judged a great success. As Dick Conklin remembered, the Secret Service were on edge, and especially so after the attempt on Pope John Paul's life the week before the commencement. Reagan attracted a considerable number of protestors, many of them from places far from South Bend. Their presence elevated the tension. All who entered the convocation center did so through metal detectors, and invitees were limited to only the graduates and their families. The event proceeded flawlessly. Reagan received an enthusiastic welcome and so too did his fellow honoree, Pat O'Brien. As Conklin remembered: "When Pat O'Brien received his honorary degree, Reagan rose from his chair and the two robed men embraced center stage to what I would still argue was the most sustained applause ever recorded in the campus convocation center. The president was seen whispering something to O'Brien, and he later said his words were: 'I guess they like the movie.'"[63] After his speech the president left the stage as the ceremony continued. Father Ted had no chance to exchange farewells, although Father Joyce presented the president with a certificate making him an honorary member of the Monogram Club, along with a Notre Dame monogram blazer, which Reagan immediately donned, revealing his bulletproof vest as he did so. His whole visit to the campus took barely three hours, but Reagan enjoyed the day and wrote of it in his diary.[64] To Hesburgh's disappointment, he had minimal opportunity to share any thoughts with Reagan, and Reagan did not ask him to do so—then or ever. Instead, Reagan delivered a speech that was filled with food for thought, although not exactly to Hesburgh's taste.

Reagan delivered a memorable speech that revealed well why he earned his label as the "Great Communicator." He played his Notre Dame connections to the hilt and initially evoked the life and legend of Rockne and his "win one for the Gipper" speech to emphasize the moral of men who "joined together in a common cause and attained the unattainable." After this sentimental but characteristically effective lead-in the president deftly moved to touch upon the two overarching themes of his presidency—the need to correct the excessive government intervention in people's lives and in the economy as well as the obligation to overcome the communist challenge. It was on the latter subject that Reagan spoke most forcefully and in a way that echoed some of the themes William F. Buckley had addressed three years previously. The president uttered the memorable lines: "The years ahead will be great ones for our country, for the cause of freedom and for the spread of civilization. The West will not contain communism; it will transcend communism. We will not bother to denounce it; we'll dismiss it as a sad, bizarre chapter in human history whose last pages are even now being written."[65]

A wide gap separated the views of President Reagan and Father Hesburgh. Reagan's abhorrence of communism and his profound recognition that communists were inveterate enemies of Western democracy allowed him to escape the trap that well-meaning but naïve individuals like Father Hesburgh fell into during much of the Cold War. Such individuals tended to ignore much of the reality of the Soviet system and to focus instead on efforts to bring the two adversaries together. Ideological differences and the malevolent nature of the communist regime were downplayed, and especially after the dangers of the nuclear arms race began to dominate attention in the 1970s and 1980s. Hesburgh once told the Soviet minister of higher education that the best way to avoid war "was to help the Russian and American people get to know each other better."[66] He found Reagan's rejection of such recommendations disturbing. The new president rightly viewed conciliatory gestures like those proposed by Hesburgh as soft-headed. By contrast his approach emphasized putting pressure on the Soviet Union to bring the nation to the bargaining table. In order to do so he pushed through an enormous peacetime military buildup and embraced the Strategic Defense Initiative—popularly known as Star Wars—a missile defense program that especially troubled the Soviets. The distinguished diplomatic historian John Lewis Gaddis summed up the Reagan objective as being to push the Soviet system "to the breaking point."[67] Father Ted was reading from a very different script.

The Catholic bishops as a group laid the groundwork for Hesburgh's deepened involvement on the nuclear issue. In November 1980, and immediately after Reagan defeated Carter, the bishops gathered for their general meeting and decided to prepare a statement on the issue of nuclear war and peace. In January 1981, Archbishop John Roach, the president of the bishops' conference, announced the creation of an ad hoc committee on war and peace charged with drafting such a statement. He asked then archbishop of Chicago Joseph Bernardin to chair the committee. The Bernardin committee adopted a quite open process in preparing its initial draft by soliciting input from a variety of experts—scientists, theologians, military and government officials. Undertaken in the context of Reagan's defense buildup, the work of the bishops' committee attracted substantial public interest and attention, and it made the nuclear issue a prominent one in Catholic circles. The issue began to be much discussed on Catholic campuses, including at Notre Dame. Those discussions provided the background for Father Hesburgh's epiphany on the nuclear issue that occurred on November 11, 1981. On that day he celebrated a Mass and preached a homily on what was designated as "Nuclear Day." He then listened to a lecture in which a Notre Dame alumnus, Dr. James Muller of Harvard University and Physicians for Social Responsibility, "spoke to our students on the effect of a one-megaton bomb exploding over South Bend." The lights dramatically went on for Father Ted. It was a powerful experience. "Suddenly," he remembered, "the dire facts became clear in a local context." Rather like a modern-day Saint Paul undergoing an abrupt conversion experience, Hesburgh changed his whole perspective on his priorities. As he walked back to his office he focused on the horrendous consequences of a nuclear war. He concluded that all the other issues he had worked on "would be irrelevant if there were no more human beings left to have problems." Indeed, he reasoned, "all the progress I had worked so hard for could be easily obliterated in a few minutes if the nuclear weapons, now existing, were unleashed." So he decided to reduce his other commitments and to focus on this one. He left the chairmanship of the Rockefeller Foundation, the Overseas Development Council, and even resigned from the board of Chase Manhattan Bank. He planned to do what he could to address the nuclear issue and to arrest "the nuclear threat to humanity."[68]

Hesburgh revealed a genuine passion on this subject. As he saw it: "This is not a Soviet or an American problem. It is a human problem. We may continue creation or utterly destroy it. What sin could be greater? To reverse creation must be the worst blasphemy imaginable." He saw the issue through a moral lens as he worked to "avert disaster." He focused his efforts in 1982 and 1983 on building collaboration between scientists from both sides of the Iron Curtain with religious leaders from various faith traditions. Working in conjunction with his old friend Cardinal Franz König of Vienna he organized a number of international meetings bringing representatives of both groups together.[69] No doubt they seemed important gatherings at the time, but like so many earnest meetings around this issue their import in practice seems minimal. In addition to his own special efforts Hesburgh gave his full support to the Bernardin committee's work. Just weeks after the U.S. bishops gave their final approval to their pastoral letter, The Challenge of Peace: God's Promise and Our Response, at their plenary session in Chicago in May 1983, Hesburgh invited Cardinal Bernardin to Notre Dame to receive an honorary degree and to serve as the commencement speaker to explain and promote the pastoral letter.[70] Hesburgh fully supported the bishops' work. He was broadly cognizant of the direct efforts both of the Reagan administration officials and of the Vatican to temper the earlier versions of the letter that treated nuclear pacifism more favorably.[71] He hardly welcomed this "outside" pressure on the bishops, but he had no major reservations about their final draft.

Father Hesburgh wished to exert some influence on Reagan himself on the nuclear issue, but he gained no access to the president. The best he managed was a meeting with the courteous but noncommittal vice president, George H. W. Bush.[72] Lack of engagement with the Reagan administration failed to dampen Hesburgh's commitment. He continued writing and speaking on the issue through the mid-1980s, associating himself with The Challenge of Peace and warning of the dangers of a nuclear conflagration in hyperbolic terms. In 1984 he sparred with William F. Buckley on Firing Line and rejected his host's suggestion that the bishops were meddling in prudential areas where they had no competence. For him the danger of the unleashing of nuclear weapons demanded the bishops' involvement.[73] In 1985, as noted earlier, he held that "we are not far from utter disaster. We are in proximate danger of destroying everything we hold dear."[74] Such overhyped rhetoric came to be seen as ill founded when Reagan proceeded through his second term to pursue successful arms control negotiations. With Mikhail Gorbachev in place and fully cognizant of Soviet economic weakness, a firm basis existed for genuine negotiations over arms reductions. It turned out that Ronald Reagan even favored the abolition of nuclear weapons, and that he deemed the doctrine of mutual assured destruction as literally mad. In Washington in December 1987, Reagan and Gorbachev signed a treaty eliminating intermediate-range missiles from Europe.[75] The Reagan approach to peace through strength appeared vindicated, although it proved very hard for the Reagan critics to concede this.

Because Father Hesburgh devoted so much of his energies in the 1980s to the nuclear issue, he did not play as prominent a role in another of the major foreign policy issues that attracted critical attention from the U.S. bishops, namely the Reagan administration's policy toward Central America and the Caribbean. Reagan and his advisers took an ideologically inspired approach to the region, and viewed it essentially through the lens of East–West conflict. The Reagan policymakers made some of the Central American nations—most notably El Salvador and Nicaragua—focal points in an anticommunist crusade. The U.S. bishops objected to the militarization of American policy, and instead recommended that political and diplomatic solutions be sought for the region's vast problems. The assassination of San Salvador's Archbishop Oscar Romero in March 1980, and the vicious rape and murder of three American Catholic nuns and a lay missionary later that year, gave a poignant intensity to the bishops' claim that violence was not the answer. In November 1981, the U.S. Catholic Conference issued a statement that rejected Reagan's hard-line focus on military threats to the region, and pointed to the need to address the deep-seated social and economic roots of much of the conflict.[76] The Catholic Church emerged as a restraining influence on the Reagan administration, and various Church groups applied substantial public pressure against the military emphasis of U.S. policy.

Father Hesburgh sympathized fully with the approach of the bishops. He too later criticized the "emphasis on military solutions" in Central America. He believed that there was no ultimate military answer "to the basic problem, which is the historical cancer of social injustice, the crass denial of human rights, the shattered economy, the wanton and cruel killings on both sides, the almost total lack of the most basic human aspirations for dignity and personal development." He argued that "violence is not eliminated by more violence, injustice by more injustice."[77] Yet he tempered his criticisms of American policy, because he had a very personal connection to the turmoil in Central America—his friendship with José Napoleón Duarte, the Christian Democratic leader in El Salvador.

Hesburgh initially met the Salvadoran man he referred to as "Napo" in one of the first classes he ever taught at Notre Dame, where the young man had come to study engineering. They stayed in touch thereafter, and in the 1960s Hesburgh encouraged Duarte to turn from his successful career as a civil engineer to serve as a "social engineer" to construct a more just political and economic order in his country. This Duarte did by helping found the Christian Democratic Party with the encouragement of noted Latin American leaders such as Eduardo Frei of Chile and Rafael Caldera of Venezuela. He served three successful terms as mayor of San Salvador from 1964 to 1970, and in 1972 ran for the presidency of El Salvador. The Salvadoran military not only stole that election from him but also arrested him after he had sought refuge in a Venezuelan diplomatic residence. They brutally beat him and seemed determined to kill him. In this dire situation Duarte's brother, Rolando, called "Padrecito" Hesburgh and begged him to arrange for American intervention to save his brother's life. Duarte's old teacher, proud of his onetime student's commitment and courage in running for the presidency, doubted that either the Nixon administration or the Vatican could act quickly and forcefully. So he cold-called John McCone, the former director of the CIA and his friend from IAEA days, and asked him for help. McCone still had good contacts in "the Company," and as Father Ted related the story, they went quickly to work. President Caldera and others were enlisted to threaten Colonel Arturo Molina—the authoritarian ruler of El Salvador—and they forced him to recognize that his interest lay in exiling rather than killing the badly beaten Duarte. His torturers spared his life but expelled him, and he spent the next seven years in Venezuela.[78]

Having helped save Duarte's life, and knowing him to be a decent man who wanted genuine social justice for his country, Hesburgh was understanding when Duarte returned to El Salvador in 1979 as part of a joint military-civilian junta. He knew him to be a centrist battling against the dark forces of both the Left and the Right. He believed that Duarte wanted to move his nation toward more democratic rule, but his friend's presence in the government gave it a patina of respectability during the very time when elements of the Salvadoran security forces sponsored savage death squad murders against thousands of citizens, of whom Archbishop Romero

President Eisenhower meets in the Oval Office with members of the Civil Rights Commission, September 8, 1959. (Left to right: George M. Johnston, Theodore M. Hesburgh, Robert G. Storey, President Eisenhower, John R. Hannah [chairman], Doyle E. Carlton, John S. Battle.)

President John F. Kennedy and Fr. Hesburgh examine the Laetare Medal, Notre Dame's highest honor, presented by Hesburgh to Kennedy at the White House, November 22, 1961.

President Lyndon B. Johnson shakes hands with Fr. Hesburgh after presenting him with the Presidential Medal of Freedom in a White House ceremony, September 14, 1964.

Fr. Hesburgh with Martin Luther King Jr., Rev. Edgar Chandler, and Msgr. Robert Hagarty at the Illinois Rally for Civil Rights in Chicago's Soldier Field, 1964.

Football Game Day—Notre Dame vs. USC, November 1952; Vice President-Elect Richard Nixon, Patricia Nixon, and Fr. Hesburgh in the stands.

President Gerald Ford waving to the assembly at a special convocation at Notre Dame, where Fr. Hesburgh presented him with an honorary degree, March 17, 1975.

Holy See delegates to the International Atomic Energy Agency, Rev. Theodore Hesburgh and Mr. Frank Folsom report to Pope Pius XII at the Vatican, 1957.

Fr. Hesburgh meeting with Pope Paul VI at the Vatican, c. 1960s.

Fr. Hesburgh reporting to Pope John XXIII at the Vatican with Frank Folsom, c. 1960.

Pope John Paul II meets with Fr. Hesburgh, c. 1978.

Fr. Hesburgh in a flight suit and Colonel Franklin D. Shelton at Beale Air Force Base in California after Hesburgh's flight in the SR-71 Blackbird reconnaissance jet, February 1979.

Fr. Hesburgh meeting with President Jimmy Carter in the White House, prior to the 1979 UN Conference on Science and Technology for Development.

Fr. Hesburgh and Edmund Stephan presenting President Ronald Reagan with an honorary degree, 1981.

President José Napoleón Duarte of El Salvador, a former student of Fr. Hesburgh, talking with his former teacher prior to the Commencement ceremony, May 1985.

Fr. Hesburgh receiving the Congressional Gold Medal from President Bill Clinton, Senator Strom Thurmond, and House Speaker Dennis Hastert, 2000.

President Barack Obama and Fr. Hesburgh meet prior to the Commencement, May 2009.

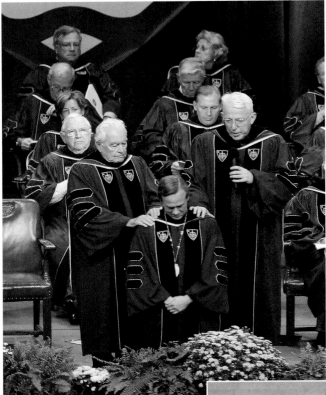

Fr. Ted Hesburgh and Fr. Edward "Monk" Malloy pray over Fr. John Jenkins at his inauguration as president of Notre Dame, 2005.

Fr. Hesburgh and administrative assistant Melanie Chapleau near the steps of the Main Building, Notre Dame, October 13, 2014.

was but one. Hesburgh's decision to support Duarte put him at odds with the many critics of U.S. support for El Salvador. Instead, Hesburgh aligned with those elements in the American government who believed that the Marxist guerrillas could be defeated only if El Salvador engaged in political reform, moved to hold genuine elections, and improved its human rights record. He supported the pressure they applied on the Salvadoran military to relinquish some of its control.[79] For this reason and because, as Father Ted explained, Duarte "was my former student and I wanted to go down and bolster him," he accepted an appointment from the Reagan administration to join a bipartisan delegation to observe national assembly elections, which were conducted in March of 1982.[80] Republican Senator Nancy Kassebaum of Kansas headed the U.S. delegation, which also included Democratic Congressman John P. Murtha of Pennsylvania.[81] Presumably the Reagan administration recruited Hesburgh knowing well both his sympathy for Duarte and the respect in which he was held by liberal and church groups in the United States. Father Ted valued the assignment. The U.S. ambassador initially designated him to work at a rather safe observer post in the capital, but he objected and insisted that he be allowed to accompany the former Marine Murtha, who was traveling by helicopter to outlying communities where the risk of attack by guerrilla forces was much higher. In a manner similar to his flying in the SR-71, he welcomed the sense of danger and adventure, and the chance to demonstrate his physical courage. He recalled with considerable glee Murtha's instruction to him not to put his flak jacket on while riding in the helicopter but to sit on it so as to protect "the family jewels" while the chopper flew at low heights. Both the elections and the observer mission went relatively smoothly, although Father Ted, always ready to serve as priest, was called upon to perform a brief ceremony for a soldier killed by guerrillas while defending a polling station. The soldier had been shot and his face had been mutilated with a machete, which clarified for Hesburgh the harsh realities on the ground. Praying for the dead soldier and comforting his mother in Spanish added to the emotion he felt as he observed the people of El Salvador struggling through the birth pangs of becoming a genuine democracy.[82]

The national assembly elections gave Duarte's Christian Democrats real representation, and they were a forerunner to Duarte's election to the presidency in 1984—the first civilian freely elected president of his country in half a century. Hesburgh rejoiced in Napo's political success. His student was the first graduate of Notre Dame to become a head of state. Duarte's supporters, like Hesburgh, portrayed him as "the father of Salvadoran democracy," struggling to bring justice to his troubled nation. Critics pointed out what they saw as his failure to introduce effective social and economic reforms, to curb the brutal human rights abuses of the security branch of the Salvadoran military, and to end the civil war by pursuing negotiations with the FMLN revolutionaries. To boost Duarte's stature, Hesburgh invited him to give the commencement address at Notre Dame in 1985, and Duarte made his case both to his Notre Dame audience and beyond that he would continue his struggle for democracy and peace.[83] Hesburgh ignored the impassioned objections to his inviting Duarte, from on and off campus, and he kept the substantial number who protested Duarte's visit at a far distance.[84] His pride in and almost fatherly love for Duarte was in evidence for all to see at the graduation ceremony. In 1986 he penned a moving tribute as a preface to Duarte's biography. Here he noted that "in a world of violence, injustice and strong ideological convictions, Duarte can seem compromised by his own deeply held convictions." Hesburgh testified that his friend had walked the "difficult path" of Christian virtue "with more risk than I, and with at least equal virtue." As it turned out, advanced stomach cancer rather than brutish violence took Duarte's life. Hesburgh visited him in 1989 and celebrated Mass in his room at Walter Reed Army Medical Center, where he received emergency treatment. Father Ted later was part of the U.S. delegation led by Vice President Dan Quayle that attended Duarte's funeral in El Salvador in February 1990. He always remembered Duarte as a man who tried "to make a difference, despite the heavy odds against him." He held him up as an exemplar for other Notre Dame graduates and was proud that Duarte, when inscribing a copy of his 1986 biography, identified him as his teacher, the shaper of his ideals ("*mentor de mes ideales*"), and his beloved friend.

Although Father Hesburgh celebrated Duarte's 1984 presidential victory, the results of the U.S. presidential race that year brought him little joy. Not surprisingly, he favored Walter Mondale, whom he had known when Mondale served as a senator from Minnesota, and with whom he had worked well during the Carter administration. Whatever his friendship with Mondale, Hesburgh adopted a low profile in the 1984 election. Abortion remained a very sensitive issue among Catholics in particular. Reagan's pro-life stance contrasted markedly with Mondale's standard pro-choice position, and Hesburgh's prudence guided him away from any public embrace of the Democratic nominee. Nonetheless, he was excited to join in the welcome that Dick McBrien extended to Mario Cuomo in 1984 as the New York governor responded to Archbishop John J. O'Connor's vigorous criticisms of both him and Mondale's running mate, Congresswoman Geraldine Ferraro, for their pro-choice positions. At the time, Cuomo seemed to hold a special place for Catholics. He appeared ready to revoke the sad relegation of his religion to the private sphere that John F. Kennedy embraced during the 1960 campaign, and behind which many a Catholic politician subsequently hid. Cuomo's religion appeared to be of such importance to him that he fearlessly related it to issues of public policy and morality. His principled opposition to the death penalty symbolized his stance. But in his Notre Dame address Cuomo, despite accepting the teaching authority of his church and its doctrine on abortion, refused to concede that being a Catholic should lead him to support legislation or a constitutional amendment to limit abortion in any way. As noted earlier, he appealed to "Catholic realism" and insisted that public morality needed to be endorsed by broad consensus. Cuomo gave no indication that he felt any obligation to build such a consensus. His speech simply contributed further to the Democratic Party's commitment to abortion rights. On reflection, Father Hesburgh found the speech troubling.

While liberal Catholics celebrated Cuomo's rhetorically skillful retort to O'Connor and the governor basked in the glow of favorable attention from the establishment media, Hesburgh felt the need to make his own contribution to the debate. In an extended op-ed entitled "Reflections on Cuomo: The Secret Consensus," he made a ritual genuflection by writing that Cuomo's talk at Notre Dame was "brilliant," but then in a deceptively placid manner he demonstrated the moral insolvency of Cuomo. He referenced the civil rights accomplishments of the 1960s and observed of them that "neither the consensus nor the change just happened; both were made to happen." He posed the question: "If it was patriotic, just and noble to work for the repeal of *Plessy v. Ferguson* and apartheid," he asked, "why should it now seem un-American to work for fewer legally sanctioned abortions when there is already a moral consensus in our country that finds our present legal permissiveness on abortion excessive and intolerable?" He called for Catholics to "cooperate with other Americans of good will and ethical conviction to work for a more restrictive abortion law" as a worthy waystation to the complete elimination of the practice he compared to

Herod's butchering of the Holy Innocents.[85] His words left one in no doubt of Father Ted's beliefs regarding abortion, but they reflected his pragmatic approach to addressing the issue.

Reagan's landslide victory over the decent but hapless Mondale put paid to Hesburgh's hopes that he might play some consequential role at the national level during his final years as president of Notre Dame. He had little influence on the broad direction of Reagan's second term agenda and policies with the exception of his continued lobbying for the passage of the Simpson-Mazzoli bill.[86] Nonetheless, he played a notable role in a specific case deemed important by the administration. In February 1986 Reagan nominated Daniel Manion to serve on the U.S. Court of Appeals for the Seventh Circuit. Manion graduated from Notre Dame in 1964 and then served in Vietnam immediately thereafter. He returned and got his law degree from Indiana University before establishing a law practice in South Bend. Manion was the son of Clarence Manion, the onetime dean of the Notre Dame Law School and the founder of the conservative *Manion Forum*. Strong opposition emerged to the Manion nomination. Senators like Edward Kennedy and Joseph Biden—rather ironically given their past and future records—attacked Manion's character and his abilities. At bottom, however, it seems clear that Manion's conservative political leanings caused most offense to the groups that opposed him. Nonetheless, when thirty prominent law school deans charged that Manion did not meet the needed criteria for "scholarship, legal acumen, professional achievement, wisdom, fidelity to the law and commitment to our Constitution," momentum appeared to be building to deny him a place on the bench.[87]

Hesburgh already had waded into this confirmation battle, and he did so in favor of Manion. Whatever his own liberal leanings, he knew when someone was being unfairly treated. His regard for the Manion family, and his loyalty to a Notre Dame graduate whom he had known since he was a boy, moved him to write to Indiana senators Richard Lugar and Dan Quayle, who had sponsored Manion's nomination. He described Manion as "a fine Notre Dame student . . . who has shown himself dedicated to service for his country and his fellow human beings." He assured the Indiana senators and all the readers of the letter, which was made public, that Manion "will bring dedication, integrity and a keen knowledge of the law" to the position. He stated plainly that Manion's "life has been one of service and commitment to justice."[88] Reagan specifically referenced Hesburgh's "strong endorsement" of Manion in a radio address the weekend before the Senate voted on the nomination.[89] He knew Hesburgh's word provided reassurance to wavering senators and helped in the battle to sway public opinion. In the end Manion was narrowly confirmed, and Hesburgh rightly took some satisfaction in the result. He knew he had helped the Gipper win that vote.

Reagan's affection for his role as the Gipper brought him back to Notre Dame in March of 1988 for a dedication ceremony to unveil a U.S. Postal Service commemorative stamp honoring Knute Rockne, deemed "American football's most renowned coach." The Reagan public relations machine wanted to emphasize the football dimensions of the occasion, and even asked both that the football team attend the event wearing their jerseys and that the Fighting Irish Leprechaun present the president with a shillelagh. Notre Dame politely declined these requests. The Gipper didn't seem to mind, especially after he threw a decent spiral pass from the stage straight into the arms of Notre Dame's Heisman Trophy receiver Tim Brown. The crowd of over ten thousand students, faculty, and South Bend residents lapped up Reagan's sentimental address, which paid full tribute to the Rockne legend. Reagan spoke as if he had known Rockne personally, and assured his audience that the great coach "stood for fair play and honor." Yet, "most of all," he continued, "the Rockne legend meant this: on or off the field, it is faith that makes the difference, it is faith that makes great things happen." Present on the stage to thank the U.S. president for his visit was the new president of Notre Dame, Edward "Monk" Malloy. Joining him as part of the official party was the popular former athletic director Moose Krause, along with Mary Jean Kochendorfer, Rockne's daughter, and Postmaster General Anthony M. Frank. Missing from this lineup was the man who had welcomed Reagan to campus seven years before—the recently retired Theodore Hesburgh. No longer was he the host for a presidential visit. He had passed the baton for such duties to his successor. At the time Reagan visited Notre Dame in 1988, Father Ted and Father Ned Joyce were midway through a hundred-day cruise aboard the ocean liner *Queen Elizabeth 2*, which took them all over the Pacific. Hesburgh had now moved to "president emeritus" status.

CHAPTER 9

A RESTIVE RETIREMENT

THEODORE MARTIN HESBURGH'S RETIREMENT WAS NEITHER easy nor peaceful. He filled the final decades of his life with a host of activities that would have exhausted a person half his age. After being at the center of attention at Notre Dame for decades as well as involved in a range of important matters away from campus, he found it hard to step out of the spotlight, and, whatever his claims to the contrary, he made little effort to do so.

Father Hesburgh titled the final chapter of *God, Country, Notre Dame* "Starting the Future." In it he made clear that he was not about to be pensioned off to a life of quiet reflection but was determined to continue working on his varied commitments, and that he would accept new challenges. He associated to some degree or other with all the presidents who served during these years—George H. W. Bush, Bill Clinton, George W. Bush, and Barack Obama. He took on new assignments with his usual enthusiasm. He thrived on being needed. His temperament and inner constitution were wired so that he virtually required being in demand. He explained that he would "rather go out with the flags flying and the sails flapping than be sitting on a beach contemplating my umbilicus."[1]

SERVING IN MONK'S NOTRE DAME, AND AT HARVARD AND BEYOND, 1988–1998

Notre Dame was unstinting in its effort to thank Father Hesburgh for all he had done to develop the university during his long administration. The various celebrations throughout 1987, the naming of the library in his honor, and the final commencement ceremony, at which he received the Laetare Medal, were capped off by his own moving valedictory. A month later a hundred or so well-wishers gathered to see Ted Hesburgh and Ned Joyce embark on a year of travels. The initial phase took them "Out West," where over the course of almost three months they visited numerous national parks, forests, and monuments. They traveled in a recreational vehicle that Art Decio of Skyline Corporation generously provided for their use. Along the way they met with alumni friends and families. They also adjusted to living with each other in rather close quarters. The two men had seldom vacationed together, nor had they traveled together much on university business. They handled their new living arrangements quite easily, and this augured well for future trips. They took lengthy travels in Central and South America in the fall of 1987. Then the traveling duo took to sea aboard the *Queen Elizabeth 2* ocean liner. As a warm-up drill the two priests took a three-week cruise on the Caribbean over the Christmas period of 1987. Then it was on to what Father Ted called "the main event," a trip covering 30,000 nautical miles during the months from January to May of 1988, which took them to Tahiti, New Zealand, Australia, the Seychelles, India, Malaysia, Singapore, China, Korea, Japan, and back across the Pacific via Hawaii.

The Cunard Line provided for these trips, but as Father Ted noted in his account of their travels, "they were not exactly free." The two priests served as the ship's chaplains, celebrating Mass each day and counseling passengers and crew members alike. On the crowded Caribbean trip they were assigned an inside cabin with no porthole, which Father Ted described as "a little bit like living in a closet." It was more comfortable for them on the longer cruise because they occupied "an outside cabin with two portholes." Just as they were able to work well together so too were they able to travel well together. [2] When the QE2 docked in Fremantle in Western Australia, Hesburgh and Joyce met a group of dedicated lay Catholics led by Dennis Horgan and Peter Tannock who asked their counsel on establishing a Catholic higher education institution. Hesburgh, always thinking big, encouraged them to start a university right away and to model themselves on Notre Dame. He gave an important boost to the project of founding what became the University of Notre Dame, Australia, which now enrolls close to ten thousand students on its Fremantle and Sydney campuses.[3]

With their travels completed, the two priests returned to campus in the early summer of 1988. Hesburgh desired to be back in action, both on campus and away from it. On their return to Notre Dame he and Father Joyce moved into a spacious suite of offices on the thirteenth floor of what was now the Theodore M. Hesburgh Library. Hesburgh loved his new postpresidential home and always enjoyed spending time there. He explained, "My new office fulfilled all my desires, with bookshelves from floor to ceiling and a window giving the best possible panoramic view of the Notre Dame campus with the gold dome and the Sacred Heart Church spire in the center."[4] He resumed something of his old daily regimen. He slept late in his familiar room in Corby Hall, and then walked to the library, perhaps after enjoying a lunch at the Morris Inn with a friend or faculty member. In the interests of fitness he took the elevator to the eighth floor but climbed the last five flights, exactly a hundred steps. Helen Hosinski, his faithful secretary for forty years, was still there to greet him. She remained with Father Ted until 1990 when arthritis forced her to retire and the gracious Melanie Chapleau took over her responsibilities. Helen, then Melanie, worked with their boss on correspondence, on returning phone calls, and receiving visitors through the afternoon. After a break for vespers and dinner with the Holy Cross community at Corby Hall, he returned to his office, where he worked until around 2:00 a.m. He smoked cigars and listened to classical music while reading and writing. He gave initial attention to his memoirs, which he cowrote with Chicago writer Jerry Reedy, based on the extensive interviews that he had completed with Dick Conklin. *God, Country, Notre Dame* was published by Doubleday in 1990 and proved a best seller, much to his pleasure. Reedy again helped him with his travel memoir, *Travels with Ted and Ned*, also completed under the editorial guidance of Bill Barry at Doubleday, with whom Father Ted formed a good friendship. He soon began accepting invitations to say Masses in the chapels of resident halls across campus, and during the regular academic year he also gave guest lectures in a number of classes, where he invariably impressed his student audiences with the immense range of his experiences and contacts stretching back to the age of Eisenhower.

Father Hesburgh did not want to be restricted to reflecting on the past, and he could not rest on his laurels. He wanted to have some influence in the present and on the future. He outlined "five ideas" that he planned to work on going forward, because he believed they "could change the world and profoundly affect all of humanity." These included peace, human rights, economic and social development, ecology and the environment challenge, and the work of ecumenism and interfaith dialogue.[5] Each of the institutes and centers he had established as his distinct legacy broadly covered one of these areas—the Kroc Institute for International Peace Studies and the Center for Civil and Human Rights focused on the challenges of peace and justice in the world. The Kellogg Institute gave increased attention to development issues, while the Hank Family Environmental Research Center at Land O'Lakes worked to solve some of the ecological problems of the day. Finally, he hoped that the Ecumenical Institute for Theological Studies in Tantur would bring Jews, Christians, and Muslims into better conversation. Each of these entities attracted his involvement; he sat on the advisory boards of each and chaired a number of them. He gave special attention to the activities of the peace institute and the Ecumenical Institute in Tantur. He was not involved in the daily work of these institutes, but he was much more than a mere figurehead. He discussed programs with the directors and staffs, attended their major events, and contributed effectively to their fund-raising efforts. He proved to be something of a godfather to each in ensuring that they obtained appropriate resources and attention within the university.

As if this involvement with Notre Dame academic bodies was not sufficient, he also retained membership on more than fifty boards and committees. His 1994 curriculum vitae lists a number of appointments that were largely honorary, but other appointments required a significant commitment of time. He served on the board of the Teachers Insurance and Annuity Association (TIAA), the retirement fund and financial services firm that controls billions of dollars in assets, and he chaired its board from 1990 to 1991. He remained on the board of the Overseas Development Council and gave time to it. These entities held regular board meetings, which he attended. He also took on new assignments. He succumbed to the entreaties of Creed Black, the president of the Knight Foundation, to serve as co-chairman of the Knight Commission on Intercollegiate Athletics with his old friend William Friday, the president emeritus of the University of North Carolina. The commission was charged with developing a reform agenda to clean up big-time college sports, especially men's football and basketball. This was a herculean assignment, but Hesburgh roused himself to take it on.[6] His dogged efforts to address problems on the home front did not diminish his energies to contribute overseas. In the summer of 1989 he participated as part of a twelve-person delegation, called the Commission on Independence for Namibia, which was funded jointly by the Ford and Rockefeller Foundations. The group traveled to the state in southwest Africa and worked to establish ground rules for Namibia to conduct a plebiscite to confirm its movement to gain independence from South African control. Hesburgh had no particular expertise in this region, but he could not resist the opportunity for an on-the-ground experience in a troubled area.[7]

Father Ted also rejoined the honorary degree circuit and began accepting at least some of the many invitations to address commencement exercises that came his way. In 1988 the AFL-CIO bestowed its Murray-Green-Meany Award on him in recognition of his "outstanding contribution" to the general welfare of the nation. The peak body of American labor looked beyond his role in breaking the efforts of the Notre Dame groundskeepers to join the Teamsters union a decade before. In the fall of 1991, President George H. W. Bush appointed him to serve on the board of directors of the U.S. Institute of Peace in Washington, D.C., his fifteenth presidential assignment. Hesburgh reveled in his board membership and the quarterly meetings that brought him regularly to Washington. He was very pleased when Bush's successor renewed his appointment.

All this was an amazingly full and varied agenda. But these activities and the awards and accolades that came to him seemed not to fulfill him. He felt anxious and discontented. The source of his difficulty lay not in what he was doing but in what he had not been asked to do. The heart of his angst was that he believed that he was being marginalized by Monk Malloy at a time when he still had constructive input to provide for the university.

Following a legend is rarely an easy task, as Harry S. Truman came to appreciate well after Franklin Roosevelt's death. But like Truman and without any dramatic flair, Malloy simply assumed the position as president of Notre Dame and gave his best effort to fulfilling its duties. Malloy was a marked contrast to Hesburgh in personality and style. A former varsity basketball player at Notre Dame with a doctorate in Christian Ethics from Vanderbilt, Malloy was more reserved and stolid. He loved all sports, and he still played "Monk hoops" basketball with the undergraduate students of Sorin Hall, where he resided even after having assumed the presidency. But he possessed none of Hesburgh's charisma, nor did he enjoy the kind of renown that Hesburgh had earned outside of Notre Dame. Malloy simply had a reputation as a dedicated teacher and a thoughtful moral theologian. He was a competent but not especially exciting speaker, and a man not given to the extended socializing that some university administrators pursue in an effort to gain favor with trustees and wealthy donors. He shared this latter quality with his new executive vice president, Bill Beauchamp, who took over Father Joyce's responsibilities. Beauchamp approached his new duties with a plain, no-nonsense willingness to get on with the job and to get the work done. Malloy and Beauchamp both appeared to be at a peace with who they were as men and priests, and each resisted the temptation to try to outdo their predecessors. Instead, each of them saw his work as building on the inheritance he had received. Neither appeared intimidated to be following a legend.

Malloy recalled that "one of the great gifts that Ted Hesburgh gave me as he left office was to travel around the world for about a year with Ned Joyce, leaving the field free for me to begin my administration without him physically present on the campus."[8] Malloy appreciated the time, and he and Beauchamp settled in to the offices in the Main Building that Hesburgh and Joyce had previously occupied. Hesburgh's parting advice to Malloy had been "Be yourself."[9] By the time Hesburgh and Father Joyce returned to campus in June of 1988, Malloy and Beauchamp had found their sea legs, and the newcomers made no systematic moves to consult their elders. Malloy only invited Hesburgh to an occasional pro forma lunch. There was no real connection between them, and Hesburgh deemed Malloy to be not particularly engaging. In retrospect, Monk Malloy admitted that it was a mistake on his part not to have met more often with Father Ted. His explanation is for many understandable: "Part of my reason was that I wanted to chart my own path and to manifest that I was not a lackey or dependent on the old regime. I figured that the greatest compliment I could pay Ted was to build on what he had helped to establish over thirty-five years and to sustain the momentum."[10] Malloy welcomed Father Ted's continued involvement with the various institutes and centers that the older man had helped establish. He assumed that these gave the president emeritus significant opportunities to meet his declared need to be involved at Notre Dame. He never fully appreciated that not being kept close to the major decision making of the university troubled Hesburgh.

In many ways the transition from Hesburgh/Joyce to Malloy/Beauchamp proceeded quite smoothly. Malloy pursued no sudden reversals in policy nor instituted any major new initiatives in his first years as president. Tim O'Meara continued as provost, for the most part maintaining his dominance over academic matters. Bill Sexton continued as vice president for development, and under his expert guidance the fund-raising effort proceeded more successfully than ever. New buildings were planned and constructed, including the Hesburgh Center for International Studies. The endowment grew. Malloy aimed to bring "evolutionary change" to Notre Dame, and to build on the impressive foundation that he had inherited from Hesburgh. Malloy shared broadly the liberal Catholicism that Hesburgh had embraced. The two men certainly were on the same page regarding *Ex Corde Ecclesiae,* and Malloy continued Hesburgh's efforts to resist any move by the institutional Church to exercise a role in the affairs of a Catholic university. He enunciated the same concerns about academic freedom that Father Ted had articulated from the time of Land O'Lakes. Malloy also wanted to continue shaping Notre Dame with a distinct social justice emphasis, and to continue the effort to address major issues and problems in the world. In this regard, he began to tweak aspects of Hesburgh's approach. He paid more attention to issues closer to home and gave much greater attention to the South Bend community than Hesburgh had. The university's generous support for a new homeless center in South Bend notably demonstrated this enhanced local commitment. Like Hesburgh, Malloy had a deep commitment to civil rights, but he aimed to manifest his concern primarily at Notre Dame. He moved far beyond anything his predecessor had ever undertaken to increase the minority student enrollment by significantly increasing available financial aid. He also declared 1988–1989, his second year in office, as "the Year of Cultural Diversity," during which various notable minority speakers and performers were brought to campus. Malloy also tackled elements of the difficult situation for women at Notre Dame. When Hesburgh left office only a third of undergraduate students were female and barely 10 percent of the full-time faculty. The new president set in place measures to improve these numbers; he also appointed Patricia O'Hara, a professor in the Law School, as vice president for student affairs, thereby making her the first woman to serve as an officer in the history of the university.[11]

Father Hesburgh had no particular objection to any of these decisions, although the sense that Malloy was addressing "problems" regarding minority and women representation left to him by his predecessor grated a little. So' too did the favorable attention given Malloy's emphasis on the role of the Congregation of Holy Cross at the university, which Father Ted thought merely replicated his own. Malloy encouraged the academic appointment of Holy Cross priests at Notre Dame, and during the early years of his presidency Tim Scully took up an appointment in political science, as did Mark Poorman in theology, Austin Collins in art, just as I did in history. But Malloy spoke out more vigorously than had Father Ted about the crucial importance of the Holy Cross order at Notre Dame. In 1990 he bluntly commented that "if Holy Cross were not centrally involved in the administration and other units of the university, there would be a very difficult time sustaining its Catholic mission and identity."[12] Tensions over the Catholic identity and character of Notre Dame had simmered mainly out of the public eye during the final years of Hesburgh's reign, but the lid now came off the debate. Questions were raised about whether Notre Dame was on a trajectory toward secularization, especially in light of the declining percentage of Catholics on the faculty, a trend that had begun during the Hesburgh administration. Would Notre Dame traverse the same path away from its religious foundation that the leading Protestant schools had trod over the past century? The contentious issue of faculty hiring notably attracted some animated attention. Malloy gave the issue some treatment in the deliberations of his Colloquy for the Year 2000, his institutional self-study and planning exercise, but it also provided the focus for much of the occasionally disputatious discussion in the Conversation on the Catholic Character of Notre Dame group, which was initiated in 1992. Father Hesburgh felt frustrated that Malloy never brought the Catholic identity and faculty hiring matters to him for his advice and possible assistance.

Malloy's hesitation in going to Hesburgh resulted primarily from his desire to forge his own path, but he presumably also felt some hesitation because of Father Ted's continued close friendship with Dick McBrien, who emerged as a critic of the new administration. McBrien had voiced concern in 1990 about Malloy's closeness to the Holy Cross order—rather strangely given that Malloy was a member of the order—as compared to Father Hesburgh. He raised the concern that "people think the order sees an opportunity under Malloy to reassert its presence" in the academic areas of the university.[13] The implication was that things were better done the Hesburgh way.

Hesburgh also worried about the place of Tim O'Meara in the new administration. O'Meara's relationship with Malloy could hardly be the same as the one he had enjoyed with Hesburgh. There were no longer the late-night meetings in Father Ted's office where major decisions for the university were made. Malloy attempted to institute more regular planning and budgetary procedures, and Beauchamp implemented the latter with more energy than Father Joyce had undertaken in his final years as executive vice president. Inevitably there were some tensions as O'Meara's power was modestly trimmed. O'Meara handled the changes quite well, but Hesburgh fretted that his friend and key lieutenant, on whom he had relied so heavily, was in some way being disrespected by Malloy and Beauchamp. Nonetheless, Hesburgh felt more reassured about Malloy's administration while O'Meara remained as provost. O'Meara always kept him briefed on key issues. He felt further isolated from the heart of university decision making when O'Meara retired in 1996 and was replaced by the historian Nathan Hatch, with whom Malloy was close.

Somewhat ironically, Hesburgh criticized Malloy in one instance not for restricting O'Meara's role, but for asking him to take the lead on a sensitive matter. The issue concerned Father James Burtchaell and the charges against him of sexual misconduct with male students. In Malloy's telling, "whenever serious accusations concerning faculty were forthcoming, it was my practice to ask Tim O'Meara to lead an investigation." In 1991 O'Meara took on the difficult assignment of examining charges raised against Burtchaell. He interviewed the accusers, gathered all the facts, and eventually confronted Burtchaell. "After considerable consultation," Malloy summarized, "and with the agreement of the accusers, Burtchaell agreed to resign publicly and was forbidden from remaining on the Notre Dame campus."[14] Malloy thought the matter had been handled appropriately, but Hesburgh viewed the matter differently. He noted in 1998 that "Monk didn't touch it [the Burtchaell case]. He dumped it on Tim O'Meara. And Tim had to gather the evidence, he had to call Jim in and he had to make him . . . sign the letter [of resignation], and he didn't particularly want to do it all." Hesburgh made clear that although he personally had "absolutely zero to do with any of this because no one asked me," he felt Malloy should have dealt directly with Burtchaell.[15] Malloy's reliance on established procedures seemed more prudent in this instance, but that Father Ted still raised this criticism of his successor in 1998 is an indication of the critical attitude he had toward the man who had taken his place at the helm of Notre Dame.

While his concerns regarding individuals like O'Meara caused Father Hesburgh to have reservations about the Malloy administration, they did not exhaust his list of grievances. More mundane though very important matters, including such cherished Domer topics as athletics, money, architecture, and buildings, also made it onto his complaint docket. While continuing to employ Ellerbe and Company on most projects during the 1990s, the relevant decision-makers in Malloy's administration began to receive pressure to vary the architectural firms with whom the university dealt.[16] Eventually they decided to end the longtime exclusive relationship with Ellerbe. Initially this was done for the extensive renovations on Sacred Heart Basilica and the Main Building, which required specialist expertise, as did the Marie DeBartolo Performing Arts Center later on. But after working with different architectural firms on these important projects, Malloy and Beauchamp authorized more competitive bidding for future projects, and even allowed for a return to the more attractive Collegiate Gothic style instead of the plain function-over-form approach of Ellerbe. Hesburgh and Ned Joyce believed the relationship with Ellerbe had served the university very well, and they regretted the fraying of the relationship with the Minnesota firm and the eventual end of the special connection with it. Rather amusingly, however, Father Ted allowed himself to play the architectural critic of buildings constructed in the Malloy era, including those designed by Ellerbe. He lambasted the huge DeBartolo classroom building, suggesting that it possessed "the dullest wall of the whole university" when approached from the north. He further held that the "damn cream brick" should not have been used, but observed that it would be okay "when they get some ivy on it."[17]

Hesburgh and Joyce were more disturbed by changes that came in the 1990s in the closely related areas of money and athletics at Notre Dame. While Father Ted labored away on the Knight Commission, money came to dominate big-time college athletics more than ever, and Notre Dame was front and center in this picture. The trend was well under way, of course, before Father Hesburgh left office. Father Joyce, after all, had helped found the sixty-four-member College Football Association (CFA) back in 1986, and he remained close to its executive director Chuck Neinas. He also had turned down opportunities in 1984 and in 1987 "for Notre Dame to negotiate separate agreements with the television networks out of loyalty to the CFA and its [group] television package." This commitment to the sixty-four-school combine seemed to be an enduring one as Notre Dame participated in 1990 in CFA negotiations with the ABC and ESPN networks to extend their contracts. But Notre Dame had been meeting secretly with another network, NBC, while the CFA negotiations were being pursued. Bill Beauchamp and his athletic and financial counselors led by the new athletic director Dick Rosenthal decided to break with the

Hesburgh-Joyce relationship with the CFA, and to enhance the revenue Notre Dame could earn from its football team. Just weeks after a new CFA deal was announced, as Allen Sack has outlined, "Notre Dame sent shock waves through the world of sports by announcing that it was out of the CFA and had closed its own separate package with NBC for $38 million dollars."[18] Some CFA members were stunned and criticized Notre Dame for its "greed" and deception.

Father Hesburgh had mixed feelings about the NBC contract deal. He resented that both he and especially Ned Joyce had been kept completely in the dark on the matter. He worried when Notre Dame's new deal immediately attracted unfavorable media attention, and that it only seemed to highlight that Notre Dame was a "football school." Yet as the media criticism died down he began to accommodate himself to the new arrangement. He later noted the obvious point that "the new crowd" undertook a "very intensive raising of funds through athletics" and that "some people gripe about it." Yet he readily acknowledged the beneficial impact of the athletics money. He noted that "it's an incredible thing that they get six million bucks a year that goes mostly into student scholarships."[19]

Hesburgh found himself more troubled by the willingness of the Malloy-Beauchamp administration to borrow money to fund their new projects, especially the expansion of the football stadium. He had blocked Father Joyce's earlier plans for a stadium expansion, arguing that it would draw too much attention to football and away from the academic progress the university had made. But he accepted with good grace the Malloy administration's decision, which emerged from the Colloquy for the Year 2000 process, to expand the famous "House that Rockne Built." But what drove both him and Ned Joyce into some level of anxiety was the decision to borrow money to complete the stadium renovation and expansion. It confirmed that they were no longer in charge.

In 1998 Father Hesburgh complained that Monk Malloy had only called him "for advice twice in eleven years."[20] One of his favorite nieces, Mary Flaherty, captured his sentiments well when she told Michael O'Brien some years earlier that she thought her uncle "misses . . . running the big picture. . . . It is probably difficult for him that things are not done exactly the way he may have done them."[21] His thoughtful niece sensitively voiced the reality for Father Hesburgh. He deeply missed being president of Notre Dame, and the passing of years barely diminished his angst at not being in command. To understand Father Hesburgh in the 1990s one must appreciate that he found it very difficult to let go and to allow his successors to take his beloved institution in directions they charted without consulting him.

A certain relief came to him from his involvement at another university. Harvard University sought his assistance. Harvard's president Derek Bok called Father Hesburgh in late 1989 and asked him to stand for election to the board of overseers, the governing body that exerted influence over the strategic direction of the university and advised the university's leadership on priorities and plans. Bok explained to Hesburgh that he was eligible to serve because he was an alumnus as a result of the honorary doctorate he had received when he delivered the commencement address in Harvard Yard in 1973.[22] So began Hesburgh's association with Harvard, and it proved not only a consequential one but also a rewarding one for the Notre Dame priest. He accepted appointments to the academic affairs and nominations committee of the board and soon found himself traveling to Cambridge for meetings every six weeks or so. He racked up many thousands of miles with US Airways traveling back and forth between Boston and South Bend from 1990 to 1996. He enjoyed very much his work with his fellow board members and with Harvard's officers and faculty, whose capacities and credentials impressed him. He quickly got into a pattern of staying at the Harvard Faculty Club, where he would offer Mass early in the morning of the days of the committee and full board meetings.

After Hesburgh's first year on the board of overseers Derek Bok announced his intention to resign and so a presidential search began. Father Ted participated energetically in the process and endorsed the majority decision to offer the position to a mild-mannered Renaissance literature professor and experienced educational administrator named Neil Rudenstine, who took up his duties in mid-1991. Hesburgh established a friendly relationship with Rudenstine and gladly offered him formal and informal counsel when requested.[23] While Rudenstine settled in as president and devoted himself to much travel to meet alumni and to raise money, Father Hesburgh saw his duties on the board of overseers enlarged. Hanna Holborn Gray, who chaired the nominations committee of the overseers (as well as serving as president of the University of Chicago), orchestrated his election to chair the board. According to Father Ted, he tried to persuade her that he should not take on the role, offering as reasons his age (now seventy-six), his failing eyesight, his living in rather distant South Bend, and his being a Catholic priest. The formidable Hanna Gray—whom Hesburgh fondly described as a "tough German gal"—quickly dismissed all his objections. Soon Ted Hesburgh, Roman Catholic priest, was announced as president of the board of overseers. Neil Rudenstine described him as "among the most extraordinary and accomplished educational leaders of our time," and said that it was "Harvard's privilege" to have him serve in the role.[24] As an encomium from the American educational establishment this was hard to beat, and Hesburgh basked in it.

Hesburgh soon faced a particular challenge involving the leadership of the school. In November 1994 Neil Rudenstine suffered some kind of breakdown brought on by exhaustion and sleep deprivation. Hesburgh went into what might be deemed crisis management mode. He already had arrived in Boston to attend a committee meeting, so he went directly to Rudenstine's home and met with him, one of only a few people who gained admission. He could see that Rudenstine was in no shape to quickly resume his duties. He consulted immediately with Dr. Daniel C. Tosteson, the forceful dean of the Harvard Medical School, who also served as Rudenstine's personal physician. They agreed to run Rudenstine through every conceivable medical test to get to the bottom of what ailed him. Hesburgh then began his own investigation of Rudenstine's circumstance. He determined after speaking to his immediate staff that the Harvard president maintained an impossible work schedule with long and endless days filled with donor meetings, fund-raisers, extensive correspondence, overseeing a vast and bloated administration, and efforts to get the wealthier schools at Harvard to share some of their largesse with the poorer ones. He determined that he would need to help Rudenstine get some control over his life and his job.[25]

Naturally the overseers worried about whether Rudenstine could return to perform his presidential duties effectively. At the next board meeting, Father Ted had Dr. Dan Tosteson available for questioning and one of the overseers, Dr. Bernardine Healy, a former director of the National Institute of Health, probed the Harvard Medical School dean at length to get at Rudenstine's true situation. After her interrogation she declared that Tosteson's diagnosis and prognosis were convincing and all her board colleagues agreed. Then Hesburgh took the reins at the meeting. He explained that Rudenstine would need some months off and that during that time there would need to be some reorganization of his duties to cut down on the number of officers reporting directly to him and to establish better control of his schedule. He made it clear that he would assist in that task, and his fellow overseers endorsed his plans. In the interim Hesburgh explained that the provost, Al Carnesale, would act as president and Harvard would move forward. The board of overseers seemed reassured by the guarantees of the elderly priest, and the crisis surrounding Rudenstine's leadership of Harvard soon subsided. The Harvard president got some rest, returned to his duties, and served until 2001.

Rudenstine remained very grateful to Hesburgh for his assistance during a distressing personal ordeal. He knew that there had been some agitation that he should resign, but Hesburgh had played a crucial role in steadying the Harvard ship to give him the time to recover and then to return to take the helm. Rudenstine's gratitude was shared by the board of overseers. Hesburgh was approached to stay on as chair after the difficult 1994–1995 academic year, although it was the normal practice for the chair to serve but one year. His reassuring firmness throughout Rudenstine's health crisis merited the regard of his colleagues. His continued presence in the chair's seat seemed a guarantee of stability, and he gladly agreed to stay on. The 1995–1996 academic year at Harvard passed more smoothly for Rudenstine and for Hesburgh. His contribution on the Harvard Board of Overseers certainly must be measured well above and beyond those of most who serve on it or similar bodies, and he rightfully took some pride in his six years of service amidst the Harvard Crimson.[26]

While he made a genuine contribution in Cambridge, Massachusetts, Hesburgh had little of major consequence to contribute in Washington, D.C., in the 1990s. He was well disposed to President George H. W. Bush and much admired the judicious way he and Secretary of State James Baker cooperated with Mikhail Gorbachev to wind down the Cold War, thereby reducing the threat of nuclear confrontation. Hesburgh also expressed satisfaction that Bush traveled to Notre Dame to deliver the commencement address in May of 1992. He took pleasure in Bush's willingness to quote him in his speech when the president told the graduates that "you would do well to consider the simple but profound words of Notre Dame's own Father Hesburgh when he said, 'The most important thing a father can do for his children is to love their mother.'"[27]

The American people acknowledged Bush's competence in foreign policy, but they preferred a president more focused on domestic affairs to lead them in the post–Cold War era. In 1992 Bill Clinton, a baby boomer, defeated the last of the World War II generation to lead the country. Hesburgh didn't know the new young president, but he quickly recognized Clinton's gifts as a politician and his mastery of policy details. Hesburgh's affection and regard for Clinton grew demonstrably after his first meeting with the president on June 24, 1993, his ordination anniversary. Hesburgh was in the capital for a meeting of the U.S. Institute of Peace board when he received a call to come immediately to the White House. When ushered into the Oval Office, Clinton asked him, "Is it true that you were ordained a priest fifty years ago today?" When Hesburgh confirmed the point, he remembered to Robert Schmuhl that Clinton said, "Then I think it is proper you should be in this house and in this office so I can congratulate you on what you have done for your church as well as what you have done for your country."[28] Clinton's charm and flattery won over Father Hesburgh rather easily. Thereafter he became a Clinton supporter, and not simply of Clinton administration policies, but of Clinton personally in certain struggles of his turbulent presidency.

In November 1993 Hesburgh joined a long list of notable Americans in endorsing the North American Free Trade Agreement and was publicly singled out by Clinton for doing so.[29] Sometime later and after Republicans led by Newt Gingrich won control of the House of Representatives, Hesburgh wrote an op-ed piece complaining of the proposed House budget cuts in various programs, especially AmeriCorps.[30] There was no doubt that his sympathies lay with Clinton. But he made this patently clear in 1994 when he signed on as co-chair of the Clinton's Presidential Legal Expense Trust, which was "established to raise money for the personal legal expenses of Bill and Hillary Clinton related to [their] pre–White House business and conduct." Stung by criticism of his action, Father Ted claimed high-minded motives. He explained, "I agreed to do this for the presidency, not necessarily for this president. I would have done it for any president."[31]

Although Father Hesburgh willingly put his good name on the line for the Clintons this hardly gained him any real influence in return. In October 1994 Hesburgh wrote to the Democratic governor of Pennsylvania, Robert P. Casey, in reply to Casey's sending him one of his proudly pro-life speeches. He told Casey that he had spoken to Clinton on the abortion issue and "its ultimate divisiveness" prior to the UN-sponsored Cairo International Conference on Population and Development. Hesburgh reported that he told Clinton "that the 'A[bortion]' word should be left out of any statement of the United States delegation."[32] At the Cairo meeting the Clinton administration and some of the more "advanced" nations sought to define a universal human right to abortion on demand under the guise of reproductive health services, but they were blocked by an international coalition in which John Paul II and his Vatican diplomats played an important part.[33] Hesburgh remained largely silent as the Democratic administration not only entrenched its commitment to the wide abortion license of *Roe v. Wade*, but sought to internationalize it.

Hesburgh expended much greater energy and personal emotion on a very specific case, trying to win release for Jonathan Jay Pollard, who had been convicted in 1987 of supplying vast quantities of secret information to Israel.[34] Pollard was the son of Morris Pollard, who had taught at Notre Dame since 1961 when he arrived to direct LOBUND. Hesburgh had known the family since that time and he shared the anguish that Morris Pollard and his wife, Mildred, felt for their son. He began his lobbying effort to win clemency for Jonathan Pollard during the Bush administration but got nowhere. He pushed more strongly with Clinton, writing letters, making calls, and importuning administration officials. He was hardly alone in doing so. American Jewish groups and Israeli leaders also pressured Clinton to reduce the life sentence imposed on Pollard. The convicted spy maintained that he had compromised neither U.S. agents overseas nor American intelligence gathering methods (e.g., ciphers and codes), and Father Hesburgh believed that should be taken into account. But the combined weight of the Defense and Justice Department recommendations along with forceful lobbying by the CIA prevented Clinton from granting clemency, whatever his personal sympathies. Pollard remained in federal prison until 2015. He gained release and left for Israel some months after Father Hesburgh's death. The old priest regretted to the end of his life that he had not been able to do more for the son of his good friends.

Father Hesburgh also expressed regret at the tawdry scandals that affected Bill Clinton's second term in office. The revelations of the president's affair with the young White House intern Monica Lewinsky surprised him as much for Clinton's stupidity as for his immorality. He acknowledged that a faculty member who engaged in similar behavior with a student intern would probably have been fired from a university post, but he retained sympathy for Clinton. He stated in an interview that Clinton's character was flawed, and that he lacked a moral compass, but he blamed this on his sad family background and the absence of a true father in his life. Two years after Clinton left office Father Ted went further and told Robert Schmuhl that Clinton's problem was not "his brains. It's his gonads."[35] Whatever his diagnosis of the root causes of Clinton's problems, Hesburgh remained restrained in any comment on the Lewinsky scandal and the subsequent impeachment. He sympathized with Clinton's political predicament but held off making any offer of assistance to the embattled president. In the early summer of 1998, when the possibility of Clinton's impeachment was strongly mooted, Hesburgh explained in an interview that he normally would never say "no" if an American president asked for his help, but that "if Clinton wanted help on Monica Lewinsky, I'd say, 'I'm sorry. That ain't my bag.'"[36] Clinton didn't need Father Hesburgh's help. He relied on the loyalty of Democratic senators to fend off the charges of perjury and obstruction of justice brought against him in the impeachment trial early in 1999. Hesburgh admired Clinton's ability to slither out of trouble and to survive politically, even as he worried that the president's behavior had demeaned the office.

ENDLESS HONORS AND SEEKING PEACE, 1999–2009

During the second decade of Father Hesburgh's restive retirement he gradually slowed down and reduced his commitments. In 1999 he joined a delegation organized by the U.S. Association for the UN High Commissioner for Refugees, and he traveled to inspect refugee camps in Kosovo, Macedonia, and Albania, where victims of the brutal terror of Slobodan Milošević's Serbian troops had fled during the appalling conflict in the Balkans. He met with various officials and with refugees, to whom he offered encouragement. His role revealed his continuing commitment to alleviate suffering in the world, and to encourage forgiveness and reconciliation. He gladly undertook the trip but on his return he commented, "By the end of it, I really felt my age." It was one of the first times that he admitted to being troubled by his advanced years.

The now eighty-two-year-old slowed the amount of international travel that he undertook thereafter, but he hardly slacked off in other areas. He continued to write forewords and book chapters as well as to offer endorsements for books. He also continued his role as an occasional lecturer on campus and made guest appearances in many classes. He maintained his schedule of presiding and preaching at Sunday Masses both in the dorm chapels and at more formal liturgical occasions. Not surprisingly as his retirement years progressed he found himself called upon to preach or to eulogize at many funerals. He had performed this essential priestly role from the earliest days of his ministry, and delivered the homily at the funerals of his parents, his sisters, and at those of older friends like "Doc" Kenna and I. A. O'Shaughnessy. But during the decades of his retirement he was called upon to speak words of remembrance and consolation at the funerals of some of his closest collaborators, most of whom he outlived. In February 1995 he donned long red robes and climbed into the pulpit of the Episcopalian Cathedral Church of St. John the Divine in New York City to eulogize his friend Jim Grant. In front of twenty-five hundred people including such dignitaries as First Lady Hillary Clinton, he described Grant as "my conscience when justice was needed in this great unjust world of ours," and he praised the UNICEF director's ability to get "all of us to do things we didn't really want to do."[37]

Closer to home, he presided in October 2000 at the funeral of the woman who had kept order in his office throughout his whole presidency, Helen Hosinski. Father Ted had demonstrated his good understanding of the meaning of friendship by staying in close touch with Helen after her retirement, and through visiting her regularly at the Holy Cross Care and Rehabilitation Center after her ailments caused her to reside there. He preached with deep affection and admiration for this quiet and discreet woman who had aided him in his many and varied endeavors. Less than four year later, in May 2004, he returned to Sacred Heart Basilica for the funeral of his other great collaborator throughout the entire term of his presidency, Father Edmund P. Joyce. Father Ted had demonstrated his brotherhood to Ned Joyce during his confrere's difficult final years after Father Joyce suffered a stroke and was confined to Holy Cross House, the priests' retirement home at Notre Dame. Hesburgh visited his longtime partner in the running of Notre Dame almost daily, and took steps to make life as comfortable as possible during very difficult circumstances for Ned Joyce. In his homily Hesburgh referenced their long association and paid a handsome tribute to the priest who he said "more than carried his half of the load" of their joint labors. Hesburgh told the mourners in the packed church, "He never let me down once. He was always there when I was missing and managed to fill in the gap and probably do better than I could have. He was always loyal, and faithful, and hardworking, and wonderful. I guess I'd have to say more than anything else he was a good friend—in the best sense of the word *friend* that we care well for each other." Toward the end of his homily he began to speak directly to Ned Joyce, and he thanked him for being such a good brother and great priest. And he moved to his conclusion, linking himself with Joyce: "I guess all we can say, Ned, is we'll be seeing you. And I truly believe that. There will be more days when we can get around and talk about the glories of this wonderful place and all its wonderful people. There will be days ahead when we can look back and thank God we got through without too many scrapes and bruises. But especially, I think we'll look back with great gratitude on that wonderful grace that Jesus gave us both in making us priests."[38]

Sometimes Hesburgh was called to be with colleagues and friends as they faced death, and he never refused to answer a call if he could be of help. He had long appreciated his friendship with Eppie Lederer/Ann Landers, despite the very liberal direction in which the advice columnist had headed on issues like abortion and homosexuality since they had first met almost a half-century before. Eppie Lederer had once joked to the writer Christopher Buckley that her relationship with Ted Hesburgh was "the greatest unfertilized romance in the history of the world," and Hesburgh had shared a running gag with her that he would extend his fraternal love to her but not his kisses. The Notre Dame president had sent the famous columnist a framed triptych "showing him on the day he began at Notre Dame, during the middle of his reign, and on the last day, cleaning out his desk." According to Buckley's account it was signed "To Eppie, L[ove] but no K[isses], Devotedly, Ted."[39] He always had loved that Eppie Lederer was so "bright and feisty," but in the early summer of 2002 her zest was spent. She lay dying in her beautiful Chicago apartment on Lake Shore Drive with its wonderful view of Lake Michigan. According to Carol Felsenthal, the Chicago writer and biographer, Hesburgh was one of the last people she called to her bedside. Suffering from multiple myeloma, she had decided against chemotherapy. Although she was receiving heavy doses of morphine she still experienced excruciating pain. Hesburgh spoke words of reassurance and consolation to the woman who had imparted advice to so many. He knew she would have a Jewish funeral, but he promised her "a few requiem masses, you can count on that." And he left his friend a rosary during his visit "so that there's something physical you can hang on to." Apparently "when the pain was at its most intense, she grasped the rosary," and perhaps she thought gratefully of the priest-friend who had given it to her.[40]

Hesburgh's sadness during the early years of the new century was not rooted only in his losing friends like Ned Joyce and Eppie Lederer. These were also the years when the priesthood he so prized was dreadfully besmirched in the ordeal now known somewhat banally as the clergy sexual abuse crisis. This purgatorial ordeal for the Catholic Church did not catch Hesburgh completely by surprise. He knew of cases like Burtchaell's where priests had abused their ministerial trust and preyed on those they were called to serve. In 1996 while traveling by train from Union Station in Washington, D.C., to Baltimore, a 1977 Notre Dame graduate named John Salveson had engaged Father Ted in conversation and revealed to him that he had been abused while at Notre Dame by a priest of the Diocese of Rockville Centre on Long Island. This priest had held an assistant rector's position at Notre Dame while studying for a graduate degree in the mid-1970s. According to Salveson's account, Hesburgh looked "angry and disturbed" on hearing his heartrending story. The president emeritus told the abuse survivor that he wished that Salveson had alerted him to the situation when he was a student as he "would have removed the priest immediately." Hesburgh also apologized for what had happened, which provided Salveson some modest solace.[41]

Such personal encounters only stoked a more general disquiet Hesburgh felt regarding the health and well-being of the priestly ranks. His concern emerged from an awareness of the sizable percentage of homosexual priests and seminarians in the United States. Both Richard McBrien and Andrew Greeley had raised this matter as a concern in articles published in the late 1980s with attention-grabbing titles such as "Homosexuality and the Priesthood: Questions We Can't Keep in the Closet" (McBrien's), and "Bishops Paralyzed over Heavily Gay Priesthood" (Greeley's).[42] McBrien hoped that Catholic apprehensions about the high numbers of "gay" clergy would pressure Church authorities to permit a married priesthood, and he occasionally made this case to Hesburgh. More regularly he simply provoked the older priest's concerns about the numbers of homosexual priests and seminarians, and he gossiped with him about what members of the hierarchy might be of homosexual disposition. Yet the clergy crisis and the media storm that surrounded it still caught Father Ted by surprise when it broke open early in 2002. Hesburgh was taken aback by the extent of clerical abuse as well as the scope of episcopal incompetence and malfeasance.

A less dispiriting issue to which Hesburgh gave attention at this time was the failure of the new generation of university presidents to speak out publicly on matters of broad consequence. Hesburgh had been much taken by a lively piece by the journalist/historian David Greenberg entitled "Small Men on Campus: The Shrinking College President," featured in the *New*

Republic in the summer of 1998.[43] Three years later he took his inspiration from Greenberg and penned an essay for *The Chronicle of Higher Education* whose title posed the sharp question "Where Are College Presidents' Voices on Important Public Issues?"[44] He lamented that "where we once had a fellowship of public intellectuals, do we now have insulated chief executives intent on keeping the complicated machinery of American higher education running smoothly?" He regretted that the modus operandi of current university leaders seemed to be to avoid controversy, to build up bloated bureaucracies, and to raise money. His article read as both an implicit indictment of contemporary presidents such as Rudenstine and Malloy and as an exercise in retrospective congratulation for the presidential endeavors of individuals like Kingman Brewster, Bill Friday, Clark Kerr, and himself.

He still intended to play a public role and to comment on public issues, whatever the increased restraints that his failing eyesight imposed on him. In 2001 he accepted his last presidential appointment when he agreed to President George W. Bush's request that he serve on the Commission on Presidential Scholars, the body that met annually to select high school students from across the nation for recognition as "presidential scholars."[45] It was his sixteenth presidential appointment and one he probably should not have accepted because he was incapable of reading the dossiers of the students nominated for this recognition.

Although what Robert Schmuhl called his "condition of near-blindness" soon thereafter led him to conclude that he must end most of his board and commission commitments, it did not interfere with his involvements on the Notre Dame campus. He remained available and accessible for students, faculty, and alumni who were willing to seek him out on the thirteenth floor of the library. And many did come to see him and they drew inspiration from him. An aura of sorts now surrounded him. He shared willingly his advice and his blessings. He loved to bless children and babies, and if a pregnant mother visited him she was certain to receive a blessing for her and her unborn child. He still said Mass regularly in the small chapel in his office suite, and if Melanie Chapleau was absent he would wander out on the floor and seek out a student working in a library carrel or at an open table and enlist help to do the Scripture readings of the day. He had memorized the second Eucharistic Prayer, so he only needed modest help for the Liturgy of the Word. He enjoyed a greater inner peace as the years progressed. He was grateful that he could still undertake his ministry on campus and touch the lives of others for the good. The resentments of his first postpresidential decade dissipated somewhat and were replaced by a genuine gratitude.

Although he gradually experienced life in a more peaceable way, he surrendered nothing of his interest in developments at Notre Dame. These years gave him much material for reflection and reaction. In 1998 Jim Burtchaell published his massive *The Dying of the Light: The Disengagement of Colleges and Universities from Their Christian Churches*, and Hesburgh followed its reception with interest, although he could not read the whole book. Burtchaell's book provided seventeen case studies of colleges and universities of various denominations whose Christian identities had sadly deteriorated or even disappeared. In a book that one reviewer labeled "a jeremiad, a lamentation for what has been lost," Burtchaell asked whether "the story within the [seventeen distinct] stories" that he told "meant the end of Christian colleges and universities." Notre Dame's onetime provost regretted that there had been such "little learned rage against the dying of the light" as these colleges surrendered their Christian identities.[46] The weighty tome barely mentioned either Notre Dame or Hesburgh, but Burtchaell's incisive understanding of Notre Dame's experience under Hesburgh provided a kind of searing inspiration for his project. The very use of "disengagement" in the book's subtitle hinted strongly at the indictment Burtchaell launched against Land O'Lakes and what followed it in Catholic colleges and universities. Burtchaell criticized the presidents of the various institutions, who in their supposed desire to strengthen the academic reputation of their schools sought independence from their churches to allow their autonomy.

Hesburgh learned the essence of Burtchaell's thesis from various sources. He reacted defensively toward the implied criticisms launched at him and at what he had undertaken at Notre Dame. His knowledge that Burtchaell had suffered disgrace and banishment for his moral transgressions did not lead him to simply ignore the arguments his former provost outlined. He knew that the thesis of *The Dying of the Light* might influence how future historians would portray him and his legacy at Notre Dame. In informal conversations about Burtchaell's book he contested the extent to which Notre Dame had disengaged from the Church, while still holding his ground on the necessity of the Land O'Lakes formula. He also noted the steps he had taken to strengthen Catholic identity, especially the hiring of Richard McBrien and his "rescue mission" of the theology department.

Father Ted held that when he left office approximately two-thirds of the faculty had identified as Catholic, and he noted that the precipitous decline in Catholic hiring had occurred on Monk Malloy's watch. This argument ignored that the very faculty hired under his quest for excellence largely oversaw the hiring during the decade after he left office. In the end, Hesburgh worried that there might be something to Burtchaell's "slippery slope" thesis regarding the secularization of Catholic universities, but he absolved himself of responsibility for any movement at Notre Dame in that direction.

While the larger questions prompted by books such as Burtchaell's attracted his interest, Father Hesburgh found himself much more drawn to the turbulent developments in the leadership of Notre Dame that characterized the years from 2000 to 2005. The turmoil emerged at the winter meeting of the board of trustees in Palm Beach, Florida. There the trustees forced the resignation of the athletic director, Michael Wadsworth, and removed the executive vice president, Bill Beauchamp, from of his oversight responsibilities for athletics. The two men took the proverbial fall for a number of mishaps in the athletic department that had landed Notre Dame on NCAA probation. The fact that the Notre Dame football team had a mediocre record under Bob Davie's tenure as coach hardly helped the prospects of either man. At the board's spring meeting at Notre Dame the trustees voted to remove Beauchamp as executive vice president and to replace him with Father Tim Scully. At the same time they elected Father John Jenkins to fill the vacancy as vice president and associate provost created by Scully's promotion.

Hesburgh watched these maneuvers with great interest. Some of his friends among the older trustees such as Jerry Hank kept him informed of developments inasmuch as they knew of them themselves. Hesburgh regretted the unceremonious dumping of Beauchamp, for whom he always retained regard, but he was more troubled by the appointment of Scully. Hesburgh admired Scully's sharp intellect and the impressive work he accomplished in founding the Alliance for Catholic Education. Yet he found himself uneasy at the prospect of Tim Scully's ascending to the presidency of the university. He had earlier described Tim as acting "like the Mayor of Chicago," who "overdoes the development thing." Given that Father Ted had helped define a major part of the Notre Dame president's job as raising money, this criticism of Scully's undoubted ability to elicit financial support from donors seemed a little odd. But Hesburgh had other concerns about

Scully. He saw Scully as "the favorite boy of Dick Warner," and he felt Warner worked as a gray eminence to facilitate Scully's rise. Furthermore, he resented Scully's supposed willingness to play favorites. In response to my supportive comments about Tim Scully's capacity to be president, he simply expressed the hope that Tim would "grow up" before Malloy passed the presidential keys to him.[47]

As it turned out Tim Scully did not succeed Monk Malloy. Some tension existed between Malloy and Scully from the outset, but matters came to a head in late February 2003. Tim Scully had an unfortunate dispute with a female TV reporter one evening when he returned to his residence, Fisher Hall, for a Mass for a missing student. The rather minor episode sparked a larger controversy and the airing of a number of grievances against the talented executive vice president for his aggressive management style. Malloy eventually made it clear "that it was in the best interests of the university that he [Scully] not continue in his role."[48] Thereafter the Holy Cross provincial administration asked Scully to resign his appointment, and Scully did so on May 1. Some of the leading university trustees resented the interference of the Holy Cross order in this matter. It was clear that some of them would have preferred to have Malloy resign, and to elevate Scully to the presidency. At the next meeting of the trustees held later in May some of the trustees took the opportunity to excoriate the mild-mannered Holy Cross provincial Father William Dorwart for daring to intervene in a dispute that he worried might seriously damage both of the men involved. Hesburgh also worried about both Scully and Malloy and, most of all, the university. He rarely had spoken during trustee meetings prior to this one, but on this occasion he intervened and spoke calmly and reassuringly that almost forty years had passed since the formal transfer of ownership, and that this was the first major flare-up between the Holy Cross and the lay members of the board. He expressed the hope that the waters would calm and that the university would continue to progress.[49] Father Hesburgh wanted peace to prevail.

On the surface the tensions on campus subsided, but the powerful trustees led by Patrick McCartan and Andrew McKenna wanted Malloy gone. Concern about the faltering state of the football program under the Malloy-appointed Tyrone Willingham, Notre Dame's first African American head football coach, only added fuel to the fire. Malloy held to the notion that Willingham should be allowed to serve the full five years of his contract, but anxious trustees concerned that Notre Dame's "brand" required that it always stand among the elite of college football saw such a view as distinctly old school. In late March McCartan, a lawyer with the firm of Jones Day and then the chair of the board of trustees, informed Malloy that his term would not be renewed at the end of June 2005. No public announcement was made of this decision nor was a public search process undertaken to select a successor. Instead a predetermined "search process" was undertaken. The powerful inner core of trustees had determined from the outset that John Jenkins should succeed Malloy. On the day before the Friday, April 30, board meeting at which Jenkins was formally elected, McCartan and McKenna made a visit to Father Hesburgh's office, where they briefed him on their decision and on what would transpire the next day. Hesburgh was a little surprised at the news that Jenkins would replace Malloy, and that the decision was being made a full year before Malloy would complete his service. He did not know Jenkins well and had not been greatly impressed by his introverted personality. But the assurances of Jenkins's backers that their candidate would need Father Ted's help and would consult regularly with him gained the older priest's acquiescence. The next day he was on hand to add his imprimatur to the board's decision to appoint Jenkins, who would serve as president-in-waiting for a full year.

The turmoil of these years, especially the episode involving Tim Scully, caused Father Ted some anxiety about Notre Dame's well-being and future, but these same years also brought him a cascade of honors and recognition. The 1990s had brought him various awards, and in 1998 he reclaimed the world record for holding the most honorary degrees from Thailand's King Bhumibol. But the new decade got off to an especially notable start when he was awarded the Congressional Gold Medal in a moving ceremony in the Rotunda of the U.S. Capitol in July 2000. Hesburgh always had treasured the Medal of Freedom that Lyndon Johnson awarded him in 1964, but he gave the gold medal awarded by virtual unanimous vote of the Congress almost equal regard. The fact that he was the sole recipient at the ceremony, and that it had been awarded only 122 times previously, added to the cachet he accorded it. So too did the presence of Bill Clinton, who broke away from Mideast peace talks at Camp David with Israeli Prime Minister Ehud Barak and Palestinian Authority Chair Yasser Arafat to attend the ceremony. Clinton gave an affecting tribute, which included the line Hesburgh cherished most: "I would say that the most important thing about you and the greatest honor you will ever wear around your neck is the collar you have worn for fifty-seven years."

In 2001 Father Ted valued the tribute President George W. Bush paid to him in the commencement address he gave at Notre Dame. Bush assured the graduates and their families that Hesburgh's tenure had "in many ways defined the reputation and values of Notre Dame." In 2002 the University of San Diego awarded him his 150th honorary degree with considerable celebration. Not to be outdone by external awards, Notre Dame sustained a steady stream of initiatives to honor the man who increasingly held an iconic status on campus. In summary form here we might note that to add to the Hesburgh Library, the Hesburgh Center for International Studies, the Hesburgh Program in Public Service, and the Hesburgh Lecture Series of the Alumni Association came the Keough-Hesburgh Professorships in 2006 and the Hesburgh-Yusko Scholarship Program in 2009.[50]

In 2007 Hesburgh celebrated his ninetieth birthday. Various celebratory events occurred, and the extended Notre Dame family honored him by undertaking numerous service projects throughout the country and abroad. During the year a number of other initiatives also recognized him. The Smithsonian Institution's National Portrait Gallery unveiled the photo of Hesburgh and Martin Luther King Jr., cropped to exclude the men on either side of them, taken over forty years before at Soldier Field, and added it to its permanent exhibits. On the day of the unveiling Father Ted visited the White House to receive congratulations from President Bush, and later attended a gala dinner in the Donald W. Reynolds Center for American Art and Portraiture with Speaker of the House Nancy Pelosi and other dignitaries. Secretary of State and Notre Dame alumna Condoleezza Rice paid tribute to the man she had known since she was a fourteen-year-old. At the year's end Congressman Joe Donnelly of Indiana's Second District, in which Notre Dame was located, secured a unanimous resolution recognizing "Reverend Theodore M. Hesburgh, C.S.C., for his contributions to the civil rights movement in the United States, his tireless work to reduce the threat of nuclear conflict, and his efforts to secure the peaceful resolution of international conflicts." House Resolution 687 naturally went on at greater length describing the priest's "life of distinguished public service and deep faith," and Hesburgh was gratified by the gesture.[51] He also appreciated the films made about his life and work and in which he appeared, especially Family Theater Productions' *God, Country, Notre Dame: The Story of Father Ted Hesburgh, C.S.C.* Occasionally he gave some indication that he thought it was all a bit much, but not sufficiently so as to discourage further recognition.

By the time of his ninetieth birthday celebrations, Father Ted had moved from his familiar room in Corby Hall to Holy Cross House, his order's nursing home and assisted living facility where he had so faithfully visited Ned Joyce. A fall in his room at Corby that opened a cut in his head requiring stitches prompted his journey to the other side of St. Joseph's Lake on campus. He moved into a comfortable room on the second floor that had a view back across to the campus. In the evenings the lit Golden Dome remained somewhat visible to him. He handled the move with considerable grace and settled in to the rhythm of life at Holy Cross House. As the years progressed he benefited from assistance in dressing in the mornings. He concelebrated at the late morning community Mass, where he sat in his assigned seat in the front row right in front of the lectern. Thereafter he maintained a schedule of journeying in a Notre Dame security cruiser to his office, where Melanie Chapleau was on hand to meet him and to assist him with his work and meetings. He maintained his disposition that he would "wear out rather than rust out," and retained a great interest in university and current events. To assist him a wonderful group of volunteer student readers visited him and read to him from the *Observer*, the Notre Dame student paper, and from the *New York Times*, which he still thought of as containing all the news that's fit to print. The student readers also found themselves regaled with stories from the priest, whom they regarded as a grandfather of sorts. On normal evenings he returned to Holy Cross House for dinner, but there were still many instances where university events and social occasions called for his presence. Dick McBrien and Bev Brazauskas remained frequent dinner companions and sources of gossipy information. He also enjoyed dinner gatherings at Parisi's, an Italian restaurant near campus, where Melanie Chapleau and Father Austin Collins would take him to meet friends like Digger Phelps and to enjoy his favorite pasta with Alfredo sauce and a now watered-down Manhattan.[52] Most important, his brother Jim and sister-in-law Mary had moved back to South Bend and lived in a nearby retirement complex. They, along with the extended Hesburgh family, visited him often, and had him visit them.

The Notre Dame property at Land O'Lakes remained a place that he truly loved to visit. As always he found great personal peace there, as he had throughout his life. He needed Fr. Paul Doyle's help to travel to northern Wisconsin on the university plane, and then to settle in to the familiar space of the honeymoon cottage. He still tried to fish and was able to utilize a special boat on Plum Lake that Jerry Hank had used for his wheelchair-bound son. His fisherman's reflexes were such that he could still cast effectively toward the shore. He felt a particular closeness to God surrounded by the beauty and sounds of nature in this place he loved. But nothing replaced the centrality of the Mass in his spiritual life.[53] With his capacity to read so impaired, Father Ted replaced the reading of the breviary with the recitation of three rosaries a day. Whatever his progressive political and social views, his traditional devotion to the Blessed Mother never wavered, and he loved the beautiful Marian prayer that allowed him to reflect on the joyful, sorrowful, and glorious mysteries. When at Notre Dame he still loved to visit the Grotto. Whenever he was driven on campus at night he always asked the driver to stop in front of the Grotto. There, as he watched the flames of the candles flickering in the wind, he would offer his own petitionary prayers and seek Mary's intercession.

Among those Hesburgh prayed for at the Grotto was John Jenkins. After being named as Malloy's successor, Jenkins spent a full year assembling his administration and preparing himself for his new responsibilities. In December 2004, over six months before he formally took office, he acted under the prompting of his powerful trustee backers and forced the firing of Tyrone Willingham as head football coach. The move prompted an outburst by Malloy, who opined that "in my 18 years, there have been only two days that I've been embarrassed to be president of Notre Dame: Tuesday and Wednesday of last week [when Willingham was fired and the decision announced]." Malloy explained: "I thought we were going to abide by our precedent, which was a five-year window for a coach to display a capacity to be successful within our system and to fit."[54] Although he was still president of the institution he washed his hands of the decision. Father Ted told me in private conversation later that he shared some of Monk Malloy's reservations. The memory of his dismissal of Terry Brennan still resounded for him, and he took some pride in the fact that he and Ned Joyce had allowed Gerry Faust to serve out his five-year contract. But Hesburgh made no public comment. He sympathized with Jenkins and recognized both the pressures he was under and the legitimate concerns about Willingham's ability to succeed as Notre Dame's head coach. He wanted to do his part to assist Jenkins succeed as president.

Father Hesburgh participated fully in John Jenkins's inauguration as president of Notre Dame. Father Ted and Monk Malloy extended a poignant blessing to the Holy Cross priest who would be just the third president of Notre Dame in half a century. John Jenkins proved good to the word of his influential supporters, and he consulted Hesburgh regularly in his initial years in office. After just a year of the Jenkins presidency Father Ted assured me that "John has spoken with me more in the past year than Monk did in his whole time in office." Jenkins also skillfully utilized Hesburgh's support and presence. Hesburgh began to attend such events as the president's annual address to the faculty, which he had not done for Malloy. He was featured more in fund-raising and development initiatives. He flew with Jenkins to Atlanta to make the pitch to Don Keough and his family that led to the large donation that created the Keough-Hesburgh endowed professorships. Hesburgh appreciated being more directly involved in university matters and felt grateful to Jenkins for drawing him back more fully into the affairs of Notre Dame. His gratitude to Jenkins led him to be understanding when Jenkins made decisions for which he held reservations. This was the case when the new Notre Dame president retreated from assurances given prior to his formally taking office that he would cancel performances of *The Vagina Monologues*, a play that attacked Catholic sexual ethics. Hesburgh had expected Jenkins to make good on his assurances to cancel the play, but he excused Jenkins's bowing to faculty pressures and reversing his decision as a case of growing pains as Jenkins settled into his presidency. He contributed all he could to the circling of the wagons in defense of John Jenkins on this issue and others. This was especially so regarding the decision to invite President Barack Obama to give the address to the graduates at the 2009 commencement.

Hesburgh warmly welcomed the election of the first African American president. He saw Obama's comfortable victory over John McCain in 2008 as a validation of the civil rights efforts he had begun over a half century before. He also greeted favorably the decision of the University of Notre Dame to award the new president an honorary degree at its May 2009 commencement exercises, although he was well aware of Obama's fulsome proabortion record, and his undisguised determination to extend the abortion regime in the United States and outside it. Such concerns were trumped for him, as for the Jenkins administration, by the prestige involved in hosting a presidential visit. His deep regard for the presidency weighed in to his calculations.

The decision to honor Obama provoked enormous criticism of Notre Dame, including public statements from over eighty bishops. It damaged Notre Dame's reputation and standing within sizable parts of the American

Catholic community, as well as among the active members of the pro-life movement. These critics simply found fatuous the university's presentation of the graduation exercises as an opportunity for "dialogue." The critics recognized instead that Notre Dame naïvely provided an occasion and a forum for Obama to make a play for Catholic support. This off-campus opposition to the honoring of Obama was complemented by a thoughtful and prayerful challenge on campus led by students of ND Response, an umbrella group that organized prayer vigils and various protests with the support of sympathetic faculty who gravitated around the Notre Dame Center for Ethics and Culture. Father Hesburgh was somewhat taken aback by the extent and the passion of the opposition to Obama's visit, as was the Jenkins administration. But Father Ted assured John Jenkins of the soundness of his decision, and he gave him personal support in light of the heavy criticism directed at the Notre Dame president.

On commencement day, President Obama was cheered wildly inside the Joyce Athletic and Convocation Center. His speech included a number of flattering references to Father Hesburgh, and he concluded his address by recalling Father Hesburgh's bringing the Civil Rights Commission members to Land O'Lakes to settle on the recommendations for their 1960 report. He placed Father Ted at the center of the story and highlighted Hesburgh's reply to Eisenhower that he had gathered six fishermen together as an explanation for their agreement. The deft account received generous approval and laughter. The president then asked the graduates to grasp on to the example of Father Hesburgh as they left Notre Dame, and specifically to "remember that in the end, in some way, we are all fishermen."[55] Father Hesburgh saw the whole event as a wonderful success. Yet the criticism it had provoked bothered him as did the division the event triggered within the Notre Dame community. He wanted to help restore some peace and to that end he wrote a letter to the Notre Dame alumni magazine in which he congratulated the university because it "didn't duck the big issue of our times and the horrendous fact of so many millions of unborn children being coldly killed that brought this to a head." He even expressed the hope that the Notre Dame imbroglio might have an effect on the national debate so that there might be efforts "to lower the number of abortions."[56] The old priest wanted something good to come from the angst and acrimony surrounding the honoring of Obama, but his wishes were hardly fulfilled during the Obama presidency.

THE FINAL LAP AND A MOVING FAREWELL, 2010–2015

The final five years of Father Hesburgh's life were rather tranquil. He was a living legend on campus and much celebrated off it. He retained his reason and remained interested in current events. He had developed at an earlier point a tendency to repeat stories, and while aware of it, he hardly refrained from harkening back to treasured episodes from his past and sharing the details again. After 2007 he gave up alcohol on his doctor's advice but continued to enjoy puffing on large cigars. He allowed himself to smoke within the confines of his thirteenth floor office in the library when he worked there, but he was forbidden to smoke inside Holy Cross House. This was bearable during the warmer months when he could enjoy a good cigar out on the porch area, but it was a real burden during the cold winter months. To remedy that situation he obtained a benefaction from a generous donor to build a heated smoking shack at the end of the building. There he and confreres like Fr. Jim Riehle would gather to smoke and swap stories.

Fr. Bill Botzum's death in 2006 left Hesburgh as the last living member of his 1943 ordination class, and as the years progressed he became the oldest person in the entire U.S. Province of Priests and Brothers both in terms of age and in terms of years lived under religious vows. He continued to be kind and generous in his daily interactions, and maintained a quite buoyant spirit. The prospect of death seemed to cause him no special fear, although he worried about either a possible debilitating physical impairment as had beset Ned Joyce or the loss of his mind, as he now witnessed daily when he encountered Jim Burtchaell, whose dementia was such that he no longer recognized him. He prayed that he would be able to say Mass even on the day he died. Soon after Ned Joyce's death, Fr. David Tyson, who had once been his assistant but now served as the Holy Cross provincial, took him to lunch and raised the matter of his death and funeral. To Tyson's relief Hesburgh requested a "typical Holy Cross funeral" and that it should take place in the Basilica of the Sacred Heart, the very church in which he had been ordained.[57] He rested secure knowing these details were settled.

Hesburgh felt at some peace with whatever the future might hold, but he also remained very much involved in the present, and sometimes controversially so. In March 2010 at the request of House Speaker Nancy Pelosi, Father Hesburgh called Representative Joe Donnelly and encouraged him to vote for the Obama health care legislation. Donnelly, a graduate of both Notre Dame and the Notre Dame Law School, was a member of the small pro-life Democratic faction in the House of Representatives led by Representative Bart Stupak. They had withheld their support from the bill because of their objection to the legislation's inclusion of federal subsidies for abortion. The U.S. Conference of Catholic Bishops had opposed the legislation because of this provision. The National Right to Life organization had warned explicitly that "a lawmaker who votes for this bill is voting to require federal agencies to subsidize and administer health plans that will pay for elective abortion, and voting to undermine longstanding pro-life policies in other ways as well." Hesburgh's intervention at Pelosi's prompting apparently swayed Donnelly, and he succumbed to the pressure and voted in favor of what came to be called Obamacare with its provisions to mandate birth control and abortifacient coverage in health care plans. Father Hesburgh defended his position by clarifying that he told Donnelly to "vote his conscience," but the fact that the priest didn't seek to strengthen Donnelly in his pro-life convictions, or to encourage him to hold out for genuine concessions from the Obama administration, disappointed many.[58]

Most of Father Ted's other public stances caused less controversy. In March of 2010 he contributed an opinion piece, ghostwritten for him, to the *Wall Street Journal* defending the voucher system that operated in the District of Columbia, which allowed poor students to escape the failing public schools and to attend private (including Catholic) schools.[59] He could have expected that his help on the health care issue might gain some reciprocity on this issue, but Democrats led by Senator Richard Durbin of Illinois worked to defund the program. Durbin had no interest in the opinion of Ted Hesburgh on this matter. He answered to other and more powerful lobbies. In 2011 Father Ted wrote in the *Washington Post* to defend the funding of the U.S. Institute of Peace from Republican legislators who were eager to reduce government spending. He argued with still notable passion that the Institute "should have a permanent home in the nation's capital from which to teach, inspire and prepare current and future generations of peacemakers."[60] He genuinely believed in this cause.

Hesburgh's resilience and stamina were tested in May of 2011 when he underwent kidney surgery, but the ninety-three-year-old came through the operation well and returned to his varied activities. He continued to receive honors and recognition. In 2012 Enda Kenny, the Irish Taoiseach (prime minister), traveled to Notre Dame and conferred Irish citizenship on Father Ted. In 2013 Father Ted had his dream of serving as a Navy chaplain fulfilled at last. In a ceremony in the auditorium of the Hesburgh Library, Rear Admiral Mark Tidd, the chief of Navy chaplains, formally named Father Theodore M. Hesburgh an honorary U.S. Navy chaplain. The audience included all the Navy ROTC midshipmen at Notre Dame, and they were moved as the new chaplain told them, "I will cherish this and I hope I will continue to serve the Navy as well as our country in every way possible. Anchors aweigh."[61]

Then came yet another lionizing tribute to him in Washington, D.C., on May 23. House minority leader Nancy Pelosi took the lead in organizing the event and enlisted House Speaker John Boehner's endorsement to give the occasion a bipartisan gloss. She billed it as a national celebration of Hesburgh's ninety-sixth birthday, but due note was taken also of the upcoming seventieth anniversary of his ordination to the priesthood. The now disgraced and former cardinal Theodore McCarrick gave the invocation at the event held in the Rayburn Room of the Capitol. It was a smaller affair than the Congressional Gold Medal award ceremony. Nonetheless, lavish accolades were paid to Hesburgh's life and work. Before the event Father Ted had visited with President Obama in the White House for what turned out to be his final visit to the famous residence on Pennsylvania Avenue. Vice President Joe Biden made a surprise visit to the Capitol Hill gathering and spoke with typical enthusiasm and exaggeration. "You're one of the most powerful unelected officials this nation has ever seen," he assured Father Ted, presumably overlooking such towering figures as George C. Marshall, Louis Brandeis, Paul Volcker, and Henry Kissinger in the emotion of the moment. Father Hesburgh drank it all in, and, with assistance, he took the podium and dismissed "all the story-telling with an Italian saying he translated for the benefit of his all-American audience: 'By golly, it may not be true, but it sure sounds good.'"[62]

Father Ted flew straight back to Notre Dame after the Washington festivities and was on hand the next day to participate in the Jubilee Mass at Sacred Heart Basilica to celebrate the ordination anniversaries in the Congregation of Holy Cross. He vested fully, and, although seated, he was able to concelebrate at the Mass. In the company of Jim and Mary Hesburgh and other family members he then attended the combined reception for all the jubilarians, where he received the congratulations of many well-wishers on his remarkable seventy years of priesthood. The next day, May 25, he marked his ninety-sixth birthday with a further, if less public, celebration with family and friends.

During the next year, however, aging and some illness brought further slowing to his once sturdy body. In December he decided he couldn't travel to Chicago to attend a gala dinner in his honor hosted by Governor Mike Pence and the Indiana Society of Chicago. Yet with the help of Melanie Chapleau and a devoted nurse's aide from Holy Cross House, Amivi Gbologan, he tried to continue something of his old pattern. He made occasional visits to his office, taking obvious satisfaction from the surrounds of his books, photos, and memorabilia. He enjoyed a cigar and conversing with family and friends. He continued to concelebrate at daily Mass in the chapel at Holy Cross House, and to take some of his meals in the regular dining room. He was aware that Sister Death, as Saint Francis might put it, was approaching for him, but he navigated forward calmly. He was saddened to learn on January 25, 2015, of the death of his friend, Fr. Richard McBrien, who had waged a courageous battle against cancer. Dick McBrien had returned to his home in Connecticut during the final stages of his life, and his funeral was held in Hartford. It was not possible for Father Ted to attend, yet he still managed to offer Mass for his controversial friend.

Just one month later, on February 26, God granted Father Hesburgh the happy death that the priest could not have scripted better. Although quite weak, he came to the chapel that day in a wheelchair, and with a stole around him he concelebrated at Mass. He greeted a few friends and fellow religious, and then returned to his room. Family members, Holy Cross confreres, close friends, and staff members spent the ensuing hours with him as his breathing grew more labored. He died around 11:30 p.m. In the late evening Amivi Gbologan—originally from Togo and a native French speaker—had recited the Rosary with him in French. The praying of the powerful Marian devotion seemed most fitting for Father Ted, who had devoted his life to building up Our Lady's University. He had often entrusted the university to the Blessed Mother's care. Now, he assuredly trusted that she would be his gracious advocate as he passed over from this earthly life.

The news of his death prompted an outpouring of tributes. Lengthy obituaries listed his many appointments and accomplishments. On campus he was remembered with wide admiration and deep affection, bordering in some quarters on veneration. The university had prepared well for his farewell, and it proceeded with taste and precision. Over twelve thousand people paid their respects to Notre Dame's famous priest during the hours of public visitation in Sacred Heart Basilica. Monk Malloy remembered Hesburgh in a warm and humorous eulogy at the wake service on March 3. The solemn funeral Mass took place on the next afternoon. John Jenkins preached a homily that focused on Father Ted's achievements, and Jim Hesburgh offered a reflection on his brother after communion. The Mass concluded with the singing of the alma mater and then the funeral procession began the slow walk from the basilica, round past the Grotto, up the road beside the ice-covered St. Mary's Lake to the Holy Cross cemetery. On a frigid day well-dressed Notre Dame students lined the route in a moving tribute. The procession passed the site of the minor seminary where a teenager from Syracuse had arrived to begin his journey in the Congregation of Holy Cross over eighty years before. Then Theodore Martin Hesburgh was laid to rest in a grave that soon would have mounted over it a simple stone cross. After the burial service family members and friends lingered around the gravesite, but eventually they dispersed only to regather for a celebratory memorial tribute to Father Ted that evening. Over ten thousand members of the extended Notre Dame family filled the Joyce Center and heard from a range of speakers including Senator Joe Donnelly, Governor Pence, and Coach Lou Holtz. Harris Wofford, Alan Simpson, Condolezza Rice, Theodore McCarrick, and Jimmy and Rosalyn Carter all spoke with warm esteem and occasional humor of their noteworthy associations with Father Hesburgh. President Obama delivered a video tribute. The evening ended with a pre-recorded message of blessing from Father Hesburgh. His familiar voice movingly recited the familiar Irish blessing which ended with the request, "And until we meet again, may God hold you in the very palm of his hand." It was the prayer he would have wanted to pray for all present.[63]

GOD, COUNTRY, NOTRE DAME

A TTENTIVE READERS MAY REMEMBER THAT FOLLOWING HIS OR-dination in June 1943 Father Hesburgh stopped by the east door of Sacred Heart Church and read the dedication above it—"God, Country, Notre Dame." He recalled that right there he committed his life to serving that "trinity." Surely the contours of his story revealed in this book speak to the fidelity with which he kept this pledge. He poured out his energies to serve his nation and his Church, and to build up the university with which he was integrally linked for over seven decades. His remarkable life and notable contributions made him unquestionably the most significant figure in the modern history of Notre Dame. His broad vision for the university and for himself led to his endlessly looking outward to take on assignments far beyond the campus he loved so much. Hesburgh's myriad activities un-doubtedly allowed him to impress an indelible stamp on the presidency of Notre Dame.

Yet, when we more closely examine Hesburgh's portrait, the glowing picture portrayed in most general commentary about him becomes some-what more blurred and the exact nature of his accomplishments more de-batable. Although the aura that surrounds Father Hesburgh, especially at Notre Dame, makes it difficult to criticize his actions and inactions, the historian's task is not to simply burnish the image of a charismatic individ-ual, but rather to examine a mortal life in its complexity. I hope the reader has gained from this study a richer appreciation of Father Ted's character and motivations, as well as a more comprehensive and accurate under-standing of his activities and their impact on his Church, his country, and his university.

Theodore Hesburgh possessed a powerful belief that he was meant to lead Notre Dame to greatness as a Catholic university. He was blessed with rare self-assurance and a zealous energy, which he utilized effectively in performing his leadership role. He possessed some good measure of the qualities of vision, integrity, and courage that are the usual requisites for greatness, and he had that special charismatic quality that drew others to him to share his vision. His pragmatism and ability to seize opportunities equipped him well to lead his university in a time of change and expansive growth. He was a man of action willing to make decisions. Such personal attributes made it possible for him to accomplish much. He believed that he personally could make a difference wherever he applied his talents and energies. He also possessed a strong compulsion to break free of the restraints of those whom he judged might thwart his ambitions. His desire for greater independence from his religious order and from the institutional Church certainly shaped how he led the university. Ironically, however, he developed a virtual dependence on the regard and esteem of the liberal establishment in America. This partially concealed but very real craving imposed fetters of a different sort on him. He personified the push for assimilation and acceptance in America just as notably as did JFK, and his membership in the upper echelons of the American establishment came to mean a great deal to him. The desire to be part of the elite circles of power and influence colored how he led Notre Dame as well as what causes he pursued. He especially sought the regard of the higher education elite for his university and his leadership of it. But this recognition and regard came with a cost as is evident to all who have traced his story to this point. Might it be said of him that he did too much "kneeling before the world"?[1]

Hesburgh's contributions as priest, public servant, and university president overlapped and impacted one another. Yet it is still possible—at least to some extent—to separate the strands of these roles, and to evaluate the nature of his contributions. We must begin with his service as a priest in the Congregation of Holy Cross. He always held his priesthood as the very center of his life. It was "the ground of [his] being," and inseparable from his identity. He surely did throughout his life what good priests have always done over the centuries: proclaimed the Word of God and preached about it with authenticity, ministered devoutly the sacraments (especially the Eucharist), and spoke words of forgiveness, consolation, compassion, and encouragement. Literally thousands benefited from his ministry. Over the decades he assisted and inspired many members of the extended Notre

Dame family—students, faculty, alumni, friends—to live their faith more truly. He spoke with genuine care to individuals in all kinds of difficulties and proved a steadying force for many on their earthly journeys.

His understanding of the priesthood was of a profound and very traditional sort and he had no doubts about himself in the role. He was a mediator who stood between God and humanity, a veritable man in the middle who bridged the gap between the human and the Divine. He served as a priest during very turbulent times, but his sense of vocation never wavered. He was a priest forever, and one who never called for any radical changes in the priestly role. He experienced his celibacy as of "great value" because it freed him to serve others more efficaciously. He was sustained by a simple spirituality and prayer life. There was no hint of the mystical about his prayer. He was not given to powerful spiritual experiences, but relied deeply upon the Mass, the breviary, his devotion to Our Lady, and the endless recitation of his all-purpose prayer: "Come Holy Spirit." For him the Holy Spirit was a friend who would give him "the light and strength to do the right thing." Furthermore, he held that "the Holy Spirit has never failed to show me the way, and to give me the strength of purpose to struggle on in the face of all kinds of adversity," as he ranged widely in his priesthood. He took pride in the fact that he often was the only priest in gatherings in which he participated. He once explained that "my beat, apart from Notre Dame, has been on the outer fringes of Christianity. You don't find many priests in the Antarctic or in the Kremlin or in the United Nations or in the company of people like Gorbachev."[2] He saw himself as representing the Church in engaging a changing and complex world. His understanding of the call of the Second Vatican Council sustained him in his efforts to serve in the world. He was a notable part of the public face of American Catholicism for decades, and undoubtedly he presented a favorable image of priesthood to many non-Catholics, who were impressed by his public service just as he was a source of pride for fellow Catholics.

Father Ted's renown, however, owed much more to his actions in the public sphere and to his leadership of his university than to any particular contributions in the broad Church. He played no significant role in Vatican II. His relations with the popes he served aside from Paul VI were quite limited. His service for the Vatican at the International Atomic Energy Agency and his work with Paul VI in developing the ecumenical institute at Tantur were useful but modest contributions when seen in the whole context of the last half century of Church history. Ironically, his most consequential role was in helping lead the effort of American Catholic universities to distance themselves from ecclesial oversight. Through the combination of the transfer of Notre Dame's ownership from the Congregation of Holy Cross, the Land O'Lakes Statement, and his efforts with IFCU, he effectively established his independence from Church authority. This fraying in the formal relationship between Catholic universities like Notre Dame and the Church that provided their raison d'etre reflected no desire on Father Ted's part to secularize his school. Rather he wanted to make it more consonant with and acceptable to the reigning approach in American higher education. Such efforts ultimately prompted a response from the Church in the form of John Paul II's *Ex Corde Ecclesiae,* an apostolic constitution that Father Hesburgh viewed with jaundiced eyes.

By the time *Ex Corde Ecclesiae* appeared in 1990, Father Ted identified with liberal or progressive Catholicism in America. From the time of his dissent over *Humanae Vitae* he moved firmly into the camp of those who argued for greater reform in the Church. His work for nuclear disarmament and social justice led him to identify primarily with liberals within and outside the Church, and to associate himself with the notable pastoral letters issued by the U.S. bishops in the 1980s. His motives were pure as he saw them. He wanted to work to bring about the kingdom of God here on earth. But his being tethered to the liberal establishment prevented him from reading well the signs of the times. He never sufficiently grasped, as did Pope John Paul II, how the individualism, utilitarianism, and secularism of late modernity represented such a threat to his religion. Nor did he grasp how some of the very liberal elites who lionized him bore a deep-seated hostility to the faithful living out of religious principles.

Father Hesburgh's influence proved much more noteworthy in his efforts to serve his nation than his Church. No other priest served so effectively in the public sphere over such a long period spanning presidential administrations from Eisenhower's through to Clinton's. His involvements are all the more extraordinary in that he pursued them while still actively leading his university. His role was not one of spiritual guide or religious counselor to American leaders as in the manner of Billy Graham. Instead, he toiled tirelessly to aid the United States in resolving some of the major issues and challenges it confronted during this tumultuous time. He carried an optimistic temperament into his various engagements, always holding to the conviction that if good people worked together they could solve even the most difficult of problems. This was the approach he brought to the issue that had bedeviled the United States from its founding—to provide justice for African Americans. Hesburgh labored on this issue through his important service on the Civil Rights Commission from 1957 until 1972. His sustained commitment to secure civil and voting rights for African Americans who had suffered long years of shameful discrimination suffices in and of itself to win him a place of honor for his public service. He played a valuable part in aiding his country to at long last make good on the promises of its foundational charter.

Ted Hesburgh readily and rightly acknowledged that he was a true American patriot. He held strongly that the United States possessed a special and God-given destiny. He loved the country, its Constitution, governmental system, and especially the office of the presidency. He viewed the American experiment as a work in progress, and it remained for him always "the most exciting human experiment in the world." In some ways we might understand him as playing his part in upholding and defending the "American Project" of which John Courtney Murray had written in We Hold These Truths. Hesburgh's untiring civic engagement covered in this book surely testifies to his commitment to America. He never gave up on the country or its leaders, and he especially relished aiding the various occupants of the Oval Office. He contributed meritoriously through agencies such as the Civil Rights Commission, the Peace Corps, and the Presidential Clemency Board. He energetically addressed major issues like Cambodian relief, human rights, international development, and immigration. His work reveals a man giving of his best so as to make his country better.

Hesburgh's assignments to formal and consequential governmental roles largely ended with the arrival of the Reagan administration in Washington, D.C., but that did not mean he ended his efforts to influence national policies. His dogged activism to foster nuclear arms control occupied much of his energies in the 1980s, although it had virtually no impact on American policy. Hesburgh's engagement in the public sphere had from early days been pursued through non-governmental agencies and institutions as well as through formal presidential appointments. He savored the experience of working with the doyens of the establishment to discern the correct course for the country. Even after elements of the establishment, best personified by Robert McNamara, imploded over Vietnam, Father Ted sustained his involvement in hopes of addressing issues like world hunger and global development. Yet he became caught in the embrace of an increasingly secular liberal establishment especially through his membership on the board of the Rockefeller Foundation. Sadly, he influenced the establishment much less than the technocratic and utilitarian establishment swayed or manipulated him. He was the accommodating and acceptable priest. The powerful grip of the establishment upon him is evidenced in his ambivalence regarding the extensive population control efforts supported by the Rockefellers. Membership in the establishment exacted a painful price because he tempered his commitment on key moral issues that attracted establishment disapproval—most notably opposition to abortion. Father Hesburgh's refusal to put at risk the status and acceptance he had gained in elite circles must be seen as an Achilles heel of sorts. Far from shaping public attitudes in key areas where his voice might have made a difference, he increasingly either reflected the liberal political and social agenda or downplayed the areas where he dissented from it.

Father Ted pursued his public service while also serving as president of Notre Dame. This was the position that he deemed "the biggest thing that I could possibly do in my life." It was much more significant to him than serving as a bishop. Even the possibility of directing NASA could not tempt him to relinquish the reins of the school that he wanted to forge into a "great Catholic university." Hesburgh's efforts over thirty-five years in the president's chair certainly warrant Marvin O'Connell's designation of him as the "Second Founder of Notre Dame."[3] He was an extraordinary institution builder who dramatically enhanced Notre Dame's size and reputation by most secular measures such as student enrollment, faculty growth, endowment, operating budget, and physical facilities. He oversaw the major decisions to transfer ownership from the Congregation of Holy Cross to the board of fellows and to admit undergraduate women to the university. He set Notre Dame on the course to becoming a significant research university in the United States. He recognized from the outset the importance of raising money for the development of the university, and he proved a prodigious fund-raiser. He had natural strengths for leadership and enlisted the aid of dedicated benefactors to support his mission. He led Notre Dame in a modern direction more in the mode of the reigning Harvard-Berkeley paradigm for American universities.

Yet readers will appreciate that he did not succeed fully in his ambition to create a great *Catholic* university. His initial plan was clear and admirable. He did not want to be a mere follower in American higher education, but promulgated a vibrant incarnational vision of Catholic higher education. This was the time period when he tried to recruit Catholic intellectuals like Christopher Dawson to come to campus to help form an even more distinctive Catholic university, making Notre Dame a new center of Christian culture. He dreamed of sparking a Catholic intellectual revival that would redeem the time. But shaken by John Tracy Ellis's and others' harsh criticism of the mediocrity of Catholic higher education, Hesburgh lost confidence in the possibilities of the Catholic intellectual tradition. He gave up on working for a distinctive institution. He played his part in overthrowing the neoscholastic synthesis without having a distinctively Catholic approach to replace it. Instead he settled for making his university more modern and more American. Because he was influenced by his deepening associations with the important foundations and the elite of higher education, the pursuit of excellence as defined by the secular academy came to dominate his actions. Father Hesburgh continued to talk of building a great Catholic university throughout his presidency, but he failed both to fashion and to implement a viable model for it. He neither recruited effectively nor empowered academic collaborators who might have aided him to do so. His attempts to articulate a new approach such as in his emphasis on applied research to address the world's problems when he criticized Cardinal Newman in 1962 or in his explication of Notre Dame's serving as a beacon, as a bridge, and as a crossroads in 1967, were simply inadequate.

Father Hesburgh never achieved his grand goal of constructing a great Catholic university because he never developed a grand strategy that identified and developed the appropriate means to secure that good end. While he surely did his part to raise the finances and to erect the (functional) buildings to fulfill his goal, he never gave sufficient attention to the crucial matters of faculty hiring and the content of the curriculum. He failed to effectively address the crucial questions at the heart of a university—namely, who teaches and what is taught? Hesburgh's desire that Notre Dame fit comfortably into the American academic milieu and win the respect of the leading American universities won the day. This sentiment contributed to his desire to declare his independence from Church authority as revealed in the Land O'Lakes Statement. The pressures for assimilation and conformity proved too powerful in the central academic domain of the university. Yet, while Father Hesburgh never managed to successfully develop a coherent model for a modern Catholic university he did preserve some distinct elements. And he gave Notre Dame a notable Catholic gloss by maintaining the religious neighborhood on campus that so impresses most visitors—the basilica and its liturgies, dorm communities and service activities, the Lady on the Dome, the Grotto, and the many religious symbols that adorn the campus. At least outside the classroom and laboratory Notre Dame still has the atmosphere of a Catholic school.

Over the three decades since Father Hesburgh left the presidency of Notre Dame, discussions and debates have ensued about the Catholic mission and identity of the university. Those who follow Notre Dame and the broader debates about Catholic higher education know that the Hesburgh legacy is a contested one. Was the price paid for enhanced academic prestige worth it? Is Notre Dame an instantiation of the institution that gained much in the world but lost its soul? Certainly the debates at Notre Dame over its Catholicity during the Malloy and Jenkins administrations reveal that these question are live ones. How the Hesburgh legacy is viewed has clear implications for how the present and future are to be navigated. This brings to mind the much-quoted observation from William Faulkner: "The past is never dead. It's not even past." How Father Hesburgh will ultimately be regarded lies partly in the hands of those who follow him. If Notre Dame's present and future is one of continuing secularization, then elements of the course Hesburgh charted surely must be deemed as flawed, at least by those who hold that its legitimate destiny will be fulfilled only when it truly is a great Catholic university.

On the dedication page of his biography of Edward Sorin, where he deemed Hesburgh "the Second Founder of Notre Dame," Marvin O'Connell included a Latin aphorism: "*Nisi Dominus aedificaverit domum, in vanum laborant quie aedificant eam.*" He drew on the opening verse of Psalm 127: "If the Lord does not build the house, in vain do its builders labor." As O'Connell made clear, Sorin was not a great educational theorist or intellectual. Instead he was a practical institution builder and a decisive leader whose courage and iron will ensured that Notre Dame survived despite the many crises that beset it during its formative decades. From the outset Father Sorin hoped that Notre Dame would develop as a "most powerful means for good" by preparing young Catholics to go forth and serve well in the world. But he also unflinchingly held that Catholic education was not only about training minds, but also about forming character and shaping souls. He wanted to prepare good citizens for this world and, much more importantly, for the next. Father Hesburgh deeply admired his legendary predecessor and believed deeply that Sorin had not labored in vain. He described him as "my hero," and he saw himself always as fulfilling Sorin's vision for the university.[4] He further believed that he too had not labored in vain but had engaged in the Lord's work. He went to his death confident that the Lord would judge kindly his efforts. How the heavenly judgment should be rendered is not within our purview, but the details provided in this book suggest that the verdict of history should be a mixed one. Guided by his conscience Father Hesburgh sought to serve his Church, his nation, and his university according to his own lights. He contributed much in that endeavor, but there are sizable limitations in his record. Comprehending the full details of his life and work can provide valuable lessons for the present and future as to what to do and, even more importantly, what not to do. Perhaps a new generation of courageous educators in the faith might draw from the story of Theodore Martin Hesburgh an even better way to serve God, Country, and Notre Dame.

ACKNOWLEDGMENTS

I HAVE ACQUIRED DEBTS TO BOTH PEOPLE AND INSTITUTIONS IN the course of completing this study of Father Hesburgh's life and legacy. I wish to acknowledge them here, although the responsibility for the book's contents belongs solely to me. My first debt is to Father Ted Hesburgh himself for living the absorbing life about which I have written. I remain grateful to Father Ted for his support of my work, for his agreeing to sit for extensive interviews with me, and for his candor in them. May he enjoy eternal peace.

Madeline (Gillen) Bradley worked with me on this project from the time I made it my writing priority. She worked on everything from transcribing the taped interviews through to selecting photos for the book, as well as on other projects besides. During that time she became both a wife to Michael and a mother to Anastasia and Helena Rose. I am deeply grateful for all her labors and her friendship. I doubt that reading this book to her children will be of benefit in the short term, but perhaps a day will come when they might be interested in the project on which their mother served as such a sterling research assistant! Michael Skaggs took over the research assistant duties down the final stretch and gave excellent service as the book moved through the production process.

I am very grateful to those generous friends who read either all or part of the manuscript and offered helpful comments on it—David and Lou Solomon, Bill and Mary Dempsey, Bill Rooney, Stephen Koeth, C.S.C., George Weigel, and the late Don Briel. Each of them provided encouragement for me to write a book that addressed serious questions. I also am indebted to a number of scholars whose important published work influenced me in writing the book. I must mention Philip Gleason, Michael Baxter, Thomas Blantz, C.S.C., Donald Critchlow, Michael O'Brien, Thomas Schlereth, Robert Schmuhl, Fred Freddoso, and the late Dick Conklin.

Over the years a number of kind individuals either have provided me with specific research assistance or passed along archival materials and

other unpublished work relevant to this study. Let me express my grati-
tude to Steven Brady, Duane Jundt, Christopher Temple, Thomas Blantz,
C.S.C., Claire Cousino, Timothy Scully, C.S.C., Greer Hannan, Thomas
Schwartz, Kate Sullivan, Jack Pratt, Bradley Birzer, Daniel Boland, Fritz
Heinzen, and Dolores Fain.

Archivists and librarians have made my work possible, and I acknowledge my debts to the staffs of the libraries and archives listed in the bibliog-
raphy. I must recognize and thank the cooperative team at the University
of Notre Dame Archives, especially Wendy Schlereth, Kevin Cawley, Peter
Lysy, and Joseph Smith. Elizabeth Hogan and Charles Lamb gave excellent assistance in assembling the photos included in the book. Fr. Christopher Kuhn at the Holy Cross Provincial Archives gave me access to the
materials that helped me understand better the events of 1966–1967.

I was very fortunate to enlist the support of Bill Barry as my literary
agent. Bill had worked with Father Hesburgh on his memoir *God, Country,
Notre Dame,* and he understood the potential of this book from the start.
I am grateful to him for his wise counsel and encouragement. I trust our
association will extend well beyond this book.

Institutional debts that I must note are to the History Department of
the University of Notre Dame and to the International Security Studies
program at Yale University, which gave me an academic home during my
2016–2017 sabbatical. I also must thank all the fine people at Crown Image
books who contributed to the preparation and production of the book. Executive editor Gary Jansen led the team, and his editorial guidance has
made this a more accessible and agreeable book. Maggie Carr served as an
exceptionally diligent copy editor. Ashley Hong and Mark Birkey also made
important contributions.

I have benefited greatly from the support of good friends in completing
this book. Henry Smith and Sun-Joo Shin encouraged me throughout, extended wise counsel to me, and allowed me to use their New Haven home,
where I wrote most of the book. My sabbatical year at Yale was blessed by
the fraternity of John Young, C.S.C., Fr. John Brinsmade, Fr. Dan Sullivan,
and the good people of Our Lady of Mt. Carmel Parish in Hamden. I was
fortunate to enjoy the continued friendship of John Lewis Gaddis, Toni
Dorfman, Charlie Hill, and Norma Thompson. (How I miss the Sunday
evening meetings of the "conclave" at L'Orcio!) Colin and Becca Devine
lifted my spirits whenever we got together. Others whose support aided me
along the way include Bishop Robert Barron, Ed Campion, Tom Schwartz,

Peter Robinson, Gerry Bradley, Jim McAdams, Semion Lyandres, Mark Noll, Fred Freddoso, Patrick Deneen, Dan Philpott, Kate Riley, and the late Fr. Marvin O'Connell. I thank my *confreres* in the Congregation of Holy Cross, especially the men of Moreau Seminary, for their brotherhood.

Of course, I also must thank my immediate family, who have supported me over a long period on this and all else I have undertaken. My mother as well as my sister and brother, Jenny and Phillip, have maintained a special interest in this book, as each of them met Father Ted at some point. Jenny read a number of chapters in draft form, and my dear Mum read drafts of every chapter even while she recovered from a stroke. They are absolved from reading the final version.

This book is dedicated with deep gratitude to some loyal friends who have generously supported my work over the years. Dan and Mary Ann Rogers were present at my ordination and have assisted me on matters great and small throughout my priestly ministry at Notre Dame. I came to know Brian and Nancy Sullivan through their support of the seminary program of the Congregation of Holy Cross. They have proved true friends through thick and thin over the past fifteen years in my various endeavors, and they gave special assistance on this project. I connected with Terry Seidler over our shared commitment to the cause of life to which she and her wonderful family are so devoted. Terry has been a source of spiritual and practical support that aided this book in important ways, and I am deeply grateful to her.

Finally, let me thank all those who have expressed interest in this book over the years that I have worked on it, especially members of the extended Notre Dame family. I trust the book will deepen their understanding of Father Hesburgh and the university he led for so long.

Wilson D. (Bill) Miscamble, C.S.C.
Feast of the Exaltation of the Holy Cross—September 14, 2018

NOTES

PREFACE

1. Original copy in author's possession. Ultimately, I revised the title slightly as the reader would note.
2. See University of Notre Dame's Mission Statement.
3. See Theodore M. Hesburgh, ed., *The Challenge and Promise of a Catholic University* (Notre Dame, IN: University of Notre Dame Press, 1994). My essay entitled "Meeting the Challenge and Fulfilling the Promise: Mission and Method in Constructing a Great Catholic University" is found on pp. 209–23.
4. The transcripts of these extensive interviews are held in the University of Notre Dame Archives.
5. Hesburgh, interview by author, June 16, 1998.
6. Hesburgh, interview by author, June 21, 1998.
7. Hesburgh to author, June 26, 1998, in author's possession.
8. Notation from Father Hesburgh, in author's possession. Attached to it was a copy of Sister Alice Gallin's review of Michael O'Brien's biography, which appeared in the *Catholic Historical Review* 85, no. 4 (October 1999): 673–74.
9. Hesburgh to author, June 26, 1998, in author's possession.

CHAPTER 1

1. Hesburgh, interview by author, June 16, 1998.
2. Hesburgh, interview by author, June 16, 1998.
3. Michael O'Brien, *Hesburgh: A Biography* (Washington, DC: Catholic University of America Press, 1998), p. 16.
4. Hesburgh, interview by author, June 16, 1998.
5. Edward Sorin to Basil Moreau, December 5, 1842, cited in Edward L. Heston, trans., *Circular Letters of the Very Reverend Basil Anthony Mary Moreau*, 2 vols. (Notre Dame, IN: Ave Maria Press, 1943), vol. 1, pp. 58–60.
6. Hesburgh, interview by author, June 16, 1998.
7. Grantland Rice, quoted in Arthur J. Hope, *Notre Dame: One Hundred Years*, rev. ed. (Notre Dame, IN: University of Notre Dame Press, 1950), p. 387.
8. For a full account of Rockne's halftime address, see Ray Robinson, *Rockne of Notre Dame: The Making of a Football Legend* (New York: Oxford University Press, 1999), pp. 211–12.
9. On the development of the campus I rely on the wonderful study by Thomas J. Schlereth, *The University of Notre Dame: A Portrait of Its History and Campus* (Notre Dame, IN: University of Notre Dame Press, 1976).
10. Hesburgh, interview by author, June 16, 1998.
11. Father Hesburgh gave over ten pages of *God, Country, Notre Dame* to his novitiate experience. See Theodore M. Hesburgh, with Jerry Reedy, *God, Country, Notre Dame* (Notre Dame, IN: University of Notre Dame Press, 1999), pp. 14–24.
12. I have used here the variation of Ward's comments that Father Hesburgh provided in

God, Country, Notre Dame, p. 14, rather than the version that he recalled to me, which ended with Father Ward proclaiming he needed to either change his style or end up "a monumental bore."

13. Thomas Stritch, "A Short Biography of Theodore M. Hesburgh," in Charlotte A. Ames, *Theodore M. Hesburgh: A Bio-Bibliography* (New York: Greenwood Press, 1989), p. 6.

14. Hesburgh, "Election of Pius XII," *Ave Maria*, August 10, 1940, pp. 175–76.

15. Hesburgh, interview by author, June 16, 1998.

16. Ibid.

17. Hesburgh, "Reflections on Priesthood," address at the commencement exercises, Immaculate Conception Seminary, Darlington, NJ, September 11, 1983.

18. Hesburgh, *God, Country, Notre Dame*, p. 38.

19. Hesburgh, interview by author, June 16, 1998.

20. Theodore M. Hesburgh, *The Theology of Catholic Action* (Notre Dame, IN: University of Notre Dame Press, 1946), pp. 185–86.

21. Hesburgh, interview by author, June 16, 1998. Also see Hesburgh, *God, Country, Notre Dame*, pp. 42–45.

22. Hope, *Notre Dame: One Hundred Years*, pp. 476–77.

23. Hesburgh, *God, Country, Notre Dame*, p. 46.

24. Stritch, "A Short Biography of Theodore M. Hesburgh," p. 9.

25. Hesburgh, interview by author, June 17, 1998.

26. Hesburgh, *God, Country, Notre Dame*, p. 54.

27. Hesburgh, "Department of Religion: Mid-Century Report," *Notre Dame Alumnus*, September-October, 1949, p. 5.

28. Hesburgh, *God, Country, Notre Dame*, p. 53.

29. Hesburgh, interview by author, June 17, 1998.

30. Ibid.

31. Ibid.

32. On the Crowleys and the Christian Family Movement, see Jeffrey M. Burns, *Disturbing the Peace: A History of the Christian Family Movement, 1949–1974* (Notre Dame, IN: University of Notre Dame Press, 1999).

33. Hesburgh, interview by Richard Conklin, transcript, p. 265. (Father Ted sat for lengthy interviews with Dick Conklin of Notre Dame's public relations department to provide the basic material for his memoir.)

34. See for further details Doug Hennes, *That Great Heart: The Life of I. A. O'Shaughnesssy* (Edina, MN: Beaver's Pond Press, 2014), pp. 131–37.

35. Hesburgh, interview by Conklin, transcript, p. 267.

36. Schlereth, *The University of Notre Dame*, p. 177.

37. Hesburgh, interview by Conklin, transcript, p. 268.

38. Hesburgh, interview by author, June 17, 1998.

39. Hesburgh, *God, Country, Notre Dame*, p. 77.

40. Waldemar Gurian, "Football Capital or Intellectual Community?," *Commonweal* 51, no. 1 (October 14, 1949): 17–18.

41. Schlereth, *The University of Notre Dame*, p. 180.

42. On this story in detail, see Murray Sperber's *Shake Down the Thunder: The Creation of Notre Dame Football* (New York: Henry Holt, 1995).

43. Hesburgh's speech to the Annual Football Banquet, December 1951, in Robert E. Pruett, ed., *Words Have Meaning: The Selected Speeches of Father Theodore Hesburgh* (Bloomington, IN: First Books, 2002), pp. 272–73.

44. Hesburgh, *God, Country, Notre Dame*, p. 81.

CHAPTER 2

1. Philip Gleason, "A Half-Century of Change in Catholic Higher Education," *U.S. Catholic Historian* 19, no. 1 (Winter 2001): 1–4.

2. Theodore M. Hesburgh, *Patterns for Educational Growth: Six Discourses at the University of Notre Dame* (Notre Dame, IN: University of Notre Dame, 1958), p. xv.

3. Hesburgh, *God, Country, Notre Dame*, pp. 60–61.

4. Ibid., p. 61.

5. Ibid., p. 64.

6. David Gergen, *Eyewitness to Power: The Essence of Leadership, Nixon to Clinton* (New York: Simon & Schuster, 2000), p. 262.

7. Richard Conklin, "Edmund P. Joyce, CSC, 1917–2004," *Notre Dame Magazine*, Summer 2004, p 18.

8. Hesburgh, *God, Country, Notre Dame*, pp. 72–73.

9. Hesburgh described her as such in *God, Country, Notre Dame*, p. 73.

10. Hesburgh, interview by author, June 18, 1998.

11. Hesburgh, *God, Country, Notre Dame*, p. 64.

12. Hesburgh, interview by Conklin, transcript, p. 260.

13. On Catholic higher education, see Philip Gleason's *Contending with Modernity: Catholic Higher Education in the Twentieth Century* (New York: Oxford University Press, 1995).

14. Gurian, "Football Capital or Intellectual Community?," p. 17.

15. John Tracy Ellis, "American Catholics and the Intellectual Life," *Thought* 30, no. 3 (Fall 1955): 351–88.

16. Hesburgh, interview by author, June 17, 1998.

17. Hesburgh, *God, Country, Notre Dame*, p. 65

18. Ibid., p. 66. Note that Hesburgh does not mention Manion by name.

19. For the direct quotations and subsequent detail on Manion, see the fascinating essay by Kyle Burke, "Radio Free Enterprise: The *Manion Forum* and the Making of the Transnational Right in the 1960s," *Diplomatic History* 40, no. 1 (January 2016): 111–16.

20. For more detail on Keller and his critics, see the insightful chapter "Sanctifying American Capitalism," in Craig R. Prentiss, *Debating God's Economy: Social Justice in America on the Eve of Vatican II* (University Park: Pennsylvania State University Press, 2008), especially pp. 164–74.

21. Hesburgh, interview by author, June 16, 1998.

22. Philip Gleason, "A Question of Academic Freedom," *Notre Dame Magazine*, Spring 2013, p. 31.

23. Minutes for Faculty Meeting, October 28, 1952, University of Notre Dame Archives, quoted in Jack Pratt's unpublished history of the Notre Dame Law School, kindly shared with the author.

24. See the fine article by Richard Gribble, C.S.C., "Thomas T. McAvoy, C.S.C.: Historian, Archivist and Educator," *American Catholic Studies* 115, no. 1 (Spring 2004): 25–43.

25. Hesburgh, interview by author, June 21, 1998.

26. Hesburgh, *Patterns for Educational Growth*, p. ix.

27. Ibid., pp. 18–19.

28. Ibid., pp. 30–31.

29. Ibid., pp. 47, 38–44.

30. Ibid., pp. 49–54.

31. I quote directly from Michael J. Baxter, "God, Notre Dame, Country: Rethinking the Mission of Catholic Higher Education in the United States," *Nova et Vetera* 9, no. 4 (2011): 899. Michael Baxter summarizes the intellectual agenda of neoscholasticism from Gleason's *Contending with Modernity*, pp. 118–23.

32. Theodore Hesburgh, *God and the World of Man* (Notre Dame, IN: University of Notre Dame Press, 1950), pp. 1–7.

33. On the impact of this intellectual renaissance in the United States, see Arnold Sparr, *To Promote, Defend, and Redeem: The Catholic Literary Revival and the Cultural Transformation of American Catholicism, 1920–1960* (New York: Greenwood Press, 1990).

34. Christopher Dawson, "Education and Christian Culture," *Commonweal* 59 (December 4, 1953): 216–220.

35. See Hesburgh to Christopher Dawson, January 20, 1954. Bradley Birzer generously provided me with a copy of this letter. Birzer brilliantly addresses Dawson's significance in his *Sanctifying the World: The Augustinian Life and Mind of Christopher Dawson* (Front Royal, VA: Christendom Press, 2007).

36. Hesburgh, interview by author, June 18, 1998. Much of the following discussion relies on this interview.

37. Press release, January 14, 1955, University of Notre Dame Archives.

38. Hesburgh, interview by Conklin, transcript, pp. 342–43.

39. Ibid., p. 296.

40. John Courtney Murray, "On the Structure of the Church-State Problem," in *The Catholic Church in World Affairs*, ed. Waldemar Gurian and M. A. Fitzsimons (Notre Dame, IN: University of Notre Dame Press, 1954), pp. 11–32.

41. On Murray and his theological battles with opponents like Monsignor Joseph Clifford Fenton and the Redemptorist priest Francis Connell, see Barry Hudock, *Struggle, Condemnation, Vindication: John Courtney Murray's Journey Toward Vatican II* (Collegeville, MN: Liturgical Press, 2013).

42. Hesburgh, interview by author, June 17, 1998.

43. Hesburgh, *God, Country, Notre Dame*, p. 226.

44. Hesburgh, interview by Conklin, transcript, p. 312.

45. "Fr. Hesburgh Names Eleven New Advisors," *Scholastic*, October 30, 1953, p. 12; *Scholastic* articles are available through the University of Notre Dame Archives.

46. On this extraordinary woman, see Gail Porter Mandell, *Madeleva: A Biography* (Albany: State University of New York Press, 1997).

47. Ibid., p. 216.

48. Hesburgh, interview by Conklin, transcript, p. 342.

49. Hesburgh, interview by author, June 18, 1998.

50. Cavanaugh acknowledged both effusively. See Cavanaugh to Kennedy, October 27, 1949, and August 29, 1950, Box 249, Joseph P. Kennedy Papers, John F. Kennedy Library.

51. On Kennedy's honorary degree given at January commencement exercises at Notre Dame, see "January Graduates Hear Kennedy Speak," *Scholastic*, February 10, 1950, 16.

52. Hesburgh, interview by author, June 16, 1998.

53. Kennedy to Hesburgh, May 21, 1951, Box 249, Joseph Kennedy Papers, John F. Kenendy Library.

54. David Nasaw discusses the episode in *The Patriarch: The Remarkable Life and Turbulent Times of Joseph P. Kennedy* (New York: Penguin, 2012), pp. 647–51. For the accounting of tuition charged, see the memo from G. E. Harwood to Edmund P. Joyce, April 5, 1954, Box 250, Joseph Kennedy Papers, John F. Kennedy Library.

55. Hesburgh to Joseph Kennedy, July 9, 1952, Box 250, Joseph Kennedy Papers, John F. Kennedy Library.

56. Hesburgh to Joseph Kennedy, March 16, 1954, Box 250, Joseph P. Kennedy Papers, John F. Kennedy Library.

57. The account given here relies upon my notes and recollections of conversations with Father Hesburgh, June 16 and 17, 1998.

58. Hesburgh to Joseph Kennedy, August 23, 1954, Box 250, Joseph P. Kennedy Papers, John F. Kennedy Library. Also see Theodore M. Hesburgh, "The True Spirit of Notre Dame," *Sports Illustrated*, September 27, 1954, pp. 16–20, 30–32.

59. Hesburgh to Joseph Kennedy, May 18, 1955, Box 250, Joseph P. Kennedy Papers, John F. Kennedy Library.

60. Hesburgh, interview by author, June 18, 1998.

61. Edwin M. Yoder Jr., "Knowledge Industry: The Lowdown on Higher Learning in America," *Weekly Standard*, July 18, 2016, p. 38.

62. Hesburgh, *God, Country, Notre Dame*, p. 81.

63. Jim Dent, *Resurrection: The Miracle Season That Saved Notre Dame* (New York: Thomas Dunne Books, 2009), p. 8.

64. Hesburgh, *God, Country, Notre Dame*, p. 84.
65. Hesburgh, interview by author, June 20, 1998.
66. Hesburgh, "The True Spirit of Notre Dame," p. 30.
67. Stritch, "A Short Biography of Theodore M. Hesburgh," p. 15.
68. Hesburgh, "The True Spirit of Notre Dame," p. 32.
69. Hesburgh, interview by author, June 20, 1998.
70. Arthur Daley, "The Unsmiling Irishman," *New York Times*, December 31, 1958, p. 21.
71. Hesburgh, interview by author, June 17, 1998.
72. Ibid.
73. Marvin R. O'Connell, unpublished memoir, in author's possession.
74. Ralph McInerny, *I Alone Have Escaped to Tell You: My Life and Pastimes* (Notre Dame, IN: University of Notre Dame Press, 2006), pp. 32–33.
75. Hesburgh, interview by author, June 16, 1998. The material in the following paragraph is also drawn from this interview.
76. See "Education in a World of Science," in Hesburgh, *Patterns for Educational Growth*, pp. 57–71.
77. Mehling's re-appointment of Hesburgh was announced in a press release dated April 26, 1958, University of Notre Dame Archives.
78. Hesburgh, interview by author, June 17, 1998.
79. The appointment of Grimm and Soleta is noted in *Notre Dame Alumnus*, August-September 1958, p. 3.
80. James T. Burtchaell, *The Dying of the Light: The Disengagement of Colleges and Universities from Their Christian Churches* (Grand Rapids, MI: Eerdmans, 1998), p. 586.
81. For the dual editorials by Jim Steintrager and John Galvin, see *Scholastic*, May 2, 1958, p. 7.

CHAPTER 3

1. Theodore M. Hesburgh, "What Notre Dame Really Is," *Dome* (Notre Dame yearbook), Notre Dame, IN: University of Notre Dame, 1961), p. 23.
2. Jerry M. Brady, "Ted and Jerry See Africa," *Notre Dame Magazine, Rev. Theodore M. Hesburgh, C.S.C., Priest, President, Citizen of the World, 1917–2015 (Special Edition)*, April 2015, pp. 24–27; hereafter *Notre Dame Magazine*, 2015 Hesburgh Special Edition. All subsequent quotations by Brady are from this article.
3. Press release, March 2, 1958, University of Notre Dame Archives. (All quotations are from the press release.)
4. Philip S. Moore, *Academic Development, University of Notre Dame: Past, Present and Future* (Notre Dame, IN: University of Notre Dame, 1960). See his "Conclusion," pp. 163–78.
5. For McCone's speech on "The Atomic Energy Commission and the University," see Wilson D. Miscamble, ed., *Go Forth and Do Good: Memorable Notre Dame Commencement Addresses* (Notre Dame, IN: University of Notre Dame Press, 2003), pp. 144–51.
6. Press release, September 25, 1960, University of Notre Dame Archives.
7. Hesburgh, interview by Conklin, transcript, pp. 438–41.
8. On the number of donors, see press release, December 19, 1963, University of Notre Dame Archives.
9. Stritch, "A Short Biography of Theodore M. Hesburgh," p. 16.
10. Hesburgh, interview by Conklin, transcript, pp. 345–46.
11. Hesburgh, interview by author, June 18, 1998.
12. Margaret M. Grubiak, "Visualizing the Modern Catholic University: The Original Intention of 'Touchdown Jesus' at the University of Notre Dame," *Material Religion* 6, no. 3 (October 2010): pp. 346–47.
13. Press release, September 11, 1960, University of Notre Dame Archives.
14. Schlereth, *The University of Notre Dame*, p. 210.

15. On his regrets and on Sheedy's role and other matters regarding the library, I rely on Hesburgh, interview by author, June 18, 1998.

16. Bill Schmitt, *Words of Life: Celebrating Fifty Years of the Hesburgh Library's Message, Mural, and Meaning* (Notre Dame, IN: University of Notre Dame Press, 2013). I rely on this book for the account of the opening ceremonies that follows in this paragraph, including the direct quotations. See pp. 1–16 especially.

17. Hesburgh's introductory reflections and Kenneth Thompson's comment are included in the booklet published on the symposium proceedings. See *The Person in Contemporary Society: A Symposium on the Occasion of the Dedication of the Memorial Library* (Notre Dame, IN: Memorial Library, University of Notre Dame, 1964), pp. 3–10.

18. Hesburgh, interview by author, June 18, 1998.

19. Theodore M. Hesburgh, *Thoughts for Our Times* (Notre Dame, IN: Office of the President, University of Notre Dame, 1962).

20. Theodore M. Hesburgh, *More Thoughts for Our Times* (Notre Dame, IN: Office of the President, University of Notre Dame, 1964).

21. Theodore M. Hesburgh, *Still More Thoughts for Our Times* (Notre Dame, IN: Office of the President, University of Notre Dame, 1966).

22. Richard Norton Smith uses this as an epigraph in his biography *On His Own Terms: A Life of Nelson Rockefeller* (New York: Random House, 2014).

23. Kenneth L. Woodward, "Man of the Church," *Notre Dame Magazine*, 2015 Hesburgh Special Edition, pp. 62–67.

24. See Thomas E. Blantz, *George N. Shuster: On the Side of Truth* (Notre Dame, IN: University of Notre Dame Press, 1993). I draw on Blantz's study in this brief overview of Shuster.

25. Hesburgh, interview by Conklin, transcript, p. 436.

26. Theodore M. Hesburgh, foreword to *On the Side of Truth: George N. Shuster: An Evaluation with Readings*, ed. Vincent P. Lannie (Notre Dame, IN: University of Notre Dame Press, 1974), pp. ix–x.

27. Hesburgh, interview by author, June 18, 1998.

28. Blantz, *George N. Shuster*, p. 331

29. "Why Not 'Chancellor' Hesburgh?," *Scholastic*, February 22, 1963, pp. 7–8.

30. See Shuster's "Concerning the University Administration," *Scholastic*, March 1, 1963, pp. 7–8.

31. Hesburgh, interview by author, June 17, 1998.

32. For these vivid descriptions, see the lively study of student life and struggles with the administration at Notre Dame during the 1960s by Joel R. Connelly and Howard J. Dooley, *Hesburgh's Notre Dame: Triumph in Transition* (New York: Hawthorn Books, 1972), pp. 6, 26. The following paragraphs draw heavily on this book.

33. Ibid., p. 42

34. Hesburgh, *Dome* (1961), p. 19.

35. Schlereth, *The University of Notre Dame*, p. 213.

36. Substantial extracts of Hesburgh's long letter are included in Connelly and Dooley, *Hesburgh's Notre Dame*, pp. 54–58.

37. Rockefeller Brothers Fund, *The Pursuit of Excellence: Education and the Future of America* (Garden City, NY: Doubleday, 1958); Gleason, *Contending with Modernity*, p. 295.

38. Gleason, *Contending with Modernity*, p. 295.

39. Hesburgh address quoted from Connelly and Dooley, *Hesburgh's Notre Dame*, pp. 30–31.

40. "God and Man at Notre Dame," *Time*, February 9, 1962, p. 54.

41. I borrow these words from Bishop Robert Barron. See his *The Priority of Christ: Towards a Postliberal Catholicism* (Grand Rapids, MI: Brazos Press, 2007).

42. Gleason, *Contending with Modernity*, p. 296.

43. Hesburgh, "Looking Back at Newman," *America*, March 3, 1962, pp. 720–21.

44. Kenneth M. Sayre, *Adventures in Philosophy at Notre Dame* (Notre Dame, IN: University of Notre Dame Press, 2014), p. 84.

45. See McInerny, *I Alone Have Escaped to Tell You*, pp. 99–101.

46. Robert Pelton's views are captured in "Campus at a Glance," *Scholastic*, March 8, 1963, p.11; and in his article "Theological Dynamism at Notre Dame," *Notre Dame Alumnus*, April-May 1962, p. 6.

47. Hesburgh, interview by author, June 18, 1998.

48. On O'Malley, see the wonderful study by John W. Meaney, *O'Malley of Notre Dame* (Notre Dame, IN: University of Notre Dame Press, 1991), pp. 52–54.

49. Hesburgh, *God, Country, Notre Dame*, pp. 93–103.

50. Morris Pollard, quoted in Michael Garvey, "In Memoriam: Notre Dame Scientist Morris Pollard," Notre Dame press release, June 19, 2011, https://news.nd.edu/news/in-memoriam-notre-dame-scientist-morris-pollard/.

51. Hesburgh gives his account of the Shapiro case in *God, Country, Notre Dame*, pp. 101–2.

52. Paul R. Ehrlich, *The Population Bomb* (New York: Ballantine Books, 1978), p. xi.

53. Donald T. Critchlow, *Intended Consequences: Birth Control, Abortion, and the Federal Government in Modern America* (New York: Oxford University Press, 1999), p. 62. I rely on Critchlow, pp. 62–64, for my analysis here.

54. Hesburgh, interview by author, June 19, 1998.

55. For these observations on Father Kenna, see Edward A. Malloy, *Monk's Tale: The Pilgrimage Begins, 1941–1975* (Notre Dame, IN: University of Notre Dame Press, 2009), pp. 177–78.

56. Sermon delivered by Rev. Theodore M. Hesburgh at Funeral Mass for Howard Kenna, Sacred Heart Church, Notre Dame, September 17, 1973, University of Notre Dame Archives.

57. Ibid.

58. Hesburgh, interview by author, June 17, 1998.

59. On this episode, see Alice Gallin, *Negotiating Identity: Catholic Higher Education Since 1960* (Notre Dame, IN: University of Notre Dame Press, 2000), pp. 14–17.

60. Hesburgh, *God, Country, Notre Dame*, p. 171.

61. For an effort to make the alumni more aware of the role and composition of the lay advisory board, see "The Trustees: Who They Are and What They Do," *Notre Dame Magazine*, Summer 1965, pp. 6–8.

62. I rely on Hesburgh's account here. See *God, Country, Notre Dame*, pp. 172–73

63. O'Brien, *Hesburgh: A Biography*, p. 97, summarizes the Lalande position well.

64. Minutes of the meeting of the Steering Committee of the Development Committee, Board of Lay Trustees, Land O'Lakes Lodge, Land O'Lakes, Wisconsin, June 23–25, 1966, University of Notre Dame Archives.

65. See Blantz, *George N. Shuster*, pp. 333–36.

66. This relies on my own knowledge and on correspondence with Dr. Daniel Boland, in author's possession. (Boland served as a Holy Cross priest at the time.)

67. Hesburgh, interview by Conklin, transcript, p. 193.

68. Hesburgh, *God, Country, Notre Dame*, p. 186.

69. Anne O'Grady, quoted in O'Brien, *Hesburgh: A Biography*, p. 216.

70. Joyce, quoted in Dent, *Resurrection*, p. 25.

71. On Ara Parseghian's appointment, see Hesburgh, *God, Country, Notre Dame*, pp. 85–87. Father Ted repeated much the same story to me in Hesburgh, interview by author, June 20, 1998. Also see Terry Wolkerstorfer, "Parseghian: A New Ara in Notre Dame Football," *Scholastic*, January 17, 1964, pp. 27–28; and Dent, *Resurrection*, pp. 65–80.

72. Wolkerstorfer, "Parseghian: A New Ara in Notre Dame Football," p. 27.

73. Dent's *Resurrection* provides a fascinating account of this remarkable season.

74. Ara Parseghian, quoted in Wolkerstofer, "Parseghian: A New Ara in Notre Dame Football," p. 28.

75. Dent, *Resurrection*, pp. 245–46.

76. Hesburgh, "The Football Season: Fantasy and Reality," *Scholastic*, 1966 Football Review, December 9, 1966, p. 9. This article was reprinted as "College Football: The True Meaning of the Game," *Sports Illustrated*, December 12, 1966, pp. 56–57.

CHAPTER 4

1. Theodore M. Hesburgh, "The Vision of a Great Catholic University in the World of Today," included in Theodore M. Hesburgh, *Thoughts IV: Five Addresses Delivered During 1967* (Notre Dame, IN: University of Notre Dame Press, 1968), pp. 1–16.
2. Hesburgh, foreword to *Thoughts IV*, p. ii.
3. Hesburgh, "Vision of a Great Catholic University," pp. 1–2.
4. Edmund Stephan, oral history interview by Richard W. Conklin, Evanston, IL, May 2, 1983, transcript, p. 11, University of Notre Dame Archives.
5. See the press release on Hesburgh's letter, which quotes from it, January 19, 1967, University of Notre Dame Archives.
6. John L. Reedy, C.S.C., and James F. Andrews, "Control of Catholic Universities," *Ave Maria*, January 28, 1967, pp. 16–19, 30–31.
7. Minutes of Indiana Province Chapter, January 25, 1967, Box B-10, Holy Cross Archives.
8. Hesburgh, interview by author, June 18, 1998.
9. Minutes of Indiana Province Chapter, January 25, 1967, Box B-10, Holy Cross Archives.
10. Minutes of Indiana Province Chapter, January 26, 1967, Box B-10, Holy Cross Archives.
11. Press release, May 6, 1967, University of Notre Dame Archives.
12. Stephan, oral history interview, transcript, p. 11.
13. O'Brien, *Hesburgh: A Biography*, p. 98.
14. Hesburgh, *God, Country, Notre Dame*, p. 177.
15. Burtchaell, *The Dying of the Light*, p. 595.
16. Land O'Lakes statement, "The Nature of the Contemporary Catholic University," in Alice Gallin, ed., *American Catholic Higher Education: Essential Documents, 1967–1990* (Notre Dame, IN: University of Notre Dame Press, 1992), pp. 7–12.
17. For my account of the details of the lead-up to the Land O'Lakes meeting, I rely on the fine account by Neil G. McCluskey provided in the introduction to Neil G. McCluskey, S.J., *The Catholic University: A Modern Appraisal* (Notre Dame, IN: University of Notre Dame Press, 1970), pp. 1–28.
18. Grennan, quoted in Burtchaell, *Dying of the Light*, p. 593.
19. McCluskey, *The Catholic University: A Modern Appraisal*, p. 4.
20. Hesburgh, interview by author, June 18, 1998.
21. Hesburgh, preface to the Land O'Lakes Statement, in Gallin, ed., *American Catholic Higher Education*.
22. McCluskey, *The Catholic University: A Modern Appraisal*, p. 6.
23. Hesburgh, interview by author, June 18, 1998.
24. On this point see Joseph A. Komonchak, "Where Does the Church Do Her Thinking?," *Commonweal*, April 7, 2006, https://www.commonwealmagazine.org/where-does-church-do-her-thinking.
25. On this George Marsden is deeply insightful. See his *The Soul of the American University: From Protestant Establishment to Established Nonbelief* (New York: Oxford University Press, 1994).
26. Hesburgh, "The Vision of a Great Catholic University in the World of Today," pp. 15–16.
27. See Rome Statement, "The Catholic University and the Aggiornamento," in Gallin, ed., *American Catholic Higher Education*, p. 17.
28. "The Catholic University in the Modern World," in Gallin, ed., *American Catholic Higher Education*, pp. 37–57; quotation from p. 37.
29. See "A Letter from Gabriel Marie Cardinal Garrone, Prefect of the Sacred Congregation for Catholic Education," April 25, 1973, in Gallin, ed., *American Catholic Higher Education*, pp. 59–61; quotation from p. 60.
30. Father Ted gives a description of his efforts, especially with regard to academic freedom, in *God, Country, Notre Dame*, pp. 232–45.
31. Christopher Jencks and David Riesman, *The Academic Revolution* (Garden City, NY: Doubleday, 1968), p. 405.

32. Hesburgh, "The 'Events': A Retrospective View," *Daedalus: American Higher Education: Toward an Uncertain Future*, Fall 1974, pp. 67–68.
33. Hesburgh, interview by author, June 19, 1998.
34. O'Brien, *Hesburgh: A Biography*, p. 100.
35. See "Father Hesburgh On: The Dow Protest, the Kennan Article, Student Activism and ROTC," *Scholastic*, February 16, 1968, p. 20.
36. Hesburgh, "In Defense of the Younger Generation," June 6, 1968, in *Thoughts for Our Times: V*, pp. 12–19.
37. "Blacks Demonstrate at the Game," *Observer*, November 18, 1968, p. 2.
38. Hesburgh, interview by author, June 19, 1998.
39. O'Brien, *Hesburgh: A Biography*, p. 102.
40. "Hesburgh Hits CIA Lie-in," *Observer*, November 25, 1968, p. 1.
41. O'Brien, *Hesburgh: A Biography*, p. 106.
42. This all relies on Tara Hunt, "The Damnedest Experience We Ever Had: The Pornography and Censorship Conference of 1969," *Notre Dame Magazine*, Spring 2015, pp. 14–16.
43. O'Brien, *Hesburgh: A Biography*, p. 106.
44. Hesburgh, interview by Conklin, transcript, p. 628.
45. "The Hesburgh Letter on Student Unrest," February 17, 1969, University of Notre Dame Archives. Father Ted deemed the letter of such importance that he included a sizable part of it in *God, Country, Notre Dame*, pp. 113–18.
46. In his interview with Dick Conklin he explained, "I just felt we were at a point where by and large the university presidents were gutless at this point. Not gutless, it's the wrong word probably, but they were scared to death of students. Everything the students wanted they were caving in on." Hesburgh, interview by Conklin, transcript, p. 629.
47. Nixon to Hesburgh, February 22, 1969, "Nixon" folder, Hesburgh Papers, University of Notre Dame Archives; and Nan Robertson, "Nixon Letter Hails Notre Dame for Tough Stand on Disruption," *New York Times*, February 25, 1969, p. 29.
48. Hesburgh, *God, Country, Notre Dame*, pp. 113, 118.
49. Hesburgh gives details in *God, Country, Notre Dame*, pp. 123–25.
50. Hesburgh, quoted in O'Brien, *Hesburgh: A Biography*, p. 114.
51. "Fifteen Minute Rule Enacted for the First Time," *Observer*, November 19, 1969, p. 1.
52. Robert Schmuhl, *Fifty Years with Father Hesburgh: On and Off the Record* (Notre Dame, IN: University of Notre Dame Press, 2016), p. 12.
53. Hesburgh, interview by author, June 19, 1998.
54. Hesburgh, interview by Conklin, transcript, p. 664.
55. O'Brien, *Hesburgh: A Biography*, p. 121. I rely on O'Brien (pp. 117–22) and on Robert Schmuhl, *Fifty Years with Father Hesburgh*, pp. 17–23, for my overview of these events of May 1970. See also Schmuhl's "May 1970," in his *In So Many Words: Arguments and Adventures* (Notre Dame, IN: University of Notre Dame Press, 2006), pp. 167–77.
56. See the press release of November 10, 1967, on the conference The Changing Woman: The Impact of Family Planning, scheduled for November 20–22, 1967, University of Notre Dame Archives.
57. Connelly and Dooley, *Hesburgh's Notre Dame*, p. 274.
58. Hesburgh, "The 'Events': A Retrospective View," p. 70.
59. Alfred J. Freddoso, introduction to *What Happened to Notre Dame*, by Charles E. Rice (South Bend, IN: St. Augustine's Press, 2009), p. xii.
60. See Don Briel, "The University and the Church," *Logos* 18, no. 4 (Fall 2015): 29.
61. See Greer Hannan, "The Role of Philosophy and Theology in Catholic Universities" (senior thesis, University of Notre Dame, 2009).
62. Connelly and Dooley, *Hesburgh's Notre Dame*, pp. 273–74.
63. For a somewhat later defense, see James T. Burtchaell, C.S.C., "In Loco Parentis: Life With(out) Father," *Notre Dame Magazine*, August, 1972, pp. 21–23.
64. Hesburgh, interview by author, June 19, 1988.

65. On the changes, see "Notre Dame Charts New Leadership Course," *Notre Dame Alumnus*, July-August 1970, pp. 1–3. Also see "Administrative Structure Revised," *Observer*, September 4, 1970, p. 1.

66. Hesburgh, interview by author, June 19, 1998.

67. On the COUP committee and report, see Schlereth, *The University of Notre Dame*, pp. 228–29.

68. Hesburgh, interview by author, June 19, 1998.

69. Ibid.

70. Stephan, oral history interview, transcript, p. 19.

71. This all relies on Hesburgh, interview by author, June 19, 1998.

72. Stephan, oral history interview, transcript, p. 19. Stephan added, "I guess in the fifteen years that I have had my position, it's the episode that saddened me the most and that stays with me to this day."

73. Hesburgh, *God, Country, Notre Dame*, pp. 182–83.

74. See Nancy Weiss Malkiel, *"Keep the Damned Women Out": The Struggle for Coeducation* (Princeton, NJ: Princeton University Press, 2016). Brewster is quoted in Malkeil, p. 66.

75. Susan L. Poulson and Loretta P. Higgins, "Gender, Coeducation, and the Transformation of Catholic Identity in American Catholic Higher Education," *Catholic Historical Review* 89, no. 3 (July 2003): 494. (The subsequent quotation is also from p. 494.)

76. On Shuster's important role in the early stages of negotiations, see Blantz, *George N. Shuster*, pp. 336–41. (I rely heavily on Blantz's careful reconstruction of events regarding the merger for the material in this paragraph.)

77. Statement quoted in Blantz, *George N. Shuster*, p. 338.

78. Burtchaell, "A Proposal to the Trustees of the University of Notre Dame and Saint Mary's College," February 1971, quoted in Poulson and Higgins, "Gender, Coeducation, and the Transformation of Catholic Identity in American Catholic Higher Education," p. 498.

79. Hesburgh, *God, Country, Notre Dame*, p. 181.

80. Stephan, oral history interview, transcript, p. 25.

81. Hesburgh, *God, Country, Notre Dame*, p. 181.

82. Hesburgh, interview by author, June 20, 1998.

83. Ibid.

84. For this love and loyalty, see Ann Therese Darin Palmer, ed., *Thanking Father Ted: Thirty-Five Years of Notre Dame Coeducation* (Kansas City, MO: Andrews McMeel, 2013).

85. Hesburgh, interview by author, June 19, 1998.

86. Ibid.

87. See "Brandt Sent Plea by Yale Strikers," *New York Times*, June 3, 1971. Hesburgh remembered the Yale ceremony as a raucous event and told me that every single person, including Willy Brandt, got booed and hissed. He was the lone exception and he suspected that it was "because of [his work for] the Civil Rights movement." Hesburgh, interview by author, June 19, 1998.

88. Hesburgh, "A New Vision for Spaceship Earth," Harvard University commencement address, June 13, 1973, University of Notre Dame Archives.

89. Hesburgh, *The Humane Imperative: A Challenge for the Year 2000* (New Haven, CT: Yale University Press, 1974), p. 33.

90. Hesburgh, interview by author, June 21, 1998.

91. Some of the papers from these conferences are gathered in *Abortion: New Directions for Policy Studies*, ed. Edward Manier, William Liu, and David Solomon (Notre Dame, IN: University of Notre Dame Press, 1977). David Solomon, oral history interview by author, February 8, 2016.

92. Theodore M. Hesburgh and Edmund A. Stephan to Leo A. Pursley, Bishop of Fort Wayne–South Bend, October 11, 1973, quoted in the preface to *Abortion: New Directions for Policy Studies*, ed. Manier, Liu, and Solomon, p. viii.

93. Hesburgh, interview by author, June 20, 1998.

94. Ibid.
95. For Parseghian's fervent denials as to the substance of the rumors of racial tensions, see Allen Sack, *Counterfeit Amateurs: An Athlete's Journey Through the Sixties to the Age of Academic Capitalism* (University Park: Pennsylvania State University Press, 2008), p. 77. Sack quotes Parseghian telling him that the rumors were "a joke, an absolute zero."
96. Hesburgh, interview by author, June 20, 1998.
97. Hesburgh, *God, Country, Notre Dame*, p. 87.
98. Hesburgh, foreword to *Thoughts IV*, p. ii.
99. Hesburgh sermon, "Year of Faith," in *Thoughts IV*, pp. 37–39.
100. Andrew M. Greeley, *Furthermore! Memories of a Parish Priest* (New York: Forge, 1999), pp. 263–64.
101. See "Decree on the Appropriate Renewal of Religious Life (*Perfectae Caritatis*)," in Walter M. Abbott, S.J., ed., *The Documents of Vatican II* (New York: America Press, 1966), pp. 466–82.
102. Hesburgh, interview by author, June 18, 1998.
103. Minutes of Indiana Province Chapter, June 13, 1967, Box B-10, Holy Cross Archives, Notre Dame, IN.
104. Hesburgh, interview by author, June 18, 1998.
105. Hesburgh, Sermon, Funeral Mass for Howard J. Kenna, September 17, 1973, Sacred Heart Church, Notre Dame, IN, online version, University of Notre Dame Archives.
106. "Letter from Campus: Autumn Rituals," *Notre Dame Magazine*, Winter 2005–2006, pp. 2–3.
107. On Hellmuth's deep involvement with the CIA, see James T. Fisher, *Dr. America: The Lives of Thomas A. Dooley, 1927–1961* (Amherst: University of Massachusetts Press, 1997), pp. 215–19.
108. Blantz, *George N. Shuster*, p. 341.
109. Connelly and Dooley, *Hesburgh's Notre Dame*, pp. 277 and 293.
110. Kingman Brewster Jr., preface to *The Humane Imperative*, by Hesburgh, pp. ix–xi.
111. Hesburgh's address to the fifty-ninth annual meeting of the American Council on Education, October 7, 1971, Washington, DC, quoted in Connelly and Dooley, *Hesburgh's Notre Dame*, p. 278.
112. Hesburgh, *The Humane Imperative*, p. 2.
113. See Don Briel, "A Reflection on Catholic Studies," in Matthew T. Gerlach, ed., *Renewal of Catholic Higher Education: Essays on Catholic Studies in Honor of Don J. Briel* (Bismarck, ND: University of Mary Press, 2017), p. 28.
114. For a notable example, see the case of Mr. Richard Notebaert, who served as chair of the board of trustees from 2007 to 2013. See my "Mr. Notebaert, *Ex Corde Ecclesiae*, and the Future of Notre Dame," in Wilson D. Miscamble, *For Notre Dame: Battling for the Heart and Soul of a Catholic University* (South Bend, IN: St. Augustine's Press, 2013), pp. 153–58.
115. I rely for details of this incident on the excellent history paper by Stuart Mora, "Notre Dame vs. the Teamsters: A Case Study of the Decline of the American Labor Movement" (History honors thesis, Notre Dame, April 2008).
116. John Fitzgerald, quoted in *Observer*, October 14, 1977, p. 1.
117. Hesburgh, "An Open Letter to the University," published in *Observer*, October 14, 1977, p. 1.
118. Hesburgh, interview by author, June 21, 1998.

CHAPTER 5

1. "Meet the Provost," *Scholastic*, September 8, 1978, p. 7.
2. For an autobiographical portrait, see Timothy O'Meara, "The Idea of a Catholic University: A Personal Perspective," in *The Challenge and Promise of a Catholic University*, ed. Hesburgh, pp. 257–65.

3. Edward A. Malloy, C.S.C., *Monk's Tale: Way Stations on the Journey* (Notre Dame, IN: University of Notre Dame Press, 2011), pp. 261 and 269.

4. Hesburgh, interview by author, June 20, 1998.

5. Ibid.

6. Ibid.

7. Gleason, "A Half-Century of Change in Catholic Higher Education," p. 15.

8. I draw here on an essay I wrote a quarter century ago entitled "Meeting the Challenge and Fulfilling the Promise: Mission and Method in Constructing a Great Catholic University," in *The Challenge and Promise of a Catholic University*, ed. Hesburgh, pp. 209–23.

9. Briel, "A Reflection on Catholic Studies," p. 6.

10. The factual details here draw upon "1973–1976: Founding a Civil Rights Center," on the website of the Center for Civil and Human Rights, University of Notre Dame, http://humanrights.nd.edu/the-center/history/.

11. See Hesburgh, *The Humane Imperative*, p. 33.

12. Hesburgh, interview by author, June 20, 1998.

13. All the above including the quotations from Peter Walshe relies on O'Brien, *Hesburgh: A Biography*, pp. 164–67.

14. Hesburgh, interview by author, June 18, 1998

15. See "Ministers of Justice," *Notre Dame Magazine*, Summer 2016, pp. 14–15. Hesburgh loved that the center now was training human rights lawyers who would use their Notre Dame educations to fight for basic rights and freedoms in various parts of the world. With the permission of subsequent provincials he channeled most of his speaking fees and various honorariums to Bill Lewers and the center. This still left it a rather poor relative among the institutes Hesburgh supported, but his actions spoke loudly about his own personal sympathies.

16. Hesburgh, interview by author, June 20, 1998.

17. Hesburgh, quoted in Robert Schmuhl, *The University of Notre Dame: A Contemporary Portrait* (Notre Dame, IN: University of Notre Dame Press, 1986), p. 20.

18. See "Hesburgh Urges Curbing of Arms Race," *Observer*, April 16, 1985, p. 1.

19. Hesburgh, quoted in Schmuhl, *The University of Notre Dame: A Contemporary Portrait*, p. 24.

20. Hesburgh, interview by author, June 20, 1998.

21. See Hesburgh, *God, Country, Notre Dame*, pp. 307–8; and Hesburgh, interview by author, June 20, 1998.

22. See Hesburgh, *God, Country, Notre Dame*, p. 308; and Hesburgh, interview by author, June 20, 1998.

23. This was but one of a number of major bequests made by Joan Kroc. For details on her life and remarkable generosity, see Lisa Napoli, *Ray and Joan: The Man Who Made the McDonald's Fortune and the Woman Who Gave It All Away* (New York: Dutton, 2016). For Napoli's discussion of Joan Kroc and Father Hesburgh, see pp. 211–14.

24. Hesburgh, foreword to *Abortion Parley: Papers Delivered at the National Conference on Abortion*, by James Tunstead Burtchaell, C.S.C. (Kansas City: Andrews and McMeel, 1980), p. vii.

25. Hesburgh, sermon, Respect Life Mass, Sacred Heart Church, Notre Dame, January 22, 1975, quoted in the preface to *Abortion: New Directions for Policy Studies*, ed. Mannier, Liu, and Solomon, p. viii.

26. For an example of Hesburgh's modest support, see Janet E. Smith's letter, "Care Center Owes Much to Campus Community," *Observer*, April 16, 1985, p. 5.

27. "Hesburgh Sought Ratzinger for Spot on ND Faculty," *South Bend Tribune*, April 20, 2005, p. A4.

28. See R. R. Reno, "The Public Square: Rahner's New Church," *First Things*, March 2017, p. 7.

29. See Karl Rahner, S.J., *The Shape of the Church to Come*, trans. Edward Quinn (New York: Seabury Press, 1974).

30. Stanley Hauerwas, *Hannah's Child: A Theologian's Memoir* (Grand Rapids, MI: Eerdmans, 2012), p. 107.

31. See Stanley Hauerwas, "Pilgrim in the Promised Land," *Notre Dame Magazine*, Winter 1994–1995, p. 19.

32. Hesburgh, interview by author, June 19, 1998.

33. Ibid.

34. See "Rev. Richard McBrien Assumes Newly Established Theology Chair," *Observer*, April 11, 1980, p. 16.

35. Hesburgh, interview by author, June 20, 1998.

36. See the dedication in Richard P. McBrien, *Lives of the Popes: The Pontiffs from St. Peter to John Paul II* (New York: HarperCollins, 1997).

37. I borrow the white hats/black hats distinction from Michael Novak's review of McBrien's *Lives of the Popes*, "The Keys to the Papacy," *Weekly Standard*, January 19, 1998, p. 35.

38. For a good summary of McBrien's positions, see his "The Hard-Line Pontiff," *Notre Dame Magazine*, Spring 1987, pp. 27–29.

39. Cuomo, quoted in Wilson D. Miscamble, "The Tragedy of Mario Cuomo," *Notre Dame Magazine*, Autumn 1993, pp.41–43.

40. John Paul II's address to the presidents of Catholic colleges and universities, Catholic University of America, Washington, DC, October 7, 1979, quoted in Alice Gallin, *Negotiating Identity*, p. 147.

41. Gallin, *Negotiating Identity*, p. 148.

42. Ibid., p. 149.

43. Ibid., p. 152.

44. See Malloy's discussion in *Monk's Tale: The Presidential Years, 1987–2005* (Notre Dame, IN: University of Notre Dame Press, 2016), pp. 291–95.

45. The listings in Ames, ed., *Theodore M. Hesburgh: A Bio-Bibliography*, provide a guide to some of his many lectures, publications, and interviews.

46. Elie Wiesel, *Four Hasidic Masters and Their Struggle Against Melancholy*, with a foreword by Theodore M. Hesburgh (Notre Dame, IN: University of Notre Dame Press, 1978).

47. See Marit Hogan, "University Announces Campaign," *Observer*, April 15, 1977, p. 1.

48. Hesburgh, interview by author, June 18, 1998.

49. Ibid.

50. Ibid.

51. I borrow here from Carlos Lozada, review of *Billion-Dollar Ball: A Journey Through the Big-Money Culture of College Football*, by Gilbert M. Gaul, *Washington Post*, August 21, 2015, https://www.washingtonpost.com/news/book-party/wp/2015/08/21/college-football-isnt-about-college-and-its-barely-about-football-its-about-money/?noredirect=on&utm_term=.99d65fa0e5ba.

52. Theodore M. Hesburgh, speech at the Annual Football Banquet, Notre Dame, IN, 1981, in *Words Have Meaning: The Selected Speeches of Father Theodore Hesburgh*, ed. Pruett, pp. 286–90.

53. Hesburgh, interview by author, June 18, 1998.

54. Fr. James Riehle, oral history interview by author, Notre Dame, IN, December 11, 1997.

55. Hesburgh, *God, Country, Notre Dame*, p. 87.

56. For Faust's story, see Gerry Faust and Steve Love, *The Golden Dream* (Champaign, IL: Sagamore Publishing, 1997).

57. For Lou Holtz's account of his own career, see Lou Holtz, *Wins, Losses, and Lessons: An Autobiography* (New York: William Morrow, 2006).

58. Letter quoted in Lou Holtz, with John Heisler, *The Fighting Spirit: A Championship Season at Notre Dame* (New York: Pocket Books, 1989), pp. 7–8.

59. Hesburgh, interview by author, June 20, 1998.

60. "Hesburgh Interview: 'The Fact Is, I'm Not Eternal by Any Means,'" *Observer*, February 15, 1979, p. 6.

61. Hesburgh, interview by author, June 19, 1998. (I must note that my friend Fr. Thomas Blantz has no recollection of this conversation with Father Hesburgh, but Hesburgh's memory on this episode was very clear.)

62. "Hesburgh Remains at Helm," *Observer*, October 27, 1981, p. 1.

63. For his series of cartoons on the subject, see *Observer*, October 27–30, 1981.

64. See "Hesburgh Announces Administrative Posts," *Observer*, October 28, 1981, p. 1.

65. Hesburgh, interview by author, June 20, 1998.

66. "Monk Chosen," *Observer*, November 15, 1986.

67. Hesburgh, interview by author, June 17, 1998.

68. See especially the special issue of *Observer* dedicated to "The Hesburgh Years," Spring 1987.

69. Kelly had been raising concerns about Notre Dame since the publication of his *The Battle for the American Church* in 1979. See especially George A. Kelly, *The Battle for the American Church* (Garden City, NY: Doubleday, 1979), pp. 82–88.

70. Theodore Hesburgh, "Charge to the Graduating Class of 1987," in Miscamble, ed., *Go Forth and Do Good*, pp. 282–83.

CHAPTER 6

1. Patrick Carey, *The Roman Catholics* (Westport, CT: Greenwood Press, 1993), p. 103.

2. George R. Marsden, *The Twilight of the American Enlightenment: The 1950s and the Crisis of Liberal Belief* (New York: Basic Books, 2014), pp. 25–32.

3. Paul Blanshard, *American Freedom and Catholic Power* (Boston: Beacon Press 1949). See John McGreevy, *Catholicism and American Freedom: A History* (New York: W. W. Norton, 2003), pp. 166–69.

4. Christopher Temple, "Father Hesburgh and Science: Transforming the University of Notre Dame into a Preeminent American Catholic Research University, 1952–1967," paper delivered at Saint Louis University, St. Louis, MO, September 21, 2017.

5. Hesburgh revealed his presidential votes in Hesburgh, interview by author, June 17, 1998.

6. O'Brien, *Hesburgh: A Biography*, p. 65.

7. See, of course, David Halberstam's classic study *The Best and the Brightest* (New York: Random House, 1972).

8. Richard Norton Smith, *On His Own Terms: A Life of Nelson Rockefeller* (New York: Random House, 2014), p. 197.

9. Niall Ferguson, *Kissinger*, vol. 1, *1923–1968: The Idealist* (New York: Penguin Press, 2015), p. 395.

10. Hesburgh, interview by Conklin, transcript, p. 867.

11. Hesburgh to Nelson Rockefeller, March 20, 1957, RG V4C, Box 20, Folder 218, Special Studies Project papers, Rockefeller Archives Center.

12. Ferguson, *Kissinger*, vol. 1, p. 398.

13. Hesburgh to Nelson Rockefeller, April 21, 1958, RG V4C, Box 24, Folder 262, Special Studies Project papers, Rockefeller Archives Center.

14. For this section of Report III, "Foreign Economic Policy for the Twentieth Century," initially issued on June 16, 1958, see Rockefeller Brothers Fund, *Prospect for America: The Rockefeller Panel Reports* (Garden City, NY: Doubleday, 1961), pp. 167–71.

15. For Hesburgh's brief comments on his relationship with each of the Rockefeller brothers, see Hesburgh, interview by Conklin, transcript, p. 868.

16. See Critchlow, *Intended Consequences*, especially pp. 25–33; and Matthew Connelly, *Fatal Misconception: The Struggle to Control World Population* (Cambridge, MA: Belknap Press of Harvard University Press, 2008). Connelly is terrific on the overseas population control measures undertaken by the Rockefeller Foundation.

17. Hesburgh's name does not appear in the edited papers of Martin Luther King Jr. until 1961, and then only as the commissioner who employed a young lawyer named Harris Wofford. See Clayborne Carson and Tenisha Armstrong, eds., *The Papers of Martin*

Luther King, Jr., vol. 7, *To Save the Soul of America, January 1961–August 1962* (Oakland: University of California Press, 2014), p. 170.

18. Robert Fredrick Burk, *The Eisenhower Administration and Black Civil Rights* (Knoxville: University of Tennessee Press, 1984), pp. 229–30.

19. Harris Wofford, *Of Kennedys and Kings: Making Sense of the Sixties* (Pittsburgh: University of Pittsburgh Press, 1992), p. 462.

20. Ibid., pp. 463–64.

21. For the Hesburgh account, see *God, Country, Notre Dame*, pp. 199–201.

22. Foster Rhea Dulles, *The Civil Rights Commission: 1957–1965* (East Lansing: Michigan State University Press, 1968), p. 63. What follows relies on Dulles's chapter "The First Report—1959," pp. 64–80.

23. Dulles, *The Civil Rights Commission*, p. 80.

24. Robert B. McKay, "Review of *Report of the United States Commission on Civil Rights*," *Columbia Law Review* 60, no. 5 (May 1960): 759.

25. Burk in *The Eisenhower Administration and Black Civil Rights* mentions Hesburgh only as a member of the Civil Rights Commission, p. 230. Branch mentions Hesburgh twice in his one-thousand-page book, and both references concern the Kennedy administration. See Taylor Branch, *Parting the Waters: America in the King Years, 1954–63* (New York: Simon & Schuster, 1988), pp. 398 and 721.

26. Hesburgh, *God, Country, Notre Dame*, p. 251.

27. Ibid., p. 247; Hesburgh, interview by author, June 17, 1998.

28. John Cornwell, *Hitler's Pope: The Secret History of Pius XII* (New York: Viking Penguin, 1999).

29. Photo of Father Hesburgh and Pope Pius XII, Holy Cross General Chapter, July 19, 1956, GCSC 2/38, University of Notre Dame Archives (GCSC, 2/38).

30. Hesburgh, *God, Country, Notre Dame*, p. 282.

31. On "The Conference on the Statute," see David Fischer, *History of the International Atomic Energy Agency: The First Forty Years* (Vienna: International Atomic Energy Agency, 1997), pp. 46–49.

32. Hesburgh, interview by Conklin, transcript, p. 388.

33. This relies on Fischer, *History of the International Atomic Energy Agency: The First Forty Years*.

34. Hesburgh, *God, Country, Notre Dame*, pp. 290–95.

35. In a conversation in February 1960, McCone encouraged President Eisenhower to accept Hesburgh's invitation to speak at Notre Dame's commencement and recalled that Hesburgh "had been instrumental in composing the differences between McCone and Emelyanov two years ago when they had a violent argument over charges made by Emelyanov in an open meeting." Memorandum of conversation, February 3, 1960, White House Records, Dwight D. Eisenhower Presidential Library. (I am grateful to Duane Jundt for sharing this document with me.)

36. Eamon Duffy, *Saints and Sinners: A History of the Popes* (New Haven, CT: Yale University Press, 2002), p. 268

37. "Commentary," *Scholastic*, October 31, 1958, p. 5.

38. Hesburgh, *God, Country, Notre Dame*, p. 249

39. John XXII, *Gaudet Mater Ecclesia* (Mother Church Rejoices), speech at the inauguration of the Second Vatican Council, October 11, 1962. For the official Latin text see, http://w2.vatican.va/content/john-xxiii/la/speeches/1962/documents/hf_jxxiii_spe_19621011_opening-council.html.

40. Hesburgh, interview by author, June 17, 1998.

41. Hesburgh, *God, Country, Notre Dame*, pp. 103–4.

42. Kenneth L. Woodward, "Man of the Church," *Notre Dame Magazine*, 2015 Hesburgh Special Edition, p. 63.

43. Wofford, *Of Kennedys and Kings*, p. 44.

44. Hesburgh, interview by author, June 17, 1998.

45. Photo, GPHR 45/1960, University of Notre Dame Archives.

46. This relies on Wofford, *Of Kennedys and Kings*, pp. 37–38.

47. Nasaw, *The Patriarch*, p. 715.

48. Joseph Kennedy to O'Toole, November 11, 1959, Box 250, Joseph P. Kennedy Papers, JFK Library.

49. On this see John Cavanaugh to Joseph Kennedy, January 27, 1960, Box 250, Joseph P. Kennedy Papers, JFK Library.

50. Fletcher Knebel, "The Democratic Forecast: A Catholic in 1960," *Look* (magazine), March 3, 1959, p. 17.

51. Nasaw discusses the matter in *The Patriarch*, pp. 721–23.

52. "Editorial: Catholics and the Presidency," *Ave Maria*, March 7, 1959, p. 18.

53. Various press clippings on the Kennedy visit, University of Notre Dame Archives.

54. Hesburgh, interview by author, June 17, 1998.

55. Wofford, *Of Kennedys and Kings*, p. 43.

56. James E. Murphy to Theodore Hesburgh, November 11, 1960, Hesburgh Papers, University of Notre Dame Archives.

57. Branch, *Parting the Waters*, p. 398.

58. The above paragraph and direct quotations rely on Wofford, *Of Kennedys and Kings*, pp. 129–33. Also see Branch, *Parting the Waters*, pp. 397–99.

59. See Robert G. Carey, *The Peace Corps* (New York: Praeger Publishers, 1970), p. 3.

60. Wofford, *Of Kennedys and Kings*, pp. 259–60.

61. Hesburgh, *God, Country, Notre Dame*, pp. 92–93.

62. For details see Carey, *The Peace Corps*, pp. 13–15; and Gerard T. Rice, *The Bold Experiment: JFK's Peace Corps* (Notre Dame, IN: University of Notre Dame Press, 1985), pp. 35–39.

63. Hesburgh, quoted in Scott Stossel, *Sarge: The Life and Times of Sargent Shriver* (Washington, DC: Smithsonian Books, 2004), p. 114. (Stossel interviewed Father Hesburgh in 2002.)

64. Hesburgh provides details in *God, Country, Notre Dame*, pp. 94–95.

65. Hesburgh to John F. Kennedy, February 14, 1961, "Theodore Hesburgh" folder, John F. Kennedy Papers, President's Office File, Special Correspondence Series, JFK Library.

66. Ibid.

67. Hesburgh, interview by author, June 17, 1998.

68. Hesburgh to John F. Kennedy, March 3, 1961, "Theodore Hesburgh" folder, John F. Kennedy Papers, President's Office File, Special Correspondence Series, JFK Library.

69. See the citation accompanying the Laetare Medal presented to President John F. Kennedy, November 22, 1961, University of Notre Dame Archives.

70. The details of the Laetare presentation rely on Jim Murphy's interesting account prepared for his family, November 22, 1961, University of Notre Dame Archives.

71. All this relies on Hesburgh, *God, Country, Notre Dame*, pp. 95–97.

72. Hesburgh, *God, Country, Notre Dame*, pp. 97–99.

73. See the touching recollection by one of the first group of Peace Corps volunteers trained at Notre Dame, Evadna Smith Bartlett, "Volunteering for Justice and Peace," *Notre Dame Magazine*, 2015 Hesburgh Special Edition, p. 54.

74. Hesburgh, oral history interview by Joseph E. O'Connor, March 27, 1966, transcript, pp. 7 and 9, JFK Library.

75. Theodore M. Hesburgh, "The Presidency of Notre Dame During the Vietnam Era," November 3, 1997, transcript in author's possession.

76. Hesburgh, quoted in Lawrence J. McAndrews, *What They Wished For: American Catholics and American Presidents, 1960–2004* (Athens: University of Georgia Press, 2014), p. 28.

77. Hesburgh, interview by Conklin, transcript, p. 718.

78. Hesburgh, *God, Country, Notre Dame*, p. 104.

79. For a good overview, see Dulles's "The Second Report—1961," in *The Civil Rights Commission, 1957–1965*, pp. 132–51.

80. See Hesburgh's use of "national conscience" in his personal statement appended to the Civil Rights Commission report. The *Scholastic* proudly published the statement in full. See *Scholastic*, December 15, 1961, pp. 24–26.

81. Hesburgh, oral history interview, transcript, p. 20, JFK Library.

82. Hesburgh, personal statement for the Civil Rights Commission report, in *Scholastic*, December 15, 1961, pp. 24–26. The *New York Times* included excerpts of both the commission's report and Father Hesburgh's statement. See "Excerpts from Civil Rights Unit's Report and Statement by Hesburgh," *New York Times*, November 17, 1961, p. 22. Also see "Civil Rights: Dawdling on the Corner," *Time*, November 24, 1961, pp. 15–16.

83. Wofford, *Of Kennedys and Kings*, p. 161.

84. Robert F. Kennedy, interview, quoted in Arthur M. Schlesinger Jr., *Robert Kennedy and His Times* (Boston: Houghton Mifflin, 1978), p. 314.

85. Wofford, *Of Kennedys and Kings*, p. 420.

86. For an example of these tactics in Greenwood, Mississippi, see Branch, *Parting the Waters*, pp. 711–25.

87. See Dulles, *The Civil Rights Commission, 1957–1965*, pp. 179–82.

88. Branch, *Parting the Waters*, p. 721.

89. Marshall, quoted in Branch, *Parting the Waters*, p. 721.

90. Branch, *Parting the Waters*, p. 746.

91. I rely for all this on Dulles, *The Civil Rights Commission, 1957–1965*, pp. 182–83.

92. For an explanation of why Hesburgh and Joyce did not attend King's speech, see the letter to the editor from Thomas F. Broden in *Voice*, November 6, 1963, p. 2.

93. See the letter to the editor of Thomas Vitullo in *Voice*, October 23, 1963, p. 2. Vitullo noted that "hundreds of students were shamed and angered Friday night by the very conspicuous absence of the official representative of the University at the Martin Luther King lecture."

94. Hesburgh, oral history interview, transcript, p. 11, JFK Library.

95. David L. Holmes, *The Faiths of the Postwar Presidents: From Truman to Obama* (Athens: University of Georgia Press, 2012), p. 66.

96. James Wolfe, "Exclusion, Fusion, or Dialogue: How Should Religion and Politics Relate?," *Journal of Church and State* 22 (Winter 1980): 93–94.

97. Statement by Rev. Theodore M. Hesburgh on the occasion of the assassination of John F. Kennedy, November 22, 1963, University of Notre Dame Archives.

98. This passage relies on Hesburgh, interview by author, June 17, 1998.

99. See John Cavanaugh, oral history interview by Joseph E. O'Connor, March 27, 1966, transcript, pp. 17–20, JFK Library.

100. Hesburgh, interview by author, June 17, 1998.

101. Ibid.

102. For extensive details of the funeral, see the classic account by William Manchester, *The Death of a President: November 20–November 25, 1963* (New York: Harper & Row, 1967), pp. 581–93. (Manchester does not mention Father Hesburgh's presence at the funeral.)

103. Theodore M. Hesburgh, "The Road," *Scholastic*, extra edition, November 26, 1963, p. 3.

104. See Johnson's quotation in Doris Kearns Goodwin, *Lyndon Johnson and the American Dream* (New York: Harper & Row, 1976), p. 178.

CHAPTER 7

1. Duffy, *Saints and Sinners*, p. 276.

2. Robert Dallek, *Flawed Giant: Lyndon Johnson and His Times, 1961–1973* (New York: Oxford University Press, 1998).

3. Hesburgh, *God, Country, Notre Dame*, p. 252.

4. On this point see George Weigel, *The End and the Beginning: Pope John Paul II—The Victory of Freedom, the Last Years, the Legacy* (New York: Doubleday, 2010), pp. 61–65, and 168–69.

5. Hesburgh, interview by author, June 17, 1998.

6. Hesburgh, *God, Country, Notre Dame*, p. 257.

7. All this relies on Hesburgh, *God, Country, Notre Dame*, pp. 257–58.

8. Hesburgh, interview by author, June 21, 1998.

9. Ibid.

10. See "Decree on Ecumenism (*Unitatis Redintegratio*)," in Abbott, ed., *The Documents of Vatican II*, pp. 341–70.

11. Hesburgh, *The Humane Imperative*, p. 15.

12. Hesburgh to I. A. O'Shaughnessy, August 4, 1964, quoted in Hennes, *That Great Heart*, p. 203.

13. Hesburgh Memorandum on meeting with Pope Paul VI at Castel Galdolfo on August 29, 1964, memo dated September 1964, quoted in Hennes, *The Great Heart*, pp. 203–4.

14. Robert McClory, *Turning Point: The Inside Story of the Papal Birth Control Commission, and How* Humanae Vitae *Changed the Life of Patty Crowley and the Future of the Church* (New York: Crossroad, 1995), p. 2.

15. The Crowleys "were convinced change was coming," as "all signs pointed that way." Ibid., p. 75.

16. This majority report of the Birth Control Commission, entitled "Responsible Parenthood," is included as an appendix in McClory, *Turning Point*, pp. 171–87.

17. This relies on Critchlow, *Intended Consequences*, pp. 62–64.

18. William V. D'Antonio, "Fr. Ted Hesburgh: A Reflection on His Impact," March 13, 2015, http://www.catholicsinalliance.org/fr_hesburgh.

19. Critchlow, *Intended Consequences*, p. 123.

20. D'Antonio, "Fr. Ted Hesburgh: A Reflection on His Impact."

21. See stories from *South Bend Tribune*, October 9, 1967, and January 28, 1969, in the "Planned Parenthood of Northern Indiana" press clippings folder, South Bend Public Library, South Bend, IN.

22. On Rockefeller's meeting with Paul VI and McGeorge Bundy, see Critchlow, *Intended Consequences*, pp. 64–65.

23. For Bundy's address entitled "American Power and Responsibility," see Miscamble, ed., *Go Forth and Do Good*, pp. 172–75.

24. See McGreevy, *Catholicism and American Freedom*, pp. 243–45.

25. Paul VI, encyclical, *Humane Vitae* (Of Human Life), July 25, 1968.

26. Critchlow, *Intended Consequences*, p. 131.

27. Hesburgh, interview by author, June 18, 1998.

28. Ibid.

29. The details rely on Hesburgh, *God, Country, Notre Dame*, pp. 260–61.

30. Hesburgh, *God, Country, Notre Dame*, p. 262.

31. Ibid., pp. 262–63.

32. Robert Dallek, *Lone Star Rising: Lyndon Johnson and His Times, 1908–1960* (New York: Oxford University Press, 1991), p. 589.

33. Robert Schmuhl quotes Father Hesburgh as saying of the 1964 Civil Rights Act: "Johnson was absolutely ruthless in this pursuit. I have to applaud his ruthlessness because it was in a cause where nobody else could have gotten that law through." Robert Schmuhl, "Extreme Measures," *Notre Dame Magazine*, Autumn 2016, p. 28.

34. See Dulles, *The Civil Rights Commission, 1957–1965*, pp. 214–16.

35. See Erwin Griswold to Hesburgh, September 4, 1973, included as a prefatory note to Hesburgh, oral history interview by Paige E. Mulholland, February 1, 1971, Lyndon Johnson Oral History Collection, Lyndon B. Johnson Library, Austin, Texas; hereafter LBJ Library.

36. See Lyndon B. Johnson's Daily Diary, February 12, 1964, LBJ Library.

37. The full list is included in Johnson's Daily Diary, July 4, 1964, LBJ Library.

38. D'Antonio, "Fr. Ted Hesburgh: A Reflection on His Impact."

39. On the student criticism, see the letter entitled "Disgusting Disguise," by Philip F. O'Mara and Ralph Martin, *Scholastic*, May 15, 1964, p. 9.

40. "Memorial March," *Scholastic*, May 22, 1964, p. 14.
41. Taylor Branch, *Pillar of Fire: America in the King Years, 1963–65* (New York: Simon & Schuster, 1998), pp. 359–60.
42. On Dr. King's 1966 campaign, see "Chicago, July–August, 1966," in Taylor Branch, *At Canaan's Edge: America in the King Years, 1965–68* (New York: Simon & Schuster, 2006), pp. 501–22.
43. On the 1964 rally, see the online entry "Illinois Rally for Civil Rights, 1964, University of Notre Dame Archives.
44. Lyndon B. Johnson, Remarks at the Presentation of the 1964 Presidential Medal of Freedom Awards, September 14, 1964, LBJ Library.
45. Hesburgh, oral history interview, transcript, p. 14, LBJ Library.
46. See Robert Mann, *The Walls of Jericho: Lyndon Johnson, Hubert Humphrey, Richard Russell, and the Struggle for Civil Rights* (New York: Harcourt Brace, 1996).
47. This relies on Schmuhl, *Fifty Years with Father Hesburgh*, pp. 7–8.
48. The Selma campaign can be tracked in detail in Branch's *At Canaan's Edge*, pp. 5–115.
49. Dulles, *The Civil Rights Commission: 1957–1965*, p. 245.
50. Hesburgh, "The Moral Dimensions of the Civil Rights Movement," speech given at the American Academy of Arts and Sciences, Boston, MA, November 1964, in Hesburgh, *More Thoughts for Our Times*, pp. 1–24.
51. Daniel P. Moynihan, *The Negro Family: The Case for National Action* (Washington, DC: Office of Policy Planning and Research, U.S. Department of Labor, 1965).
52. Hesburgh to Patrick Moynihan, February 3, 1966, "Moynihan" folder, Hesburgh Papers, University of Notre Dame Archives.
53. On the conference and its outcome, see Kevin L. Yuill, "The 1966 White House Conference on Civil Rights," *Historical Journal* 41, no. 1 (March 1998): 259–82.
54. Johnson's Daily Diary, January 20, 1967, LBJ Library.
55. Johnson's Daily Diary, February 13, 1967, LBJ Library.
56. Lyndon B. Johnson, Statement by the president on the "Message on Equal Justice," February 15, 1967, LBJ Library.
57. Johnson's Daily Diary, August 17, 1967, LBJ Library.
58. Hesburgh, oral history interview, transcript, p. 19, LBJ Library.
59. Ibid., pp. 21–24.
60. Hesburgh, interview by author, June 21, 1998.
61. See William Westmoreland to Hesburgh, December 24, 1966, reproduced in *Scholastic*, February 17, 1967, p. 31. (This references Hesburgh's letter.)
62. Hesburgh, oral history interview, transcript, p. 27, LBJ Library.
63. See Wilson D. Miscamble, "Francis Cardinal Spellman and 'Spellman's War,'" in David L. Anderson, *The Human Tradition in the Vietnam Era* (Wilmington, DE: Scholarly Resources Books, 2000), pp. 3–22.
64. On Shannon's reasoning and for details of the letter, see James Patrick Shannon, *Reluctant Dissenter: A Catholic Bishop's Journey of Faith* (New York: Crossroad, 1998), pp. 114–16.
65. See "Father Hesburgh On: The Dow Protest, the Kennan Article, Student Activism and ROTC," pp. 20–21.
66. Clark Kerr, *The Gold and the Blue: A Personal Memoir of the University of California, 1949–1967*, vol. 2, *Political Turmoil* (Berkeley: University of California Press, 2003), pp. 289–90.
67. See Schlesinger, *Robert Kennedy and His Times*, pp. 778–800.
68. For the visit of RFK, see "Kennedy Kicks Off Indiana Campaign with Stepan Center Speech," *Observer*, April 5, 1968, p. 1; and for McCarthy, see "McCarthy Campaigns on Campus, Draws Small Crowd to Conference," *Observer*, April 29, 1968, p. 1.
69. Kenneth Woodward, "Man of the Church," *Notre Dame Magazine*, 2015 Hesburgh Special Edition, p. 56.
70. See *Observer*, January 24, 1973, p. 1.

71. "LBJ Eulogized by Hesburgh," *Observer,* January 25, 1973, p. 1.
72. Tom Wicker, "Richard M. Nixon," in James M. McPherson, ed., *"To the Best of My Ability": The American Presidents* (New York: Dorling Kindersley, 2000), p. 266.
73. Hesburgh, interview by author, June 17, 1998.
74. See Stephen M. Koeth, "The Strengths and Limits of American Catholic Confidence: Reverend John F. Cronin, S.S., and His Political Friendship with Richard M. Nixon, 1947–1960," *Journal of Church and State* 56, no. 4 (Autumn 2013): 711–31.
75. Nixon to Hesburgh, January 27, 1969, "Nixon" folder, Hesburgh Papers, University of Notre Dame Archives.
76. Nixon to Hesburgh, February 4, 1969, "Nixon" folder, Hesburgh Papers, University of Notre Dame Archives.
77. Hesburgh, *God, Country, Notre Dame,* pp. 206–07.
78. Ibid., p. 207.
79. Hesburgh to Nixon, February 17, 1969, "Nixon" folder, Hesburgh Papers, University of Notre Dame Archives.
80. Nixon to Hesburgh, February 22, 1969, "Nixon" folder, Hesburgh Papers, University of Notre Dame Archives. (The letter was written on February 22 and publicly released on February 24, 1969.)
81. Hesburgh to Nixon, March 6, 1969, "Nixon" folder, Hesburgh Papers, University of Notre Dame Archives.
82. Nixon to Hesburgh, March 7, 1969, "Nixon" folder, Hesburgh Papers, University of Notre Dame Archives. See also Hesburgh to Nixon, March 4, 1969, "Nixon" folder, Hesburgh Papers, University of Notre Dame Archives.
83. Hesburgh discussed this matter at some length in the lecture "Presidency of Notre Dame During the Vietnam Era," November 3, 1997, transcript in author's possession.
84. Richard M. Nixon, Daily Diary, February 21, 1970, Nixon Papers, Richard M. Nixon Presidential Library.
85. Hesburgh discussed this matter at some length in the lecture "Presidency of Notre Dame During the Vietnam Era."
86. O'Brien, *Hesburgh: A Biography,* p. 125.
87. Hesburgh, interview by author, June 19, 1998.
88. Daniel P. Moynihan, "Politics as the Art of the Impossible," commencement address, University of Notre Dame, May 1969, in Miscamble, ed., *Go Forth and Do Good,* p. 186.
89. Hesburgh to Nixon, April 1, 1969, "Nixon" folder, Hesburgh Papers, University of Notre Dame Archives.
90. Hesburgh, interview by author, June 19, 1998.
91. Telegram from Hesburgh and five commissioners to Nixon, June 26, 1969, "Moynihan" folder, Hesburgh Papers, University of Notre Dame Archives.
92. Moynihan to Hesburgh, June 26, 1969, "Moynihan" folder, Hesburgh Papers, University of Notre Dame Archives.
93. On Nixon's "Southern strategy" and the Philadelphia Plan, see James T. Patterson, *Grand Expectations: The United States, 1945–1974* (New York: Oxford University Press, 1996), pp. 723–24 and 730–32.
94. See John Herbers, "U.S. Rights Panel Finds Breakdown in Enforcement," *New York Times,* October 13, 1970, pp. 1 and 28. Also see "Commission Report Urges Leadership," *Observer,* October 14, 1970, p. 1.
95. For the details here, I rely on Hesburgh, *God, Country, Notre Dame,* pp. 208–10; and O'Brien, *Hesburgh: A Biography,* pp. 126–30.
96. O'Brien, *Hesburgh: A Biography,* p. 130. (O'Brien was able to interview Garment.)
97. See *Observer,* October 14, 1969, p. 3.
98. Nixon to Hesburgh, February 25, 1970, "Nixon" folder, Hesburgh Papers, University of Notre Dame Archives.
99. For the remarks and a copy of the "Hesburgh Declaration," see *Observer,* May 5, 1970, p. 1.

100. Hesburgh to Nixon, May 13, 1970, "Nixon" folder, Hesburgh Papers, University of Notre Dame Archives.

101. See the letter from David Parker, staff assistant to the president, in which he passed on Nixon's thanks for the invitation and declined to accept it. Parker to Hesburgh, October 21, 1971, "Nixon" folder, Hesburgh Papers, University of Notre Dame Archives.

102. O'Brien gives details in *Hesburgh: A Biography*, pp. 130–32.

103. Hesburgh, quoted in O'Brien, *Hesburgh: A Biography*, p. 132.

104. O'Brien, *Hesburgh: A Biography*, p. 132.

105. "Civil Rights Series Begins with Warren," *Observer*, April 6, 1972, p. 1.

106. See Theodore M. Hesburgh, "The Price Is Very High, the Price of Delay Is Vastly Higher: Father Hesburgh's Program for Racial Justice," *New York Times Magazine*, October 29, 1972, pp. 20–21 and 76–83.

107. White House Conversation, Tape 799, October 16, 1972, Richard M. Nixon Library.

108. Hesburgh to Nixon, August 28, 1972, "Nixon" folder, Hesburgh Papers, University of Notre Dame Archives.

109. "Shriver Speaks at Stepan," *Observer*, October 12, 1972, p. 1.

110. Author's private conversation with Hesburgh.

111. Stoessel, *Sarge: The Life and Times of Sargent Shriver*, pp. 579–89.

112. Hesburgh, interview by author, June 17, 1998.

113. White House Conversation, Tape 824, December 15, 1972, Richard M. Nixon Library.

114. Nixon to Hesburgh, December 20, 1972, "Nixon" folder, Hesburgh Papers, University of Notre Dame Archives.

115. Hesburgh, *God, Country, Notre Dame*, p. 212.

116. Editorial, "First Out," *New York Times*, November 18, 1972, p. 36.

117. See Daniel K. Williams, *Defenders of the Unborn: The Pro-Life Movement Before Roe v. Wade* (New York: Oxford University Press, 2016).

118. Hesburgh, *The Humane Imperative*, p. 33.

119. See Father Hesburgh's sermon at Respect Life Mass, Sacred Heart Church, Notre Dame, January 22, 1975, quoted in preface to *Abortion: New Directions for Policy Studies*, ed. Manier, Liu, and Solomon, p. viii.

120. Richard Conklin, "The Maker of Notre Dame," *Notre Dame Magazine*, 2015 Hesburgh Special Edition, p. 22.

121. See Hesburgh to Nixon, April 23, 1985, "Nixon" folder, Hesburgh Papers, University of Notre Dame Archives.

122. Hesburgh, interview by Conklin, transcript, p. 868.

123. Hesburgh, interview by author, June 17, 1998.

124. This relies on the recollections of Father Richard V. Warner and Father Timothy Scully, shared with author.

125. Ford to Hesburgh, August 19, 1974, Box 1432, "Hesburgh, Theodore" folder, White House Central Files, Gerald R. Ford Presidential Library, Ann Arbor, Michigan; hereafter Ford Library.

126. Gerald Ford, Proclamation No. 4313, Announcing a Program for the Return of Vietnam Era Draft Evaders and Military Deserters, September 16, 1974, Ford Library.

127. "Pres. Ford Appoints Hesburgh," *Observer*, September 17, 1974, p. 1.

128. Hesburgh to Ford, September 23, 1975, Box 1432, White House Central Files, Ford Library.

129. See the excellent chapter "Presidential Clemency Board: Eloquent Conscience," in John C. Lungren Jr., *Hesburgh of Notre Dame: Priest, Educator, Public Servant* (Kansas City, MO: Sheed & Ward, 1987), pp. 79–91. I rely on this work for the following paragraphs.

130. Hesburgh references their disagreements in *God, Country, Notre Dame*, pp. 266–67.

131. Lungren, *Hesburgh of Notre Dame*, p. 86.

132. James Maye, quoted in Lungren, *Hesburgh of Notre Dame*, p. 87.

133. Lungren, *Hesburgh of Notre Dame*, p. 84.

134. Hesburgh, *God, Country, Notre Dame*, p. 268.

135. See the schedule, texts, and briefing papers sent to Father Hesburgh by Nia Nickolas of the Presidential Clemency Board in "Clemency Board" folder, Hesburgh Papers, University of Notre Dame Archives.

136. For example, the Clemency Board met with President Ford on November 29, 1974, for a signing ceremony for the first warrants for clemency. See Ford's Daily Diary, November 29, 1974, Ford Library. Also see Ford's Farewell Greeting with the members and staff of the Clemency Board, September 16, 1975, Ford's Daily Diary, September 16, 1975, Ford Library.

137. Hesburgh, interview by author, June 16, 1998. (Hesburgh was incorrect in suggesting Ford had not visited any other campus. He delivered a commencement address at Ohio State on August 30, 1974, an event that had been arranged when he was still Nixon's vice president.)

138. Gerald R. Ford, Address at Notre Dame Convocation, March 17, 1975, *Public Papers of the President: Gerald R. Ford, 1975* (Washington, DC: U.S. Government Printing Office, 1976), pp. 353–61.

139. Ford to Hesburgh, March 27, 1975, Box 1432, White House Central Files, Ford Library.

140. See Ford to Hesburgh, May 17, June 24, July 15, 1975, Box 1432, White House Central Files, Ford Library.

141. On Hesburgh's letter, see "Hesburgh Urges More Food Aid," *Observer*, November 25, 1974, pp. 1 and 3, for the text of the letter.

142. Ford to Hesburgh, December 6, 1974, Box 1432, White House Central Files, Ford Library.

143. Ford to Hesburgh, March 18, 1975, Box 1432, White House Central Files, Ford Library.

144. Ford to Hesburgh, May 28, 1976, Box 1432, White House Central Files, Ford Library.

145. Theodore M. Hesburgh, *Three Bicentennial Addresses* (Notre Dame, IN: Office of the President, University of Notre Dame, 1976), pp. 3, 10, 28, 30–31, 32.

146. Hesburgh, interview by author, June 21, 1998.

147. Ford to Hesburgh, November 30, 1976, Box 1432, White House Central Files, Ford Library.

CHAPTER 8

1. "Jimmy Carter Visits South Bend," *Observer*, April 7, 1976, pp. 1 and 5.

2. The details of Carter and the Catholic bishops on the abortion issue rely on McAndrews, *What They Wished For*, pp. 184–87. (Quotations from p. 185.)

3. Hesburgh, *God, Country, Notre Dame*, pp. 271–72.

4. "Carter Cites Need for Voluntarism, New Commitment to Civil Rights," *Observer*, October 11, 1976, p. 1.

5. Jack Colwell, "Carter Likes Idea of Abortion Conference," *South Bend Tribune*, October 11, 1976, p. 1.

6. Hesburgh, *God, Country, Notre Dame*, pp. 269–71.

7. Stoessel, *Sarge: The Life and Times of Sargent Shriver*, p. 646.

8. See Memorandum, "National Advisors Group for Presidential Appointments," Folder: "Cabinet Selection-Political Problems, 11/76–1/77," Office of Staff Secretary, 1976 Campaign Transition File, Jimmy Carter Presidential Library; hereafter Carter Library.

9. See Robert Ajemian, "Picking the Team with Ham and Fritz," *Time*, December 20, 1976, pp. 10–11.

10. For Carter's commencement address, see Miscamble, ed., *Go Forth and Do Good*, pp. 196–203.

11. Hesburgh to Brzezinski, May 24, 1977, Zbigniew Brzezinski name files, 1977–81, Box 2, Records of the Office of National Security Adviser, Carter Library.

12. Carter's Daily Diary, September 7, 1977, Carter Library.

13. For the list of participants, see Hamilton Jordan to Carter, August 30, 1977, Folder: "Panama Canal Treaty 9/77," Container 36, Office of Chief of Staff Files, Hamilton Jordan's Confidential files, Carter Library.

14. Details of the Carter administration's efforts can be gleaned from Hamilton Jordan's briefings of Carter, Folder: "Panama Canal Treaty 10, 11, 12/77 [2]," Container 36, Office of Chief of Staff Files, Hamilton Jordan's Confidential files, Carter Library.

15. Frank Press to President Carter, May 20, 1977, Folder: "5/22/1977," Container 21, Office of Staff Secretary Series, Presidential Files, Carter Library.

16. James B. King to President Carter, July 11, 1977, Folder "7/11/77 [3]," Container 30, Office of Staff Secretary, President's Files, Carter Library.

17. For Wilkowski's account, see Jean M. Wilkowski, *Abroad for Her Country: Tales of a Pioneer Woman Ambassador in the U.S. Foreign Service* (Notre Dame, IN: University of Notre Dame Press, 2008), pp. 300–18.

18. Hesburgh, interview by Conklin, transcript, pp. 802–3.

19. Elizabeth Crump Hanson, *The United Nations Conference on Science and Technology for Development*, American Universities Field Staff Report, vol. 10 (Hanover, NH: American Universities Field Staff, 1980), p. 1. (I rely on Hanson for further details of the conference.)

20. Wilkowski, *Abroad for Her Country*, p. 317.

21. The details of the conference along with the Hesburgh quotations are drawn from Hanson, *The United Nations Conference on Science and Technology for Development*, pp. 1–14.

22. Hesburgh, interview by Conklin, transcript, pp. 802–3.

23. Hesburgh to Carter, September 10, 1977, attached to President's Address to Faculty, October 10, 1977, *Notre Dame Report*, University of Notre Dame Archives.

24. See Joseph A. Califano Jr., *Inside: A Public and Private Life* (New York: PublicAffairs, 2004), pp. 347–48.

25. William F. Buckley Jr., commencement address at University of Notre Dame, May 21, 1978, *Notre Dame Report*, June 2, 1978, pp. 420–23.

26. Transcript, *Meet the Press*, December 25, 1977, Folder "H2/10.01," Notre Dame Information Service Records, University of Notre Dame Archives.

27. See President's Commission on the Holocaust, November 8, 1978, *Public Papers of the Presidents of the United States: Jimmy Carter, 1978* (Washington, DC: GPO, 1979), pp. 1973–75; and "United States Holocaust Memorial Council," May 2, 1980, *Public Papers of the Presidents of the United States: Jimmy Carter, 1980* (Washington, DC: GPO, 1981), pp. 820–23.

28. Hesburgh, *God, Country, Notre Dame*, p. 274.

29. On the debates and legislative twists and turns, see Lawrence J. McAndrews, *Refuge in the Lord: Catholics, Presidents, and the Politics of Immigration, 1981–2013* (Washington, DC: Catholic University of America Press, 2015), pp. 60–75. Also see Hesburgh, *God, Country, Notre Dame*, pp. 277–79.

30. On Grant's efforts on Cambodian relief, see Andrew Fifield, *A Mighty Purpose: How Jim Grant Sold the World on Saving Its Children* (New York: Other Press, 2015), pp. 22–33.

31. Don Oberdorfer, "$69 Million Cambodian Aid Pledged," *Washington Post*, October 25, 1979, p. 1.

32. See the remarks of President Carter on "Aid for Kampucheans," followed by remarks by Father Hesburgh in which he recounts the details of the earlier meeting and Carter's response, November 13, 1979, *Public Papers of the Presidents of the United States: Jimmy Carter, 1979* (Washington, DC: GPO, 1980), pp. 2112–15.

33. Hesburgh, interview by Conklin, transcript, p. 806.

34. See Robert J. Stein and Deborah A. Harding, ". . . To Humanitarian Aid in Cambodia," *Notre Dame Magazine*, 2015 Hesburgh Special Edition, p. 61.

35. Hesburgh to Friends, September 1980, attached to Travel Diary from July 1980, Hesburgh Papers, University of Notre Dame Archives.

36. On the complications and mistakes made in getting aid to the Cambodians, see William Shawcross, *The Quality of Mercy: Cambodia, Holocaust and Modern Conscience* (New York: Simon & Schuster, 1984).

37. Michael O'Brien discussed this exchange well in *Hesburgh: A Biography*, pp. 155–56.

38. Ibid., p. 156; and Hesburgh, *God, Country, Notre Dame*, p. 311.

39. George Weigel, *Witness to Hope: The Biography of Pope John Paul II* (New York: Cliff Street Books, 1999), pp. 304–20.

40. George Weigel, *The Final Revolution: The Resistance Church and the Collapse of Communism* (New York: Oxford University Press, 1992), p. 16.

41. Hesburgh, interview by Conklin, transcript, p. 806.

42. Hesburgh to Carter, October 10, 1979, and Carter's handwritten note on Hesburgh's letter, Folder: "10/10/79 [1]," Container 134, Office of Staff Secretary, Presidential Files, Carter Library.

43. John Brademas to President Carter, September 4, 1979, Folder: "9/5/79," Container 129, Office of Staff Secretary, Presidential Files, Carter Library.

44. All this relies on Hesburgh, *God, Country, Notre Dame*, pp. 142–53.

45. For the transcript of the Presidential Debate in Cleveland, Ohio, October 28, 1980, which includes the Carter and Reagan quotes, see http://www.presidency.ucsb.edu/ws/index.php?pid=29408.

46. Photographs of Carter and Hesburgh with inscription, August 1979, Hesburgh Papers, University of Notre Dame Archives.

47. Hesburgh, interview by Conklin, transcript, pp. 803–4.

48. Hesburgh, interview by author, June 21, 1998.

49. See Hesburgh, preface to John Brademas, *Washington, D.C., to Washington Square: Essays on Government and Education* (New York: Weidenfeld & Nicolson, 1986), p. 10.

50. Hesburgh, interview by author, June 21, 1998. (I rely fully on Father Ted's recollection here. I have not been able to verify his remarks at this meeting.)

51. Hesburgh, interview by Conklin, transcript, p. 564.

52. Hesburgh, interview by author, June 18, 1998.

53. Ibid.

54. Ibid.

55. Hesburgh, interview by author, June 20, 1998.

56. John A. McCoy, *A Still and Quiet Conscience: A Life of Raymond Hunthausen* (Maryknoll, NY: Orbis Books, 2015), p. 226.

57. McBrien, "The Hard-line Pontiff," pp. 27–29.

58. Father Hesburgh endorsed Richard McBrien's evaluation of John Paul II. Hesburgh, interview by author, June 18, 1998.

59. This relies on George Weigel's work, especially in *The End and the Beginning*, but I quote directly from a brief essay of his entitled "An Eminent Distortion of History," *First Things*, July 16, 2014, https://www.firstthings.com/web-exclusives/2014/07/an-eminent-distortion-of-history.

60. In addition to Weigel's work, I draw here on Andrew Nagorski, "The Power of John Paul II," *Notre Dame Magazine*, Winter 2002–2003, p. 20.

61. "Haleys Greet the Gipper," *South Bend Tribune*, May 4, 1976, p. 1. Clipping in University of Notre Dame Archives.

62. Hesburgh, interview by Conklin, transcript, p. 804.

63. Richard W. Conklin, "Memories of the Gipper and Notre Dame," June 13, 2004, Notre Dame News and Information Press Release, University of Notre Dame Archives. (This piece was published originally in the *St. Paul Pioneer Press*.)

64. Diary entry, May 17, 1981, in Douglas Brinkley, ed., *The Reagan Diaries* (New York: HarperCollins, 2007), p. 19. Also see Daily Diary of President Ronald Reagan, May 17, 1981, Ronald Reagan Presidential Library; hereafter Reagan Library.

65. Ronald Reagan, Address at the Commencement Exercises at the University of Notre Dame, May 17, 1981, *Public Papers of the Presidents of the United States: Ronald Reagan, 1981* (Washington, DC: GPO, 1982), pp. 431–35.

66. Hesburgh, *God, Country, Notre Dame*, p. 301.

67. John Lewis Gaddis, *Strategies of Containment: A Critical Appraisal of American National*

Security Policy During the Cold War, rev. ed. (New York: Oxford University Press, 2005), p. 354.

68. Hesburgh outlined his epiphany experience in his foreword to *Catholic and Nuclear War: A Commentary on the Challenge of Peace*, ed. Philip J. Murnion (New York: Crossroad, 1983), pp. xi–xii.

69. For an illustration of the outcome of one of the meetings held in Bellagio, Italy, see the statement by thirty scientists and religious leaders issued November 24, 1984, entitled "Nuclear War: Its Consequences and Prevention," *Origins*, November 29, 1984, p. 415.

70. For Cardinal Bernardin's speech, "The Challenge of Peace," see Miscamble, ed., *Go Forth and Do Good*, pp. 216–23.

71. On the revisions to the earlier drafts of the pastoral letter, see Jared McBrady, "The Challenge of Peace: Ronald Reagan, John Paul II, and the American Bishops," *Journal of Cold War Studies* 17, no. 1 (Winter 2015): 129–52. Also see McAndrew, *What They Wished For*, pp. 198–217.

72. Hesburgh, interview by Conklin, transcript, p. 805.

73. "Is There a Crisis in the Catholic Church?," *Firing Line*, Program No. S0579, January 6, 1984.

74. "Hesburgh Urges Curbing the Arms Race," *Observer*, April 16, 1985, p. 1.

75. Gaddis, *Strategies of Containment*, p. 377.

76. U.S. Bishops' Statement on Central America, November 19, 1981, *Origins*, December 3, 1981, pp. 393–96.

77. See Hesburgh's preface to *Duarte: My Story*, by José Napoleón Duarte (New York: G. P. Putnam's Sons, 1986), p. 12.

78. Hesburgh, interview by author, June 21, 1998. Also see Duarte, *Duarte: My Story*, especially pp. 18–27.

79. For a favorable treatment of U.S. policy, see Russell Crandall, *The Salvador Option: The United States in El Salvador, 1977–1992* (New York: Cambridge University Press, 2016).

80. Hesburgh, interview by author, June 18, 1998.

81. Richard J. Meislin, "Salvador Trying Public Relations," *New York Times*, March 27, 1982, p. 17.

82. Hesburgh, interview by author, June 21, 1998.

83. José Napoleón Duarte, "The Struggle for Democracy," in Miscamble, ed., *Go Forth and Do Good*, pp. 226–35.

84. "Demonstrations Planned in Protest of Duarte Policies," *Observer*, May 17, 1985, p. 1.

85. This op-ed was published in various places. For its fullest expression see Theodore M. Hesburgh, "Reflections on Cuomo: The Secret Consensus," *Notre Dame Journal of Law, Ethics, and Public Policy* 1, no. 1 (1984): 53–56.

86. McAndrews, *Refuge in the Lord*, p. 67.

87. Philip Shenon, "Law Deans Oppose Naming of a Judge," *New York Times*, June 24, 1986, p. 1.

88. See Jack Colwell, "Hesburgh Lends Support to Manion," *South Bend Tribune*, May 21, 1986, p. B1.

89. Ronald Reagan, Radio Address to the Nation on Federal Judiciary, June 21, 1986, *Public Papers of the Presidents of the United States, Ronald Reagan, 1986*, Book 1 (Washington, DC: GPO, 1988–1989), pp. 818–19.

CHAPTER 9

1. Hesburgh, interview by author, June 21, 1998.

2. For further details, see Theodore M. Hesburgh, *Travels with Ted and Ned* (New York: Doubleday, 1992).

3. See Peter Tannock, *The Founding and Establishment of the University of Notre Dame Australia, 1986–2014* (Fremantle, Western Australia: University of Notre Dame Australia, 2014), p. 3.

4. Hesburgh, *God, Country, Notre Dame*, p. 304.
5. Ibid., p. 305.
6. Ibid., p. 310.
7. For some details of this commission, see the recollections of another participant, John W. Douglas, oral history interview, November 30, 2005, Miller Center, University of Virginia (accessed online).
8. Malloy, *Monk's Tale: The Presidential Years*, p. 418.
9. Hesburgh, *God, Country, Notre Dame*, p. 304.
10. Malloy, *Monk's Tale: The Presidential Years*, p. 63.
11. This all relies on Denise K. Magner, "With a New President, 'Evolutionary' Change Comes to Notre Dame," *Chronicle of Higher Education*, July 11, 1990, p. A3.
12. Ibid.
13. McBrien, quoted in Magner, "With a New President," p. A3.
14. Malloy, *Monk's Tale: The Presidential Years*, p. 136.
15. Hesburgh, interview by author, June 19, 1996.
16. Malloy discusses this in *Monk's Tale: The Presidential Years*, pp. 18–19.
17. Hesburgh, interview by author, June 18, 1996.
18. Sack, *Counterfeit Amateurs*, pp. 131–32.
19. Hesburgh, interview by author, June 20, 1998.
20. Ibid.
21. Mary Flaherty, quoted in O'Brien, *Hesburgh: A Biography*, p. 309.
22. Hesburgh, interview by author, June 21, 1998.
23. Ibid.
24. Rudenstine, quoted in Notre Dame press release, April 21, 1994, University of Notre Dame Archives.
25. Hesburgh, interview by author, June 21, 1998.
26. Ibid.
27. George H. W. Bush, Remarks at the University of Notre Dame Commencement Ceremony, May 17, 1992, in *Public Papers of the Presidents of the United States: George H. W. Bush, 1992, Book 1, January 1 to July 31, 1992* (Washington, DC: GPO, 1993), pp. 785–88.
28. Schmuhl, *Fifty Years with Father Hesburgh*, p. 118.
29. Clinton's Remarks on Endorsements of the North American Free Trade Agreement, November 2, 1993, *Public Papers of the Presidents of the United States: William J. Clinton, 1993* (Washington, DC: GPO, 1994), p. 1882.
30. Theodore M. Hesburgh, "Cuts Will Destroy the Core of American Values," *Chicago Tribune*, March 23, 1995, p. 19.
31. I rely on Robert Schmuhl for the details here, including the Hesburgh quotations. See his *Fifty Years with Father Hesburgh*, pp. 116–18.
32. Hesburgh to Robert P. Casey, October 10, 1994. This letter is in the author's possession and was supplied to me by Governor Casey.
33. George Weigel provides lots of details in *Witness to Hope*, pp. 715–27.
34. O'Brien gives more details on the Pollard case and I rely upon him. See *Hesburgh: A Biography*, pp. 306–7.
35. Schmuhl, *Fifty Years with Father Hesburgh*, p. 91.
36. Hesburgh, interview by author, June 17, 1998.
37. Fifield, *A Mighty Purpose*, pp. 384–86.
38. Father Hesburgh's homily is included in "Rev. Edmund P. Joyce: Obituary," *Indiana Province Review*, May 2004, pp. 21–24.
39. Christopher Buckley, "You Got a Problem?" *New Yorker*, December 4, 1995, pp. 83–84.
40. These details of Father Hesburgh's visit to the dying Eppie Lederer rely on Carol Felsenthal, "Father Hesburgh and His Close Friendship with Ann Landers," *Chicago Magazine*, February 28, 2015, http://www.chicagomag.com/Chicago-Magazine/Felsenthal-Files/February-2015/Fr-Hesburgh/.
41. John Salveson, "I Was Abused . . . ," *Notre Dame Magazine*, Summer 2003, p. 29.

42. These articles are referenced in the chapter "Considering Orientation," in Donald B. Cozzens, *The Changing Face of the Priesthood: A Reflection on the Priest's Crisis of Soul* (Collegeville, MN: Liturgical Press, 2000), p. 98.

43. David Greenberg, "Small Men on Campus: The Shrinking College President," *New Republic*, June 1, 1998, pp. 16–21.

44. Hesburgh, "Where Are the College Presidents' Voices on Important Public Issues?," *Chronicle of Higher Education*, February 2, 2001, p. B20.

45. For the Notre Dame press release announcing his appointment, see https://news.nd .edu/news/father-hesburgh-receives-16th-presidential-appointment/, University of Notre Dame Archives.

46. Burtchaell, *The Dying of the Light*, p. 851.

47. Hesburgh, interview by author, June 19, 1998.

48. Malloy, *Monk's Tale: The Presidential Years*, p. 354.

49. Father Hesburgh reported on this meeting to me in an informal conversation some months thereafter.

50. See Schmuhl, *Fifty Years with Father Hesburgh*, pp. 128–29.

51. The full text of House Resolution 687 is included in *Observer*, December 3, 2007, p. 3.

52. Digger Phelps, with Tim Bourret, *Father Ted Hesburgh: He Coached Me* (Chicago: Triumph Books, 2017), pp. 50–51.

53. "Nearly 91, Hesburgh Finds Time for Visitors," *Observer*, May 16, 2008, p. 5.

54. Malloy, quoted in Darren Rovell, "Malloy 'Embarrassed' by Move," *ESPN.Com:College Football*, December 8, 2004, http://www.espn.com/college-football/news/story ?id=1941810.

55. Barack Obama, "Commencement Address at the University of Notre Dame," May 17, 2009, *Public Papers of the Presidents of the United States: Barack Obama, 2009* (Washington, DC: GPO, 2010), pp. 658–63.

56. Hesburgh letter, *Notre Dame Magazine*, Fall 2009, p. 3.

57. David T. Tyson, "Thoughts of Ted," *Pillars*, Spring 2015, p. 15.

58. Joseph Lawler, "Fr. Hesburgh and Joe Donnelly's Vote," *American Spectator*, March 27, 2010, https://spectator.org/22277_fr-hesburgh-and-joe-donnellys-vote/.

59. Theodore M. Hesburgh, "A Setback for Educational Civil Rights," *Wall Street Journal*, March 18, 2010, p. 19.

60. Ted Hesburgh, "The U.S. Can't Turn Its Back on Peace," accessed February 27, 2011, http://www.washingtonpost.com/wp-dyn/content/article/2011/02/25/AR2011022506347 .html.

61. Hesburgh, quoted in "Seen & Heard," *Notre Dame Magazine*, Summer 2013, p. 17.

62. John Nagy, "His National Birthday Party," *Notre Dame Magazine*, 2015 Hesburgh Special Edition, pp. 78–79.

63. In addition to my own memory from my participation in these events, I rely on "Requiem," *Notre Dame Magazine*, 2015 Hesburgh Special Edition, pp. 84–85.

CONCLUSION

1. I borrow the words of the aging Jacques Maritain. See his *The Peasant of Garonne: An Old Layman Questions Himself About the Present Time* (New York: Holt, Rinehart and Winston, 1968), p. 53.

2. Theodore M. Hesburgh, untitled essay in Francis P. Friedl and Rex Reynolds, *Extraordinary Lives: Thirty-Four Priests Tell Their Stories* (Notre Dame, IN: Ave Maria Press, 1997), p. 266.

3. Marvin R. O'Connell, *Edward Sorin* (Notre Dame, IN: University of Notre Dame Press, 2001), p. v.

4. Hesburgh, interview by author, June 21, 1998.

SELECT BIBLIOGRAPHY

I. PRIMARY SOURCES

A. Manuscript Collections

ARCHIVES OF U.S. PROVINCE OF HOLY CROSS, NOTRE DAME, IN
Records of Provincial Chapter 1967

GERALD R. FORD PRESIDENTIAL LIBRARY, ANN ARBOR, MI
Goldwin Papers
President's Daily Diary
White House Central Files

JIMMY CARTER PRESIDENTIAL LIBRARY, ATLANTA, GA
Hamilton Jordan's Confidential files
President's Daily Diary
Presidential Files

JOHN F. KENNEDY PRESIDENTIAL LIBRARY, COLUMBIA POINT, BOSTON, MA
John F. Kennedy Papers
Joseph P. Kennedy Papers

LYNDON B. JOHNSON PRESIDENTIAL LIBRARY, AUSTIN, TX
Papers of Lyndon B. Johnson
President's Daily Diary

RICHARD M. NIXON LIBRARY, YORBA LINDA, CA
President's Daily Diary
White House Conversation Tapes

ROCKEFELLER ARCHIVES CENTER, SLEEPY HOLLOW, NY
Records of the Special Studies Project

RONALD REAGAN PRESIDENTIAL LIBRARY, SIMI VALLEY, CA
President's Daily Diary

UNIVERSITY OF NOTRE DAME ARCHIVES, NOTRE DAME, IN
Board of Trustees Minutes, University of Notre Dame, 1966
Notre Dame Press Releases, 1952–2015
Papers of Theodore M. Hesburgh
Notre Dame Archive News and Notes

B. Documents

Abbott, Walter M., S.J., ed. *The Documents of Vatican II*. New York: America Press, 1966.
Benestad, Brian, and Francis J. Butler, eds. *Quest for Justice: A Compendium of Statements of the United States Catholic Bishops on the Political and Social Order, 1966–1980*. Washington, DC: USCCB, 1981.

Carter, Jimmy. *Public Papers of the Presidents of the United States: Jimmy Carter, 1977–1981.* Washington, DC: U.S. Government Printing Office, 1977–1981.

———. "Presidential Debate in Cleveland," October 28, 1980. Online by Gerhard Peters and John T. Woolley, *The American Presidency Project.* http://www.presidency.ucsb.edu/ws/?pid=29408.

Ford, Gerald R. *Public Papers of the Presidents of the United States: Gerald R. Ford, 1975–1977.* Washington, DC: U.S. Government Printing Office, 1977–1978.

Gallin, Alice, ed. *American Catholic Higher Education: Essential Documents, 1967–1990.* Notre Dame, IN: University of Notre Dame Press, 1992.

Nixon, Richard M. *Public Papers of the Presidents of the United States: Richard M. Nixon, 1969–1974.* Washington, DC: U.S. Government Printing Office, 1971–1975.

O'Brien, David J., and Thomas A. Shannon, eds. *Renewing the Earth: Catholic Documents on Peace, Justice and Liberation.* Garden City, NY: Image Books, 1977.

Reagan, Ronald. *Public Papers of the Presidents of the United States: Ronald Reagan, 1981–1989.* Washington, DC: U.S. Government Printing Office, 1982–1990.

U.S. Catholic Bishops. Statement on Central America. November 19, 1981. *Origins,* December 3, 1981, pp. 393–96.

United States Commission on Civil Rights. *With Liberty and Justice for All.* An abridgment of the Report of the United States Commission on Civil Rights, 1959. Washington, DC: U.S. Government Printing Office, 1959.

University of Notre Dame. *The Person in Contemporary Society: A Symposium on the Occasion of the Dedication of the Memorial Library.* Notre Dame, IN: Memorial Library, University of Notre Dame, 1964.

C. Oral Histories and Interviews

JOHN F. KENNEDY LIBRARY ORAL HISTORY COLLECTION
Cavanaugh, John. Interviewed by Joseph E. O'Connor, March 27, 1966.
Hesburgh, Theodore M. Interviewed by Joseph E. O'Connor, March 27, 1966.

KROC INSTITUTE
Värynen, Raimo. Interview with Rev. Theodore M. Hesburgh. *Kroc Institute Report,* Spring 1996, pp. 11–13.

LYNDON JOHNSON LIBRARY ORAL HISTORY COLLECTION
Theodore M. Hesburgh. Interviewed by Paige E. Mulholland, February 1, 1971.

MEDIA INTERVIEWS
"Is There a Crisis in the Catholic Church?" *Firing Line,* Program No. S0579, January 6, 1984.
Transcript, *Meet the Press,* with Theodore M. Hesburgh, December 25, 1977. Folder "H2/10.01." Notre Dame Information Service Records. University of Notre Dame Archives.

PERSONAL INTERVIEWS
Hesburgh, Theodore M., C.S.C. Interviews by author. Land O'Lakes, Wisconsin, June 16–21, 1998.
Riehle, James, C.S.C. Interview by author. Notre Dame, IN, December 11, 1997.
Solomon, David. Interview by author. Notre Dame, Indiana, February 8, 2016.

UNIVERSITY OF NOTRE DAME ARCHIVES
Hesburgh, Theodore M., C.S.C. Interview by Richard Conklin. Notre Dame and Land O'Lakes, Wisconsin, 1982 and 1989.
Stephan, Edmund. Interview by Richard Conklin. Evanston, IL, May 2, 1983.

D. Newspapers and Periodicals

America, 1952–1987

Chicago Tribune, various years 1952–1987

New York Times, various years 1952–2015

Notre Dame Alumnus, 1952–1971

Notre Dame Magazine, 1972–2016

Notre Dame Report, various years 1970–2007

Observer, 1966–2015

Origins, various issues 1980–1987

Scholastic, 1952–2015

South Bend Tribune, various years 1952–2015

Time, 1955–1975

E. Published Memoirs, Diaries, and Papers

Brademas, John. *Washington, D.C., to Washington Square*. New York: Weidenfeld & Nicolson, 1986.

Brinkley, Douglas, ed. *The Reagan Diaries*. New York: HarperCollins, 2007.

Califano, Joseph A., Jr. *Inside: A Public and Private Life*. New York: PublicAffairs, 2004.

Carson, Clayborne, et al. *The Papers of Martin Luther King Jr*. Vol. 7, *To Save the Soul of America, January 1961–August 1962*. Oakland: University of California Press, 2014.

Duarte, José Napoleón. *Duarte: My Story*. New York: G. P. Putnam's Sons, 1986.

Ehrlichman, John. *Witness to Power: The Nixon Years*. New York: Simon & Schuster, 1982.

Faust, Gerry. *The Golden Dream*. Champaign, IL: Sagamore Publishing, 1997.

Greeley, Andrew M. *Furthermore! Memories of a Parish Priest*. New York: Forge, 1999.

Haldeman, H. R. *The Haldeman Diaries: Inside the Nixon White House*. New York: G. P. Putnam's Sons, 1994.

Hauerwas, Stanley. *Hannah's Child: A Theologian's Memoir*. Grand Rapids, MI: Eerdmans, 2012.

Heston, Edward L., trans. *Circular Letters of the Very Reverend Basil Anthony Mary Moreau*. 2 vols. Notre Dame, IN: Ave Maria Press, 1943.

Holtz, Lou. *Wins, Losses, and Lessons: An Autobiography*. New York: William Morrow, 2006.

Kerr, Clark. *The Gold and the Blue: A Personal Memoir of the University of California, 1949–1967*. Vol. 2, *Political Turmoil*. Berkeley: University of California Press, 2003.

Lannie, Vincent P., ed. *On the Side of Truth: George N. Shuster: An Evaluation with Readings*. Notre Dame, IN: University of Notre Dame Press, 1974.

Malloy, Edward A., C.S.C. *Monk's Tale: The Pilgrimage Begins, 1941–1975*. Notre Dame, IN: University of Notre Dame Press, 2009.

———. *Monk's Tale: The Presidential Years, 1987–2005*. Notre Dame, IN: University of Notre Dame Press, 2016.

———. *Monk's Tale: Way Stations on the Journey*. Notre Dame, IN: University of Notre Dame Press, 2011.

McInerny, Ralph. *I Alone Have Escaped to Tell You: My Life and Pastimes*. Notre Dame, IN: University of Notre Dame Press, 2006.

Nixon, Richard. *RN: The Memoirs of Richard Nixon*. New York: Warner Books, 1978.

Pipes, Richard. *Vixi: Memoirs of a Non-Belonger*. New Haven, CT: Yale University Press, 2003.

Shannon, James P. *Reluctant Dissenter: A Catholic Bishop's Journey of Faith*. New York: Crossroad, 1998.

Wilkowski, Jean M. *Abroad for Her Country: Tales of a Pioneer Woman Ambassador in the U.S. Foreign Service*. Notre Dame, IN: University of Notre Dame Press, 2008.

Wofford, Harris. *Of Kennedys and Kings: Making Sense of the Sixties*. Pittsburgh, PA: University of Pittsburgh Press, 1992.

F. Hesburgh Publications

Hesburgh, Theodore M., C.S.C. *God and the World of Man.* Notre Dame, IN: University of Notre Dame Press, 1950.

——. *God, Country, Notre Dame.* Notre Dame, IN: University of Notre Dame Press, 1999.

——. *The Humane Imperative: A Challenge for the Year 2000.* New Haven, CT: Yale University Press, 1974.

——. *More Thoughts for Our Times.* Notre Dame, IN: Office of the President, University of Notre Dame, 1964.

——. *Patterns for Educational Growth: Six Discourses at the University of Notre Dame.* Notre Dame, IN: University of Notre Dame Press, 1958.

——. *Still More Thoughts for Our Times.* Notre Dame, IN: Office of the President, University of Notre Dame, 1966.

——. *The Theology of Catholic Action.* Notre Dame, IN: University of Notre Dame Press, 1946.

——. *Thoughts IV: Five Addresses Delivered During 1967.* Notre Dame, IN: University of Notre Dame Press, 1968.

——. *Thoughts for Our Times.* Notre Dame, IN: Office of the President, University of Notre Dame, 1962.

——. *Thoughts for Our Times V.* Notre Dame, IN: University of Notre Dame Press, 1969.

——. *Three Bicentennial Addresses.* Notre Dame, IN: Office of the President, University of Notre Dame, 1976.

——. *Travels with Ted and Ned.* New York: Doubleday, 1992.

Hesburgh, Theodore M., C.S.C., ed. *The Challenge and Promise of a Catholic University.* Notre Dame, IN: University of Notre Dame Press, 1994.

Pruett, Robert E., ed. *Words Have Meaning: The Selected Speeches of Father Theodore Hesburgh.* Bloomington, IN: First Books, 2002.

II. ARTICLES AND ADDRESSES

Hesburgh, Theodore M., C.S.C. "An Open Letter to the University." Published in *Observer*, October 14, 1977, p. 1.

——. "Another Part of the Kingdom," *Notre Dame Magazine*, Spring 1985, pp. 65–67.

——. "College Football: The True Meaning of the Game," *Sports Illustrated*, December 12, 1966, pp. 56–57.

——. "Department of Religion: Mid-Century Report," *Notre Dame Alumnus*, September-October 1949, pp. 5–6.

——. "Election of Pius XII," *Ave Maria*, August 10, 1940, pp. 175–76.

——. "The 'Events': A Retrospective View," *Daedalus: American Higher Education: Toward an Uncertain Future*, Fall 1974, pp. 67–71.

——. "The Facts of the Matter," *Sports Illustrated*, January 19, 1959, pp. 16–17.

——. "Father Hesburgh's Program for Racial Justice," *New York Times Magazine*, October 29, 1972, pp. 20–21, 76–83.

——. "The Football Season: Fantasy and Reality," *Scholastic's* 1966 Football Review, December 9, 1966, p. 9.

——. "Looking Back at Newman," *America*, March 3, 1962, pp. 720–21.

——. "Reflections on Cuomo: The Secret Consensus," *Notre Dame Journal of Law, Ethics, and Public Policy* 1 (1984): 53–56.

——. "Reflections on Priesthood." Address at Commencement Exercises. Immaculate Conception Seminary, Darlington, NJ, September 11, 1983.

——. Sermon delivered by Rev. Theodore M. Hesburgh at Funeral Mass for Rev. Howard Kenna, C.S.C. Sacred Heart Church, September 17, 1973, University of Notre Dame Archives.

———. "The True Spirit of Notre Dame," *Sports Illustrated*, September 27, 1954, pp. 16–20, 30–32.

———. "Why Are We a Catholic University?," *Notre Dame Alumnus*, May-June 1967, pp. 8–9.

II. SECONDARY SOURCES

A. Books

Ames, Charlotte A. *Theodore M. Hesburgh: A Bio-Bibliography*. New York: Greenwood Press, 1989.

Avella, Steven M. *This Confident Church: Catholic Leadership and Life in Chicago, 1940–1965*. Notre Dame, IN: University of Notre Dame Press, 1992.

Barron, Bishop Robert. *The Priority of Christ: Toward a Postliberal Catholicism*. Grand Rapids, MI: Brazos Press, 2007.

Birzer, Bradley J. *Sanctifying the World: The Augustinian Life and Mind of Christopher Dawson*. Front Royal, VA: Christendom Press, 2007.

Black, Edwin. *War Against the Weak: Eugenics and America's Campaign to Create a Master Race*. New York: Four Walls Eight Windows, 2003.

Blanshard, Paul. *American Freedom and Catholic Power*. Boston: Beacon Press, 1949.

Blantz, Thomas. *George N. Shuster: On the Side of Truth*. Notre Dame, IN: University of Notre Dame Press, 1993.

Branch, Taylor. *At Canaan's Edge: America in the King Years, 1965–68*. New York: Simon & Schuster, 2006.

———. *Parting the Waters: America in the King Years, 1954–63*. New York: Simon & Schuster, 1988.

———. *Pillar of Fire: America in the King Years, 1963–65*. New York: Simon & Schuster, 1998.

Burk, Robert Fredrick. *The Eisenhower Administration and Black Civil Rights*. Knoxville: University of Tennessee Press, 1984.

Burns, Jeffrey M. *Disturbing the Peace: A History of the Christian Family Movement, 1949–1974*. Notre Dame, IN: University of Notre Dame Press, 1999.

Burtchaell, James T. *Abortion Parley*. Kansas City, MO: Andrews and McMeel, 1980.

———. *The Dying of the Light: The Disengagement of College and Universities from Their Christian Churches*. Grand Rapids, MI: Eerdmans, 1998.

Carey, Patrick. *The Roman Catholics*. Westport, CT: Greenwood Press, 1993.

Carey, Robert. *The Peace Corps*. New York: Praeger, 1970.

Christ, Frank L., and Gerard E. Sherry, eds. *American Catholicism and the Intellectual Ideal*. New York: Appleton-Century-Crofts, 1961.

Connelly, Joel R., and Howard J. Dooley. *Hesburgh's Notre Dame: Triumph in Transition*. New York: Hawthorn Books, 1972.

Connelly, Matthew. *Fatal Misconception: The Struggle to Control World Population*. Cambridge: MA: Belknap Press of Harvard University Press, 2008.

Connor, Jack. *Leahy's Lads: The Story of the Famous Notre Dame Teams of the 1940s*. Rev. ed. Lakeville, IN: Diamonds Communications, 1997.

Cornwell, John. *Hitler's Pope: The Secret History of Pius XII*. New York: Viking, 1999.

Cozzens, Donald B. *The Changing Face of the Priesthood: A Reflection on the Priest's Crisis of Soul*. Collegeville, MN: Liturgical Press, 2000.

Crandall, Russell. *The Salvador Option: The United States in El Salvador, 1977–1992*. New York: Cambridge University Press, 2016.

Critchlow, Donald T. *Intended Consequences: Birth Control, Abortion, and the Federal Government in Modern America*. New York: Oxford University Press, 1999.

Dallek, Robert. *Flawed Giant: Lyndon Johnson and His Times, 1961–1973*. New York: Oxford University Press, 1998.

——. *Lone Star Rising: Lyndon Johnson and His Times*. New York: Oxford University Press, 1991.

Dent, Jim. *Resurrection: The Miracle Season That Saved Notre Dame*. New York: Thomas Dunne Books, 2009.

Diggins, John Patrick. *The Proud Decades: America in War and Peace: 1941–1960*. New York: W. W. Norton, 1989.

Duffy, Eamon. *Saints and Sinners: A History of the Popes*. 2nd ed. New Haven, CT: Yale University Press, 2002.

Dulles, Foster Rhea. *The Civil Rights Commission: 1957–1965*. East Lansing: Michigan State University Press, 1968.

Ehrlich, Paul R. *The Population Bomb*. New York: Ballantine Books, 1978.

Ferguson, Niall. *Kissinger*. Vol. 1, *1923–1968: The Idealist*. New York: Penguin, 2015.

Fifield, Andrew. *A Mighty Purpose: How Jim Grant Sold the World on Saving Its Children*. New York: Other Press, 2015.

Fischer, David. *History of the International Atomic Energy Agency: The First Forty Years*. Vienna: International Atomic Energy Agency, 1997.

Fisher, James T. *Dr. America: The Lives of Thomas A. Dooley, 1927–1961*. Amherst: University of Massachusetts Press, 1997.

Friedl, Francis P., and Rex Reynolds. *Extraordinary Lives: Thirty-Four Priests Tell Their Stories*. Notre Dame, IN: Ave Maria Press, 1997.

Gaddis, John Lewis. *Strategies of Containment: A Critical Appraisal of American National Security Policy During the Cold War*. Rev. ed. New York: Oxford University Press, 2005.

Gallin, Alice. *Negotiating Identity: Catholic Higher Education Since 1960*. Notre Dame, IN: University of Notre Dame Press, 2000.

Gergen, David. *Eyewitness to Power: The Essence of Leadership, Nixon to Clinton*. New York: Simon & Schuster, 2000.

Gerlach, Matthew T., ed. *Renewal of Catholic Higher Education: Essays on Catholic Studies in Honor of Don J. Briel*. Bismarck, ND.: University of Mary Press, 2017.

Glazer, Nathan, and Daniel P. Moynihan. *Beyond the Melting Pot*, 2nd ed. Cambridge, MA: M.I.T. Press, 1970.

Gleason, Philip. *Contending with Modernity: Catholic Higher Education in the Twentieth Century*. New York: Oxford University Press, 1995.

Goldhagen, Daniel Jonah. *A Moral Reckoning: The Role of the Catholic Church in the Holocaust and Its Unfulfilled Duty of Repair*. New York: Knopf, 2002.

Goodwin, Doris Kearns. *Lyndon Johnson and the American Dream*. New York: Harper & Row, 1976.

Halberstam, David. *The Best and the Brightest*. New York: Random House, 1972.

Hanson, Elizabeth Crump. *The United Nations Conference on Science and Technology for Development*. American Universities Field Staff Report. Vol. 10. Hanover, NH: American Universities Field Staff, 1980.

Hennes, Doug. *That Great Heart: The Life of I. A. O'Shaughnessy, Oilman and Philanthropist*. Edina, MN: Beaver's Pond Press, 2014.

Herberg, Will. *Protestant, Catholic, Jew: An Essay in American Religious Sociology*. Rev. ed. Garden City, NY: Anchor Books, 1960.

Holmes, David L. *The Faiths of the Postwar Presidents: From Truman to Obama*. Athens: University of Georgia Press, 2012.

Holtz, Lou, with John Heisler. *The Fighting Spirit: A Championship Season at Notre Dame*. New York: Pocket Books, 1989.

Hope, Arthur J. *Notre Dame One Hundred Years*. Rev. ed. Notre Dame, IN: University of Notre Dame Press, 1950.

Horton, Thomas R., ed. *"What Works for Me": 16 CEOs Talk About Their Careers and Commitments*. New York: Random House, 1986.

Hudock, Barry. *Struggle, Condemnation, Vindication: John Courtney Murray's Journey Toward Vatican II*. Collegeville, MN: Liturgical Press, 2013.

Jencks, Christopher, and David Riesman. *The Academic Revolution.* Garden City, NY: Doubleday, 1968.

Kabaservice, Geoffrey. *The Guardians: Kingman Brewster, His Circle, and the Rise of the Liberal Establishment.* New York: Henry Holt, 2004.

Kelly, George A. *The Battle for the American Church.* Garden City: NY: Doubleday, 1979.

Kengor, Paul A. *A Pope and a President: John Paul II, Ronald Reagan, and the Extraordinary Untold Story of the 20th Century.* Wilmington, DE: Intercollegiate Studies Institute Books, 2017.

Kotz, Nick. *Judgment Days: Lyndon Baines Johnson, Martin Luther King Jr., and the Laws That Changed America.* Boston: Houghton Mifflin, 2005.

Lungren, John C., Jr. *Hesburgh of Notre Dame: Priest, Educator, Public Servant.* Kansas City, MO: Sheed & Ward, 1987.

Malkiel, Nancy Weiss. *"Keep the Damned Women Out": The Struggle for Coeducation.* Princeton, NJ: Princeton University Press, 2016.

Manchester, William. *The Death of a President: November 20–November 25, 1963.* New York: Harper & Row, 1967.

Mandell, Gail Porter. *Madeleva: A Biography.* Albany: State University of New York Press, 1997.

Manier, Edward, William Liu, and David Solomon, eds. *Abortion: New Directions for Policy Studies.* Notre Dame, IN: University of Notre Dame Press, 1977.

Mann, Robert. *The Walls of Jericho: Lyndon Johnson, Hubert Humphrey, Richard Russell, and the Struggle for Civil Rights.* New York: Harcourt Brace, 1996.

Maritain, Jacques. *Integral Humanism: Temporal and Spiritual Problems of a New Christendom.* Translated by Joseph W. Evans. New York: Scribner, 1968.

——. *The Peasant of Garonne: An Old Layman Questions Himself and the Present Time.* New York: Holt, Rinehart and Winston, 1968.

——. *The Person and the Common Good.* Translated by John J. Fitzgerald. New York: Charles Scribner's Sons, 1947.

Marsden, George R. *The Soul of the American University.* New York: Oxford University Press, 1994.

——. *The Twilight of the American Enlightenment: The 1950s and the Crisis of Liberal Belief.* New York: Basic Books, 2014.

Mason, Linda, and Roger Brown. *Rice, Rivalry, and Politics: Managing Cambodian Relief.* Notre Dame, IN: University of Notre Dame Press, 1983.

McAndrews, Lawrence J. *Refuge in the Lord: Catholics, Presidents, and the Politics of Immigration, 1981–2013.* Washington, DC: Catholic University of America Press, 2015.

——. *What They Wished For: American Catholics and American Presidents, 1960–2004.* Athens: University of Georgia Press, 2014.

McBrien, Richard. *Catholicism.* Vols. 1 and 2. Minneapolis: Winston Press, 1980.

——. *Catholicism.* Study edition. Minneapolis: Winston Press, 1981.

——. *Lives of the Popes: The Pontiffs from St. Peter to John Paul II.* New York: HarperCollins, 1997.

McClory, Robert. *Turning Point: The Inside Story of the Papal Birth Control Commission, and How* Humanae Vitae *Changed the Life of Patty Crowley and the Future of the Church.* New York: Crossroad, 1995.

McCluskey, Neil G., S.J., *The Catholic University: A Modern Appraisal.* Notre Dame, IN: University of Notre Dame Press, 1970.

McCoy, John A. *A Still and Quiet Conscience: A Life of Raymond Hunthausen.* Maryknoll, NY: Orbis Books, 2015.

McGreevy, John. *Catholicism and American Freedom: A History.* New York: W. W. Norton, 2003.

McPherson, James, ed. *"To the Best of My Ability": The American Presidents.* New York: Dorling Kindersley, 2000.

Meaney, John W. *O'Malley of Notre Dame.* Notre Dame, IN: University of Notre Dame Press, 1991.

Miscamble, Wilson D., C.S.C. *For Notre Dame: Battling for the Heart and Soul of a Catholic University*. South Bend, IN: St. Augustine's Press, 2013.

———, ed. *Go Forth and Do Good: Memorable Notre Dame Commencement Addresses*. Notre Dame, IN: University of Notre Dame Press, 2003.

Mitchell, Peter M. *The Coup at Catholic University: The 1968 Revolution in Catholic Education*. San Francisco: Ignatius Press, 2015.

Moore, Philip S. *Academic Development, University of Notre Dame: Past, Present and Future*. Notre Dame, IN: University of Notre Dame, 1960.

Moynihan, Daniel P. *The Negro Family: The Case for National Action*. Washington, DC: Office of Policy Planning and Research, U.S. Department of Labor, 1965.

Murnion, Philip J., ed. *Catholic and Nuclear War: A Commentary on the Challenge of Peace*. New York: Crossroad, 1983.

Napoli, Lisa. *Ray and Joan: The Man Who Made the McDonald's Fortune and the Woman Who Gave It All Away*. New York: Dutton, 2016.

Nasaw, David. *The Patriarch: The Remarkable Life and Turbulent Times of Joseph P. Kennedy*. New York: Penguin, 2012.

Neustadt, Richard E. *Presidential Power and the Modern Presidents: The Politics of Leadership from Roosevelt to Reagan*. New York: Free Press, 1991.

O'Brien, David J. *American Catholics and Social Reform: The New Deal Years*. New York: Oxford University Press, 1968.

O'Brien, Michael. *Hesburgh: A Biography*. Washington, DC: Catholic University of America Press, 1998.

O'Connell, Marvin R. *Edward Sorin*. Notre Dame, IN: University of Notre Dame Press, 2001.

Patterson, James T. *Grand Expectations: The United States, 1945–1974*. New York: Oxford University Press, 1996.

———. *Restless Giant: The United States from Watergate to Bush v. Gore*. New York: Oxford University Press, 2005.

Phelps, Digger. *Father Ted Hesburgh: He Coached Me*. Chicago: Triumph Books, 2017.

Posner, Gerald. *God's Bankers: A History of Money and Power at the Vatican*. New York: Simon & Schuster, 2015.

Prentiss, Craig R. *Debating God's Economy: Social Justice in America on the Eve of Vatican II*. University Park: Pennsylvania State University Press, 2008.

Rahner, Karl, S.J. *The Shape of the Church to Come*. Translated by Edward Quinn. New York: Seabury Press, 1974.

Rice, Charles E. *What Happened to Notre Dame?* South Bend, IN: St. Augustine's Press, 2009.

Rice, Gerald T. *The Bold Experiment: JFK's Peace Corps*. Notre Dame, IN: University of Notre Dame Press, 1985.

Riebling, Mark. *Church of Spies: The Pope's Secret War Against Hitler*. New York: Basic Books, 2015.

Robinson, Ray. *Rockne of Notre Dame: The Making of a Football Legend*. New York: Oxford University Press, 1999.

Rockefeller Brothers Fund. *Prospect for America: The Rockefeller Panel Reports*. Garden City, NY: Doubleday, 1961.

———. *The Pursuit of Excellence: Education and the Future of America*. Garden City, NY: Doubleday, 1958.

Sack, Allen. *Counterfeit Amateurs: An Athlete's Journey Through the Sixties to the Age of Academic Capitalism*. University Park: Pennsylvania State University Press, 2008.

Sandbrook, Dominic. *Eugene McCarthy: The Rise and Fall of Postwar American Liberalism*. New York: Knopf, 2004.

Sayre, Kenneth M. *Adventures in Philosophy at Notre Dame*. Notre Dame, IN: University of Notre Dame Press, 2014.

Schlereth, Thomas J. *The University of Notre Dame: A Portrait of Its History and Campus*. Notre Dame, IN: University of Notre Dame Press, 1976.

Schlesinger, Arthur M. *Robert Kennedy and His Times*. Boston: Houghton Mifflin, 1978.

Schmitt, Bill. *Words of Life: Celebrating Fifty Years of the Hesburgh Library's Message, Mural, and Meaning*. Notre Dame, IN: University of Notre Dame Press, 2013.

Schmuhl, Robert. *Fifty Years with Father Hesburgh: On and Off the Record*. Notre Dame, IN: University of Notre Dame Press, 2016.

———. *In So Many Words: Arguments and Adventures*. Notre Dame, IN: University of Notre Dame Press, 2006.

———. *The University of Notre Dame: A Contemporary Portrait*. Notre Dame, IN: University of Notre Dame Press, 1986.

Schultz, Kevin M. *Tri-Faith America: How Catholics and Jews Held Postwar America to Its Protestant Promise*. New York: Oxford University Press, 2011.

Shawcross, William. *The Quality of Mercy: Cambodia, Holocaust and Modern Conscience*. New York: Simon & Schuster, 1984.

Smith, Gary Scott. *Faith and the Presidency: From George Washington to George W. Bush*. New York: Oxford University Press, 2006.

———. *Religion in the Oval Office: The Religious Lives of American Presidents*. New York: Oxford University Press, 2015.

Smith, Richard Norton. *On His Own Terms: A Life of Nelson Rockefeller*. New York: Random House, 2014.

Sparr, Arnold. *To Promote, Defend, and Redeem: The Catholic Literary Revival and the Cultural Transformation of American Catholicism, 1920–1960*. New York: Greenwood Press, 1990.

Sperber, Murray. *Shake Down the Thunder: The Creation of Notre Dame Football*. New York: Henry Holt, 1995.

Stern, Seth, and Stephen Wermeil. *Justice Brennan: Liberal Champion*. Boston: Houghton Mifflin, 2010.

Stoessel, Scott. *Sarge: The Life and Times of Sargent Shriver*. Washington, DC: Smithsonian, 2004.

Tannock, Peter. *The Founding and Establishment of the University of Notre Dame Australia, 1986–2014*. Fremantle, Western Australia: University of Notre Dame Australia, 2014.

Tocqueville, Alexis de. *Democracy in America*. Abridged edition. New York: New American Library, 1956.

Van Allen, Rodger. *The Commonweal and American Catholicism: The Magazine, the Movement, the Meaning*. Philadelphia: Fortress Press, 1974.

Wedgwood, C. V. *William the Silent: William of Nassau, Prince of Orange*. New York: W. W. Norton, 1968.

Weigel, George. *The End and the Beginning: Pope John Paul II—The Victory of Freedom, the Last Years, the Legacy*. New York: Doubleday, 2010.

———. *Evangelical Catholicism: Deep Reform in the 21st-Century Church*. New York: Basic Books, 2013.

———. *The Final Revolution: The Resistance Church and the Collapse of Communism*. New York: Oxford University Press, 1992.

———. *Witness to Hope: The Biography of Pope John Paul II*. New York: Cliff Street Books, 1999.

White, Theodore H. *The Making of the President, 1972*. New York: Bantam Books, 1972.

Wiesel, Elie. *Four Hasidic Masters and Their Struggle Against Melancholy*. Notre Dame, IN: University of Notre Dame Press, 1978.

Williams, Daniel K. *Defenders of the Unborn: The Pro-Life Movement Before Roe v. Wade*. New York: Oxford University Press, 2016.

Zelizer, Julian E. *The Fierce Urgency of Now: Lyndon Johnson, Congress, and the Battle for the Great Society*. New York: Penguin, 2015.

B. Articles

Ajemian, Robert. "Picking the Team with Ham and Fritz," *Time*, December 20, 1976, pp. 10–11.

Bartlett, Evadna Smith. "Volunteering for Justice and Peace," *Notre Dame Magazine, Rev. Theodore M. Hesburgh, C.S.C., Priest, President, Citizen of the World, 1917–2015 (Special Edition)*, April 2015, p. 54. Hereafter *Notre Dame Magazine*, 2015 Hesburgh Special Edition.

Bauman, Robert. "'King of a Secular Sacrament': Father Geno Baroni, Monsignor John E. Egan, and the Catholic War on Poverty," *Catholic Historical Review* 99, no. 2 (April 2013): 298–317.

Baxter, Michael J. "God, Notre Dame, Country: Rethinking the Mission of Catholic Higher Education in the United States," *Nova et Vetera* 9, no. 4 (2011): 893–929.

Brady, Jerry M. "Ted and Jerry See Africa," *Notre Dame Magazine*, 2015 Hesburgh Special Edition, pp. 24–27.

Briel, Don J. "A Reflection on Catholic Studies." In *Renewal of Catholic Higher Education: Essays on Catholic Studies in Honor of Don J. Briel*. Edited by Matthew T. Gerlach. Bismarck, ND: University of Mary Press, 2017, pp. 3–18.

——. "The University and the Church," *Logos* 18, no. 4 (Fall 2015): 15–31.

Burke, Kyle. "Radio Free Enterprise: The *Manion Forum* and the Making of the Transnational Right in the 1960s," *Diplomatic History* 40, no. 1 (January 2016): 111–39.

Burtchaell, James T., C.S.C. "In Loco Parentis: Life With(out) Father," *Notre Dame Magazine*, August 1972, pp. 21–23.

——. "Notre Dame and the Christian Teacher," *Notre Dame Journal of Education* 4, no. 3 (Fall 1973): 239–42.

Cogley, John. "Catholic Universities: The Future of an Illusion," *Commonweal*, June 2, 1967, pp. 310–16.

Colwell, Jack. "Carter Likes Idea of Abortion Conference," *South Bend Tribune*, October 11, 1976, p. 1.

——. "Hesburgh Lends Support to Manion," *South Bend Tribune*, May 21, 1986, p. B1.

Conklin, Richard. "Edmund P. Joyce, C.S.C., 1917–2004," *Notre Dame Magazine*, Summer 2004, p. 18–19.

——. "The Maker of Notre Dame," *Notre Dame Magazine*, 2015 Hesburgh Special Edition, pp. 14–22.

——. "Memories of the Gipper and Notre Dame," June 13, 2004, Notre Dame News and Information Press Release, University of Notre Dame Archives.

D'Antonio, William V. "Fr. Ted Hesburgh: A Reflection on His Impact," March 13, 2015. http://www.catholicsinalliance.org/fr_hesburgh.

Dawson, Christopher. "Education and Christian Culture," *Commonweal*, December 4, 1953, pp. 216–20.

Doino, William. "Pius XII's Duel with Hitler," *First Things*, September 12, 2016. https://www.firstthings.com/web-exclusives/2016/09/pius-xiis-duel-with-hitler.

Donnelly, Doris, and John Pawlikowsk. "Lovingly Observant," *America*, June 18–25, 2007, pp. 10–13.

Donovan, Elizabeth. "Meet the Provost," *Scholastic*, September 8, 1978, p. 7.

Ellis, John Tracy. "American Catholics and the Intellectual Life," *Thought* 30, no. 3 (Fall 1955): 351–88.

Gleason, Philip. "A Half-Century of Change in Catholic Higher Education," *U.S. Catholic Historian* 19, no. 1 (Winter 2001): 1–4 and 12.

——. "A Question of Academic Freedom," *Notre Dame Magazine*, Spring 2013, pp. 29–31.

——. "Thomas T. McAvoy, C.S.C.: Some Informal Recollections," *American Catholics Studies* 115, no. 4 (2004): 59–68.

Gribble, Richard, C.S.C. "Thomas T. McAvoy, C.S.C.: Historian, Archivist, Educator," *American Catholic Studies* 115, no. 4 (Winter 2004): 25–43.

Grubiak, Margaret M. "Visualizing the Modern Catholic University: The Original Intention of 'Touchdown Jesus' at the University of Notre Dame," *Material Religion* 6, no. 3 (October 2010): 336–69.

Gurian, Waldemar. "Football Capital or Intellectual Community?," *Commonweal*, October 14, 1949, pp. 17–18.

Hauerwas, Stanley. "Pilgrim in the Promised Land," *Notre Dame Magazine*, Winter 1994–1995, pp. 17–19.

Hunt, Tara. "The Damnedest Experience We Ever Had: The Pornography and Censorship Conference of 1969," *Notre Dame Magazine*, Spring 2015, pp. 14–16.

Imbelli, Robert P. "A Pure Distillation of 1970s Catholicism," *The Catholic Thing*, August 28, 2016. https://www.thecatholicthing.org/2016/08/28/a-pure-distillation-of-1970s-catholicism/.

Ingals, Zoe. "For God, for Country and for Notre Dame," *Chronicle of Higher Education*, October 13, 1982, p. 7.

Jaroff, Leon. "Surrender at Notre Dame," *Sports Illustrated*, January 5, 1959, pp. 12–14.

Koeth, Stephen M. "The Strength and Limits of American Catholic Confidence: Reverend John F. Cronin, S.S., and His Political Friendship with Richard M. Nixon, 1947–1960," *Journal of Church and State* 56, no. 4 (2014): 711–31.

Komonchak, Joseph A. "Where Does the Church Do Her Thinking?" *Commonweal* online entry, April 7, 2006.

Lozada, Carlos. Review of *Billion-Dollar Ball: A Journey Through the Big-Money Culture of College Football* by Gilbert M. Gaul, *Washington Post*, August 21, 2015. https://www.washingtonpost.com/news/book-party/wp/2015/08/21/college-football-isnt-about-college-and-its-barely-about-football-its-about-money/?utm_term=.c054a07b5d97.

McBrady, Jared. "The Challenge of Peace: Ronald Reagan, John Paul II, and the American Bishops," *Journal of Cold War Studies* 17, no. 1 (Winter 2015): 129–52.

McBrien, Richard. "The Hard-Line Pontiff," *Notre Dame Magazine*, Spring 1987, pp. 27–29.

McKay, Robert B. "Review of *Report of the United States Commission on Civil Rights*," *Columbia Law Review* 60, no. 5 (May 1960): 759.

Miscamble, Wilson D. "Francis Cardinal Spellman and 'Spellman's War.'" In David L. Anderson, *The Human Tradition in the Vietnam Era*. Wilmington, DE: SR Books, 2000, pp. 3–22.

——. "Sectarian Passivism?" Contribution to a symposium on the work of Stanley Hauerwas. *Theology Today* 94, no. 1 (April 1987): 69–77.

——. "The Tragedy of Mario Cuomo," *Notre Dame Magazine*, Autumn 1993, pp. 41–43.

Murray, John Courtney. "On the Structure of the Church-State Problem." In *The Catholic Church in World Affairs*. Edited by Waldemar Gurian and M. A. Fitzsimons. Notre Dame, IN: University of Notre Dame Press, 1954.

Nicgorski, Andrew. "The Power of John Paul II," *Notre Dame Magazine*, Winter, 2002–2003, pp. 18–21.

Novak, Michael. "The Keys of the Papacy," *Weekly Standard*, January 19, 1998, p. 35.

O'Shaughnessy, Brendan. "Ministers of Justice," *Notre Dame Magazine*, Summer 2016, pp. 14–15.

Pelton, Robert. "Theological Dynamism at Notre Dame," *Notre Dame Alumnus*, April-May 1962, p. 6.

Piereson, James. "Castro and the Kennedy Assassination," *Real Clear Politics*, November 28, 2016. http://www.realclearpolitics.com/articles/2016/11/28/castro_and_the_kennedy_assassination_132442.html

Poulson, Susan L., and Loretta P. Higgins. "Gender, Coeducation, and the Transformation of Catholic Identity in American Catholic Higher Education," *Catholic Historical Review* 89, no. 3 (July 2003): 494.

Reedy, John L., C.S.C., and James F. Andrews. "Control of Catholic Universities," *Ave Maria*, January 28, 1967, pp. 16–19 and 30–31.

Reno, R.R. "The Public Square: Rahner's New Church," *First Things*, March 2017, p. 7.

———. "Theology After the Revolution," *First Things*, May 2007, pp. 15–21.

Roberts, Tom. "Reporter Recalls Rocky Friendship with Fr. Theodore Hesburgh," *National Catholic Reporter* (online edition), May 2, 2015.

Schmuhl, Robert. "Extreme Measures," *Notre Dame Magazine*, Autumn 2016, pp. 26–29.

Short, Carolyn P. "Time for Me," *Notre Dame Magazine*, 2015 Hesburgh Special Edition, pp. 34–35.

Shuster, George. "Concerning the University Administration," *Scholastic*, March 1, 1963, pp. 7–8.

Stein, Robert J., and Deborah A. Harding. ". . . To Humanitarian Aid in Cambodia," *Notre Dame Magazine*, 2015 Hesburgh Special Edition, p. 61.

Temple, Kerry. "Letter from Campus: Autumn Rituals," *Notre Dame Magazine*, Winter 2005–2006, pp. 2–3.

———. "The Man for the Times," *Notre Dame Magazine*, Summer 2014, pp. 2–3.

———. "The Priest at Şelma," *Notre Dame Magazine*, Summer 2015, pp. 4–5.

Weigel, George. "An Eminent Distortion of History," *First Things*, July 16, 2014. https://www.firstthings.com/web-exclusives/2014/07/an-eminent-distortion-of-history.

———. "John Paul II and the Priority of Culture," *First Things*, February 1989, pp. 19–25.

Wolfe, James. "Exclusion, Fusion or Dialogue: How Should Religion and Politics Relate?," *Journal of Church and State* 22 (Winter 1980): 93–94.

Wolkerstorfer, Terry. "Parseghian: A New Ara in Notre Dame Football," *Scholastic*, January 17, 1964, pp. 27–28.

Woodward, Kenneth L. "Man of the Church," *Notre Dame Magazine*, 2015 Hesburgh Special Edition, pp. 62–67.

Yoder, Edwin M., Jr. "Knowledge Industry: The Lowdown on Higher Learning in America," *Weekly Standard*, July 18, 2016, p. 38.

Yuill, Kevin L. "The White House Conference on Civil Rights," *Historical Journal* 41, no. 1 (March 1998): 259–82.

C. Unpublished Materials

Hannan, Greer. "The Role of Philosophy and Theology in Catholic Universities." Senior thesis, University of Notre Dame, 2009.

Mora, Stuart. "Notre Dame vs. the Teamsters: A Case Study of the Decline of the American Labor Movement." Senior thesis, University of Notre Dame, 2008.

O'Connell, Marvin R. Unpublished memoir. In author's possession.

Temple, Christopher. "Father Hesburgh and Science: Transforming the University of Notre Dame into a Preeminent American Catholic Research University, 1952–1967." Paper delivered at Saint Louis University, September 21, 2017.

PHOTOGRAPHY CREDITS

INDEX

ABOUT THE AUTHOR

REVEREND WILSON D. (BILL) MISCAMBLE, C.S.C., joined the permanent faculty of the history department at Notre Dame in 1988. He chaired the department from 1993 to 1998. He also served as rector and superior of Moreau Seminary (2000 to 2004), the principal formation site for the Congregation of Holy Cross in North America. Fr. Miscamble's primary research interests are American foreign policy since World War II and the role of Catholics in twentieth-century American public life.